MODERN PERSONNEL MANAGEMENT

PAUL S. GREENLAW

Professor of Management
College of Business Administration
The Pennsylvania State University

WILLIAM D. BIGGS

Associate Professor of Management
School of Business and Administration
Alfred University

1979 · W. B. SAUNDERS · Philadelphia · London · Toronto

W. B. Saunders Company: West Washington Square
Philadelphia, PA   19105

1 St. Anne's Road
Eastbourne, East Sussex BN21 3UN, England

1 Goldthorne Avenue
Toronto, Ontario M8Z 5T9, Canada

Modern Personnel Management   ISBN   0-7216-4259-4

Last digit is the print number: 9   8   7   6   5   4   3   2   1

PREFACE

Personnel management is visualized becoming less and less as providing a simple "human relations" approach to the "people problems" of organizations. Rather, it is being increasingly seen as a complex decision-making process involving the management of human resources within an organizational *system* geared to meeting both individual needs and organizational objectives. It is to emphasize this latter concept of personnel management that we have written this text.

More specifically, we have oriented *Modern Personnel Management* around managerial decision making with respect to four broad areas—the acquisition, development, rewarding, and maintenance of human resources. We have focused attention on the functional decision areas typically handled by personnel departments (e.g., recruiting, selection, and training) rather than on such broad behavioral issues as leadership styles or span of control, since these subjects are taught so widely in organizational theory and behavior courses. We have, however, drawn considerably upon those social science concepts and research which may provide a basis for choosing better personnel decision-making strategies. For example, we illustrate how different leadership styles may affect performance appraisal and how learning theory can be useful in helping to choose among alternative training and development decision strategies.

Personnel management, as emphasized in this text, is a multifaceted discipline, drawing on many other social science fields than those already noted. At the present time, when both individual organizations and society as a whole are facing serious economic problems, many economic issues germane to modern personnel management emerge as highly significant. These range from providing economic incentives to executives that will be most cost-beneficial to the firm and the individual in light of existing tax laws to designing safe and sound, yet viable, pension strategies in an era in which total pension fund assets in the United States have reached several hundred *billion* dollars. We have given more consideration to the economic aspects of modern personnel management than many other texts.

A trend which has become extremely pronounced in recent years is increasing governmental legislation, rulings by administrative agencies, and court decisions that have constrained the strategy space of those making decisions relative to the management of human resources. Examples of such key legislation are the Civil Rights Act of 1964, with its "affirmative action," and the complex Employee Retirement Income Security Act of 1974 (ERISA). In examining legal issues we have attempted to provide depth without trivia, e.g., examining the major provisions of key legislation and the basic substantive issues in important Supreme Court decisions without delving into the myriad of minor administrative rulings promulgated by various federal agencies.

In *Modern Personnel Management* we have also taken, where feasible, a "contingency" approach to human resource decision making—one that attempts to identify the conditions under which different types of decisions appear most effective. Further, going back to the Ford and Carnegie Foundation reports of the 1950's, which strongly urged that more emphasis be placed on quantitative analysis in business education, we have presented a number of management science models used by organizations in human resource decision making. In doing so, we have avoided all sophisticated mathematical notation and have presented simple examples and descriptions understandable by students who have not gone beyond *basic* college algebra and statistics courses. We have also segmented our discussion of these models so that instructors who do not wish to cover certain ones can omit consideration of them without impairing the logical flow of thought in any chapter.

Modern Personnel Management has been designed not only for those individuals who aspire to be personnel managers but rather for all persons who assume or expect to assume decision-making responsibilities in organizations. For example, all managers need to be familiar with many basic facets of performance appraisal, as all members of organizations should know something about their rights under such federal legislation as the National Labor Relations Act or ERISA.

We have placed considerable emphasis on human resource *decision making* as a core notion in modern personnel management. In light of this emphasis, we were especially gratified when the 1978 Nobel Prize in Economics was awarded to Dr. Herbert A. Simon of Carnegie-Mellon University for pioneering work in examining such phenomena as the decision-making processes within organizations. As a result of this event, we hope to see even more emphasis placed on decision making as a core focus in modern personnel management in the future.

PAUL S. GREENLAW
WILLIAM D. BIGGS

ACKNOWLEDGMENTS

We have been assisted in our writing efforts by many individuals. We are grateful to the following people, who provided us with many constructive suggestions for improvement of the text: Karl Price, Temple University; Steven Kerr, University of Southern California; Robert Van Auken, University of Oklahoma; William Cornelius and Leonard Davidson, University of Florida; Dan McGill and Lawrence Hrebiniak, University of Pennsylvania—Wharton School; Robert Smith, Kent State University; Joseph Foerst, Jr., Georgia State University; Allan Nash, University of Maryland; Donald Jarrell and Rodger Collons, Drexel University.

We would also like to thank the following professors at The Pennsylvania State University: Bart Basi, James Farr, Gary Kochenberger, Benjamin Niebel, Richard A. Olsen, and John Schmidman. We owe a special debt of gratitude to Bert L. Metzger, President of the Profit Sharing Research Foundation of Evanston, Illinois; to Merl Douglas, Executive Director of the Sears, Roebuck Savings and Profit Sharing Fund of Sears Employees; and to Richard S. Sabo, Manager of Publicity and Educational Services of the Lincoln Electric Company, for their careful analysis and suggestions for improving Chapter 11. Of course, we assume full responsibility for the adequacy of the materials in all chapters of this text.

There are many others who assisted us in many ways. We would like to thank Dr. M. William Frey, President of the North American Contracting Corp., of Sanibel Island, Florida, for providing us with secretarial support. We also deeply appreciate the support of Dr. Eugene J. Kelley, Dean of the College of Business Administration of The Pennsylvania State University, Dr. Wilford G. Miles, Dean of the School of Business and Administration of Alfred University, and Dr. Michael P. Hottenstein, Chairman of the Department of Management Science and Organizational Behavior in the College of Business Administration of The Pennsylvania State University, during the period in which this text was written.

We would also like to thank our wives, Shirley Greenlaw and Cathy Biggs, and Mrs. Hilda Greenlaw for assisting us in proofreading, and Diane Greenlaw for helping us with some of the artwork. We would further like to express appreciation to our secretaries and typists for their high quality of work and dedication in helping us with our manuscript—Lorraine Fies, Ildiko Takacs, Cindy Puglisi, and Tricia Harrison of The Pennsylvania State University, and Gail Aguglia and Linda Keim of Alfred University. Last, but not least, we would like to acknowledge the support of the many librarians at both The Pennsylvania State University and Alfred University who provided us with various types of assistance.

PAUL S. GREENLAW
WILLIAM D. BIGGS

CONTENTS

Part I
INTRODUCTION... 1

Chapter 1
INTRODUCTION 3

Chapter 2
THE PERSONNEL DEPARTMENT.. 31

Part II
THE ACQUISITION OF HUMAN RESOURCES 67

Chapter 3
HUMAN RESOURCE PLANNING... 69

Chapter 4
RECRUITING AND SELECTION 120

Part III
THE DEVELOPMENT OF HUMAN RESOURCES.................... 179

Chapter 5
PERFORMANCE APPRAISAL.. 181

Chapter 6
EMPLOYEE DEVELOPMENT: BASIC CONSIDERA-
TIONS IN PLANNED ORGANIZATIONAL LEARNING............... 214

Chapter 7
EMPLOYEE DEVELOPMENT: DESIGN DECISIONS 255

Chapter 8
EMPLOYEE DEVELOPMENT: CURRENT PROBLEMS
AND ISSUES... 311

Part IV

THE REWARDING OF HUMAN RESOURCES.........................353

Chapter 9
WAGE AND SALARY ADMINISTRATION...............................355

Chapter 10
INDIVIDUAL INCENTIVE SYSTEMS.......................................395

Chapter 11
SYSTEM INCENTIVES 435

Part V

THE MAINTENANCE OF HUMAN RESOURCES 475

Chapter 12
EMPLOYEE BENEFITS 477

Chapter 13
OCCUPATIONAL SAFETY AND HEALTH..............................522

Chapter 14
EMPLOYEE MANAGEMENT RELATIONS...............................580

Part VI

EPILOGUE...633

Chapter 15
PERCY'S PARADOXES AND THE "FEAST OF FOOLS".........634

Name Index...647

Subject Index 653

I

INTRODUCTION

1

INTRODUCTION

Basic to the success of all organizations is the effective use of human resources. Such use has increased in importance in this century as organizations have grown in size, number, and complexity, have developed new technologies and work environments, and have come to be viewed by society as providers of safe, meaningful, and satisfying work as well as monetary rewards.

We have named this book *Modern Personnel Management*. By "modern" we do not intend to imply that most of the approaches presented in this text are "new." As a matter of fact, some of them are quite old. Suggestion systems, for example, date back to the nineteenth century; while the use of tests for selection can be traced back to 1115 B.C. at the beginning of the Chan Dynasty in China.[1] Rather, what we intend to do is to look at certain more modern ways of viewing the field of personnel. We will primarily consider the work of those engaged in personnel management as centering around making decisions in a systems context. In making these decisions, personnel managers may be aided by two relatively new approaches:

1. Applying certain so-called "contingency" views in analyzing personnel problems.
2. Giving adequate attention to newer "management science" tools and methodologies and computers as they have been applied to the field of personnel administration.

Although these two aids to personnel decision making have not been fully developed and researched and cannot be applied to all types of personnel problems, there are numerous areas in which they can help sharpen our analysis.

This chapter has been designed to achieve four purposes: (1) to define the scope of personnel management as we view it; (2) to provide a brief history of personnel management; (3) to give an overview of the organization of the text; and (4) to spell out in detail the nature of personnel decision making viewed in a systems sense, in which the manager may be aided by contingency views and management science tools and computers.

THE SCOPE OF PERSONNEL MANAGEMENT

Personnel management in its broadest sense involves all matters in an organization regarding "people decisions." This broad view focuses attention on three distinct but interrelated topics. The first is that of *human relations*, in which such matters as individual motivation, leadership, and group relationships and behavior are covered. The second is the field of *organization theory*, which considers job design, managerial spans of control, the flow of work through the organization, and so forth. The third consists of the specific kinds of *decision areas* for which the personnel manager or personnel department is directly responsible—acquisition, development, rewarding, and maintenance of human resources.

The broad definition of personnel management illustrates that the scope of personnel management pervades the organization. Every person in an organization is involved with personnel decisions. For example, all managers in any organization will need to know how to train their employees, appraise their performance, and so forth. Similarly, nonmanagerial employees will be exposed to performance appraisals, selection interviews when hired, and so on.

We recognize the interdependencies and importance of the three topics included in the broad definition of personnel management. We prefer, however, to define personnel management in the narrower sense of the third topic. Thus, this text will focus attention on personnel management in terms of the specific kinds of decision areas for which the personnel manager or personnel department is directly responsible. These decision areas include the personnel functions of human resource planning, recruiting and selection, performance appraisal, training and development, wage and salary administration, incentives, employee health and safety, employee benefits, and employee-management relations. Depending upon the size of an organization, it should be emphasized, there may not be a formalized personnel department. Rather, one individual might perform all personnel functions. Or in a very small organization, one person may spend only part of his time on personnel matters and the rest on other types of decision problems.

It should be pointed out that human relations and organization theory are very legitimate fields for study by themselves. We consider it desirable, however, to treat personnel management as described here, because human relations and organization theory are so often taught in separate behavioral science and organizational behavior—theory courses. Thus, covering these areas extensively in this text would create redundancies for many readers. We will, however, draw on numerous behavioral science concepts as bases for the analysis of particular personnel problems. In fact, some of the "contingency" approaches to the study of personnel management mentioned here represent ideas and notions drawn directly from individuals working in the field of organization theory and behavior.

THE HISTORY UNDERLYING MODERN PERSONNEL MANAGEMENT

One of the first major thrusts toward modern personnel management in the United States occurred in the public sector. The assassination of President James Garfield in 1881 by a disappointed office seeker led to the passage in 1883 of the Pendleton Act. This Act established the Federal Civil Service Commission, geared, among other things, to meet the objective of selecting federal employees on the basis of merit rather than on political grounds — the so-called patronage system.

Organized personnel work appears to have emerged in business organizations about 1900.[2] The first employment department (which was only a hiring bureau) appeared at that time at the B.F. Goodrich Company, while as early as 1902 the National Cash Register Company had a fairly broadly conceived "labor department," which dealt with worker grievances, wage administration, working conditions, employment, record keeping, discharges, education, and improvement of workers and foremen.[3] The emergence of personnel management has been attributed to two diverse fields of endeavor: (1) the industrial welfare movement and (2) Frederick W. Taylor's scientific management. The industrial welfare movement, derived from religion and philanthropy, led some managements to set such humanitarian objectives as providing facilities such as libraries, financial assistance for education, recreational facilities, and medical care. These functions were sometimes performed by welfare secretaries, who were conceived as a point of contact between the company and its employees. Although the status of "welfare" declined, these types of endeavors continued, and industrial welfare "clearly contained the beginning of personnel administration . . . . The line from the social and welfare secretaries to the employment manager is a direct one."[4]

The second, and quite different, field that led to the emergence of modern personnel administration was "scientific management," fathered by Frederick W. Taylor.[5] Taylor's basic objective was to develop more efficient ways of performing work at the lowest level in organizations — with workers at the shop level. Taylor emphasized: (1) researching ways of performing tasks, such as studying jobs with the objective of eliminating unnecessary motions; (2) applying the best methods devised to all jobs; (3) selecting workers suited to perform the jobs; and (4) training them in the one best method developed. Taylor's work attracted many followers, such as Frank and Lillian Gilbreth and Henry Gantt. The time and motion study methods and other worker efficiency techniques developed and used by Taylor and his followers are still widely used in industry and taught today in industrial engineering (and other) departments in colleges and universities.

Certain other aspects of the early history of the personnel field are also of significance. These were developed during the period 1910–1920. First, although the significance of unions was apparent by this time, managements suddenly "discovered" labor turnover as a costly proposition and turned to personnel managers to help meet the objective of reducing turnover by the proper selection and placement of workers (along with adequate training). Second, World War I created a labor shortage, which made turnover a calamity and tardiness and absenteeism serious problems. This led many organizations to develop personnel departments to deal with these problems. Further, in many cases the powers of foremen, such as hiring and discharging employees, were seriously curtailed by centralizing personnel hiring and giving personnel departments powers to override supervisors' discharge decisions.[6] World War I also triggered the development of the Army Alpha as a group intelligence test for military selection. "It was so constructed as to measure all gradations of intelligence and was by far the most highly standardized test of this sort at that time."[7] The Army Alpha has also been widely used by civil service commissions.

Beginning in the 1920's, the nature of the American labor force began to change considerably. Among the reasons for this change were: (1) the slowdown in immigration due, in no small part, to new federal immigration laws passed in the 1920's; (2) the continued rise in educational levels of American workers; and (3) the increase in urbanization. With the American worker's knowledge and abilities becoming more fully developed than ever before, he began to expect and demand more dignified and respectful treatment.[8] In the 1920's many business firms tried to "be good" to their employees, on the assumption that their workers would consequently be more satisfied and work harder. Incorporated into this approach (often referred to as "paternalism") were such activities as company cafeterias and planned recreation programs. Significant research at Western Electric's Hawthorne plant indicated that interpersonal relationships and group behavior were indeed important in organizations. This research stimulated the so-called "human relations" approach to management beginning in the 1930's, when it was documented for general consumption.

In the 1930's, with protective legislation enacted under President Franklin D. Roosevelt's New Deal, the growth and power of unions was enhanced considerably. Such union power provided a strong check on personnel decisions, and forced firms to place considerably more emphasis on union-management relations. This situation, quite naturally, enlarged the power of those organizational specialists specifically dealing with unions — labor relations and personnel managers.

Moving to the 1940's, the spotlight on personnel management was increased during World War II. With large numbers of persons engaged in active military service, the labor market again became tight. In addition, the need developed for intensive skill training programs for those workers (including many women) who replaced the individuals in the military services. Further, the freezing of wages by the federal government led unions to demand compensation in the form of benefits (such as pension plans) that further enlarged the scope of the personnel department.

In the 30 some years since the end of World War II, the personnel department has continued to grow in at least three ways. First, it has been faced with an increasingly expanding and complex technology. Among such technological changes, computerization and automation stand out as probably the most important to the personnel manager. Computers have not only created problems that personnel managers face today (e.g., retraining displaced employees) but also have served as an important record keeping and problem solving tool. The automation of production processes has not only required layoffs and retraining, it has also created quite different social systems in which different types of interpersonal relationships and human problems have arisen. In addition, in some instances automation has resulted in jobs becoming so routine that employee dissatisfaction has resulted.

Second, personnel managers have been forced more and more to deal with the monumental social and economic objective of providing minority groups with protection from unequal treatment. Following the passage of the Civil Rights Act of 1964, firms have had to be careful not to discriminate with respect to selection, promotions, training, wage and salary administration, and other types of managerial decisions.

Finally, personnel management is becoming increasingly circumscribed by federal and state legislation. For example, in addition to the Civil Rights Act, the Equal Pay Act of 1963 was geared to the objective of providing women with the same pay as men for doing the same work; the Occupational Safety and Health Act (OSHA) of 1970 was passed as a means for government stimulation of safer and more healthy job environments; and the Employee Retirement Income Security Act (ERISA) of 1974 was primarily designed to ensure that individuals would not lose their pension rights as members of company retirement plans.

ORGANIZATION OF THIS TEXT

As is evident from our preceding discussion of the history of personnel management, the scope, depth, and nature of personnel management in general and personnel departments in particular have expanded in many ways since around 1900. The purpose of this section is to help crystallize and organize the reader's thinking about the many different types of work performed today by personnel managers.

Basically, we have organized this text on a functional basis, with each chapter dealing with one or more related personnel functions. Within each functional area, specific problems, concepts, tools, and techniques are discussed. Numerous topics that cut across functional areas — such as civil rights legislation — are covered in part in more than one chapter.

Introduction

We have divided this text into six separate parts. This chapter and the next are introductory. They are intended to provide a background for discussion of the specific objectives, problems, and decisions of personnel management in later chapters. Chapter 2 focuses attention on the extremely important question of the role personnel should play as a staff department in organizations. Here we will delve into such areas as the different types of work performed by personnel, and the problems and ways of overcoming them in personnel's relationships with other departments in the organization.

The Acquisition of Human Resources

Part II consists of two chapters dealing with the acquisition of human resources. Before a firm can begin to operate, it must determine the specific work that needs to be carried out by members of the organization and the number of employees that will be required for each job defined. Chapter 3 focuses on the problems involved and some of the decision approaches used in the forecasting of and planning for specific human resources requirements. Once the organization has defined its human resource needs, it will be able to proceed to recruiting and selecting the organization's employees. This will be the primary focus of Chapter 4. Sources of human resources, recruiting methods, the use of application forms, tests, and interviews in the selection process, and the highly significant implications for selection of such legislation as the Civil Rights Act of 1964 are among the content areas covered in our discussion of recruiting and selection.

The Development of Human Resources

Once its human resources have been obtained, the organization will need to appraise the performance of its employees and train and develop them so they will be able to perform specific jobs and, in many cases, be prepared to deal with higher level jobs involving more responsibilities in the future. It is upon such development that Part III of this text focuses. The organization must appraise the performance of its employees not only as a basis for compensation increases but also to supply feedback to employees so they may improve their performance. Such information may also provide an indication to the organization's training department as to what kinds of training programs would be of most value in meeting the firm's objectives. Various approaches to decision making in the field of performance appraisal are covered in Chapter 5.

Chapters 6 to 8 each cover both management and nonmanagement training and development, rather than segregating these two topics as is done in some texts. Chapter 6 deals with determining the need for training and development programs, designing these programs in light of our knowledge from learning theory, and means of evaluation of these efforts. In Chapter 7, our coverage of the design phase of training and development programs continues, and we discuss decisions concerning where training will take place and what training methods should be used. In this chapter, we discuss the advantages and limitations of on-the-job as opposed to off-the-job training and treat several training methods, such as computer assisted instruction, simulation, and case studies. In Chapter 8 we turn our attention to some topics of current interest in training and development. Among these are: orientation training, training and development for special groups such as the hard-core unemployed, assessment centers, and organizational development.

The Rewarding of Human Resources

Although members of organizations work for many reasons, providing them with fair and equitable monetary rewards is of great importance. Part IV of this text emphasizes ways in which monetary reward systems may be designed, and also focuses attention on certain nonmonetary rewards. In Chapter 9 we discuss money as a motivator and indicate some of the many ways in which organizations may design effective wage and salary systems. In addition to being rewarded with his basic wage or salary, the organization member may receive additional monetary rewards either (1) on the basis of his own or work group's output; or (2) indirectly as a result of company-wide or system performance. In Chapter 10, emphasis is placed on such "individual" rewards. Here, attention is given first to hourly wage incentives. We discuss both (1) "traditional" wage incentives and (2) special means of providing direct financial incentives in automated operations. We also cover one of the older and widely used methods of rewarding employees for creative thinking — suggestion systems — as well as executive incentives and the relatively new flexible "cafeteria" compensation.

In addition to these individual incentives, numerous companies have provided employees with additional system incentives. With the objective of stimulating both employee production and creativity with such incentives, individuals are rewarded on the basis of the organization's financial success rather than on their own specific output. In Chapter 11 we discuss three of the more prominent "system" plans. First we examine the popular profit-sharing plan, on which the basis for incentives is the firm's profits. Then we will cover another well-known incentive plan — the Scanlon Plan. This type of plan provides rewards to an individual based on suggestions made by all employees that reduce company costs as well as on increases in worker output as a whole. Finally, we examine the extremely successful "system" incentive plan in effect for several decades at the Lincoln Electric Company of Cleveland, Ohio.

The Maintenance of Human Resources

In addition to acquiring, developing, and rewarding employees, it is necessary to maintain these valuable human resources. This objective of maintenance provides the focus for Part V of this text. We use the word "maintenance" in a very broad sense here. We include programs designed to meet the objectives of: (1) providing organization members with benefits such as health insurance and pensions; (2) maintaining employee health and safety; and (3) maintaining effective employee management relationships.

In the course of their development, personnel departments have assumed the responsibility of providing employees with many kinds of benefits and services to meet a variety of objectives — company cafeterias, recreational programs, life and health insurance, pensions, and so forth. In Chapter 12 we assess some of the more important of these benefit programs. Firms are constrained in many ways in making employee benefit decisions by governmental legislation, and we consider such legislation as the Social Security Act, unemployment compensation, and the extremely complex but highly significant federal law passed in 1974 — ERISA. In light of a growing interest in economic security after retirement, we focus considerable attention on the subject of pension plans in Chapter 12 and indicate some of the more important decisions involved in pension plan management.

Chapter 13 focuses attention on various aspects of employee health and safety. Decision strategies that are effective in maintaining a healthy and safe work environment are discussed along with such other subjects as (1) evaluating the benefits of health and safety programs in light of their costs and (2) federal and state legislation aimed at requiring organizations to comply with adequate health and safety standards. Special attention is given to the major piece of federal health and safety legislation in effect today—OSHA.

The importance of maintaining effective employee management relations, the subject of Chapter 14, is obvious. We discuss such basic labor legislation as the Wagner Act, the Taft-Hartley Act, and the Landrum-Griffin Act, each of which opened opportunities and imposed restrictions or constraints on union management relations. We also delve into the two major decision making processes involved in union management relations — collective bargaining and grievances, which may need to be ultimately resolved by means of arbitration.

Epilogue

Part VI of this text (Chapter 15) provides an epilogue. Some of the problems and paradoxes facing the modern personnel manager are pointed out.

PERSONNEL DECISION MAKING

In this text we conceive of the personnel functions described above as centering around decision making. The purpose of this section is to (1) describe this decision-making process as it exists in an interrelated systems sense and (2) indicate how the two approaches mentioned at the beginning of this chapter — contingency views and management science and computers — may aid such decision making.

Decision Making and Systems

Fundamental to personnel management is the meeting of organizational objectives.[9] In personnel, these objectives often involve both economic and noneconomic "social," "humanitarian" aspects. For example, by providing the organization's employees with a safe and healthy work environment, "humanitarian" goals are met. Economic goals may be met at the same time, however, since a better safety record may help reduce a firm's workmen's compensation costs. Implicit in these statements is that personnel decisions attempt to meet individual needs as well as organizational objectives.

If any of his objectives are *not met* or are *inappropriate*, we consider that the personnel manager has problems. For example, a large number of accidents might indicate that the firm's safety goals are not being met, while an objective of a company *never* having a single accident would be unrealistic, and hence inappropriate.

To overcome any problems he faces, the personnel manager needs to generate possible courses of action, evaluate the merits of each, make a decision or decisions as to how to overcome the problems, and implement the decision(s). If the firm's safety objectives are not being met, for example, personnel management might:

1. Generate such possible courses of action as increasing expenditures for safety training, instituting a safety contest, or replacing its present safety director with a hopefully more effective one.
2. Evaluate the costs, probable effectiveness in reducing the number and seriousness of accidents, etc. of each alternative.
3. Select one or more of these alternatives (say expanding safety training).
4. Actually implement this course of action by setting up a particular training program.

Personnel decisions such as these are not made in isolation. Rather, like all management decisions, they affect and are affected by other management decisions and actions and by forces outside the organization. Looking at decisions in such an inter-related sense is often referred to as taking a *systems view* of decision making.

The concept "system" has been defined in many different ways. We will consider a system to represent a complex of elements interacting with each other to form a unified whole. Scholars have classified systems into two "pure" types: *closed* and *open*. Closed systems, theoretically, are isolated from any external environment and over time become more and more dis-organized.

Open systems, on the other hand, consist of both elements mutually interacting within the system and those which mutually interact to varying degrees with their *external* environment. Fur-ther, they may exhibit tendencies toward increasing order rather than disorder. These systems are of much greater concern to the personnel manager, because his organization, his own and other departments, groups within such departments, and individuals within such groups all represent systems "open" to varying ex-tents and in mutual interaction with their environments. By "mu-tual interaction" we mean situations in which one change in a system or its environment will lead to another, which in turn, will "come back" to influence the one originally modified. For exam-ple, within the organization establishment of a new retirement system may influence certain production managers to retire sooner, which may, in turn, make it necessary for personnel to develop a speeded-up training program for their replacements; or, with respect to a firm's external environment, the personnel department may raise the educational requirements for a particu-lar job. This action may lead to job applicants increasing their salary demands, which would in turn, require personnel to modi-fy starting salaries for that job. From these two examples, we can see that when viewed in systems terms, there is considerable interdependence among decisions made in the different personnel functions already described.

Personnel decision making in a systems sense may also be thought of as comprising several different kinds of elements. Essentially, the systems view conceives of decisions as *trans-forming* informational *inputs* into *outputs* or courses of action. For example, personnel managers may be required to make a decision to transform information about a job applicant into an output recommendation, such as to hire the individual, not hire him, or run a further background check on him. Informational inputs are especially important to the personnel manager because the environment with which he is in mutual interaction is a probabilistic one, and he needs to be able to predict future events to some extent. The entire human resource forecasting function, for example, provides management with information upon which to base recruiting, selection and other decisions. The use of statistical data concerning the probable on-the-job success of job applicants obtaining certain psychological test scores provides another example of the need for and value of predictive information in the selection function.

Personnel management also requires the establishment of a *control* element to guide organization members' information-gathering and decision-making behavior. Such control may be provided by corporate policies, e.g., a policy of granting a one week vacation for workers who have been with the firm more than one year but less than five, two weeks vacation from five but less than ten years service, etc. Such controls provide at least two functions. First, they relieve individual managers of making decisions. With our example, first line supervisors would not have to decide as to how long each of their employee's vacations should be — it is predetermined for them. Second, policies controlling organization member behavior may help ensure that all individuals receive equitable treatment. Everyone with seven years' service will get a two weeks vacation — supervisors cannot play "favorites" with certain subordinates. Finally, with respect to controls, it should be reemphasized that government legislation such as OSHA, ERISA, and the Civil Rights Act of 1964 controls the behavior of organizations to a much larger extent than in years past, introducing a greater need for personnel managers to understand the legal aspects of their profession.

All open systems need a *feedback* element. This element informs them as to the appropriateness of their previous actions so that they may learn how to correct prior mistaken decisions and improve their performance or continue the correct performance in the future. For this reason, one of the primary functions of the personnel department (or manager), as indicated earlier, is helping to develop a viable performance appraisal system for the organization. Under such systems, the organizational member's performance is periodically reviewed by his superior, and information is often fed back to him to help him in improving his performance in the future.

Those engaged in personnel management need to have a *memory* element to function properly. Such an element provides for the storage of information from the past that can be used in guiding them in making future decisions. Data may be stored in the human mind, in the organization's manual files or in computerized information storage and retrieval systems. The latter, of course, is being used more and more frequently, as our computer technology continues to improve in cost and effectiveness.

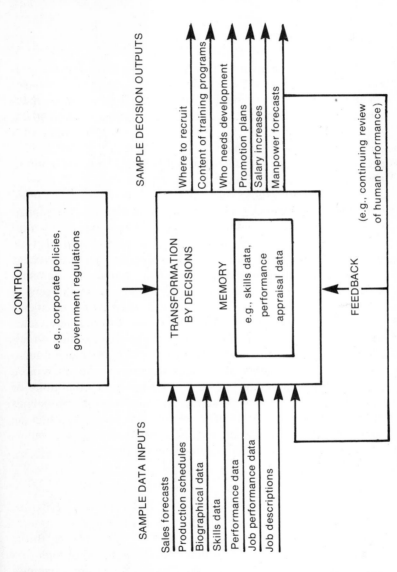

Figure 1-1 *Personnel-Information-Decision System (PIDS). (Adapted from Paul S. Greenlaw and Robert D. Smith, eds., Personnel Management: A Management Science Approach (Scranton, Pa.: International Textbook Company, 1970), p. 2.*

From this discussion, we can see that personnel management centers around interdependent decisions in which information plays a critical role. This conceptualization is illustrated in Figure 1–1. We will delve more deeply into the role of the computer in personnel information-decision systems in Chapter 2.

Contingency Views

In years past many management theorists tended to overgeneralize about the ways in which management should manage. Some individuals, for example, stressed the importance of maintaining effective human relations in organizations,[10] while others prescribed organizational behavior characterized by formal rules and relationships, a rigid hierarchy, a "rational" decision-making process in which personal desires and feelings would be ignored, and a high degree of worker specialization.[11]

More recently, those studying management have taken more balanced "contingency" views of the ways in which organizations, including personnel functions, should be managed. Contingency views all begin with the premise that there is no single type of organizational structure, design, or decision-making process that is best for all organizations in general. Rather, they emphasize that the effectiveness of any particular management decision *all depends* on the *specific* conditions faced by a particular organization existing in a particular environment. Contingency views are important to personnel decision making because they do not ask the general, unanswerable, question: "What personnel techniques are best?" Rather, they focus attention on the much more specific and answerable question: "Under *what* conditions or contingencies will *which* personnel decision-making approaches be most appropriate?" In this section, we focus attention on some of the more important contingencies found to have important implications for personnel decision making.

Degree of Certainty

One important contingency in determining what types of management systems are most effective is the degree of *certainty* under which they operate. As early as 1961, for example, Burns and Stalker took the position that under conditions of high certainty in the environment of organizations (or their departments), rigid hierarchies, rules, and regulations seemed to be most effective.[12] When an organization is operating under high environmental uncertainty, on the other hand, human relations orientations seem more appropriate. Burns and Stalker viewed "certainty" and "uncertainty" as opposite poles of a continuum, with degrees of certainty-uncertainty existing in between. They referred to the most appropriate form of organizational structure at the certainty end of the continuum as "mechanistic" and that most effective at its "polar" opposite of uncertain as "organic." The mechanistic form of structuring in its "pure" form has several characteristics. Among the more important of these are:

1. A precisely spelled out definition of rights, obligations, and methods for each organizational member.
2. A hierarchical structure of control, authority, and communications.
3. A tendency toward a high degree of task specialization for employees.

On the other hand, the organic structure in its pure form is characterized by such human relations–behavioral science orientations as:

1. A movement away from the idea that responsibility is a limited area of rights, rules, obligations, methods, etc.
2. A more lateral form of communication to individuals in a collegial type of relationship, rather than precisely defined "orders" received from the top down in the organization.
3. In general, a more "democratic" flexible free flowing internal environment as opposed to a more "authoritarian" one that emphasizes orders, commands, rights, rules, regulations, and other "bureaucratic" features.[13]

Several comments are in order concerning environmental certainty, the organic-mechanistic framework, and personnel management. First, the organic-mechanistic continuum is quite logical in relation to certainty-uncertainty when one gives it a little thought. When organizations do operate under fairly certain conditions, it is possible for them to spell out clearly specific rules of behavior for their members to follow. On the other hand, when operating conditions are not very certain and the organization does not know what the future will bring, it is difficult to prescribe behavior, and the organization is almost forced to give more decision-making latitude to its members to handle uncertainty as it arises as they think most appropriate. For example, psychological tests cannot be developed to guide the personnel manager's selection of job applicants who will be successful on any particular job five years in the future if organizational conditions are so uncertain that management is unsure of what the jobs will entail at that time. Rather, under such conditions the personnel manager may only be able to make an "intuitive" appraisal of job applicants' future performance based on his own experience and judgment.

Second, historically, the organization's technology has been emphasized as a key factor contributing to the degree of certainty it faces, and hence the appropriateness of organic as opposed to mechanistic management styles.[14] Today, however, it is recognized that uncertainty and technology are not the only variables that may influence the organization's choice as to where to operate along the organic-mechanistic continuum. For example, the following internal and external variables have been considered as important with respect to this decision: the education and skills of organization personnel, the firm's customers, suppliers, and competitors, manager personalities, and the perceptions of and tolerance for ambiguity and uncertainty of organization members.[15]

Third, we should emphasize that different organizational units within a firm may be exposed to different degrees of uncertainty and, hence, desire to take a more organic or mechanistic approach to management than other units within the organization. For example, organizations often attempt and are able to protect their "core technologies" from uncertainty — e.g., by decoupling or making independent their manufacturing process from the direct influence of customer demand by introducing inventories. On the other hand, there may be no way whatsoever to reduce uncertainty in a firm's research department.[16]

Finally, and of special importance to us, is the fact that with such wide differences in organizational "climates" as described, we will find different types of personnel decision-making techniques most appropriate under different conditions. For example, as we will indicate in Chapter 5, the so-called Management by Objectives approach to performance appraisal is theoretically more congruent with an organic climate than a mechanistic one. Or as will be pointed out in Chapter 9, the so-called curve approach to wage and salary administration was especially designed to deal with scientists working in highly organic situations. Certain types of management training, especially sensitivity training (discussed in Chapter 8) also are more congruent in an organic organizational environment. Finally, we should reiterate the general point made earlier regarding personnel and certainty-uncertainty: As personnel problem situations become clouded with more uncertainty, the formalization of policies and procedures becomes less feasible.

Change

A second key contingency influencing the types of personnel decision-making approaches that will be effective under different conditions is the degree of *change* faced by an organization or one of its units. Some organizational situations are relatively stable or static, while others are highly dynamic.

The degree of change existing in organizations has certain basic implications for personnel decision making. First, any formalized policies, procedures, or programs established must be *updated* more frequently in dynamic organizational situations than in static ones. All other factors being the same, the more frequent the updating is required the more costly it will be for the organization, up to a point. These costs may be relatively high or low, depending upon the particular programs or policies needing updating. To the extent that updating costs are substantial, there will be pressures existing in organizations to choose more organic types of personnel systems where there will be (1) a lesser degree of formalization and (2) greater latitude to make decisions for individuals dealing with personnel problems. For example:

1. In a relatively static environment, the personnel manager may supervise the development of a formalized training program for new employees in a department, which can be used over and over again because organizational conditions do not change much.

2. On the contrary, a formalized program for new employees in a highly dynamic research and development department, for instance, may become obsolete in a few months, and its development costs not be justified in terms of usage. In such a department, it might well be much more feasible to have the department head or a senior employee conduct the necessary training for new employees on a more "fluid" basis, changing the content of the training informally as organizational conditions change.

In a related manner, the updating of personnel procedures may help create human problems in an organization leading managers in dynamic operations to avoid formalization for this reason as well as on a pure cost basis. As we will point out in Chapter 10, for example, establishing wage incentives based on work standards developed by time study and other techniques often leads to considerable "haggling" between management and workers. For this reason, frequent changes in such standards may create more problems than benefits, and one will find this personnel approach generally more appropriate in stable rather than dynamic organizational settings.

Size

Another contingency that we have found to be of importance in personnel decision making is organizational "size." There has been an increased amount of attention given to this variable, although it has been defined in many different ways and care must be exercised in its discussion.[17]

We will focus attention on one facet of the complex phenomenon of "size." We will examine it in terms of the *number* of employees who will be *exposed* to any particular personnel technique or program. With respect to this variable, two general observations may be made:

1. The number of persons exposed to a personnel technique or program may vary widely within any given firm, depending on the particular employees involved and the technique or program in question. For example, the number of blue-collar job applicants given a psychological test in a large manufacturing company during any given year may be much greater than the number of its management trainees who are exposed to a computer assisted instruction program in that same period.

2. For any particular job, firms employing smaller numbers of people will generally need to expose fewer people to any given personnel program or technique than firms employing more people on that job. For example, assuming the same selection procedures and employee turnover, a small commercial airline would not have to train as many newly hired stewardesses as the nation's largest airline in any given year.

Our concern with the "exposure" aspect of organizational size as being important to personnel decision making has two basic facets. First is a cost-benefit one. With many personnel programs such as those illustrated above, the firm will often incur a set of relatively fixed costs, regardless of the number of program exposures up to a point, in addition to a per unit (variable) cost for each exposure. In such cases, economies of scale will take place, and the organization's average costs per person exposed to any personnel program or technique will decrease up to a point as the number of individuals exposed increases. For example, suppose it costs $5000 to develop a particular psychological test and $10 to give the test to each job applicant and interpret his test results. If a company were to use the test with only 10 people, its average cost/applicant would be:

$$\frac{\$5000 \text{ fixed cost} + \$10 \ (10)}{10} = \$510.$$

For a firm examining a much larger number of job applicants (say, 1000), its average cost would only be:

$$\frac{\$5000 \text{ fixed cost} + \$10 \ (1000)}{1000} = \$15000/1000 \text{ or } \$15.$$

Although this example is somewhat oversimplified for purposes of illustration, it does point up a basic reason why firms cannot afford to use certain costly types of personnel techniques and programs *themselves* unless they are going to expose a sufficient number of their employees to these personnel efforts. We emphasize the word "themselves" since some firms with a relatively small number of employees may hire outsiders to do personnel work for them and hence avoid the high fixed costs. For example, we know of one small home fuel oil distributor that employed a local college professor as a consultant when needed to handle its testing of job applicants at a fee of $50 per applicant. Large firms in terms of *total* number of employees may also have to resort to the same strategy if only a few of their employees need to be exposed to a particular personnel program or technique. For example, if only a handful of a large company's executives needed to become familiarized with a new piece of governmental legislation, it would probably be much cheaper to send these individuals to a training program conducted by an outside organization such as the American Management Association, rather than attempt to train these few executives itself.

The exposure aspect of size also has another important impact on personnel decision making. In operations in which only a few individuals will need exposure, certain types of personnel work cannot be performed because the firm can never obtain an adequate sample size. For example, if a small supermarket is only going to test four applicants per year for meatcutting jobs, it would be years before it could obtain a large enough sample of test scores to validate the test statistically, rendering any such validation out of the question. The same problem could be faced by a large firm, of course, which only examined a very small number of applicants for a *particular job* that required a low-exposure specialized type of test—e.g., a mechanical comprehension test in a firm with only a few engineers and low engineer turnover.

Contingencies: Overview

We have found the three contingencies indicated of considerable importance in determining which types of personnel programs, techniques, and other decision-making tools are effective under varying conditions. These are not the only key variables, of course, that affect personnel management. Other factors, such as the philosophy of top line management, the financial position of the firm, the actions competitors are taking, and the state of the economy, are all of significance to personnel decision making. For example, in times of high firm profits in an expanding economy, much more personnel efforts are often directed toward management development than during recessionary periods, in which top management believes it has to make numerous budgetary cuts. Of key importance is not only recognizing these contingencies, as well as the three major ones discussed in detail, but rather developing a contingency *mode of thinking* as we view the various personnel functions covered in this text. As a decision maker, the personnel manager must choose from among alternative strategies, as indicated earlier. Under what conditions should which strategies be chosen? This question lies at the heart of contingency thinking.

Management Science and Computers

For many years, personnel managers have used traditional statistical analyses such as regression and correlation to help deal with personnel problems. More recently, personnel management has begun relying on various "management science" approaches as an aid to decision making. This field has been defined in many different ways. With respect to personnel management, we will conceive of management science as encompassing mathematical, statistical, and other so-called "operations research" models used for decision making in personnel management.[18] Computers have often been utilized with such models as well as for other purposes relevant to personnel decision making.

Before discussing either mathematical models or computerization, it is important to spell out the knowledge that will be required by the reader to understand our treatment of these materials in this text. In dealing with the quantitative management science models, we will *not* delve into any mathematics above college algebra. Rather, our prime focus will be to illustrate how these models have been applied to various problems in personnel management. Thus, the reader will *not* need any sophisticated mathematical background to understand any part of this text. Similarly, we will also discuss numerous aspects of personnel-related problems that have been computerized but will *not* delve into any of the aspects of computerization that would require knowledge of computer languages or other technical facets of computer operation.

For many years managers have used mathematical models in helping them to make decisions. The economic lot size model, designed to meet the objective of minimizing total costs in inventory management, for example, dates back to before 1920. It was not until World War II, however, when mathematical techniques were developed for determining the location of British interception radar, that operations research became an organized approach. In more recent years, the development of electronic computers opened up vast opportunities for dealing with quantitative decision-making models so complex that they could not have been dealt with previously by means of manual calculations. The use of computerized models has had its major thrust in areas such as production management, where it has been possible to quantify many variables. In the behavioral science–oriented areas, such as personnel management, where the quantification of human variables has often been elusive, however, only a relatively small amount of attention has traditionally been given to these models. Although still lagging behind the areas easier to quantify, progress has been made in the use of certain types of management science models in dealing with personnel problems.

Chapter	Network Models	Mathematical Programming	Simulation
3. Human Resource Planning		X	X
4. Recruiting and Selection	X	X	X
7. Employee Development: Design Decisions	X		X
8. Employee Development: Current Problems and Issues			X
9. Wage and Salary Administration	X	X	X
10. Individual Incentives		X	
11. System Incentives		X	
12. Employee Benefits	X		X
14. Employee Management Relations			X

This matrix is intended to be suggestive rather than exhaustive. For a fuller description of the application of these models, see: Paul S. Greenlaw, "Management Science and Personnel Management," *Personnel Journal*, 52 (November 1973), pp. 946–954.

Figure 1–2 *Utilization of basic three types of management science models in personnel.*

The computer, in addition to its utilization with the mathematical models, has served to facilitate the use of traditional statistical techniques in personnel management. It has also been used in many different ways to store and retrieve information, both quantitative and qualitative, to aid in decision making in many of the functional areas of personnel. We will discuss examples of computerization at various places throughout this text. We will also focus special attention on computerized personnel information-decision systems in Chapter 2 after we have examined the role of the personnel department in organizations.

Many quantitative management science models used in personnel are unique to one function and will be discussed as appropriate later when we deal with that function. We have, however, found three basic types of these models which have been used in a variety of personnel functions: (1) network models, (2) mathematical programming, and (3) simulation. These are shown in Figure 1–2. We will now discuss briefly each of these more widely used types of models

Network Models

Two basic types of network models have been utilized for planning and controlling *project type* endeavors in the field of management. One is called the Program Evaluation and Review Technique (PERT) and the other, the Critical Path Method (CPM). We will not describe the differences between these two types, especially since one authority has indicated that "the recent versions of the two original methods have become increas-

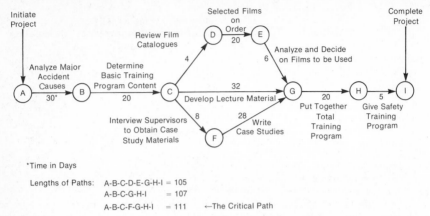

*Time in Days

Lengths of Paths: A-B-C-D-E-G-H-I = 105
A-B-C-G-H-I   = 107
A-B-C-F-G-H-I   = 111   ←The Critical Path

Figure 1-3 *Illustrative project network, safety training program. The activity arrows are not to scale as is also true with real network charts.*

ingly alike."[19] What the network approaches call for is spelling out of all activities that need to be accomplished to complete a project; the relationships between activities; and the development of a schematic diagram such as the simple one illustrated in Figure 1–3 for a training program in the personnel function of safety.

Each arrow in Figure 1–3 represents an activity and each circled letter an event, i.e., the completion of an activity. The numbers next to each activity arrow represent the length of time needed to complete that activity. It must be noted that some activities cannot be undertaken until other prior activities have been completed. In Figure 1–3, for example, activity F-G (writing up case studies) cannot begin until after activity C-F (gathering case materials) has been finished. Of special importance is that all PERT/CPM models will have one or more *critical paths*. The critical path is that path in the network which is the longest. In Figure 1–3, this path is A→B→C→F→G→H→I, which requires 111 days. This means that (1) any delay on the critical path will always delay the whole project and (2) to shorten the time required to complete the project, the critical path must be shortened. This objective may be accomplished by transferring some resources from other paths to the critical path. For instance, in Figure 1–3 the individual or individuals assigned to analyze the training films (E-G) might be asked to spend some time (say two days) to help with final editing of the case studies (F-G), which could shorten the critical path and hence completion time for the whole safety training project. It should be noted that all paths must be completed in any network.

PERT and CPM methods have been utilized historically to deal with highly complex projects — PERT in the development of the Polaris Fleet Ballistic Missile Program, and CPM for large construction projects at the du Pont Company. Of importance to us is the fact that network techniques are also applicable to smaller projects of the types more frequently undertaken in personnel management. In many such projects of lesser magnitude, it may not be necessary to use a computer with network models.

Mathematical Programming

Mathematical programming is the second type of management science model that has been utilized with a variety of personnel problems. There are many different types of mathematical programming. All are similar in that they deal with scarce resources and attempt to minimize or maximize some objective subject to the existence of a number of constraints. We will illustrate this approach briefly by reference to a problem in assigning personnel to different jobs. This type of problem illustrates in a simple manner the notion of maximizing a quantitatively stated goal or objective with the existence of scarce resources and constraints. Our illustrative problem is as follows:[20]

A personnel placement test was given to 100 job applicants to determine their ability in performing on each of three different jobs. The test was scored on a 10-point basis with 10 representing the greatest ability. Analysis of test results showed that three distinct applicant groups existed, as is shown in Figure 1–4. All 40 people in applicant group 1, for example, had the same scores of 1, 4 and 9 for jobs X, Y, and Z, respectively. Also shown in Figure 1–4 is the number of job openings for each of the three jobs in question. Our problem is to assign the individuals to jobs so as to maximize the total of all applicants' test scores.

On a purely logical basis, we might expect that to meet this objective we would surely have to assign people to the two highest valued cells in Figure 1–4 — Z1 and X2. Mathematical programming methods[21] indicate that this is not the case and that the solution shown in Figure 1–4 assigning no one to X2 is the best possible solution.

Because of its simplicity, this mathematical programming example can quickly be solved manually. Practically all "real life" applications of mathematical programming today, however, are complex enough to require, for all practical purpose, the use of computers. In succeeding chapters we will see how such applications have taken place in personnel management in such diverse areas as providing equal employment opportunities for minorities and women to the establishment of work standards for jobs.

		Applicant Group			Job
Job Type	1		2	3	Openings
X	1* / 0		8 / 0	6 / 30	30
Y	4 / 20		7 / 25	2 / 5	50
Z	9 / 20		3 / 0	5 / 0	20
Number of Applicants	40		25	35	100

*Test Scores are the numbers above the diagonal line in each cell; the number of applicants assigned to each cell are indicated below each diagonal line.

Total Points: X3: $30 \times 6 = 180$
Y1: $20 \times 4 = 80$
Y2: $25 \times 7 = 175$
Y3: $5 \times 2 = 10$
Z1: $20 \times 9 = 180$
TOTAL $\overline{625}$

Figure 1-4 *A personnel assignment problem: an illustration of mathematical programming.*

Simulation

The third basic management science technique that has been applied to personnel management is simulation. Simulation has sometimes been referred to as the "unsophisticated mathematician's friend," because it can often be utilized without involving complex mathematics. In simulation, "real life" situations are replicated usually by means of a computer program. That is, the highlights of a real problem are "copied" or represented in one way or another on a computer model. For example, as we will show in Chapter 4, the thought processes of a psychologist in making personnel selection recommendations have been simulated on a computer program, so that the computer can be used as a substitute for a human decision maker. As we will illustrate in Chapter 14, both managements and unions have used computer simulation in collective bargaining negotiations.

SUMMARY AND OVERVIEW

In this chapter we have explored the history of modern personnel management from its origins at about 1900 up to the present. We have seen how personnel management has expanded to encompass a broad and complex set of decision-making problems. Social welfare, scientific management, union growth, manpower shortages in two world wars, and more recently, an expanded technology, the problem of civil rights, and increased governmental constraints have all contributed to this expansion.

Increasingly, management has become more aware of the fact that its most important resources are its people and that the personnel manager's job is to make human-resources decisions designed to meet both the organization's economic and social (or humanitarian) objectives by means of acquiring, developing, rewarding, and maintaining its human resources.

In spite of these advances, the personnel manager in some companies is viewed as a "second-class citizen" and in some cases rightly so, for he performs mostly "routine chores" rather than making key decisions to meet organizational objectives. For example, more than two decades ago, Peter Drucker, a noted management thinker, entitled one chapter of his classic *The Practice of Management*: "Is Personnel Management Bankrupt?"[22] Although his answer to this question was no, he did indicate that personnel managers tended to be "fire fighters" and that the human relations approach avoided the economic dimension of management. These criticisms are still valid today for some firms. Other personnel managers, however, are now developing sophisticated types of long-range planning (such as human resource planning) and are looking at the economic dimension of both the dollar costs and benefits of their programs in light of organizational objectives.

Further, as we have noted in this chapter, increased emphasis is being given to personnel decision making in a systems sense. Two relatively new intellectual thrusts in the last few decades have also sharpened the personnel manager's ability to make effective decisions. Contingency views have helped focus attention on the conditions under which various personnel decision-making approaches will be most effective. Management science techniques and computerization have also made it possible to make better personnel decisions.

In short, personnel management has come a long way since its inception around 1900 but must still overcome many challenges ahead before it becomes a truly mature discipline. In light of these perspectives, we will next turn our attention to personnel's basic role operating within the total organization.

DISCUSSION AND STUDY QUESTIONS

1. In what ways have the following types of variables had an influence on personnel administration?

     a. Chance events.

     b. Federal legislation and/or other actions.

     c. Technological advances in our society.

     d. Changing social and cultural forces in our society.

2. The "Maintenance of Human Resources" should not be considered as a major section of the book. Providing organizational members with benefits should be considered as a "reward." Employee-management relations should also be placed in the "reward" category because especially in unionized firms the main objective of unions is to get more money. Discuss.

3. The text talks of the *meeting* of organizational objectives as fundamental. Isn't the establishment of objectives to be met an even more basic objective? Or, isn't determining *how* to establish objectives which are later to determine which objectives the firm should try to meet even more fundamental? Discuss.

4. Draw a simple flow diagram of the stages in the managerial decision making process. Under what conditions, if any, in your flow diagram would you have *no* problems?

5. A manager is faced with the task of developing an annual performance appraisal for one of his subordinates. Give a specific example of one of each of the following system elements that might be involved in such an appraisal.

     a. Informational inputs.

     b. Memory.

     c. Outputs.

     d. Control.

     e. Feedback.

6. In which of the following operations do you believe that mechanistic rather than organic personnel systems might be more appropriate? Why?

     a. An assembly line.

     b. A research and development department.

     c. A college or university department of management.

     d. A local bank.

7. Larger organizations inherently possess certain characteristics that permit them to utilize more sophisticated personnel techniques in most areas. Discuss.

8. A firm can hire a full-time trained psychologist at an annual salary of $45,000 to analyze and interpret its psychological tests. Additionally, the firm would incur a variable cost of $5/test. The firm also has the option of hiring a local college professor of personnel management to analyze its tests at a cost of $50 per applicant. How large does the firm have to be to justify hiring the trained psychologist, assuming that both he and the college professor are equally competent? Show all calculations.

9. Of the three types of management science models being used across personnel functions, which do you believe would be most practical for the small businessman? Why?

10. Which of the three types of management science models mentioned in the chapter would be most applicable in each of the following situations? Give your reasons why.

     a. A firm has a number of geographically dispersed recruiting offices, recruits from different areas coming to these offices for visits, and wants to minimize the visit costs of all job applicant trips.

b. A firm, taking into account such variables as birth rate, technology, and percentage of the population using its products, wants to determine how large its work force must be 10 years hence.

c. A new option to a firm's retirement program has just been arranged, and employees will have four months in which to decide whether or not to take the new option. In the meantime, personnel must get mimeographed brochures describing the new plan written, printed, and distributed; personnel plans to have special meetings for various employee groups to answer any questions about the plan; and personnel must get special forms on which each employee will "vote" yes or no on the new option to each employee three weeks prior to the final day for their deciding on this issue.

11. Your father has just retired from managing a nonunionized soft drink bottler and distributor, which has been in operation for 30 years. You have served as vice president of the firm for the last two years (and in this capacity have been handling all personnel matters). The distributorship covers a five-county area, and the firm employs 36 full-time and eight part-time employees. These include clerks, bottlers, eight deliverymen (who truck your soft drink bottles to customers), and two district supervisors, each of whom supervises four deliverymen. Turnover among the deliverymen has been high (60 per cent last year), and their accident rates are well above the industry average. What concepts, ideas and techniques presented in Chapter 1 might be useful to you as the new president of this firm?

Notes

[1]*New York Times*, May 29, 1966, Section 4.

[2]The materials in this paragraph were drawn heavily from Henry Eilbert, "The Development of Personnel Management in the United States," *Business History Review*, 33 (Autumn, 1959), pp. 345–364.

[3]Ibid., pp. 352–353.

[4]Ibid., p. 351. Eilbert does not explain why welfare work so declined.

[5]For more information on Taylor's work, see his *Principles of Scientific Management* (New York: Harper & Bros., 1911).

[6]See Eilbert, op. cit., pp. 359 ff. It should also be noted that following World War I, when the wartime labor shortages ceased to exist, the activities of personnel departments were curtailed and a considerable amount of authority was restored to the supervisor.

[7]William E. Mosher, et al., *Public Personnel Administration*, 3rd ed. (New York: Harper and Brothers Publishers, 1950), p. 113.

[8]Cyril Ling, *The Management of Personnel Relations* (Homewood, Ill.: Richard D. Irwin, Inc., 1965), p. 32.

[9]Many of the basic concepts presented in this section are drawn from Max D. Richards and Paul S. Greenlaw, *Management: Decisions and Behavior*, rev. ed. (Homewood, Ill.: Richard D. Irwin, Inc., 1972), Chapters 2–4.

[10]The so-called "human relations" movement is generally considered to have

begun with experiments undertaken at the Hawthorne Plant of the Western Electric Company. For a discussion of these experiments, see Elton Mayo, *The Human Problems of an Industrial Civilization* (New York: The Macmillan Co., 1933); and F. J. Roethlisberger and W. J. Dickson, *Management and the Worker* (Cambridge, Mass.: Harvard University Press, 1939).

[11]This thinking was put forth in Max Weber's so-called "bureaucratic" model of organizations. For a discussion of this model see Max Weber, *The Theory of Social and Economic Organization*, trans. by A. M. Henderson and Talcott Parsons (London: Oxford University Press, 1947).

[12]Tom Burns and G. M. Stalker, *The Management of Innovation* (London: Tavistock, 1961).

[13]Ibid. A discussion of precisely what is meant by "environment" and "certainty" is beyond the scope of this text. One interesting way of viewing environmental certainty may be found in Robert B. Duncan, "Characteristics of Organizational Environments and Perceived Environmental Uncertainty," *Administrative Science Quarterly*, 17 (September, 1972), pp. 313–327.

[14]A classic work on the impact of technology on organizational behavior is Joan Woodward, *Industrial Organization: Theory and Practice* (London: Oxford University Press, 1965). For a general overview of several researchers' positions on the importance of technology on organization design, see: Robert T. Keller, "A Look at the Sociotechnical System," *California Management Review*, 15 (Fall, 1972), pp. 86–91.

[15]For a discussion of some of these factors see, for example, Y. K. Shetty and Howard M. Carlisle, "A Contingency Model of Organizational Design," *California Management Review*, 15 (Fall, 1972), pp. 38–45.

[16]Lorsch and Lawrence have found, for example, that in the plastics industry the techno-economic sector of firms tended to exist in a "highly certain" environment while the scientific sector had a "very uncertain" environment. See Jay W. Lorsch, "Introduction to the Structural Design of Organizations," in Gene W. Dalton, et al., *Organization Structure and Design* (Homewood, Ill.: Richard D. Irwin, Inc., and the Dorsey Press, 1970), p. 6. For a concise summary of some of the findings of Lawrence and Lorsch, see Charles J. Coleman and David D. Palmer, "Organizational Application of Systems Theory," *Business Horizons*, 16 (December, 1973), pp. 80–81.

[17]For a discussion of organizational size, see John R. Kimberly, "Organizational Size and the Structuralist Perspective: A Review, Critique, and Proposal," *Administrative Science Quarterly*, 21 (December, 1976), pp. 571–597.

[18]One technical point deserves consideration here. "Operations research" and "management science" are often thought of as being synonymous terms, although some individuals have held that management science is broader than operations research since it deals with human behavioral variables to a greater degree. We will use these terms interchangeably when referring to quantitative decision models in the field of personnel.

[19]Joseph J. Moder and Cecil R. Phillips, *Project Management with CPM and PERT*, 2nd ed. (New York: Van Nostrand Reinhold Co., 1970), p. 337.

[20]This example is patterned after one presented in Richards and Greenlaw, op. cit., pp. 527–528.

[21]This problem was solved by application of the transportation method of linear programming.

[22]Peter Drucker, *The Practice of Management* (New York: Harper & Bros., 1954), Chapter 21.

2

THE PERSONNEL DEPARTMENT

The personnel department in organizations is in a unique position. If well managed, it may become involved in a wider range of activities than any other function in the organization. At the same time, every person in the organization is a "personnel man" in the sense that they are dealing with personnel decision problems on a day-to-day basis. For example, a first line supervisor training or disciplining his employees, inducing them to follow safety standards, and so forth, is engaged in personnel decision making.[1]

In this chapter, we will focus attention on several key facets of the operation of the personnel department and consider some of the more important problems it faces. This chapter is divided into six sections. First, we will make some observations about individuals occupying personnel positions and the work that they perform. Second, we will view personnel as a staff department and show what roles it performs and what problems it may face assuming such roles. Third, we will turn our attention to the power and stature of today's personnel department. Fourth, we will indicate some of the ways in which personnel departments may be managed so as to meet organizational objectives. Fifth, we will explore the role of the computer in personnel management, with a specific focus on personnel information-decision systems. Finally, we will assess the impact of government on personnel management and the personnel department.

THE PERSONNEL MANAGER AND PERSONNEL WORK

Personnel work is heterogeneous, with involved individuals having many different backgrounds and performing many different kinds of work. In North America, for example, we would find in personnel departments people with backgrounds as "lawyers, engineers, psychologists, teachers and accountants."[2] Turning our attention to Europe, differences in education and work background are strikingly diverse and it is "far from clear what it takes to be a good personnel man."[3] In Europe, most personnel managers have had one of several backgrounds. These include academic degrees in law, economics, business administration, or in one of the social sciences or a career in the military services or in the company as an accountant, wage and salary administrator, or in a "technical" area such as production.[4]

Such differences are not hard to explain, considering the diversity of personnel work. Training and development activities call for backgrounds in learning theory and psychology; backgrounds in both psychology and engineering would be useful in safety management, while labor relations work is highly legalistic and economic in orientation.

It should also be pointed out that there is considerable diversity with respect to the degree of specialization involved in the work of individuals in personnel. Some people doing personnel work are generalists, who deal with many diverse problems and work with many different people on a day-to-day basis. For example, the personnel manager in a geographical division of a supermarket chain might be engaged on any single day in such activities as placing an advertisement in a newspaper for clerical help to work in a new store soon to open, explaining to an employee who is about to retire what his pension rights are, or handling a medical insurance claim for another employee.

At the other extreme, in many larger organizations, we find (in addition to personnel generalists) a number of highly specialized personnel professionals. For example, in one company there were around 30 managers and professionals in the firm's corporate headquarters, each performing specialized personnel functions. One individual dealt with nothing but wage and salary administration for the company; another individual, who was not a manager, spent much of his time developing training materials for the firm's management development programs; and so forth.

Two final observations concerning the degree of specialization in personnel work are in order. First is that the top personnel manager of any operating unit must be a generalist. The specialists indicated in the last example all reported to managers who were under the direction of a "generalist" personnel vice president. This individual was responsible for all personnel work undertaken in the company just as the supermarket personnel manager was responsible for all personnel work in his geographical division.[5]

The second observation is that this discussion should quickly dispel the notion held by some individuals not familiar with personnel work that they would "like to get into personnel because they like *dealing with people.*" As we have seen, the supermarket personnel manager had numerous daily contacts with people. The individual developing training materials, however, spent many weeks at a time working on projects, often alone, and with only moderate interaction with others. Thus, people with quite different interests and personality characteristics may find satisfaction in some type of personnel work.

Another important point that has received much less attention than those made thus far in this chapter is that personnel work in certain types of firms may vary over time as the firm goes through product (or project) *life cycles.* In such firms, operational "activities — and personnel programs — revolve around a succession of market phases of major products. Defined uniquely by each industry's experience, this pattern of changes is caused by such factors as volatile tastes of buyers, competitive encroachments, technological developments, and new governmental regulations."[6] Five key stages in a product's life style, for example, have been identified by Fox:[7]

1. Precommercialization,
2. Product introduction,
3. Growth of product sales,
4. Maturity in which the product's sales trends is level, and
5. Decline in sales.

That the personnel manager's focus of attention will vary as the firm goes through such cycles may be illustrated by a few examples. As a new product is introduced, manufacturing processes need "debugging" and personnel may be required to help industrial engineers set methods and time standards. Once the product has reached the growth stage, considerable effort will be needed to recruit and train additional workers. At the decline stage, on the other hand, personnel may aid displaced workers in finding other jobs in the firm, and in some cases may encourage workers who are unable to be relocated to take an early retirement.

Although there has not been a great deal of research on the personnel department's role in life-cycle analysis, certain hypotheses of a contingency nature may be made. In some industries, such as department stores, there are relatively few if any major "products" being developed, although such industries may experience growth, maturity, and decline. Therefore, the life-cycle type of analysis may not be highly relevant for personnel managers in such operations. At the other extreme, however, explicit recognition even to the extent of developing special types of organizational structures[8] to meet project life-cycle needs has occurred in industries such as aerospace. Here, during the life cycle of many projects, such as a five year ballistic missle project, " the bulk of the engineering efforts required might be expended during the first two years . . . [and then] . . . at a later time, the number of production man hours required for the project would be at its maximum."[9]

The important point to be gained from this discussion is that personnel managers should be familiar enough with their organization's operations that they can plan ahead to meet the human resource requirements of all phases of product life cycles. Unfortunately, some surveys have shown that a majority of corporate personnel managers have not known such key operational variables as what the dollar volume of their company's sales was or what their firm's profit level was. In light of this, it is not surprising that one chief executive officer of a firm "when asked what qualifications he would like to see in his personnel director, replied, 'The ability to read and understand the company's financial statement.'"[10]

Another characteristic of personnel work that has received insufficient attention is the impact of economic conditions on the personnel department. From a historical standpoint it appears that interest in personnel management often has been highest when economic conditions are good or expanding and labor is in short supply. When economic conditions are poor or contracting and there is an oversupply of labor, however, the interest in personnel management frequently appears to fade. Three reasons for such conditions can be put forth. First, much of the work of the personnel department cannot be shown directly to affect sales and profits. The absence of a production worker or a salesperson, on the other hand, often can be seen to result directly in reduced production or sales. In bad times, therefore, persons in marketing and production are more likely to be retained than are those in the personnel department. Second, organizations may believe that they can hire more freely in bad times because of the oversupply of labor. Therefore, they may be less concerned with such personnel functions as recruiting, selection, and training and development. Third, there may be a real decrease in the need for certain types of personnel work. For example, if the firm is *not* hiring, it may make sense to curtail its recruiting activities, or if workers have been laid off, there may not be much of a need for training and development programs, particularly if the retained workers are experienced.

In spite of poor economic conditions from time to time, however, the personnel department's scope of activities has continued to expand historically (See Chapter 1). Even in poor times, most established personnel programs are not completely eliminated — they are only cut back. For example, in the 1974-1975 recession, many training and development programs were reduced, but generally they were not completely eliminated.

In spite of economic downturns and the fact that some personnel managers do not exert a very strong influence in their firms, personnel, as we have pointed out, can become involved in a wider range of activities than any other function in an organization. This being the case, today's personnel manager can wield considerable power as a staff officer and also can be in a favorable position to move up in his organization to a top-level managerial position. For example, it was pointed out in 1974 that the chairman of Delta Airlines came from a labor relations and personnel background; the board chairman of Tenneco started his career as a personnel manager; "for many years Eli Lilly has given its top people the opportunity to spend some time in key personnel jobs"; and, interestingly, personnel departments in Japan were frequently seen as a route to the top in organizations.[11]

THE PERSONNEL DEPARTMENT

At the beginning of this chapter we indicated that everyone in organizations is involved in personnel-type activities. Why, then, it may be asked, do firms centralize such functions as psychological testing or wage and salary administration into one personnel department? One basic answer to this question is that organizational efficiency may be achieved through specialization. It would be extremely inefficient to train all the organization's employees to administer and interpret psychological tests, engage in wage and salary surveys, and so on. Further, centralization of personnel activities permits the development and application of consistent policies and rules throughout the organization.

Personnel as a Staff Department

Personnel is considered a *staff* department within the organization rather than a line one. Line operations in firms are normally those that deal directly with the organization's output — sales and production in manufacturing — while staff helps support these functions with professional expertise.

Traditionally, line managers were considered able to exercise command power over their subordinates, while staff managers could only advise or counsel line members in an orgainzation. According to this view, in a manufacturing plant of 1500 to 2000 employees headed by a production manager, the latter would wield command power over his supervisors, who in turn would have command power over the production workers reporting to them. Personnel as a staff department, however, would report to the production manager and only have the power to render advice and counsel to the line organization. Such a relationship is illustrated in Figure 2–1. Personnel managers do, of course, have direct line relationships with their *own* subordinates and, hence, have command power over them.

Of key significance is that this dichotomy of line and staff has been found to be an inadequate way of describing organizational relationships. In actual practice, the distinction between line and staff is a blurred one. In some situations, for example, the personnel staff may technically only provide advice, but the advice would be so overwhelmingly strong that line management would have no choice but to make the decision "recommended" by personnel. For example, the personnel manager depicted in Figure 2–1 might have engaged in research that showed conclusively that a high percentage of newly hired employees performing a job in one department who are 35 years of age or older do not have the required finger dexterity for learning how to do a particular job, while the probabilities for success on the job are considerably higher for newly employed workers 30 years or less in age. If he presents this informational input to the production manager and the latter accepts the personnel manager's advice to set up a

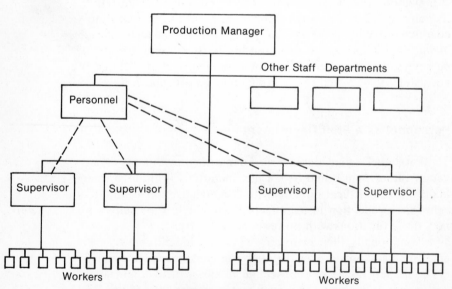

Figure 2–1 *Illustrative line-staff relationships.*

maximum age limit on this job, who is really making the decision? Overtly, it would be the plant manager, but the individual wielding the real power in this situation would be the personnel manager. This situation results because the personnel manager has *control over basic information,* a staff characteristic that we will examine more thoroughly later in this chapter.

We should emphasize here that in actual practice the personnel manager may also wield direct "command power" over supervisors such as shown in Figure 2–1, even though they do not report to him. For example, in a company emphasizing safety, the personnel manager may see that a safety violation exists in a particular supervisor's department, and may "advise" the supervisor to correct the situation. Here, the supervisor, although not reporting to the personnel manager, may take the "advice" as a command, knowing that if any injury occurs subsequent to this warning, he will have to account for his actions to his superior, the production manager.

Personnel Functions and Line-Staff Problems

The personnel department has been perceived as having many different kinds of relationships with other organizational units. The personnel manager has been viewed as a planner, a change agent, an educator to line managers, and so forth. Among the many role relationships attributed to the personnel department, four stand out as being commonly accepted by students of personnel. First is the function of providing advice and counsel, as indicated earlier. Second, personnel managers as staff officers are frequently called on to provide *services* for the other functions in the organization. Among the services that personnel can provide is everything from screening job applicants with psychological tests and other selection techniques to managing the company's cafeteria. Third, the personnel manager may be called on to develop policies, rules, and regulations with the approval of top line management that are binding on other managers and organizational members. For example, with line management's blessing, personnel may prescribe that a particular battery of psychological tests must be given to all applicants for managerial or professional jobs. Although this role results in personnel developing policies that control organization members' behavior, we will refer to it as "policy formulation" rather than "control." We will reserve this latter term for the fourth role personnel assumes as a staff department. This fourth role, which has been referred to as both "audit" and "control," calls for personnel to look at certain company performance standards, compare actual performance with these standards, and attempt to correct any deficiencies between actual and desired performance. For example, the personnel manager may examine absenteeism rates in a particular production department, observe that the rates are well above acceptable standards set by management, and discuss the problem with the departmental supervisor in an effort to reduce absenteeism.

These four role relationships may lead to interorganizational frictions. With regard to the providing of services, line management may ask staff to provide too many services or services which are ill-advised; there may be conflicts over scarce services; or some line departments may want to do certain types of work themselves and resist staff performance of services. To illustrate one of these points — line's asking for ill-advised services — one training director in a good sized manufacturing operation ran into the following situation: Both his supervisor, the personnel manager, and the latter's superior, the plant manager, would frequently run across articles in professional management or personnel journals suggesting new types of training programs, and bring them to his attention. In many cases, such training programs were theoretically unsound in his opinion. For this reason, the training director considered as one important facet of his position the ability of influencing line management to say "no" to the establishment of poor programs such as oversimplified human relations training.

Perhaps even more serious than these service-type problems are the *inherently* contradictory roles of advisor and auditor. The personnel manager is expected to be a trusted advisor to line managers. Effectiveness in this role "requires that line feel free to discuss the problems being confronted."[12] The personnel staff at the same time is expected to inspect and evaluate line performance. Many observers "contend that it is unrealistic to expect line to confide in a staff helper who also monitors his performance."[13] One approach developed to help alleviate such conflict situations is for the personnel manager to go directly to the line manager whose operation has become out of control and help him improve his performance without going to the manager's boss with the negative information which would put the line manager "on the spot." One author was involved in a situation in which the "direct help" approach worked quite effectively. This example does not concern staff-line relationships but rather staff-staff relationships, on which we will focus our attention later. The basic principle and psychodynamics involved, however, are essentially the same as would be found in a line-staff relationship so that this example provides a clear picture of the source of help approach:

For years, a large supermarket chain had had personnel managers in each of its geographically dispersed divisions administer psychological tests for college degree job applicants but required the field personnel managers to send the tests to a specialized department in its central office for test interpretation. This approach worked fairly well until a period in which the labor market got tight. In such cases, the divisional personnel managers could not make any recommendations to their superiors (divisional vice presidents) until after the tests had been sent to and returned from the centralized corporate staff for interpretation — which in some cases took a week or ten days. Thus, no job offers could be made to college graduates on the spot when they made their trip to the division and were tested and interviewed by the divisional management. Top management believed that the whole college recruiting effort could be improved if psychological test interpretation as well as administration were to be delegated to the divisional personnel managers. This would enable the company to tender immediate offers to promising job seekers who might well accept an offer with another firm if they had to wait a week or ten days before receiving an offer from the supermarket chain.

The firm's centralized staff personnel department was asked to develop manuals explaining how its tests should be interpreted, and held training sessions to teach all divisional personnel managers how to interpret the tests.

Even though the interpretation work had been decentralized, the corporate personnel staff was still responsible for ensuring that test interpretation would be handled properly throughout all divisions in the company. This required a control mechanism to be established by corporate personnel. Initially, each divisional personnel manager was required to send a copy of all his test interpretations to corporate personnel for inspection. Then, if the centralized staff found any division personnel managers who were not making correct interpretations, it would phone the personnel manager who was having problems. A trip would be arranged for one of centralized personnel's members to visit the division, spending a day going over the interpretation problems with the divisional personnel manager. Following the source of help concept, none of the divisional vice presidents were told that their personnel manager was performing poorly in test interpretation. They were simply informed that the centralized personnel staff representative was visiting the division to "talk over the new testing program" with the field personnel manager.

With this approach all division personnel managers were handling the test interpretation properly within a few months. If this approach had not worked and numerous poor candidates had been hired, the divisional vice-presidents, of course, would have had to eventually be informed of the situation.

Finally, we should indicate that the policy formulation role may also create line-staff problems. Personnel may generate a new policy with the approval of top management that is not completely compatible with other goals set for other organizational units. For example, a new safety policy may lead to lower production per employee in certain manufacturing departments and hence conflict with the department's output objectives.

In one research study, it is interesting to note that the attitude of line management toward these four personnel role relationships was as follows: "Managers did not indicate a desire to have the personnel staff more actively involved than it is. In most instances, fewer managers, rather than more, are requesting involvement by the personnel department."[14] This study also found that more line managers would welcome advice from personnel, but fewer wanted personnel involvement in policy, and even fewer wanted personnel performing service and control activities.[15]

In addition to the conflicts involved in personnel's role relationships, there exist certain status incongruencies that may interfere with effective staff-line relationships. By status incongruencies we mean that there are a number of characteristics that individuals possess which gave them status within the company — e. g., education, work experience, seniority in an organization, and so forth. When two people interact and one of them has more status, according to most indicators, status congruency exists and the individuals tend to be aware of the proper roles they should assume in interacting with each other. However, if one individual has, for example, more education, but considerably less seniority in the organization we have some status incongruency and it may be difficult for the individuals to relate to each other. As one authority has pointed out, such ambiguity

. . . tends to result in stress and various other reactions . . . . For example, a college educated assembler might disturb other assemblers in a department who would then either ignore him or behave in an unfriendly way toward him and thus cause him to be uncomfortable.[16]

In the personnel line-staff relationship, a number of incongruencies often exist. For example, personnel managers (and professional nonmanagers) often have more education than many line officials in the company, they may be closer than middle-line managers in reporting to top management, and they may have specialized information that their line counterparts do not possess. At the same time, however, they may well have less seniority in the organization than many of the line managers with whom they interact and make less money than line. A particular problem of status incongruency in today's organization concerns the recently employed, young, college-educated female, who must interact with the more senior, noncollege-educated male. Under such conditions, it is not hard to see why personnel as a staff department may find it uncomfortable to relate to some line managers and vice versa.

In light of the line-staff problems discussed thus far, some writers have attempted to view personnel in different ways than the traditional staff role. For example, certain individuals have taken a much broader conception of personnel:

. . . total human resources [should] be controlled through a central point via the vehicle of the human resources programming, planning and budgeting . . .[and] . . . it is recommended that the director of human resources management be given a major role in guiding the structuring of the organization and control of the people aspects.[17]

In making such a recommendation, this author did recognize that with such a dominant role, the personnel manager might easily undermine superior-subordinate relations.

The role of line and staff in an organization has also been viewed in decision-making and systems terms. Two authors who have taken such a perspective have indicated that the systems view rejects the development of any new "global prescriptions for the ills between line and staff."[18] They contend that to foster line-staff effectiveness in any organization an analysis of interpersonal work flows and interaction patterns existing in that organization is required; and, "since the goal of line-staff interaction is effective decision making, . . . decision-making roles [should] be defined according to the best interests of the organization with regard to the problem in question."[19] Such a systems view emphasizing work flow analysis dates back at least to the 1960's,[20] and may be an effective way of analyzing staff-line problems. This type of analysis will often require developing new patterns of role relationships and different supporting organizational structures and processes before it can be operationalized.[21] For example, an important goal is to increase the legitimacy of each decision maker as perceived by his colleagues, i. e., that his right to make decisions is "proper." We will discuss some of the ways that the role of personnel managers may be legitimatized later in this chapter.

Staff Parallelism

As in the previous example of decentralizing test interpretation, a large firm may have personnel staff paralleling each other — one at the corporation level and one at each of the operational levels in the organization.[22] This situation is commonly referred to as "staff parallelism," and often will lead to the evolution of relationships somewhat different from typical line-staff ones. An example of staff parallelism is indicated in Figure 2-2.[23]

As indicated previously, personnel managers (except the top manager) in the corporate headquarters perform specialized types of personnel work, while their divisional counterparts are personnel generalists. A basic task of many corporate staff members is to formulate company policies, which are then administered by the operating divisions. Traditionally, the central staff may en-

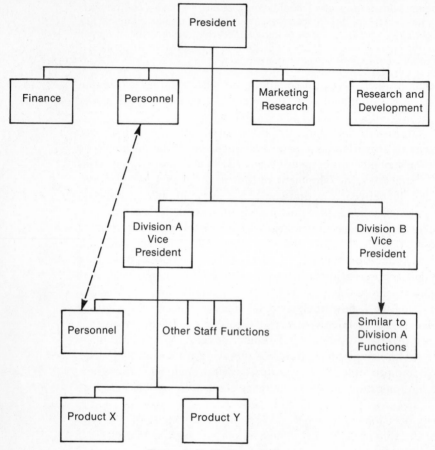

Figure 2-2 *Staff parallelism.*

gage in research activities, serve as consultants to the divisions, and, as with our previous test interpretation example, assume the audit or control role to ensure that all divisional personnel managers are following corporate policies.

In such situations, the operating personnel managers are "men in the middle" in the sense that they report directly to their divisional manager yet are called on to follow personnel practices developed by the corporate staff. Their continued employment, merit raises, and possibly promotion into a line position in the operating unit are all primarily determined by their immediate superior. On the other hand, possible promotions to the central office personnel department and promotions to personnel management positions in other larger divisions where more responsibilities are called for require them to be in the good graces of the corporate personnel staff. In some cases, the operating vice president may resist certain corporate personnel policies and the division personnel manager may find himself in a conflict situation. In such a man-in-the middle position, the divisional personnel manager's proper role has been well described by Osgood, who deals with a situation in which a field personnel manager reports to a district marketing manager:

He has a mutual responsibility with the district marketing manager for employee welfare . . . [etc.] . . . within the district, but he also has the corporate responsibility of keeping the district manager advised about all company personnel matters, including the reasons behind new releases and changes in policy. It is imperative that he make specific recommendations for changes within the district. When he sees that something is being done in his district that is contrary to company personnel policies or practices, it is up to him to appraise his own manager. He is to keep the district manager out of "personnel trouble," but he must go beyond a passive role in supporting his district manager, even to the point of disagreeing with him about a particular personnel policy and making an active attempt to change it.[24]

Osgood's point that the personnel manager must take an active rather than passive role leads us to the next question we will cover in this chapter — just what is the power and stature of personnel management?

THE POWER AND STATURE OF PERSONNEL MANAGEMENT

Personnel departments and managers from different organizations differ considerably in the amount of power and stature they hold. One important reason for this is that there is little consensus among firms as to exactly what kinds of work the personnel manager should do. At one extreme, we find

. . . low-status "personnel departments" doing little more than wage and salary administration, and on the other end, high-status groups carrying the same name but deeply involved in the organization's long-term objective setting and the development of its management structure, with all kinds of possibilities in between.[25]

A basic reason for these differences is the degree to which top management gives support to the personnel function. There seems to be almost unanimous agreement among personnel management thinkers that the "leadership displayed by top executives cannot be overemphasized because they are the ultimate determiners of personnel philosophy."[26] From an "organizational climate" point of view, if an organization is static and mechanistic, if its overall approach to management is one of reaction instead of action, if it focuses attention only on short-term problems, and if its managers are rewarded only for dealing with problems but not opportunities, personnel will probably not perform effectively.[27] Even with top management support and a favorable organizational climate, of course, the personnel manager *himself* must be proactive rather than simply waiting for problems to come to him instead of seeking out new and creative personnel opportunities. This is especially true since many managers in organizations do not have a "clear understanding of the responsibilities and relationships within the personnel function."[28]

Today, more than ever before, there exists an opportunity for many personnel managers to assume more of a proactive and dynamic role if they choose to. More knowledge about personnel management is available to them today than ever before, and they can use new technological developments to increase their possession of information and expertise, which will, in turn, enhance their power and influence in relating to line managers and others in organizations. As Coleman and Rich have phrased it:

> The new techniques that have developed in such areas as manufacturing, accounting and computer applications have often put staff personnel into a position in which they possess more of the data and skills relevant to critical organizational problems than line officials.[29]

Especially relevant here for the personnel manager is the computer, which can be developed to provide rather sophisticated personnel information-decision systems, particularly in larger firms. Regardless of such possibilities, however, it may take other specific kinds of action to enhance the power and status of the personnel manager so that he will be able to effectively help meet organization goals and individual needs.

Enhancing Power and Stature

There are a number of ways in which the organization may make decisions explicitly aimed at enhancing the power and stature of its personnel department. One of the most important of these is the assignment of the personnel manager to a high level in the organizational hierarchy — preferably as a vice president reporting directly to the president of the firm. This action will not only provide status to the personnel department; it will also provide a vehicle for bringing good ideas for personnel programs directly to the organization's top executive officer rather than having them get lost in the organization, as is often the case if personnel reports to low-level executives.

Several companies have attempted to enhance the power of

personnel in just such a manner. It was reported in 1975 that the United California Bank, for example, established not just a vice president but rather a senior vice president of personnel, while RCA had an executive vice president for industrial relations. In each of these two cases, the vice presidents reported directly to their respective presidents.[30] Further, in some unionized companies in which labor relations historically have assumed more importance than many other phases of personnel, these two tasks have been split, and a vice president for personnel has been established with the same hierarchical status as his labor relations counterpart. Such an approach was taken by General Motors in 1971, and since that time it has also been adopted by such companies as Weyerhaeuser, AT&T, and Burlington Industries.[31] To carry this notion even further, some individuals have emphasized that not only should personnel report directly to the president of the firm, but it also should be represented on the board of directors, When insiders are on the board of directors, one of them may be the top personnel staff member. This approach, while rare, has been utilized by such firms as Brown and Williamson, United Parcel Service, and RCA.[32]

If the personnel manager has been placed in a top-level position, his status and role may be made to appear more legitimate through such techniques as providing him with an impressive title (such as vice president for human resources), giving him attractive office space and equipment, and placing him in close physical proximity to the president of the firm to enhance interpersonal relations between the two. "However, to be vested with legitimacy, the decision-maker must be accepted by others on the basis of competence."[33] A key variable, which bears directly on the perception of competence by others in the organization, is the possession of information. As mentioned, the possibility of developing computerized information-decision systems affords the personnel manager an excellent opportunity to have considerable pertinent information to aid in making personnel decisions.

Enhancing the power and influence of personnel may also be undertaken by what is called the cross-training approach. This approach involves sending out personnel professionals to take over line jobs they can handle while at the same time bringing line officials to take over certain duties in the personnel department. This arrangement provides not only a broadening of the experience of the personnel person, but also gives line managers a better understanding of personnel work that may render them more supportive of personnel in the future. Such an approach, of course, is feasible only to the extent that the cross-training can be effected without having to provide either the personnel individual or the line official with too lengthy and costly training.[34]

The Implications of Personnel Power

Should personnel continue to gain more decision-making responsibilities and be vested with greater power, two important implications are evident. First, the training of personnel managers will have to be updated. In discussing the impact of automation upon personnel, one authority has stated that:

> Future personnel executives would have difficulties to perform their functions without a graduate degree in personnel administration, the curriculum of which should include such subjects as linear programming, game theory and organization planning.[35]

The second implication of a more influential personnel department is that it may assume too much power, which can undermine the authority of line managers. For example, in one company the personnel manager and his staff made all the final selection decisions for its largest plant. This gave the supervisor an excellent chance to "pass the buck" to the personnel department if the new employees' performances were poor — even though such performance turned out this way largely because the supervisor did not bother to train the employees properly. The supervisor could simply say that the personnel department had given him a "poor worker" and this was why the performance was inadequate. To overcome this problem, the selection process was modified so that personnel continued to interview, test, and make recommendations on all new employees, but the supervisors were given the power to make all final selection decisions. Having chosen the new employees themselves, the supervisors could no longer shift the blame back to personnel if a worker's performance was below par.

Even though personnel has been gaining more power and stature, there are dangers in giving it too much power. What is needed most is some type of balance of line-staff power that will meet the objectives of the organization most fully. This balance may be a delicate one; how far to go in either direction must be viewed in situational terms with respect to each decision type and the particular organization with which one is dealing.

THE PERSONNEL DEPARTMENT: MANAGEMENT AND RESOURCE ALLOCATION

As indicated in Chapter 1, personnel managers make decisions to meet organizational (and individual) objectives. In doing so they are confronted with various alternative courses of action but are constrained by scarce resources. In some cases, personnel departments have not paid adequate attention to meeting organizational goals, nor to the economic implications of their decisions. In some personnel departments, many of the activities undertaken have become ends in themselves. Some individuals have become so "ultraspecialized and punctilious that they end up knowing everything about nothing . . . [which] results, of course, in serious goal-displacement behavior in many organizations."[36] Further, different activities carried out within personnel departments themselves have often not been integrated and may be working at cross-purposes with respect to the attainment of organizational objectives. For example, those concerned with personnel's functions of compensation and employee benefits may be dealing with adjusting compensation and benefits to meet both internal and external pressures but seldom are "specifically aware of the relevance of organization development plans, long-range manpower plans, and organization change programs to the optimum design of a compensation system."[37]

To help ensure that departmental activities will meet organizational objectives, a management philosophy and approach called "Management by Objectives," or MBO, has been developed. Further, as an aid to determining how economic resources should be allocated to various activities so that organizational objectives will be better met, a resource allocation technique called program budgeting has been designed. One tool that may be useful in program budgeting is an approach called "cost-benefit" analysis. In the following sections, we will treat each of these approaches and indicate their application to the personnel department and its mission of meeting organizational objectives.

Management By Objectives (MBO)

For a number of years, many organizations have successfully been following a philosophy of management called MBO. This philosophy was first brought to the attention of managers in the 1950's by Peter Drucker.[38] MBO has been perceived both as a general approach to managing organizations and as a specific performance appraisal method making up one part of this general approach. We will focus attention on these performance appraisal aspects in Chapter 5. Here, we will give attention to the more general aspects of MBO as a viable managerial approach within the personnel department.

Although there are many different forms of MBO, the approach may be seen as one that focuses attention on the achievement of organizational objectives rather than the performance of activities per se. Essentially, MBO provides the link between individual job performance and the departmental goals, which are in turn linked to higher-level and ultimately overall organization objectives. For example, a manufacturing plant's personnel manager might develop a new selection procedure for job applicants that would lead to better performance and lower turnover in the plant, which would reduce manufacturing expenses, which in turn would contribute to greater profitability for the firm as a whole.

The MBO process usually involves the following basic steps: First, managers meet with their subordinates and together set objectives for the subordinates for a specific time period. Second, the objectives set are translated into action plans and implemented. Finally, individuals receive feedback regarding the extent to which their objectives have been met so that they can modify their behavior if necessary.

Several advantages have been claimed for the MBO approach. First, by focusing the attention of all managers on objectives and goals, MBO, if carried out properly, may increase the probability of linking individual performance to organizational objectives. As Hellriegel and Slocum have pointed out: "MBO may reduce the tendency for goals or objectives to be displaced because of an undue emphasis on rules, conformist behavior, and rigid behavior in light of changed or special job circumstances."[39] Second, by giving individual managers an opportunity to participate in goal setting, certain advantages may accrue:

1. Participation in goal setting may lead some managers to become more committed to the goals set.
2. The participation may enhance such managerial skills as problem solving.
3. The feedback given to individuals in MBO discussions with their supervisors lets them know better how they stand and provides an integral part of the performance appraisal process (which we will discuss in Chapter 5).

Implementing MBO successfully, however, requires facing certain problems. First, it may be very difficult in some cases to link individual efforts clearly and specifically to higher level goals. For example, suppose that a training specialist in a large corporate personnel department is developing a case study for use in a two-week management development program to be held for 25 of the firm's middle-level managers with the immediate objective of improving their "decision-making skills." How can we be sure that developing the case study will contribute toward "bettering" the training program? How can we be sure that the training program itself will really help improve the trainees' "decision-making" skills so that they will be more effective managers? So many variables influence all of these links that it would be extremely difficult to measure whether the individual writing the case study is really doing work that ultimately better helps to meet overall organizational objectives.

Second, although most supporters of MBO believe that goals should be quantified as much as possible, there is a danger that if too much emphasis is put on quantification, very important but hard to quantify goals may never be established because managers will shy away from them. This problem may be a more serious one in the personnel department than in organizational units such as production, where output levels are easier to quantify. For example, management training and development objectives may be ignored because of the difficulty in measuring the outputs of these efforts, as in the preceding example.

Third, in some cases, organizational goals will conflict with each other, so that undertaking one activity may lead to the greater attainment of one objective but only at the expense of another. For example, as indicated earlier in this chapter, a new safety policy put forth by personnel may conflict with the firm's production output objectives.[40]

In spite of such implementation problems, MBO has been utilized effectively in many firms and the approach has many supporters. Further, some authorities believe that MBO problems are often created *not* by the approach itself but rather by "how it is actually applied in organizations."[41] Although there may be more difficulties in using MBO in personnel departments than in other organizational units because of the intangible nature of personnel's objective, it may be a viable approach for personnel managers to consider. This may be especially so if MBO can be supplemented by an approach designed to evaluate both quantitative and qualitative programs designed to meet organizational objectives—program budgeting.

Program Budgeting

In the past, as is still true today, budgets of many organizations have focused attention on expenditures for such items as salaries, office equipment, and transportation without considering what objectives are being met by the allocation of these resources. To help overcome this problem, program budgeting has been designed toward knowing what the organization is spending on each program, as well as the benefits of each in terms of meeting organizational objectives. The basic idea underlying program budgeting

. . . is that the organization's budget be directly related to its objectives and major programs *rather* than represent simply a classification of financial obligations and expenditures by object class — i.e., by categories such as personnel, travel expenses, printing and reproduction of company brochures.[42]

This program budgeting emphasis does not ignore these object class items. With program budgeting, however, all expenditures should be related to the organization's overall objectives and subobjectives as much as possible.

There are three basic types of cost information needed for program budgeting:

(1) A system for budgeting and coding nonstaff expenses as they occur, by program and by type of expenditure; (2) monthly estimates of staff time devoted to each program; and (3) annual assumptions regarding the allocation of overhead expenses by program.[43]

In some cases, nonstaff expenses may all be allocated to one program budget. When this is not the case, they may be assigned on the basis of the primary program served. When expenditures cannot clearly be assigned to one program, however, they may be placed in an administrative expense category.

The largest expenditures in the personnel department are the costs of salaries and benefits of the members of the department. When any staff members work on more than one program, program-oriented time reporting can be utilized, in which employees provide estimates of the time spent on each program, say on a monthly basis. Such breakdowns need not be very fine—units of half days are usually adequate. Finally, overhead costs such as rent and utilities may be prorated to each personnel unit, and then, by means of reasonably good estimates, may be assigned to each program carried out by the unit.[44]

Even though the costing aspects of program budgeting are simple enough to understand conceptually, there are a number of obstacles for their implementation. As Borgeson has pointed out, for example:

1. It is time consuming and difficult to pinpoint, predict, and measure the costs of many of the personnel department's activities.
2. Many important personnel activities require working on more than one program at a time and also require collaboration with other organizational units, so that it is difficult to allocate staff costs among programs.
3. Many personnel managers do not have a fully developed awareness of costs, as is true with many staff departments.[45]

In light of such difficulties, cost allocation to programs to meet organizational objectives requires considerable skill and judgment on the part of the personnel manager.

Thus far, our emphasis has been on program costs. Although sometimes very difficult to ascertain and allocate, costs are usually much more determinable than are the benefits to be gained from any particular program. This is particularly true in the personnel department, as many of its outputs are intangible and difficult to deal with. As one observer has noted:

There are special and sometimes insuperable difficulties in measuring the effectiveness of most personnel activities in terms of dollar value received; . . . most can be "justified" only on the basis of necessity, logic and experience (or even faith), rather than in terms of how they made or saved money for the company.[46]

In spite of the difficulties in dealing with both program costs and benefits, many business firms and governmental organizations have utilized program budgeting approaches in personnel work in which both costs and benefits have been estimated and measured and the programs developed have been related to overall organization objectives. As an example, one such approach was first implemented in the Xerox Corporation in 1971 as part of a long range human resource planning effort.[47] The first of four basic procedural steps incorporated in this program budgeting approach was simply to define and describe various program alternatives. Then, the legal requirements, if any, associated with each program were examined. Since legal requirements such as "affirmative action" to ensure nondiscrimination in selection programs had to be met lest the firm be penalized, Xerox adopted the decision rule that "legally required efforts are handled separately from all other proposals and assigned the highest priority."[48]

Next, the feasibility of the programs being evaluated was examined in terms of four different questions. The first had to do with the "state-of-the-art" requirements. That is, had the program type characteristics become sufficiently well known and were there experts in the company who could effectively design such a program? Second, the question was raised as to how easy it would be to get line management to accept and implement the program. This was considered the most critical stage of feasibility evaluation. Third, it was asked what the net economic benefits of the program would be. Here, both tangible and intangible benefits were identified, and another decision rule was employed: "When a choice must be made between two programs of almost equal merit, the intangible — if properly framed — may become key factors that swing the decision."[49] Finally, the overall feasibility of proposed programs was evaluated. Programs were classified from "very desirable" to "not worthwhile" and ranked according to their benefits. Here, another decision rule was employed: a high rating on any factor would not conclusively lead to adopting the program, but a low rating on any single aspect of the program could eliminate it from further consideration. Following these four steps, programs were ranked and the most worthwhile of these undertaken.

The Xerox budget, like any program budgeting effort, has been by no means perfect. Further, one of its strongest supporters expressed doubts that "an optimal [program budgeting] approach will ever be developed—particularly for staff projects."[50] Nonetheless, programs such as Xerox's may encourage staff to "rigorously assess their programs' benefits and to evaluate the likelihood of achieving them,"[51] and such an evaluation may make it more possible for personnel departments to contribute to overall organizational objectives.

Cost-Benefit Analysis

In choosing most organizational decision alternatives, some resources (costs) must be given up in order to obtain certain returns (benefits). These benefits may be returns accruing: (1) to the firm, such as greater profitability, or (2) to the individual, such as greater income after taxes. We will use the term cost-benefit analysis to refer to both types of situations. In this section, we will restrict our attention to examining costs and benefits obtained by the organization in the context of program budgeting.

There are certain situations in which costs and benefits are relatively easy to ascertain. These determinations are easy when both the resources required for the program and the benefits obtained from it can be framed in tangible direct-dollar terms. This may sometimes be accomplished when the cost of an existing program can be directly compared with that of a proposed program. For example, if a personnel department can do its own managerial recruiting by hiring a professional recruiter at $25,000 per year and incurring traveling expenses of $5,000 per year in doing so—whereas it now utilizes employment agencies to assume this work at an average annual cost of $40,000—it would save approximately $10,000 in each year of the program's existence, assuming all these costs remained the same. Additionally, carrying out pilot tests of a program on a small group of employees may provide a basis for projecting dollar savings for the total organization. Both of these approaches were utilized in the cost-benefit analysis carried out by the Xerox personnel program budgeting described earlier.

Sometimes ratio analysis can be utilized in helping to develop meaningful direct-dollar cost and expenditure data. Such an effort has been undertaken in the U.S. Forest Service, in which both accident and accident prevention costs have been related to injury frequency ratios. This approach rejected zero accidents as an unrealistic goal and developed a program "based on the economically prudent goal of the lowest possible combined cost of accidents and accident-prevention work."[52]

When direct dollar-cost–dollar-effectiveness cannot be used in determining program effectiveness, measures of efficiency other than dollars may be utilized. Efforts have been made to use such measures (as well as the whole program budgeting approach itself) in governmental as well as business organizations for many years. Here, one approach to cost benefit analysis is to use lower level measures as substitutes for unavailable measures of ultimate objectives. Such substitute measures are often referred to as proximate or "proxy" criteria. For example, in governmental programs "the observed 'going' price of narcotics may be used as a proxy for the effectiveness of efforts to reduce narcotics flow."[53] As another example, with respect to education in the field of business administration, the average starting salary offered to a College of Business Administration's recently graduated M.B.A. student may serve as one proxy in evaluating the effectiveness of its graduate program.

It is beyond the scope of this text to delve further into proxy criteria or other techniques to handle cost-benefit situations where direct dollar-effectiveness cannot be used.[54] We should indicate, however, that as there is a danger in searching too much for the highly quantifiable in MBO, so also does this danger exist with the use of proxy criteria in cost-benefit analysis. As one observer has pointed out, there is a tendency for analysts to overdo the use of proxy criteria by "accepting a proxy criterion that is readily quantifiable . . . [rather] than to attempt the difficult task of finding vital, but less quantifiable, relations."[55]

PERSONNEL INFORMATION DECISION SYSTEMS (PIDS)

In Chapter 1, we indicated the importance of information in personnel decision making. For many years before the advent of the computer, organizations had personnel information systems capable of data storage and retrieval. Information inputs were manually stored in personnel folders, and this information was retrieved to provide a basis for better decisions in the personnel department. In recent years, more and more firms have developed computerized systems to aid personnel decision making. Some of these have simply stored information for retrieval as in the traditional manual systems. Others, however, have gone beyond simple information storage and retrieval and have been programmed to create decision rules for application within the organization—e.g., decisions concerning optimum human resource allocation.

Although the computer is an "idiot," being able to supply only what humans provide as programs and other inputs, it has three basic characteristics that make it such a valuable tool for personnel decision making. First, the computer can both store and retrieve huge amounts of information at an almost unbelievably fast pace. Second, it can carry out both preprogrammed arithmetic and logic operations at fantastically quick speeds. Finally, the computer can perform these two functions with an accuracy of less than one error in a million operations.[56]

The Scope of PIDS

Several observations are in order concerning the scope of PIDS. First, information-decision systems are generally utilized less in personnel than in many other organizational units. Second, rarely, if ever, has a firm initially installed a computer designed especially for personnel. The usual pattern is for organizations to obtain computer facilities for work in other departments, and at some later time use them for PIDS. Further, although some observers have presented notions about extremely encompassing PIDS, covering virtually all of the personnel functions discussed in Chapter 1,[57] surveys have shown that electronic data processing has tended to be used much more in certain personnel functions than others. Surveys reported in 1966 and 1969, for example, both indicated that electronic data processing was used most frequently in dealing with wage and salary administration and in keeping records.[58] In the 1966 study, EDP was used least with safety, while in the 1969 study, the area of least computer usage was in technical training. Both studies indicated that firms were planning to rely more and more on computerization in future years, but neither study clearly distinguished to what extent decisions were being based on computer output.

Advantages of PIDS

Several advantages of PIDS have been cited. In many cases, use of the computer as a substitute for human effort has resulted in reduced clerical costs. In 1969, for example, one study reported that among some 25 organizations, the cost of processing personnel information was reduced each year by between $6 and $12 per employee by use of the computer.[59] The real savings from computer utilization, however, according to this study, came from "increased efficiency and effectiveness."[60]

The significant reductions in cost are likely to be found in other ways—computerization allows the company to use the talents of its people more fully, to their own advantage and to the company's advantage.[61]

Many companies have realized such savings, while other organizations have found their personnel computer systems not paying for themselves. Probably the most basic reason for the success of PIDS is that they must be related to one or more specific organization objectives. As one observer has pointed out, *"a system that is irrelevant to corporate performance objectives is likely to generate a problem of nonacceptance."*[62]

One observation is in order concerning the obvious advantages of computers with respect to speed. With earlier computers we were able to create a program, wait for the computer to finish other programs submitted earlier, wait then for our program to be executed, and then receive our output in a standardized format as prescribed by our program. This was referred to as "batch processing." Today, however, with modern computers it is possible to probe the computer on an on-line real-time basis for information that we need. By "on-line, real-time" we mean that an individual—at his computation center or through remote job entry (RJE) at a computer terminal—can probe the computer for answers and get immediate responses to his questions. For example, if a company's president were going to give an after-dinner speech at his alma mater, he could request his PIDS to inform him of the names and positions of all other members in his firm that were also graduated from the same college. Outside of the personnel field, airlines have long been capable of probing the computer to determine the number of seats remaining unfilled at any time for any flight, so they could know when a flight had reached its seating capacity. These systems are in real time because each time a ticket is sold, the computer data are updated.

Another task the computer can obviously perform for the personnel department is record keeping. Traditionally, the record keeping task of personnel has been looked down upon as a routine chore that almost anyone could perform. We suggest, on the contrary, that personnel record keeping is extremely important and becoming more and more important. One reason for this is that with increased government regulation of personnel management, keeping accurate records for reporting to such agencies as the Equal Employment Opportunity Commission (EEOC) concerning the status of the firm's affirmative action program is very important.

Computers have had an influence on personnel managers and the personnel department in other ways. By giving the personnel manager more and better expertise, his power and influence in the organization may be enhanced. Further, computerized PIDS can relieve the personnel manager of routine decision making and give him more time for original and creative thinking. Decentralizing decision making from corporate staff personnel to field personnel managers is one specific way in which the delegation of responsibilities to lower levels in the organization may be accomplished. At the Northern Natural Gas Company of Omaha, for example, the

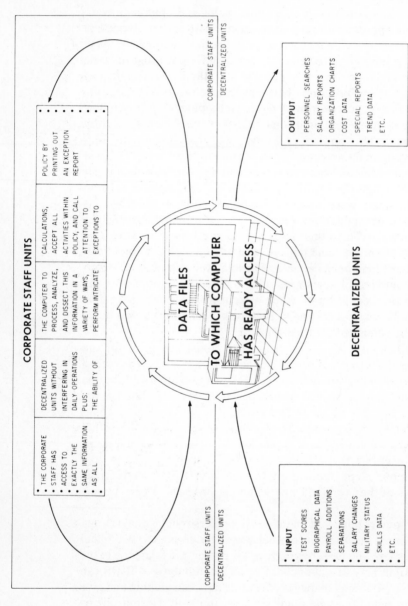

Figure 2–3 *Computers, decentralization and corporate control. From L. G. Wagner, "Computers, Decentralization and Corporate Control," California Management Review, 9 (Winter, 1966), p. 26. Copyright 1966 by the Regents of the University of California. Reprinted by permission of the Regents.*

decentralization of personnel (and other) decision making was made more manageable in the 1960's by the creation of a computerized system. This system provided the central corporate personnel department with a wide variety of data, including information about the operations of the field personnel managers, so that it could monitor their activities to ensure that the decentralized decision making was appropriate. Information stored in the computer was also available to the field staff, which could help them directly improve their decision making. This PIDS is illustrated in Figure 2–3. In this system, centralized personnel used multiple measures in monitoring the activities of the field personnel staffs and quantified as many variables as possible, even the "soft" variables in the system. For example, concerning job descriptions, the computer could inform central personnel if there were written descriptions of all jobs in a unit, and how up to date they were. "From these basic data, two 'indices' or measurements were developed: the percentage of descriptions unwritten in any unit and the percentage of descriptions not reviewed within policy time requirements."[63]

The Northern Natural Gas computer system was also set up so that various types of probes could be undertaken. In addition to the possibility of querying the computer concerning such specific areas as human resource planning, the system was designed to provide a general question-answering capability:

... miscellaneous requests which are so time-consuming ... can be handled with ease—questions such as: How many employees speak French? What is the average salary of nonexempt employees in the maintenance man classification in all locations?[64]

At Northern Natural Gas the continuous monitoring of the operations provided a two-fold benefit. First, the decentralized units obtained the benefits of having access to a PIDS. Second, the central corporate personnel staff was able to have a monitoring system which: (1) did not interfere in the operations of the field staffs and (2) provided for "exception" reporting, i.e., providing information about the field operations only when the performance of these parts of the system were "out-of-control."

PIDS: Limitations and Implementation Problems

We have already indicated that PIDS may be irrelevant if they are not specifically aimed at meeting the objectives of the organization. Thus, for a PIDS to be successful, it follows that organizational objectives need to be spelled out and related to personnel management. This relationship cannot be done effectively unless the personnel manager has the support of top management in the organization.

Another prerequisite for the development of an effective PIDS is that personnel managers be able to relate appropriately to the systems specialists who are performing the actual design of the system. As one writer has pointed out, "the abstract terminology that systems architects use to describe their work is so far divorced from the day-to-day realities the personnel man deals with that it is almost impossible for them to communicate at first."[65] He also indicated that because of such difficulties there has occurred both an overselling and overbuying of PIDS. With systems people unfamiliar with the complexities of the personnel manager's job, they are inclined to oversimplify the system, while the personnel manager burdened with the current demands of his own job may be "too ready to believe that the computer can lift or at least substantially ease that burden."[66]

There have been other problems in designing PIDS, one of which is updating. In some companies, more than 200 separate items about each employee are kept in their computer system and must be updated whenever data on employees have changed. Two points concerning this problem should be mentioned. First, companies should be alert to the updating problem and not put too many items in the system. Second, even without a computerized system, personnel management will be required to keep up to date many items about employees in their personnel folders, so that updating may not be much more of a problem with a PIDS than with a manual system.

Finally, questions have been raised with respect to both security and privacy when items about employees are kept in computerized PIDS. As Westin has pointed out, privacy involves: (1) what kinds of information are essential to be stored in the system, (2) who has the right to use the information in (or outside of) the organization, and (3) what do employees know about what is in their records and are they given procedures for contesting and correcting data about themselves. Security, on the other hand, "involves the ability of an organization to keep its promises of confidentiality—to protect its informational facilities against unauthorized access or disclosure, alteration or destruction."[67] Westin also indicated in 1974 that in one large survey it was found that "organizations that have been computerized are *not* yet collecting more intrusive types of information about their employees than they did under a manual record-keeping system."[68]

Westin presented a case in which a "colossal fraud" was perpetuated with a computerized system. In this case, a young man had a $2.5 million payment credited to his bank, which was carried out by telling his fiancée, who worked in the bank to type in the computer console some "funny little numbers" so that he could say hello to a buddy of his who worked in a Midwest bank.[69] Computer systems security has posed real, serious problems for organizations, and elaborate efforts have been developed to design organizational computer systems to permit only authorized personnel to obtain access to them and to audit these personnel. No practical way has yet been developed to audit the work of these individuals sufficiently, however, "because of the increasing complexity of computer systems and the lack of standards, discipline, and structured practices in their design and construction."[70]

GOVERNMENT AND THE PERSONNEL DEPARTMENT

In Chapter 1, we mentioned the increasing role of government in regulating and circumscribing personnel activities. We will now make some general observations with respect to the implications of such intervention into the firm's personnel activities. Specific governmental legislation is discussed throughout the text where appropriate.

As indicated, the effective personnel manager of today needs to be better trained than ever before because of the growing importance the personnel department may assume. One key area in which the effective personnel manager must keep himself up to date is in compliance with governmental regulations that affect the organization's handling of and dealing with its human resources. In fact, one could take the position that one of the basic functions of the personnel manager of today is that of a compliance officer. As Lewis has pointed out: "In no area of management is the Personnel Executive more vulnerable than in that of the law."[71] He went on to indicate that failure to comply with applicable laws and regulations may put the firm in the position of having to appear "before the courts or governmental agencies as a defendant—unwelcome prospects indeed."[72] Such legal proceedings may be extremely costly to a company, with adverse rulings sometimes running into millions of dollars. For example, the American Telephone and Telegraph Company had to "pay $38 million in back pay and provide raises to thousands of women, blacks, and others considered discriminated against. . . ."[73]

If the personnel manager does keep up with the "compliance jungle," he will possess knowledge and skills that are vital to the firm, and hence—as we indicated was the case of computer-derived expertise—be able to increase his power and influence within the organization. If he fails, however, to keep up with federal legislation and executive orders, court rulings, and state laws, a void will be left in the organization that will invite governmental intervention. As one individual has pointed out, the failure of the personnel director to be proactive in complying with governmental regulations

. . . leaves a void that invites several alternatives. Imposition of policy on the firm from external agencies may be one of these and will prevent the firm from establishing policies that serve its needs and purposes. Personnel departments must . . . protect the firm and permit it to serve social and economic needs with . . . freedom and responsiveness to change . . . .[74]

Governmental regulation treats the organization as a total system. For example, a single ruling made under the Civil Rights Act of 1964 may affect the firm's selection, training, promotion, performance appraisal, and wage and salary functions. As one individual has pointed out with respect to equal opportunity employment guidelines, these

. . . treat the employment and development process as a system . . . if they did not, we would now have six or seven separate sets of guidelines— one for each of the possible decision-making points in the employment process—and compliance efforts would be complicated beyond belief.[75]

What implications do the above observations have for personnel management and organizational objectives? Without question, government legislation has constrained the strategy space of the firm's decision making; compliance with governmental regulations usually results in additional costs. Further, as opposed to becoming more important, as we indicated earlier, some authorities have made much more gloomy predictions about the role of the personnel manager in the future. For example, Patten had indicated the belief that the personnel manager:

. . . stands to be clericalized, and his potential contribution . . . [to his firm] reduced to a very low level. . . . It looks like the . . . 1970's means the obliteration of the last traces of *laissez-faire* in personnel work . . . and the elimination of chances for the personnel manager to become "effective.". . .[76]

On the other hand, some authorities have argued that such a "gloomy prognosis" is not justified. Rather, they indicate that a "spinoff" of compliance with governmental regulations may well lead to the development of better personnel management. It has been pointed out that executives often have failed to recognize their responsibilities to their human assets as much as those of money, equipment, and good will. It seems unfortunate that only when an organization is being threatened in this area does the human assets responsibility obtain the attention it should have had all the time.[77]

To resolve these conflicting opinions the following may be stated. Government *is* constraining the scope of organizational decisions, but these constraints may afford the proactive personnel manager additional opportunities for influencing management decisions; and in many cases governmental regulations may ultimately lead to the development of better personnel practices.

SUMMARY

Many different kinds of work are done in personnel departments, which are staff departments. As a staff department, personnel assumes four basic role relationships — advisory, service, policy formulation, and control. Various conflicts may emerge between personnel and line departments, and the power that personnel wields is an important organizational variable. In recent years, the stature of personnel has been enhanced in many organizations with good reason; yet there is always the possibility that personnel may wield too much power.

One of the problems facing personnel departments is how to decide which activities to undertake to meet organizational objectives. Following an MBO approach may be useful in helping tie personnel activities to objectives. Further, program budgeting and cost benefit analysis may be utilized to help allocate resources aimed at the meeting of organizational objectives.

Two other general areas of concern are important to personnel managers today—PIDS and governmental regulation. PIDS provide the personnel manager with a powerful tool to aid him in decision making, although computerization has presented certain knotty problems as security. Governmental legislation is constraining the personnel manager in his decision making to a greater extent than ever before. Such regulation, however, may enhance the power of the personnel manager by giving him greater opportunities to influence organizational decisions. Further, many governmental regulations may help lead to more progressive personnel practices.

DISCUSSION AND STUDY QUESTIONS

1. As personnel manager for the Ajax Corporation, a chemical manufacturer in the midwest, you want to hire an intelligent college graduate to be your assistant in the following three areas: labor relations, wage and salary administration, and safety. You have narrowed your search down to the following three applicants, all of whom had cumulative college grade point averages of above 3.0 on a 4.0 basis at reputable institutions. Which applicant would you choose to be your assistant, and why?

a. A major in business administration who has taken one personnel course using a book like this one, a senior level personnel course in which case studies were utilized, a basic course in both macro- and microeconomics, and three credits of industrial psychology.
b. A liberal arts candidate who majored in economics, with six credits in labor economics, and six credits in basic psychology.
c. An industrial engineering major, who also had two courses in mechanical engineering, and who has taken a course in time and motion study, numerous credits in operations research courses, and six credits in industrial psychology.

2. Why do personnel positions often provide experience valuable for managers moving up to higher level line management positions?

3. You are the personnel manager in a manufacturing plant of about 1500 employees, and, as you walk through the plant one day, you see three workers performing their job without using their safety guards. You do not see their supervisor present in the department. You "advise" the workers that they are violating safety regulations and they respond that their boss, the first line supervisor, has ordered them specifically not to use the guard because the batch of work he is dealing with is part of a "rush order," and work on the order is already behind. They also tell you that you have no authority to tell them how to do their jobs. The workers' supervisor reports to a general foreman (with whom you are personally friendly) who, in turn, reports to the plant manager. You know that both the general foreman and plant manager would not condone such unsafe practices. What actions, if any, should you take?

4. Personnel managers should not be as proactive as suggested in the chapter. If they are so, they will end up making too many decisions, thus undermining the authority of many line managers. Discuss.

5. National Enterprises Incorporated is a large firm with both a corporate personnel staff and personnel managers in each of its 32 geographically dispersed manufacturing plants. For each of the following activities, indicate whether it should be corporate personnel or one of the plant personnel managers who should deal with the problem. In each case give your reasons why.
a. Determining which of the three permissible vesting rules under ERISA (see Chapter 12) that the company should choose for its new pension plan.
b. Explaining to an employee about to retire what his benefit options would be.
c. Recruiting college graduates for managerial positions.
d. Orienting newly hired individuals to work in personnel to the company's basic personnel policies.
e. Determining lower cutoff scores for mental alertness tests to be used in selection of college graduates as managers.
f. Interpreting psychological tests.

6. You are the personnel vice president of a large corporation headquartered in the east, with 18 geographically dispersed plants throughout the nation. You have approximately 40 employees working for you in specialized corporate personnel departments: training, selection, performance appraisal, human resource planning, wage and salary administration, employee benefits, and so on. All members of your corporate staff have college degrees; 10 of 40 have some graduate education, including three with Master's degrees and one with a Ph.D, and there are several highly motivated professionals who have high career aspirations in your firm. Some of the work carried out by your corporate personnel staff is "continuous" in nature, not of a project type nature; e.g., executive recruiting, interpretation of psychological tests administered by your field divisions, and handling claim problems arising under the administration of your company's relatively new major medical health insurance plan. Other work performed by some of your personnel specialists is more of a project-type nature. For example, your training department gears up for four two-week in-company classroom management development programs a year, and one individual was given prime responsibility for developing your major medical plan and spent about 90 per cent of his time on it over a four-month period. Do you believe MBO would be an appropriate management approach for your department? Why? What problems might you run into in utilizing MBO?
7. Assuming you decide to manage your corporate personnel department as in Question 6 using an MBO approach, do you think program budgeting would be of value to you?
8. The personnel vice president in the last two questions is also interested in applying cost-benefit analysis to his operation, and is trying to pin down some proxy criteria that might be utilized in the operation. Give two proxy criteria that you think he might use, and indicate their limitations.
9. There are simply too many "soft" variables in personnel to make a computerized PIDS very valuable. For example, in the company cited in the chapter, simply knowing whether all job descriptions in a unit had been written and up to date provided no hard quantitative evidence as to how good the job descriptions were. Discuss.
10. The statements in the chapter summarizing views on the expanding role of government and its effects on personnel management are sheer nonsense. Government regulations are often so confusing that either (1) the personnel manager will also be so confused that no one in the organization will know what to do, or (2) he will become such a proactive "legal beagle," speaking only in "legalese" that no line managers in the organization will fully understand him and accept his recommendations solely on the basis of his advice. Further, one cannot force "better personnel practices" by governmental legislation; top management must want to improve personnel practices or they never will be improved. Discuss.

Notes

[1]The notions in this paragraph are drawn from: John Paul Jones, "Today's Role and Scope of Personnel Administration in Management," in Joseph J. Famularo, ed., *Handbook of Modern Personnel Administration* (New York: McGraw-Hill, Inc., 1972), p. 1–4.

[2]David N. Campbell, "The Personnel Director, His Staff, and Structure of the Department," in ibid., p. 4–8.

[3]Geert Hofstede, "Frustrations of Personnel Managers," *Management International Review,* 13 (1973/4–5), p. 127.

[4]Ibid. Hofstede has also pointed out that there are differences in qualifications from country to country in Europe. For example, he indicated that a 1966 survey showed lawyers to be particularly popular in France, Spain, Austria and Germany, with economists predominating in personnel work in Italy.

[5]Two comments are in order here. First, we will discuss the relationships between specialized headquarters personnel staffs and divisional personnel later in this chapter. Second, we have dichotomized here between "generalist" and "specialist" for purpose of simplification. In some personnel departments, for example, the personnel manager may be a generalist, with assistant personnel managers who report to him generalists to a degree but specializing in particular areas. These individuals may be rotated among the specialties to give them a broad background in personnel. For an example of this so-called "Assistant Personnel Manager" approach, see Campbell, op. cit., pp. 4–9 and 4–10.

[6]Harold W. Fox, "Early Signals for Personnel Administration," *Personnel Journal,* 53 (March, 1974), p. 202.

[7]Ibid., pp. 201–204.

[8]See, for example, Max D. Richards and Paul S. Greenlaw, *Management: Decisions and Behavior,* rev. ed. (Homewood, Ill.: Richard D. Irwin, Inc., 1972), pp. 272–276, for a discussion of these organization types, which are called project and matrix organizations.

[9]Ibid., pp. 273–274.

[10]Fred K. Foulkes, "The Expanding Role of the Personnel Function," *Harvard Business Review,* 53 (March-April, 1975), p.73.

[11]Ibid., p. 75.

[12]Charles Coleman and Joseph Rich, "Line, Staff and the Systems Perspective," *Human Resources Management,* 12 (Fall, 1973), p. 21.

[13]Ibid.

[14]Robert E. Boynton and Harold C. White, "Functions of Personnel Administration: Management's View in a Federal Installation," *Public Personnel Management,* 2 (January-February, 1973), p. 32.

[15]Ibid., p. 33.

[16]J. G. Hunt, "Status Congruence: An Important Organization Function," *Personnel Administration,* 32 (January-February, 1969), p. 22.

[17]Rossall J. Johnson, "The Personnel Manager of the 1970's," *Personnel Journal,* 50 (April, 1971), p. 304.

[18]Coleman and Rich, op. cit., p. 24.

[19]Ibid., p. 25.

[20]See Elliot V. Chapple and Leonard R. Sayles, *The Measure of Management* (New York: Macmillan, 1961), especially pp. 19–45.

[21]Coleman and Rich, op. cit., pp. 25–26.

[22]In some companies more than two parallel personnel staffs may exist. At the Northern Natural Gas Company of Omaha, for example, there were, as reported in 1966, 18 personnel administrators headed by a corporate personnel manager, but operating at four different levels of the firm's organizational hierarchy. This situation is described in L. G. Wagner, "Computers, Decentralization and Corporate Control," *California Management Review,* 9 (Winter, 1966), pp. 25–32.

[23]This is referred to as a divisionalized structure, which is common to many corporations. An alternative form of staff parallelism, which is referred to as a "functional" structure, exists, and in it the personnel department would report in a

straight line from botton to top. An organization chart illustrating this type of structure is shown in Campbell, op. cit., p. 4–12.

[24]Donald W. Osgood, "The Personnel Manager's Front-Line Role in the Marketing Field," *Personnel,* 50 (November-December, 1973), p. 43.

[25]Hofstede, op. cit., p. 127.

[26]Charles R. Milton and James M. Black, "Theory X, Theory Y, or Something in Between?" *Personnel,* 50 (May-June, 1973), p. 49.

[27]Drawn from Robert R. Guthrie, "Personnel's Emerging Role," *Personnel Journal,* 53 (September, 1974), pp. 657–658.

[28]George Ritzer and Harrison M. Trice, *An Occupation in Conflict: A Study of the Personnel Manager* (Ithaca, New York: Cornell University Press, 1969), p. 66.

[29]Coleman and Rich, op. cit., p. 22.

[30]Foulkes, op. cit., p. 77.

[31]Ibid.

[32]Ibid., p. 78. Foulkes has also pointed out that when corporations have "outsider" boards of directors, it is equally rare to find one of them specifically representing the human resource point of view.

[33]Coleman and Rich, op. cit., p. 26.

[34]This approach to training is discussed in James M. Mitchell and Rolfe E. Schroeder, "Future Shock for Personnel Administration," *Public Personnel Management,* 3 (July-August, 1974), pp. 267–268.

[35]Julius Rezler, "Automation and the Personnel Manager," *Advanced Management Journal,* 32 (January, 1967), p. 81. We would agree with Rezler with the exception of game theory. This is a highly complex branch of mathematics which has not proved practical for dealing with managerial problems.

[36]Thomas H. Patten, Jr., "OD, MBO and the R/P System," *Personnel Administration,* 35 (March-April, 1972), p. 19.

[37]Fred Schuster, "A Systems Approach to Managing Human Resources," *The Personnel Administrator,* 16 (March-April, 1971), p. 28.

[38]Peter Drucker, *The Practice of Management* (New York: Harper & Bros., 1954).

[39]Don Hellriegel and John W. Slocum, Jr., *Organizational Behavior: Contingency Views* (St. Paul: West Publishing Co., 1976), p. 418.

[40]For other problems encountered in using the MBO approach, see for example, ibid., p. 422 and William F. Glueck, *Management* (Hinsdale, Ill.: The Dryden Press, 1977), pp. 358–359.

[41]Hellriegel and Slocum, op. cit., p. 422.

[42]Richards and Greenlaw, op. cit., p. 456.

[43]Roger D. Borgeson, "Planning the Personnel Function and Budget," in Famularo, op. cit., p. 6–9.

[44]The materials in this paragraph are drawn largely from ibid., pp. 6–9, 6–10, and 6–11.

[45]Ibid., p. 6–8.

[46]Ibid.

[47]The materials describing the efforts at Xerox have been drawn from: Logan M. Cheek, "Cost Effectiveness Comes to the Personnel Function," *Harvard Business Review,* 51 (May-June, 1973), pp. 96–105.

[48]Ibid., p. 98.

[49]Ibid., p. 102.

[50]Ibid., p. 105.

[51]Ibid.

[52]James T. Sykes, "Defining an Injury-Frequency Goal," *National Safety News,* 100 (October, 1969), p. 53.

[53]Harry P. Hatry, "Measuring the Effectiveness of Nondefense Public Programs," *Operations Research,* 18 (September-October, 1970), p. 779.

[54]For a more thorough, but not overly complex discussion of this topic, see Richards and Greenlaw, op. cit., pp. 412–416.

[55]Hatry, op. cit., p. 779.

[56]Drawn from Orman R. Wright, Jr., "Computerization of the Employment Process," *Personnel Administration/Public Personnel Review,* 1 (November-

December 1972), p. 48. For a somewhat more sophisticated treatment of the characteristics of computers relative to personnel administration, see Rolf E. Rogers, "An Integrated Personnel System," *Personnel Administration,* 33 (March-April, 1970), pp. 22–28.

[57]See, for example, Gerald E. Connally, "Personnel Administration and the Computer," *Personnel Journal,* 48 (August, 1969), pp. 605–611.

[58]Charles E. J. Cassidy, "Electronic Data Processing and the Personnel Function: The Present and the Future," *Personnel Journal,* 45 (June, 1966), pp. 352–354; and Frederick H. Black, Jr., "The Computer in the Personnel Department," *Personnel,* 46 (September-October, 1969), pp. 65–71.

[59]John V. MacGuffie, "Computer Programs for People," *Datamation,* 15 (November, 1969), p. 216.

[60]Ibid.

[61]Ibid.

[62]Logan M. Cheek, "Personnel Computer Systems," *Business Horizons,* 14 (August, 1971), p. 71.

[63]L. G. Wagner, op. cit., p. 28.

[64]Ibid., p. 31.

[65]Glenn Bassett, "EDP Personnel Systems: Do's, Don'ts and How-To's," *Personnel,* 48 (July-August, 1971), p. 22.

[66]Ibid.

[67]Alan F. Westin, "The Problem of Privacy and Security With Computerized Data Collection," *The Conference Board Record,* 11 (March, 1974), p. 31.

[68]Ibid., p. 32.

[69]Ibid.

[70]Donn B. Parker, "The Increasingly Binary Nature of Crime," *New York Times,* July 11, 1976, Section 3, p. 12.

[71]Willard A. Lewis, "The Personnel Manager-as-Compliance-Officer," *Personnel Journal,* 50 (December, 1971), p. 907.

[72]Ibid.

[73]Thomas H. Patten, Jr., "Personnel Management in the 1970's,: The End of Laissez Faire," *Human Resource Management,* 12 (Fall, 1973), p. 10.

[74]W. F. Rabe, "The Role of the Personnel Administration Department in Creating and Controlling Personnel Policy," in Famularo, op. cit., p. 7–10.

[75]Herbert P. Froehlich and Dennis A. Hawver, "Compliance Spinoff: Better Personnel Systems," *Personnel,* 51 (January-February, 1974), p. 64.

[76]Patten, "Personnel Management in the 1970's," p. 19.

[77]Drawn from Froechlich and Hawver, op. cit., p. 62.

II

THE ACQUISITION OF HUMAN RESOURCES

3

HUMAN RESOURCE PLANNING

To function successfully, organizations need people, just as they need raw materials, equipment, and other resources. In fact, it is not uncommon to find human resources regarded as a firm's most important asset, even though they do not appear on its financial statement. Therefore, organizations need human resource planning to enable them to meet their future "people" needs, just as they need to plan for nonhuman resources. In light of our perspective in the previous two chapters, we will define human resource planning as an information — decision — making process designed to ensure that enough competent people with appropriate skills are available to perform jobs where and when they will be needed.

In this chapter we will first make some introductory comments concerning the goals of and trends in human resource planning; then we will discuss a basic set of information necessary for human resource planning — job analysis. We will next cover forecasting both the demand for and the supply of human resources. Finally we will turn our attention to making human resource decisions such as filling job vacancies and reducing the number of the firm's human resources when necessary. A model of this conceptualization of the human resource planning process is shown in Figure 3-1.

INTRODUCTION

Goals and Objectives

To the extent that human resource planning is effective, numerous organizational subgoals can be met, that can, in turn, help meet both overall firm objectives such as profitability and the

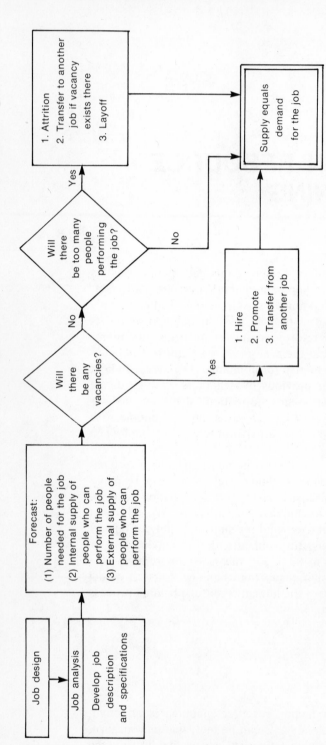

Figure 3–1 Human resource planning model for any particular job at any particular time.

needs of members of the organization. For example, effective human resource planning may:

1. Serve to stabilize employment levels when demand for a firm's product is variable. Such stabilization, in turn, may: (a) reduce the firm's unemployment compensation liability costs incurred due to layoffs; (b) provide more job security to the organization's employees; and (c) minimize the costs of overtime during peak periods of demand.

2. Prevent young college recruits from leaving the firm after expensive training has been given them because there are no really challenging positions for them to be promoted into.

3. Reduce the problems of managerial succession by permitting plans for replacements to be drawn up in advance in case key executives leave the firm suddenly due to resignation or death.

4. Make it possible to allocate financial resources so that departments will not be restricted in having available the people they need to produce the firm's desired output.[1]

This employment stabilization situation illustrates a fundamental problem in managerial decision making — suboptimization. Suboptimization means that some organizational objectives may be achieved more fully only at the expense of impairing or sacrificing the attainment of other goals. With an employment stabilization objective in a fluctuating-demand organization, larger inventories would have to be built up in slack periods to provide for later peak periods, which would result in sacrificing the firm's objective of minimizing inventory carrying costs. In such a case, management might find that hiring on an overtime basis during peak periods while laying employees off in slack periods would minimize total organization economic costs, although it would not necessarily maximize its humanitarian objectives. We can also see from this example that human resource planning cannot be looked at in isolation; rather, it must be considered in light of mutual interactions with other aspects of organizational operations in a systems sense.

From a systems view, human resource planning is mutually interrelated with many of the organization's other endeavors. The strongest direct relationship exists between human resource planning and selection. In fact, *all* selection efforts really serve as an integral part of the whole human resource planning process. Organizations that have either stable or increasing human resource needs must go into the external labor market and hire individuals to fill some positions, *even though* they generally follow a promotion-from-within policy (as we will indicate later). Further, human resource planning is related to both performance appraisal and training and development. Performance appraisals can pinpoint the skills that will be required if individuals are to move into higher level positions via promotion while training and development efforts may then be designed to provide these skills.

To meet the organizational goals, a basic objective involved in human resource planning itself is to ensure that the organization's desired demand for individuals for each job at any particular time will be *just met* by available human resources. This view assumes that both "stockpiling" employees at levels greater than demand and having available a number of employees less than needed are undesirable. This assumption represents a major difference between the planning for human resources and that for nonhuman resources. It is generally considered unacceptable for organizations to stockpile or build inventories of human resources whereas raw materials and finished goods inventories are common, as is backup production equipment. It is unacceptable to hold human resource inventories for three reasons. First, human resources are often scarce, and taking potentially productive people out of the economy's labor pool is often considered socially unacceptable. Second, human resources are costly and it may be difficult economically to justify excess personnel. Finally, excess people not engaged in productive work are likely to be bored and frustrated by the lack of anything constructive to do. Such boredom and frustration can create problems because "excess" people may make unnecessary work for or get in the way of productive employees. It is equally undesirable for an organization to have too few employees. As with "stockpiled" employees, individuals may feel frustrated, but in this case because of overwork rather than a lack of productive work.[2]

Trends in Human Resource Management

Often the human resource planning efforts of organizations have been feeble, not emphasizing any truly systematized approach geared toward meeting overall objectives. As Mason Haire has put it:

. . . we have typically taken up a little selection, a little motivation, and a little training, and not dealt either with their interaction or with their implications for a broad organization-wide view of the process of managing human resources.[3]

In recent years, however, both personnel practitioners and scholars have emphasized some of the basic facets of personnel decision making that we stressed in Chapters 1 and 2: (1) taking systems and contingency approaches; (2) developing more sophisticated mathematical human resource forecasting and planning models; and (3) using computers to a greater extent. Two observations are in order concerning these approaches. First, as with the application of many sophisticated personnel approaches, more complex human resource planning systems have generally been used in larger companies in which human resource planning *is* more complex and in which the higher cost of such approaches can be afforded. Second, there has been a wide range of mathematical human resource models developed. In terms of applicability, some of these models have assumed away so many "real-life" personnel variables that they have had virtually no practical application. On the other hand, there have been other quantitative models that have been very useful to organizations. In this chapter, we will focus attention on the basic concepts involved in some of these more useful models.

Why have human resource planning models, which are systems oriented, quantitatively based and/or computer oriented, been increasing in recent years? There are many reasons. Some of the more important include:

1. Organizations simply have been growing larger and/or more complex, requiring more sophisticated approaches. This has been especially true in those organizations in which task interdependencies have increased.[4]

2. The invention and development of the computer has made possible analysis of complex human resource problems which would previously have been so time consuming as to be cost prohibitive or virtually impossible to deal with by manual computations.

3. "The manpower mix in organizations had gradually come to focus around highly skilled managerial and technical talent."[5] Such personnel have at times been in short supply, and more of a lead time has been required for their training and development.

4. Once an integrated, well-thought out human resource planning program has been initiated, managers tend to appreciate its benefits and work together with the firm's human resource specialists in developing viable programs—"they are more than willing to plan in this area, if only they are shown how to begin."[6]

In spite of these reasons for the growth in organizational human resource planning, certain basic problems face such endeavors. Aside from the inherent mathematical complexity often required to model human resource systems, there are two basic problems which are interrelated, though this is often not obvious. These are: (1) a lack of certainty surrounding future human resource needs, *coupled with* (2) the existence of an acquisition lead time for meeting these needs. If the firm's human resource planning experts were *completely uncertain* about the number of operations researchers that would be required on July 28 in the year 2000, for example, it would face *no* problems *if* it could, at that future time, instantaneously obtain any number of such personnel needed to meet its objectives.[7] With lead times needed to recruit and train personnel from outside the firm and to train and promote existing personnel for any new positions, however, real forecasting problems arise.[8] As indicated, acquisition lead times have become more of a problem in recent years because of needs for more highly skilled managerial and technical personnel — a trend that is expected to continue in future years. Finally, and somewhat relatedly, human resource plans must be *updated* much more quickly and often in firms (or any of their subsystems) in which greater *uncertainty* exists. As one observer has pointed out:

> . . . increasing instability and the greater uncertainties associated with certain job environments (e.g., research and development or marketing) indicate a requirement for more up-to-date information on emergent needs. This manpower data is increasingly subject to change, and organizational needs dictate timely information with appropriate system support.[9]

JOB ANALYSIS

Before any human resource planning can be carried out, management must first define what work is to be performed and how the many tasks to be carried out can be divided and allocated into manageable work units, which we call jobs. Such an assignment of tasks to jobs is commonly known as "job design."

Once jobs have been defined, it is important to maintain current information about their content. This information-gathering process is called job analysis and may serve several useful functions in the organization. First, since tasks comprising many jobs will change from time to time due to technological or other reasons, up-to-date job analysis may provide the firm with an indication of when jobs need redesigning because of task content changes. For example, technological change may reduce by 50 per cent the time required to perform the tasks comprising one job, making it necessary to give the job occupant additional duties to keep him busy doing a full day's work. Second, identifying the work to be performed in each job provides an extremely important basis for planning for the firm's human resources, the subject of this chapter. Such planning obviously cannot be undertaken by management until it first knows fairly precisely what a "sales," "engineering," or any other type of job actually consists of. Third, describing accurately what each job entails is essential for recruiting and selection. For this reason, job analysis involves not only describing what the content of jobs is to be, but also job specifications — i.e., what characteristics the individual needs to possess to be qualified for any given job. Fourth, job analysis provides valuable data for performance appraisal, since it helps permit a comparison between an individual's *actual* job performance and the tasks required to be carried out as specified in the design of the jobs. Fifth, job analysis data provide a basis for training and development. In order to train an individual to perform a particular job effectively, we need to define for him (and the trainer) just what tasks he is expected to carry out. Sixth, job analysis data are extremely valuable in wage and salary administration. Through job evaluation, which is discussed in Chapter 9, jobs in the organization must be compared with each other and differential levels of pay established for jobs calling for greater or lesser skills than others. Basic to evaluating and comparing jobs for wage and salary purposes is a clear statement of what each job entails. Finally, job analysis has become increasingly important as the federal government has sought to compel firms to end discriminatory hiring, promotional, wage and salary, and other personnel practices. For example, accurate description of a job may represent a prime defense for proving that a woman performing one job and being paid less than a man performing another is really working at a lower skill level, so that, as a consequence, she is not being discriminated against on the basis of her sex as prohibited by the Equal Pay Act of 1963.

Undertaking Job Analysis[10]

There are a number of techniques available for gathering information about different jobs. In some cases, the job analyst may interview the employee performing a job, the supervisor or both. This technique may be quite time-consuming, and there is the danger that employees will exaggerate the importance of their jobs.

Probably the least costly method of collecting job analysis data is by using questionnaires. A well-designed questionnaire has been claimed to be:

. . . the most efficient way to collect a wide array of job information in a short period of time. There is, however, the danger that a respondee will either not complete it, complete it inaccurately, or take an excessively long time to return it.[11]

A third approach to information gathering in job analysis is having the analyst actually observe the individual performing a job and record observations while doing so. In some cases this method may be very useful while under certain conditions it beomes difficult if not impossible. This is especially true with jobs in which some elements of the complete job cycle occur at infrequent (and perhaps unpredictable) intervals. Here, the analyst cannot simply record the performance of a job all at one time.

Although it is difficult to generalize, one authority has indicated that probably the most effective way of obtaining job analysis data is "the combination of observation and the interview."[12] Whatever technique or combination of techniques is chosen, it is important to determine just what objectives among those mentioned are to be met by the analysis. For example, if the job data are *not* to be used for wage and salary administration, discriminating among jobs in terms of levels of difficulty for salary differential purposes would not be required.

Job Descriptions and Specifications

Almost universally, job analysis provides two types of information — job descriptions and job specifications. Turning our attention to job descriptions first, job analysis describes the characteristics of jobs to be filled. In larger organizations, job descriptions are often done by personnel specialists, while in smaller ones, supervisors usually develop descriptions for the jobs in their department, if descriptions are developed at all. In general, job descriptions tend to be less specific at higher level positions in any organization. The reason for this is that lower level jobs (such as ones on a highly repetitive assembly line) are preprogrammed to a much greater extent than that of marketing vice president, which may involve everything from entertaining visiting "dignitaries" to supervising the development of marketing projections of a particular product over the next three to five years.

It is also important to recognize that most jobs are more "dynamic" than are their descriptions, from two points of view. First, activities in most organizations will gradually change, owing to technological advances or other reasons. As a consequence, job descriptions need periodic updating. Second, regardless of the description of a job (except possibly highly programmed repetitious production jobs), the human personalities of individuals currently filling it will moderate the job description. This fact, unfortunately, is often not taken into account in organizations.

These two points may be seen in Figure 3–2, a description for a secretarial job in a large eastern organization. The incumbent has held this position since 1970, and the job description was updated in 1973 to account for expanded responsibilities. For example, with a larger department, the individual holding the Secretary A position directs the work of three other full-time secretaries, whereas in 1972 the position only required direction of work of two others. With the firm having expanded its efforts abroad in 1974, the responsibilities for item 10 — making travel arrangements — have been complicated by much more foreign

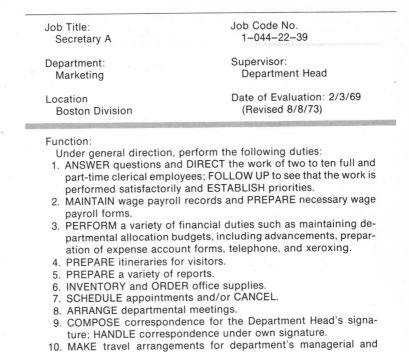

Job Title: Secretary A	Job Code No. 1–044–22–39
Department: Marketing	Supervisor: Department Head
Location Boston Division	Date of Evaluation: 2/3/69 (Revised 8/8/73)

Function:
Under general direction, perform the following duties:
1. ANSWER questions and DIRECT the work of two to ten full and part-time clerical employees; FOLLOW UP to see that the work is performed satisfactorily and ESTABLISH priorities.
2. MAINTAIN wage payroll records and PREPARE necessary wage payroll forms.
3. PERFORM a variety of financial duties such as maintaining departmental allocation budgets, including advancements, preparation of expense account forms, telephone, and xeroxing.
4. PREPARE itineraries for visitors.
5. PREPARE a variety of reports.
6. INVENTORY and ORDER office supplies.
7. SCHEDULE appointments and/or CANCEL.
8. ARRANGE departmental meetings.
9. COMPOSE correspondence for the Department Head's signature; HANDLE correspondence under own signature.
10. MAKE travel arrangements for department's managerial and professional staff.
11. TAKE and TRANSCRIBE dictation, also by machine.
12. TYPE correspondence, reports, forms, lists, records, schedules, etc.
13. ANSWER telephone; PROVIDE information or REFER.
14. GREET visitors; PROVIDE information or REFER.
15. PLACE long distance telephone calls.
16. FILE correspondence, reports, forms.
17. OPEN, SORT, and DISTRIBUTE mail.
18. ASSEMBLE, COLLATE duplicated material.
19. PROCESS outgoing mail.
20. PERFORM other duties as assigned by supervisor.

Information Supplied By: Smith	Analyst: W. N. Frey

Figure 3–2 *The Jones Corporation, clerical job description.*

travel among the managerial and professional members of the department.

The fact that human responsibilities may well have an important bearing on how jobs are *actually* performed may also be illustrated by a situation that took place for over two years in the department in which the Secretary A position existed.

One of the three secretaries (Susan) who was supervised by the person holding the Secretary A position was an excellent typist and could take her own shorthand but sometimes could not read it very well. On the other hand, Susan could read the current Secretary A's shorthand quite well. In consequence, from time to time the managerial and professional personnel dictated a letter to Secretary A, which she in turn gave to Susan to type up. An interesting arrangement — but one which, on several occasions, helped get necessary typing completed in time.

Along with job descriptions, job analysis generates job specifications, which represent a statement of the human qualifications required to perform the job. Among the categories of human qualifications that may be specified in job analyses are:[13]

1. Educational standards which may spell out, for example, degrees attained, such as a B.S. in engineering.
2. Experience requirements, such as two years of general clerical experience for the job described in Figure 3–2. This job, as may be noted, calls for *directing* the work of from two to ten clerical employees, and hence, would normally require some prior experience in actually performing clerical activities.
3. Skills requirements, such as typing and dictation skills for the clerical position described in Figure 3–2.
4. Physical requirements, which might include such factors as the ability to lift 100 pounds intermittently.
5. Certification or licensing requirements, such as a license to practice medicine for a job as an orthopedic physician in a health center in a particular state.

Although job specifications may be extremely valuable for human resource planning, recruiting and selection, and so forth, there is one problem in their development which should be mentioned. Some human requirements are fairly easy to translate into specific well-defined skills, e.g., typing and dictation. Other human requirements, however, such as "personality," "the ability to get along with others," or "leadership skills" may be much less amenable to specification in job analysis.

Job description and specification information may be stored in computers (primarily with larger organizations) to aid in providing data to help make promotional (and employee transfer) decisions. Stored along with an inventory of the skills possessed by each member of the organization, both sets of data can be probed to determine which, if any, individuals in the organization have the skills to fill specified job vacancies. We will discuss these "skills inventories" to a greater extent later in this chapter.

HUMAN RESOURCE FORECASTING

To make effective decisions, managers need to be able to forecast both *what* their human resource needs will be in the future and *from where* these resources will be obtained. Thus, there is both a "demand" and "supply" side of human resource forecasting. From the demand side, the organization will need to predict the number of managers, technicians, etc., that it will need at particular times in the future. It will also need to forecast what its own internal supply of human resources is, i.e., its current members available for promotion or transfer to other organization positions as they become vacant.

Organizations also need to be concerned with forecasting "external" human resource demand and supply, i.e., the demand of other firms for various classes of human resources, as well as the supply of these resources in the external labor market. For example, both the external supply of accountants graduated by business schools five years hence as well as other firms' demand for these human resources would have to be considered by any organization seeking to be actively hiring these graduates at that time.

In the following sections we will examine a number of forecasting techniques that have been developed to cope with the firm's human resources demand, its internal supply, and both external demand and supply. As we will note, some of the same forecasting techniques are useful for each of these different types of situations.

Forecasting the Demand for Human Resources

As indicated earlier, human resource plans must be updated more frequently in firms operating in more uncertain environments. In addition, regardless of the degree of uncertainty faced by any firm, the farther into the future that it makes its human resource demand forecasts, the greater the uncertainty will be with respect to their accuracy. Some observers, for example, have gone as far as to indicate that, regardless of firm, long-term forecasts generally are not too accurate, even in companies using reasonably sophisticated human resource planning techniques. They have considered it feasible to develop relatively accurate forecasts for a year or so ahead but believe that human resource demand forecasts will decline rapidly in accuracy after such a time period.

Regardless of organizational type, length of planning period, or degree of certainty faced, organizations must focus their human resource demand forecasting on three related factors linked by two conversions. First, an organization must examine variables, both internal and external, that will enable it to make a reasonably accurate projection of its output. Externally, for example, the nation's birth rate has been declining, which has resulted in a smaller potential market for the sale of baby food and, in the longer run, declining enrollments in colleges and universities (assuming that a constant percentage of the population continues to go to college). Internally, a firm already may have developed a new product and started construction on a new plant for producing the product.

Knowledge of factors such as these will be of value in forecasting the demand for its output. For example, the baby food manufacturer must convert birth rate statisitics into the number of jars of baby food of each flavor it will be able to sell each year. Colleges and universities must convert these birth statistics (along with numerous other variables) into projections for future student demand in each department for each academic year. The personnel manager may not be asked to participate in such output forecasting in some firms. In more personnel-proactive firms, however, the organization's top personnel officer may participate in the firm's output decision making. When this is the case, the personnel manager may provide valuable data on the available supply of human resources (both internal and external) to meet projected output levels.

When sales forecasts have been developed, they must be converted into specific human resource needs for specific jobs throughout the firm. In some cases, such a conversion is relatively simple; in other cases it may be quite difficult. For example, it may be fairly straightforward to predict the number of *direct* employee hours required to build a tire, cure it, inspect it, etc. In such a case, based on previous production data, the firm can simply take the time required in each stage of producing one P195/75R-14 tire; and multiply these figures by its sales forecast for P195/75R-14 tires to arrive at a prescribed number of work hours required for building, curing, etc. Taking these data, along with similar information on the manufacture of all of its tires of other sizes, the firm can then arrive at the number of direct-labor jobs required at each stage of the manufacturing process.

Somewhat more difficult would be the establishment of indirect-to-direct labor hour ratios. For example, the number of setup men required on a production line might increase if the firm's output level increased by 10 per cent, but not necessarily by this same percentage. Even more difficult is the projection of the numbers of clerical workers and managerial, technical, and professional personnel. If total sales increased by 10 per cent in the tire situation, the number of first-line supervisors might not be increased at all — each supervisor might simply have his span of control increased instead. Even if a supervisor or two is added to the work force, their supervisors (general foremen) might be able to handle this increase in the same fashion.

In discussing such output–human resource–demand conversions, two additional points deserve attention. First, many companies rely heavily on historical data in making their projections. These data may be of various types — a relatively constant percentage increase in sales each year, stable employee absenteeism rates, etc. These data are only valuable to the extent that the relevant variables remain the same in the future as in the past. In some situations, the historical data may represent good predictors of the future, but in many cases they will not. Second, because of uncertainties in the future, some organizations will develop a *range* of output and human resource forecasts contingent on the overall economic outlook for the firm's output, e.g., a human resource projection for next year if sales remain the same, or a projection with a 10 per cent sales increase or decrease.

Several different forecasting techniques have been used to cope with the problems involved in human resource demand forecasting. We will now focus our attention on four of these: (1) traditional statistical projections, (2) logarithmic learning curve analysis, (3) computer simulation and other related mathematical models, and (4) the Delphi technique.

Traditional Statistical Projections

Traditional statistical techniques such as correlation and regression analyses have been found very useful by many firms in converting output forecasts to specific human resource needs along the lines suggested. Rowland and Sovereign, looking at ways of forecasting demand, have described one firm's experience with statistical projections as follows:

> The manpower forecast was based on a correlation of employment to number of major product units shipped.
> The initial forecast was derived from a seven-year trend line relating manpower to amount of major product shipped and from an estimate of orders for the next time period obtained from market research.[14]

The human resource demand forecasts were then broken up into divisional requirements, and the firm was able to use this method of forecasting with considerable success. The company did recognize the limitations of historical data indicated above and made adjustments in its final forecasts periodically to reflect changing conditions in the economy and firm. This firm was deemed typical of many companies, especially those in a rapid growth period where demand for human resources would be increasing, rather than decreasing.

Logarithmic Learning Curve Analysis

In 1936, T. P. Wright published an article specifying how direct labor hours would decrease in the aircraft industry as additional units of aircraft were produced.[15] This decrease in labor hours reflects *organizational* learning rather than individual learning. Wright's model has been referred to as describing "manufacturing progress curves," "experience curves," "learning curves," or more descriptively as "logarithmic learning curves" since the model is based on logarithmic calculations.

Wright's model indicated that as the number of units of production *doubles*, the number of direct labor hours it takes to produce a unit *decreases* by a *constant percentage*. Thus, if it takes 10,000 hours to produce the first unit, and the learning percentage is 80 per cent, it would take 8000 hours to produce unit two, 6400 to produce the fourth unit, etc. This relationship for both 80 per cent and 70 per cent curves is illustrated in Figure 3–3. Regardless of the number of direct manhours required to produce the *first* unit, all 80 per cent curves have the same shape, all 70 per cent curves the same shape, etc. Thus, we have a family of logarithmic learning curves. Figure 3–4 shows both the 80 and 70 per cent curves for purposes of illustration. We illustrate these percentages because most logarithmic learning curves found to exist fall within this range.

As can be seen from Figures 3–3 and 3–4, once the learning

	y = Number of Hours of Direct Labor to Produce Any (xth) Unit		x =
	80% Curve	70% Curve	Unit Number
y_1	1000	1000	1
y_2	800	700	2
	•	•	•
y_4	640	490	4
	•	•	•
	•	•	•
	•	•	•
y_8	512	343	8
	•	•	•
	•	•	•
	•	•	•
	•	•	•
	•	•	•
y_{16}	409.6	240.1	16
	↓	↓	↓

Figure 3–3 Log-learning curve data. This figure emphasizes the decreasing times needed to produce additional (doubled) units, but not the fact that *cumulative* direct labor hours *increase* as more units are produced. For the 80 per cent curve, for example, 1000 plus 800 or 1800 hours would be required to produce the first two units; another 702.1 hours (not calculated here) would be required for the third unit; and 640 for the fourth unit; so that cumulative labor hours for the first four units would be 3142.1. From C. Richard Anderson, OSHA and Accident Control through Training, p. 8. © 1975 and published by the Industrial Press, Inc., New York. Reprinted with permission.

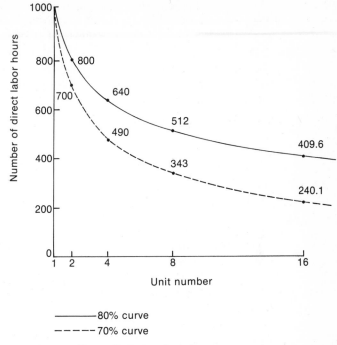

Figure 3-4 *Log-learning curve graph.*

percentage is established it is an elementary matter to determine the number of direct labor hours for the second, fourth, eighth, or sixteenth units produced. For the third, fifth through seventh, and ninth through fifteenth, however, the number of direct labor hours required in their manufacture cannot be precisely defined by simple arithmetic. For these numbers of units, we need a mathematical model to determine the number of direct labor hours required. The mathematics of the model, which will give us these numbers of direct labor hours, is provided in the Appendix to this chapter for readers interested in pursuing the quantitative aspects of the model more fully.

One other quantitative aspect of the logarithmic learning curve model is of critical importance — all points in *real life* will rarely, if ever, fall exactly on any logarithmic learning curves such as those shown in Figure 3–4. This problem may be overcome by using a statistical approach — logarithmic least squares linear regression analysis — to fit a line to the data points. A discussion of this approach is beyond the scope of this book, but there are numerous sources where the statistical model is described.[16]

Among the more important human resource planning objectives that the logarithmic learning curve model may help meet are:

1. Effecting more efficient production scheduling since approximate improvement in work performance is predictable.

2. Making possible the more efficient control of hiring and laying off human resources over the life of a contract.

Further, the model may be used to meet other organization objectives such as establishing production goals and evaluating performance in meeting these goals, and as a negotiation tool in purchasing.[17]

Although originally geared to aircraft production, the logarithmic learning curve has been applied to many other industries. For example, in a survey of nonaircraft companies reported in 1958, 61 per cent of the respondents indicated that they made use of it in manufacturing planning, while 64 per cent reported that it was very useful or necessary.[18] Among the specific kinds of industries mentioned in discussions of learning curve applications are metalworking, textile, candy making,[19] automobile assembly, apparel manufacture and in the production of large musical instruments.[20]

The learning curve has not been utilized without criticism. Young, for example, has indicated that for a number of reasons aerospace firms' learning curves have sometimes initially been poorly formulated. In such cases, using such curves once actual production was underway posed a real danger of obscuring problem areas. In these cases: "Being 'on the curve' implies that all is as it should be, when in fact it may be far from it."[21] More recently however, it has been concluded that:

. . . the relevance of the learning curve in labour-intensive manufacture extends beyond the aerospace and related defence industries . . . the learning curve phenomenon is *not an artifact of defence-contracting procedures* or a self-fulfilling prophecy, since two of the firms studied had never attempted learning curve analysis.[22]

Two final observations are in order here. First, from a contingency point of view, logarithmic learning curve analysis is most amenable to labor intensive industries — one would not find the model applicable in most continuous processing operations, where, for example, the rate of automated chemical manufacture may be relatively constant. Second, with wide acceptance as a tool that can help firms not only deal with human resource planning problems but with others as well, research on the applications of this tool continues, with further refinements of the basic model being developed.[23]

Computer Simulation and Other Quantitative Models

There has been a considerable number of simulation and other types of quantitative models developed to forecast human resource needs. These models will vary to a greater extent from organization to organization than the logarithmic learning curve model. We will describe one such successful computer model.

The model which we will discuss is MANPLAN, which was developed at the General Electric Company.[24] MANPLAN, as described by Bassett, was developed to overcome human resource modeling problems, such as the nonexistence of clean clear-cut models, and the overwhelming mathematical complexity that can be brought into human resource planning efforts. While recognizing the fact that for human resource planning it would be best for each firm to develop a model to fit its own business, it was decided to develop a "general purpose" simulator (MANPLAN) to be made available to users of the GE computer time-sharing service. This computer program interrogates its human user for the information it needs for its forecast, asking such questions as follows:

1. How many different product lines do you manufacture?
2. How many months does your sales forecast cover?
3. How many units of refrigerators, washers, dryers, air conditioners, and fans do you forecast for the next 10 months?[25]

These questions, when answered by the human and fed back into the computer, produce average human resource levels required to meet product demand. MANPLAN also provides for ranges of possible human resource needs for any period. With the model, the personnel manager can test the impact of various human resource decision making strategies. For example:

. . . possible changes in current manning levels of various employee classifications by means of promotion or downgrading could be tested to locate minimum lay-off strategies . . . . Any number of experiments with various numbers of upgrades and downgrades are permissible until you have finally reached an optimum schedule.[26]

One final merit of MANPLAN is that running the computer model is extremely inexpensive. An average forecast and schedule on the computer could be made for a total cost of about $2.00, as reported in 1973.

The Delphi Technique

The Delphi technique for forecasting is different from the human resource planning models we have discussed thus far, in that it is basically subjective in nature. For this reason, it is often viewed with suspicion by members of the quantitative school. The basic objective of the Delphi technique is to predict future situations by integrating the *independent* opinions of *experts*.

With the Delphi technique, a major objective is to avoid

direct confrontation of experts, since individuals in group discussions may be influenced unduly by others because of status differences and may compromise on some of their good ideas. This lack of direct confrontation is accomplished by having an intermediary provide the experts with a sequential series of questionnaires concerning the forecasting along with the controlled written feedback to each expert. More specifically, in each round of written interrogation each expert making forecasts independently:

1. Specifies his assumptions concerning the forecasting problem.
2. Identifies source material that would be helpful in revising his forecast estimates.
3. Is given these kinds of information developed by each of other experts, whose names are *not* associated with these data.

The intermediary:

. . . gathers the data requests of the experts and summarizes them along with the experts' answers to the primary question. . . .The developers of the delphi argue that the [above] procedures are more conducive to independent thought and allow more gradual formulation to a considered opinion.[27]

Successive revisions of these procedures are continued until a composite forecast is obtained.

These rounds of information–decision making provide each expert with an iterative (or step-by-step) feedback loop in which he gets successive rounds of reactions of others which may be helpful in forecasting. Such successive rounds usually result in the experts' opinions *converging* so as to provide a viable composite forecast.

The Delphi technique, which supposedly obtained its name from the widely celebrated Oracle of Delphi, who lived in the 4th century A.D., dates back at least to the late 1940's at the famed "think tank"—the RAND Corporation in Santa Monica, California. It has become more and more popular, and as reported in 1970, an estimated 50 to 100 companies had started Delphi forecasting projects to gain insights as to how future events might affect industry, and the world in 25 years.[28] Among the firms which have utilized the Delphi for various types of projections are McDonnell Douglas, Weyerhaeuser, Smith Kline and French, and TRW, Inc.[29]

Of special interest to us here is that a one-year human resource forecast utilizing Delphi has been carried out successfully by a retailing firm concerned with the number of buyers needed "one year from now."[30] Comparisons of the Delphi projections were made with linear regression equations, and the composite Delphi forecast came closer to ascertaining the number of buyers in the following year than did the regression analysis.

The researchers who did this study pointed out that there are certain limitations to the Delphi technique; e.g., the experts are instructed not to discuss their Delphi problem, but they may well do so, and the summaries of intermediaries are brief and omit some of the richness of detail in the experts' written reports. Problems have also occurred in other organizational uses of Delphi. For example, problems have arisen in integrating the forecasts of the experts, who are able to make no decisions, with the regular decision-making processes of top management. Further, some authorities indicate that one-year human resource demand forecasts are often easy to make, but longer range projections than this become increasingly difficult. In light of this we must ask how successful Delphi would be, for example, in developing 10-year human resource forecasts.

In spite of these limitations, the popularity of Delphi appears to be increasing, and there is no reason to expect that this trend will reverse itself. "At the minimum the delphi appears to be highly useful in generating preliminary insights into highly unstructured or undeveloped subject areas such as manpower planning."[31]

Forecasting the Internal Supply of Personnel

Assuming that an organization has developed a reasonably accurate human resource demand forecast for each job, it will next want to determine what persons having which skills will be available within the organization to meet this demand. Traditional statistical analyses may be used in this internal supply forecasting process, e.g., correlating turnover of various occupational groupings within the firm with individuals' age and years of company experience. Additionally, a number of other techniques have been developed for forecasting internal supply. In this section, we will examine three of these: (1) skills inventories, (2) replacement charts, and (3) Markov models.

Skills Inventories

A skills inventory is a device for pinpointing information concerning an individual with respect to his suitability for different jobs. For example, it may consist of the following data: age, address, health, education, willingness to travel, experience in present and previous jobs, and foreign languages spoken. If management has quick access to the skills of all of its employees, the organization will gain by being able to pick the "best" qualified individual within the organization for promotion or transfer. Specific skill requirements needed to perform available jobs competently may be obtained from job specifications developed in the job analysis process. Organization personnel may benefit in at least two ways from skills inventories. First, they will know that there is an *ongoing mechanism* for filling positions by promotion that *includes them*. This will enable them to know that they will not simply get "lost in the shuffle," especially in large organizations, and be overlooked for a better job when a vacancy for which they are qualified opens. Second, being chosen for a higher level position can mean the satisfaction of more human needs such as power, achievement, and esteem. Thus, skills inventories may serve to meet simultaneously both the firm's objectives and the individuals' needs.

Manual skills inventories have been utilized for many years with success. However, when computer capabilities for filing personnel inventories became operational, personnel management had a tool that permitted data to be obtained quickly for examination of all possible employees.

In the remainder of this section we will consider some of the mechanics of developing skills inventories, some of the many more specific goals that skills inventories can help meet, and some of the limitations and implementation problems faced with this human resource planning tool.

With respect to computerized skills inventory design, there are several steps involved. First, it will be necessary to structure an information-gathering instrument specifying the skills to be included in the inventory. In some cases, forms with provided "vocabularies" of words describing skills for the employee to check off if applicable are utilized. For example, in one IBM skills inventory form, major fields such as "photography" and "reproduction-printing," as well as numerous subfield vocabulary words (e.g., movie photography), were included for possible checkoff. A more flexible modification of this technique is to provide the employee with a defined checkoff vocabulary with an open-end-provision, i.e., giving him the opportunity to also list words describing his skills not found in the fixed vocabulary. Second, management must decide how to elicit information from employees. Interviews with individual employees, group interviews, or the questionnaire approach may be utilized. The most costly of these approaches, the individual interview, is also the most advantageous, in that the employee is led step by step through the interview, increasing the accuracy of the data. Finally, once the skills data have been collected, they must be coded for processing by the computer, and certain technical aspects of arranging the data for computer storage and retrieval, which we will not discuss, must be undertaken.[32]

Important in this whole design process is the *precise* and *brief* definition of each skill so that the computer can do a quick and accurate job of providing the skills inventory outputs desired. For example, at the Douglas Missile and Space Systems Division, copies of biographies of individuals suited for promotion according to the criteria desired could be received from the computer within 30 minutes to an hour.[33] With respect to accuracy, when IBM developed its skills inventory system, it found many errors in its original data, as well as errors that occurred in putting the data on the computer. These errors were pinpointed both by human review and by the computer itself, e.g., the computer was programmed so that it could detect that Seattle is not in the Eastern Regional Area, while a human auditor was faced with the question: "is a man likely to have graduated from college at the age of eight?"[34]

A number of large companies have reported successes with their skills inventories, e.g., IBM, RCA Service Company,[35] and Douglas Missile. Some of the values realized by such systems, in addition to the basic objective of quick human resource, individual-job matching include:

1. Data from the human, precomputerized information system has often been redundant, discovered, and corrected as the computerization process takes place. In IBM, for example, it was found that "over 2000 pieces of personnel information were being maintained but only 145 of these were unduplicated."[36]

2. Valuable special studies may be undertaken quickly by probing the computer skills inventory data on the computer. For example, the RCA system provided for special studies "on a moment's notice — such as military reserve status, payroll data, seniority, or the potential effects of possible wage increases."[37]

3. Skills inventories can provide data of value in the utilization of replacement charts, a human resource planning tool discussed later.

4. Skills inventories can also constitute an important ingredient of an effective "affirmative action" program. The federal government has taken more and more of an active role in forcing organizations to do away with discriminatory actions with respect to both hiring and promotional decisions. If an organization has taken affirmative action to provide equal employment opportunities in making its human resource decisions, having information to clearly indicate this in its skills inventories data bank can serve to make its case more "court proof," should its policies be questioned.

A number of conditions are essential for successful skills inventories. Extremely important among these is that the organization must have clear-cut objectives *and* viable procedures to attain these goals when developing such a system. In one company, World Equipment and Machinery, for example, a prime goal of the skills inventory system was that of identifying candidates for promotion. Here, it was claimed that the skills inventory was not adequate in identifying individuals for promotion to positions of "significant responsibility" because relevant current skills were not found to be valid predictors of potential at these higher levels. The validity of this claim must be questioned, however, since procedurally this inventory "in many cases, could not accurately represent currently available skills because controls on input were weak."[38]

Some other success conditions for skills inventories include:

1. The system cannot be perceived by employees as impersonal. This perception may be overcome if individuals actually *see* the system working, e.g., if they observe one of their colleagues being promoted as a result of the system. Further, a careful explanation about the system to employees when it is first developed may be helpful in relieving concern.

2. As with virtually every personnel program, the support of top management is required for a successful skills inventories system.

3. All skills inventory systems need *updating* from time to time. From a contingency point of view, this presents extra problems for dynamic organizations in which change is rapid.

4. Again from a contingency viewpoint, it has been argued that skills inventories would be less successful in firms organized by function (such as engineering, production, and sales) than in those organized along product lines: "All similar skills, such as circuit design, stress analysis. . . etc., would be in specialized, segregated units and, thus, the location of most skills would be reasonably well known" without a skills register.[39] Somewhat relatedly, it has been argued that it is easier to match individual skills to jobs when the jobs are comparatively well-defined (e.g., a personnel interviewer) as compared to more ambiguously defined, top level line managerial positions.

5. There has been a concern among many employees who believe that skills inventories represent an invasion of privacy. As we indicated in Chapter 2, privacy may be a real problem with computerized PIDS, even with care taken in limiting access to computer probing to only authorized personnel.

6. The user of a skills inventory system must apply judgment concerning *how many* skills requirements are necessary to obtain a list of qualified employees for a job vacancy. If too many attributes are required, the probabilities may be very low or zero for finding any qualified employees in the organization; e.g., if the job calls for a physicist with a Ph. D. degree, at least five years of experience in solid state physics, the ability to speak French fluently, who is under 30 years of age, and is willing to travel abroad. Conversely, if the manager's requirements are too few, a computer printout of 200 qualified individuals may result, e.g., if the description specified only someone with a B.S. degree in engineering and three years of experience in this field. How many biographies are desirable is a matter of judgement. In the Douglas Missile and Space Systems skills inventory system described earlier, for example, a skills search in a functional area at one time produced about 30 to 60 biographies.[40]

To summarize, we have indicated some real values that may be provided by skills inventories. Especially important in larger firms, skills inventories may foster an "open systems" human resource movement approach, i.e., capable employees in one division of a company are not closed off from promotional opportunities in other parts of the organization simply because they are not known to be available. At the same time, a number of conditions must be met if skills inventories are to be successful. In general, many of the potential limitations of skills inventories apply to both manual and computerized systems. What the effective personnel manager must do in deciding whether to recommend the adoption of skills inventories is to consider both their values and limitations with respect to the conditions both existing or potential in his own organization.

Replacement Charts

As indicted earlier, skills inventories may provide the data for replacement charts. Replacement charts, unlike skills inventories, are *visual display* devices that focus attention on such factors as the ages, current levels of performance, and potential promotability of managers. An example of a replacement chart is illustrated in Figure 3–5.

A replacement chart can *complement* skills inventories by presenting *summary data* to management in a *different form*. It does not show all the information about employees that may be obtained from skills inventories. Rather, it condenses and summarizes data, as shown in Figure 3–5. Unlike skills inventories, replacement charts generally do not include data on all organizational employees — they are concerned primarily with managerial and professional personnel.

The replacement chart may also indicate which specific individuals are ready *now* for promotion. If such individuals are not promoted in the near future, there is often a high probability that they may search for employment with another organization. It also can enable the executive to visualize career patterns for different individuals. For example, as shown in Figure 3–5, Joe Jones is performing in his present position in an outstanding manner and therefore might be a logical candidate for plant manager. Additionally, he has a backup man for his position whose performance and promotion potential are both excellent. Sam Elkins' performance, on the other hand, needs improvement, and there are no backup men for his position who are ready now for promotion into his position.

Although the names of promotable individuals may result from a skills inventory probe, a replacement chart — often kept by the top line manager in each major organizational department or division of an organization — can serve to bring human resource planning needs and problems continuously and conspicuously to the attention of line management. Replacement charts also indicate when an individual's performance is below average, which may call for training to improve his performance. If it is not

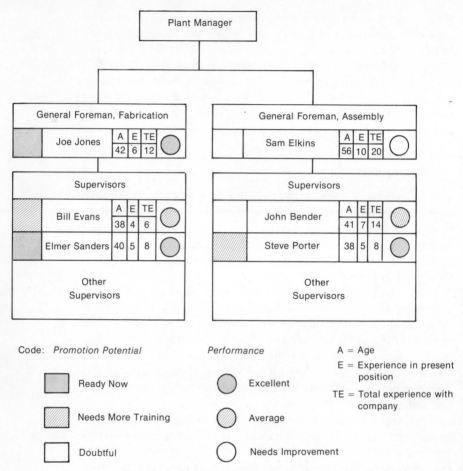

Figure 3–5 Hypothetical replacement chart.

believed that training will correct the problem, a demotion or dismissal may be called for.

Unlike a centrally located computerized skills inventory systems, large organizations may well require numerous replacement charts, one for each division. This need results because replacement charts would become unmanageable if data on all 300 to 400 managers and professional employees in a large firm were visually displayed together. This would not render immediate information on possible promotable individuals available as a whole, but this function could be accomplished by a computerized skills inventory.

Finally, the value of replacement charts is contingent on several of the same conditions as skills inventories. If they are to be successful, line management must use them, top management support is called for, and the same kinds of updating problems exist as with skills inventories. In short, an appropriately designed and updated replacement chart continuously provides management with a current summary visual display of its human resource conditions, while skills inventories can provide a rapid probe for eligible individuals, providing much more information on these individuals.

Markov Models

Another technique used by an organization to determine the numbers and classes of individuals in its internal labor supply is the Markov model. Essentially, a Markov model is used in human resource planning to indicate the probabilities of movement of organization members from one job to another over time.

Markov models are developed as follows. Similar jobs are clustered together at a particular time to get an initial "state;" then employee movements from state to state are determined.[41] For example, suppose at the beginning of 1975, 20 individuals had been in one job state (e.g., production supervisor), and that 18 of these 20 people remained in that state after a year, with the other two members of the state having been promoted to a "general foreman" state. In such a case, we should say that the probabilities (called *transition* probabilities) of the supervisors remaining as supervisors would be 0.90 and of them being promoted to the general foreman state, 0.10.

As an illustrative example of a Markov model, suppose we had only 50 people in a firm at the beginning of 1977 distributed as follows among three different positions: 20 junior engineers, 20 engineers, and 10 senior engineers. If at the end of this year 16 junior engineers, 18 engineers, and all of the 10 senior engineers remained in their same position, while four junior engineers were promoted during the year to engineers, and two engineers promoted to senior engineers, we would have the data shown in Figure 3–6. (Such data may be obtained from skills inventories.) As indicated in Figure 3–6, the rows showing the number of engineers in each of the three positions at the beginning of both 1977 and 1978 are called row vectors, and the bracketed nine transition probabilities are called a transition matrix. This is a very simplified example and does not account for people leaving the organization or being newly hired.[42] A more extensive and realistic transition matrix which does consider these probabilities as shown in Figure 3–7. It is important to note that the sum of all probabilities in *each row* of transition matrices equals 1.0. This is because "something happens" to everyone, whether they remain in the same state or move into another—all personnel must be accounted for. This characteristic may be observed in Figures 3–6 and 3–7.

Markov models may serve either or both of two distinct functions in human resource planning. They can be used to *predict* human resource movements in the future and to *describe* current human resource distributions and movements.

Predictive functions. Markov process data such as shown in Figure 3–6 can enable us to predict the number of organization members that will be in each job state at future times by some simple calculations involving matrix algebra. The number of engineers in each of the three job states in Figure 3–6 at the beginning of 1979 may be obtained by multiplying the beginning year 1977 row vector by the transition matrix *squared*; the number in each state at the beginning of 1980 is found by multiplying this same row vector by the transition matrix *cubed*, etc.[43]

This sounds straightforward enough, but there are two limiting assumptions (or conditions) necessary to make these predic-

A. Row Vector Showing Distribution of Engineers at Beginning of Year 1977

$$
\begin{array}{ccc}
\text{JE} & \text{E} & \text{SE*} \\
[20 & 20 & 10]
\end{array}
$$

B. Probabilities of Movement During Year 1977: The Transition Matrix

From   To

$$
\begin{array}{c}
 \\
\text{JE} \\
\text{E} \\
\text{SE}
\end{array}
\begin{array}{ccc}
\text{JE} & \text{E} & \text{SE} \\
.80 & .20 & 0 \\
0 & .90 & .10 \\
0 & 0 & 1.0
\end{array}
$$

C. Movements During the Year 1977

```
JE Remaining JE   (20 ×  .80) = 16
JE Promoted to E  (20 ×  .20) =        4
E Remaining E     (20 ×  .90) =       18
E Promoted to SE  (20 ×  .10) =              2
SE Remaining SE   (10 × 1.0 ) =             10
                                ──  ──  ──
                                16  22  12
```

D. Row Vector Showing Distribution Distribution of Engineers at Beginning of Year 1978 $[16 \quad 22 \quad 12]$

---

*JE = Junior Engineers; E = Engineers; SE = Senior Engineers

Figure 3–6 *Illustrative Markov model.*

Time II

Time I	MGRL	PROF B	PROF A	TRNE	SEC	TYP	CLK	CLER	CRFT	LA C	LA B	LA A	POOL	EXIT
MGRL	.92	0	0	0										.08
PROF B	.10	.78	0	0										.12
PROF A	.06	0	.80	0										.14
TRAINEE	0	.35	.30	.15										.20
SEC					.82	0	0	0						.18
TYPIST					.16	.64	0	0						.20
CLERK					0	.05	.75	0						.20
CLERICAL					0	.18	.10	.52						.20
CRAFT									.92					.08
LABOR C										.68	0	0	.10	.22
LABOR B										0	.80	0	0	.20
LABOR A										0	0	.70	.06	.24
LABOR POOL										0	.30	.15	.30	.25
RECRUIT	0	0	0	.14	0	0	0	.25	.01	0	0	0	.60	

Figure 3–7 Markovian matrix.

Source: Thomas A. Mahoney and George T. Milkovich, "Internal Labor Markets: An Empirical Investigation," Technical Report 7006, Industrial Relations Center, University of Minnesota, July 1972, p. 8.

tions. First, the validity of the model requires that the chances of moving to each possible state during some time interval depends entirely on the current state. In most human resource situations this condition does not exist if the states are defined *solely* on the basis of *position*.

It may be possible, however, to define the states so as to meet the current state assumption. For example, the probability of moving from one managerial level to another may depend "not only on being in the lower-level position but also on the length of service at that level."[44] A state redefinition that would include both level and length of service may permit the development of a valid Markov model. We could, for example, have three states instead of only one for the junior engineers in Figure 3–6: (1) junior engineers with less than three years of experience; (2) those with from three to five years of experience, and (3) those with more than five years of experience. Such a redefinition might well result in realistic higher promotional transition probabilities for the longer service states, and hence a viable predictive model.

Second, Markov models as predictive tools depend upon the transition probabilities remaining constant (or stable) over each time period. In many cases, such probabilities do not remain stable, although in some they do. For example, in one study of a single department in a large firm in the steel industry:

Employment over the total period studied was relatively stable with the exception of a period of reduced demand following increased sales in anticipation of a strike which did not occur.[45]

The degree of stability depends on the nature of the actual work force being analyzed and the manner in which the states are defined. It also depends on the time intervals chosen between periods. If the periods are defined very closely (for example, each day) one may or may not find the same human resource pattern as in the previous day. By lengthening these time periods to six months or a year, however, we are more likely to find stable transition probabilities "since minor economic or policy changes will then tend to cancel out."[46]

Descriptive functions. In addition to predicting human resource movements, Markov models can often give us much valuable descriptive information as to what has been going on during the two time intervals chosen for application of the model, e.g., in our example at the beginning of 1977 and the beginning of 1978. Such information when analyzed may help answer many important questions:

1. What are the organization's entry positions? Do most newly hired people enter the organization at very low level jobs? What about intermediate and higher level jobs?[47]

2. What are the organization's mobility channels? For example, do many people hired as production supervisors eventually move up to become general foremen in their departments? Do they get promoted to positions in other departments such as marketing? In one firm in which there were manufacturing, marketing, engineering, and service positions, for example, the interfunctional mobility was highest from 1964 to 1965 from engineering and marketing.[48]

3. What are the firm's mobility clusters? There exist in organizations classes or clusters of jobs within which mobility is restricted, i.e., individuals move more readily among these jobs than between jobs within and outside the clusters. Reference to the Markovian matrix in Figure 3–7 illustrates extremely clear-cut mobility clusters in the firm studied.

4. Are the internal job clusters and career paths for whites different for those who are nonwhites? If so, the firm may have problems meeting governmental equal opportunity regulations.

5. Where is turnover the highest? In one study it was found that the turnover rates for women were consistently lower than for men.[49] In the model mentioned above, which included marketing, manufacturing and engineering, and service jobs, the highest turnover from the beginning of 1964 to the beginning of 1965 was in the highest level service positions (personnel, finance, etc.).

6. Do men predominate in the highest paid job clusters? If so, the firm may be discriminating against women and must be concerned with equal employment opportunity problems with the government.

Markov models: Overview. Markov models represent an interesting approach to describing and sometimes predicting human resource movement within a firm. Unlike skills inventories, which are concerned with specific individuals having specific skills, Markov models use quantitative techniques, which simply give us numbers of personnel in various job states. They are also limited to use to larger organizations. In very small ones there would simply be too few personnel to provide an adequate sample size.

External Demand and Supply

As indicated earlier, it is not enough for a firm to predict only its own human resources demand and internal supply — it must also be concerned with demand and supply conditions externally in its industry and in the economy.

Several comments are in order concerning external forecasts. First, a number of information sources to improve human resources decision making are available for external demand and supply forecasts that do not exist for its own demand and internal supply projections. Both some unions and industrial trade associations publish reports concerning supply and demand projections in the labor force. Additionally, a wide variety of occupational data are continuously published by the U.S. Department of Labor and other governmental sources. For example, the *Monthly Labor Review,* published by the Bureau of Labor Statistics, concerns itself with occupational projection data;[50] the demand for various occupational groups was projected for 1980 in 1971 in the *Manpower Report of the President.*[51] Second, some of the same types of forecasting techniques useful in projecting a firm's human resource demand and internal supply may be applicable for external human resource forecasting. The Delphi technique, for example, can be utilized to project occupational supply and demand trends just as well as for forecasting human resource demand for the firm. Traditional statistical techniques such as regression or correlation, as well as simulation and other types of management science models often provide the basis for human resource reports published by the government. For example, the Office of Civilian Manpower Management in the Department of the Navy has published a number of mathematical research reports oriented toward human resource forecasting and planning. One of its 1976 reports indicated how a mathematical model can aid in establishing a realistic set of equal employment opportunity goals.[52] This model: (1) had an *objective* to be maximized (meeting certain quantifiable goals for integrating women and minority group members into the Department of the Navy's work force); and (2) included certain *constraints,* such as supply limitations determined by external labor market projections. As may be recalled from Chapter 1, problems in which there are scarce resources and which attempt to maximize some objective subject to constraints are often amenable to solution by the management science technique of mathematical programming; this type of model was at the heart of this endeavor. Management science models have also been utilized for external supply and demand projections outside of the federal government. For example, in 1971, Whybark reported on a mathematical model simulating certain key variables in predicting 1980 human resource requirements for an entire industry—pilots and mechanics in civil aviation.[53]

Third, the supply of human resources in the external labor market is generally forecast with special attention to enrollments in various educational institutions and anticipated losses in an occupation due to retirement, transfer elsewhere, or death. Thus, looking at graduation figures and the age distribution of individuals in different occupations become very important.

Finally, firms may employ specific strategies to meet their own human resource needs based on cues derived from external demand and supply conditions. For example, in spite of the disadvantages of stockpiling mentioned earlier, a firm may engage in this practice and offer very high starting salaries to this year's crop of graduates in electrical engineering, if external supply and demand analysis indicates that the economy's demand for individuals in this profession will start exceeding the supply being graduated beginning in the next two or three years. In a somewhat different vein, organizations may contribute to scholarship funds at colleges and universities to encourage more students to study in specific disciplines in which there is a shortage of human resources.

FORMULATING HUMAN RESOURCE PLANS

Once an organization has forecast human resource supply and demand it will be in a position to deal with either or both of the following types of conditions:

1. The projected number of employees available for any given job is less than the demand for the personnel, i.e., one or more job vacancies is anticipated.

2. The forecast number of people working at any given job is greater than the number of personnel needed to perform that job, i.e., internal supply is greater than demand.

In this section, we will: (1) discuss these two situations and indicate various strategies, problems, and characteristics of each, and (2) specifically consider the impact of governmental equal opportunity employment constraints on human resource planning decisions.

Filling Job Vacancies

Filling job vacancies in organizations involves many considerations: deciding to what extent to promote from within; analyzing internal career movement patterns; and informing employees of their opportunities for betterment by internal movement. Many such actions, it should be emphasized, are closely related to performance appraisal and training decisions. Also involved in internal human resource movement decisions are actions taken by the government to ensure equal opportunity employment.

Introduction

When vacancies are forecast for any job in an organization, basically two strategies may be undertaken to overcome this problem. First, the firm may hire an outsider to fill the position. This approach falls in the area of selection and is discussed at length in the next chapter. The second strategy is to promote or transfer someone already in the organization to fill the position *and to hire*. We emphasize the words "and to hire" because, unless the organization is going to reduce the number of its total human resources, the job of the individual being moved into the vacant position will then become *vacant itself*. In fact, any such move may kick off a "chain-reaction" of human resource flows. For example, if a firm's marketing vice president is to retire, his assistant may take his job, the firm's marketing manager for its Eastern Division may be moved up into the assistant's job, the marketing manager's assistant may be moved into his job, and so on, until we come to a point at which there is (1) no one within the organization who is capable of being moved up (or transferred), and (2) hence, the firm is forced to go into the external labor market.

It is important to recognize that such movements may represent "lateral transfers" as well as promotions on the firm's organization chart. In such cases, the individuals moved may assume different "broadening" responsibilities and obtain increases in pay.

If an organization is to emphasize movement from within to fill job vacancies, it must have effective training and development efforts so that members of the organization will be capable of moving into higher-level positions or those calling for differing responsibilities.

It should also be emphasized that although there are some differences among firms as to the extent that the placement-from-within decision strategy is chosen over the hire-from-outside strategy, a majority of companies adhere to placement-from-within policies. In one study:

Almost universally (96 percent), the companies . . . believed in filling positions from within their own organizations. The most frequent estimate was that at all levels of management, at least 90 to 95 percent of managers had come from internal sources.[54]

The authors of this study also found that organizations that did *not* place mostly from within were usually *forced* to adopt the "hire" strategy out of necessity — they were in rapid growth situations, where internal personnel were taxed so greatly that there simply were not enough qualified personnel in the firm to fill all needed job vacancies.[55]

Thus far, we have been referring primarily to managerial and professional transfers and promotions. In nonmanagerial situations, where there is a union contract, management may often be forced to promote from within. It may be required to "post" notices of all job vacancies; then, members of the collective bargaining unit are permitted to "bid" for the jobs. Probably the most common decision rule written into labor-managment contracts for handling this type of situation is that the employee with the most *seniority* who "bids" gets the higher level job, *providing* he has certain skills necessary for the job.

As we will indicate later, it has been suggested that managerial and professional jobs also be "posted," but this practice is not too common. On the other hand, many firms do give attention at managerial and professional levels to both the seniority and ability criteria inherent in unionized job bidding. Many organizations, for example, follow the decision rule: "Promote the most able; but if two or more individuals are about equally able, promote the one with the greatest seniority." The primary problem with such a rule is that, especially at managerial and professional levels, it may be extremely difficult to determine the "most able" individual. It is very difficult to objectively measure executive and professional performance in individuals' present positions, to say nothing of predicting the individual's *ability* to succeed at a higher level position or one calling for different responsibilities.

Finally, in discussing the hire vs. promote (or transfer) decision alternatives, some of the basic reasons to support each of these strategies are worthy of attention. With respect to providing promotion opportunities in an organization:

1. Many employees may be more highly motivated and satisfied if they can see promotions awaiting them when they increase their skills and abilities.

2. Promoting a *known* insider rather than a usually not as well known outsider may decrease the risk of making a poor human resource decision. This is because we have a greater amount of valid information to provide a basis for the decision when we move from within, e.g., performance appraisal data developed over several years of previous work with the firm.

On the other hand, hiring from the outside for jobs above those at beginning or "entry port" levels can be said to have the following merits:

1. At the managerial and professional levels, incumbent personnel may grow "stale" and ultraconservative, and hiring new employees from outside the firm may provide much needed "new blood" for the organization.

2. The hire-from-the-outside strategy at these levels does not create the strong need for training and developing managers and professionals, and the firm will not face any upheavals due to promotional chain reactions as discussed above.

Career Paths

Many of the points just discussed dealt with subjective, judgmental managerial decisions. One of the reasons for this is that both promotional and external job market selection have not been subject to a high degree of quantification. In recent years, however, quantitative models (such as Markov models) have been utilized to identify entry level positions, job clustering in organizations, and definition of career paths.

Analyzing such phenomena is of value both to the organization and to individuals within it. Career path analysis can be useful in human resource forecasting and also as feedback to individuals to give them data about possible career routes they might follow in the organizaiton.

Career path analysis.   More and more researchers are studying the flow of human resources through different paths in the organization. Our previous discussion of Markov models is a prime illustration of career path analysis, so that by referring to Figure 3–7, we can see several facets of this endeavor. For example:

1. The three primary "entry ports" were managerial trainees, clerical positions, and in the labor pool.
2. The managerial and professional, clerical, craft, and labor groupings were discrete job families, between which *no* mobility existed.
3. The management trainees had: (1) the greatest probability of any entry-level individuals to be promoted by Time II, and (2) only two possible paths open to them (trainee to professional A or trainee to professional B). There was *no movement at all* between the two professional positions.

Such data could be useful to management in several ways. Management could, for example, indicate to managerial trainee job applicants that 65 percent of the trainees hired during the previous one-year time period studied were promoted to either a professional A or professional B job.

Career path counseling.   As far back as the 1920's, Western Electric employed professional counselors to help advise its employees on career and other problems important to them. The employment of such counselors created many problems, and their use has declined. One of the major limitations of this approach was that employees could bypass their supervisors and point out supervisor deficiencies to a counselor, who was not in the normal managerial hierarchy. This placed the counselors in a difficult position—they had obligations to management yet at the same time if they betrayed confidences placed in them by employees they would lose the trust of the latter. Today's employee, however, should be able to obtain career guidance and support from his supervisor, both in daily contacts and formal performance appraisals—especially managerial and professional personnel. Career guidance is probably needed today more than ever, because of such problems as concerns for equal opportunity, altered markets for professional people, the development of paraprofessional occupations, rapid changes in technology, and emerging patterns for a "second" career among many middle-aged persons.[56]

We have already discussed some key types of questions that organization members might ask with respect to careers and career paths in our previous discussion of replacement charts and Markov models, e.g., what career paths are available to them?

Most individuals would also like to obtain an estimate as to how long they will have to remain in their present job before being promoted. This question almost invariably has to be answered in probabilistic terms; and there may be considerable variation from job to job. For example, in the 1964–1965 Markov model analysis illustrated earlier, it was estimated that the average number of years that a person would have to remain in the lowest level manufacturing positions was 7.8, while this same figure was only 4.8 years for lower level marketing personnel.[57] Closely related, most individuals would probably like to know what training they would need for each of the various career paths that might be open to them. Employees may also like to know if they will be locked into a dead-end job. In the 1964–1965 example just referred to, for instance, 13 percent of the personnel in the highest level "service" job class left the company from 1964 to 1965, thus indicating a good possibility that this was a dead-end job.[58]

One should not infer from these statements that having dead-end jobs is necessarily wrong. There are some individuals who have strong dependence needs, do not want too much responsibility, and, consequently, do not aspire for top executive positions. For such individuals, "dead-end" positions may be desirable. Further, no organization, to use the old saying, can have "all Chiefs and no Indians." There will be only so far that each person can (and in many cases, wants to) go. Rather obviously, not everyone can reach the position of president or vice president of a large organization.

In some cases, however, firms have kept people in positions that do not really tap the individual's skills, knowledge, and abilities. In one study undertaken in analyzing careers in the Boston area, it was found that there was a "roadblocking" of minority older persons whose skills, talents, and college education were largely untapped after years of employment — these individuals were "career disadvantaged."[59] This study, which was reported in 1974, indicated that 23 percent of older minority college graduates were employed at low-level jobs paying less than $10,000, while there were *no* minorities among those surveyed holding jobs paying $25,000 or more annually.[60]

Two other types of career counseling situations should be discussed. The first is the case in which the individual is obviously ready *now* for a promotion but is blocked because there are no higher-level vacancies open for which he is qualified. In some such situations in which the company really wants to keep the individual, it may, for example, create a "temporary position" (or give him a satisfactory salary increase) so as to try not to lose him to another company. Further, in career planning discussions, the individual's supervisor may reassure the individual that he *is ready* for promotion, that top management is aware of this and that he will be promoted as soon as a vacancy at the desired level occurs. From a contingency point of view, in some types of work it may be relatively easy to promote a worker "ready," *regardless* of the existence of current vacancies. This would be the case in such organic situations as research departments, where an individual can be promoted to "senior" researcher and be given more responsibilities regardless of whether a "vacancy" exists. This would also be true in many university situations, where promotion, for example, from Assistant to Associate Professor takes place.

Second, there may be cases in which an individual's supervisor indicates that the worker has *no* career path opportunities, i.e., that the person does not have the *capability* to be promoted anywhere higher up in the organization. In some such cases, there may be no problems — the individual himself may concur with this indication and may not want to be promoted. In other cases, however, the individual may perceive his abilities to be much greater than has been indicated by his supervisor, and a delicate situation may arise. In such cases, the individual may sometimes simply accept the situation portrayed by the supervisor and remain on the job, possibly because he cannot find a better job elsewhere. In others, on the contrary, he may leave the organization (if he can) to seek greater opportunities with another organization. Such an action frequently follows an individual's having been "bypassed" in the organization — someone has just been promoted into the position he wanted himself. Such a move may be either desirable or undesirable for either the man or the organization. For example, if the individual's performance does not compare favorably (as perceived by the supervisor) with that of his peers, the firm may be pleased to see him leave. In other situations, it may be desirable for both the company and the individual, even when a *competent* person leaves for greater opportunities elsewhere, if there are *real* lengthy roadblocks to promotion. For example, a highly competent personnel manager was in a position in which his superior indicated that he did not envision any vacancies that would be available to meet manager's desires in the foreseeable future. Obviously unhappy, this person took a position elsewhere, commanding a higher salary and calling for greater responsibilities. Such a move bettered the individual. It was also privately admitted by some managers in the company he left that the exit move was probably desirable for the organization as well, since the individual's frustrations were beginning to impair his motivation and ability to work effectively toward organizational objectives.

Open and Closed Systems

In the last discussion, we used the phrase "*real* roadblocks to promotion." This statement opens the door to many questions that management should ask when job vacancies exist above entry-port positions in the organization. Are supervisors correct in concluding that one or more of their subordinates does not have the capability for greater responsibilities or that no promotional opportunities will emerge in the near future? The supervisor might be (1) wrong in his assessment of the subordinate's capabilities, (2) unaware of promotional opportunities in other departments that would meet the desires and capabilities of his subordinates, or (3) selfish and trying to "hoard" subordinates for himself rather than encouraging their promotion elsewhere because they really *are* competent.

The use of skills inventories and replacement charts is specifically designed to help create an "open promotional system" — one in which information is developed and transmitted where necessary in the organization so that all employees with the necessary skills will be considered when any vacancies do open.

Although recognizing the value of replacement charts and skills inventories, in some organizations, certain observers believe that "procedures for bringing candidates up for review . . . is . . . [a] problem area which . . . has been too often overlooked."[61] Many such situations may occur that lead to a "closed" promotional system. Some of the key characteristics of this type of system as indicated by Alfred are:[62]

1. In many organizations, the system is so structured as to make it easy to hoard good people.
2. It is also common for managers to be permitted to hire from within their own departments "without considering others in the organization."[63]
3. A person's chances of being considered for promotion depend too heavily on his own supervisor's *opinion,* which as we indicated earlier, may be erroneous.
4. When a promotion has been announced, those who are bypassed are not informed as to whether they were considered, or, if so, why *they* did not get the job.

As an extreme case of a closed system, this observer has noted that one company had its interdivisional manpower flows so cut off that "men were quitting the company to be rehired again by another division."[64]

Underlying these characteristics of a closed system, according to Alfred, are two basic factors:

1. There is not enough information available in the system.
2. Supervisors have "*unnecessary authority*" over their subordinates' careers.[65]

If a firm is large enough, wants to develop a *high quality* skills inventory system, does so, and indoctrinates its managers as to the benefits of the system, Alfred's first factor may be lessened considerably.[66] Managers should have it clearly pointed out to them that not only will situations arise in which they may lose good personnel to other departments; but that the converse will also occur — they themselves will have opportunities to take highly qualified talent from other departments. With respect to the second factor, supervisors in some organizations may well have too much power in controlling their subordinates' careers. In some organizations, however, subordinates actively participate in their performance appraisals (see Chapter 5). Further, other higher level members of the organization than just a subordinate's immediate supervisor may participate in the appraisals where career planning may be considered. In addition to the two methods we indicated earlier — skills inventories and performance appraisals — which Alfred also recognized, he suggested the advertising of all jobs. Such jobs would be posted, and individuals would be given a chance to bid on them, a practice which, as mentioned earlier, exists in many union contract situations today.

Open systems for promotion (and transfer) are congruent with the advantages and limitations of the movement-from-within philosophy itself. Openness provides individuals with greater opportunities for advancement. Such a system, however, requires better (and probably more costly) information generation, transmittal, and retrieval systems as well as a commitment on the part of the organization to active training and development processes at all levels of the organization to ensure that its personnel may become capable of assuming more or different responsibilities.

The Reduction of Unnecessary Personnel

Most organizations have invariably had periods in which there were more employees on its payroll than were currently needed. This may occur regularly each year, as has happened in the automobile industry with new model changes. Excess employees may also exist when there are recessions in the economy or when technological changes reduce or eliminate the number of employee hours required to perform a particular job. This has often been the case in some automated and computerized operations, e.g., office computerization may result in a reduced demand for typists.

In some excess human resource situations, workers themselves have agreed to reducing their work hours each week so that the lesser amount of work could be spread among all of the existing personnel requiring no one to be laid off. This has generally occurred to a greater extent in blue collar jobs than at professional and managerial levels. With declining college enrollments in the mid-70's, however, each faculty member in one department of a major university agreed to take a cut in pay so that no one in the department would have to be laid off.

Basically, there are three ways in which excessive human resources may be reduced: (1) by attrition; (2) by transfer to another job, and (3) by layoff. We will now discuss each of these.

Attrition

Employees leave organizations due to retirement, death, for a better job elsewhere, and so on. Except for retirement, an organization may have no idea of exactly which employees in each specific job will leave the firm. The organization may have turnover data by job or department,[67] but not knowing specifically who will leave renders the attrition approach highly uncertain.

Transfers

Employee transfers may be utilized to fill job vacancies both when the firm's demand for human resources is increasing and when reductions-in-force occur. If a decreased need for employees in *one* job category in an organization occurs *simultaneously* with an increased need for employees in another, it may be possible to retrain people and transfer them. This strategy has been particularly useful as technological changes such as computerization and automation have simultaneously reduced or eliminated the number of human resources in certain traditional jobs while creating new jobs in other areas. For example, a no-longer-needed typist might easily be trained as a key punch operator with the advent of computerization. Important here is that management invariably has advance notice of the technological change, and thus can plan an orderly transition of personnel from one job to another.

Layoffs

It is usually difficult for firms to predict the need for laying off personnel in the future. Still, in periods of declining sales, some human resource projections can be developed and layoffs can be planned to a certain extent, rather than being made on a completely haphazard basis. Haphazard human resource planning practices often occur, as was pointed out by one observer in 1971 with respect to economic downtrend at that time:

Many organizations are now [laying off workers]. . . . While some reduction in the work force may be a direct result of loss of sales, some of it was based on an edict from above: cut your personnel by 10% or 15% or some other set figure.[68]

At managerial, professional, and other nonunionized levels of organizations, individuals have no protection with respect to who will be laid off in these kinds of situations. The layoff of workers covered by many union contracts, on the other hand, is based on seniority — with the least senior employees in any seniority unit being laid off first. The impact of seniority systems on human resource flows when layoffs are called for is considerable, and we will now turn our attention to such systems.

Seniority and bumping. Many union contracts provide that if an employee is to be laid off, he may "bump" the next least senior employee and take his job; that the latter can, in turn, bump the person with the next least seniority, and so on until it is the least senior employee in the unit who actually loses his job. In many cases, some jobs are "protected" from bumping to the extent that another employee needs certain job qualifications to bump into the job. Without such protection, production could be reduced drastically, e.g., on a highly skilled job in which it would take an employee without any prior experience 10 to 20 weeks before he could reach a standard level of production. In one plant no such protection existed at a time when over 400 workers were laid off. If the union contract had been followed, the lower production of workers newly bumped into positions calling for experience would have resulted in a smaller number of units to be processed in *other* departments. This would, in turn, have meant fewer employee work hours required, and created an additional series of bumps. These would have shortly meant bumping the newly bumped workers on the original unprotected higher skill jobs, etc., until the plant would have been forced to shut down. This ultimate consequence of the contract was realized by both the union and management. Both sides agreed to modify the contract so that only a portion of the called for bumps into the highly skilled jobs would be made each month over a period of six months. This permitted a fairly high level of production to be maintained on the highly skilled jobs, so that additional bumping to other jobs as described above would not occur.

There are many types of seniority systems written into union contracts. The implications for human resource planning of three "pure" types of systems include:

1. Job seniority units, where seniority is based on the length of time the individual has been on the job.
2. Department-wide units, in which the employee's seniority is based on the length of time he has worked in the department.
3. Plant (or company) seniority units. Here seniority is based on the

length of time the individual has worked in the plant (or firm as a whole).

The choice of units ranging from narrow (job) to wide (plant or company) has a number of implications for human resource planning. These may be grasped most easily by examining a specific situation, as illustrated in Figure 3–8. Here we see what flow of human resources would take place should a hypothetical employee, who came to work in 1966, hold a position where there would be a temporary layoff or permanent termination. We have also indicated for each type of seniority unit the starting years of those laid off should three layoffs occur.

From these data two points are evident. First, as seniority units widen from job to department to plant, the number of bumps increases. This increased flow of human resources can be disruptive, and more efforts may well be required for training bumped workers.

Second, where a number of layoffs (or terminations) takes place, the firm will lose more recently hired employees as seniority units widen. To expand on the data in Figure 3–8, if a manufacturing plant with 2000 workers lays off 50 of them, with plant-

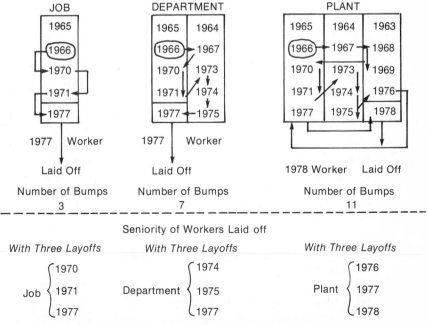

Figure 3–8 *Alternative seniority systems.*

wide seniority it would be the 50 most recently hired employees who would be "bumped" off the payroll. Contrast this with the same sized plant and number of layoffs, with job seniority units. If the layoffs were *concentrated* on one or two jobs, the company might well have to lose workers with five, ten, or more years seniority, since they could not bump anyone outside of their own narrowly defined job unit. This raises questions both of an ethical and efficiency nature:

1. Is it fair to have a system in which admittedly qualified employees with long years of service are laid off while younger, less senior people are retained on the payroll?
2. Are the firm's most senior employees in general more efficient and highly skilled? If so, the firm would be losing some of its better people with narrow units.

One other point of significance that arises is that with wider units it is much easier for management to request and gain acceptance of transfers by workers from one job to another. If our 1966 employee in Figure 3–8 was asked by supervision to move into another job where it felt he could contribute more toward meeting the objectives of the organization:

1. Working in a job seniority unit, he would lose this seniority, and, having just been transferred, would become the individual with the *least seniority in any other job unit*.
2. On the other hand if the whole plant constituted a single large seniority unit, he could move to *any* other job in the plant and retain his 1966 seniority in the wider unit.

Because of this, wider seniority units greatly increase management's probability of obtaining an individual's willingness to move from one position to another.

Just which type of seniority system is most efficient or fair to the employees depends on many variables. How many employees hold the same job, i.e., how many total employees would be in each job seniority unit if this strategy were chosen? How often do layoffs occur? What percentage of the total number of employees in the bargaining unit are subject to layoffs? Is the firm one in which temporary layoffs are required each year due to uneven demand patterns? Is the firm a technologically stable one as opposed to one where continuing advances in technology require the elimination of old jobs and the creation of new?

Equal Opportunity Employment and Human Resource Planning

Equal opportunity employment has become an extremely important organization and social concern, and government efforts aimed at forcing organizations to take affirmative action to end discriminatory practices have increased considerably in recent years. In this section we will illustrate some ways in which equal employment opportunity efforts on the part of the federal government have affected human resource planning and decision making.

A basic piece of legislation affecting human resource planning was the Civil Rights Act of 1964. Title VII of this Act prohibited discrimination against employees on the basis of race, color, religion, national origin, or sex. Title VII of the act specifically gave firms the right to utilize psychological tests as long as they were not discriminatory. This act also established an Equal Employment Opportunity Commission (EEOC), which was set up as a fact-finding and conciliatory agency. The Civil Rights Act was amended in 1972 by the Equal Employment Opportunity Act, which extended the scope of the EEOC's jurisdiction (e.g., to state and local governments). The 1972 Act also gave the EEOC the power to *bring suits* against organizations when any patterns of discrimination were found.

In 1971 a unanimous landmark Supreme Court decision was handed down which involved psychological testing and both initial selection and internal human resource movements. In this case, *Griggs, et al., vs. Duke Power Company,* the court ruled that the company was discriminating against blacks by requiring two psychological tests[69] and a high school education as prerequisites for promotion. Discrimination was ruled because these two criteria for promotion could not be shown to be related to successful performance on the job. As the Court phrased it: "What Congress has commanded is that any tests used must measure the person for the job and not the person in the abstract."[70]

The courts have also interceded in the realm of job seniority, which, as we have seen, affects both bidding for better positions and bumping when layoffs or terminations occur. With respect to minority groups and women moving up in organizations, at least 30 lower court decisions rendered seniority systems illegal "if they locked racial minorities and women into a lower-paying job specialization while white males moved up a better-paying separate seniority ladder."[71] Further, in 1974, nine steel companies faced with the threat of court suits, agreed to a consent decree giving back pay totaling $30.9 million to minority groups and women and a "drastic restructuring of the seniority system to permit freer movement from job to job."[72] In the 51-page consent degree, the new rules "opened up new 'lines of promotion' to blacks, enabling them to bid on jobs on the basis of plant-wide seniority."[73]

Equal employment opportunities, job seniority, and human resource movements also have important implications from a somewhat different point of view. Since more and more minority members and women have been employed in recent years under EEOC and other affirmative action pressures, it is also among these groups where the highest percentages of employees with less seniority exist. Hence, many minority and women workers have been the first to be bumped out of their jobs during adverse business conditions. In essence, this has meant a basic conflict between two philosophies and mechanisms, each geared toward providing equitable treatment to the citizens of a democratic society. If traditional seniority systems are allowed to exist, as agreed to by both labor and management, gains made in equal opportunity employment will be negated. On the other hand, if changes are made in seniority provisions, a number of older workers who took employment 20 to 25 years ago under explicit legal agreements protecting them against being laid off as their seniority increased, would lose this protection.

There have been a number of court tests evoked with respect to seniority, as noted, and the issue reached the Supreme Court in 1976 (which ruled in favor of equal opportunity employment).[74] Then, however, on May 31, 1977 the Supreme Court in an important 7 to 2 decision made a ruling supporting the existence of "bona fide" seniority systems that perpetuate the effects of discrimination that occurred before Title VII of the 1964 Civil Rights Act went into effect, as long as there was no *intent* to discriminate. In an opinion rendered by Justice Potter Stewart, the court said:

Although a seniority system inevitably tends to perpetuate the effects of pre-act discrimination in such cases, the Congressional judgment was that Title VII should not outlaw the use of existing seniority lists and thereby destroy or water down the vested seniority rights of employees simply because their employer had engaged in discrimination prior to the act.[75]

Although there are numerous complexities involved in this case not fully analyzed at the time of this writing, the decision, which involved the Teamsters and the T. I. M. E-DC, Inc., a trucking company, was generally considered a setback for equal employment opportunities for women and minority groups.[76]

SUMMARY

In this chapter attention has been focused on several aspects of human resource forecasting and planning. In engaging in this activity, which is closely interrelated with other personnel functions such as selection, training and performance appraisal, the firm must develop job descriptions and specifications for each job. Then, it must project its demand for human resources, develop an inventory of existing personnel, and look at external human resource supply and demand projections. If it is determined that additional personnel are needed for any particular job, promoting or transferring employees may take place, with the concomitant necessity of hiring from outside the firm certain personnel who will enter the positions of those transferred or promoted. Such decisions are now constrained considerably more than in the past due to equal opportunity employment pressures from the government.

Under conditions in which there are too many human resources, firms may rely on attrition to reduce the size of their labor force, transfer of personnel should any other jobs be simultaneously vacant, or laying off employees. Layoffs at managerial and other nonunion levels may be effected utilizing any criteria management wishes. For most unionized employees, seniority will be the basis for retention. Different types of seniority systems exist with different implications for human resource planning. Further, there is a fundamental conflict between seniority and equal employment opportunities since so many groups traditionally discriminated against have been hired most recently and thus, would be the first to be layed off under union-management seniority agreements.

DISCUSSION AND STUDY QUESTIONS

1. There is a department store in a mall in the suburbs of a college town isolated from any major cities which is trying to upgrade its image by carrying higher quality items. A sales-clerk job in the store that calls for working in departments with both hardware and household goods items (e.g., electric toasters, blenders) has been described to include the following duties: answer questions from customers, demonstrate how certain items work, sell items to customers both on a cash and charge basis, rearrange items on shelves when instructed to do so by the supervisor, help take inventory at periodic intervals under the supervision of the department supervisor, and handle customer complaints and inform the department supervisor of any such complaints when deemed necessary. Develop a job specification for this job.
2. What are some variables that have an effect on output that must be considered by manufacturers of color television sets in determining output levels and ultimate human resource requirements for 1989?
3. Which of the following types of operations would be amenable to using logarithmic learning curve analysis for human resource demand forecasting? In each case, give your reasons why.
   a. An automated petroleum refiner.
   b. An assembly line in which 98 percent of the time required

to turn out each item is determined by machine speed and the other 2 percent by worker proficiency.
c. The manufacture of electronic computers.
d. A supermarket.
e. The construction of standardized, precut homes.

4. Given the following Markovian transition matrix, which was derived from data in two departments of a firm during the year 1978, what problems do you see? What do you think some of these causes might be, and how might you overcome them?

	M_1	M_2	M_3	S_1	S_2	S_3	Exit
M_1	.82	.05	0	.08	0	0	.05
M_2	0	.88	.04	0	.02	0	.06
M_3	0	0	.90	0	0	0	.10
S_1	.10	0	0	.82	.06	0	.02
S_2	0	.09	0	0	.76	.11	.04
S_3	0	0	.06	0	0	.88	.06
Exit	0	0	0	0	0	0	1.0

Note: M_1 to M_3 are manufacuring positions, from the lowest level to the highest and S_1 to S_3 are sales positions from the lowest level to the highest in the organization.

5. If you were the president of an aerospace firm and wanted to determine the number of direct labor hours that will be required of your firm in manufacturing aircraft in 1989, which of the following human resource forecasting techniques do you feel might be useful? In each case give your reasons why.
a. Simulation models.
b. The Delphi technique.
c. The logarithmic learning curve model.
d. Skills inventories.
e. Markov models.

6. If you were a 23-year-old college graduate with two years experience as an assistant supermarket manager in a large food retailing chain that had 23 geographically decentralized divisions, each averaging about $100,000,000 in sales each year, would you want your firm to have a computerized skills inventory? Would you answer the question the same way if you were a 59-year-old store manager? A middle-aged store manager with 10 years experience in a small chain with only eight supermarkets?

7. You are the plant manager of an industrial goods manufacturing firm, and in your plant there are approximately 1400 rank-and-file employees; eight general foremen, 55 first line supervisors, and about 50 managerial and professional employees in your firm's various staff departments, e.g., ac-

counting, quality control, production control, industrial engineering, and personnel. Your firm is in a very competitive industry, and your managerial and professional turnover is somewhat higher than you like. Your personnel manager has recommended that a replacement chart be developed to aid you in keeping up-to-date data on managerial performance and potential. Would you follow his recommendation? Why?

8. Career path analysis and counseling are both of little value in dynamic organizations — conditions are changing so rapidly that no meaningful plans may be made. Discuss.

9. To encourage "open systems," it should be company policy that managers who train their subordinates to assume managerial positions in other divisions of a firm should, for each individual trained and "lost," be "paid" for the man taken by the other division (on an interdepartment budget transfer). Discuss.

10. You are the manager of a plant that is characterized by stability; and your supervisors rarely ask their production workers to move from one job or department to another. In a plant next door to yours, conditions are highly dynamic, there are frequent layoffs and "bumps," and production workers are often asked to move from one job or department to another. Which types of seniority system, narrow (job) or wide (plant), would be most appropriate for your plant? For the plant next door? Why?

11. Everyone is a loser with affirmative action programs, since if well established seniority agreements are eliminated to provide equal employment opportunities, loyal long-service employees may be bumped off their jobs; on the other hand, if such systems are maintained, it is going to be the more recently hired women and minorities that will lose their jobs in case of a recession. Discuss.

12. *Assuming an 80 percent learning curve and the number of direct labor hours required to manufacture the first unit to be 1000 hours, determine, by means of using the equations in the Appendix of this chapter, how many hours would be required to produce the third unit. Show all calculations.

Notes

[1]The examples were largely drawn from Kenneth R. MacCrimmon, "Improving Decision Making with Manpower Management Systems," *The Business Quarterly,* 36 (Autumn, 1971), p. 32, and Glenn A. Bassett, "Elements of Manpower Forecasting and Scheduling," *Human Resource Management,* 12 (Fall, 1973), p. 35.

[2]In spite of the general undesirability of having unused human resources, many firms have, in fact, "stockpiled" engineers and scientists, for example, so that they could show adequate human resource support in bidding for government contracts. Further, some companies have "slack" in their systems (i.e., extra personnel) to handle emergency assignments. Either of these strategies may be least costly ones for the organization as a whole.

*Optional mathematically oriented question, which requires knowledge in manipulating the mathematical model given in the Appendix to the chapter.

[3]Mason Haire, "Approach to an Integrated Personnel Policy," *Industrial Relations,* 7 (February, 1968), p. 107.

[4]Elmer Burack, *Strategies for Manpower Planning and Programming* (Morristown, N. J.: General Learning Corporation, 1972), p. 95.

[5]James Walker, "Forecasting Manpower Needs," *Harvard Business Review,* 47 (March-April, 1969), p. 153.

[6]Ibid.

[7]This situation is very much the same as that in dealing with inventory models. For a discussion of this problem in inventory management see Max D. Richards and Paul S. Greenlaw, *Management: Decisions and Behavior,* rev. ed. (Homewood, Ill.: Richard D. Irwin, Inc., 1972), p. 547.

[8]The lead time–uncertainty problem applies to periods of human resource expansion. In periods of a declining demand for human resources, individuals may, for example, be laid off rather quickly after management has decided to follow this course of action.

[9]Burack, op. cit., p. 95.

[10]Much of the discussion in this section is drawn from Richard I. Henderson, *Compensation Management* (Reston, Va.: Reston Publishing Company, Inc., 1976), pp. 103–106.

[11]Ibid., p. 105.

[12]Ibid., p. 106.

[13]This categorization was drawn from ibid., p. 147.

[14]Kendrith M. Rowland and Michael G. Sovereign, "Markov-Chain Analysis of Internal Manpower Supply," *Industrial Relations,* 9 (October, 1969), p. 89.

[15]T. P. Wright, "Factors Affecting the Cost of Airplanes," *Journal of Aeronautical Sciences,* 3 (February, 1936), pp. 122–128.

[16]See, for example, Rocco Carzo, Jr. and John N. Yanouzas, *Formal Organization* (Homewood, Ill.; Richard D. Irwin, Inc. and the Dorsey Press, 1967), pp. 300–305; or S. A. Billon, "Industrial Learning Curves and Forecasting," *Management International Review,* No. 6 (1966), pp. 65–79.

[17]See W. Bert Bowers, "Who's Afraid of the Learning Curve?" *Purchasing,* 60 (March 24, 1966), pp. 77–79, 134. In this article, Bowers showed how the learning curve was used as a negotiation tool with a subcontracter and saved the Perkin-Elmer Corp. approximately $30,000.

[18]Reno R. Cole, "Increasing Utilization of the Cost-Quantity Relationship in Manufacturing," *The Journal of Industrial Engineering,* 9 (May-June, 1958), pp. 173–177.

[19]Frank J. Andress, "The Learning Curve as a Production Tool," *Harvard Business Review,* 32 (January-February, 1954), p. 87.

[20]Nicholas Baloff, "Extension of the Learning Curve — Some Empirical Results," *Operations Research Quarterly,* 22 (December, 1971), pp. 329–340.

[21]Samuel L. Young, "Misapplications of the Learning Curve Concept," *The Journal of Industrial Engineering,* 17 (August, 1966), p. 414.

[22]Baloff, op. cit., pp. 339–340. The italics are ours.

[23]For example, one researcher has indicated that one of the major problems in learning curve applications is the potential error of unrecognized *constant* unit costs, and has developed a modification of the learning curve approach taking into account this problem. See Wayne J. Morse, "Learning Curve Cost Projections with Constant Unit Costs," *Management Planning,* 22 (March-April, 1974), pp. 15–21.

[24]This plan is described in Glenn A. Bassett, op. cit., pp. 35–43.

[25]These questions were taken from an illustrative computer printout in ibid., p. 41.

[26]Ibid., p. 40.

[27]George T. Milkovich, et al., "The Use of Delphi Procedures in Manpower Forecasting," *Management Science,* 19 (December, 1972), p. 381.

[28]"Forecasters Turn to Group Guesswork," *Business Week,* March 14, 1970, p. 130.

[29]Ibid., p. 132.

[30]Milkovich, et al., op. cit. Most of the materials in the remainder of our discussion of Delphi were derived from this source.

[31]Ibid., p. 387.

[32]For a discussion of some of the technical mechanics involved in designing skills inventions, see William Bryce, "Skills Inventories," MBA Paper, College of Business Administration, The Pennsylvania State University, 1970.

[33]Richard A. Kaumeyer, Jr., "Automated Skills Retrieval: One Company's Program," *Personnel,* 44 (January-February, 1967), p. 20.

[34]W. J. Pedicord, "Advanced Data Systems for Personnel Planning and Placement," *Computers and Automation,* 15 (September, 1966), p. 21.

[35]See T. I. Bradshaw, "Computerized Employee Search Program," *Data Processing Magazine,* 7 (November, 1965), pp. 48–50.

[36]Pedicord, op. cit., p. 20.

[37]Bradshaw, op. cit., p. 48.

[38]Logan M. Cheek, "Personnel Computer Systems," *Business Horizons,* 14 (August, 1971), p. 72.

[39]Robert A. Martin, "Skills Inventories," *Personnel Journal,* 46 (January, 1967), p. 28.

[40]Kaumeyer, op. cit., p. 19.

[41]The model must be designed so that an individual is a member of only one state at any given time.

[42]For a simple introduction to Markov models see both John W. Merck, "A Markovian Model for Projecting Movements of Personnel Through a System," PRL-TR-65-6, 6570th Personnel Research Laboratory, Aerospace Medical Division, Air Force Systems Command, Lackland Air Force Base, Texas, March, 1965, as reprinted in Paul S. Greenlaw and Robert D. Smith, eds., *Personnel Management: A Management Science Approach* (Scranton, Pa.: International Textbook Company, 1970), pp. 100–116; and Paul S. Greenlaw and Robert D. Smith, "Some Notes on Merck's Markovian Model for Those Without Matrix Algebra," in ibid., pp. 117–120.

[43]A description of how a row vector is multiplied by a transition matrix is shown in Merck's paper as reprinted in ibid., p. 111.

[44]Victor H. Vroom and Kenneth R. MacCrimmon, "Toward a Stochastic Model of Managerial Careers," *Administrative Science Quarterly,* 13 (June, 1968), p. 29.

[45]Thomas A. Mahoney and George Milkovich, "Internal Labor Markets: An Empirical Investigation," Technical Report 7006, Industrial Relations Center, University of Minnesota, July, 1972, p. 10.

[46]Vroom and MacCrimmon, op. cit., p. 30.

[47]Many of these questions were stimulated by reference to Mahoney and Milkovich, op. cit., pp. 25–26.

[48]Vroom and MacCrimmon, op. cit., p. 36.

[49]Mahoney and Milkovich, op. cit., p. 25.

[50]See for example, S. Swerdloff, "How Good Were Manpower Projections for the 1960's," *Monthly Labor Review,* 92 (November, 1969), pp. 17–22.

[51]See: *Manpower Report of the President* (Washington, D.C.: Government Printing Office, 1971), p. 297.

[52]J. A. Burroughs and R. J. Niehaus, "An Application of a Model and Control System to Equal Employment Opportunity Planning," Research Report No. 26, Office of Civilian Manpower Management, Department of the Navy, Washington, D.C.: July, 1976.

[53]D. Clay Whybark, "Forecasting Manpower Requirements in Civil Aviation," *Personnel Administration,* 33 (March-April, 1970), pp. 45-51.

[54]John P. Campbell, et. al., *Managerial Behavior, Performance and Effectiveness* (New York: McGraw-Hill Book Company, 1970), p. 23.

[55]Ibid.

[56]Jack Brewer, et al., "A New Dimension in Employee Development: A System for Career Planning & Guidance," *Personnel Journal,* 54 (April, 1975), p. 228.

[57]Vroom and MacCrimmon, op. cit., p. 41.

[58]Ibid., p. 34.

[59]Philip Crotty and Jeffry Timmons, "Older Minorities — 'Roadblocked' in the Organization," *Business Horizons,* 17 (June, 1974), pp. 27–34.

[60]Ibid., p. 34.

[61]Theodore M. Alfred, "Checkers or Choice in Manpower Management," *Harvard Business Review,* 43 (January-February, 1967), p. 161.

[62]Ibid., 158.

[63]Ibid.

[64]Ibid., p. 163.

[65]Ibid., pp. 160–161.

[66]In small organizations, every managerial or professional employee may know all others personally, and thus promotional information may in effect be transmitted more informally.

[67]Turnover has been defined in a number of ways. We prefer the following definition:

$$\frac{\text{Total Number of Separations per Month}}{\text{Average Number of Employees on the Payroll}} \times 100.$$

[68]Rossall J. Johnson, "The Personnel Administrator of the 1970's," *Personnel Journal,* 50 (April, 1971), p. 301.

[69]The Wonderlic Mental Alertness test and the Bennett Mechanical Comprehension test.

[70]*The United States LAW WEEK,* 39 (March 9, 1971), p. 4321.

[71]"The EEOC Retreats After a Seniority Ruling," *Business Week,* June 20, 1977, p. 28.

[72]Ibid.

[73]Harvey Shapiro, "'Business' Equal Opportunity Albatross," *The Commercial and Financial Chronicle,* 220, No. 7478, July 7, 1975, p. 24.

[74]See, for example, *Time,* April 5, 1976, p. 65.

[75]Cited in the *New York Times,* June 1, 1977, p. 1.

[76]For an analysis of some of the more important reactions to this case, see Stephen C. Swanson, "The Affect of The Supreme Court's Seniority Decisions," *Personnel Journal,* 56 (December, 1977), pp. 625–627.

APPENDIX TO CHAPTER 3

THE LOGARITHMIC LEARNING CURVE MODEL

Wright's mathematical formula, which will express a constant percentage decline in direct labor hours as the number of units of production doubles, is as follows:

$$y = ax^b$$

where y = the number of direct labor hours needed to produce the xth unit
a = the number of direct labor hours needed to produce the first unit
x = the unit number
b = a constant representing the rate of learning. The parameter b must be ≤ 0; and is *not* the learning percentage (for instance, 80 per cent) as discussed in this chapter.

The number of labor hours required for the first unit (*a and also* y_1), as well as the first unit ($x = 1$) are known, so that the parameter that must be found is b. This parameter may be determined most easily by transforming the basic equation given above into logarithmic form:

(1) $y = ax^b$

(2) $\log y = \log a + b \log x$; and

(3) $b = \dfrac{\log y - \log a}{\log x}$

For example if we let $a = 1000$ hours, y_2, 800 hours and $x = 2$, b would become:

$$b = \frac{2.9031 - 3.0000}{.3010}$$

$$= -.3219$$

To calculate the number of direct labor hours required to produce the fifth unit, for example, we would take the above data and proceed as follows:

$$y = 1000 \ x_5^{-.3219}$$

$$\log y = \log 1000 - .3219 \log 5$$

$$= 3.0000 - (.3219)(.6990)$$

$$= 3.0000 - (.2250)$$

$$= 2.7750; \text{ and}$$

$$y = 595.71 \text{ hours}$$

We should also note that the reason why *linear* least squares regression can be utilized if all of the points do not fall exactly on the learning *curve* shown in Figure 3–5 is, when transformed into a logarithmic function indicated above ($\log y = \log a + b \log x$), we have a linear equation of the very simple linear form $y = a + bx$.

4

RECRUITING AND SELECTION

Extremely important to the organization is the selection of competent personnel. In the previous chapter, we indicated the need to select individuals from both inside and outside the firm. In this chapter, we will focus attention on recruiting and selecting job applicants from outside the organization. There are, of course, some elements of these functions that also apply to internal selection for promotion. For example, the internal promotional candidate will be interviewed by his prospective superior and any data obtained about him when he originally came with the company may be examined.

"Recruiting" and "selection" are closely interrelated parts of a multistage decision process. For purposes of exposition, however, we will view recruiting as *searching for* and *obtaining* job candidates and selection as *evaluating* and *deciding* whether to hire candidates once they have been obtained. It should be emphasized, however, that these two endeavors overlap in many respects. For example, college recruiters, when visiting campuses, both obtain prospective job applicants and also evaluate students whom they have interviewed.

In this chapter, we will first discuss the objectives and major characteristics of recruiting and selection systems and the role of personnel in this process. Next, we will consider the very important constraints placed on selection decision making today by governmental equal employment opportunities and affirmative action pressures. Then we will turn our attention to the recruiting process. Finally, we will consider selection, including the major selection instruments, such as interviews and psychological tests.

THE OBJECTIVES OF RECRUITING AND SELECTION

A basic goal of recruiting and selection is to hire at the least cost as many competent individuals as needed to fill job openings in the organization. The aim of organizations should be to avoid hiring of both:

1. Underqualified individuals, who will likely experience frustration on the job and who may have to be terminated by the organization.

2. Overqualified individuals, who will not have an opportunity to utilize fully their abilities and hence also experience frustration. With such individuals, turnover rates tend to be high unless they are promoted into higher-level positions.

In discussing competence, two questions arise: (1) How can an organization measure an employee's competence or "success" on the job? (2) How can recruiting and selection procedures predict just which job applicants are the most likely to succeed?

With routine, highly programmed jobs such as those on the assembly line it may be relatively easy to define success. For example, the number of good pieces a worker turns out each day may provide a very concrete measure of success, although other variables such as absenteeism may also be relevant. For example, a "high" producer who is frequently absent without notice or excuse may disrupt production schedules and have to be dismissed.

With managerial and professional employees, the determination of successful performance is much more difficult because of its greater complexity and lack of preciseness. With these employees supervisory ratings of the individual are often utilized. In other cases tenure alone is used as a "success" measure — is the individual still with the firm after two years? In a somewhat more complicated case, an organization doing $1 billion sales annually defined success when analyzing its use of psychological tests for managerial and professional personnel as follows. Any individual was considered successful if he remained with the firm for two years, either (1) staying in his same position, (2) having been laterally transferred, or (3) promoted into a higher-level position.

Regardless of the success criterion chosen, organizations aim to develop selection tools that measure what they are supposed to measure. For example, do high scores on a mental alertness test actually predict success on the job? When selection tools actually measure what they are supposed to, we say that they are *valid*. For a selection tool to be a valid predictor of success, it must also be *reliable*. Reliability means that there is a high probability that an individual who is exposed to the same selection tool at different times would score about the same each time. If a selection tool is not reliable, it cannot serve as a valid predictor. On the other hand, just because a selection tool *is* reliable does *not* make it valid; e.g., individual scores on a mental alertness test may be about the same each time it is taken, but they may not predict successful job performance at all.

Two additional observations are in order here. First, both reliability and validity are complex subjects. With respect to reliability in test development, for example:

> Traditionally, all measurement error . . . has been encompassed by the term *reliability*. Today it is recognized that many factors influence and contribute to measurement "error" and that there is no best way of talking about or estimating test reliability.[1]

Among the factors that may lead an individual to respond differently on the same measuring instrument at different times are different environmental conditions (such as lighting), or personal changes over time such as mood or physical health.[2] Validity has many facets, too; when discussing the validation of psychological tests later in this chapter we will consider several types of validation.

Second, reliability and validity in psychological measurement are used to describe "tests" defined in a very broad sense — as a wide variety of sets of standardized stimuli. For example, we ask whether patterned interviews or weighted application forms as well as tests are valid. In the field of performance appraisal, we are concerned with interrater reliability in using a performance appraisal technique. In other words, is the probability high that different raters of an individual's performance will substantially agree with each other?

BASIC CHARACTERISTICS OF RECRUITING AND SELECTION SYSTEMS

To meet selection objectives, information-decision systems are often viewed as multistage in nature and invariably involve decision making under risk. We will now describe these two characteristics.

Multistage Systems

One common and convenient way of viewing the recruiting-selection information process is to conceive of it as a multistage one, in which a number of decision points exist. This process may vary considerably from firm to firm, with organization size a major contingency. In a small 20-person firm, recruiting and selection may involve nothing more than the manager placing an advertisement in the local newspaper, interviewing several respondents, and selecting the one whom he subjectively "feels" would make the best worker. In large organizations, on the other hand, a multitude of policies and procedures may be developed to meet the firm's selection objectives. A conceptual model of the multistage recruiting and selection process that assumes a "successive hurdle" approach for larger organizations is presented in Figure 4–1. By "successive hurdle," we mean that if an applicant does not do well on (or "clear") any of the five selection tool "hurdles" shown in Figure 4–1, he or she will not be considered further for selection.

Several observations are in order concerning this model. First, in some cases it may not be possible to make a simple "yes" or "no" decision at a particular decision point. For example, a member of the personnel department may be unsure about a candidate after only having given him an application form, and therefore have him proceed to take some psychological tests before making a final recommendation. On the other hand, the simple yes-no branching may often be easily accomplished and quite appropriate. For instance, if the personnel department is searching for an electronic engineer with a college degree and three years' experience, a quick glance at an individual's application form can determine whether he has the appropriate education and experience.

Second, the sequencing of selection tools may not always follow the order indicated in Figure 4–1. For example, in college recruiting, the recruiter may first interview the candidate and then, if the applicant looks promising, encourage him to fill out and send in an application form. This form may help provide a basis for a later plant trip. We will discuss sequencing in the multistage recruiting and selection process from both a cost and an information-effectiveness point of view later in this chapter.

Third, in some cases a firm may continue to put a candidate through later stages of the selection process, even though it has already come up with a "no hire" decision at an earlier stage. This is often the case in situations in which a managerial applicant is visiting the firm for a day, has taken some psychological tests early in the morning, and done extremely poorly on them. To maintain good public relations, it probably would not be advisable to send the applicant immediately "back home," indicating to him that he did so poorly on the tests that he has been rejected for the job. Rather, many personnel managers provide the candidate with courteous treatment for the remainder of the day. One

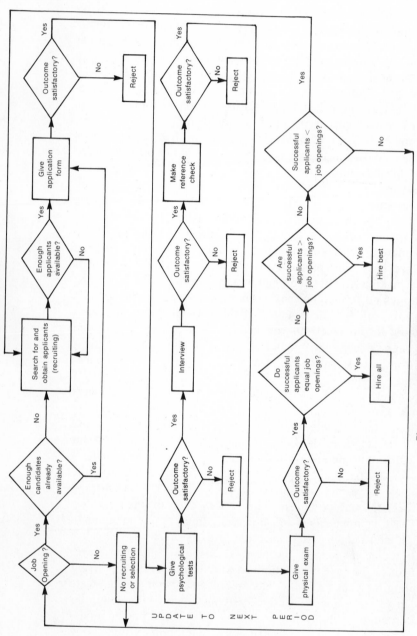

Figure 4–1 *The recruiting-selection process.*

or two interviews, however, might be dropped from the originally planned schedule in light of management's previous decision to reject the candidate.

Finally, we should mention that even though multiple decisions are involved in personnel selection as described, in some cases an approach is used that calls for looking at *all* data concerning a job applicant before deciding whether or not to hire him. This "composite" approach is based on the assumption that an applicant's "falling down" slightly on any one measure can be more than *offset* by his doing very favorably on another. For example, if the firm's lowest "favorable" cut-off score on a mental alertness test is 28, and an applicant scores only a 26 but has some special related work experience that is valued very highly, this latter factor might be considered as more than offsetting the slightly lower than desired test score. This composite approach is used mainly in situations in which falling down slightly on any measure is not associated with a high probability of failure on the job. Otherwise, high performance on other measures could not be "more than offsetting" factors.

Decision Making Under Risk

General Observations

It is important to recognize that recruiting and selection involve decision making under risk. That is, the results of the recruitment and selection process are *probabilistic*. Owing to both the complexity of human behavior and the predictive limitations of our selection instruments, all we can do is make probability estimates regarding the success or failure of any particular job applicant. In any *single case,* an individual who is hired may still fail even though selection measures indicate a high probability of success on the job. It is only in the *long run* with *many cases* of individuals who have similar characteristics that we can predict with some degree of confidence that a certain proportion of them will succeed in a particular job.

With respect to recruiting and selection decisions, one basic aim is to *increase the probabilities* of choosing "successful" job applicants. This objective, however, must be constrained by the additional costs of improving the predictability of the selection instruments. Sometimes, we may be able to improve our predictions of success by 10 or 15 per cent for only a nominal cost. In other cases, however, we may find that the cost of improving our success-prediction probabilities is so great in comparison with the advantages of doing so that it would not be a wise economic step for the organization to take.

A Cost-Benefit Model

In Chapter 2, we indicated that firms sometimes use cost-benefit analysis in decision making. Many probabilistic models using costs and benefits have been developed to help make better selection decisions. We will now present a cost-benefit selection model that reemphasizes the probabilistic nature of selection decision making and stresses some of the *economic* implications of selection decisions — implications that are too often ignored. To help understand this example, it is useful first to recognize that involved in all selection decisions are four possible outcomes, as shown in Figure 4–2. The positive signs in Quadrants 1 and 3 indicate that we would like to hire people who will turn out to be successes and reject "would-be" failures. The negative signs in Quadrants 2 and 4, on the other hand, represent the desire to avoid hiring people who might fail and rejecting people who might have succeeded.

To illustrate probabilistic cost-benefit analysis in selection, we will use the data in Figure 4–2 and assume that the probabilities represent the outcomes generated from a firm's current selection procedures. These data show that in the *long run* for every 50 job applicants examined on the *average:* (1) the firm's selection tools would *predict* success 80 per cent of the time (40 hires per 50 applicants); and (2) if we chose 40 such individuals, they would *actually* be successful $7/8$ of the time (35 of 40).

Next, let us assume that our organization is expanding and needs to hire 35 new clerical employees (the number in Quadrant 1 in Figure 4–2), and that it has estimated that *on the average* it costs $500 to recruit and select each job applicant and $600 in training and "other costs" for each applicant hired.[3] Since we are

Total Number of Job Applicants Being Considered for Selection
(n = 50)

	Reject (n = 10)	Hire (n = 40)
Success (n = 38)	(2) Type 1 Error — ($p = .06$) ($n = 3$)	(1) + $p = .70$ $n = 35$
Failure (n = 12)	(3) + ($p = .14$) ($n = 7$)	(4) Type 2 Error — $p = .10$ $n = 5$

Notes: (1) p = the conditional probability that a person will succeed or fail given that he has been selected or rejected.

(2) The data in Quadrants 2 and 3 have been put in parentheses since the most we can do is to infer the success or failure of individuals who were not hired by the organization.

Figure 4–2   *Selection decision outcomes.*

dealing with clerical positions, we will assume zero rejection costs for Quadrant 2 because many observers agree that it is not meaningful to associate any costs to the rejection of lower-level employees (Quadrant 2 in Figure 4–2), although the rejection of successful executives may be very costly.[4] Thus, in order to obtain 35 successful employees with present selection methods, *on the average* we will need to examine 50 applicants at a cost of $500 each, and hire 40 of these, incurring training and other costs of $600 each, for a total cost of $49,000:

Average Recruiting and Selection Costs 50 × $500 = $25,000
Average Training and Other Costs   40 × $600 = $24,000
$$\overline{\$49,000}$$

It should be emphasized that these calculations are based on probabilities and that in any specific case we might need to hire more or less than 40 persons to obtain the 35 needed successes. For the same reason, we might need to examine more or fewer than 50 applicants to obtain 35 such people.

Now, let us suppose that we want to raise our selection standards so as to hire fewer failures (Quadrant 4) and that we can do this by adding another selection tool at an additional cost of $10 per applicant. Let us assume that the probabilities associated with using the additional tool represent "guesstimates" based on a similar analysis done previously elsewhere and are as shown in Figure 4–3. These data indicate that on the average, again we would need to examine 50 applicants, but now we would need to hire only 38 to meet our goal of obtaining 35 successful hires. We are assuming here that *only* hired "failures" would decrease, with hired "successes" *remaining the same*. This is done for purposes of simplification, since in some situations we would

Total Number of Individuals Being Considered for Selection
(n = 50)

	Reject (n = 12)		Hire (n = 38)	
Success (n = 38)	(2) Type 1 Error		(1)	
	(p = .06)	(n = 3)	p = .70	n = 35
Failure (n = 12)	(3)		(4) Type 2 Error	
	(p = .18)	(n = 9)	p = .06	n = 3

Notes: (1) p = the conditional probability that a person will succeed or fail given that he has been selected or rejected.

       (2) The data in Quadrants 2 and 3 have been put in parentheses since the most we can do is to infer the success or failure of individuals who were not hired by the organization.

Figure 4–3   Modified data with additional selection tool.

expect hired "successes" to *increase* along with a decline in hired "failures." Our total average costs would be increased to $510 recruiting and selection costs per applicant times 50, or $25,500 plus $600 in training costs for the 38 to be hired ($22,800). The total expected costs would be $48,300 or $700 less using the additional selection tool.

We emphasize again that all figures, as those given here, are probabilistic. With our probabilistic data in Figure 4–3 for 38 hires, in *any given group* 33, 34, 36, or 37 or some other number of these might actually be successful, rather than 35, which would represent an average number expected in the *long run*.

THE ROLE OF PERSONNEL IN RECRUITING AND SELECTION

In Chapter 2, we discussed line-staff relationships in general. We will now illustrate these in more detail by looking at some of the staff and line activities of a large eastern corporation recruiting and selecting college graduates. Top line management and the personnel vice-president of the company had set two basic objectives:

1. The company should develop a strong affirmative action program to provide equal employment opportunities for all of its employees.

2. The firm should hire only college graduates for all entry-level management positions since they would hopefully advance to higher level positions. In order to make this objective congruent with the affirmative action one, the company had taken special efforts to recruit at several predominantly black colleges.

With these two objectives in mind, each year a college recruiting effort was undertaken. Annually, the personnel department analyzed its previous college recruiting efforts, decided which colleges were yielding the best candidates, and made the decision as to which colleges should be visited in the current year. Experienced recruiters from the personnel department visited the campuses decided upon, interviewed prospective applicants, and asked the most promising ones to submit applications to the firm's personnel department. Based on the applications received and the recruiters' reports, the candidates deemed best were invited to visit the firm for a day.

During the visit each candidate was interviewed by members of the personnel department and members of line management. (To help ensure that the line managers would be skilled in interviewing, it had been a practice for several years for the personnel department to train all managers in how to interview.) Although the personnel department provided line management with written recommendations about each college student who had visited the firm, line management made the final hiring decision.

This example illustrates recruiting and selecting as a multi-stage process, which involves line-staff relationships of the types described in Chapter 2. In the firm just described, there was no clear-cut distinction between line and staff — both participated in the selection process. Further, the personnel department did more than simply advise. Its information and expertise gave it power actually to make many decisions. The recruiters made preliminary screening decisions during their campus visits, the personnel department decided which applicants should be invited for the firm trip, and so forth. Finally, to improve the selection process, the personnel department performed work in another functional area, training. Managers were trained by personnel to interview by use of the technique of role playing, which we will discuss in a later chapter. This example points up another example of the interrelatedness of personnel activities undertaken and roles performed in relation to line management in the organizational system.

EQUAL OPPORTUNITY EMPLOYMENT

One of the most complex and significant constraints placed on organizations' decision-making capabilities concerning recruiting and selection is governmental "equal employment" pressures. We discussed some of the promotional and seniority aspects of this problem in Chapter 3. We will now elaborate on the problem of providing equal opportunity employment, placing primary emphasis on selection from *outside* the firm.

It is very commonly accepted that for years minority groups and women have been discriminated against in employment. Several efforts prior to 1960 such as state fair employment practice laws and Presidential executive orders putting forth a policy of nondiscrimination in the executive branch of the federal government dealt with this problem, but were not highly successful in providing equal employment opportunities.[5] As indicated in Chapter 3, however, landmark steps were taken to provide such opportunities by Title VII of the Civil Rights Act of 1964 as amended in 1972. With the Equal Employment Opportunity Commission (EEOC) established with conciliatory powers in the 1964 Act, and given stronger powers to initiate suits against employers by the 1972 Amendment, a new avenue was open to remedy any discriminatory policies of organizations. If an individual complains of discrimination by an employer under Title VII, he may go to the EEOC, which first investigates the complaint and if it finds it valid, attempts are then made to work out a voluntary conciliation agreement with the employer. If the conciliation effort is not successful, the EEOC may go to court and obtain an affirmative action ruling against the employer. Court suits may also be brought against employers by individuals or the U.S. Attorney General.[6] If the employer is found guilty of discriminating on the basis of race, color, religion, sex, or national origin, the court may:

. . . enjoin the respondent from engaging in such unlawful employment practice, and order such affirmative action as may be appropriate, which may include, but is not limited to, reinstatement or hiring of employees, with or without back pay . . . or any other equitable relief as the court deems appropriate.[7]

In addition to the prohibition of discriminatory employment practices in the Civil Rights Act, President Lyndon B. Johnson signed Executive Order 11246 in 1965, which called on government contractors not to discriminate on the basis of race, color, religion, national origin, or sex.[8] This order was designed to be enforced by the Office of Federal Contract Compliance (OFCC) and government contracting agencies themselves. With respect to the OFCC and contracting agencies, conciliation attempts are first made and if conciliation fails, contractors' progress payments can be withheld, or contracts can be suspended or cancelled. Severe sanctions have been "rarely used," however, under Executive Order 11246.[9]

With both the original Civil Rights Act and its 1972 Amendments, executive orders, EEOC and OFFC equal employment guidelines, and decisions rendered in cases that have reached the courts, the whole area of equal employment opportunity is extremely complex. In the following sections, we will cover some of the major aspects of equal opportunity employment. First, we will spell out some of the selection practices that have been considered discriminatory. Then we will turn our attention to an area of increasing concern — the establishment of employment goals and quotas and "reverse discrimination." Next, we will discuss a lesser used piece of legislation aimed at prohibiting discrimination on the basis of age (the Age Discrimination in Employment Act of 1967), and "Bona Fide Occupational Qualifications" (BFOQ), a doctrine that may permit firms to refuse to hire individuals because of their religion, sex, or national origin. Finally, some of the problems faced by employers in meeting equal opportunity objectives will be discussed.

Discriminatory Actions

A number of employer actions have been considered discriminatory. As indicated in Chapter 3, Title VII of the Civil

Rights Act permits the use of psychological tests as long as they do not discriminate, and the Supreme Court ruled in *Griggs vs. Duke Power* that tests must be specifically *related to the job* in making promotion and selection decisions if they are to be used.

A sample of some other employment practices that have been held to be discriminatory follows. In recruiting, for example, an employer cannot "let an employment agency do his screening and thus circumvent the requirements of the law."[10] In selection, the validity of even "unscored or casual interviews, unscored application forms, etc.,"[11] may fall within the scope of governmental equal opportunity employment examination as have psychological tests. It has been considered to be an unfair equal employment practice to require submission of a photograph with the job application form, although companies may ask an applicant to do so at his own option.[12] With respect to the job interview, there are a number of questions that may lead to answers which may be interpreted as discriminatory. For example, asking an individual if he is a member of the Knights of Columbus might raise the question of discrimination with respect to religion. Because interviews are highly subjective, one writer has expressed the opinion that the scope of the interview be limited to "the gathering of information that can be obtained in no other way."[13] Finally, and extremely important, firms are considered to be discriminating if minority groups or women are "underrepresented" in their work forces (either because of selection or promotion decisions). This has led to the establishment of affirmative action quotas and goals, which we will discuss shortly.

Two different types of discrimination have been described, *overt* and *systemic,* both of which are illegal:

1. Overt discrimination refers to a "specific act of discrimination against one individual."[14]

2. Systemic discrimination results from personnel practices that "over the years, have unintentionally led to the different treatment" of minority (or women) employees.[15]

Organizations are believed to be more widely affected by systemic than by overt discrimination. At least some systemic discrimination, for example, has resulted from honest attempts by organizations to comply with existing governmental legislation. For instance, numerous states have passed laws to protect certain classes of people. Some states limited the number of hours that a woman could work in a day or the amount of weight she could be asked to lift. Companies conscientiously developing explicit policies and practices to meet the requirements of these laws have found that such efforts have been considered incongruent with the Civil Rights Act and must be abandoned.[16] Thus, organization selection policies excluding women from positions requiring heavy lifting, even though they conform to laws intended to be progressive, may be considered discriminatory.

Quotas and Reverse Discrimination

Affirmative action programs arising from governmental pressures have often included the establishment of affirmative action goals or quotas[17] aimed at ensuring parity between the percentage of minorities and women in the firm's labor market and the percentage employed in the organization. For example, "a city or state may have to fill its policeman or fire fighter vacancies on a 2:1 minority-to-white quota until the force is 25% minority."[18] This type of hiring is also referred to as *ratio hiring.*

Several important facets of the establishment of affirmative action goals (or quotas) deserve attention. First, ratio hiring favoring minorities or women was not meant to be required by Title VII of the Civil Rights Act, and this philosophy was reaffirmed strongly in the *Griggs vs. Duke Power* decision. According to Section 703(j) of the Civil Rights Act:

> Nothing contained in this title shall be interpreted to require any employer . . . to grant preferential treatment to any individual or to any group because of the race, color, religion, sex, or national origin of such individual or group on account of an imbalance which may exist with respect to the total number or percentage of persons of any race, color, religion, sex, or national origin employed by any employer . . . in comparison with the total number or percentage of persons of such race, color, religion, sex, or national origin in any community, State, section, or other area, or in the available work force in any community, State, section, or other area.[19]

In the *Duke Power* decision, the court continued to follow this reasoning with these comments:

> Congress did not intend by Title VII . . . to guarantee a job to every person regardless of qualifications. In short, the Act does not command that any person be hired simply because he was formerly the subject of discrimination, or because he is a member of a minority group. Discriminatory preference for any group, minority or majority, is precisely and only what Congress has proscribed.[20]

Second, ratio hiring has become a highly debatable subject because, in effect, it discriminates against white males. Such a practice has been commonly referred to as reverse discrimination and is considered by many to be as unjust as discriminating against minority groups and women.

Third, in spite of the Title VII and *Griggs* language presented above, when confronted directly with the question of reverse discrimination, the Supreme Court evaded the issue completely in the case of *DeFunis vs. Odegaard* in 1974. Marco DeFunis was denied entry into the University of Washington Law School in 1971 while "blacks and other minority students were admitted under special lower academic requirements."[21] DeFunis filed suit, he was admitted to the school under court order, and the legal process took so long that DeFunis was expected to graduate in 1974 *regardless* of how the Supreme Court ruled. The justices "seized on this factual quirk and declared the case moot because DeFunis' law school status no longer presented a controversy."[22] Four justices dissented, and Justice William Douglas wrote that the Fourteenth Amendment "commands the elimination of racial barriers, not their creation in order to satisfy our theory as to how society ought to be organized."[23]

The reverse discrimination issue was raised again when Allan Bakke was denied admission to the University of California, Davis, medical school in both 1973 and 1974, even though he had excellent credentials. The medical school had developed special admissions policies (with lower standards) for applicants "from economically disadvantaged backgrounds,"[24] and minority groups. Bakke took his case to court, charging that he had been discriminated against, and in September 1976, the California Supreme Court upheld Bakke. One of the points made by the court was that the admission spots for the economically disadvantaged were, in fact, a quota based on race.[25] The university decided to appeal the case, and the United States Supreme Court agreed to hear the appeal.

The Supreme Court heard this case (*The Regents of the University of California vs. Bakke*) in October, 1977, and in what may be an historic decision, ruled in favor of Bakke on June 28, 1978, in a lengthy, complex and close (5 to 4) decision. The court ordered Bakke to be admitted to the Davis medical school on the grounds that its affirmative action program was inflexibly and unjustifiably biased against white applicants like him. This school, which did *not* have any record of past discrimination against minorities to "correct," had set aside 16 special admissions seats just for minority applicants of 100 available, so that white applicants could compete for only 84 seats in the entering class. In the *Bakke* decision, Justice Lewis Powell indicated that whether "this limitation is described as a quota or a goal, it is a line drawn upon the basis of race and ethnic status" which is in conflict with the equal protection clause of the Fourteenth Amendment. Said Powell: "The guarantees of equal protection cannot mean one thing when applied to one individual and something else when applied to a person of another color." The court, however, *very importantly,* did go on to say that *more flexible* affirmative action programs (such as that at Harvard) *were* admissable and that race could be considered as *one* factor in affirmative action programs.

The Fourteenth Amendment, it must be emphasized, provides a prohibition against *states,* but *not* private employers. Further, considered in the *Bakke* decision was Title VI of the Civil Rights Act of 1964, which prohibited discrimination "under any program or activity receiving Federal financial assistance" (78 Stat. 252), and the Davis medical school was receiving such assistance. Section 703 (j) of Title VII of the Civil Rights Act cited above does not apply to Title VI. Hence, in spite of its possible historical significance, the much awaited *Bakke* case did not deal directly with goals, quotas, or affirmative action with respect to private employers, and it currently appears that the meaning of "reverse discrimination" is still clouded and may be so for many years.[26]

Age Discrimination in Employment

In addition to the legislation we have discussed with respect to minority groups and women is the Age Discrimination in Employment Act of 1967. This Act, which prohibits discrimination against employees based solely on age (from 40 to 65), has resulted in two types of actions. Companies have been successfully sued by workers laid off because of age and been forced to reinstate them with back pay. For example, the Standard Oil Company of California, in a consent decree, agreed to pay $2 million in back pay to workers discriminated against on the basis of age.[27]

With respect to *selection,* under this act, many individuals 40 or over who were refused empolyment because of age have filed complaints with the U.S. Labor Department's Wage-Hour Division, responsible for administering the law. Such pressures have further constrained management's selection strategy alternatives. For example, firms have been banned from using words such as "young person" and "youthful" in their advertisements for job candidates. A real critical issue with respect to discrimination by age is the extent to which human beings "deteriorate" both physiologically and mentally as they reach ages of 35, 40 or 45. In some job situations, older employees may perform better than younger ones because they have more experience. On the other hand, for certain jobs, hiring people on the basis of age may be justified. For example, the Greyhound Company set a maximum age of 35 for newly hired bus drivers. This policy was first prohibited by a lower court, which challenged Greyhound to prove that drivers over 35 constituted a risk to their passengers.

This decision, however, was later reversed by higher courts on Greyhound's successful defense of the position that human beings begin to degenerate at 35.

Bona Fide Occupational Qualifications (BFOQ)

Title VII of the Civil Rights Act provided that an employer could hire employees in "certain instances where religion, sex, or national origin is a bona fide occupational qualification reasonably necessary to the normal operation" of the firm.[28] This provision has had special significance with respect to discrimination against women in employment. Prior to 1971, some lower courts held that while women could not be barred from employment because of their sex alone, they could be rejected because of their sex *plus* one other factor, e.g., age, weight, marital status, or parental responsibilities.[29] This position was commonly referred to as the "sex-plus" doctrine. The Martin Marietta Company, using this doctrine, refused to hire a mother of small children, although it did hire men in a similar situation. In January 1971, Martin Marietta's policy, which had been challenged, reached the Supreme Court.[30] The court unanimously ruled that Martin Marietta could only refuse to hire women with small children if it did the same with men. The court rejected the "sex-plus" doctrine but did dim "the women's rights victory by suggesting that the bar against hiring mothers of young children might be justified as a 'BFOQ'."[31] BFOQ is a somewhat vague concept and some civil rights advocates have insisted that it does not mean much more than that a firm can require a woman to model new female fashions and a man to play Julius Caesar in a Shakespeare play. Regardless of this belief, in general, courts have interpreted BFOQ since the Martin Marietta case quite narrowly. For example:

Certain generally held beliefs that line managers usually present as the rationale for disparate effects against females ("Customers will not accept advice from female salespersons" or "We would need separate facilities") have been found invalid.[32]

Equal Opportunities: Objectives and Problems

It is important to recognize that the basic objectives of legislation such as the Civil Rights Act of 1964 and the Equal Employment Act of 1972 parallel progressive personnel policies — the hiring of competent individuals to meet both organizational goals and individual needs regardless of their race, religion, sex, or national origin. Developing selection approaches designed to meet equal employment objectives, however, may pose problems to an organization in several different ways.

As we have noted before, there are federal and state legislation, EEOC actions, OFCC actions, and numerous court decisions affecting equal employment opportunities. With all these groups involved, and with sometimes conflicting rulings coming from different sources, a great deal of confusion has arisen as to exactly what constitutes "affirmative action." This has discouraged many firms from developing effective affirmative action programs.

For a firm that does have discriminatory policies and would like to remedy them, the costs and time involved in doing so might be prohibitive. Effective validation of psychological testing, for example, may take many years and cost thousands of dollars. With respect to the size contingency mentioned in Chapter 1, validation may not be statistically possible for small firms — there may never be enough employees in a particular job to obtain the necessary sample size required for validation.

Simply to provide data to governmental compliance organizations such as the EEOC may be very time consuming. As of 1975, for example, one writer indicated that "employers are finding it may take 400 to 500 man-hours to generate the data requested by visiting compliance investigators."[33]

Even though it may be morally just to require firms to pay for past or present discriminatory actions, some back pay awards have been exceptionally costly. Further, some courts have added punitive damages to these awards, and additionally, firms have incurred substantial costs in maintaining legal staffs to keep up with equal opportunity employment court rulings and governmental guidelines.

Firms have found it costly and sometimes not possible to take affirmative action by establishing quotas or goals. Engaging in such "ratio hiring" involves a rather complex utilization analysis, in which firms must: (1) compute how many minorities and women are currently employed in various classes of jobs, (2) determine how many such employees should be employed to end underutilization, and (3) compute the difference between these two and then take appropriate actions.[34] Especially difficult here is step two — determining what percentage or number of minorities or women need to be employed to obtain parity with respect to the firm's labor markets.

Regardless of goals, firms may not be able to *find* enough competent minority applicants for open positions. As the reader is undoubtedly aware, blacks, for example, have been discriminated against in many ways for years. The United States Supreme

Court's ruling in 1896 *(Plessy vs. Ferguson)* that "separate but equal" schools for black and white children would be adequate led to a situation in which whites were generally given a better education than blacks. It was not until 1954 *(Brown vs. Board of Education of Topeka)* that the Supreme Court struck down this earlier doctrine and called for desegregation in school systems. Blacks today still are often culturally and educationally disadvantaged. In addition, black males sometimes live in a "matriarchal family unit," in which the responsible wage earner is the mother and it is not a sign of manliness to accept steady work. Other minority groups such as Spanish-speaking Americans also are often raised in family and environmental conditions that lead to cultural disadvantages.

Women, on the other hand, regardless of education or ability, have worked in industry for many decades. Often, however, they have been confined to jobs not allowing them to assume responsibilities commensurate with their capabilities. The women's rights movement has gained in strength, and although the number is still small, more and more women are being provided with managerial and professional responsibilities. For example, *Business Week* reported that as of early 1976, 202 women were directors of 239 major corporations — almost all of them appointed in the few years immediately preceding. This movement began slowly in 1972 and increased "tremendously" in 1975.[35]

These observations lead to a final problem with respect to providing minorities and women with equal employment opportunities — assimilating them into the organization. With culturally deprived minority groups, their attitudes and the attitudes toward them must often be changed if they are to be assimilated into an organization that requires people to come to work on time steadily and abide by many work rules and regulations. Women, somewhat differently, have often not had the training for managerial level jobs nor the responsibility for supervising male managers. Here also, both the attitudes of women as career managers or professionals and male attitudes toward them as colleagues and sometimes superiors must be modified for viable assimilation into the organization. We will delve into the problems of training and assimilating special groups such as the hard-core unemployed and women in Chapter 8.

RECRUITING

Recruiting involves searching for and obtaining job applicants. There are several facets of and approaches utilized for recruiting. We will now turn to some of the more important of these.

Labor Markets, Information Transmission, and Decision Making

In searching for candidates, a firm must be aware of the external "labor market" and direct its recruiting efforts for different classes of personnel to the appropriate markets. Basically, an external labor market refers to those individuals outside the firm seeking work in some defined geographical area.

In general, most blue collar, clerical, and other nonmanagement or nonprofessional individuals do not move frequently from city to city. Thus, most of the potential employees for these kinds of work may be sought out locally. A much broader labor market usually exists for managerial and professional employees. These individuals are much more mobile and may be willing to move any place in the United States (and sometimes abroad) for another job.

Within each labor market we have persons seeking (or willing to accept) jobs and organizations seeking individuals. Bringing these groups together are many different *media,* through which these individuals and organizations may transmit information to each other. If this process were perfect, the "rational individual would maximize his probability of gaining the best job and minimize his costs of search."[36] Similarly, management would attempt to hire the most competent individuals at a minimum cost. In both cases, owing to having imperfect information, the individuals and organizations are engaged in decision making under risk. Further, both individuals and organizations are inclined to satisfice rather than optimize. That is, the firm will look at applicants until it finds a "competent" one, but will not continue its search indefinitely to find the "very best" one in the whole United States. Similarly, individuals will look for a "good" job, but will not keep searching indefinitely until they find the "very best" job. Time may also be a significant constraint on both the individual (who may be unemployed) and on the firm, which needs to fill a position quickly.

There are many different types of information transmission media used in recruiting, including individual newspaper advertisements, organization newspaper advertisements, the union hiring hall in some trades, college placement offices, public and private employment agencies, professional meetings, trade magazines, computerized resume placement services, friends and relatives, and an individual's direct application to the organization.

Three general observations may be made concerning recruiting decision making. First, there seems to be some evidence that the two most common search strategies chosen by individuals are direct application and through friends and relatives. For example, in a mail survey of 5000 scientists and engineers in the United States from 1950 to 1970, it was found among those responding that of a list of 14 recruiting media, direct application led to the greatest percentage of jobs (36.3 per cent), with friends or relatives a close second (30.6 per cent). Newspaper advertisements came in third and private employment agencies fourth.[37] When this study was compared with two other nonmanagerial studies, it was found that the same two strategies were most commonly used among production workers. A New Haven, Connecticut, study of production workers showed that 31 per cent of all jobs came via direct application and 27.5 per cent via friends or relatives;[38] a Nashua, New Hampshire, study showed 17.5 and 38.5 per cent respectively for these two categories.[39] It should be noted that "direct application" as indicated in these studies may be used in conjunction with other search alternatives. For example, a person may learn from a friend about a job and then apply directly to the firm.

Second, many recruiting sources are geared in specific directions so that the organization (and knowledgeable individuals) have some media source guidelines. College placement offices would obviously be used only for positions requiring education beyond the high school level and they deal mostly with beginning level managerial and professional positions. Certain private employment agencies, on the other hand, deal more with experienced managers and professionals and are often used by individuals who still have good jobs but are looking for something better elsewhere. In contrast, many individuals who utilize the services of state employment offices are unemployed and may be looking for any reasonable position by means of which they can support themselves.

Third, there are a number of contingencies involved in recruitment decision making. One of these is organization size in terms of number of "exposures" as discussed in Chapter 1. A firm needing to hire 50 to 100 individuals at once would normally be expected to engage in more extensive and formalized recruiting procedures than if it had only one vacant position. An aerospace firm requiring 50 engineers to work on a new government contract, or a retail food chain opening a new supermarket in which 60 new nonmanagerial employees are needed provide examples of where more formalized efforts would be needed.

The state of the labor market also represents an important contingency. In the late 1950's some firms recruited to "stockpile" engineers to have them available to support contract bids with the government. At the other extreme, with the recession in 1974, many firms completely dropped their college recruiting efforts, while a number paid "courtesy" visits simply to maintain good public relations. Such public relations are also important. In the academic market, for example, the Harvard Business School, Carnegie-Mellon, MIT, or UCLA will find it much easier to recruit highly competent newly graduated Ph.D's than will small state teachers' colleges. Likewise, companies with good "images" tend to find recruiting easier than those without such an image. Another contingency of importance may be the degree of uncertainty and complexity facing the organization. It has been hypothesized that

. . . there may be a degree of self-selection of the individuals with various personality types . . . in relation to types of organizations. Persons with high dependence needs may tend to be attached to organizations designed for stability and simplicity. Individuals with high autonomy needs, conversely, would tend to be less comfortable in structured situations and would seek out organizations offering relatively more opportunity for individual expression.[40]

Whether this hypothesis is valid is open to speculation; we will reserve such a discussion question until the end of this chapter.

Recruiting and Management Science

Three types of management science efforts have been used in recruiting to help managers make better decisions — simulation, linear programming, and network models. We will now give attention to some of these as well as to computerized man-job matching systems.

Simulation

Employment offices in larger firms are generally responsible for attracting and screening many job applicants every day. In one firm, a computer simulation was developed to test the effects of three types of conditions upon two dependent variables in a corporate employment office. In eight simulation runs made, the employment office's operations were replicated for:

1. Easy and busy days in terms of numbers of applicants processed (75 and 150 respectively).
2. Management's utilization of either two or four interviewers.
3. A testing schedule then being used in the office as well as a "proposed schedule which was expected to speed up the flow of applicants through the office."[41]

Each of the eight possible combinations of conditions — easy days with two interviewers with the present schedule, busy days with two interviewers with the present schedule, and so forth — were observed with respect to the average waiting time and the average transit time of the applicants going through the operation as the two dependent variables. The results of the simulation showed that cutting the number of interviewers in half increased the waiting time at least *tenfold,* while doubling the number of applicants increased it at least *eight times.*[42] The simulation results showed, however, that the proposed change in the test schedule had "little, if any, effect on either the average waiting time or average transit time of the applicants."[43] This simulation model has been of value in helping to plan and make decisions in an employment office. As we indicated in Chapter 1, the mathematics are often not complex in simulations, which is the case with the employment office simulation. Whether the costs of conducting such a simulation outweigh the advantages of creating a better alternative to a particular decision problem, however, is another question that must be asked in utilizing this (as well as other) management science approaches.

Mathematical Programming

The management science technique of mathematical programming has been applied to recruiting at IBM. Here, the simplex technique of linear programming was utilized in college recruiting. Facing an increasing demand for college graduates in the late 1960's, IBM set up a "National Recruiting Organization" (NRO) and divided up its NRO activities by delineating four geographical areas in the United States, each with an NRO office. With *scarce resources* (dollars), and subject to certain *constraints,* the linear programming model attempted to *minimize* the total visit and moving costs of all the college recruits. These costs included travel and visit expenses (motel, meals, etc.) for job applicants visiting NRO offices in the recruiting process, and moving expenses for those recruits who were hired.[44] Minimizing such expenses by calculating and analyzing them for each job applicant in each location in the United States would have been extremely difficult, if not impossible. Therefore, the linear program was designed to incorporate:

1. A center of supply for each NRO area that was the "geographical point at which the total supply of graduates of the NRO area can be considered to be located."[45]
2. A center of demand for each NRO area that was "the geographical point at which the total requirements of the NRO area can be considered to be located."[46]

By using these geographical center points, total *average* visit and moving expenses could be calculated and minimized (within the capability of the program model). The description of this center of supply and demand model developed by IBM requires careful study to fully understand. It has, however, proven to be quite useful to IBM:

> The order and logic that it brings to the area of recruitment planning was very much needed. It is now possible to quickly distribute the college requirements of the corporation and analyze the effects of the allocation on the NRO areas.[47]

PERT

Another college recruiting effort using newer decision-making techniques was a CPM/PERT network developed by Sandia Corporation for recruitment planning.[48] An adaptation of this Sandia network is shown in Figure 4–4. The critical path in the Sandia recruiting effort was the 1-2-17 path—comprising the two activities "make salary projections" and "establish salary guides"—which projected a time of 16 days.

PERT networks such as the Sandia one serve several purposes. First, they set up a formalized visual plan, which permits management to pinpoint problem areas. They also indicate *where* changes will be required should problems arise during the course of the project. They may show dramatically that such inappropriate managerial strategies as "putting the whole project on a crash basis" are unnecessary, and that it is only on the critical (and perhaps the next-to-most critical) paths that attention needs to be placed. Finally, it should be pointed out that a simple PERT/CPM network such as the one in Figure 4–4 is not costly to develop, may help spell out more clearly for each manager what his responsibilities are, and may have applications to many different types of personnel projects.

Computerized Man-Job Matching Systems

In addition to utilizing the three management science techniques above, organizations have developed computerized man-job matching systems. These are *conceptually similar* to skills inventories, but are systems *external* to the firm in which employment agencies (or groups) use the computer to match up job applicants with firms having job openings. This approach was hailed as a major advance in the late 1960's by some,[49] and one report published in 1969 indicated that 14 computerized man-matching systems were in existence, some of which were privately operated while others were government operated.[50] One of the more successful of these systems was called Graduate Resource Accumulation and Distribution (GRAD), and was developed and

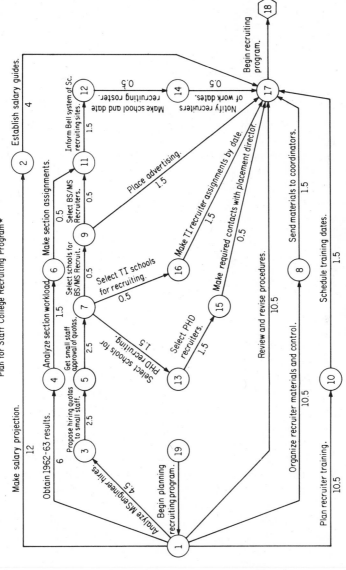

CHART I

Plan for Staff College Recruiting Program*

* Adapted from a PERT program used by Sandia Corporation. While not complete, this should give the reader some idea of how PERT or CPM networks can be used by personnel managers.

Figure 4-4 PERT recruiting network. Reprinted from Lawrence L. Steinmetz, "PERT Personnel Practices," Personnel Journal, 44 (September, 1965), pp. 422–3. Reprinted with permission of Personnel Journal, Copyright, September, 1965.

run by the nonprofit organization the College Placement Council, Inc. This service was designed for college graduates who had at least one year's work experience. The system was so effective that by September 1969, the Council was mailing out some 6000 resumes a month. At the time, however, "the recession began to influence the job market at such a rapid rate that employer requests dwindled and the system had to be discontinued in June 1973."[51] The recession apparently contributed to the termination of other man-job systems as well, for when we wrote late in 1975 to the 14 organizations which were reportedly in existence in 1969: (1) three responses (including GRAD) reported discontinuance; (2) five letters were returned, not forwardable; and (3) no response was obtained from the other six. This is what one would expect as a size contingency in terms of "exposures" as discussed in Chapter 1. Since the number of firms using the system decreased rapidly, there were not enough job applicants to enable these systems to continue to operate economically.

The United States Manpower Administration in the Department of Labor has run a number of experimental man-job matching systems within the U.S. Employment Service that may be more successful than the ones mentioned earlier. Further, the individual responsible for these programs indicated in 1976 that plans have been made to extend what are called Job Service Matching Systems (JSMS) to all states "within the next 3 to 4 years."[52]

Evaluating Recruiting Performance

How can one evaluate the effectiveness of the firm's recruiting efforts? One approach is to look first at a particular recruiting medium, such as newspaper advertising, and calculate all costs associated with it (e.g., company costs for applicants' plant visits and, should they take the job, possible moving expenses). Next, the firm would obtain an average cost per successful hire for each medium for each class of worker (blue collar, clerical) and select the medium that provides the most successful hires at the least cost. There are problems involved in such an evaluation, however. One problem is that labor market characteristics and media attraction may change before a firm has had a chance to determine whether or not its earlier hires have been successful. Second, as indicated previously, recruiting is part of an interdependent information-decision system. Therefore, it may be hard to isolate the attractiveness of employment agencies, for instance, from the image that candidates referred from such agencies obtain from the specific interviewers which the firm chooses to talk with them in a plant visit. Carleton Dukes has suggested measuring the efforts of different recruiters by looking at and comparing their efforts by the number of initial contacts made, the percentage of those whom the interviewer referred to the firm, the percentage of those whom the firm actually invited for a visit, the percentage of those actually interviewed, and the percentage of offers given, accepted, and refused.[53] Although this effort was a laudable one in that it dealt with a difficult systems problem, one can question the validity of the approach. Some interviewers may make fewer referrals because their standards are higher than others. Is this desirable or undesirable? Further, factors beyond the control of the recruiters enter into the picture. Different candidates, for instance, may be interviewed by different managers when visiting the firm and may come away from their visits with quite different images of the organization — a situation that may be almost completely beyond the control of the recruiters who made the referrals. We are not suggesting that the above approach is without merit. We do wish to emphasize, however, that these kinds of data need to be looked at carefully and that the existence of systems interdependencies be recognized. For example, if four of five of a firm's college recruiters refer from 20 to 25 per cent of candidates contacted, while the fifth only refers 10 per cent, a problem may well exist and be pinpointed by further analysis. Perhaps this one interviewer has standards that are too high. On the other hand, analysis may indicate that the interviewer has been visiting poorer colleges from which a smaller number of candidates would normally be referred.

SELECTION

In this section, we will first make a number of general observations about the decision-making processes in evaluating and deciding whether to hire any given job applicant. We will then treat each of the five decision techniques indicated in Figure 4–1: application forms, psychological tests, interviews, reference checks, and physical examinations.

Selection: Some General Observations

Line management should make final hiring decisions. However, the personnel department really makes many decisions of an evaluative nature as the job candidate progresses through the selection process and therefore influences greatly what the final decision will be. The line manager will not even see certain job applicants because they have already been rejected for employment by personnel.

In the progression through the stages of selection, several considerations are important. The whole selection process should be viewed as a *two-way* communications process. It is not only important for the firm to obtain the necessary information from the candidate to make its selection decision — it is also important for the candidate to obtain information from the firm for *him* to make a good accept-or-reject decision should a job offer be made. The applicant may be able to obtain easily much financial and other overall information about the firm from its annual report and other published information. Other information, which may be of more significance, however, may be difficult to obtain. For example, it may be extremely difficult in an hour interview for the candidate to really obtain a good picture of a potential supervisor's personality in order to know how well the two would get along. This knowledge is especially important at those levels at which there may be few clear-cut measures of performance and an individual's future may strongly be influenced by the supervisor-subordinate relationship and his supervisor's opinion of him.

We also believe that honesty on the part of both candidates and the firm is important. With subjective selection techniques, a sophisticated graduating college senior may lie his way through an interview, enter dishonest responses on certain psychological tests and "con" the company into giving him a job not really suited to his personality. If he does, he will probably be unhappy on the job, not excel on it, and quit or be dismissed before long, representing a waste of resources both for him and the organization. Similarly, if the firm conveys the false impression to the college graduate that in most cases promotions from entry-port managerial positions to higher levels take about a year, whereas actual experience indicates an average time of 3.1 years, the employee may well become disturbed by the false impressions and leave the organization or not work as hard.

Another key fact that should be considered by the firm in making selection decisions is that once an individual reaches adulthood, many *basic* behavioral patterns will usually be firmly established and difficult to change. Selecting individuals who appear questionable in the pious hope that "Joe's behavior will somehow change if we hire him" is rather naive. This is not meant to infer that people do not change, for all of us are learning all the time. Rather we are talking about *basic* behavioral dispositions. Because many adult behavioral patterns do remain fairly constant, previous behavioral patterns are one of the best predictors of future behavior and should be examined carefully. As emphasized at the beginning of this chapter, however, we are talking in a probabilistic sense with decision making under risk.

Further, we should qualify these remarks by pointing out that there is disagreement among psychologists as to the ease of changing adult behavior; some believe that although basic adult patterns may be modified, it is questionable as to how effective the organization can be in doing so.

In selection, personnel departments look for both good and bad points with respect to an individual, recognizing that there is no such creature as the "perfect person." In looking at these characteristics, it is extremely important to identify patterns of behavior. For instance, if an individual indicates on his application form that he has left one of four previous jobs because he "disliked the boss," it may be that the supervisor was a difficult person to get along with. On the other hand, if the job applicant indicates that he left all four jobs because of a poor supervisor, we might infer with a fairly good probability of being correct that he is basically hostile toward all authority and probably would not get along too well with any supervisor. There is, however, a real danger of jumping to conclusions and overgeneralizations based on a single fact. As pointed out by William H. Whyte, Jr., more than two decades ago, simply because a man married a woman two years older than himself (a fact), whereas men generally marry women younger than themselves (another fact), one cannot jump to the general conclusion that he married seeking subconsciously a "mother-surrogate," and would be inclined to be passive-dependent on the job.[54]

Considerable importance should be given not only to patterns of behavior but also the reasons why such patterns may exist. Some firms, for example, are concerned if a managerial applicant is heavily in debt. There may be two reasons for this concern: (1) the individual may have to take on a second job to meet these obligations, which would result in too much stress being placed on him; and (2) if he cannot manage his own finances, how can we expect him to manage any of the firm's financial problems satisfactorily? But why is he in debt? Because he "can't leave the horses alone" or because his spouse had a very serious illness two years ago and all the medical debts have not yet been paid off? With answers to such questions, a much better decision can be made as to the suitability of the applicant.

Such probing raises another *fundamental issue* in personnel selection: Are we infringing on the rights of individuals to have privacy? When we discussed equal opportunity employment earlier, we indicated that questions such as those which would reveal a person's religion would be in conflict with EEOC policies. But what about other questions, such as those concerning the individual's drinking habits? Although such writers as Whyte[55] have been very much concerned with the individual's right to privacy, our position is that a firm facing a selection decision that may involve thousands of dollars has the right to ask many "personal" questions as long as they are: (1) relevant to on-the-job behavior and (2) discreetly done. For example, since alcoholism is a major problem in American life today, one large midwestern manufacturing firm probed drinking habits in interviews with managerial candidates. The interviewer would not ask bluntly, however, any such inappropriate questions as "Are you a drunk?" Rather, the questions would be phrased more subtly: "How often do you drink?" "When did you have your last drink?" "What was the occasion?"

Two final general observations about selection deserve elaboration here. First, the organization will often use different selection techniques for managerial and professional applicants than for rank-and-file ones. The application form may be more sophisticated, different psychological tests may be given, and more interviews and interviewing time may be devoted to the managerial and professional candidate. The basic reason for this is that managers and professionals are usually going to be making many more key decisions in the organization, and hence, have to be screened more carefully.

Second, the sequencing of selection tools has an effect on both costs and information inputs to decision making. With respect to costs, it is much cheaper to have someone fill out an application form first and be given a physical examination later. This is true because of not only the absolute costs involved but also the probabilistic outcomes of the use of each tool. For example, it may cost only $5 to quickly scan an application form and screen out all but 30 per cent of the applicants for a job, while it would cost $50 for a physical examination which is "passed" by job applicants 80 per cent of the time. If these were the *only* two selection tools, processing 100 applicants with the application form given first would cost:

$$\$5/\text{applicant} \times 100 \text{ applicants} = \$\ 500$$
$$\$50/\text{applicant} \times\ 30 \text{ applicants} = \underline{\$1500}$$

Total Costs $2000

If this sequence were reversed, on the other hand, total costs would be:

$$\$50/\text{applicant} \times 100 \text{ applicants} = \$5000$$
$$\$5/\text{applicant} \times\ 80 \text{ applicants} = \underline{\$\ 400}$$

Total Costs $5400

Irrespective of costs, there is disagreement as to whether psychological tests (if they are used) should be given prior to or after the interview. Some personnel managers believe that giving an interviewer the applicant's psychological test data may bias his attitudes in the interview. On the other hand, it can be argued that the interviewer should possess all available information to provide a better basis for decision making. We prefer the latter strategy even though both test and application form data may bias an interviewer, especially if he or she is inexperienced. Our preference is based on the benefits to be derived from having these inputs available to the interviewer. This information may provide some indication of a candidate's strong and weak points, which can serve as a very useful guide to the interviewer for determining what types of questions would be most appropriate to ask in the interview.

The Application Form

The application form is a quick and inexpensive means of screening out obviously unqualified applicants for a job. It can also provide much valuable information for future use and serve as a test of the applicant's ability to read, write, and follow instructions. Typical types of questions on application forms concern: age, previous work experience, education, marital status, leadership experiences, and hobbies. For managerial and professional employees, some application forms ask the candidate to write a 100 word autobiography, to indicate what he would like to be doing ten years in the future, and to describe what he likes and dislikes most about other people. Some responses are interpreted similarly by different personnel managers. For example, extensive job hopping is usually viewed negatively, while having both the education and experience required for the position open would be a positive factor. More subjective tasks such as writing the autobiography, however, may be interpreted quite differently by different analysts, and a real question can be raised concerning the predictive validity of such items. In light of affirmative action regulations, the safest strategy on application forms would be to ask only questions of fact directly relevant to the individual's ability to perform the job for which he is applying.

In an effort to develop application forms that can predict probabilities of success on the job, "weighted application forms" have been used successfully by organizations as far back as the 1920's. Weighted application forms assume that the applicant's personal history is predictive of success on the job, and that statistical analysis can indicate the degree of relatedness of *specific* application form *items* to some job success criteria such as tenure. On weighted application forms those items which are most strongly predictive are given more weight than those of lesser importance. For any job candidate, the item weights (which may be both positive or negative) are summed to provide a total score. Then a firm develops a "cut-off" score that will help make correct hiring decisions — i.e., a score that results in maximizing the probability of applicants falling in Quadrants 1 and 3 in Figure 4–2. If the candidate's summed score is equal to or above the cut-off score, he or she is considered further for selection. If not, the applicant is rejected. The cut-off scores may have to be changed due to economic conditions. In recessionary times, an organization can increase its cut-off score and be more selective than in times of full employment.

Historically, the weighted application form has been generally used for job positions that are unskilled, semiskilled, or service-oriented. However, weighted application forms have also been used for scientists, air force officers, engineers, and service station managers.[56]

A brief description of some of the results of one study in which tenure was used as a criterion for success among clerical workers at Yale University in 1960 will illustrate specifically how the weighted application blank works.[57] Local address (within city vs. suburban) was found to be a good predictor, and a weight of +2 was given to living in the city and a −2 for living in outlying suburbs. Previous salary was found to have no relationship to success, and therefore was given a weight of zero. Age was found to be a key predictor, with individuals aged 35 and over assigned a +3 weight, and those under 20 a −3 weight. Age of children was also a significant variable, with women with children of preschool and grade school ages given a weight of −3 and those whose children were of high school age or older given a +3 weight. In general, the weightings obtained were what one would have expected at that time. For example, it was more difficult to get to work from the outlying suburbs than from in the city, and workers who were 35 and over tended to be more likely to stay with the university than those under 20. Appropriately validated weighted application blanks have provided management with good (probabilistic) prediction instruments for making personnel selection decisions. From a contingency point of view, the more dynamic the organization, the more frequently weighted blanks as well as other selection tools such as tests must be updated and revalidated. Inskeep, for example, has expressed the opinion that: "Weighted application forms are seldom valid for more than two years."[58] Finally, size represents an important contingency, because a weighted application form must be given to a large enough sample of applicants within a "reasonable" period of time to be statistically sound. Using a sample spread over many years leads to problems in obtaining a sample from a stable population.

Psychological Tests

Psychological tests have been used for over half a century as selection tools. Sometimes firms develop tests of their own; in other cases, they purchase tests developed by firms specializing in test design and development. In 1974, it was estimated that there were about 2600 tests available to employers.[59]

Tests have been controversial for many years. A basic assumption underlying all of them is that there are differences in individual abilities, attitudes, and behavior that can be measured and are related to successful job performance. In many cases, this assumption has not proved valid.

In the years immediately following the passage of the Civil Rights Act of 1964, tests were seen as a means of providing compliance with this Act, and test sales zoomed. In the year immediately following passage of the Act, it was estimated that 6 million copies of one test—the Wonderlic Personnel Test—were sold.[60] With later EEOC guidelines and the *Griggs vs. Duke Power* decision, however, many firms looked more closely at their psychological testing.

More recently, many firms have dropped tests because they did not believe the tests would meet government compliance standards. Other firms, however, have continued to use tests in selection. There are three basic types of tests in use — aptitude and ability, interest, and personality. Before discussing these, a discussion on validating tests is necessary, since this is basic to the understanding of test use.

Test Validation

Validity, as indicated earlier, refers to the ability of any instrument to measure what it is supposed to measure. Validation of many types of measurement instruments is important in personnel management; e.g., weighted application forms and patterned interviews (which we will discuss later). Here we will focus special attention on the validation of psychological tests, long a major area of validation research. Two basic types of validation are frequently used by the personnel manager: *predictive* and *concurrent*. The use of both types assumes that the firm has developed job descriptions and job specifications. Predictive validation is the most scientific of the two and calls for:

1. Giving tests to all job applicants but not using the test scores in hiring any of these applicants.
2. "Hiding" the test scores of the applicants who were hired for some period of time after hiring (e.g., six months to two years).
3. At this later time analyzing the relationship between the individual test scores and a criterion measure such as actual performance on the job.

The basic reason for "hiding" the test results is to avoid *contamination*. This means that if supervisors know what subordinates' test scores are, they may be biased and both treat and rate the performance of those with the higher scores more favorably. To the extent that this occurs, we would have test scores influencing the behavior they are supposed to predict, and there would be no solid basis for scientific validation.

Although predictive validation is the most "scientific," it has its limitations. Basically, it is both expensive and time consuming, which would pose special problems for smaller companies. The smaller firm might not be able to afford the statistical analysis required for validation, and it might take an inordinate amount of time before it was possible to hire a large enough sample size of any particular class of employees to permit statistical analysis. Further, in all firms, by not using the tests to start with, many individuals who are *not competent* for the jobs for which they apply would be hired. This poses not only an economic problem, but an ethical one as well — what does the firm do with employees who are not competent to perform their jobs? Their performance would lead to neither the meeting of organizational objectives nor many human needs.

Concurrent validation means giving tests to *current* employees and concurrently obtaining criterion data, e.g., supervisor ratings of performance. This approach permits using the results of this analysis without any great delay, unlike predictive validation. Further, concurrent validation gets around the problem of having to put poor performers on the payroll to obtain adequate statistical data. It is limited, however, by a phenomenon known as *range restriction*. This results because only qualified employees who have stayed with the firm are being given the tests and, therefore, a smaller range of behavior is being evaluated; also, the motivation of present employees in taking tests might be quite different from that of job applicants.

It should be also noted that two newer types of validation have been developed, each looking at different *tasks* involved in jobs, rather than the job as a whole. The first of these is *synthetic* validity, which involves "the inferring of validity in a specific situation from a logical analysis of jobs into their elements, a determination of test validities for these elements, and a combination of elemental validities into a whole."[61] This approach has been held in high regard by many authorities on test validation. Dunnette, for example, has stated that this "validity approach fits perfectly into our model for selection research, particularly at the point of calling for the discovery and the separate validation of predictors against specific job behaviors."[62]

The second approach is *content* validity, in which jobs are broken down into specific tasks and a panel of experts is asked to judge how well each test item measures performance, e.g., how essential is each item on an arithmetic test to the performance of mathematical computations required for a certain job? This approach does not call for statistical validation of test items, as does a synthetic validity approach. Although businesses have not focused too much attention on content validity:

> Civil rights legislation, the attendant actions of compliance agencies, and a few landmark court cases have provided the impetus for the extension of the application of content validity from academic achievement testing to personnel testing in business and industry.[63]

With respect to validation, firms have various alternative strategies open to them. There are a number of organizations that develop, provide statistical data on, and sell tests to business firms. Among these are the Psychological Corporation, Science Research Associates, and E. F. Wonderlic and Associates, Inc. Thus, a firm may not have to go through the laborious and costly process of developing its own tests. It may simply buy one or more of the tests developed by firms specializing in this kind of work. In doing so, however, it must be extremely careful that the jobs for which statistical data are available from the test developers are very similar to or the same as those jobs for which the test is to be used. This illustrates another value of job analysis.

In light of the above there are five widely used strategies open to firms with respect to psychological test evaluation:

> 1. Buy test(s) and utilize norms developed by the test designers. For example, in one company, the Wonderlic Personnel Test was utilized for all managerial candidates. The minimum score considered to be favorable was the "central tendency" score for "manager and manager trainees" from a study of the test involving data supplied by 703 companies.[64]
> 2. Use purchased test(s) but carry out its own concurrent validation study to develop its own standards.
> 3. Use purchased test(s) and carry out a predictive validation study.
> 4. Develop its own test(s) and carry out a concurrent validity study.
> 5. Develop its own test(s) and carry out a predictive validity study.

These five alternatives are listed in order of least costly to most costly. We hypothesize that the organization's size and resources would represent important contingencies in choosing from among them.

Two final points are in order concerning test validation. First, regardless of the validation approach chosen, continuous review of the test process and updating norms, when necessary, are essential. Second, as noted, affirmative action is interrelated with the validation process. As an illustration, suppose blacks are underrepresented in clerical positions in a company, which may have to lower its selection standards to overcome this problem and wants to utilize a mental alertness test for *all* of its clerical job applicants. It might utilize a widely used mental alertness test, the Wonderlic Personnel Test. In addition to determining norms for whites, the developers of this test have developed black norms based on a large study of 38,452 job applicants for use in affirmative action programs.[65] If a company wanted to examine only clerical applicants who scored above the 50th percentile on the test, a raw score of 23 for whites would be required (50.2 percentile rank), while a raw score of 17 would be required for blacks (53.0 percentile rank).[66] These test data do not mean that a black applicant scoring 17 would be as likely to succeed as the white applicant scoring 23. Since the norms have been validated for blacks, however, a black scoring 17 would have a greater probability of success as a clerical worker than, for example, a black scoring 14. Thus, the use of the test would enable the firm to identify which individuals would have the greatest probabilities of being successful.

Ability and Aptitude Tests

Numerous tests have been developed to measure a person's ability to do a specific job, or aptitude (potential ability) to undertake some task successfully.

Ability tests (sometimes referred to as achievement) can be geared to testing either a candidate's assumed knowledge or skills. An example of an ability test for an employee who claims previous meat-cutting experience would be a written test about various cuts of meat and how to make such cuts. An example of a skills test would be having a secretary take a dictated letter, transcribe it, and type it up. Most such tests are for nonmanagerial jobs, where skills and abilities are more precisely definable. In general, of all psychological tests, the greatest confidence can be placed upon ability tests, for they are measuring something fairly concrete.

Aptitude tests may measure the applicant's general mental ability or certain special abilities. Widely employed (both at managerial and professional, as well as lower level position jobs) are the mental alertness or mental ability tests. Among the most common of these are the Thurstone Test of Mental Ability and the Wonderlic Personnel Test. Tests such as these frequently measure three types of reasoning: verbal, symbolic, and numerical. For instance, on the Wonderlic test, examples of these three types of questions are shown in Figure 4–5.

Unfortunately, some mental alertness tests may be "culturally biased." It is not possible to "fake" such tests, however. One either knows the answer to the questions or does not. However, since some of these tests are so widely used there may be a test familiarity problem. To help overcome this, alternative forms have been developed for some tests. These are given to job applicants who indicate that they have taken a particular test previously. Most of the well-known mental alertness tests are relatively inexpensive to administer and interpret, and considerable statistical data concerning their validity are often available from the publishers. This does not mean that a firm should not conduct its own validity study.

How are such tests utilized in personnel selection decision making? The current situation is clouded because of affirmative action issues, but historically with respect to the mental alertness tests, the following may be said:

1. They have been given more weight than interest and personality profiles.

2. Firms have developed either from a publisher's statistical data or their own validation data a lower cut-off point or points. For example, one firm had predictively validated the Wonderlic test for managerial applicants and found that four fifths of those scoring in a "favorable" area (32 to 50) were successful, while of those scoring 21 or less, five sixths were failures on the job. It used this data to set up the following decision rules:

29. REPRIMAND   REPROVE—do these words have
    1. similar meanings
    2. contradictory
    3. mean neither the same or opposite?

30. Four of the following five parts can be fitted together in such a way as to make a triangle. Which four are they?

31. Which number in the following group of numbers represents the smallest amount?
    10   3   2   .8   .888   .96

Figure 4–5 *Mental alertness test questions. (Taken from Form EM of the Wonderlic Personnel Test, with permission of the publisher: E. F. Wonderlic and Associates, Northfield, Illinois.)*

a. If the applicant's score is 32 or above, he appears to have the degree of mental alertness required of him, so move on and go to examining him on other selection criteria.

b. If his score is from 22 to 31, raise a caution about hiring him. If other data obtained about him are very favorable, however, consider him further.

c. If his score is below 22, do not consider the applicant for employment.

3. In some cases, primarily in nonindustrial sales positions, an upper cut-off point may be established, on the rationale that an extremely bright person would not find such a job challenging. Upper cut-off points (in the high 40's) have been used on the Wonderlic test in sales positions with firms in the hearing aid industry, and in manufacture of women's lingerie.

All selection decision rules, it should be emphasized, are ones that improve the firm's *probabilities* of hiring employees who will be successful and rejecting those who would have failed. Thus, we are dealing with selection decision making under risk.

Interest Profiles

Vocational interest profiles have been utilized for a number of years in vocational guidance work and in personnel selection. Unlike the mental alertness tests, such profiles can sometimes be "faked." Some of them, however, do attempt to overcome this problem by asking essentially the same question more than once, but phrased differently. The questions and answers are then compared. Among the more widely known interest profiles are the Kuder Preference Record and Kuder Occupational Interest Survey. In these two profiles, individuals are given triads of questions, and asked to indicate for each triad the activity they like most and the one they like the least. Two illustrative triads from the Kuder are shown in Figure 4–6.

With the Kuder Preference Record, triad responses are grouped into various broad occupational areas, such as artistic, literary, numerical, and scientific. The scoring is such that an individual cannot obtain a high score on all categories. For example, in the first of the above two triads, the least liked art gallery visit would not contribute to the "artistic" category, but the visit to the museum might contribute to the "scientific." If the most liked choice had been browsing in a library, this would have contributed to "literary" instead of "scientific."

The following may be said with respect to decision making in one firm that used the Kuder profile with candidates for managerial and professional jobs. First, lesser weight was usually placed on the Kuder in comparison to the mental alertness test that accompanied it in a battery of tests. One of the reasons for this was its possibility of being "faked." No one was rejected

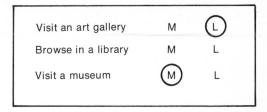

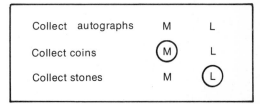

Figure 4-6 *Illustrative Kuder profile triads. From Kuder Occupational Interest Survey, Form DD by G. Frederic Kuder. © 1965, 1968, 1970 Science Research Associates, Inc. Reprinted by permission of the publisher.*

outright because of a Kuder score. However, *glaring incongruencies* between any Kuder scores and other information about an individual would be probed in an interview with the applicant. For example, a low "numerical" score in the 15th percentile for a college senior applying for a job in accounting would raise a serious question, since so much numerical work is done in this particular profession. A major advantage of many interest profiles such as the Kuder is that they are not difficult to interpret, so that persons with some personnel or related background can be trained in their interpretation.

Personality Profiles

Personality profiles were the most controversial types of tests long before the Civil Rights Act of 1964 was passed and the term "affirmative action" ever coined. They have been criticized on the grounds of invasion of privacy, because some of them are easily faked,[67] because of their often questionable validation, and because they have supposedly led firms to hire "organization men," i.e., individuals who would conform to the organization rather than somewhat "different" but more creative individuals.[68]

There are basically two types of personality tests. The first is the objective, which asks specific questions calling for "yes," "no," "sometimes" or "?" responses. Among the better known objective personality inventories are the Thurstone Temperament Schedule, the Edwards Personality Inventory, and the Minnesota Multiphasic Personality Inventory.

The second type is the projective personality test, which

provides the individual with ambiguous stimuli, and asks the individual to project his or her personality upon the stimuli. The grandfather of this type of test is the well-known Rorschach Inkblot Test. Also well known is the Thematic Apperception Test (TAT), which involves showing the individual a series of pictures, and asking him or her to write stories about the pictures. For example, an individual shown a picture of a person sitting at a desk with both work and a family photograph on top of it could respond with a story:

1. Describing the picture as being one of a business person leisurely doing some work at home, and pleasantly reminiscing about a recent family outing while looking at the photograph; or

2. Describing the picture as an engineer thinking hard about the amount of stress that can be accepted as tolerable on a bridge being designed.[69]

In general, objective personality tests are easier and less expensive to interpret, and have been used more frequently in industry than projective tests. Many projective tests require interpretation by a clinical psychologist, while interpretation of many objective tests can be taught to someone working in personnel in a relatively short period of time. One reason for the "fakeability" problem on objective profiles is that often they pose questions to which certain answers constitute *socially unacceptable* responses. For example, even though a person's father had been one of the most reputable "bookies" in town, to respond "no" to the question: "My father was a law abiding citizen," would represent a negative one to anyone familiar with testing. Even with the simpler "yes" and "no" pencil and paper personality profiles, interpretation is usually much more difficult than with mental alertness tests.

Basically, the objectives of personality tests are twofold. First, the firm hopes to "weed out" any applicants with psychological problems serious enough that they could not perform well in general. Second, a skilled interpreter will attempt to ascertain how well the personalities of individuals not exhibiting such psychological problems match the psychological characteristics of the jobs for which they are being considered. For example, the Thurstone Temperament Schedule consists of 140 questions to be answered "yes," "no," or "don't know." The responses to these questions are designed to measure seven personality characteristics: active, vigorous, impulsive, dominant, sociable, stable, and reflective.[70] A skilled interpreter might interpret this profile thusly, depending upon the individual's responses:

1. There are certain *patterns* of *extremely* high or low scores on the seven personality characteristics that indicate a good probability of the individual having psychological problems. Depending on the degree of

severity, the interpreter might recommend rejecting the individual out-right or probing further into certain areas in more depth when he or she is interviewed.

2. The applicant's test scores may be such that he or she is very low on sociability, but quite high on reflective thinking. If a graduating college senior in business administration is applying for a job as a production supervisor, such scores may provide negative indications. The production supervisor has to carry on many interpersonal relationships daily, and devotes much time to daily problems that do not require a high degree of reflective thinking. On the other hand, these same profile scores might indicate an ideal match in an operations research position. This type of position calls for more individual work with fewer social interactions than a production supervisor's position but does require a high degree of reflective thinking. In such a situation, the interpreter might point out that the latter might be quite sound psychologically, at least according to the Thurstone profile.

Regardless of their limitations, a skilled interpreter will not simply recommend only those whose personality profile scores fall "right down the middle," leading to the hiring of "organization men," as Whyte has indicated.[71]

Computerized Test Interpretation

If human psychological test interpreters can develop decision rules such as those indicated in the preceding sections, the question may be raised: "Why can't decision rules be programmed on a computer for interpreting psychological tests?" Actually, this has been done. As far back as 1962, the Mayo Clinic reported that it had developed effective computerized interpretation of the Minnesota Multiphasic Personality Inventory (MMPI).[72] Patients at the clinic responded to the questions on this personality profile, these data were fed into the computer, and an interpretation was printed out to serve as preliminary diagnostic information for clinicians. Dr. Howard Rome, of the Clinic's Section of Psychiatry, expressed considerable faith in the computerized MMPI program, indicating that it had "a reliable usefulness comparable to that of the electrocardiogram, the electroencephalogram, and the basal metabolic rate. . . ."[73]

Shortly thereafter, Kleinmuntz simulated the thought processes of a psychologist, using the same MMPI personality profile.[74] This was accomplished by having the psychologist verbalize his thoughts as the MMPI was interpreted for various individuals, tape recording his comments, developing decision rules from them, and building these rules into a computer program. This verbalization-recording approach is called the *protocol* method. Kleinmuntz's objective was to be able to distinguish between "adjusted" and "maladjusted" college students. He also used statistical techniques to improve on the protocol-based decision rules, so that his program represented more than just a simulation (or replication) of human thought processes.

Smith and Greenlaw extended the idea of computerized thought process simulation directly into the field of personnel selection. They dealt with a psychologist interpreting not only one test but:

1. A battery of five tests (mental alertness, ability, and personality).
2. Personal information about the individual, such as age and number of years of previous relevant experience.
3. An indication of the relative importance of six job requirement variables including verbal fluency, accuracy and speed.[75]

All applicants being analyzed were being considered for clerical and clerical-administrative positions. The program output included both: (1) recommendations to hire, hire as a fair risk, check background further, or reject, and (2) a number of interpretative comments about the individual. Although not enough applicants were available for validating the program, several measures indicated that it did fairly effectively simulate the psychologist's decision processes.[76]

Two other observations concerning computerized psychological test interpretations are in order. First, all three of these efforts are based on the same basic assumption — that complex thought processes can be broken down into relatively *simple* decision rules and represented by networks of simple decision branches. As an example, suppose that, for a particular job, a mental alertness score of from 30 to 40 is considered favorable, and that individuals scoring over 40 on the test would probably be too bright and become quickly dissatisfied with the job, while individuals scoring less than 30 would have problems coping with the job. This decision rule branch could be programmed on a computer based on a flow diagram, as illustrated in Figure 4–7. The number of such decision rules in computerized interpretations is large, and there are many interrelationships among branches. All branching, in essence, is broken down into simple "if-yes," "if-no," "go to" statements.

Finally, what are the values and limitations of computerized test interpretation? First, if organizational size in terms of "exposures" is sufficiently large relative to the initial investment of developing the program, the costs of test interpretation may be reduced. In the Smith and Greenlaw study, in spite of a heavy initial investment, once the program was developed, the cost of computer time was less than 5 cents/applicant interpretation. With human interpretations much more costly, such a program could reduce personnel costs *if* enough applicants were processed so that the present value of savings for all applicants would exceed the initial investment costs. Additionally, on a contingency basis, all

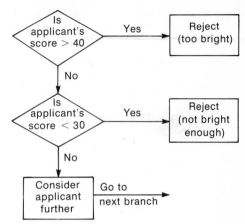

Figure 4–7 Simple decision rule branch.

jobs in the organization would need to have a relatively stable content. In dynamic organizations, many jobs might significantly change before the computerized program had been developed and validated. Computer interpretations, *once perfected,* would also be more consistent than human ones, for the computer, unlike us humans, does not have its good days and "not so good days." Further, if the thought processes of two or more psychologists were pooled and then incorporated into the program, we might well expect better interpretations than could be expected from any single human interpreter. We emphasize "once perfected," because with poor human input in the design of computerized programs, one would have consistency — consistently *poor* output.

Interviewing

Employment interviews are used by virtually all firms as an integral part of the selection process. In spite of this wide use, they are extremely subjective in nature. Research studies on interviewing have reported: (1) incongruent findings, (2) low validities when related to successful job performance, and (3) lack of inter-rater reliability.

There are a number of reasons for the generally poor predictive nature of interviews. First, interviewers tend to have well-defined stereotypes of the "ideal" applicant. Second, they tend to rate an applicant on one factor by the kinds of rating they give him on another factor. (This is often referred to as the "halo effect.") Additionally, interviewers may be biased by a host of other factors. An applicant interviewed after a very poor candidate, for instance, may be more highly rated than if he or she had been interviewed immediately after a very good candidate.

Such problems may be overcome to varying extents. A number of research studies have indicated that a more highly structured interview is more effective than a less structured one. Goodale has indicated two reasons why unstructured interviews may not be reliable:

> Systematic biases and selective perception can affect interviewers in different ways, thus resulting in lack of agreement between them. Further, if the interview is unstructured, entirely different topics may be covered by one interviewer than by another. . . .[77]

There are, however, other research studies that have shown that the degree of structure is not a key variable in interviewing,[78] and one highly unstructured form of interviewing (nondirective) has been found effective by many interviewers trained in its use.

Suggestions have also been made that interviewing an applicant with respect to the *specific job* for which he or she is applying is more effective than "interviewing in the abstract," and that, therefore, providing the interviewer with adequate job description information will help improve interviewer decisions.[79] This suggestion has been supported by one study, which found that the availability of job information "reduced the effect of irrelevant attributes on decisions but did not eliminate it."[80]

Finally, it is often recommended that interviewers spend more time listening and less time talking. The listening should encompass two dimensions, "the content of the response and the *attitude-feeling* underlying the content."[81] We have seen such nonverbal changes in behavior during an interview as sweating, blushing, or a sudden change in the speed or pitch of the applicant's voice. These may indicate that the interviewer has opened up an area of discussion that is anxiety-producing for the applicant. However, such interpretations should be very cautiously made. An applicant may start sweating, for example, when the interviewer asks him about his drinking habits. This may, however, be due more to the fact that the air conditioner has just broken down and the room is extremely hot and humid than anything else! As the interviewer listens and watches, it may be desirable for him to take written notes, for if he does not, much information may be lost.

In addition to "ordinary" interviewing, in which both interviewer and interviewee engage in "two-way" communications, there are at least three specially defined types of interviews available to the decision maker: patterned, nondirective, and stress. In addition, firms, especially at managerial and professional levels, usually conduct more than one interview, and these three strategies may be "mixed" from interviewer to interviewer.

The Patterned Interview

For many years, some firms have utilized what is called the "patterned" interview. The patterned interview provides a form for each interviewer to follow, so that all interviewers ask basically the same questions in the same sequence to all applicants. The patterned interview form asks questions with respect to marital status, previous education, previous jobs, etc. Portions of the "work history" part of one firm's patterned interview are shown in Figure 4–8. Claimed advantages of the patterned interview are that the interviewer works from definite job specifications, he knows what questions to ask, and there is a definite interview plan. With all interviewers asking the same questions, the patterned inter-

WORK HISTORY *** LAST PREVIOUS JOB	
Company (*Same as on application?*)	Address
Employment dates (*If unemployed, how long?*) 19 TO 19	
Starting Assignments (*How much responsibility, judgment?*)	
Assignments when left job (*How much growth, maturation?*)	
Name and title of supervisor (*How close was supervision?*)	
How was he to work for? (*Attitudes towards supervisors*)?	
Number people supervised	(*What supervisory problems arose?*)
What policy decisions responsible for? (*Has he had management responsibilities?*)	
What did you like most about this job? (*Satisfaction? Maturity?*)	
What did you like least about this job? (*Dislikes justified?*)	

Figure 4–8 *Patterned interview form.*

view is claimed to provide greater interrater reliability. More than three decades ago, McMurry successfully used the patterned interview with workers at the Link-Belt Company, truck drivers at the White Motor Company, and workers at the York Knitting Mills.[82] Length of service and supervisor ratings were used as criterion measures. In McMurry's study, all interviewers received *training* in how to use the patterned interview technique.[83] The training raises an interesting question: To what extent was it interviewer expertise (having been specially trained) or the patterned interview which led to successful validation? Without taking anything away from McMurray's research, the question must be raised as to whether the same interviewers trained extensively in how to use a different approach (e.g., nondirective) would have accomplished more or fewer successful outcomes. The patterned technique is compatible with a number of research studies that have shown that better success is achieved in interviews with more structure. Many interviewers, on the other hand, do not like the patterned interview, since it constrains them by making them ask a prescribed set of questions in a prescribed order. This approach provides less opportunity to explore other areas that may be more relevant.

The Nondirective Interview

An almost diametrically opposite interviewing strategy is the nondirective interview. Used in both counseling and selection interviews, the interviewer attempts to let the interviewee structure direction, plays a very permissive role (not exhibiting any signs of approval or disapproval) and hopes that the applicant in such a setting may "let his hair down" and discuss questions that he would not normally do with a more conventional interview. This approach requires considerable skill, and will sometimes induce the interviewee to disclose salient facts about himself that might never have come out in a patterned interview. For example, one experienced interviewer of managerial candidates in a large western firm described the following experiences with the nondirective interview:

> In many cases I've tried being nondirective and don't feel as though I'm making much progress with the applicant. I start out by asking him "Could you tell me something about yourself?"; he responds "What would you like to know?" and finally we start talking about his work experience and family relations — the same kinds of things that I could have covered with a conventional interview. But in some rare cases, *wow*! For example, once I ran into a situation like this:
> *Interviewer:* Could you tell me something about yourself?
> *Applicant:* My psychiatrist tells me that I've got my problems mostly solved now.
> *Interviewer:* (showing no surprise): Your psychiatrist?

Applicant: Yes.

Interviewer: Could you tell me more about this?

Applicant: All my problems went back to my relations with my father when I was a child.

Interviewer: (still showing no surprise or disapproval): Oh?

Applicant: Yes, my father. . . .

You may wonder whether or not we hired this applicant. The answer is "no," but you may be surprised at the reasoning behind this decision. We did not reject him because he had had psychiatric problems. Rather, what concerned us was his compulsive need to tell us about his problems. This was what convinced us that he really hadn't solved his problems yet.

As the reader may note, the nondirective approach avoids using leading questions, frequently uses the clinical "Oh?" or "Can you tell me more?" and encourages the applicant to continue talking by facing him with questions that are phrased in a non-threatening way in a permissive atmosphere.

Stress Interviews

Sometimes firms will use stress interviews, in which they attempt to obtain an idea of the applicants' reactions to stress. This approach seems especially useful when job candidates are applying for positions involving considerable pressure such as union-contract negotiators. What the stress interviewer does is to make the applicant feel uncomfortable and see how he reacts to it. For example, excerpts from a stress interview might be like this:

Interviewer: Five minutes ago you told me you did graduate work because you wanted to teach. You did that for only one year and now you say you want to get out of teaching and take a job with our firm. This appears to be _____ inconsistent!

Applicant: Well, the salary wasn't too good and I. . . .

Interviewer: (breaking in): And you what? If all you're interested in is money, you probably would leave us in another year if we did give you an offer because someone else might buy you for a few hundred more bucks. What in _____ do you want out of a job?

Applicant: But, I didn't say money was everything. I also. . . .

Interviewer (interrupting again): Well, just what did you say?

Another means of providing stress is to have one or more job applicants be interviewed by more than one interviewer at the same time. One person, for example, was placed in a situation in which he and three other interviewees were called together to reach agreement on a managerial decision problem given them, with two interviewers (one at each end of the table) observing the "group dynamics" of the problem solving but making only a few comments during this process. All interviewees expressed the opinion afterwards that this was a fairly stressful experience for them.

Just how effective stress interviews are is open to debate, as is whether those being interviewed should be informed afterwards that the stress was not intended to be personal, but rather that it was a deliberately chosen systemic technique given to all candidates for such positions. Some believe that certain applicants (especially if they are rejected) may go away with a bad impression of the firm, which would help hurt its image, if they are not "debriefed" in this manner. Others, however, believe that if firms inform applicants that the stress was planned, it would simply engender their hostility.

Multiple Interviews

Because interviewing is subjective, most large firms provide a number of interviews for the job applicant, especially at managerial and professional levels. Sometimes, in doing so, companies may deliberately mix strategies. For example, a stress interview may be followed with a very permissive nondirective one, on the theory that, with this sharp contrast, the applicant will be even more inclined to "let his hair down" in the nondirective interview.

We strongly support the use of multiple interviews based on the old notion that "two heads are better than one." Sometimes, there will be considerable agreement among interviewers and none of them will really uncover any highly significant information that the others have missed. In some cases, though, this will not be the case. In one actual situation four experienced interviewers, armed with full testing and application form data on a candidate, missed the point on his application form that he had received a medical discharge from the armed forces. The fifth interviewer, however, did note this point and in the interview the applicant indicated that this discharge resulted from his having had a nervous breakdown, among other things having "suffered the pains of the crucifixion." Multiple interviews, in spite of their advantages, utilize more managerial time and the costs of using them must be considered.

Reference Checks

Another selection tool used by firms is the reference check. Most application forms ask the job candidate to list previous employers, and some ask for names of other individuals who will provide a recommendation. The degree to which organizations rely on reference checks varies widely. At one end of the spectrum, some firms make no such checks at all. At the other extreme, a college professor who was being considered for a visiting professorship elsewhere was required to provide recommendations from five scholars with national reputations.

There are several different reference check alternatives open to the firm, each with different outcomes. Probably the poorest of all are letters sent to personal friends, for they will almost invariably provide a favorable view of the job applicant. If the personal friend is interviewed, however, much relevant information may be obtained. One person once participated in an interview in which the college roommate and close friend of the applicant was questioned. Both the applicant and his wife were being considered for positions and the interview ran along the following lines:

Interviewer: What information can you provide me on John and Mary?

Friend: John is really a great guy. He works hard and will accomplish whatever he sets out to do.

Interviewer: What about Mary?

Friend: Mary's OK. John is really fantastic. He has a really good sense of humor and everybody likes him.

Interviewer: Is Mary as well liked as John?

Friend: No, but she's OK. Now John is really a great guy. Why he. . . .

Interviewer (interrupting): What's wrong with Mary?

Friend: Well, she seems to be mentally unstable. . . .

A second strategy is to telephone the candidate's supervisor in the last job. Sometimes quite valid data can be obtained by this alternative. Previous supervisors, however, not wanting to ruin a very poorly performing individual's chances for obtaining another job, may often gloss over major performance deficiencies. Further, if the applicant is still employed elsewhere, he may express a real reluctance to have a prospective new employer talk with the current supervisor, lest the latter get angry and fire him, or make life on the job difficult.

A third source of background data may be obtained by communicating with the personnel departments of previous employers. Many firms buy or develop forms specifically designed for this purpose. One such form is illustrated in Figure 4–9. With reciprocity as a guiding principle, personnel departments will often willingly provide the data in their records. The problem here is that many key bits of data (such as an alcoholic problem) may never reach the records kept by the personnel departments.

Much information may be gained from local retail credit agencies, although their data historically have been negatively biased. These agencies keep much more information in an individual's files than credit ratings — everything from divorces to police arrests. At times, they may serve as very useful media for obtaining background information on individuals, as is illustrated in the following true story:

An employee in a manufacturing operation was about to be promoted to a managerial position, when a rumor started spreading that he had been

Applicant: Please complete top section and on the reverse side, the reference's name and address

P-6 EMPL

FORMER EMPLOYER REFERENCE
CONFIDENTIAL REPORT

The applicant described below is being considered for employment as .... by us. He(she) has authorized all previous employers to furnish any information concerning personal character, habit and employment records. We will appreciate your confidential replies to the questions below.

Name of Applicant .... Social Sec. No. ....

Stated Dates of Employment from .... to .... Leaving Position .... Leaving Earnings $ ....

TO BE COMPLETED BY FORMER EMPLOYER REFERENCE

ARE THESE FACTS CORRECT? .... If not please give correct information: ....

Reason for leaving .... Would you re-employ? .... If not, why not? ....

Major duties performed ....

Character .... Health .... Reliability ....

ANY SUSPICION OF: Dishonesty .... Gambling .... Extravagance .... Drinking ....

Is there any reason known to you why this applicant would not make an acceptable or satisfactory employee? ....

....

Signed: .... Position .... Date ....

DETACH ALONG THIS EDGE AND INSERT IN ATTACHED ENVELOPE

Figure 4–9 *Former Employer reference form. Reproduced with permission of E. F. Wonderlic & Associates, Inc.*

an embezzler in his previous line of work. Concerned, the personnel manager called the local retail credit agency and asked for any available information with respect to the matter. The credit agency had clipped from a downstate newspaper information to the effect that the individual had been arrested for embezzlement and had the name of the sheriff who had investigated the case. The sheriff was then called and indicated that, indeed, an arrest had been made with respect to the individual's handling of funds in his own small business. However, the sheriff indicated that there was no question of embezzlement, simply allegations of mismanagement of funds, and that most important of all the individual had been found *not guilty* of the charges that some of his creditors had made. The sheriff concluded by making numerous positive comments about the individual, such as his work with the local chamber of commerce, and, in fact, indicated that he thought that the individual would make a good manager.

References and recommendations data stored in either manual files or computerized systems have raised some serious questions about possible damages that a person can suffer if misleading or erroneous data are stored in these files. Historically, data kept by credit agencies have been more negative than positive. This situation has been aggravated because newspapers often indicate arrest reports about an individual, but much more rarely report on the *disposition* of the case—which many times may be an acquittal. To help protect individuals against possible erroneous and negatively misleading data being kept in their files, the Fair Credit Reporting Act, which took effect in 1971, was passed.[84] Under the Act, whoever turns down an individual for credit, insurance, or jobs must provide the name of the credit agency that made the report. The agency must then let the individual see exactly what its files say. Any data which are inaccurate or which cannot be verified must be deleted immediately. This Act, together with a trend toward including more positive data in credit files, should make this medium a more useful one in personnel selection.

Another more recent piece of federal legislation has a bearing on recommendations for employment decision making — the Family Educational Rights and Privacy Act of 1974, more commonly known as the Buckley Amendment since it was authored by former Senator James Buckley of New York. As originally written, the Act

. . . required educational institutions to permit parents and students over 18 to inspect student files and obtain the consent of the parents (or student if over 18) in most cases before releasing information in these files to third parties.[85]

The language of this Act was not completely clear and was amended to provide

. . . that confidential recommendations pertaining to admission to an educational institution, . . . [and] . . . employment applications . . . need not be disclosed to a student if they were received before January 1, 1975;

[and] provided that a student could *waive his right* to see confidential recommendations after that date. . . .[86]

The main implication of this legislation for personnel selection is that permitting parents (and students) to examine files in which confidential recommendations would be contained would tend to discourage those persons making recommendations from bringing out negative information in proper perspective. The waiver clause now permits recommendations to be made without giving the student the right to see items if a waiver statement is signed. As of the beginning of 1976, several graduate schools of business were including a waiver statement for the student to sign right on its recommendation form, thus rendering the recommendation confidential and encouraging more candid appraisals.

Physical Examination

Organizations invariably require physical examinations of all new employees. The objectives of these examinations are twofold. First are humanitarian reasons. Any responsible firm would not want an individual with a bad back placed on a job requiring lifting, or an executive candidate with a serious ulcer problem placed in a high stress decision-making position.

Second are economic reasons. If a firm hires the man with the bad back who injures himself in the near future, and must quit his job as a result, the firm's selection and training costs would be wasted. In addition, the employee would be eligible for workmen's compensation benefits. This would be costly to the firm, in that its experience affects its workmen's compensation contributions, as we will discuss in Chapter 13.

Firms employ different physical examination strategies. Some hire a doctor to give the applicant a thorough examination or have on staff a physician who handles these examinations as well as other duties such as dealing with injuries received in the firm's operations. Less reliable is the alternative of giving the job candidate a medical history form for the family doctor to complete and mail back. We believe that a good majority of licensed physicians are both reputable and competent. The family doctor, however, knowing that the individual wants the job, may well report any serious medical problems that the individual has (or has had), but may provide a less thorough examination report than a physician employed or hired by the company.

SUMMARY

Recruiting and selection represents a multistage decision-making process under conditions of risk. It is geared toward obtaining competent human resources at a minimal cost. Many different recruiting and selection decision-making techniques are available. These range from the highly subjective interview, which is as old as human organizations themselves, to newer management science and computer approaches such as simulation, linear programming, PERT, and computerized man-job matching systems. The degree to which organizations use more sophisticated techniques is contingent on two key variables. Firms that can expose only a small number of applicants to their recruiting and selection systems cannot justify the costs of more elaborate decision-making techniques. Further, firms operating under dynamic conditions will find it more difficult to validate such tools as psychological tests, compared with organizations operating as more stable systems. Finally, one major constraint imposed on recruiting and selection decision making is governmental pressure for affirmative action to provide equal employment opportunities for all employees. Although the basic objective of providing equal employment opportunities is generally considered desirable, implementing this objective has posed many problems. In numerous cases, governmental pressures have gone as far as to create controversial "reverse discrimination" against white males. Regardless of future government actions, such as legislation and court decisions, we foresee continuing problems in implementing equal employment opportunity goals in personnel recruiting and selection.

DISCUSSION AND STUDY QUESTIONS

1. The "composite" approach to selection is more appropriate than the hurdle approach in most organization settings because it gives the firm the chance to evaluate all aspects of an applicant's attitudes and behavior. The hurdle approach is likely to "cut off" potentially good employees too soon. Discuss.
2. A firm needs to hire 35 clerical job applicants, and its selection outcomes using its current tools are shown in Figure 4–2. Assuming that: (1) by investing $20 more in one additional selection instrument, the conditional probabilities that a person will succeed or fail are those given below, (2) current recruiting and selection costs are $400/applicant and that average training and other costs for all applicants hired whether they succeed or not is $500, should the firm utilize the new instrument? Show all calculations.

Total Number of Job Applicants Being Considered for Selection (n = 50)

	Reject (n = 14)	Hire (n = 36)
Success (n = 38)	$p = .06$ (n = 3)	$p = .70$ (n = 35)
Failure (n = 12)	$p = .22$ (n = 11)	$p = .02$ (n = 1)

3. American organizations face an insoluble dilemma. If "ratio hiring" is not undertaken, women and minority groups will never achieve equal employment opportunities. On the other hand, ratio hiring discriminates against other groups. Regardless of Supreme Court decisions, do you believe in "quotas," "goals," and ratio hiring? Why?

4. In light of the courts' interpretation of BFOQ, as spelled out in Title VII of the Civil Rights Act, which of the following actions do you think would be discriminatory?
   a. Refusing to hire a minority employee with a record of three arrests and one conviction for petty larceny.
   b. Refusing to hire a woman as a long-distance truck driver because the work would be too tedious for her.
   c. Refusing to hire a man to work in the lingerie department of a department store because this would offend women customers.
   d. Refusing to hire a Jewish professor to teach management at a southern Methodist college because his religious beliefs do not coincide with those of most other individuals at the institution.
   e. Refusing to hire a woman to play the role of "Mephistopheles" in Gounod's opera "Faust."

5. In the chapter, we included a quotation indicating there might be a degree of self-selection of individuals, with people trying to obtain positions in firms that fit their personalities. To what extent do you agree with this hypothesis?

6. We discussed the question of the invasion of individual privacy in the personnel selection process. Which of the following questions would you consider legitimate ones to ask a man aged 35, applying for a middle level management position?
   a. If he is a homosexual.
   b. If married, the number of children he has.
   c. If he possesses any tax-free municipal bonds or 90 day treasury bills.
   d. If he plays golf or tennis.
   e. What his mother's maiden name is.

7. A firm has a number of positions in which individuals perform fairly routine jobs on an assembly line requiring relatively little physical effort. Which of the following characteristics would you consider predictive of tenure (as a measure of success) if the firm were to develop and use a weighted application form in its selection?
   a. Educational level.
   b. Marital status.
   c. Height and weight.
   d. Home ownership.
   e. Religious faith and ethnic background.

8. In Chapter 4 we indicated five possible strategies for psychological test validation. Which strategy would be appropriate for:
   a. A small firm with a total of 50 employees?
   b. A large corporation with annual sales in the billions and 50,000 employees?
   In each case give your reasons why.

9. A department store chain gives its managerial and professional employees a mental alertness test, which it weights most, a

personality profile, which it weights second, and an interest profile, which it primarily uses not for outright rejection of any applicants but to note and probe any incongruencies as discussed in Chapter 4. Based *solely* on the following test information on an individual and ignoring appropriate age, education, experience, etc. (all of which we will assume that the job candidate has), which of the jobs listed below do you think the individual would be most suited for and least suited for? Give your reasons for each choice.

The test scores (in percentiles of the general population) are as follows:

    Mental Alertness Test: 98th
    Interest Profile:
      Computational 73rd
      Scientific 71st
      Artistic 13th
      Persuasive 60th
      Literary 29th
    Personality Profile:
      Active: Likes to be on the go: 35th
      Impulsive: Likes to make quick decisions: 53rd
      Sociable: Likes to do things with other people: 47th
      Stable: Is "even" in his work from day to day; doesn't have
        many "ups" or "downs": 31st

The five jobs are:

a. Assistant manager in one of the store's men's shoe departments.
b. Personnel manager in one of the chain's stores.
c. A senior accountant in the firm's corporate headquarters.
d. Manager of one of the chain's stores.
e. Window and floor display consultant working with four of the chain's stores in central Pennsylvania in setting up displays in the store to attract customers to certain items.

10. We indicated in the chapter that computerized test interpretation was feasible; yet we have not found firms making much, if any, use of this approach. Why do you think this is so?

11. In which type of interview — ordinary, patterned, nondirective, or stress — do you think the following questions would most likely be used? In each case, give your reason why.

a. What was your most interesting subject in college?
b. You've just indicated to me that you didn't like working for your father during high school. Could you tell me more about this?
c. You just told me that you majored in accounting because your father was an accountant and you wanted to follow in his steps, and now you say your father drank too much and you had little respect for him. This seems __ inconsistent! Just what do you mean?
d. You'd be willing to change job locations frequently to broaden your experience if we hired you as a manager, wouldn't you?
e. Oh?

12. Pretend that your instructor is being considered for the first teaching position he or she took at your educational institution,

and that you had the responsibility as department head of interviewing for this position. Interview him or her using:

a. A nondirective interview.

b. A stress interview.

c. An "ordinary" interview.

If someone else in your class is doing the interviewing, be prepared to comment on the adequacy of his interview.

13. Joe Goe graduated from one of the nation's largest leading colleges of business administration three years ago with a 3.8 average (of 4.0), took a position as assistant personnel manager of a relatively small manufacturing firm upon graduation, still has this job, and has applied for a similar position with your firm, which is larger and in which his pay and responsibilities would be greater. Joe is married and has one infant son. His application form looks very favorable. On this form, he has indicated that he does not want your firm checking his current supervisor, because the latter would become extremely angry if he thought Joe was looking for another job. Joe has given you five references to check. Which of the following six sources (including these references) would you check, and how valuable do you think the information obtained from each might be? Give your reasons why.

a. His clergyman.

b. A former boss from when he was a waiter at a seashore resort hotel restaurant, where he worked summers while attending college.

c. The professor from whom he took his basic management course as a sophomore, and who you know has a national reputation as a first-rate scholar.

d. A professor who supervised his thesis in the senior level personnel management course. (You know nothing about this professor).

e. His university's debate coach who supervised an activity in which Joe was very active.

f. His current supervisor—even though Joe has asked you not to contact him.

g. The retail credit agency in the city in which Joe now resides.

Notes

[1]Marvin D. Dunnette, *Personnel Selection and Placement* (Belmont, Calif.: Brooks/Cole Publishing Co., 1966), p. 28.

[2]For a more thorough discussion of these and other reasons for measurement error, see ibid., pp. 28–30.

[3]Certain aspects of this example were suggested by Raymond Lee and Jerome M. Booth, "A Utility Analysis of a Weighted Application Blank to Predict Turnover for Clerical Employees," *Journal of Applied Psychology,* 59 (August, 1974), pp. 516–518. The "other costs" might include those associated with a loss in production and the cost of employee benefits.

[4]See, for example, ibid., p. 517.

[5]For a brief history and evaluation of nondiscrimination policies, see, for example, Larry E. Short, "Nondiscrimination Policies: Are They Effective?" *Personnel Journal,* 52(September, 1973), pp. 786–792.

[6]James M. Higgins, "A Manager's Guide to the Equal Employment Opportuni-

ty Laws," *Personnel Journal,* 55 (August, 1976), p. 408.

7 42 USCA 2000 (e) (5) (g).

8 According to Higgins, op. cit., p. 407, sex was not originally included in Executive Order 11246, but rather was included later in Executive Order 11375.

9 Ibid., p. 409.

10 David E. Robertson, "Employment Testing and Discrimination," *Personnel Journal,* 54 (January, 1975), p. 21.

11 Ibid.

12 Lipman G. Feld, "15 Questions You Dare Not Ask Job Applicants," *Administrative Management,* 35 (June, 1974), p. 21.

13 Gerald L. Bassford, "Job-Testing — Alternative to Employment Quotas," *Business Horizons,* 17 (February, 1974), p. 40.

14 Oscar A. Ornati and Edward Giblin, "The High Cost of Discrimination," *Business Horizons,* 18(February, 1975), p. 35.

15 Ibid.

16 Cary D. Thorp, Jr., "Fair Employment Practices: The Compliance Jungle," *Personnel Journal,* 52 (July, 1973), p. 643.

17 Some authorities have argued that the mathematical ratios used to remedy discrimination are "goals" and not "quotas." It has been asserted that quotas are permanent requirements, while a goal is only in effect until it is reached. In our opinion this debate is largely semantic. For a further discussion of this subject, see Timothy T. Reese, "Reverse Discrimination 1977," M.B.A. Paper, College of Business Administration, The Pennsylvania State University, 1977.

18 Antonia Chayes, "Make Your Equal Opportunity Program Court-Proof," *Harvard Business Review,* 52 (September-October, 1974), p. 88.

19 78 Stat. 267.

20 *The United States LAW WEEK,* 39 (March 9, 1971), p. 4319.

21 "Hints on Reverse Bias," *Time,* May 6, 1974.

22 Ibid.

23 Cited in ibid. The Fourteenth Amendment was germane in the *DeFunis* case since under its "equal protection" clause: "No State shall . . . deny to any person within its jurisdiction the equal protection of its laws."

24 Robert Lindsey, "White/Caucasian — and Rejected," *New York Times Magazine,* April 3, 1977, p. 43.

25 Ibid., p. 95.

26 The direct quotations of Justice Powell were taken from "Excerpts of High Court Opinions in Bakke Case," *The Washington Post,* (June 29, 1978), p. A-25.

27 Lawrence Stessin, "The Ax and Older Workers," *New York Times,* June 23, 1974, Section 3, p. 3.

28 78 Stat. 257.

29 "Sex Equality: A Woman's Place May Be on the Production Line," *New York Times,* January 31, 1971, Section 4, p. 8.

30 *Phillips vs. Martin Marietta Corporation,* 400 U.S. 542 (1971).

31 "Sex Equality," op. cit., p. 8.

32 Ornati and Giblin, op. cit., p. 38.

33 George R. Wendt, "Questions Compliance Officers Ask," *Personnel Journal,* 54 (July, 1975), p. 385.

34 For a discussion of the problems of utilization analysis in light of federal guidelines, see, for example, James M. Higgins, "The Complicated Process of Establishing Goals for Equal Employment," *Personnel Journal,* 54(December, 1975), pp. 631–636.

35 "More Women Move into the Boardroom," *Business Week,* March 1, 1976, p. 26.

36 Ross Azevedo, "Scientists, Engineers, and the Job Search Process," *California Management Review,* 17 (Winter, 1974), p. 41.

37 Ibid., p. 46.

38 Lloyd Reynolds and Joseph Shister, *Job Horizons* (New York: Harper and Row Publishers, 1949), as cited in ibid.

39 Charles A. Myers and George P. Schultz, *Dynamics of a Labor Market* (New York: John Wiley & Sons, 1951), as cited in Azevado, op. cit., p. 46.

40 Max D. Richards and Paul S. Greenlaw, *Management: Decisions and Behavior,* rev. ed. (Homewood, Ill.: Richard D. Irwin, Inc., 1972), p. 196.

[41]Robert H. Flast, "A Computer Simulation of a Corporate Employment Office," *Personnel Journal,* 53 (January, 1974), p. 53.

[42]Ibid., p. 57. The italics are ours.

[43]Ibid.

[44]Leon Teach and John D. Thompson, "Simulation in Recruitment Planning," *Personnel Journal,* 48 (April, 1969), p. 289.

[45]Ibid., p. 288.

[46]Ibid., p. 289.

[47]Ibid., p. 292.

[48]Lawrence L. Steinmetz, "PERT Personnel Practices," *Personnel Journal,* 44 (September, 1965), pp. 419–424.

[49]Gordon K. Davies, "Needed: A National Job Matching Network," *Harvard Business Review,* 47 (September-October, 1969), pp. 63–72.

[50]George P. Huber and Charles H. Falkner, "Computer-Based Man-Job Matching: Current Practice and Applicable Research," *Socio-Economic Planning Sciences Journal,* 3 (1969), p. 387.

[51]This information was provided to the authors by Mr. Robert F. Herrick, Executive Director of the College Placement Council in a letter of November, 1975. For a brief discussion of GRAD, see Walter A. Kleinschrod, "New System Finds Job Applicants Fast," *Administrative Management,* 27 (April, 1966), pp. 28, 30.

[52]Quoted from correspondence to the authors in February, 1976 from Mr. Robert A. Dickman, Director of the Division of Manpower Matching Systems, USES, Department of Labor, Washington, D.C.

[53]Carlton Dukes, "Effective Measurement of a Professional Recruiting Effort — A Systems Approach," *Personnel Journal,* 44 (January, 1965), pp. 12–17.

[54]William H. Whyte, Jr., "The Fallacies of 'Personality' Testing," *Fortune Magazine,* 50 (September, 1954), pp. 117–120 and 204–208.

[55]Ibid. In a more recent empirical study, job applicants' attitudes toward privacy indicated that the issue of invasion of privacy is a complex one. See Bernard Rosenbaum, "Attitude Toward Invasion of Privacy in the Personnel Selection Process and Job Applicant Demographic and Personality Correlates," *Journal of Applied Psychology,* 58 (December, 1973), pp. 333–338.

[56]George W. England, *Development and Use of Weighted Application Blanks,* rev. ed. (Minneapolis: Industrial Relations Center, University of Minnesota, 1971), pp. 49–50.

[57]Edward A. Fleishman and Joseph Berniger, "One Way to Reduce Office Turnover," *Personnel,* 37 (1960), pp. 63–69. For a more recent study of the weighted application blank, see Gordon Inskeep, "Statistically Guided Employee Selection: An Approach to the Labor Turnover Problem," *Personnel Journal,* 49 (January, 1970), pp. 15–24.

[58]Ibid., p. 21.

[59]Peter Koenig, "They Just Changed the Rules on How to Get Ahead," *Psychology Today,* 8 (June, 1974), p. 89.

[60]Ibid.

[61]M. J. Balma, "The Concept of Synthetic Validity," *Personnel Psychology,* 12 (1959), p. 395.

[62]Dunnette, op. cit., p. 165.

[63]C. H. Lawshe, "A Quantitative Approach to Content Validity," *Personnel Psychology,* 28 (Winter, 1975), p. 563.

[64]E. F. Wonderlic, *Wonderlic Personnel Test Manual* (Northfield, Ill.: E. F. Wonderlic and Associates, Inc., 1966), p. 11. It should also be noted that using norms developed on the basis of validity studies conducted by test publishers may create special problems in meeting federal nondiscrimination regulations. For example, in an attempt to clarify governmental guidelines in employee selection procedures, proposed rules for uniform guidelines on employee selection procedures were promulgated by the Civil Service Commission, EEOC, Department of Justice, and Department of Labor on December 30, 1977. In this proposal the following guidelines were suggested for using validity studies developed by others:

"Users may, under certain circumstances, support the use of selection procedures by validity studies conducted by other users or conducted by test publishers or distributors and described in test manuals. While publishers of selection procedures have a professional obligation to provide evidence of validity which meets generally accepted professional standards . . . users are cautioned that they are responsible for compliance with these guidelines. Accordingly, users seeking to obtain selection procedures from publishers and distributors should be careful to determine that, in the event the user becomes subject to the validity requirements of these guidelines, the necessary information to support validity has been determined and will be made available to the user." 41 *Federal Register,* 65545.

[65]*Negro Norms* (Northfield, Ill.: E. F. Wonderlic & Associates, Inc., 1972).

[66]Ibid., p. 24. It should also be noted that the use of black norms as described here has been considered by this test's designers as a satisfactory approach to affirmative action under Federal EEOC and OFCC guidelines. Ibid., p. 2. See also footnote 64 above.

[67]Some personality profiles such as the Washburne Social Adjustment Inventory are specially geared to provide a measure of truthfulness. See J. N. Washburne, *Manual for Interpretation of the Washburne Social Adjustment Inventory* (New York: Harcourt, Brace and World, Inc., 1940).

[68]Whyte, op. cit.

[69]The TAT has been used to classify individuals by the amount of "achievement motivation" they have, by David McClelland and others. In this example, the second story would be what one would expect from a high achiever. For a brief description of achievement motivation, see Richards and Greenlaw, op. cit., pp. 150–152.

[70]*SRA Catalog for Business* (Chicago: Science Research Association, Inc., 1976), p. 20.

[71]Whyte, op. cit. For another critique of personality profiles, see Martin L. Gross, *The Brain Watchers* (New York: Random House, 1962).

[72]"Symposium on Automation Technics in Personality Assessment," *Proceedings of the Staff Meetings of the Mayo Clinic,* 37(January 31, 1962), pp. 61–82.

[73]Ibid., p. 62.

[74]Benjamin Kleinmuntz, "Personality Test Interpretation by Digital Computer," *Science,* 139 (February, 1963), pp. 416–418.

[75]Robert D. Smith and Paul S. Greenlaw, "Simulation of a Psychological Decision Process in Personnel Selection," *Management Science,* 13 (April, 1967), pp. B409–419.

[76]These are discussed in ibid., pp. B413–417.

[77]James G. Goodale, "Tailoring the Selection Interview to the Job," *Personnel Journal,* 55 (February, 1976), p. 64.

[78]Herbert G. Heneman, III, et al., "Interviewer Validity as a Function of Interview Structure, Biographical Data, and Interviewee Order," *Journal of Applied Psychology,* 60 (December, 1975), pp. 748–753.

[79]Goodale, op. cit., p. 65.

[80]Yoash Wiener and Mark L. Schneiderman, "Use of Job Information as a Criterion in Employment Decisions of Interviewers," *Journal of Applied Psychology,* 59 (December, 1974), p. 699.

[81]Claudio R. Serafini, "Interviewer Listening," *Personnel Journal,* 54 (July, 1975), p. 399. The italics are ours.

[82]Robert N. McMurry, "Validating the Patterned Interview," *Personnel,* 23 (1947), pp. 2–11.

[83]Except in the White Motor Company case, in which a trained psychologist conducted the interviews.

[84]"How to Question Your Credit Rating," *Business Week,* May 22, 1971, p. 76.

[85]*Congressional Quarterly Almanac,* 30 (1974), p. 483.

[86]Ibid., p. 484. The italics are ours.

III

THE DEVELOPMENT OF HUMAN RESOURCES

5

PERFORMANCE APPRAISAL

Performance appraisal is found throughout our modern society, not only in business organizations but also in government, schools, social groups, and the family unit. The President evaluates the actions of his cabinet members, college professors grade their students and are evaluated by their students, and fathers and mothers evaluate the behavior of their children. A basic reason for such appraisals is that humans represent open systems and must receive feedback from their environment concerning the appropriateness of their behavior if they are to correct errors, improve their performance, and continue to survive and grow.

People in organizations will always be appraising the performance of others, regardless of what top management does. This presents management with two basic choices. First, it can simply permit "natural" or "spontaneous" informal, unplanned appraisals to be made without attempting to control them in any way. Second, it can intervene and establish a planned, more systematic approach for directing the appraisal of human performance toward the meeting of both organizational objectives and individual needs.

Most organizations do have some type of formal appraisal system. There are many different types of such systems which range from very simple to quite complex. Despite these differences, many performance appraisal efforts traditionally have focused attention on each supervisor appraising the performance of all of his subordinates. Resulting improvement in performance has been geared toward meeting both organizational objectives and individual needs. In this chapter, we will first discuss several aspects of performance appraisal. Then we will focus attention on the two components of performance appraisal systems — the performance appraisal interview and the methods of performance appraisal.

PERFORMANCE APPRAISAL: SOME BASIC CONSIDERATIONS

Objectives

In today's modern organization, performance appraisal data may serve as an input to other personnel functions as well as provide feedback to individuals in order to help them improve their performance. These are illustrated in Figure 5–1, which presents a general schematic model of the whole performance appraisal process. Two sets of terms presented in Figure 5–1 need definition. By *feedback,* as opposed to *no feedback,* we mean information given to an individual in the performance process specifically geared toward improving his performance. Thus, if a supervisor simply tells a subordinate that he ranks second out of 10 members in the department but provides no information on how the latter might improve his performance, we would not consider this feedback. Second, by *comparative,* we mean systems in which an individual's performance is systematically compared with that of other employees; *absolute* systems are those in which an individual's performance is compared with one or more written standards.

As may be noted from Figure 5–1, performance appraisal data, aside from their feedback function, can provide inputs to selection, training, human resource planning, and wage and salary decisions. They may aid in selection decision making in two ways. First, as indicated in Chapter 4, supervisory ratings are often used to validate selection instruments. Second, supervisory appraisals may indicate the need for an organization to modify its current selection policies. For example, a firm may find that the performance of certain blue-collar workers who have graduated from high school is rated significantly higher by first line supervision than that of employees who have less education. Such a finding might indicate that the firm should require a high school degree for *all* individuals applying for such jobs.

Performance appraisal data may indicate a need for specific types of training and aid in the evaluation of training programs. With respect to training needs, for example, an evaluation of supervisory skills in the Tennessee Department of Public Health spelled out not only what specific kinds of supervisory training were needed but also in which particular divisions and locations

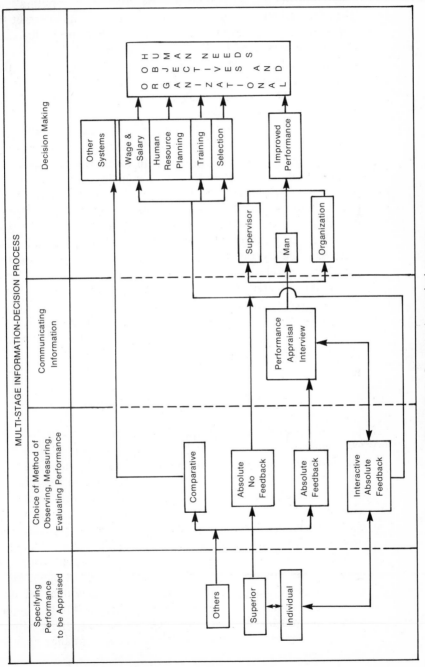

Figure 5-1 Personnel appraisal process.

in the organization the training was needed most.[1] As an example of performance appraisal data used to evaluate training, one manufacturing concern conducted two two-hour "briefing" sessions for all first line supervisors on changes in its contract that had just been negotiated with the union. When the performance of these supervisors was next appraised by their supervisors, analysis of their handling contract-related problems with their subordinates gave an indication that the briefing sessions had been fairly effective, although no statistical analysis of the appraisal data was undertaken.

Data obtained from appraisals may aid in making appropriate human resource planning decisions. Performance appraisal data can often help determine whether an individual possesses the necessary skills to be promoted to a higher level or whether current job skills are lacking. If the latter is so and it is determined that training will not help, the organization may consider demoting or firing the employee.

Finally, appraisal data may aid in making wage and salary decisions. Ideally, outstanding performance should be recognized with merit increases in pay. Since salary decisions fall so greatly within the domain of wage and salary administration, we will reserve discussion of "merit increases" for Chapter 9. Keeping in mind these multiple purposes that performance appraisal systems can meet, we will now turn to several basic characteristics of effective appraisal systems.

Basic Characteristics of Appraisal Systems

The effective functioning of any performance appraisal system depends, first of all, on establishing realistic performance standards for each position in the organization. Jobs have to be analyzed, job descriptions must be developed, and performance standards must be set. Performance standards will be defined differently from one job to another in the organization. On an assembly-line job, the standard might be 80 good pieces an hour or a monthly sales quota might be $100,000 for an industrial selling job. Then, individuals need to be informed about the specific types and levels of performance expected of them. Finally, in the performance appraisal process: (1) individual behavior needs to be monitored; (2) corrective actions need to be planned should desired levels of performance not be met; and (3) future plans for improving already satisfactory performance may be spelled out.

It is important to recognize that the effectiveness of any appraisal effort depends upon an appropriate *mutual interaction* among techniques, human appraiser and organizational objectives. If we utilize an appraisal technique that provides no feedback to a subordinate while our objective is to improve performance, our efforts will fail regardless of how expert the supervisor is in appraising performance. Conversely, suppose that a firm has developed an appraisal technique that is highly appropriate for providing feedback to its members. If managers are inept in and indifferent toward using this technique in dealing with their subordinates, no effective appraisals can be expected. In short, effective appraisal requires both an appropriate system in light of its objectives and managers who are *proficient* in using the system. We will indicate later how appropriate various appraisal systems in use today are in meeting different organizational objectives.

It is not uncommon for performance appraisal interviews to be held at fixed period intervals, frequently once a year. This approach, however, fails to recognize individuals' varying needs for feedback, the need to reinforce positive behavior and negate undesired behavior immediately, and that different jobs require different amounts of time to complete. Because of these factors, some observers believe that variable-interval appraisals may be more effective than fixed-interval ones. Among the ways that variable-interval appraisals can be structured, the most appropriate one, when feasible, is probably tailoring the timing of the measurement and feedback of performance "to the completion of an assigned or agreed upon project."[2] For example, under the management by objectives (MBO) approach to appraisal, which we will cover later, a supervisor and subordinate may agree that it should take six months to complete one project and 14 months for another, and the appraisal periods for these projects would be set at six and 14 months respectively. Subobjectives of projects of such duration may be set with earlier time limits, so that more frequent appraisals on these subgoals may be appropriate. Further, if an individual is to maintain and possibly increase proficiency in the organization, much more frequent feedback will usually be necessary. In fact, a manager's day-in and day-out on-the-job coaching and counseling of subordinates is often more important for individual growth and development than either periodic appraisal interviews or participation in off-the-job training and development programs.

Effective performance appraisal systems additionally require top management support. As we will indicate more fully later, conducting appraisals and communicating appraisal data to their subordinates is a difficult task, which many supervisors dislike and attempt to avoid. One effective decision strategy utilized by a top management that wants to see a truly effective appraisal program in operation is to have the president appraise vice presidents on how well they appraise their general managers, who in turn will be evaluated on how well they appraise their middle-level managers, and so on all the way down the organizational hierarchy. If such continuous reinforcement throughout the organization is not provided, excellent performance appraisal systems, first greeted with enthusiasm, may soon lose their appeal and effective use.

A further development leading to more effective performance appraisal systems in recent decades has been a switch away from assessing personality *traits* and toward appraising actual *behavior*. There are basically two reasons why emphasis on behavior rather than traits is more effective. First, by telling a subordinate that he or she is "not aggressive enough" will often be perceived as a threat and arouse defensive attitudes and behavior. On the other hand, telling him or her about things that are factually based can often be used as the basis for a mature discussion. Second, indicating to a subordinate that he or she has a trait deficiency (such as the one mentioned above) will in no way help indicate to the individual just *how* to *improve* performance. Behaviorally oriented appraisal feedback, on the other hand, will tend to both minimize defensiveness and lead toward constructive suggestions for performance improvement. Contrast the "you're not aggressive enough" trait message from a sales manager to one of his salesmen, for example, with the following behaviorally oriented feedback:

I have analyzed sales data in our division and found that 35 per cent of our dollar sales volume comes from repeat calls to customers who would not buy our product when first called upon by one of our salesmen. In looking over your sales records, I find that only 5 per cent of your dollar sales volume comes from repeat calls. If you gave more attention to such calls, I think you could increase your sales record considerably.

Here there is no reference to any possibly defective personality trait. Rather, a specific problem has been focused upon with a specific suggestion as to how performance may be improved.

It is also fairly widely agreed today that salary discussions between superiors and subordinates should be conducted *separately* from performance appraisal interviews. A basic reason for this is that the economic issues will typically "dominate the interview to the extent that neither the supervisor nor the employee is in a proper frame of mind"[3] to discuss possibilities for improved subordinate performance. Further, in some organizations, pay raises are automatic, not depending on performance, so that there could be no logical performance appraisal–merit increase linkage.

There are certain common appraisal rating errors that should be minimized if an effective appraisal system is to be maintained. Among the more important of these are the following:

Halo. As in selection interviews, some managers let their rating of a subordinate as either good or poor on one factor excessively influence their ratings on all other measures of performance.

Bias. It is only too easy to be biased either toward or against another individual, perhaps due considerably to basic differences in personality characteristics. To do an effective job in appraising the performance of subordinates, a manager should attempt to identify and set aside any such biases as much as possible.

Leniency and Strictness. In colleges and universities, some professors develop reputations as "real easy" graders, while others are noted for the lack of A's and B's they give as grades. This same problem exists in performance appraisal in all organizations. Some managers will tend to be lenient in rating all of their subordinates, while others may be extremely strict. Such differences can create difficult problems for the organization. This might be the case, for example, in comparing the performance of individuals working in different departments for a promotion into a higher level position that has just opened up.

Central Tendency. Some appraisers are reluctant to rate individuals as either very good or very poor. This may occur when the appraiser does not know too much about the behavior of the individuals being rated and considers rating them "average" as a safe strategy. This problem is sometimes referred to as the *central tendency* error.

Favorable Impressions. Somewhat related to the preceding two errors, some authorities have indicated that with most companies "appraisal ratings cluster around the better-than-average classification."[4] This may occur because superiors want to impress others with their ability to pick and train good subordinates.

Recency. One reason for providing day-to-day performance appraisal feedback is that appraisers tend to remember recent events, more than events in the more distant past. Thus, with a six-month or yearly performance appraisal, there may be a tendency for the supervisor to remember more about what subordinates did in the period just prior to the appraisal, which could distort the appraisal.

Other Aspects of Appraisal Systems

Three general aspects of performance appraisal warrant consideration — contingencies, the role of the personnel department in the appraisal process, and the utilization of management science techniques and computers in this process.

Contingencies

In looking at different types of performance appraisal systems and techniques, we are confronted with contingencies of the same type discussed in Chapter 4 with respect to recruiting and selection. Of these, three stand out as most important.

First is that of organization size. The more complex performance appraisal techniques require so much analysis that small firms cannot afford the time and cost.

Second, if a firm is very dynamic, it may want to utilize simpler appraisal techniques, which can be changed more easily than the more complex ones. Stable firms of sufficient size, on the other hand, may be able to allocate resources to developing more complex approaches, which are likely to be valid for a longer period. If the organization is so dynamic that there is a high proportion of unique problems for an individual to deal with, "the proficiency measure must reflect the individual's ingenuity in making the system operative, rather than his performance at preselected tasks."[5]

Third, different appraisal approaches are usually developed for managerial and professional personnel than for rank and file workers because the complexity of professional and managerial jobs is so great compared with that of many rank and file employees. As an example of the relative simplicity of the latter, let us consider job behavior with respect to annealing ovens, which require a minimum number of items passing through them to maintain the proper temperature.[6] In such a case, a minimum worker requirement, below which the system will not operate as planned, may be established — perhaps 20 units during a particular period. If a worker is supplied with 40 items during each such period, his proficiency could be quite easily measured and appraised. For example, if his output was 20 units (the minimum permitted) and the system's maximum possible output rate was 40 units, we could say that his proficiency level was 50 per cent. Further, from a total systems view, both with respect to performance appraisal and training, if he could handle more than the 40 units given him each period, say 50 or 60, this further proficiency would serve no useful purpose, since it exceeds the system's maximum output rate. In such a case, a training program to improve performance would be a wasted effort.

For most higher level positions in organizations, however, there may be no precisely defined "minimum performance," and for many managerial and professional positions there is no upper limit with respect to proficiency. Further, the outcomes of managerial and professional decisions may not be known for months or even years, which further complicates the appraisal process. Additionally, some variables that affect performance are beyond the control of the individual in managerial and professional work. A salesman's performance, for instance, might fall off significantly if his firm's major competitor comes out with an improved product at a lower price. It is because of complexities such as these that evaluating and communicating information about a manager's performance makes such appraisal a troublesome and difficult task.

Role of the Personnel Department

The personnel department participates in the performance appraisal process in many ways. First, as indicated earlier, personnel aids in developing job descriptions and specifications necessary for the development of standards of performance for jobs. Second, and of key importance, personnel chooses, usually with the approval of top management, the particular type of performance appraisal system or systems that the firm is going to use. Without effective supervisory appraisals, no system can be effective. Hence, a third central role that personnel plays in performance appraisal is that of training supervisors in how to appraise performance and conduct performance appraisal interviews. Other functions of personnel are to: (1) train employees in how the system works, (2) take various steps in implementing the system (such as designing, disseminating, and seeing that enough copies of performance appraisal forms are available), and (3) monitor the system by checking to see whether superiors are actually conducting appraisals when and how they should be doing so.

Finally, personnel departments must provide security to protect the privacy of any performance appraisal information stored in either its manual or computer files. Hayden has argued that performance data:

. . . must be available to all persons who have a need to know that information in the course of making decisions concerning salary adjustments, transfer and promotion decisions, reduction-in-force decisions, etc.[7]

He has indicated, however, that data derived for employee development and counseling should not be disseminated, since constructive suggestions for improvement may be interpreted as destructive criticisms when they become a matter of "public record" in the employee's personnel folder.[8] Our position is that some "constructive suggestions" may be quite relevant to such decisions as promotional ones and therefore are needed in the employee's data base. However, it is the responsibility of the personnel department to permit only authorized persons access to these records in order to minimize the possibility of misuse of this information by individuals not responsible for making such decisions.

Management Science, Computers, and Performance Appraisals

Very few attempts have been made to use more quantitative, management science–oriented techniques in making performance appraisal decisions. This is probably due to the highly subjective nature of the performance appraisal process. It is worth noting one quantitative effort undertaken in this area, however, to provide some notion of how performance appraisal might be looked at more "quantitatively."

In a certain firm, an "operations research" model was designed to evaluate the performance of four research managers by means of a *double weighting* method. An operations research procedure described in one well-known text in this field was used to *weight* the importance of company *objectives*.[9] The weighting method yielded the following: profit, 0.5; diversification, 0.2; growth, 0.2; and welfare, 0.1. The *activities* performed in the departments headed by each manager were *then weighted* for their relative contribution to each of the four company objectives. Then some mathematical calculations were undertaken to provide "indices of contribution" for each of the four managers for each of the four objectives; for each department the four indices were summed to provide an overall single index or measure of performance. The authors of this procedure claimed that this technique permitted "convenient quantification of research-manager performance . . . [and that the] . . . results suggest that the validity of the clinical, subjective approach to management evaluation should be questioned."[10]

Another observer, however, openly criticized this method, indicating, among other things, that the degree of sophistication built into the model such as the double weighting was both unnecessary and unsound.[11] Our analysis of the double weighting method supports the observations of its critic. The lesson from this analysis is that it is only too easy to assume that a personnel technique is "scientific" because it involves the manipulation of numerical values. Quantification is only as valid as the logic behind the numerical analysis, and in the highly subjective area of performance appraisal one must be especially wary of mathematical manipulation.

As with management science efforts, we have not found much emphasis on computerization per se with respect to performance appraisal. As one writer has put it:

> . . . computer systems have not been fully used to compare performance between departments and locations or to provide management information as to which kinds of employees best perform the work for which they have been hired.[12]

In this company, Texas Instruments, however, the computer handled for employees the type of comparisons mentioned above, rank order performance ratings of each first line supervisor's workers, and two and a half year performance reports for them.[13]

THE PERFORMANCE APPRAISAL INTERVIEW

In the performance appraisal process the interview is the central communications medium through which feedback is provided to individuals to help them improve their performance. In understanding this medium, which has been both "cussed and discussed" extensively, attention needs to be given to three basic questions: (1) Who is to conduct the interview? (2) What kinds of problems are encountered in traditional interviews? and (3) What different types of decision strategies may the appraiser and appraisee take to improve the performance of the latter?

Who Is to Be the Appraiser[14]

Performance appraisal interviews may be conducted by the employee's supervisor, peers of the supervisor, peers of the employee, or the employee's subordinates. By far the most commonly utilized type of appraisal is one in which the individual's immediate superior is the appraiser. This is a logical approach from the point of view that the organizational hierarchy legitimizes the right of the supervisor to evaluate, help develop, and reward (or punish) subordinates.

Sometimes the superior is joined by other managers in the organization who (1) are at the same hierarchical level or above and (2) are also familiar with the subordinate's work. Although these other managers may observe behavior not apparent to the individual's superior, some evidence indicates that "the immediate supervisor's appraisal is highly related to the average evaluations across several appraisers," and that consequently, he may "function adequately in the absence of other assessments."[15] Further, involving other managers in the appraisal process is more time consuming and costly to the organization. The other rater(s) may simply provide information to the supervisor, who digests the data and presents it to the subordinate; or others may actually join in the interview itself. This latter strategy may make subordinates feel even more defensive than they often do with just their supervisor present. We will discuss the whole problem of feelings of threat and defensiveness in traditional superior-subordinate interviews in the next section.

Peer rather than (or in addition to) supervisory ratings are also sometimes used by organizations. They are appropriate, however, only under certain conditions. For example, a high level of interpersonal trust and knowledge about the person being appraised, as well as a noncompetitive reward system, seems essential for peer appraisals. Peers tend to "rate down" each other if they function in a closed (or zero-sum) system in which only a *specified number of dollars* is available for merit rating distribution. In such cases, the better anyone can present himself as compared with his peers, the greater would be the rewards he would attain.

In a small number of cases, managers will be rated by their subordinates, although the subordinates may not have a performance appraisal interview per se. For example, in one university, the department head developed a simple rating form and gave it to each professor in his department. Then, a three-man committeee of subordinate professors analyzed the ratings from each professor, added their own ideas, and presented a summary of results to the department head.

While subordinate ratings may provide supervisors with valuable feedback, they pose some problems. First, such feedback is potentially stressful to the supervisor. Further, subordinates may fear that their superior may punish them if they make a candid but unfavorable appraisal. This problem was not present in the university cited above because all professors' responses on the department rating form were kept anonymous. Finally, according to Cummings and Schwab, there is some evidence to indicate that subordinates will rate their superior primarily on how well he has met *their own* needs.[16]

In a growing number of cases, subordinates are being asked to participate more fully in the appraisal interview, both in examining their own previous performance and in helping to set goals for performance improvement. This approach is referred to as "performance analysis" or "management by objectives" (MBO) and will be discussed more fully later in this chapter.

Problems with Traditional Interviews

There are a number of problems often encountered with traditional superior-subordinate interviews. Some of the appraisal problems already discussed (leniency, bias, halo, etc.) may easily slip into the appraisal interview. We will now turn to other aspects involved in feeding back appraisal data to subordinates in the interview.

In the performance interview situation both positive and negative feedback are required if a fair assessment of performance is to be expected. Many supervisors find it difficult to *provide* tactfully negative feedback, and many individuals find it difficult to *accept* their limitations as described by their supervisors. Further, even though a supervisor may not find it unpleasant to provide an employee with positive feedback, being held formally and constantly responsible for performance appraisals may place him or her in a situation in which he or she may have to give the individual less favorable or outright negative feedback sometime in the future. It is for reasons such as these that supervisors often resist holding performance appraisal interviews and find successful interviews often difficult to achieve.

In a classic article, Douglas McGregor spelled out in 1957 some of the basic reasons why supervisors find performance appraisals so difficult.[17] McGregor pointed out that supervisors are uncomfortable when they are placed in a position of "playing God" in judging subordinates' performance. One basic reason for this, according to McGregor, is that the inherent respect held for the individual makes it difficult to judge personal worth. He also indicated that with more modern emphasis in management thinking, managers are being called on to help subordinates meet both their own and organizational goals. He and others have emphasized that being put in the position both of helper and judge represents an incongruency. Hayden, for example, has stressed that supervisors cannot assume these conflicting roles simultaneously and that it is this conflict of roles "which probably causes the supervisor the most difficulty in the appraisal process."[18]

The appraisal interview may also create problems for the subordinates receiving feedback. In a classic study conducted at the General Electric Company, several specific subordinate reactions were brought out. First, praise from the superior had little or no effect on the subsequent performance of the individuals being evaluated, "perhaps because it was regarded as the sandwich which surrounded the raw meat of criticism."[19] Criticism in appraisal interviews, on the other hand, was frequently met with defensiveness, which led, in turn, to poor performance. The average employee reacted defensively about 54 per cent of the times he was criticized, constructive responses to criticism were rare, and 75 of the 92 employees studied viewed their supervisor's evaluation of their performance as less favorable than they themselves had viewed it.

One reason why criticism was believed to have evoked negative reactions was that with individuals being appraised on an annual basis, an information overload phenomenon took place. Employees became "clearly more prone to reject criticisms as the number of criticisms" mounted.[20] A basic question that can be raised here, however, is that if the managers were providing their subordinates with day-to-day feedback, which, as we indicated earlier, is essential to effective performance appraisal, how could criticisms build up so much during an annual period? A better approach would be to give small doses of criticism throughout the year which would represent more immediate feedback. These smaller doses would not represent such an "overload." Rather, they would put the appraisee in the position wherein he could hopefully overcome some of his weaknesses prior to, and anticipate many of the criticisms still valid in, the annual review, which would make it less threatening. Further, with periodic appraisals, some experienced managers will often explicitly take the strategy of only focusing attention on a few items, to try to induce subordinates to take a few steps at a time towards performance improvement, rather than overloading them with criticism.

From a more philosophical view, based on the literature of the humanities, Wallace has viewed the problem of subordinates receiving negative feedback in a somewhat different light.[21] He has argued that those performing in the lower 50th percentile of any group find it more difficult than better performers to accept negative feedback and change, even though they need it the most. According to Wallace, this problem derives from our American philosophy of life, with its Protestant ethic and capitalistic system. He has indicated that the Protestant ethic with its earthly values, demanding hard work, industry, and thrift, and influenced by Calvin's conception of "predestination [which] used the yardstick of material success to equate actual after-life destination,"[22] has put us in a position where we cannot perceive ourselves as successful if our performance is in the lower 50th percentile. Yet, no matter how excellent the performance of any work group may be, 50 per cent of its membership has to fall into this range by definition. Hopefully, subordinates falling in the lower 50 per cent in "excellent" departments will view their performance in light of the *total organization* as a reference group, and receive appropriately supportive feedback from their supervisors in their performance appraisal interviews.

One other reason for negative subordinate reactions in performance appraisal interviews is the method used by the supervisor to communicate performance appraisal data. One approach that has often been used in traditional interviews and may create problems is what Maier calls the "tell and sell approach."[23] Using this approach, the superior dominates the interview, tells his subordinates which of their faults should be corrected, and tries to "sell" each subordinate on making these improvements.

This approach has its greatest potential "with young and/or new employees," and with individuals "who are easygoing, uncritical and somewhat unimaginative, and who accept authoritarian leadership."[24] In many cases, however, the approach has two distinct disadvantages. It may (1) very easily evoke defensive reactions and (2) create a face-saving situation once the subordinate questions the supervisor's evaluation. Unless "the interviewer is very patient or something happens to break the chain of events that naturally comes from this [latter] type of conflict, the relationship continues to deteriorate."[25]

Appraisal Interview Strategies

Peformance appraisal interviews may be improved by modifying both the method used in communicating information to subordinates and the content of the communications. As far as method is concerned, there is much to be gained in many appraisal interviews if the superior dominates less, listens more to his subordinates, and lets them know that he or she understands their viewpoints. Moving more toward the "listening" direction (which Maier has referred to as the "tell and listen" approach), the supervisor permits subordinates to release frustrated feelings, which tends to reduce them. Further: "The unpleasant aspects of the appraisal interview are reduced when the superior has a method for dealing with defensive responses and when he is in a better position to understand and respect feelings."[26] Moving toward the "tell and listen approach" parallels moving from a more to a less structured selection interview; and it requires considerable skill and patience. Improvement in listening skills is one important facet incorporated into management training programs in many companies.

Content-wise, the supervisor in the appraisal interview can help guide the subordinate toward *specific* improved performance by focusing attention on behavior rather than traits and involving not only the employee but also himself and the organization in the change efforts. This strategy is illustrated in Figure 5–2. This involvement of the worker, supervisor, and organization may be aimed at improving two dimensions of the subordinate's behavior and skills: (1) specific job performance and (2) self-development. These two categories may overlap to a certain degree, but the following examples should help clarify the differences in these two behavioral dimensions.

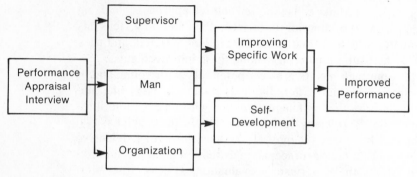

Figure 5–2 *Feedback-performance improvement strategies.*

Specific Job Performance. Here we refer to improving such specific performance measures as sales dollars, number of rejects, net operating profit, subordinate absenteeism rates, and so forth. In many such cases, performance improvements can be effected to a certain extent by the employee but help may also be needed from the superior and the organization. For example, in a manufacturing plant, the reject rate for items in one general foreman's department may be 6 per cent, which he would like to reduce to 4 per cent. One possible reason for this problem may be that two new supervisors are not fully aware of correct quality control procedures. In his appraisal interview with his own superior, the plant manager, agreement between the two may be reached that the general foreman should spend more time training the two new supervisors in quality control procedures. There may be other problems, as well, however, with respect to quality control. Perhaps the general foreman is not getting reject-rate feedback quickly enough to initiate corrective actions before the system goes out of control. Here, the plant manager may agree and, working with the firm's computer personnel, help get this information to the general foreman more quickly.

Self-Development. A young middle manager may have real difficulties in making oral presentation to groups of peers, and higher level managers. His or her supervisor might suggest taking an evening course in public speaking, the manager might agree, and the organization might agree to refund full tuition for the course upon successful completion. The net effect of this effort might well be not only improved communication abilities before groups but also a parallel improvement in the individual's self-esteem.

As indicated earlier, many performance appraisal systems have been utilized in organizations. Some of these do not provide an opportunity for the individual to obtain feedback information about his performance in a formalized interview, while others do.

In the remainder of this chapter we will discuss the more widely recognized performance appraisal techniques used in organizations today.

PERFORMANCE APPRAISAL TECHNIQUES

There are basically two types of performance appraisal techniques, comparative and absolute. None of the comparative techniques generate developmental feedback data for performance appraisal interview purposes. Among the absolute techniques, two provide no developmental feedback data to individuals; several provide superior-subordinate feedback mechanisms, which may be traditional in nature; and one fosters an interactive appraisal situation in which both the superior and subordinate participate actively in the appraisal process. These methods are illustrated in Figure 5–3; their relationship to other personnel decision-making systems is illustrated in Figure 5–1.

Comparative, Nonfeedback Techniques

Rankings

There are three basic ranking approaches used in performance appraisal. The simplest of these is ordinary ranking, in which the supervisor simply ranks subordinates from highest to lowest, generally based on overall performance rather than on numerous dimensions of performance.[27] With only a few employees to rank, this approach is easy to implement. With large numbers of subordinates to evaluate, however, ordinary ranking is difficult to carry out. With larger numbers of employees, ranking may be facilitated by the use of *alternation* ranking. Here a supervisor is given a list of his employees, thinks of and records

Comparative, Nonfeedback	Absolute, Nonfeedback	Absolute, Feedback	Absolute, Interactive Feedback
Rankings	Forced Choice;	Rating Scales; Essays;	MBO
Forced Distribution	Weighted Check List	Field Reviews	
		Critical Incident; Behaviorally Anchored Rating Scales (BARS)	

Figure 5–3   Types of appraisal systems.

the best subordinate, then thinks of the poorest employee and re-cords his name, then goes on to the next best, the next poorest, the third best and poorest and so on. This approach helps avoid the error of "central tendency" discussed earlier, since the super-visor is focusing as much attention "from the bottom up" as "from the top down."

A third type of ranking is *paired comparisons*. With this approach, the manager compares each employee with every other subordinate, one at a time. This approach is easier than simple or alternation ranking because the supervisor only needs to compare employee A with employee B, employee A with employee C, etc., and then construct a ranking from this series of compari-sons. A simple example of the use of paired comparisons is shown in Figure 5–4. It should be noted, however, that the number of comparisons that needs to be made with this method will increase rapidly with the number of employees being evalu-ated; the number of comparisons required equals $\frac{N(N-1)}{2}$. That these numbers can grow rapidly is illustrated by the fact that with 20 subordinates, $\frac{20(19)}{2}$, or 190, comparisons must be made.

One of the basic objectives of rankings in general is to avoid errors of leniency, strictness, or central tendency. The manager, with rankings, cannot rate all subordinates highly — he is forced to rank them from best to poorest.

Oberg has taken the position that multiple rankings (when two or more individuals make independent rankings of a particu-lar worker, and the rankings are averaged) are "among the best available for generating valid order-of-merit rankings for salary administration purposes."[28] Cummings and Schwab, on the other hand, have indicated that it is extremely difficult to compare the

Note: Circled letters are those chosen as the better in each pair.

Ranking:

A = 4
C = 3
B = 2
D = 1
E = 0

Figure 5–4 *Paired comparisons: hypothetical example with five employees.*

rankings of two or more groups;[29] e.g., the *best* performer in group A may not be as proficient as the *poorest* performer in group B. Further, rankings are usually done on a global basis without looking at specific performance dimensions, and supervisor bias and halo may creep into these rankings. Finally, as illustrated in Figure 5–1, rankings provide no feedback for developmental purposes.

Forced Distribution

The second comparative type of performance appraisal is the forced distribution, which resembles "grading on the curve." Here the appraiser is forced to assign a certain percentage of subordinates to one of several predetermined categories. For example, the categories might be the highest 10 per cent, the next highest 25 per cent, the middle 30 per cent, the next lowest 25 per cent, and the lowest 10 per cent. Such a technique may overcome leniency, strictness, and central tendency errors. However, the manager's bias toward or against certain individuals may still exist. Further, comparisons among different groups are difficult (as with ranking) because most individuals in one department may be performing better or poorer than all individuals in another. Further, the actual performance distribution of individuals in any department may not fall into the predefined categories, and no data are generated for feedback purposes. One advantage over the rankings is that forced distributions frequently "include comparisons on several performance factors rather than on one global dimension."[30]

Absolute, Nonfeedback Techniques

There are two performance appraisal techniques that are based on absolute standards rather than comparisons of employees. These are the forced choice and weighted checklist techniques.

Forced Choice

The forced choice technique was developed by the Army during World War II. Although there are variations of it, this procedure is generally developed and utilized as follows. First, a number of groups of statements about individuals are developed, such as the following:[31]

1. Avoids responsibility.
2. Inspires pride in the operation.
3. Lacks sense of humor.
4. Offers suggestions.

Then the supervisor picks from the groups of statements the one most descriptive of a subordinate and the one which is least descriptive. The statements are so designed so that only *one* of the two favorable statements discriminates between good performers and poor ones, while the same is also true for the two unfavorable statements.[32] After the supervisor has finished choosing statements for each subordinate, the forms are sent to personnel for scoring. Several comments regarding this approach are in order here. First, it is time consuming and expensive, since statements have to be gathered, culled, scaled for their degree of attractiveness, and analyzed as to their discrimination among good and poor performers. This renders the approach inappropriate in very small organizations. Second, even though behavioral rather than trait oriented, managers cannot use this tool for feedback purposes because they *do not know* how the items have been scaled or which items have been found to discriminate among high and low level performers. In our earlier illustration, for example, the supervisor would not know whether it was "avoids responsibility" or "lacks sense of humor" which was the discriminatory item, nor how much the discriminatory item was weighted. The purpose of keeping managers "in the dark" in this manner is to overcome their biases. This is often resented by managers, however, since it leads them to think that top management does not trust their judgment. Further, the system may be "beat" by clever managers. When they want to give a good rating to an "average" employee so that he will get a raise they "simply describe the best employee they know."[33] The technique's value for generating input data for human resource planning decisions is questionable. We question, for example, whether an analysis of the statements checked for any individual or his total score can provide adequate informational inputs for making decisions to promote individuals to higher levels in the organization.

Weighted Checklist

The weighted checklist is conceptually similar to the forced choice method. Instead of indicating the most and least descriptive statement in groups of four, however, the rater simply checks which descriptive statements on a list apply to the subordinate being rated. Each statement has been weighted based on discrimination among high and low performers, and the subordinate's score is based on the average numerical value of the items checked. Again, the supervisor does not know what numerical weight is given to any statement. Thus, the purpose and limitations of this technique are similar to those for the forced choice technique.

Absolute, Feedback Techniques

Graphic Rating Scales, Essays, and Field Reviews

One of the most widely used of all performance rating techniques is the graphic rating scale, an example of which is provided in Figure 5–5. One of the basic limitations of such scales is that they generally focus emphasis on traits rather than behavior. Further, the ratings may be highly biased, and scores, from 0 to

NAME:_____POSITION: _____

DEPARTMENT: _____DATE: _____

	Poor			Average				Excellent		
	1	2	3	4	5	6	7	8	9	10
1. Job knowledge										
2. Learning ability										
3. Interpersonal relationships										
4. Organizing ability										
5. Planning ability										
6. Creativity										
7. Work accuracy										
8. Judgment										
9. Initiative										
10. Supervisory skills										

SUPERVISOR: _____TOTAL POINTS:_____

COMMENTS:_____

_____

_____

_____

_____

Figure 5–5 Hypothetical graphic rating scale.

10 on each trait, may simply be added together without any weighting. This additivity assumption is not always valid, as may be illustrated by the somewhat far-fetched example of the bank teller who has scored 10 (of 10) on 9 trait items and 0 on the tenth of "honesty" since he just was caught embezzling. His total additive score would be 90 out of a possible 100! In one study, however, graphic rating scales were shown to be as valid as the best of forced-choice forms and better than most.[34]

By itself, just a trait-oriented graphic rating scale is probably of little use in providing feedback to employees for self-improvement. Often, however, the rater, along with completing the scale, may be asked to write a paragraph or more about the individual's strengths, weaknesses, specific means of improvement, etc. Because of their variability in both content and length, essay comparisons from one employee to another are difficult. However, if the essays are behaviorally phrased, they may provide a basis for the feedback of some constructive suggestions in the appraisal interview and inputs into the human resource planning and other personnel functions shown in Figure 5–1.

Further, to help overcome bias in graphic rating scales and essays, they may be combined with a systematic review process, which Oberg calls a "field review."[35] This might involve someone from the personnel department meeting with small groups of raters from different managerial units, going over each employee's rating and pinpointing areas of interrater disagreement, and helping to determine that each rater uses the same standards. The major advantage of this approach is that it may make ratings more valid. The major limitation of the technique is that it is very time consuming. From a contingency point of view, a simple rating scale plus a behaviorally oriented essay without the field review might be a highly appropriate strategy for small firms.

Critical Incidents and Behaviorially Anchored Rating Scales (BARS)

Two performance appraisal techniques that explicitly focus attention on behavior that can be fed back to employees for performance improvement purposes are the critical incident technique and a quantitative modification of this technique called "Behaviorally Anchored Rating Scales" (BARS).

The critical incident technique was developed by John C. Flanagan and extensively tested in the Delco-Remy Division of General Motors in the 1950's. This technique was developed as follows:

1. Foremen collected more than 2500 descriptive statements called critical incidents of specific behavior which represented either outstanding or definitely detrimental behavior.

2. The incidents were analyzed, and it was found that they included about 500 different types of behavior that were grouped into 16 categories of job requirements.

3. Special forms were developed to make it easy for supervisors to record either outstanding or detrimental behaviors in the different job requirement categories.[36]

Utilizing these forms, the foremen proceeded to jot down critical incidents. The question of how frequently this should be done arose, and research indicated that foremen recording data weekly had recorded less than half as many incidents as those who engaged in daily recording. The increased frequency thus provided more information.

The basic premise underlying the critical incident technique is that it makes the supervisor more of a recorder of what actually happened as opposed to being a judge. Thus, there may be a lesser degree of role conflict (judge vs. helper) with the critical incident technique.

The technique, in addition to making behavioral data available for feedback purposes, may contribute to the selection, human resource planning, training, and wage and salary functions. For instance, in one example provided by Flanagan and Burns, an employee notified his foreman that his job would be completed in two hours. This incident fell into the category on the critical incident "Performance Record" form "Anticipated and notified foreman that he would be out of work."[37] If this individual displayed a considerable degree of such behavior in planning ahead, he might be considered for promotion to a first-line foreman position, other factors being favorable.

During the first year of use at Delco-Remy in 1951, the critical incident technique generated a high percentage of favorable incidents — 98,566 as opposed to only 7670 unfavorable ones. On the other hand, about one fourth of the subordinates being evaluated had *no* critical incidents, either favorable or unfavorable, jotted down about their behavior. According to the researchers, "Their work was satisfactory; that and nothing more."[38] There is, of course, an alternative explanation — that a number of supervisors were simply not doing their job. Further, the question has been raised as to whether or not the critical incident guidelines as developed by Flanagan "precludes the supervisor's recording incidents of employee behavior that, although not critical to effective performance, are still important and related to such performance."[39]

The critical incident technique has also been criticized on the grounds that it may be a chore for the supervisor to jot down incidents and "need not, but may, cause a supervisor to delay feedback to employees."[40] However, at Delco-Remy, supervisors learned to mention both outstanding and negative behaviors at the time they occurred and recorded them at that time. Also at this GM plant, during the first four years' experience with the system, employees submitting suggestions doubled from about 11 to 22 per cent, while disciplinary warnings were halved.[41]

In spite of its merits, the critical incident approach has limitations. First, it may tend to encourage close supervision with a supervisor watching over subordinates' work with his "little black book." Further, developing the items is time consuming and expensive, and, thus, might not be cost justified in small firms.

BARS, the second highly behaviorally oriented appraisal approach, is a sophisticated quantitative modification of the critical incident technique in that a number of critical incidents are elicited from managers and then are placed in various categories.[42] Then, judges are asked to rate each incident for each category on a scale (say from 1 to 9 points), and items upon which there is general agreement among judges are placed on such a scale for use by managers in evaluating performance. With items assigned weights based on the average of values assigned to them by the judges, we have scales for each category which are "defined and anchored at various points by . . . behavioral incidents."[43] One such BARS scale is illustrated in Figure 5–6.

Supervisors continually record observations about their subordinates' behavior and refer to these diaries of observations as the time for the periodic performance appraisal arrives:

> Each statement is assigned to the dimension it most closely fits, and is scaled on the seven or nine point scale. . . . on the basis of closeness of fit to the items originally placed on the scale. After all statements reflecting observed job performance have been scaled, the mean scale value should be calculated for each job dimension and recorded on a summary sheet.[44]

In evaluating BARS, we see a quantitatively developed technique based on actual behavior that can be utilized not only in providing feedback but also in meeting the firm's human resource planning, selection, training, and wage and salary objectives. BARS provides a number of scales based on actual job performance incidents, which reflect not a global rating but a recognition that there are several dimensions and behavioral patterns leading to success.

BARS has the same advantage of critical incidents in that it focuses attention on behavior rather than traits and the same disadvantage (but even more pronounced) of being too complex and sophisticated for use in small firms. With respect to three other factors, research on BARS has been conflicting — the extent to which it is susceptible to leniency, the independence of its various dimensions, and interrater reliability.[45] Finally, BARS

Could be expected *never* to be late in meeting deadlines, no matter how unusual the circumstances.

Could be expected to meet deadlines comfortably by delegating the writing of an unusually high number of orders to two highly rated selling associates.

Could be expected always to get his associates' work schedules made out on time.

Could be expected to meet seasonal ordering deadlines within a reasonable length of time.

Could be expected to offer to do the orders at home after failing to get them out on the deadline day.

Could be expected to fail to schedule additional help to complete orders on time.

Could be expected to be late all the time on weekly buys for his department.

Could be expected to disregard due dates in ordering and run out of a major line in his department.

Could be expected to leave order forms in his desk drawer for several weeks even when they had been given to him by the buyer after calling his attention to short supplies and due dates for orders.

Department manager job behavior rating scale for the dimension, "meeting day-to-day deadlines"

Figure 5–6 *Behaviorally anchored rating scale for the dimension "Meeting Today's Deadlines. [From John Campbell, Marvin Dunnette, Edward Lawler III, and Karl Weick, Managerial Behavior Performance and Effectiveness (New York: McGraw-Hill Book Company, Inc., 1970), p. 122. © 1970 by the McGraw-Hill Book Company, and used with permission of the McGraw-Hill Book Company.]*

appears most viable in a relatively stable environmental situation. Otherwise, desired organization behavior may have changed before all of the time-consuming work required to develop and implement BARS has been completed.

Mutually Interactive, Feedback Technique: MBO

Management by Objectives (MBO)

In Chapter 2, we focused attention on the general managerial approach of management by objectives (MBO). One significant part of this approach is the establishment of a congruent MBO performance appraisal system. Drawing on Peter Drucker's concept of "management by objectives," Douglas McGregor suggested that the *subordinate* participate to a much greater extent in the whole process of performance appraisal.[46] This approach has been considered by some as a major development in performance appraisal, and has been used by many firms. Mechanically, although there are variations in the MBO technique, it attempts to relate individual goals to organizational objectives and proceeds generally as follows:

1. At periodic intervals, the subordinate develops short run performance goals.
2. These goals are drawn up on paper and reviewed by the supervisor.
3. The two discuss these goals and their appropriateness to organizational objectives, with the supervisor cast in the role of *helping* the subordinate but always having an ultimate veto power.
4. After an agreed upon period, the subordinate *himself appraises* his or her own effectiveness in meeting the goals agreed upon and establishes goals for the following planning period, both reviewing the appraisal and new goals set with the supervisor.
5. These steps are continued year after year.

The MBO approach has other important theoretical underpinnings in addition to Drucker's "management by objectives." It is organic, involving a more collegial relationship, as discussed in Chapter 1. Second, it is based on a more optimistic philosophy regarding the motivation of individuals. Third, MBO may also be usefully viewed in terms of leadership theory, for the whole performance appraisal process generally centers around a superior-subordinate relationship. Richards and Greenlaw, for example, have, on the basis of previous research, described an authoritarian–democratic–laissez-faire continuum of leadership styles or ways of behaving:[47]

1. At one extreme is the *authoritarian* leader who makes decisions often without consulting with his subordinates, and who exercises close supervision.

2. At the other extreme is the *laissez-faire* leader who rarely sets objectives for his subordinates and who gives them little direction.

3. In the middle is the *democratic* leader who: (a) unlike the laissez-faire leader does give some directions to his followers, and (b) unlike the authoritarian does not engage in close supervision but rather encourages his subordinates to set objectives and make decisions on their own.

In light of this theory, McGregor's MBO approach to performance involves moving from a more authoritarian style of leadership to a more democratic one. Such greater participation in goal setting, as pointed out in Chapter 2, may lead to some subordinates becoming more committed to the goals set and may foster such managerial skills as problem solving on the part of the participative subordinate.

The degree to which the MBO approach is effective will depend on numerous organizational variables. One useful framework for analyzing leadership (and performance appraisal) is that posed in the late 1950's by Tannenbaum and Schmidt.[48] Their framework indicates that there are three variables of particular importance in the choice of a leadership pattern — forces in the manager, in subordinates, and in the situation.[49]

MBO is intended to be a highly interactive feedback approach, with both the supervisor *willing* to let subordinates make more decisions on their own, and the subordinates *willing* to do so. However, in some situations, a supervisor with an authoritarian personality[50] may simply not be able to "let the reins go" and permit real subordinate participation. Such individuals, additionally, may discourage subordinates from using an MBO approach with their employees, so that a "blockage" in the whole MBO process from the top of the organizational hierarchy down may occur. Further, subordinates with certain types of personality structures may be unwilling to make such decisions as are required by MBO. For example, some individuals have strong dependence needs and want a "strong" superior to make many of their decisions for them.[51] Because many people do not want self-direction and autonomy, Oberg has indicated that increasingly more coercive types of MBO are developing — "a kind of manipulative form of management in which pseudo-participation substitutes for the real thing."[52]

With respect to situational variables and the success of MBO, there are many jobs (as on a machine-paced mass production assembly line) in which the worker simply has no control over the nature or pace of the work, and thus, no objectives to plan for and meet. In some more organic manufacturing operations (e.g., in a job shop where many different product variations are turned out) the workers may be able to help management with respect to scheduling or routing. In such cases, there may be possibilities for a limited MBO approach, depending on the degree of nonrepetitiveness of jobs performed.

Several final comments are in order regarding MBO. First, a number of researchers have indicated that *goal clarity* is a very important ingredient in the success of any human motivation and hence appraisal program, and this would represent another MBO contingency. Unlike the other appraisal techniques, MBO explicitly focuses attention on goals or objectives. But how clear are the organization's goals? The MBO superior's departmental goals? The subordinate's goals? Second, with its high emphasis on behavior rather than traits, quantitative measures are often sought out to define goals. In some cases, however, one may lean too much toward explicitly stated quantitative goals and ignore important qualitative variables. Third, MBO, unlike any other appraisal technique, is based on the individual's *unique* performance goals. This may make it very difficult to compare people when, for example, merit raises are to be given out. Fourth, developing plans, putting them down on paper, and reviewing them in the performance appraisal interview may be very time consuming and involve quite a bit of paperwork. Finally, MBO is still very controversial and has been held by some critics to work best where it is needed least. For example, MBO has been criticized as a technique

. . . that requires friendly, helpful superiors, honest and mature subordinates, and a high climate of trust. *It works best for those individuals who need it least.*
. . . [it] is best suited to those static, mechanistic environments in which we already have sufficient technology to manage competently. Rapidly changing conditions and low role clarity and ambiguity render it worse than useless. *It works best in those situations where we need it least.*[53]

We cannot agree with such strong criticism, but would advise managers considering MBO to examine carefully the values, limitations, and conditions necessary for the effectiveness of the approach.

Multiple Systems

Our discussion thus far has indicated that several different objectives may be met with performance appraisal. Similarly, a firm may want to utilize more than one performance appraisal system to meet these varying objectives. It is often very appropriate to have separate discussions about feedback-performance improvement and merit increases. Further, in the *same* department, it may be optimal to utilize *different systems* with *different* subordinates. For example, a general foreman may have working for him one first-line supervisor who is 58 years old and has a highly rigid personality structure dominated by strong dependence needs. Here MBO might be out of the question, but the general foreman could use a graphic-rating scale combined with a behaviorally oriented essay, to try to induce some little performance improvement on the part of the supervisor. Another supervisor in the same department, on the other hand, might be a 25-year-old college graduate, with family responsibilities, a strong need for independence and achievement, and an ultimate goal of rising to a high level in the organization. In such a case, the young supervisor may be very favorably impressed by being given the opportunity to set and appraise his own goals via MBO. The cost and time involved in multiple techniques, of course, must be given consideration.

SUMMARY

Some type of performance appraisal system has been developed by most organizations. The appraisal data may provide feedback to the individual in an effort to improve his performance. Further, such data may be of value in the firm's selection, training, human resource planning, and wage and salary functions. Numerous systems have been developed to meet these needs. Many systems call for performance appraisal interviews, which must be handled skillfully to be effective. Some supervisors find it difficult to "play God" and judge the worth of other human beings. Further, they may become overly lenient or strict, biased, or a victim of the halo effect or other appraisal errors.

What we basically have with most appraisal approaches is an open system involving mutual interaction between superior and subordinate within the context of a specific organizational situation. As Schwab and others have pointed out:

At a more general level, future research would do well to explicitly recognize that any evaluation instrument . . . probably has a limited impact on evaluation scores. In addition to the particular instrument, evaluation scores are potentially a function of the evaluatee . . ., the evaluator, and the evaluation context . . .[54]

It is essentially for this reason that we suggested that some firms might want to have multiple appraisal systems.

DISCUSSION AND STUDY QUESTIONS

1. Performance appraisal is probably related to more other personnel activities than any other personnel function. Discuss.
2. Indicate whether you think each of the following actions

might improve (or weaken) a firm's performance appraisal system. Why?

    a. Making performance appraisals solely a line responsibility.

    b. Making performance appraisals solely a staff responsibility to be handled by the personnel department.

    c. Making sure that every employee is provided with an *honest* and *unbiased* summary of all of his performance inadequacies every six months or year.

    d. Using the "tell and listen" rather than the "tell and sell" approach in performance appraisals.

    e. Having the president of a firm appraise vice presidents' performance partly on how well they appraise their immediate subordinates' performance, having the latter do the same, continuing with this approach down the organizational hierarchy.

3. Many managers dislike conducting performance appraisals, but good managers can, with top management support, help overcome most of the major problems associated with appraisals. Discuss. If you agree with this statement, give five specific ways in which a manager can help improve appraisals.

4. Tom Wilson received a degree with honors in business administration a year ago at a major western university, and was then hired by a medium-sized manufacturing firm as a first line supervisor. Tom has 23 subordinates working for him who know much more about the technical details of departmental operations than he does. The work that the subordinates perform involves a good degree of judgment. Tom is now being called on to carry out his first performance appraisal. He is to rate his subordinates using a graphic rating scale. Which of the following two types of appraisal erros do you think Tom is most like to commit — "central tendency" or "favorable impressions." Why?

5. A supervisor has six subordinates and plans to use the paired comparison method in ranking them. His paired comparisons are as follows: A is better than B; A better than C; A over D; A over E; A over F; C over B; D over B; B over E; F over B; D over C; C over E; F over C; D over E; F over D; and F over E. How would each subordinate be ranked with the use of these paired comparisons? What advantage does the paired comparison method have over simple ranking?

6. Use the graphic rating scale shown in Figure 5–5 to rate your instructor's performance. Of what value do you think such an appraisal would be if all appraisals in class were given to him or her? Why? What problems or inadequacies would you encounter in using this scale? Why?

7. To what extent do each of the following performance appraisal approaches seem to be appropriate to the situations indicated for them?

    a. MBO used by a first line supervisor whose production employees are performing highly routine and repetitious work.

    b. MBO used by an "authoritarian" manager.

    c. BARS used by first line supervisors in a large production operation in which job content is fairly stable.

    d. Critical incidents in a locally owned three-store pharmacy operation in a university town.

e. MBO with a group of research scientists working on aerospace projects.

8. The text indicates that some authorities believe that supervisors dislike conducting performance appraisals because they do not want to "play God"; and there is basically an incongruency when supervisors are put in a position of being both helper and judge. Indicate the extent to which these dislikes and role conflicts are fostered or inhibited by each of the following performance appraisal approaches.

a. Forced choice
b. Graphic rating scale
c. Critical incident
d. MBO
e. Forced distribution

9. One of the biggest problems in performance appraisal is that we attempt to quantify the nonquantifiable, and hence base our decisions on distorted numbers. Discuss.

10. To what extent do each of the following performance appraisal techniques take an optimistic view of human capabilities? In each case give your reasons.

a. Forced Choice
b. Weighted Checklist
c. Forced Distribution
d. Graphic Rating Scales with Essays
e. BARS
f. MBO

Notes

[1]W. W. Claycombe et al., "An Evaluation of Supervisory Skills to Determine Training Needs," *Personnel Journal,* 55 (March, 1976), pp. 116–120.

[2]L. L. Cummings and Donald P. Schwab, *Performance in Organizations* (Glenview, Ill.: Scott, Foresman and Company, 1973), p. 111. Cummings and Schwab describe other possible but less effective variable-interview approaches in ibid., pp. 111–112.

[3]Robert J. Hayden, "Performance Appraisal: A Better Way," *Personnel Journal,* 52 (July, 1973), p. 606. Some authorities, however, claim that top managers will not spend the time necessary to examine a subordinate's performance on two different occasions. See, for example, Arch Patton, "Does Performance Appraisal Work?", *Business Horizons,* 16 (February, 1973), p. 84.

[4]Albert W. Schrader, "Let's Abolish the Annual Performance Review," *Management of Personnel Quarterly,* 8 (Fall, 1969), p. 23.

[5]Robert Glaser and David J. Klaus, "Proficiency Measurement: Assessing Human Performance," in *Psychological Principles in System Development,* Robert M. Gagné, ed. (New York: Holt, Rinehart and Winston, 1962), p. 434.

[6]This example is drawn from ibid., pp. 424–425.

[7]Hayden, op. cit., p. 609.

[8]Ibid.

[9]Lloyd H. Lamouria and Thomas W. Harrell, "An Approach to an Objective Criterion for Research Managers," *Journal of Applied Psychology,* 47 (December, 1963), pp. 353–357. The reputable and well-known operations research text from which Lamouria and Harrell derived their weightings was C. W. Churchman, et al., *Introduction to Operations Research* (New York: John Wiley and Sons., Inc. 1957), pp. 150–152.

[10]Lamouria and Harrell, op. cit., p. 353.

[11]Melvin R. Marks, " 'An Objective Criterion for Research Managers': A Critique," *Journal of Applied Psychology,* 49 (April, 1965), pp. 91–92.

[12]Charles W. Eisemann, "Production Performance Measurement and Analysis," *Personal Journal,* 51 (January, 1972), p. 102.

[13]Ibid. For more "far-out" suggestions as to the role that the computer might play with respect to performance appraisal, see: Gerald E. Connally, "Personnel Administration and the Computer," *Personnel Journal,* 48 (August, 1969), p. 608.

[14]We have drawn a number of ideas in this section from the excellent discussion in Cummings and Schwab, op. cit., pp. 101 ff.

[15]Ibid, p. 104.

[16]Ibid., pp. 107–108.

[17]Douglas McGregor, "An Uneasy Look at Performance Appraisal," *Harvard Business Review,* 35 (May-June, 1957), pp. 89–94.

[18]Hayden, op cit., p. 609.

[19]H. H. Meyer et al., "Split Roles in Performance Appraisal," *Harvard Business Review,* 43 (January-February, 1965), p. 127. For a more in depth treatment of the role and effectiveness of praise, see Richard F. Farson, "Praise Reappraised," *Harvard Business Review,* 41 (September-October, 1963), pp. 61–66.

[20]H. H. Meyer et al., op. cit., p. 127. The interviewees in this study were managerial, professional, and technical personnel such as foremen, engineers, and specialists in marketing and other functions.

[21]William H. Wallace, "Performance Appraisal of Nonself Directed Personnel," *Personnel Journal,* 50 (July, 1971), pp. 521–527.

[22]Ibid., p. 523.

[23]Norman R. F. Maier, *The Appraisal Interview: Three Basic Approaches* (La Jolla, Calif.: University Associates, Inc., 1976), pp. 4 ff.

[24]Ibid., p. 8.

[25]Ibid., p. 5.

[26]Ibid. p. 10.

[27]Cummings and Schwab, op. cit., pp. 81–82.

[28]Winston Oberg, "Make Performance Appraisal Relevant," *Harvard Business Review,* 50 (January-February, 1972), p. 66.

[29]Cummings and Schwab, op. cit., p. 84.

[30]Ibid.

[31]These items are taken from Reign Bittner, "Merit Rating Procedure," *Personnel Psychology,* 1 (Winter, 1948), p. 430.

[32]A somewhat different version of this method is presented in Cummings and Schwab, op. cit., pp. 87–89. In their discussion, the reader may also find a more complete description of the development of statements than we will illustrate here.

[33]Oberg, op. cit., p. 64.

[34]James Berkshire and Richard Highland, "Forced Choice Performance Rating — A Methodological Study," *Personnel Psychology,* 6 (Autumn, 1953), p. 355.

[35]See Oberg, op. cit., p. 63.

[36]John C. Flanagan and Robert K. Burns, "The Employee Performance Record: A New Appraisal and Development Tool," *Harvard Business Review,* 33 (September-October, 1955), p. 96.

[37]Ibid., p. 98.

[38]Ibid., p. 100.

[39]Robert D. Scott, "Taking Subjectivity Out of Performance Appraisal," *Personnel,* 50 (July-August, 1973), p. 46.

[40]Oberg, op. cit., p. 64.

[41]Flanagan and Burns, op. cit., p. 101.

[42]For a highly detailed explanation of all the steps involved in developing and using one version of BARS, see John P. Campbell et al., *Managerial Behavior, Performance, and Effectiveness* (New York: McGraw-Hill Book Co., 1970), pp. 119 ff. A simpler description is provided in Cummings and Schwab, op. cit., pp. 91–93.

[43]Campbell et al., op. cit., p. 123.

[44]William J. Kearney, "The Value of Behaviorally Based Performance Appraisals," *Business Horizons,* 19 (June, 1976), p. 79.

[45]Donald P. Schwab et al., "Behaviorally Anchored Rating Scales: A Review of the Literature," *Personnel Psychology,* 28 (Winter, 1975), pp. 549–562. Interrater reliability refers here to the degree to which different individuals rate a person's performance similarly. This is, of course, important in performance appraisal, since if different raters rated an individual quite differently, real questions would be raised as to how well the individual is actually performing.

[46]McGregor, op. cit.

[47]Max D. Richards and Paul S. Greenlaw, *Management: Decisions and Behavior,* rev. ed., (Homewood, Ill.: Richard D. Irwin, Inc., 1972), pp. 184 ff.

[48]Robert Tannenbaum and Warren H. Schmidt, "How To Choose a Leadership Pattern," *Harvard Business Review,* 36 (March-April, 1958), pp. 95–101.

[49]Ibid., p. 98.

[50]It is extremely important to differentiate between a leader who *chooses* an authoritarian style to fit the circumstances, and one who has an authoritarian personality. It is the latter who finds it difficult to give subordinates more latitude in decision making. The classic work on the authoritarian personality is: T. W. Adorno et al., *The Authoritarian Personality* (New York: Harper and Brothers, 1950).

[51]This enables people to "escape" from the freedom of having to make their own decisions. See Erich Fromm, *Escape from Freedom* (New York: Farrar and Rinehart, 1941). One of Fromm's interesting ideas is that the rise of Hitler in Germany can be partially accounted for by the needs of his countrymen for a "strong father figure."

[52]Oberg, op. cit., p. 65.

[53]Steven D. Kerr, "Some Modifications of MBO as an OD Strategy," *Academy of Management Proceedings,* 1971, p. 42.

[54]Schwab et al., op. cit., p. 560.

6

EMPLOYEE DEVELOPMENT: BASIC CONSIDERATIONS IN PLANNED ORGANIZATIONAL LEARNING

Once an organization has hired individuals who are able to perform jobs or are trainable, it must integrate them into the organization in order to achieve individual needs and organizational objectives. Such orientation is the employee's first exposure to training and development in the organization. Beyond orientation training, the organization needs to engage in a *continuous process* of training and development so that *all* organization members are able to perform their current jobs effectively and efficiently and are prepared to move to other jobs or assignments when needed to help meet future organizational human resource requirements. As Dooley has stated, "Training is not something that is done once to new employees — it is used continuously in every well-run establishment."[1]

The organization must recognize that if it does not explicitly plan to teach its employees to perform and behave "correctly," they will learn certain patterns of performance and behavior anyway. Such unplanned learning may be dysfunctional and difficult to correct later, particularly if this prior learning must be unlearned before any appropriate new learning can take place.

For example, suppose an employee has learned an incorrect procedure for operating a machine, and therefore safety hazards are created. Before this worker can be taught correct, safe operating procedures, the old habits may first have to be unlearned, thus contributing to a more difficult learning situation than if the safe procedures had been taught initially.

Many different types of planned organizational learning efforts have been utilized in organizations. Frequently, the terms "training" and "development" have been used to classify these efforts, with two distinctions being made between these terms. First, development has been used to refer to efforts primarily geared toward teaching skills, knowledge, and attitudes for *future* job assignments, whereas training has been used to refer to efforts with respect to *current* job performance and behavior. Second, development often has been associated with managers and training with nonmanagers, such as clerical, blue collar and other employees who do not engage in supervision. We believe that these distinctions between training and development are inappropriate, since all constructive training efforts, whether for managers or nonmanagers, or whether geared to meet current or future organizational objectives and individual needs, involve developing the individual toward higher levels of achievement and performance. It is for this reason that we have entitled Part III of this text "The Development of Human Resources." In light of our belief that the distinctions between the terms training and development are not appropriate, we will use these two terms interchangeably in this and the following two chapters. Stating that training programs involve developing individuals, whether managers or nonmanagers, however, does not mean that such diverse groups should be exposed to the same types of developmental efforts. For example, top level managers need to develop much more complex conceptual skills in order to direct the overall firm, higher degrees of interpersonal skills for directing others in handling complex decision problems, and so forth.

Planned organizational learning, regardless of whom is involved, calls for more than merely conducting a development program. Rather, it is a process composed of four basic phases, of which conducting the program is but one. This process of planned organizational learning in an information decision-making framework is presented in Figure 6–1.[2] As Figure 6–1 indicates, the planned organizational learning process involves determining the need for development and designing, implementing, and evaluating development efforts.

In this chapter, we will focus attention on the first of these four phases — need determination. The second phase, designing development programs, involves: (1) deciding what basic princi-

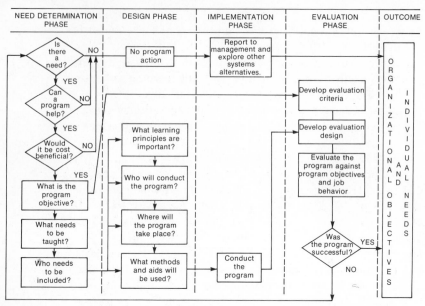

Figure 6–1 *Planned organizational learning progress.*

ples drawn from learning theory may be most effective in the training and (2) determining who should conduct the training, where it should be conducted, and what specific training techniques may be used most effectively. We find it easier to understand the total development process by considering the first of these decisions — the choice of appropriate learning principles — in this chapter, while reserving for Chapter 7 discussion of who should carry out training, where it should be conducted, and the choice of appropriate training techniques. We will touch on the third phase of development — implementation — in discussing the other three phases shown in Figure 6–1 and, hence, will devote no special section to this phase. We will discuss the fourth phase of development — program evaluation — in this chapter, as well as management science, computers and contingencies in developmental programs. We will reserve for Chapter 8 consideration of: (1) training designed for special groups, such as the hard-core unemployed and (2) selected issues in the field of training today such as that of "organizational development."

The four basic steps in the planned organizational learning process are not as sequential as implied in Figure 6–1, and for this reason are not treated as such in this three-chapter section of the text. Rather, they interact in a number of ways. For example, decisions relating to what needs to be taught and who needs to be included in training programs are likely to be considered simultaneously, as would the decisions of what is to be taught in a training effort and how that effort may best be evaluated.

NEED DETERMINATION PHASE

A basic step in the decision-making process as pointed out in Chapter 1 is to identify that problems or potential problems exist. As Goldstein has pointed out, determining the need for development programs is extremely important, since it "provides the information necessary to design the entire program."[3] The first step in determining the need for development is to ask: "Is there a problem or a potential problem in meeting organizational objectives and/or individual needs?" If the answer to this question is "no," then the personnel department can spend time on other activities. If the answer is "yes," then the question of whether training can help overcome the problem must be asked. Even if training can help correct the problem, it should be determined whether other corrective actions might be more appropriate. For example, if it is found that certain new employees lack appropriate skills to a greater extent than expected, the personnel department may choose to develop a training program or it may raise its selection standards, if such latter actions are consistent with the philosophies of the company.[4] It is also possible that the type of training necessary might not be readily apparent. For example, it may appear that a manager who is not performing at an acceptable level needs to be sent to a training program to update his skills. However, additional analysis may show that the individual already possesses the ability to engage in the required behavior but often does not do so. In such a situation, further probing might indicate that the manager has some negative attitudes created to a considerable extent by interpersonal conflicts existing between the individual and certain colleagues. Here, frank discussions between the supervisor and the individuals involved (which would represent a form of training) may be a much more appropriate way to overcome the attitude problem than to send the manager to a two-week "human relations" course.

Need Determination: Types of Analysis and Techniques

In this section we will first discuss three types of analysis which must be undertaken in determining the need for development: (1) organizational, (2) task, and (3) person.[5] While these types of analysis will be considered separately, it should be emphasized that they, in fact, overlap to varying extents. We will also discuss a number of techniques used in determining the need for development.

Organizational Analysis

Organizational analysis essentially deals with the firm's overall corporate strategy. In planning its corporate strategy, the firm will analyze its strengths and weaknesses and its environment, and decide *"on the objectives of the organization, on changes in these objectives, on the resources used to attain these objectives, and on the policies that are to govern the acquisition, use, and disposition of these resources."*[6] Likewise, organizational analysis involves looking at both short and long range goals of the organization and "consists of an examination of the entire organization, including its goals, resources, and the environment in which it exists."[7]

The organization must examine its goals and subgoals if development programs are to be designed to meet the organization's objectives and members' needs. A development program that is inconsistent with organizational or individual goals at best will have no organizational impact and at worst may be dysfunctional. For example, a firm that has no intention of utilizing newer management science tools but that sends its employees to a development program dealing with these tools might find its employees returning to the organization with views that will be rejected by top management and hence lead to frustration and possibly disillusionment on the part of the program participants.

The organization must examine both its physical and human resources in determining its development needs, since a firm's basic concern is with the allocation of its limited resources among competing alternatives. For example, with a constrained budget, management may have to decide to purchase some new equipment rather than undertake a worthwhile development program because the equipment is needed immediately, whereas the development can wait. An analysis of the organization's human resources is also a necessary portion of the organizational analysis. Specifically, the personnel department must tie the determination of development needs to future human resource requirements established by means of human resource planning, as discussed in Chapter 3.

In organizational analysis the firm must also examine its environments — external and internal. The external environment consists of the social, cultural, political, and economic systems that influence organization decisions. For example, societal attitudes and governmental legislation, such as the Civil Rights Act of 1964, have caused changes in the recruiting and selection processes. These changes, in turn, have modified many firms' needs for training programs, as they have sought to meet affirmative action goals. The internal environment consists of the philosophies, objectives, policies, leadership styles, and attitudes that create an "organizational climate," which influences the behavior of organization members. As Litwin and Stringer have stated:

> The term organizational climate refers to a set of measurable properties of the work environment, perceived directly or indirectly by the people who live and work in this environment and assumed to influence their motivation and behavior.[8]

The organizational climate helps set the stage for employee behavior and, therefore, acts as a frame of reference against which the employee can evaluate his or her own behavior.[9] In fact, Saint has stated that organizational climate may be the "most important influence affecting the development of the individual in an organization."[10] The prevailing organizational climate is a contingency with which the personnel department must deal when designing training programs. If the prevailing attitude toward development is negative, then any program is likely to fail. For example, an organization may encourage people to continue their formal education but have no formal plans to promote persons who put in such efforts. This situation has caused some persons to question the worth of continuing their education and those who do continue often do so to increase their mobility. Thus, the prevailing climate in the organization may not promote development except for an organizationally dysfunctional purpose!

Task Analysis

Task analysis is the second type of analysis in which the firm must engage in order to determine its development needs, and consists of job analysis (see Chapter 3). It involves developing job descriptions and job specifications.

Just as an organizational analysis is necessary to determine the organizational objectives, a task analysis is necessary to determine the objectives related to performance standards for skills, knowledge, and attitudes needed to successfully perform the task.[11]

The task analysis, with its job descriptions and specifications as outputs, will help to indicate what skills, knowledge, and attitudes are necessary to perform the job. For example, Loftin and

Roter have identified three levels of complexity for clerical duties from which they identify performance requirements in terms of skill, knowledge, and attitudes.[12] These duty and performance requirements are presented in Figure 6–2. From the performance requirements, the personnel department can begin to identify particular development needs by worker level. Thus, task analysis, like job analysis, deals with the job, not the individual performing the job.

Person Analysis

Person analysis is concerned with identifying specific individuals who need development. Three groups need to be considered in person analysis: (1) organization members who are performing a job, (2) organization members who will be performing some job in the future, and, (3) nonorganization members who eventually will be performing a job. For organization members, the personnel department may become aware of development needs through such means as performance appraisal analysis (see Chapter 5). For individuals to be hired, the personnel department needs to determine whether or not the new employee differs from current organization members in skills, knowledge, and attitudes. The personnel department may become aware of such differences through analysis of the information generated by the selection tools used, as discussed in Chapter 4. For example, one retailing chain hired a personnel manager who had prior experience and a good administrative record in public administration, recognizing

	Duty Requirements	Performance Requirements	
Entry level	Repetitive, routine; strict adherence to procedures	Knowledge: Basic, limited Skill: Manipulative, operative Attitude: Working environment	
Secondary level	Moderately individualized and detailed; choice between alternative actions	Knowledge: Specialized, expanded Skill: Determinative Attitude: Job satisfaction	
Senior level	Highly individualized and complicated; wider choice judgment, technical expertise	Knowledge: Cognitive, technical Skill: Analytical, research Attitude: Career opportunity	

Figure 6–2 *Illustration of how training requirements could be derived from a survey of clerical duties. [From Markus M. Loftin, III, and Benjamin Roter, "Training Clerical Employees," in Joseph J. Famularo, ed., Handbook of Modern Personnel Administration (New York: McGraw-Hill Book Company, 1972), p. 19–2. Copyright 1972 by and Used with Permission of McGraw-Hill Book Company.]*

that he would need some special orientation training with respect to the techniques of merchandising in department stores. Person analysis, it should be emphasized, is closely related to task analysis, since the skills, knowledge, and attitudes required for successful job performance as identified in task analysis must be examined in both hiring and developing specific individuals in person analysis.

Need Determination Techniques

A number of tools are available to the personnel department for determining development needs. As already indicated, job analysis and performance appraisals can be used to determine the need for development. In addition, personnel may become aware of development needs through surveys, analysis of company records, and requests from line managers.

Surveys are frequently used to identify development needs. We use the term "survey" in a broad sense to include any attempt by the personnel department to gain information that is not readily available but that is relevant to meeting development needs. Thus, we would consider psychological tests, questionnaires, and interviews with employees as survey instruments.

Surveys covering task requirements are essentially taken care of through job analysis. Since job analysis should be performed on a continuous basis, survey data relating to the task should be readily available to the personnel department. Other types of surveys, however, may need to be undertaken as special needs arise. For example, having noticed an increase in the turnover rate of the company's employees, the personnel department might decide to collect information on employee satisfaction. To gather such information it might send out a questionnaire that deals with job satisfaction such as the Job Description Index, which measures employee satisfaction on five scales (work, co-workers, pay, promotion, and supervision).[13] Analysis of the results obtained from the questionnaire might indicate the need for a development program for supervisors to help them keep their workers more satisfied. Interviewing persons leaving the firm (called "exit interviews") also constitutes a type of survey instrument that may help personnel determine the need for a particular development program. For example, a high proportion of rank and file employees leaving the firm of their own accord may complain that their supervisors "never paid attention to any of their ideas." Such information may indicate that it would be advisable to explore a developmental program for first line supervisors on ways of stimulating and encouraging creative thinking, not only for their subordinates but for themselves as well. Thus,

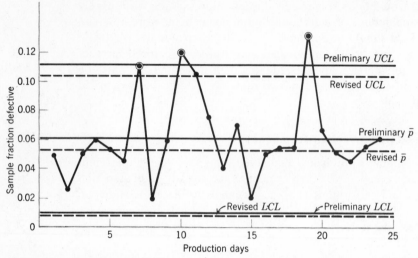

Figure 6-3 *Quality control chart. A p-chart for examining past data and establishing preliminary and revised control limits. [From Elwood S. Buffa,* Modern Production Management *(New York: John Wiley and Sons, 1973), p. 661.]*

surveys, whether of a questionnaire or interview type, and whether done continuously or on an as needed basis, may provide valuable information concerning the need for development.

Another source of information about development needs is an analysis of company records. Such items as level of output, quality, costs, accidents, absenteeism, tardiness, turnover, or grievances may indicate that training is needed. For example, in the production area, quality control charts, such as that presented in Figure 6–3, are often used to make certain that the system is under control. The variations in Figure 6–3 may be attributed to chance variations or assignable causes. Buffa has suggested that assignable causes generally are:

1. Differences among workers.
2. Differences among machines.
3. Differences among materials.
4. Differences due to interaction between any two or all three of these factors.[14]

Figure 6–3 indicates that there were control problems on the tenth and nineteenth days and perhaps on the seventh day. Buffa has reported that:

Investigation shows nothing unusual for the first point, day 7. For the second point, it appears that a logical explanation is that three new men were taken on that day. The foreman contends that the following day's defectives were also affected by the breaking in of these men. The last was explained by the fact that the die had worn and finally actually fractured that day.[15]

Thus, the quality control data may point out not only production problems but also an area in which training may be needed.

In other cases, the need for training may be established because line managers ask the personnel department to provide certain programs. Such requests need to be checked so that proper training programs are created. It is all too easy to implement a training program on the basis of a request from line without carrying out an adequate determination of a training need. For example, the plant manager in one large corporation often read about new "human relations" and other techniques, which made grandiose promises for management development. When he called the training director, the latter bluntly told the plant manager that the techniques were overly superficial and should not be undertaken. When discussing his behavior, the training director stated: "One of the most important parts of my job is saying 'NO!' to many ideas for unnecessary and poorly designed development programs that line requests me to consider."

Performance appraisal data may also be useful in the determination of development needs. First, observational data provided by the supervisor concerning employees can pinpoint *individual* development needs. Second, these data can be used to improve training programs. For example, critical incidents may be grouped into categories, poor performance areas brought to the attention of personnel, and changes made in development programs "to try to remove the causes of negative critical incidents and enhance the causes of positive ones."[16]

Of all the approaches for determining training needs, it is interesting to note that a Bureau of National Affairs (BNA) survey of approximately 350 personnel executives included in BNA's Personnel Policies Forum found that observation and analysis of job performance were the most frequently used, as shown in Figure 6–4. Thus, it appears that companies place a great deal of emphasis on person analysis for determining development needs. It is interesting to note from Figure 6–4 that the contingency of company size (large represents 1000 employees or more) does not appear to influence greatly the use of many techniques. The biggest exception is in the consideration of current and projected (organizational) changes. This approach, which relates closely to strategic planning and therefore to organizational analysis for determining development needs, is much more frequently used by larger companies. This difference makes sense, since large companies have greater resources and tend to

	All Cos.	Larger Cos.	Smaller Cos.
Observation & analysis of job performance	49%*	44%	53%
Management & staff conferences & recommendations	24	28	17
Analysis of job requirements	19	18	21
Consideration of current & projected changes	16	22	7
Surveys, reports & inventories	10	8	14
Interviews	6	6	7
Other**	15	12	21

*Percentages total more than 100 since some companies use more than one method.
**Includes experience, demand, cost figures, turnover statistics and safety records.

Figure 6-4 *Methods for determining development needs.* [*From Bureau of National Affairs, "Planning the Training Program,"* Personnel Management: BNA Policy and Practice Series *(Washington, D.C.: The Bureau of National Affairs, Inc., 1975), p. 205:103.*]

engage in much more frequent and systematic strategic planning than do smaller companies.

DESIGN PHASE: PRINCIPLES OF LEARNING

As indicated previously, the design phase of training programs involves making decisions concerning where the training will take place, what methods will be used, and who will conduct the training. Critical to all these decisions, but particularly to what methods will be used, is an understanding of numerous so-called "principles of learning," which facilitate efficient and effective learning.

When management makes the decision to undertake a development program, it does so because it expects some desired changes to occur in skills, knowledge, or attitudes. In recent years, there has been increased interest in the principles by means of which learning and transfer and retention of materials can be accomplished. Unfortunately, however, there is no general agreement concerning such principles, largely because a number of different learning theories exist. Each of these theories puts forth certain principles that may not be supported by other learning theories.[17] We do not propose to cover all the various learning theories or principles which have been suggested.[18] Rather, we will present those principles of learning and aspects of transfer and retention of learning that make the most intuitive sense to us or are supported by adequate empirical research.

Motivation

Whether or not an individual must be motivated if learning is to occur is of considerable debate.[19] It is possible to argue that learning can take place even though the individual is *not* motivated to learn. For example, a wife who is completely uninterested in football may sit down to read a book in the same room where her husband is watching the Superbowl and at the end of the game find out that she has "learned" not only who won but some of the terminology of the game as well. Likewise, the trainee in a classroom may not be interested in learning and yet at the end of the class find that there are things now known which were not known before. It appears reasonable, however, that if individuals are motivated, learning will occur more efficiently and effectively.

Since motivation is an internal process in the final analysis, the motivation to learn must come from within the trainee. However, the trainer can influence the motivation of the trainee by providing an environment that is conducive to and rewards learning. For example, since human behavior is purposeful and goal directed, the trainer can facilitate motivation to learn by showing the trainee that a particular goal can be accomplished through a development program, that the trainee is able to accomplish the goal, and that the accomplishment of the goal will in turn lead to something that is desired by the trainee, or avoid something that is not desired.[20] In terms of rewards (or sanctions) for learning (or not learning) the organization can also provide such things as promotions and merit raises or, conversely, demotions. Rewards that exist because the individual values learning per se are described as intrinsic; those provided by the trainer or the organization are referred to as extrinsic. It appears likely that given the basic ability to learn, maximum learning will occur when both intrinsic motivation and extrinsic rewards exist together and that minimal learning will result when neither is present.

It should be noted that too much motivation can be detrimental. It is possible for an individual to strive so hard that he exceeds his physiological and psychological limits and cannot perform. The college student who feels he must learn everything, ends up experiencing an information overload and finds that he "freezes" on an exam and can remember nothing represents an example of this problem. The majority of motivation-learning studies have involved animals, and the question must be raised: To what extent is it reasonable to generalize from these subjects to humans? In addition, many animal studies have involved deprivation of food or sex. As This and Lippitt have pointed out, tongue in cheek, "It may very well be that training directors have been overlooking some excellent motivational factors in this area."[21]

Individual Differences

Closely related to motivation is the consideration of the impact of individual differences on learning. Even if every person entering the training environment is highly motivated, the trainer would still need to be aware of individual differences in goals, aptitudes, past experience, and learning styles, since all these variables influence learning.

The goals of the trainee need to be assessed if learning is to occur. As noted previously, if the trainer can show the trainee that the learning will result in something desirable, motivation is likely to be increased. However, a highly motivated trainee whose goal is not consistent with those of the training program may learn a great deal but not what is desired by the organization. For example, a supervisor who receives training in how to complete performance appraisal forms provided by personnel may concentrate on how to best use the forms to ensure that one of his "favorite" subordinates obtains a raise rather than to conduct an honest appraisal. In a lighter vein, one professor asked a student in a management class, "What do you want out of this course?" The student's response, "Me!" was not anticipated but reflected the differences in the goals of the student and the instructor. A research example of training program goals that conflict with the goals of the trainees has been provided by Chowdhry.[22] He found that the goals of participants who selected themselves for a university management training program often represented attempts to escape from job stress and from planning the next phase of their career development rather than efforts to meet the goals of the training program.

The trainee's aptitude and ability to learn will influence the amount learned in any development program. Persons with greater ability will learn more quickly than persons of lesser ability. For example, in one training program in which the trainees were learning the radiotelegraphic code, it was shown that those individuals with greater aptitude as measured by the Army Radiotelegraph Operator Aptitude Tests were able to learn the code more quickly.[23] It is interesting to note that in this training the early differences between the highest and lowest aptitude groups *increased* as training progressed. This increase in differences between lower and higher ability individuals as training progresses has been found to be particularly likely when the task to be learned is relatively complex.[24]

Past learning experiences of the trainee may also influence the extent to which learning takes place. An individual who has been successful in prior learning situations will have received feedback indicating that he can be successful in such situations. This feedback may result in a favorable self-image, which will help make the individual confident in learning situations in general, and therefore, more likely to be motivated and to learn in specific programs.

It is also generally agreed that individuals possess different learning styles, which influence how they approach learning. The learning style is "uniquely personal" and involves the individual's way of "receiving, perceiving, thinking, problem-solving, and remembering."[25] For example, one classification scheme has identified four basic types of learning styles.[26] To illustrate two of these types, some people ("assimilators") tend to make use of abstract conceptualization and reflective observation in learning situations and use deductive reasoning to create theoretical models. Certain other people ("accommodators") take an opposite approach to learning and tend to use concrete experience and active experimentation in their learning. They tend to use an intuitive trial and error approach to solve problems. No particular type of learning style is inherently better or worse than any other. However, if the trainer is able to pinpoint either of these or any other distinct styles of learning with any particular trainee, he *may* be able to make the training more effective. For example, if he knows that a particular trainee learns best by thinking in terms of concrete experiences, he *may* be able to gear the training in this direction, rather than in a highly theoretical one, which may be difficult for the individual to comprehend. We emphasized the word "may" twice, since (1) some types of training may not lend themselves well to the predominant learning style of the trainee, and (2) in group training sessions there may be a heterogeneous "mix" of individuals with different learning styles, so that it would not be feasible to develop a particular training strategy that would accommodate all or even a majority of the group.

Learning Curves and Plateaus

The trainer needs to be aware that learning does not always take place nor progress at a constant rate. Such awareness is important so that he does not become discouraged if the trainee appears to be taking too long to learn or to have stopped learning. In addition, such awareness permits the trainer to tell the trainees not to be discouraged.

Rates of learning are frequently illustrated by means of learning curves such as those shown in Figure 6–5. In some instances learning may start slowly and increase at a rapid rate, as in Figure 6–5*a*. This type of situation is likely to exist when a simple but completely new skill is being learned. (The dotted line in the figure is intended to show that there is a maximum level of performance beyond which one could not progress.) Figure 6–5*b*, on the other hand, illustrates a situation in which learning progresses at a very rapid rate initially with slower rates of increase later. This type of situation may exist when the trainee comes to the training already possessing the more basic initial skills but not the more advanced ones. Figure 6–5*c* illustrates an S-shaped curve, which may represent a learning situation in which it is easy

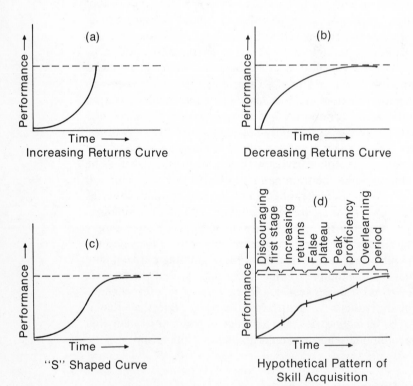

Figure 6–5 Learning curves and plateaus. [*From Theodore T. Herbert,* Dimensions of Organizational Behavior *(New York: Macmillan Publishing Company, Inc., 1976), p. 447* © MacMillan Publishing Company 1976. *(a) has been added by the authors.*]

to become partly proficient at the task but much more difficult to become highly proficient. Figure 6–5d shows a more complex learning curve and also introduces a very important concept in learning — that of *plateaus*. The trainee initially learns at a very slow rate. This stage is likely to be discouraging for both trainer and trainee. The length of this stage will depend on such factors as the complexity of task to be learned, the motivation and ability of the trainee, and the competence of the trainer. The trainee in this example next learns at an increasing rate. Following this rapid rate of increase, he reaches a plateau in which no learning appears to be taking place. In the next stage, he begins to learn at a rapid rate. Finally, the trainee reaches a final plateau, which represents his maximum performance level.

At the first plateau in Figure 6–5d a great deal of learning may be taking place, since the trainee may be subconsciously synthesizing what has previously been learned and thereby placing the parts into a meaningful whole. In fact, this gestalting process, as it is sometimes called, is one reason why plateaus occur.[27] A second reason for the occurrence of plateaus is that motivation may decline. The trainee because of his prior rapid learning rate may become bored with the learning situation or he may feel quite fatigued from the previous rapid learning. Another explanation for plateaus is that prior incorrect learning is being eliminated. For example, a person who has learned to type through the trial and error method may learn very quickly the correct method for typing, but reach a plateau period during which the old habits are being extinguished. Finally, plateaus may occur if the task requires sequential activities to be learned that increase in complexity and are dependent upon prior activities. The trainee will need time to assimilate fully the new skills so that they can be built upon. It should be noted that the first plateau in Figure 6–5d is referred to as a *false plateau* because the trainee appears to have stopped learning but, in fact, has not.

To illustrate the stages shown in Figure 6–5d, think about an individual who is trying to learn a computer language. Initially, learning is likely to be very slow, as the trainee has to learn the specific symbols and terminology used in the language. However, once these have been learned, additional ones may be learned quickly, and the individual may begin to master writing computer programs of a fairly simple nature. Next, the individual may appear to stop learning as prior steps are synthesized. The person may then suddenly begin to write more complex programs and approach peak proficiency. Finally, the individual may reach a new plateau in which everything learned previously is completely integrated and "overlearning" helps maintain peak proficiency.

If the trainer has some idea in advance of the shape the learning curve is likely to take and also understands the conditions that influence that shape, he or she will be in a better position to design the training to enhance learning. For example, knowing at what points the trainee might become discouraged or lose motivation may permit the trainer to cope with these periods by making special efforts to encourage the trainee at these times.

An attempt to use learning curves for training has been provided by Knowles and Bell.[28] Their approach involves three steps: (1) making sure existing training methods were sound, (2) finding out the average time it should take the trainee to learn the job, and (3) developing a standard learning curve for the job. Each trainee's performance was compared to the standard and those who were not performing were dropped from the program or moved into other lines of work. Those who were performing at higher levels than the standard were moved directly into full productive work sooner than the average trainees. Knowles and Bell reported that the training time was cut from between 60 and 180 days to 22 days because the quick learners were moved from training into full productive work faster, while the slow learners were dropped from the program or moved elsewhere. One problem with their analysis, however, was that plateaus appear to have been neglected. For this reason, effective learners may have been eliminated just at that point where the assimilation of material was taking place.

Knowledge of Results (Feedback)

If trainees are to learn efficiently and effectively, they must know how they are doing — they must be provided with knowledge of the results of their performance (KOR). KOR represents a feedback mechanism that "provides learners with information on how well they are doing and whether or not their responses are correct."[29] If KOR is not present, the trainee may learn the wrong skills or knowledge, thus creating a dysfunctional learning situation. For example, a trainee who is learning how to run a machine but is not told when errors have been made may learn inappropriate techniques. Further, if KOR is not present, the trainee may not learn efficiently, even though learning may ultimately take place. For example, in one study, in which subjects shot at an unseen moving target,[30] one group was told whether or not they were shooting in the vicinity of the target; the other group was not given such feedback. Not surprisingly, the feedback group outperformed the group given no feedback. However, it is interesting to note that the group not given feedback eventually did improve its performance, although it took nearly twice as long as the feedback group. Thus, the learning, while ultimately somewhat effective, was extremely inefficient.

KOR appears to influence learning because (1) it provides information to the trainee so that erroneous behavior may be corrected, and (2) it has a positive influence on motivation. The fact that corrections are made quickly means that inappropriate learning can be eliminated before it is *internalized* by the trainee. Motivation may be influenced because feedback serves to reinforce correct behavior and to provide an incentive. As noted earlier, learning is enhanced when both intrinsic motivation and extrinsic rewards are present and when the individual has a positive self-image. KOR may stimulate intrinsic motivation for individuals who value learning per se and serve as an extrinsic reward for individuals by making them aware that their learning will contribute to other goals. In addition, KOR, by making the individual aware of success, can contribute to a favorable self-image. What if the individual is *not* successful, however? Locke has suggested that in such cases KOR can be used by the trainer to help the trainees modify their goals.[31]

There is a great deal of research indicating that KOR facilitates learning. A number of generalizations based upon research concerning KOR and learning have been presented by Biel.[32]

1. KOR increases the rate and level of learning.
2. When KOR is removed, the level of learning and performance generally drops.
3. The more immediate the KOR, the greater the learning.
4. The greater the amount of relevant feedback, the greater the learning.
5. For a particular learning situation, some methods of providing KOR are better than others.
6. KOR has motivational value.

In light of these research-based generalizations, we can see that there are a number of dimensions to effective KOR. As these generalizations indicate, the timing, relevance, and accuracy of the feedback are important variables that influence the relationship between KOR and learning. The timing of feedback, for example, is important for at least two reasons. First, the sooner negative feedback is provided in a learning situation, the more likely is the trainee to see it as relevant and have an opportunity to take corrective action. For example, for the instructor in a driver training course to say: "Joe, you should have slowed down 5 miles back," is not likely to be seen as relevant by the trainee if he has been stopped and given a speeding ticket; nor is it in time for him to take appropriate corrective action. Second, the timing of feedback is related to whether the trainee receives the correct amount of feedback. Too much feedback provided at a given time relative to the complexity of the task may result in information overload; too little may be inadequate to perform effectively. Both conditions are likely to cause the trainee to become frustrated and consequently reduce the amount of learning that takes place.

Reinforcement and Conditioning

Closely related to KOR and feedback is the principle of reinforcement, which is also referred to as the *law of effect*. For effective learning, desired trainee responses must be rewarded (or positively reinforced) and negative responses ignored or perhaps punished (negatively reinforced). Psychologists once argued that positive reinforcement was superior to negative reinforcement, but in recent years they have defined *some* situations in which using a combination of both positive and negative reinforcement appears superior.[33] In training programs, as indicated earlier, extrinsic rewards for learning may be provided both by the trainer and the organization.

Research has generally shown that if a desired response is reinforced 100 per cent of the time, behavior will be learned more rapidly; at the same time, it will be forgotten (or "extinguished") more quickly. *Partial reinforcement* or reinforcing desired responses only part of the time, on the other hand, although usually resulting in slower learning, will make the behavior learned more resistant to extinction.[34]

Many of these observations relate primarily to what is called *instrumental* or *operant* conditioning, the nature of which is still very much debated by psychologists.[35] A simpler type of conditioning, called *classical* conditioning, is less controversial and may be used to facilitate certain types of learning.

In classical conditioning, the subject is taught to make a response to some *stimulus* because the response is reinforced. An association is formed between a stimulus and a response. Then, as the stimulus that created the response is modified, behavior may be changed. The classic work in this area was that of Ivan Pavlov, who observed that dogs would salivate (response) when food (a stimulus) was given to them. Pavlov further observed that he could train a dog to salivate when a bell was rung by making the bell the stimulus. He did this by presenting the dog with food immediately after ringing the bell. Eventually, the dog began to salivate in response to the bell, even when food was not presented. What had happened was that the dog had associated the sound of the bell with the presence of food. Thus, a natural response (salivation) became associated with what was previously a neutral stimulus. Pavlov also found that if the bell was rung and food was not presented, the conditioned response began to diminish and eventually would be extinguished, because the association between the bell and the food no longer existed.

Classical conditioning can be used by trainers in development programs.[36] For example, paratroopers must be trained to jump from an airplane when a signal is given. In the training program the trainer will shout "Go" (stimulus) and the trainee will pretend to jump (response). In actual conditions, however, with the aircraft door open, the paratroopers will not be able to hear the command. Therefore, in the training program when the trainer shouts "Go" he will also slap the trainee on the buttocks. The slap on the buttocks is therefore paired with the comand, "Go." Eventually the command and the slap are associated and the verbal command can be omitted. Thus, the previously neutral stimulus (slap) becomes a conditioned stimulus that elicits a response (jumping). In a similar fashion, training employees to respond to a bell when an overhead crane is moving through the plant carrying tons of steel is a stimulus that results in a response in terms of safety.

Active Versus Passive Learning

It is generally accepted that active learning (sometimes called *involvement*) is superior to passive learning. The employee who merely is told or reads how to perform a task is not likely to be as proficient as the trainee who is first shown how to do the task and then is given an opportunity to actually do it. Some passive learning must take place, since one cannot begin to perform a task of any complexity without receiving information before performing it. Therefore, "it is necessary to mix passive training methods with active ones."[37] Mixing of active and passive methods will also facilitate learning by reducing boredom and by making use of multiple sensory stimuli. The trainee who both reads and is told how to run a machine, sees the machine run, and then runs the machine is using a variety of senses in learning. Another principle of learning involved in active learning is repetition. Repetition facilitates learning when KOR is present, provided that such repetition is correct and does not continue to the point of being boring. Thus, the old adage that "practice makes perfect" appears to have application in helping trainees to learn.

Mass Versus Distributed Learning

An important consideration in designing development programs is whether the content of the program should be presented and practice sessions take place within a short time interval (mass learning) or spread out over a period of time (distributed learning).[38] In general, research suggests that distributed learning is superior to mass learning when the content is complex, there is a great deal of content, and maintaining interest for a long period is a problem.

Distributed learning is likely to be more effective than mass learning when the content is complex, because the trainee is not able to assimilate all of it in a short time period. For example, the student reading this text is probably engaged in a distributed learning situation if the text is being used in a course which is conducted over a number of weeks. It is unlikely that effective learning would take place if the student were told to read the book in one or two days. Problems would result, not only because of the complexity of the material but also because of the amount of content to be covered.

In addition to these advantages of distributed learning, there is evidence that it appears to facilitate "more rapid learning and more permanent retention."[39] If the material to be learned is very simple, however, these generalizations do not apply, and mass learning would provide more favorable results.

Despite the general superiority of distributed learning versus mass learning, distributed learning is infrequently used in industrial development programs. The lack of use of this principle is often due to practical necessity. For example, it may not be possible to have a new production employee work for one hour a day or for one day a week until he or she is trained. Further, it may not be possible for a manager to attend a management development program over an extended period of time because this would disrupt the work schedule. To overcome such problems, the personnel department has a number of alternatives.

In some cases, training may be alternated with some simple but useful activity. For example, the trainee learning how to operate a machine could be assigned some of the time to bring materials to an individual who is already an experienced machinist on that machine. This not only would give the trainee useful work to do but would constitute an extension of the training program since he would see the tasks that he was learning to do being performed by others. Different aspects of training can sometimes be alternated. For example, one young college graduate was hired to do psychological test interpretations in the corporate personnel department of a large company. He also had to become familiar with the firm's overall personnel policy manual — a very boring task. His supervisor purposely alternated his training so that part of the time he was learning about testing while spending only a couple of hours a day studying the firm's policy manual. If acceptable to both the firm and the trainees, individuals may be hired on a part-time basis during the training period. Finally, if a present employee is learning a new job, he might be permitted to spend part of each day carrying out activities on his old job while learning the new one.

Whole Versus Part Learning

Another consideration in designing development programs is whether the whole concept or skill should be presented or whether it should be broken into parts.[40] In general, two interrelated variables appear to influence whether whole or part presentation is preferable: (1) task complexity and (2) task organization. Complexity refers to the difficulty of the various subtasks; organization refers to the interrelatedness of the subtasks. Whole presentation generally appears to be more effective when organization is high, since understanding the logic of the total task would be impeded by breaking it up into parts. In addition, as task complexity increases when task organization is high, the superiority of whole presentation is generally even greater. Presentation by parts, on the other hand, tends to be superior when organization is low. This is true even if complexity exists and some parts of the total task are significantly more difficult than others. This is because under conditions of low organization, more complex units can be dealt with *separately*.

Transfer of Learning

A basic consideration in any development program is the extent to which training, when provided off the job, can be transferred to the job setting. Learning in a training environment may serve no function if it cannot be transferred to the actual job. Two theories relating to how maximum learning transfer can be facilitated frequently have been given attention. The first, referred to as the *identical element* theory, maintains that for transfer of learning to occur, identical elements must exist in the old and new settings, and that the more similar the two settings are, the more likely is the transfer. Advocates of this theory favor on-the-job training, discussed in Chapter 7, since such training would consist of identical elements.

The second theory of transfer is referred to as *transfer through principle*. This theory maintains that transfer of learning will occur even if identical elements are not present as long as principles are learned which can be *generalized* to other situations. The reader of this text, for example, should be hoping that transfer through principle can occur. This is because he or she is learning principles, concepts and tools in reading that hopefully will have application in an actual work environment in which he or she is now involved, or will be upon graduation from college. Neither of these theories can be said to be better than the other. However, having identical elements seems generally to provide the greatest likelihood of transfer.

To facilitate the transfer of learning, a number of guidelines based upon research can be made to aid the designer of development programs in decision making.[41] Since the greatest transfer results when identical elements are present in the learning and work environments, the trainer should try to maximize the similarity between the learning situation and the situation in which the trainee will actually work. The similarity should include not only the physical equipment but similar noise levels and supervisory styles. Transfer appears to be facilitated if the trainee is given adequate experience with the task in the training situation. The trainee must be permitted to learn the desired behavior completely prior to being placed in the actual work environment. Transfer of learning may be enhanced in *transfer through principle* situations if the trainee is exposed to a variety of conditions in the training environment. For example, in teaching managers about human relations in small groups, the trainer might provide a number of different situations in which the managers could try the concepts presented in the training. Each manager might be asked to apply what he or she has learned, with the other manager trainees assuming the role of managers and with them also acting as nonmanagers. Each manager trainee could then note which human relations concepts and ideas worked in both situations and which needed to be modified from the one situation to the other. This would permit him to begin to generalize from newly acquired knowledge. Finally, transfer of learning will be facilitated if a number of the principles of learning such as motivation, KOR, and reinforcement previously discussed are applied in the learning environment and on the job.

It should be noted that negative as well as positive transfer of learning can occur. What one learns in a development program could be inappropriate for on-the-job behavior. For example, in the learning environment, the pace of the work may be fairly slow and the trainer (acting as a supervisor) may interact on a personal basis with the trainees. However, when the trainee reports to his supervisor in the actual work environment and begins to work slowly and to "joke around" with the supervisor he may learn to his regret that the work environment is not the same as the training environment.

Retention of Learning

A final consideration in designing development programs, closely related to the transfer of training, is the problem of retention. As with transfer of training, it appears that retention is facilitated if a number of the learning principles are applied in the learning. For example, if the individual is motivated in the learning environment he is likely to learn more, which will result in more being retained, at least up to a point. Similarly if the material which has been learned is meaningful, more is likely to be retained.

Retention will be facilitated if what the individual has learned in the training environment is reinforced on the job. If the work environment does not support what has been learned, then the individual is unlikely to retain the learning — he certainly will not use it. For example, in a study by Fleishman, it was found that human relations training was effective in producing on-the-job behavior changes *only* if the trainees' superiors supported such behavior.[42] In short, if what the individual has learned is interfered with, retention will be diminished.

Principles of Learning: Overview

The previous discussion indicates that in designing and conducting development programs, numerous alternatives are available, and better ones may be chosen by drawing on various principles of learning. We have treated these principles separately for purposes of exposition, but the principles are interdependent. For example, task complexity is related to individual differences, learning curves, KOR, reinforcement and conditioning, and active as opposed to passive learning. The basic reason for this is that these principles mutually reinforce each other in making an impact on the individual. Further, in many cases, the use of two principles instead of only one may provide more than twice as great a positive effect on the trainee. That is, their use may be *synergistic*. Synergy is often referred to as the $2 + 2 = 5$ effect, meaning that the whole is greater than the sum of its parts. Thus, in developmental decision making, personnel must consider the many learning principles mutually interacting with each other to provide an overall effect on the trainee, rather than attempting to evaluate the impact of each principle separately and in isolation.

EVALUATION OF TRAINING

The final phase in the planned organization learning decision-making process is the evaluation of development programs. In this section we will discuss two important decisions that must be made in evaluation of development programs: (1) criterion measurement and (2) experimental design.

Criterion Measurement

As mentioned earlier, top management gives its support to the implementation of training programs because it expects some desired change to occur. "The purpose of training evaluation, therefore, should be to determine *if* such management-desired changes *did* occur as a *result* of the training."[43]

To be successful, evaluation needs to be considered an integral part of the training program.

Evaluation must be built into the training program from its very conception. Evaluation cannot be thrown in at the end of training without regard to the goals of the program, knowledge of pre-training performance of the trainees, and the methods used to present the training. A hastily or ill-planned evaluation cannot be expected to give a meaningful appraisal of the effectiveness of the training program.[44]

Evaluation of training programs must be planned, as must all managerial decisions, in light of its objectives. It is for this reason that Figure 6–1 shows evaluation criteria being generated immediately after the establishment of program objectives and preceding other evaluation considerations.

Kirkpatrick has suggested that evaluation criteria are needed at four levels: (1) reaction, (2) learning, (3) behavior, and (4) results.[45] Reaction refers to asking the participants what they thought of the program. Such measurement is essentially subjective and may often be biased. For example, in one training program the trainees (five managers) gave positive reports because they did not want to "get into trouble" with the firm's corporate personnel staff. Care also must be taken because the trainer can try to create favorable evaluations that do not relate to what has been or should have been learned.[46] The ease with which such distortion can be introduced is illustrated in a study conducted by Kelley.[47] Students were told that their regular instructor was out of town and that the class would have a substitute. The students were given information about the substitute with one group of students led to believe that his personality was "cold," while another group was led to believe it was "warm." Even though both groups then were taught by the same instructor, the group told his personality was "warm" rated him more favorably than the group told it was "cold."

The learning level criterion measures the extent to which skills, knowledge, and attitudes covered in the program are understood and acquired by the trainee. Ideally, these areas will be measured as objectively and quantifiably as possible.

The behavior level refers to the measurement of actual job performance. The important question of transfer of learning is the prime concern at this level. Unfortunately, there is ample evidence that transfer is often low.[48] At this level it is likely that both objective and subjective criteria will be utilized since some transfer of learning, such as turning out pieces on a machine, may be directly observable, while other learning, such as attitude changes, may have to be inferred.

The final level of criteria for evaluation — results — involves relating training outcomes to organizational *objectives*. Does the training pay off for the organization? Such payoff may be measured in reduced accidents, costs, grievances, absenteeism, or increases in production, satisfaction, and quality.[49] At this level, difficulty is likely to result because of ambiguous organizational objectives and the need to tie training to organizational outcomes. MBO, as discussed in Chapter 2, may help alleviate difficulties in this regard. Evaluation at all four levels is necessary so that the personnel department can ascertain whether meaningful and useful development programs are being conducted well.

The selection of criteria is not an easy decision. Criteria must be both reliable and valid. To use a criterion simply because it is available or has been used before may result in meaningless information; it must be directly related to the firm's objectives. For example, managers at different organizational levels may need to be trained in different skills. Therefore, different criteria would be needed to evaluate development programs for different levels of management. As Odiorne has suggested for evaluating managerial training, criteria should vary depending on the level of manager being trained.[50]

The criteria selected must also be measureable and be specific enough to permit assessment of successful and unsuccessful accomplishment of the objectives. For example, suppose the firm's objective is the improving of product quality. The criterion might well be percentage of rejects. However, the organization would have to specify what percentage of rejects for products would be acceptable.

The timing of the administration of the criterion measure is also important. If the criterion is administered immediately after a development program, one is looking primarily at evaluation at the reaction and learning levels, whereas a later administration is more likely to be an evaluation at the behavior and results levels. One must be careful in using evaluation at the reaction or learning levels as predictors for behavior and results levels since training can be *encapsulated* (i.e., what is learned is applied only in the training environment but not on the job). For evaluation at the behavior and results levels, longitudinal studies that provide a sufficient time for the desired changes to take effect before measurement is undertaken must be carried out. In addition, longitudinal studies are necessary to assess whether learning persists and perhaps even whether or not learning took place, if this can only be assessed on the job.

Development program evaluation, if not carried out at a relevant time, may lead to erroneous conclusions. For example, Malm has reported on a summer training program for governmental administrators in which evaluation of a reaction nature was undertaken immediately after the program each year.[51] This evaluation showed that some of the participants believed that certain materials were too theoretical and not sufficiently related to their current operating needs. Despite this feedback, the materials were kept in the program, since it was believed that they were important to long run success. Evaluation after about six years showed that certain materials that participants had at one point thought too theoretical and impractical in terms of current job needs were now believed to be most important and valuable, since they had broadened perspectives and developed insights needed for advancement to higher responsibilities.

From this discussion it can be seen that a number of decisions must be made concerning the selection of evaluation criteria.[52] None of these decisions is easy, but all are important. Failure to exercise care in either the selection of criteria or the timing of its administration is likely to result in erroneous evaluation and thereby contribute to inappropriate decisions being made in regard to future development programs.

Experimental Design

In evaluating training programs, the design of the evaluation methodology is an important consideration. Two design considerations of major importance are: (1) whether or not before and/or after criterion measures will be used and (2) whether or not control groups will be used. Answers to these questions will indicate what type of experimental design is to be chosen. In this section we will discuss the four designs shown in Figure 6–6.[53]

It is possible to conduct a training program and at the end give participants a measuring device (e.g., test, questionnaire, interview) to see if they have learned the material. This is called an after-only design. Unfortunately, such a design does not tell us whether the learning will be transferred to the job nor whether it will contribute to the achievement of organization objectives. An additional problem with the after-only design is that one cannot be certain that anything was learned as a result of the training. All

1. After-only measures without a control group.

    TP M_2

2. Before-after measures without a control group.

    M_1 TP M_2

3. After-only measures with a control group.

    Trained group: TP M_2

    Control group: TP M_2

4. Before-after measures with a single control group.

    Trained group: M_1 TP M_2

    Control group: M_1 M_2

M_1 = before measure
M_2 = after measure
TP = training program

Figure 6-6   *Four research designs for evaluation of development efforts.*

the after-only design provides is a score for each individual; we do not know what skills, knowledge, or attitudes the trainee brought to the learning situation in the first place. Therefore, an individual who scores well on a test being used to evaluate learning in the training program may be demonstrating prior expertise rather than current learning.

To overcome the problems of the after-only design, a measuring device can be given before the training and again after the training. In such a case learning may be assessed by comparing the results of the measure taken prior to the training and those after. (Hopefully, the trainees will exhibit improved behavior and attitudes after the training.) It is easy to make the invalid assumption when using the before and after design, however, that a better score on the after measure than on the before measure indicates that learning has occurred. This assumption is invalid for two reasons. First, the use of a before measure may "sensitize" the trainees so that they look, whether consciously or unconsciously, for aspects of the training situation that relate to the before measure. Thus, while learning will have occurred it may have done so primarily within the limited range of the before measure, which, like any evaluation measure, represents a sample, and would not be expected to cover the full range of material incorporated into the training program. Second, the assumption that a better score on the after measure than the before measure indicates that learning has occurred may be invalid because the learning might have resulted from uncontrolled events rather than from the development program. Suppose, for example, that while a training program is being conducted for supervisors on how to encourage employees to submit suggestions in their firm's suggestion system, a new manual is distributed to all of these supervisors on this same topic. If employees begin to submit more suggestions, can we say that the training induced the change and therefore was successful, or did the new manual contribute to the change? To compound the problem, suppose the company also changed the reward structure for adopted suggestions and publicized the change to the employees while the training program was going on. Now if employees submit more suggestions, to what extent has this behavior been influenced by better informed supervisors (whether from the training, the manual, or both), by better informed subordinates, or by both? To help overcome these problems control groups can be used.

A control group consists of individuals who do not receive the training. These individuals should be comparable to the trainee group in characteristics which might have an impact on the training.[54] If such comparability does not exist, then the trainee group might appear to have learned more or less relative to the control group than it really has. For example, if a complex manual skill has been taught in a training program, the control group and trainee group should be comparable on manual dexterity.

Control groups can be used with both after-only and before and after designs. When a control group is used with an after-only design, we can compare the two groups on the criteria established to evaluate the development program. If the trainee group performs better than the control group, we have some basis on which to say that the program was effective. This assessment must be a qualified one, however, because we do not know if the two groups differed in the skills, knowledges, or attitudes being dealt with in the training program, since no before measurement was undertaken. Further, we do not know if any uncontrollable events might have confounded the results. For example, when control groups are used, problems are created if the control and trainee groups interact while the evaluation phase is going on. In such a case the control group may receive some of the training "through" the trainee group. If so, this will distort the measure of effectiveness of the training since any differences between the two groups on the after measure will not be as great as they would have been had the two groups not interacted. In longitudinal studies, this problem of interaction increases because of the time span involved and since other system changes, such as promotions, transfers, and temporary assignment of individuals, are likely to place members of the trainee and control groups together.

The before and after design with a control group provides more information about the effectiveness of the development program than the other designs discussed thus far. This design permits us to obtain some idea of group comparability before the program begins about the material to be taught in the program, since a before measure has been used. After the training we can compare the two groups in two ways. First, we can compare them on the measuring device used after the training to see if they differ significantly. Second, we can compare each group's after measure to its before measure to see which group has changed the most. The ideal situation, from an evaluation standpoint, would be for the control group to be comparable to the trainee group prior to the training and to have the control group show no change on the after measure while the trainee group shows a major *favorable* change. We emphasize favorable here, since it is possible that the trainee group could show no change or even an unfavorable change. Such results would indicate that no learning or transfer has taken place, depending on when measurement is done, or, even more serious, that the development program has actually been dysfunctional.

We believe that, of the four designs presented in Figure 6–6, the before and after design with a control group should generally be used because of the greater information it provides. However, in some cases the use of this design may not be feasible. For example, in a small organization there may not be enough employees to permit the formation of a comparable control group. In addition, control groups represent a cost to the firm. Since the control group is not receiving training, which presumably will have a desired impact from the organization's standpoint, there is an opportunity cost associated with not having this group trained sooner. Further, since control groups are given the measuring devices, the firm must incur the cost of developing, using, scoring, and interpreting these items. Finally, control groups are costly because individuals are taken away from the job to complete the measuring devices, which again represents an opportunity cost. Thus, from a pure cost standpoint, the least expensive type of experimental design is likely to be the after-only without a control group design. The organization should recognize, however, that the dollar costs are not the only costs associated with control groups; there are psychological and sociological "costs" as well. These costs may occur because both trainee and control groups may feel they are being manipulated by management if they realize that an evaluation "experiment" is going on. In addition, in incentive pay systems the group that does not receive the training initially may believe that it has been cheated if the trainee group begins to get higher incentive pay sooner. In such a case it is possible that some members of the control group will show their dissatisfaction through absenteeism or lower productivity. Given the tradeoffs of the various costs and the additional information provided by the more complex designs, the decision maker must choose which one to use. Just because the most "scientific" design cannot be used does not mean that evaluation attempts should not be made. Rather, the most satisfactory viable design should be used, even if it may not be the most complex and "scientific."

Despite the need for evaluation of training, there is evidence that little evaluation is done at all in industry, and what is done tends to be of the reaction type. A 1953 review found only one company in 40 making any "scientific evaluation of supervisory training programs"; a 1952 review of 476 studies "failed to find any research that examined both pre-training and on-the-job performance"; a 1961 study "found that most companies spent less than 5 per cent of their time and training budgets on evaluation"; and comments made in 1970 indicated that evaluation of federally funded programs was not much more than annual reports and that there were few "sound empirical data for managerial training programs" available.[55] In 1959, Belasco and Trice stated: "Despite the fact that evaluation yields benefits to both the practitioner and the academician, probably 99 percent of all ongoing training efforts still are not systematically evaluated."[56]

There are a number of reasons for this lack of evaluation. These reasons can be classified as design, attitudinal, and cost-benefit.[57] Reasons related to design deal with the problems of criterion measurement and experimental design, which we have already discussed. When such problems exist, some people give up on evaluation because it is believed to be too difficult to carry out.

Reasons of an attitudinal nature for not evaluating training arise because some individuals believe that any and all training is good and therefore evaluation is unnecessary. Such individuals uncritically accept training as worthwhile. Another attitudinal reason for not evaluating training is the fear of evaluation on the part of the personnel department. Personnel departments often fear evaluation because it is perceived as an attack on what is being done. Frequently, this fear results because personnel fails to see that evaluation can be beneficial by providing feedback, which may be very useful in designing future development programs. This fear may result because personnel does not know why the evaluation is being done. In addition, personnel may be concerned about who will conduct the evaluation. Personnel may fear evaluation because of a lack of understanding of evaluation methodology. Finally, top management may not understand the problems involved in program evaluation and not support personnel in conducting evaluative efforts.

Reasons for not evaluating training of a cost-benefit nature may also arise. Some companies simply cannot afford the expense involved in such evaluation. In such cases the intuitive judgment of the person in charge of training is likely to be used and he may assume that he is using appropriate principles of learning. One manager, for example, in his capacity as a training director in a moderately sized company simply could not obtain funds from top management to carry out very much program evaluation, and had to rely on "intuition" in evaluating most of the firm's developmental efforts.

The personnel department should be interested in evaluation of its programs and efforts for two reasons. First, the number of dollars spent on development is large and the potential for savings may be great. For example, a 1967 report of all nonpilot and nonmanagement training being done within United Airlines revealed an annual expenditure of about $14 million.[58] Another study revealed one firm investing $30 million annually in training activities and another five firms that reported annual investments of $5 million each.[59] IBM, which began formal development programs several decades ago, had in 1975 more than 5000 full- and part-time trainers offering courses in management development, technical updating, and job retraining involving 10 million student hours which represented "the equivalent of nearly 40,000 full-time students receiving 15 hours a week in a 32-week college."[60] While IBM claimed it had no accurate estimates of the overall cost since each division handled its own training, it was estimated that it spent $80 to $90 million per year in the mid-1960's and about $100 million in 1970. Savings of only 1 percent could mean substantial amounts for any of these firms.

Second, personnel should be interested in evaluation of development because of the need to justify the value of such activities. When economic conditions are unfavorable for the firm and various subunits within the organization are fighting for scarce resources, those programs which can be best justified on a cost-benefit basis are likely to get the resources. Since the value of training programs has usually not been adequately justified in the past, such programs are often among the first to be cut in times of poor profitability. "Training budgets tend to expand in periods of company prosperity and to shrink dramatically in periods of low profits. Many training directors complain that 'when things get tough, training is the first place they cut.' "[61] Thus personnel may well need to justify the value of its planned organizational learning activities in order to ensure the continuance of such efforts.

MANAGEMENT SCIENCE, COMPUTERS, AND CONTINGENCIES

Management Science and Computers

There have been a number of attempts to apply quantitative management science techniques and computers to organizational development efforts. At the need determination stage, for example, PERT was applied to a large scale project at the Educational Testing Service designed to pinpoint for disadvantaged preschool children components of early education associated with various aspects of later development.[62] Seven initial task force networks were developed in which there were about 220 items. It took about a month to gather this information and feed it into the computer. Among the major activities in the networks were: plan, prepare, and administer exploratory pretests; designate test subjects; and plan data analysis.[63]

Mathematical and statistical techniques have been used in research involving the principles of learning discussed in this chapter and in the study of learning curves. As indicated in Chapter 3, the logarithmic learning curve model has been used extensively to predict *organizational* learning. Further, considerable research has been carried out by psychologists of a mathematical nature with respect to learning curves. It is beyond the scope of this text, however, to discuss such learning models.[64] Statistical techniques have been utilized in the evaluation stage of development, as indicated earlier. In this area the computer has had a significant impact on training, since a number of computer programs have been developed and widely used for carrying out quickly and inexpensively calculations needed in utilizing these statistical techniques.[65]

Quantitative cost-benefit analysis, as discussed in Chapter 2, although not strictly a "management science" technique, has also been used infrequently in planned organizational learning processes, especially in the evaluation of training programs. One study that used cost-benefit analysis to evaluate training was reported by Jones and Moxham.[66] The study was conducted over a five-year period and involved training machine operators.

The study identified and measured the changes in costs brought about by the change in training and then went on to identify and measure the results of this change and to relate the costs and results in money terms.[67]

The results of the study indicated an 8:1 ratio of total benefits to total costs. The authors found that costs were easier to identify and calculate than benefits. It should be noted that in this study the trainees were semiskilled workers and that the problems of identifying and calculating costs and benefits become even more difficult for management training because "there are many difficulties in relating a training investment at management levels to results."[68] As we will indicate in Chapter 7, computers and management science approaches have also been applied to specific training techniques such as business gaming (or simulation) and computer assisted instruction (CAI).

Contingencies

We have already indicated that organizational size and financial condition are key contingencies with respect to developmental efforts. In addition, the stability of the environment in which the firm operates represents another important contingency. In relatively dynamic environments, development is likely to be more difficult for the firm because of constantly changing conditions that create a need for new development programs. Thus, more novel developmental design situations are likely to be needed, and under some extremely dynamic conditions, development efforts must be carried out on an informal basis, since by the time any highly formalized efforts have been planned and developed, they will have been rendered obsolete. Finally, the evaluation of training programs will be more difficult, since longitudinal studies will be confounded to a greater extent by the changing conditions.

SUMMARY

Development will occur in organizations whether it is planned or not. In addition, individuals will require continuous training throughout their careers. Therefore, all organizations, whether formally or informally, engage in some type of development activities for their employees. Such activities are likely to be most effective when they represent planned organizational learning. The organization needs to plan its development activities by carefully identifying problems that training can overcome most effectively. This planning process should entail determining training needs and designing programs in light of well-accepted principles of learning so that efficient and effective learning takes place to meet both individual and organizational objectives. Once a development program has been conducted, the program and its results should be evaluated. All phases of planned organizational learning efforts need to be undertaken while recognizing that the contingencies of firm size, financial condition, and stability will influence the nature of development activities. Many different training techniques have been developed to meet different developmental needs, and we will focus attention on the more effective and widely used of these in Chapter 7.

DISCUSSION AND STUDY QUESTIONS

1. "The employee development process represents a series of sequential decisions." Comment. If you agree with this statement, give your reasons why. If you disagree, indicate

the specific types of decisions you believe might have to be considered together, rather than sequentially, and give your reasons why.

2. How might each of the following events influence the need for learning in the firm? In each case indicate whether organization, task, or person analysis would be primarily involved.

    a. The Employee Retirement Income Security Act (which we will discuss in Chapter 12) was passed in 1974. This was an extremely complex law affecting the management of pensions and other employee benefits, and required firms that provided benefits to disclose information to all of their employees about their benefits.

    b. The firm's Vice President of Marketing suddenly resigns, giving the firm one month's notice.

    c. The Federally established minimum wage was increased from $2.30/hour to $2.65/hour as of January 1, 1978.

    d. Joe Doakes, a senior accountant, aged 42, was divorced a month ago and since that time has been frequently late to work. His superior thinks he has noticed alcohol on Joe's breath on a couple of occasions.

3. A very profitable department store chain hires only college graduates in the upper 25 per cent of their class for managerial and professional positions. Each person hired is exposed to a year-long management development program. In this program, they are rotated from department to department in one of the chain's stores, and given a chance to observe how inventories, price markdowns, etc. are handled, and are given some opportunity to wait on customers, and to ring up both cash and credit card sales on the cash register. During the 52-week program they are also given a chance to spend about eight weeks observing the firm's managers working in its corporate offices, e.g., two weeks in accounting, one week in personnel. During the 52 weeks, three or four days are devoted to special group management development efforts. Trainers from the corporate office personnel department present full day programs to groups of all the trainees in the program in the particular geographical operating division to which they have been assigned, on subjects such as creative thinking or human relations. After the 52-week period is up, some trainees are promoted into positions as assistant managers in one of the firm's stores, department heads in a store, or in some cases into central office junior staff positions (such as an accountant or personnel specialist). The firm's pay is competitive, its management is generally progressive and receptive to new ideas, yet 32 per cent of the trainees resign from the firm during the 52-week training period, and two years after the end of the training program, only about 42 per cent of those college graduates initially hired have stayed with the company. (*Very* few have been let go because of poor performance—the vast majority of those who have left the firm have done so voluntarily.) Does the firm have a training problem? If so, how can it determine the reasons for the problem, and develop decision strategies for overcoming any problems it may have pinpointed?

4. Comment on the degree to which you agree with each of the following statements made by trainers. In each case give your reasons why.
   a. "Joe is brilliant. I can teach him the basics of computer programming in two hours."
   b. "The parts of this highly complex job are highly interrelated. Therefore, I will break the job into parts and cover them sequentially so that my trainees can grasp them better."
   c. "I find that my trainees learn best when I praise them every time they do the job right."
   d. "When I teach Mary to do a job I try to do it under conditions exactly like she's going to have to face when she actually gets on the job. I even chew tobacco and growl once in a while like Mary's potential supervisor does."
   e. "When we train our first line supervisors in such subjects as human relations, cost control, or whatever it might be, we always try to train their superiors (the general foremen) and the general foremen's boss, the plant manager, in these subjects first."

5. In one supermarket chain, the personnel department was responsible for training trainers in how to train. In one training session, which was conducted in one specially constructed training room on the second floor of one of its supermarkets, several trainees, who were all head meat cutters in their stores, took turns in training each other in how to make certain cuts from a side of beef which had been provided for the training. After each trainee taught another in making a particular cut, the other trainees and the trainer from the personnel department who was in charge of the session indicated to the individual who had played the role of the trainer those aspects of his training which were well done, and those which were not. Each of the head meat cutters was given an opportunity to train several other head meat cutters. All head meat cutters knew how to perform all tasks which they were training each other in — the purpose of the training was to make them more proficient in teaching meat cutting to their own subordinates. How effective would you consider this form of training? What principles of learning were utilized? Were any phases of planned learning omitted, or principles of learning violated?

6. What principles of learning would be involved if your instructor required you to answer orally any of the questions in this text? Would there be any additional principles involved if both your instructor and classmates responded to your analysis?

7. One large manufacturing firm periodically conducted two week management development sessions for its middle line and staff managers away from the job, often at universities where there were adequate training facilities. In these training sessions, case studies were presented, the managers were asked to engage in some role playing of human relations problems, financial analyses were delved into, organizational problems were explored, etc. When the trainees went back to their jobs, the personnel training staff

conducting the two-week sessions *never* provided the trainees' superiors with any specific comments as to how well the middle level managers had performed in the program. Do you agree with this learning strategy? If so, which principles of learning were being adhered to? If not, which available principles of learning do you believe were inappropriately ignored?

8. Teacher evaluations by students are required at many colleges and universities. Often students rate their professor on a scale of from 1 to 5 on a number of factors such as "interest in the course," "mastery of subject matter," "organization of materials," and "quality of examinations." Further, in some large universities, norms are developed so that obtaining, for example, a rating of 4.1 out of a maximum of 5 points on a particular factor might only put the professor in the 35th percentile on this factor when compared with all other professor evaluations. Finally, such evaluations invariably are made by students before they have studied for and taken their final examination; and sometimes the evaluation forms are completed by students a week or so before the semester has ended. How would you evaluate such ratings in terms of what was discussed in the chapter in light of. the evaluation of developmental efforts?

9. We indicated in the chapter that the best experimental designs available should be used in evaluating training, when conditions for more scientific design strategies do not exist. Since writing this chapter, we have been concerned about making such a statement. We have remembered the old axiom that "a little learning is a dangerous thing" and are wondering if the same is not true for evaluation— "a little evaluation can be a dangerous thing." Comment.

10. Performance appraisal, as discussed in the last chapter, may be geared to facilitate learning. How can performance appraisal utilizing the MBO approach effectively enhance employee development in terms of the specific learning principles covered in this chapter?

11. Your instructor, besides teaching personnel management, is responsible for teaching and administering the College of Business Administration's basic management course, which has an enrollment of about 400 students each semester. He lectures on Tuesdays and Thursdays in a large lecture hall to 400 students. On Fridays, each student is assigned to one "lab" section with a class size of about 40 students, conducted by a graduate assistant, in which homework and quizzes relating to the lectures and text are included along with an opportunity for students to ask the lab instructor to clarify any points not clear to them. Your professor has also developed a 40-page mimeographed "learning packet" in which additional ideas are outlined, mathematical problems which he will go over in lecture are provided (along with spaces for the students to fill in the answers to those questions as the professor proceeds through their solution showing all calculations on slides), etc. These packets are modified to a certain extent each semester and sold through the university's bookstores. Three 50-question multiple-

choice computer-scored exams are given each semester and the lab instructors: (1) help make up questions for the exams and (2) have office hours so that they can go over any student's exam with him if so desired. One of the lab instructors teaches one fewer lab section than the others, but serves as a "course coordinator." Among his duties are taking the exam answer sheet to the examination services facility for computer processing, spending five or six hours with the professor over the weekend prior to the giving of each exam going over all exam questions submitted by himself and the other lab instructors to polish them, eliminate ambiguous responses, overly easy or difficult questions, etc.

a. What principles of learning have been incorporated into this large-scale teaching effort?

b. What management science techniques do you believe would be most useful to your professor in lecturing for and administering this large course? Show *specifically* how they may be utilized.

Notes

[1] C. R. Dooley, "Training Within Industry in the United States," *International Labour Review,* 54 (September-December, 1946), p. 16.

[2] A conceptualization of the planned organizational learning process similar to that presented in Figure 6–1 is provided by Edward F. Magdarz, "Attitude Change via Curriculum in Industrial Education," *Educational Technology,* 9 (September, 1969), p. S2.

[3] Irwin L. Goldstein, *Training: Program Development and Evaluation* (Monterey, Calif.: Brooks/Cole Publishing Company, 1974), p. 19.

[4] Such consistency with the philosophies of the company is necessary because other options may be available that are unacceptable to top management. For example, a decision to eliminate the hiring of the hard core unemployed because of difficulties in integrating them into the work force might be ruled out.

[5] This classification is based upon the work of William McGehee and Paul W. Thayer, *Training in Business and Industry* (New York: McGraw-Hill Book Company, 1961). Some other writers, however, have used different terms to convey the same type of conceptual framework. For example, Bernard M. Bass and James A. Vaughan, *Training in Industry: The Management of Learning* (Belmont, Calif.: Wadsworth Publishing Company, Inc., 1966), have used the terms organizational analysis, job analysis, and manpower analysis. Goldstein, op. cit., has used the same terms as we have presented.

[6] R. N. Anthony, *Planning and Control Systems: A Framework for Analysis* (Boston: Graduate School of Business Administration, Harvard University, 1965), p. 24.

[7] Goldstein, op. cit., p. 27.

[8] George H. Litwin and Robert A. Stringer, Jr., *Motivation and Organizational Climate* (Boston: Division of Research, Graduate School of Business Administration, Harvard University, 1968), p. 1.

[9] Goldstein, op. cit., p. 31.

[10] Avice Saint, *Learning at Work* (Chicago: Nelson-Hall Company, 1974), p. 57.

[11] Goldstein, op. cit., p. 31.

[12] Markus M. Loftin, III and Benjamin Roter, "Training Clerical Employees," in Joseph J. Famularo, ed., *Handbook of Modern Personnel Administration* (New York: McGraw-Hill Book Company, Inc., 1972), pp. 19: 1–11.

[13]Patricia C. Smith, Lorne M. Kendall, and Charles I. Hulin, *The Measurement of Satisfaction in Work and Retirement: A Strategy for the Study of Attitudes* (Chicago: Rand McNally, 1969).

[14]Elwood S. Buffa, *Modern Production Management* (New York: John Wiley and Sons, 1973), p. 659.

[15]Ibid., p. 661.

[16]John P. Campbell, et al., *Managerial Behavior, Performance and Effectiveness* (New York: McGraw-Hill Book Company, 1970), p. 260.

[17]The reader who is interested in going into greater depth on the learning theories is referred to any of the following sources: R. C. Bolles, *Learning Theory* (New York: Holt, Rinehart and Winston, 1975); B. R. Bugelski, *The Psychology of Learning Applied to Teaching* (Indianapolis, Ind.: The Bobbs-Merrill Company, Inc., 1971); Laird S. Cermak, *Psychology of Learning: Research and Theory* (New York: The Ronald Press Company, 1975); Ernest R. Hilgard and Gordon H. Bower, *Theories of Learning* (Englewood Cliffs, N.J.: Prentice-Hall, Inc., 1975); Glenn E. Snelbecker, *Learning Theory, Instructional Theory, and Psychoeducational Design* (New York: McGraw-Hill Book Company, 1974).

[18]To some extent this decision is based upon the sheer number of principles of learning that have been suggested. For example, Bugelski, op. cit., pp. 294–299, suggests 59 conditions and principles of learning and Craig Eric Schneier in his "Training and Development Programs: What Learning Theory and Research Have to Offer," *Personnel Journal,* 53 (April, 1974), pp. 288–293 and 300, lists 49.

[19]Goldstein, op. cit., p. 113.

[20]The reader who is familiar with the so-called instrument-valence theory of motivation put forth by Victor H. Vroom, *Work and Motivation* (New York: John Wiley and Sons, 1964), will recognize that this situation readily fits the Vroom model. Ibid., pp. 114–118, discusses the Vroom model as it relates to training along with the Maslow model. Both of these models will be discussed in Chapter 9.

[21]Leslie E. This and Gordon L. Lippitt, "Learning Theories and Training — Part 1," *Training and Development Journal,* 20 (April, 1966), p. 4. Part 2 of the article is in *Training and Development Journal,* 20 (May, 1966), pp. 10–18.

[22]K. Chowdhry, as cited by Campbell, et al., op. cit., p. 256.

[23]This study by E. G. Boring is cited by Laurence Siegel and Irving M. Lane, *Psychology in Industrial Organizations* (Homewood, Ill.: Richard D. Irwin, Inc., 1974), p. 178.

[24]Ibid.

[25]Lee Hess and Len Sperry, "The Psychology of the Trainee as Learner," *Personnel Journal,* 52 (September, 1973), p. 781.

[26]The classification is based upon the "Learning Styles Inventory" of David A. Kolb, Irwin M. Rubin, and James M. McIntyre, *Organizational Psychology: An Experiential Approach* (Englewood Cliffs, N.J.: Prentice-Hall, Inc., 1971).

[27]The four reasons for plateaus are those put forth by Bass and Vaughan, op. cit., pp. 45–47.

[28]Alvis R. Knowles and Lawrence F. Bell, "Learning Curves Will Tell You Who's Worth Training and Who Isn't," *Factory Management and Maintenance,* 108 (June, 1950), pp. 114–115 and 202.

[29]William C. Biel, "Training Programs and Devices," in Robert M. Gagné, ed., *Psychological Principles in System Development* (New York: Holt, Rinehart and Winston, 1962), p. 375.

[30]H. C. W. Stockbridge and B. Chambers, "Aiming, Transfer of Training, and Knowledge of Results," as reported by Siegel and Lane, op. cit., pp. 182–183.

[31]Edwin A. Locke, "The Motivational Effect of Knowledge of Results: Knowledge or Goal Setting?" *Journal of Applied Psychology,* 51 (1967), pp. 324–329.

[32]Biel, op. cit., pp. 375–376. Additional studies which indicate the value of KOR have been presented by Goldstein, op. cit., pp. 123–125.

[33]Some of these conditions have been described in David Krech and Richard S. Crutchfield, *Elements of Psychology,* 3rd ed., (New York: Alfred A. Knopf, Inc., 1974), p. 382.

[34]Ibid., pp. 381–384.

[35]As has been pointed out in ibid., p. 378, "The most crucial and at the same time the most shaky element in the picture of instrumental conditioning is reinforcement."

[36]The following example was drawn from Donald R. Domm, Roger N. Blakeney, Michael T. Matteson, and Robert Scofield, *The Individual and The Organization* (New York: Harper and Row Publishers, 1973), p. 22.

[37]Norman R. F. Maier, *Psychology in Industrial Organizations* (Boston: Houghton Mifflin Company, 1973), p. 309.

[38]Much of this section is based upon ibid., p. 308; Siegel and Lane, op. cit., pp. 180–181; and Goldstein, op. cit., pp. 121–123.

[39]Siegel and Lane, op. cit., p. 181.

[40]Much of this section is based upon ibid., p. 180; Maier, op. cit., pp. 308–309; Goldstein, op. cit., pp. 120–121; and Bass and Vaughan, op. cit., p. 50.

[41]These guidelines are drawn from Goldstein, op. cit., p. 111.

[42]Edwin A. Fleishman, "Leadership Climate, Human Relations Training, and Supervisory Behavior," in Edwin A. Fleishman, ed., *Studies in Personnel and Industrial Psychology* (Homewood, Ill.: Dorsey, 1967), pp. 250–263.

[43]Warren S. Blumenfeld and Max G. Holland, "A Model for the Empirical Evaluation of Training Effectiveness," *Personnel Journal*, 50 (August, 1971), p. 638.

[44]R. Besco, J. Tiffin, and D. C. King, "Evaluation Techniques for Management Development Programs," *ASTD Journal*, 10 (1959), p. 14 as quoted by Munro H. Steel, "An Organized Evaluation of Management Training," *Personnel Journal*, 51 (October, 1972), p. 725.

[45]Donald L. Kirkpatrick, "Techniques for Evaluating Training Programs," *ASTD Journal*, 10 (November, 1959), pp. 3–9; 10 (December, 1959), pp. 21–26; 11 (January, 1960), pp. 13–18; and 11 (February, 1960), pp. 28–32.

[46]The reader may be familiar with the "Dr. Fox Effect" which has demonstrated that a lecturer who is entertaining but provides little or no content is more likely to receive better evaluations than one who has a great deal of content but is not as entertaining. This effect is one reason why many college professors become quite upset about student evaluations.

[47]Harold H. Kelley, "The Warm-Cold Variable in First Impressions of Persons," *Journal of Personality*, 18 (1950), pp. 431–439.

[48]For example, Goldstein, op. cit., p. 60, cites a study by Severin in which "the median correlation between production records and training grades was .11." Further, as one person has commented on the transferability of training in general: "Success in elementary school is an indicator of success in high school. Success in high school is an indicator of success in college. Success in college is an indicator of success in graduate school. Success in graduate school is an indicator of absolutely nothing."

[49]William R. Tracey, *Evaluating Training and Development Systems* (New York: American Management Association, 1968), pp. 19–20, cites 56 organizational benefits that might result from training.

[50]Cited by Campbell, et al., op. cit., p. 272.

[51]F. T. Malm, "Analyzing Training Needs and Results," in Paul Pigors, Charles A. Myers, and F. T. Malm, *Management of Human Resources* (New York: McGraw-Hill Book Company, 1973), pp. 441–448.

[52]It should be noted that there are many other problems relating to the selection of criteria for evaluation beside those discussed here. For a discussion of a number of these, see Goldstein, op. cit., pp. 53–58.

[53]These four designs are not the only ones that can be used to evaluate training programs and efforts. The reader who is interested in more sophisticated designs such as the Solomon four group design is referred to Goldstein, op. cit., pp. 82–83, and James A. Belasco and Harrison M. Trice, *The Assessment of Change in Training and Therapy* (New York: McGraw-Hill Book Company, 1969), pp. 27–30.

[54]Comparability can be obtained by randomly assigning individuals to the two groups or the two groups can be matched on selected characteristics. In many cases, however, it will be necessary to use intact groups so that comparability cannot be assumed. The researcher needs to be aware of such varying conditions because they influence the interpretation of the results and the determination of which statistical techniques are most appropriate.

[55]Goldstein, op. cit., pp. 49–50.

[56]Belasco and Trice, op. cit., p. 9. This harsh indictment is supported by a 1974

study which found that the best way to collect data concerning training in industry is not even known yet. See Gerald G. Somers and Myron Roomkin, "Developing Reliable Data on Training in Industry," *Monthly Labor Review,* 97 (February, 1974), pp. 33–37. This study revealed a lack of knowledge about formal programs, number of participants involved, costs, etc.

[57]The first two of these reasons, attitudinal and design, are suggested and discussed by Belasco and Trice, op. cit., pp. 9–46.

[58]Warren H. Schmidt, "How to Evaluate a Company's Training Efforts," *California Management Review,* 12 (Spring, 1970), p. 49.

[59]Jack H. Doty, "Human Capital Budgeting — Maximizing Returns on Training Investment," *The Journal of Industrial Engineering,* 16 (March-April, 1965), p. 243.

[60]"How IBM Avoids Layoffs Through Retraining," *Business Week,* (November 10, 1975), p. 112.

[61]Schmidt, op. cit., p. 49. Other examples of the tendency to drop training when economic conditions decline are provided by David Oates, "Companies Jettison Motivation and Training Programmes," *International Management,* 30 (October, 1975), pp. 23–25.

[62]C. Marston Case, "The Application of PERT to Large-Scale Educational Research and Evaluation Studies," *Educational Technology,* 9 (October, 1969), pp. 79–83.

[63]Ibid., p. 80.

[64]The reader who is interested in more detailed information on learning theory in psychological research is referred to W. K. Estes, "The Statistical Approach to Learning Theory," in S. Koch, ed., *Psychology: A Study of a Science* (New York: McGraw-Hill Book Company, Inc., 1959), Vol. 2; Robert R. Bush and Frederick Mosteller, *Stochastic Models for Learning* (New York: John Wiley and Sons, Inc., 1955); and Cermak, op. cit., particularly pp. 45–47, which deal with measures of transfer of learning.

[65]See, for example, Norman H. Nie, C. Hadlai Hull, Jean G. Steinbrenner, and Dale H. Bent, *Statistical Package for the Social Sciences* (New York: McGraw-Hill Book Company, 1975).

[66]Alun Jones and John Moxham, "Costing the Benefits of Training," *Personnel Management,* 1 (August, 1969), pp. 22–28. Another attempt to apply cost-benefit analysis to training which has certain limitations may be found in Doty, op. cit., pp. 233–252.

[67]Jones and Moxham, op. cit., p. 23.

[68]J. A. G. Jones, "The Costs and Benefits of Management Training," *Personnel Management,* 5 (September, 1973), p. 31.

7

EMPLOYEE DEVELOPMENT: DESIGN DECISIONS

The design phase of development programs involves making decisions concerning: (1) who will conduct the development program, (2) where development will take place, and (3) what specific development methods will be used. Once a program objective has been established and the specific requirements decided upon in the need determination phase, the program designer is in a position to examine who will conduct the program, where it will be conducted, what specific development techniques are "available and to choose the most appropriate for the behaviors being considered."[1]

In this chapter, alternatives in these decision areas will be described and evaluated in terms of their relative advantages and disadvantages. In addition, in evaluating where development should take place and what specific methods may be used, emphasis will be placed upon how the principles of learning presented in Chapter 6 can serve as guides in making these decisions. Such contingencies as company size, number of individuals to be trained, and cost will be discussed in terms of making development decisions. We will also examine the applications of computers and management science, where appropriate. Finally, some development approaches will be compared directly in order to highlight how the decision maker may choose from among them.

WHO SHOULD ACTUALLY CONDUCT THE TRAINING?

An important consideration in the design of any development program is "Who will actually conduct the program?" Should the trainers come from personnel or other staff, from among line employees, from outside the organization, or from a combination of these sources? It should be noted that responsibility for conducting the development program and responsibility for development (planned organizational learning) are different issues. Because of special staff expertise, the responsibility for planned organizational learning is generally considered to be a function of the personnel department.[2] For example, a Bureau of National Affairs Survey of 350 personnel executives of BNA's Forum found that "responsibility for the training program is a staff function in almost half the firms, a line function in three-tenths, and shared by line and staff in a fourth."[3] Responsibility for actually conducting the training, on the other hand, is often a line function. In this section, our concern is with the question of "Who should actually conduct various development programs?"

In making the decision as to who will conduct a particular development program, the decision maker is faced with five alternatives. A program may be conducted by: (1) line managers, (2) nonmanagerial employees, (3) staff members, (4) outside consultants, and (5) various combinations of the above. Choice of any one or more of these alternatives is related to where the program will take place — on the job or off the job — which we will discuss later.

Line Management

In on-the-job training, the line manager is very frequently the trainer. The selection of the line manager is a logical one if he has the necessary technical expertise, the ability to teach and the time to devote. In some instances, however, some or all of these conditions may be lacking. For example, a first line foreman may lack the technical expertise because his job is essentially one of coordinating activities and he is not familiar with the specifics of the operation of the equipment in his department. Or, he may have achieved his technical training on an older, obsolete version of the equipment now in use.

Even if the line manager has the technical expertise, he may not be selected as the trainer because he is not adept at explaining to others how to perform the tasks. This might be the case because the manager is so familiar with a job that he expects the trainee to understand everything he is told the first time and, in consequence, does not give the trainee a chance to ask sufficient questions. His great familiarity with the job might lead him to omit steps because they are "obvious." Further, the supervisor may have a sink-or-swim philosophy and merely show the trainee his desk or work station, give him some work to do with only a hasty explanation of how it is to be done, and tell him to "get busy." In such cases, the trainee, learning on his own, may acquire both good and poor work habits. The same thing may happen even if other employees attempt to help the trainee, with or without the supervisor's permission.

The manager who is technically competent and has the ability to train may not be selected as the trainer because he lacks the time. For example, a manager who has a large span of control may not be able to train his subordinates because of time constraints. Even a manager with a relatively small span of control may lack time to provide much training to subordinates because of the complexity of the work they perform. Another issue is whether or not the manager is rewarded for training subordinates. The manager who is told to train subordinates but then pressured to "get work out," and is rewarded for immediate operating results but not for training will not be encouraged to try to train employees. Under such conditions, the manager may believe that the training is taking time away from work that could more directly lead to a promotion or some other desired reward for himself. Finally, a line manager may not have the time because he really does have so much other work to do which must be given a higher priority.

Nonmanagerial Employees

If the line manager is not able to conduct the training for whatever reasons, a subordinate employee may be selected to do so. As with a manager, it is important that any employee selected to conduct training have the necessary technical expertise, ability to teach, and time to devote to the training. In addition, it is important to have favorable work attitudes and habits. A great deal of consideration needs to be given to the selection of a nonmanagerial employee to serve as a trainer.

There is sometimes a temptation, when selecting an experienced employee to train a new one, to pick one of the poorest performing members of the department so that the better ones will not be taken away from productive efforts. Such a decision, however, is not a good one in the long run, since the new employee may acquire the poor skills of the trainer and have to be retrained or possibly fired later. It is much better to select a proficient employee to conduct the training so that the trainee acquires the appropriate skills correctly. Selecting a proficient employee, however, does not necessarily mean selecting the very best one. The best employee may not be a good trainer because, while technically competent, he or she may not be able to teach someone else how to do the job. Just like the manager, the best worker may be too familiar with the job and therefore, skip steps or rush through them. It is for this reason that some college professors believe that the best tutors for students having difficulties in a course are often students who have received grades of "C" or "B-" rather than "A" or "B." Finally, it may be undesirable to use the most proficient employee as a trainer since this may lead to: (1) lower production in the short run, and (2) his slowing down on his own job later as a result of his need to slow down during the training. Having broken "rhythm" in the training, the highly proficient employee may find that he has some relearning to do.

In selecting an employee to train others, care should be taken to pick someone who has favorable work habits and attitudes since these may be learned by the trainees along with the specific skills he or she is attempting to master. For example, one experienced quality control clerk who was called on to train a new colleague in how to perform certain control tasks was very adept in both quality control work and in teaching it, but had a very negative attitude toward the department head. In the training, this attitude showed up, and tended to bias the new clerk against his superior.

If an employee is not rewarded for training activities, he will be unlikely to take them too seriously. In a manufacturing operation, for example, a production worker who is asked to train a new employee but then is pressured and rewarded for production will not be inclined to take the training responsibilities seriously. This problem could become acute when the worker is paid on an incentive basis, since he could produce less and thereby earn less money while conducting the training. To overcome this problem, it is a common practice to guarantee the employee-trainer his normal past incentive rate while he is training others.

Staff

Staff may be used to conduct training programs because it has special expertise, which the line does not possess. In addition, staff will typically be used when the skills, knowledge, or

attitudes to be learned are needed in a large number of organization units. For example, the personnel department frequently is
called upon to explain employee benefits such as the firm's pension plan to new employees. If the personnel department of a firm
has recently computerized its personnel records, it may be necessary for certain members of the computer department to conduct
a training program for personnel to show them how the new
system works. This illustration points out that it is not only the

(a)
Company Groups Giving Actual Instructions*

	All Companies	Larger Companies	Smaller Companies
First-line management	58%	52%	65%
Higher-line management	17	14	19
Staff-with or without line assistance	51	67	28
Qualified employees	16	15	19
Instructors & Specialists	14	13	19

*Figures total more than 100 per cent since some companies use more than one group.

(b)
Sources for Outside Specialists†

	All Companies	Larger Companies	Smaller Companies
Education institutions			
Colleges & universities	36%	30%	50%
Unspecified education institutions	16	19	11
Business, trade & high schools	15	11	22
Correspondence schools	2	3	–
Total for education institutions	69	63	83
Consultants	38	49	17
Vendors	33	38	22
Professional organizations	13	11	17
Service organizations	9	8	11
Others	10	8	12

†Percentages total more than 100 since some companies use more than one source.

(c)
Areas of Instruction Covered by Outside Specialists‡

	All Companies	Larger Companies	Smaller Companies
Management development	85%	85%	85%
Skilled crafts	57	64	45
Special skills	29	17	33

‡Percentages total more than 100 since some firms use a variety of evaluating techniques.

Figure 7-1 Groups conducting development programs. [From Bureau of National Affairs,
"Planning the Training Program," Personnel Management: BNA Policy and Practices
Series: (Washington, D.C.: The Bureau of National Affairs, Inc., 1975), p. 205:106.]

personnel staff that may be responsible for conducting a training program, but other staff members as well.

Figure 7–1a shows the results of a survey of 350 personnel executives in BNA's Forum concerning which specific groups within firms conduct the actual instruction. The results presented in Figure 7–1a permit us to make a basic observation of a contingency nature concerning firm size and who conducts the training. Larger firms use staff personnel much more frequently than do smaller firms, while smaller firms use line managers and nonmanagerial employees more frequently than do their larger counterparts. These findings make sense, since larger firms are more likely to have the resources to hire staff members competent to train employees than are smaller firms. In addition, larger firms have more organizational units in which staff specialists can be called upon to train, and therefore can more easily justify the costs involved.

Outside Consultants

Thus far we have considered only groups within the organization that might conduct development programs. A firm may also hire persons from outside to conduct training programs. For example, if a new piece of legislation is passed by Congress, a firm might hire an attorney to conduct a training program for its top executives on the impact of the law. A major variable that will influence whether or not outsiders should be used to conduct development programs is whether a particular program (or one similar to it) will be repeated. If the program will be conducted only once, it is likely to be less costly to use an outsider. On the other hand, if the program is to be repeated, it may be less costly for the company to hire a "permanent" specialist to conduct the program. The example of the new law illustrates this point. If the company will face continually changing implications from the new legislation (for example in the form of court decisions) it may be less costly to hire an attorney and use him as an "inside" consultant than to continually go outside for legal advice. If, on the other hand, it is likely that only a "one-shot" training program will cover all of the aspects of the law the firm may find it less expensive to use an outside consultant. This point is directly related to that we made in Chapter 1 concerning firm size in terms of "exposures."

A number of sources of outside training specialists are listed in Figure 7–1b, and the major training areas handled by such specialists are shown in Figure 7–1c. These figures, although from only one study, enable us to make a few speculations of a contingency nature concerning firm size and the use of outside training specialists. First, smaller firms more frequently use educational institutions as sources of consultants, whereas larger organizations use consulting firms. This difference may be partially due to cost considerations. Consultants from educational institutions are often less expensive than are consulting firms, since consulting is a supplemental source of income for the former, while it is *the* source of income for the latter. Second, larger firms more frequently obtain more training help from other firms (vendors) doing (or hoping to do) business with them than do smaller firms. This difference probably does not result from a choice on the part of the smaller firms but rather occurs because the vendor is willing to provide more training services to the larger firm due to the greater dollars involved. For example, a computer manufacturer may provide a service representative to a large firm that has just purchased one of its computers because it sees that the firm might acquire additional expensive equipment. The smaller firm, on the other hand, may be required to send (paying travel expenses) one of its employees to a short training program sponsored by the computer manufacturer at the manufacturer's own training facility. Third, smaller firms tend to use service and professional organizations (such as the Chamber of Commerce or National Association of Manufacturers) more frequently than do larger firms. This may often occur because such training is inexpensive when compared to outside consultants (or hiring an "internal" consultant) and therefore more affordable by the smaller firm. Finally, it is apparent from Figure 7–1c that outside training specialists are more frequently used by firms, regardless of firm size, to conduct development programs for management than for skilled crafts and special skills. The use of outside specialists in this area may represent an attempt to bring new concepts and ideas to managers in the organization. In addition, at the top levels of management there may be no one within the organization with the expertise to instruct them as to what to do.

Combinations of Trainers and Training the Trainers

The firm may use more than one source of trainers for a particular training program because no one group by itself can fully cover the material to be included in the program. For example, an accounting department that begins to computerize its operations may need a training program that covers not only the use of the computer but also updates the accounting skills of the members of the department. Such a program may be administered by the personnel department and conducted by computer specialists within the firm along with specialized accounting consultants from outside the firm.

It is usually recognized that trainers should have a mastery of their subject matter. Regardless of who conducts the development program, however, an important but often overlooked consideration is that it is often advisable to "train" the trainer as to how to teach others. That such training is important has been shown in a study by Bavelas.[4] In this study the trainer trained two operators prior to having received training himself. The trainer was then given four hours of training in techniques of (1) fostering "favorable social interactions," (2) motivation, and (3) guiding workers, after which he trained two more operators. The trainer was then given four additional hours of training in the areas mentioned, after which he trained two additional individuals. The basic results of this study as presented in Figure 7–2 show that training the trainer had a positive impact on the learning curves of the operators. What probably happened in this study was that the trainer became more familiar with the subject material and more adept at presenting it. Both of these possibilities, we believe, are of vital importance, regardless of who is conducting the development program.

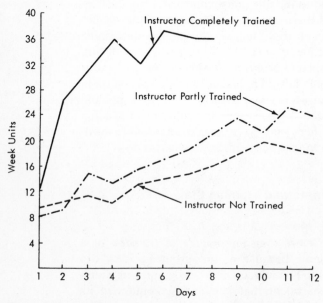

Figure 7–2 Learning curves of trainees of an instructor at various stages of the instructor's own training. [From Lawrence Siegel and Irving M. Lane, Psychology in Industrial Organizations (Homewood, Ill.: Richard D. Irwin, Inc., © 1974), p. 199.]

We can see from the previous discussion that the question of who should conduct the actual training requires the personnel department to make a number of decisions. In addition, these decisions are related to the question of where the training should take place. We will now turn our attention to this subject.

LOCATION OF DEVELOPMENT PROGRAMS

The broadest and most common classification of development techniques deals with where the development will take place: (1) on the job, or (2) off the job. On-the-job development exists when the trainee learns (i.e., acquires skills, knowledge, and attitudes) in the actual work environment. Off-the-job development, on the other hand, exists when the trainee learns in a setting other than this environment.

On-The-Job Training

On-the-job training is much more common than off-the-job training. A Bureau of National Affairs report indicated that "90 percent or more of industrial training involves on-the-job methods."[5] One reason for such a high percentage is that all employees receive at least some on-the-job training. As Bass and Vaughan have noted: "Each employee, whether he is newly hired, transferred or promoted, must be formally introduced to his specific job environment, to the people with whom he will be working, and to company policies and objectives that concern him."[6] A second reason for such a high percentage is that employees frequently need specialized training on new jobs and retraining on current jobs that can only take place on the job because of the need to work with the actual technology or environment. Such conditions might be due to unique characteristics of the technology (e.g., a computer), which are too difficult or too costly to duplicate off the job, or because interpersonal relationships are so important to successful job performance that the individual must be trained while working with colleagues. For example, the astronauts who are preparing to operate the space shuttle in the 1980's must be trained together because of the need for the development of very close interpersonal relationships necessary for the success of the mission.

On-the-job training offers a number of advantages to the trainee and to the organization when compared to off-the-job training.[7] First, it usually requires no special facilities, since the trainee is learning in the normal work environment and therefore is using existing facilities. Second, the trainee is doing some "real" work while he is learning. Such "real" work for a production worker would be useable units of output, whereas for a management trainee it might mean answering complaints about late orders. Because of these two reasons, on-the-job training is often cheaper and easier to administer than off-the-job training.

On-the-job training may make use of a number of the principles of learning discussed in Chapter 6, such as motivation, transfer, knowledge of results (KOR), and reinforcement. The trainee may be more highly motivated in on-the-job training because he is engaged in meaningful activities. The problem of transferring learning is largely overcome, since the trainee is using the same equipment, following the same procedures, and functioning in the same environment in which he will be expected to perform after becoming highly proficient. In addition, the trainee gets a chance to work with the people he will have to associate with on a day-to-day basis, which permits him to learn about the prevailing patterns of interpersonal relationships existing in the work environment. Thus, there is less of a problem in learning new patterns of behavior after a training program and perhaps having to unlearn others than if the trainee were first exposed to off-the-job training. If the trainee is provided with KOR during training, learning that is directly related to future job behavior is enhanced. Reinforcement can be facilitated because the supervisor may use some of the same rewards in the learning situation that he normally uses. For example, he might provide a basis for the occurrence of positive peer feedback by informing the trainee's colleagues that he is doing well. Thus, the link between behavior and consequences can be better established. Repetition of tasks in the actual work environment may also contribute to the retention of new materials and, hence, better performance.

There are a number of disadvantages or limitations associated with on-the-job training, however. First, in on-the-job training the trainee is utilizing existing resources, such as equipment, facilities, and the expertise of human resources, which normally would be used for productive activity. Since the trainee is just learning, it is likely that his performance will initially be low, and somewhat inefficient and ineffective. For example, in jobs involving physical production, the trainee is likely to produce fewer finished goods, at a lower quality level, and with a higher reject rate than would be the case if the equipment was used by an experienced operator. In addition, the risk of accidents and serious injury to individuals and damage to equipment is likely to be higher during training. In managerial and professional training, the trainee will probably make decisions that do not make adequate use of the resources available to him and which are of lower quality than those made by a more experienced manager. For example, one individual in learning how to interpret psychological tests, initially made a fairly large number of mistakes and had to rely on another productive organization member for guidance, lowering that employee's productivity.

A second limitation of on-the-job training exists when the trainee is under pressure to show results quickly. If such pressure (whether from the supervisor or peers) is too great, the trainee may become anxious, which will tend to interfere with learning. In addition, too much emphasis on results may lead to the trainee's "success" being evaluated almost exclusively on whether or not immediate results are achieved. This may result in his receiving much feedback as to his achievements but not enough information "about the reasons for his mistakes and failure."[8] Thus, the supposed advantage of KOR may be lacking. That the concern for results or "doing today's work" is not simply a nonmanagerial problem has been noted by Hinrichs.

. . . the emphasis in any work group tends to be on production rather then personnel development. The manager's manager has a job to do; day-to-day pressures force him or her to emphasize this, and the development, coaching, and feedback process for new managers tends to be neglected.[9]

The problems of resource utilization and pressure for work results rather than learning may lead to allocation of the poorest human and physical resources to training activities. For example, production workers may be trained on the poorest equipment so that good equipment is not taken out of service; or the new manager may be given a poor secretary on the assumption that he would not yet know how to utilize a good one effectively. Emphasizing work results rather than learning may be detrimental in the long run because the trainee will not learn properly. This may be of little interest to the manager, however, whose own performance appraisal is based upon the *current* results of his work group.

Another limitation of on-the-job training occurs because the trainers are often line employees. As indicated previously, the line manager may not do a good job of training because he is not technically competent, is not able or interested in conducting training, or lacks the time. The same types of problems may result if a line employee other than the supervisor is selected to conduct the training. Additionally, the problems of the tendency to select a worker who is not very proficient or one who has poor work attitudes may exist.

A final disadvantage of on-the-job training is that it may be inefficient, especially at nonmanagerial levels, since frequently only one person can be trained at a time. For example, there may not be enough physical space on a production job for more than one trainee along with the trainer to learn on a particular machine. In some instances, only one trainee may be hired at any given time in order to meet an existing need, and therefore only one individual is trained. In both cases the trainee to trainer ratio would be 1:1. If a number of trainees can be grouped together for training, on-the-job training may be more cost effective, in that the trainer can deal with a number of trainees together.

Off-The-Job Training

Off-the-job training has a number of advantages when compared to on-the-job training. It is often more efficient because the trainer may be able to work with groups rather than individuals, as just noted. For example, when a number of new checkout clerks must be trained for the opening of a new supermarket, several clerks may be trained together through off-the-job training. We will illustrate how this may be done realistically when we discuss "vestibule training" later in this chapter. Off-the-job training also tends to emphasize learning more than achieving immediate work results, so that the trainee can give greater attention to learning. Further, off-the-job trainers more frequently tend to have been trained in how to train, and consequently, are more able to draw upon learning theory and principles of learning to facilitate this learning. Off-the-job training may also be better planned than on-the-job training, since the person conducting the training may well be evaluated based upon the success of the trainees when they return to the job. Therefore, he or she may have a vested interest in showing the worth of the training programs and efforts. Off-the-job training additionally permits the trainee to get away from the constant pressure of the job and to concentrate more on self-development. Finally, in off-the-job training programs conducted by nonorganizational members, a company, particularly a smaller one, may be able to offer learning experiences that it could not otherwise supply due to the expense involved or the lack of individuals within the organization capable of teaching the material. For example, a company might pay the tuition of an employee who takes courses at a local university. A number of other reasons why off-the-job training may be superior to on-the-job training have been offered by Bienvenu, who has suggested that training, particularly orientation training, is best done away from the job.[10] He has argued that this is the case because off-the-job training eliminates such impediments as noise and possible embarrassment in front of other more experienced and proficient employees.

In spite of the advantages of off-the-job training, there are some drawbacks to this approach. The first and major one is the difficulty in transferring learning to the actual job situation. Too often, off-the-job training is undertaken with little concern for the effectiveness of learning other than in the training situation itself. For example, a university "operations research" course may be so theoretical that it is of little practical value to a manager back on the job. In such a case, trainees may learn much from the program, with the learning being evidenced by the use of examinations and/or other measures. The new knowledge may not be useable on the job, however, and therefore the organization's development objectives may not be met. To overcome this problem, the trainer needs to make certain that the content of the development program has current or future application and the priniciples of learning drawn upon facilitate the transfer of skills, knowledge, and attitudes to performance on the job. The support of top management for any off-the-job training and a receptive organizational climate is critical to whether learning in such programs will be transferred and retained. For example, a manager who permits subordinates to try out on the job a new "operations research" technique learned in a university course and provides KOR and positive reinforcement when appropriate, will facilitate transfer and retention of learning, assuming, of course, that the technique proves to have some applicability. In addition, a positive attitude on the part of the supervisor may help increase the chances that the employee will attempt to learn in future development programs because he has seen that he will be given a chance to apply what he has learned on the job.

A second disadvantage of off-the-job training is that expensive facilities and/or equipment may be required in order to conduct the program. Frequently, only larger companies can afford the expenses involved in having their own off-the-job facilities.

A third disadvantage of off-the-job training is that the company is not obtaining any work output while the training is taking place. This represents a cost to the firm, since it is paying the employee during the training program. The company, of course, is hoping that in the long run it will benefit because the future output of the employee will be greater.

A final disadvantage of off-the-job training relates to the learning principle of reinforcement. A problem may exist if the basis for and frequency of reinforcement in the training program is different from that existing on the job. For example, if the trainee is reinforced in the training environment by being praised every time he completes 100 units correctly, he may be disappointed on the job if he is not praised at all or if he is only praised for completing every 200 units. The employee may come to believe mistakenly that he is not doing a good job, which may lead him to become frustrated and lose motivation.

Neither on-the-job nor off-the-job training approaches can be said to be better in all instances. Rather, choosing between the two requires an examination of organizational objectives. If the primary objective of the program is to obtain some immediately productive work, then on-the-job training is usually preferable, provided it can be done safely. If, on the other hand, the objective is to expose a manager to new management concepts and approaches to problem solving, off-the-job training is generally more appropriate. A second contingency is the financial capability of the firm. Since on-the-job training of a new production worker, for example, is generally less expensive than training him off the job, firms with limited resources would be more likely to use this method in such situations. The financial capabilities of the firm are also directly related to the need for immediate work results, since firms in a poor financial position are more likely to need productive work immediately.

Finally, we should emphasize that, in many instances, it may be appropriate to combine on-the-job and off-the-job training. For example, a trainee may first be given classroom instruction, then sent to the work environment to use the training, and later be returned to the training environment for additional training. One of the best examples of a merging of both on- and off-the-job approaches is apprenticeship training, which we will discuss later in this chapter.

DEVELOPMENT TECHNIQUES

Designers of development programs have a large number of specific techniques available for use in conducting such programs. Following the approach suggested by Bass and Vaughan, we will classify the techniques as off the job or on the job as in Figure 7–3. It should be noted that the techniques are classified as on the job or off the job, based upon the location in which the technique is *primarily* used, when, in fact, some of the techniques can be used in *either* setting. For example, the lecture method is classified as off the job, even though it could be used on the job. Likewise, job instruction training is classified as an on-the-job technique, even though it can be used in some off-the-job training situations, which we will discuss later.

The designers of development programs need to select from among the various techniques those most appropriate for any program under consideration in light of their objectives, principles of learning, and numerous organizational contingencies,

Evaluation of Alternatives in Light of Principles of Learning and Other Contingencies

Alternatives	Motivation: Active Participation of Learner	Reinforcement: Feedback of Knowledge of Results	Stimulus: Meaningful Organization of Materials	Responses: Practice and Repetition	Stimulus-Response: Conditions Most Favorable for Transfer
ON-THE-JOB TECHNIQUES					
Job-Instruction Training	Yes	Sometimes	Yes	Yes	Yes
Apprentice Training	Yes	Sometimes	?	Sometimes	Yes
Internships and Assistantships	Yes	Sometimes	?	Sometimes	Yes
Job Rotation	Yes	No	?	Sometimes	Yes
Junior Board	Yes	Sometimes	Sometimes	Sometimes	Yes
Coaching	Yes	Yes	Sometimes	Sometimes	Yes
OFF-THE-JOB TECHNIQUES					
Vestibule	Yes	Sometimes	Yes	Yes	Sometimes
Lecture	No	No	Yes	No	No
Special Study	Yes	No	Yes	?	No
Films	No	No	Yes	No	No
Television	No	No	Yes	No	No
Conference or Discussion	Yes	Sometimes	Sometimes	Sometimes	No
Case Study	Yes	Sometimes	Sometimes	Sometimes	Sometimes
Role Playing	Yes	Sometimes	No	Sometimes	Sometimes
Simulation	Yes	Sometimes	Sometimes	Sometimes	Sometimes
Programmed Instruction	Yes	Yes	Yes	Yes	No
Laboratory Training	Yes	Yes	No	Yes	Sometimes
Programmed Group Exercise	Yes	Yes	Yes	Sometimes	Sometimes
Computer Assisted Instruction	Yes	Sometimes	Yes	Yes	Sometimes

```
                          CONTINGENCIES
ORGANIZATIONAL SIZE    TYPE OF DEVELOPMENT NEEDED    TYPE OF PERSON TO BE TRAINED
NUMBER OF PERSONS TO BE TRAINED    ORGANIZATIONAL FINANCIAL RESOURCES
     ENVIRONMENTAL AND TASK STABILITY AND TASK COMPLEXITY
```

Figure 7–3 *Training techniques, principles of learning and other contingencies. [Adapted from Bernard M. Bass and James A. Vaughan, Training in Industry: The Management of Learning (Belmont, California: Wadsworth Publishing Company, Inc., 1966), p. 131. Copyright © 1966 by Wadsworth Publishing Company, Inc. Used by permission of the publisher, Brooks/Cole Publishing Company, Monterey, California.] Computer Assisted Instruction and the contingencies have been added to the original figure.*

some of which are indicated in Figure 7–3. In the following sections we will describe in some detail and evaluate a number of the techniques in Figure 7–3, with the exception of laboratory (or sensitivity) training, which we will consider in Chapter 8.

On-The-Job Development Techniques

The on-the-job development techniques presented in Figure 7–3 tend to be used more frequently than the off-the-job techniques by both manufacturing and nonmanufacturing firms.[11] In this section we will discuss the following on-the-job training techniques: (1) job instruction training, (2) apprenticeship training, (3) job rotation, (4) special assignments, which include internships, assistantships, and junior boards, and (5) coaching.

Job Instruction Training

Job instruction training (JIT) was originated during World War II as a technique "to provide a guide for giving on-the-job *skill training* to white- and blue-collar employees as well as technicians."[12] Essentially, JIT involves four steps: (1) preparing the trainee, (2) demonstrating the job, (3) having the trainee perform the job, and (4) following up on the trainee's performance.

In preparing the trainee for instruction, the trainer needs to help the trainee relax, since too much anxiety is likely to result in errors. The trainer can do this by taking an interest in the individual, introducing him to his co-workers, pointing out the importance of the trainee's job and the objectives of the training, and describing the job responsibilities and duties. A formal job description and job specifications as described in Chapter 3 can help the employee know what is expected of him, which will also facilitate learning.

While demonstrating the job, the trainer should also tell the trainee how to do the job, since such parallel auditory and visual messages help to foster learning by making use of two sensory organs rather than only one. The description can be made easier to follow and learning facilitated if the job is broken down into subparts and a step-by-step sequencing followed when appropriate. In demonstrating the job, the trainee should be positioned so that he observes the demonstration from the same perspective he will have when he actually does the job. For example, when a trainer is demonstrating how to use a typewriter, the trainee should be positioned directly behind the trainer so that he does not see the job being performed "backwards." In addition, the JIT technique, utilizing the principle of repetition, calls for every job, even the simplest ones, to be demonstrated at least twice.

The JIT technique prescribes that the trainee also perform the job at *least twice*. While he is performing the job the second time, the JIT method specifies that the trainee explain to the trainer how and why he is doing each step. Such explanation serves two purposes: (1) the trainee's verbalization helps him conceptualize the task better and (2) the trainer receives feedback as to how well the trainee really understands the job. The trainer should point out errors and omissions as the trainee is doing the job and not wait until the total job is completed. One reason for this is that it provides the trainee with immediate feedback (KOR), which permits him to change his behavior before he learns incorrect procedures. A second reason for immediate correction of errors and omissions is that products may be destroyed by incorrect procedures unless they are immediately corrected. For example, in the construction of conventional tires, if air is allowed to be present when the "plies" are being put on the tire, the tire will be faulty, regardless of how well the tread is put on in a later stage of construction. When correcting the trainee, the trainer needs to do so in a nonthreatening manner so as not to create too much anxiety on the part of the trainee, which may impede motivation and learning. Further, the trainer should provide positive feedback (praise) as well as negative feedback, since positive reinforcement helps foster proper learning by rewarding desired behavior.

The fourth and final step in the JIT method is follow-up on the employee's performance. The organization needs to make certain that the individual is performing the job correctly in order to see if additional training is needed. One important aspect of this step is to let the trainee know to whom he is to go for help (supervisor, the trainer, or an experienced peer) after the "formal" training has been completed. Follow-up also provides information to the trainers and to management that may be useful for evaluating and redesigning existing training programs. Finally, follow-up, by letting the employee know how he is doing, shows him that the organization is interested in correct performance and provides him with feedback as to the effectiveness of his performance.

During World War II, thousands of individuals were trained quickly and effectively using JIT. As recently as 1970, one survey indicated that JIT was the most commonly used training technique in industry.[13] The basic reason for the popularity of JIT is that it has proved extremely successful as an on-the-job development technique. We believe its success can be accounted for because it explicitly incorporates many of the principles of learning presented in Chapter 6. Analysis of each of the four steps of JIT will show the use of such principles of learning as motivation,

KOR, repetition, reinforcement, active learning, and part learning.

Apprenticeship Training

Apprenticeship training is training in skilled crafts such as carpentry, jewelry, or upholstery, which requires a diverse range of knowledge and skills as well as independence of judgment and maturity.

The Bureau of Apprenticeship & Training in the Department of Labor has defined an apprentice as a "person at least 16 years of age who is covered by a written agreement registered with the State Apprenticeship Council (where no such Council exists, registration is with the Bureau of Apprenticeship) providing for not less than 4,000 hours of reasonably continuous employment under an approved schedule of work experience and supplemented by a recommended minimum of 144 hours per year of related classroom instruction."[14]

Each apprentice is assigned to an experienced worker who has already learned the trade, and who is referred to as a *journeyman*. As this discussion points out, apprenticeship programs are formal and lengthy, and emphasize combining off-the-job and on-the-job training under skilled supervision.

There are many trades that use apprentices and a great many persons involved in apprenticeship training. In one survey, one third of the firms that responded indicated that they conducted apprenticeship programs.[15] This same study reported that larger firms were more than twice as likely to have apprenticeship training programs as smaller firms (43 versus 20 per cent). In 1966, the Chrysler Corporation employeed 10,600 individuals in the apprenticeable skilled trades, with apprentices accounting for 2000 of these.[16] It is likely that apprenticeship programs will continue to thrive. It was estimated in 1973 that during the 1970's employment in the crafts category would reach 12.2 million, which would represent an increase of approximately 2 million over 1970, and that about 250,000 journeymen would be needed per year.[17]

Apprenticeship training is used mostly when complex skills are involved. Since the training takes place over an extended period of time, the distributed learning necessary to master such skills is able to take place. In addition, when apprenticeship training is well planned and operated, it permits the integration of the best features of on-the-job and off-the-job training. It gives the apprentice an opportunity to earn while learning, which is likely to contribute to increased motivation. Since the apprentice is working part of the time, the company receives some productive output during the training.

Apprenticeship training, however, does have a number of limitations, some of which are the same as for on-the-job training in general. Sometimes apprenticeship programs are unplanned and haphazard. Further, production, rather than learning, may be emphasized. The program may be too long for some individuals and too short for others, due to differences in learning rates. Because apprenticeship programs have fixed lengths that apply to all trainees, such differences cannot be taken into account. Additionally, unions sometimes fear that management may want to lengthen the apprenticeship period in order to get skilled but less expensive workers and therefore may oppose apprenticeship training. Finally, the apprenticeship program may become so rigid and inflexible that change becomes difficult because the journeyman wishes to protect his position, which he can do by not changing the techniques, even when technology changes.

While apprenticeship programs are restricted to skilled crafts, there is no reason why the basic idea of integrating on-the-job and off-the-job training cannot be applied to development programs for unskilled workers and in management development. In fact, the on-the-job techniques of job rotation, special assignments, and coaching, which we will discuss, all have characteristics similar to those in apprenticeship programs, even though they tend to be thought of as management development techniques rather than techniques for nonmanagerial skills development.

Job Rotation

There are a number of meanings associated with the on-the-job training technique referred to as job rotation.[18] It most frequently refers to assigning managerial trainees to different jobs in the organization in order to broaden their supervisory and nonsupervisory skills, knowledge, and experience, and to acquaint them with the work of various departments in the organization. While job rotation is most frequently associated with managerial "training," it should be emphasized that in some cases the "trainees" will be *experienced* managers being groomed for top level executive positions. Further, job rotation can be used with nonmanagers as a technique to reduce boredom brought on by specialization. For example, production workers can be taught to perform three jobs in a department and rotated from one to another every month. In addition, the nonmanager who participates in job rotation may derive satisfaction by seeing how his job relates to other jobs. Likewise, managers who are not likely to be promoted can benefit from job rotation, since it will provide them with the ability to handle more varied assignments.

The following example of a job rotation program illustrates some of the different aspects of this development technique. The purposes of the program were to give the trainee a chance to acquire specific skills, knowledge, experience, information about the work of the various functional departments, and to decide where he would prefer to work at the conclusion of training. In addition, the program permitted a number of managers to observe and evaluate the trainee in a variety of settings. The duration of the program was two years, with the trainee assigned to the organization's main office during the first year and to a field office during the second year. During the first year in the main office the trainee moved from one department to another with the time in each department varying from four to eight weeks. For example, eight weeks were spent in the staffing, training, and evaluations departments and four weeks in the appeals, investigations, and position classification departments. In addition, for about two months the trainee was loaned to another agency with which the main office worked. A number of observations concerning the assignments at the main office shed insight into the planning of job rotation programs. First, the training received was uneven. Some of the departments provided the trainee with excellent materials and opportunities to interact with their members, while others did not provide these opportunities. Second, some departments gave meaningful work to the trainee while others set up primarily "make work" projects. For example, in one department the trainee was given a procedures manual to read and told to make notes concerning its contents to discuss with the supervisor. While such an approach did provide the trainee with some new knowledge, the lack of application of such knowledge on any job meant that it was not retained for any significant period of time. Third, in departments in which the trainee was given a chance to interact with members of the department, the opportunity to observe exactly what kinds of activities individuals were engaged in at various levels of the organization was increased. Finally, in some departments unplanned training that was beneficial occurred. For example, while working in one department a special project came up to which the trainee was assigned. This assignment, which involved gathering information on a problem in another agency, permitted the trainee to see beyond the more routine work of the department and become familiar with some of the more significant activities performed by the department. The trainee was fortunate in this instance, because that department was flexible and willing to let him work on the special project. The second year of the program involved the trainee being assigned to a field office. This assignment provided him with additional information about the organization as well as providing some managerial responsibility. During the second year the trainee selected two departments in the main office to which he would like to be assigned. He was then assigned to one of these departments — a decision based both on the organization's needs and the trainee's preferences.

There are a number of positive features associated with job rotation, some of which are pointed out by this example. First, systematic job rotation helps to develop managerial generalists because it exposes them to several different types of operations and situations in many different departments. Second, job rotation programs that develop generalists and programs geared toward developing back-up personnel for specific positions may play an important role in human resource planning by creating organizational flexibility. In the event that the organization loses people or encounters rapid expansion, a number of internally trained candidates may be available to assume a variety of positions. Third, job rotation makes it possible to compare one managerial trainee with another in a variety of settings. A significant aspect of such comparisons is that evaluations of a number of managers under whom the individual being rotated has worked can be combined to get a better picture of his abilities. Conversely, the ability of the managers to train others can be evaluated by having the trainees compare the various managers under whom they have worked. Both comparisons may provide the personnel department with information on which to base future job rotation decisions in order to improve development activities. Fourth, job rotation may facilitate cooperation among various departments because those rotated will become much more familiar with each other's problems. Therefore, when they are assigned to a department on a permanent basis, they can appreciate the problems of the other departments with whom they must work, which may help foster better interdepartmental working relations. Further, the manager-trainee may bring new ideas to the departments he visits. Fifth, job rotation, within the limits indicated, permits the individual to choose the department to which he would like to be assigned on a permanent basis. Finally, it should be emphasized that job rotation draws upon many of the principles of learning mentioned in Chapter 6 and earlier in this chapter. If properly organized, job rotation may provide the trainee with active rather than passive learning, KOR, reinforcement, and distributed learning where appropriate. For example, unlike apprenticeship training, job rotation can take advantage of individual differences by structuring the program to meet the needs of each individual being trained. In the job rotation example mentioned, one trainee was assigned to a field office because the final assignment in the main office would require working with field offices; another spent two years in the main office because the final assignment would not involve working with field offices.

Job rotation does have a number of limitations. In some cases the trainee may be required to move from one geographical area to another. Such movement may be hard on the individual but refusal to move may limit his chances of moving up in the organization. Frequent movement also tends to reduce loyalty to the organization. It is possible, especially when the trainee is a practicing manager, that rotating him too frequently may lead him to focus too much attention on short range projects that have a quick payoff in order to make his performance look better. As with on-the-job training in general, this type of focus is more likely to occur if the manager is evaluated on current results. For example, he may ignore developing his own subordinates if such efforts may not reap benefits for several years, which may often be the case. The short-range focus may help induce the trainee-manager to see his supervisor as the person he must please, and consequently, he may neglect to develop peer relationships and to adequately represent his subordinates. The short-range focus is a two-sided problem in that the subordinates of managers being frequently rotated may not adopt their suggestions because they see them as temporary superiors and therefore believe that they will just have to change some of their behavior again when the next manager arrives. The unwillingness to adopt suggestions of the manager being rotated may be reasonable if he is moved from one job to another before he has sufficiently learned the job. In such cases, he may be asked to make decisions before he has learned the job adequately or he may be rotated at the point in time when he is just really beginning to master the job. Another limitation, which also comes from the emphasis on showing immediate results, is that some trainees who are quite capable may adjust slowly, have difficulty showing immediate results, and therefore be evaluated unfavorably. Such an evaluation may or may not be valid. Slow adjustment may appropriately be negatively evaluated if the organization is a dynamic one in which all managers must adapt quickly to rapid changes if they are to be effective but not necessarily represent a problem in a very stable environment. Another limitation is that the training may be uneven from one department to another. Thus, a trainee may learn a great deal in one department and very little in another. Finally, job rotation may be difficult in smaller companies because opportunities to move are limited due to the small number of positions available and the fact that individuals cannot be spared to conduct the training.

Many of these limitations may be reduced or eliminated by making certain that it is thoroughly planned. The personnel department needs to gain support for the program from the managers of the departments to which the trainees will be assigned. One way of accomplishing this is by making sure that the managers know the goals of the program and how to conduct training effectively. The trainee also must be informed of the goals of the program if he is to gain the most from job rotation. The trainee assigned to the field office in our earlier example was not initially provided with such information, received little feedback on the job and spent a number of weeks wondering if the organization was dissatisfied with his work. The fact that another trainee was assigned to the main office in this example indicates that training may be facilitated in job rotation programs when they take into account individual differences and are tailored to each trainee so that the specific types of learning needed by each individual are obtained.

Special Assignments

Many types of special assignments can be used in on-the-job training. The trainee may be given a special project on which to work in order to broaden his experience. For example, a trainee in a personnel department may be assigned to collect data on employee turnover that will enable him to learn about how to conduct such surveys. A trainee may be assigned as an assistant to a manager in order to prepare him to assume the job of the manager. For example, one of the personnel manager's professional subordinates who is considered a logical successor to him may be taken from his specialized area (testing) and work with and help his superior handle all functional areas of personnel. Such an assignment may be very valuable in helping prepare the individual for promotion to the "generalist" position of personnel manager. Further, an individual may be given committee assignments in order to broaden his experience. For example, in a unionized plant, a trainee in the personnel department might be assigned to the committee that handles employee grievances in order to let him work with both union and management representatives and see how the grievance procedure operates.

Closely related to commitee assignments is the idea of junior boards of directors or "multiple management" for management development. Under this approach, lower and middle level managers "participate formally, along with top management, in the planning and administration of corporate affairs" through what amount to permanent advisory committes.[19] Such junior boards may investigate specific problems and recommend solutions, or they may actually attempt to carry on activities representative of those undertaken by the firm's board of directors. For example, at McCormick and Company, where the multiple management concept was originally developed in 1932, a junior board of directors comprised of 10 to 20 middle managers makes recommendations to the senior board of directors. These must be unanimous, and if the senior board does not accept any recommendation, it must state in writing its reasons for not doing so to the junior board. The ability of the junior board to generate useable ideas is reflected by the fact that during the time when McCormick and Company was only a single-plant operation, more than 2000 proposals were submitted to top management over a five-year period. Most of these were adopted in whole or in part. The McCormick program is competitive, in that periodically peer ratings are made, and the three least effective members of the junior board are dropped and three new members added. Based upon the success of the junior board of directors, a number of "miniboards" were created, such as factory boards and sales boards, to deal with specific problems in various functional areas. These boards were also generally successful, and today a number of companies have adopted the multiple managment concept. In addition to generating useable ideas, multiple management permits trainees to gain skills and knowledge outside their own specialty and to engage in group decision making, which represents a basic skill requirement in most upper level managerial situations. Further, multiple management permits managers to observe the trainees and to decide which ones have the greatest potential for top management positions.

In spite of these advantages, multiple management may contribute to certain problems. The junior executives may become frustrated if their ideas are frequently not adopted or acted upon. The trainees may become tense and anxious because of the intense internal competition that can create interpersonal conflicts and interfere with motivation. Finally, while the technique is relatively inexpensive in terms of the use of facilities, it may be costly if large numbers of managers have to be taken away from their full-time jobs to devote time to the board.

Coaching

Coaching occurs when a supervisor helps his subordinates on a continuous basis by providing them with feedback on how they are doing and what is expected of them. This may take the form of answering questions, guiding the individual in finding his own answers to problems, having him participate in decision making, etc. Coaching is an important part of performance appraisal in that it helps stimulate individual growth and development. Likewise, coaching is an important ingredient in all on-the-job development techniques discussed earlier. In fact, Bass and Vaughan have suggested that job rotation and some types of special assignments simply represent coaching that has been formalized.[20]

Coaching contributes to learning and improved performance because it represents an excellent opportunity to provide KOR to the trainee on a continuous basis. With respect to performance appraisal, managers need to be careful that they do not overload subordinates with too much information, particularly of a negative nature. This same problem exists with all coaching. In a sense, coaching, if done properly, can be considered to include the better features of both on-the-job development and performance appraisal.

Off-The-Job Development Techniques

In this section we will discuss a number of the off-the-job techniques presented in Figure 7–3. We will not discuss films and television, since these media have many of the same characteristics as lectures and they are really aids to training that are "used to increase the effectiveness of a training program" rather than techniques for conducting training.[21] Discussion of the widely-used off-the-job development technique known as "laboratory," "sensitivity" or "T-group" training will be reserved for Chapter 8.

Lecture, Special Studies, and Discussion

The lecture is a traditional training technique and is probably the most commonly used method in both on-the-job and off-the-job training. The principal advantage of the lecture is that it can be used to provide *factual information* to a large number of people at one time, making it a relatively low-cost alternative. Such economy may be false, however, because merely exposing trainees to information does not mean that they will acquire knowledge.[22] A second advantage of the lecture method is that the material to be presented can be organized meaningfully, which will facilitate learning.

A number of limitations of the lecture method are frequently cited. First, in a lecture per se, communication is one way. The trainee in such a setting is passive, has no opportunity to practice, and receives no reinforcement nor KOR. In addition, individual differences in learning rates are not taken into account, so that some of the trainees may be hopelessly lost while others are bored. This results because the trainer is not receiving any feedback about whether or not the trainees understand the material being presented. Because of these limitations, a great deal of criticism has been raised against the lecture method, and it is held in low esteem by many training directors. In one study of 117 training directors the lecture method *with questions permitted* was ranked last of nine development techniques evaluated.[23] It is interesting to note that the two other "techniques" (movie films and television) included in the study that primarily involved one way communication, passive learning, lack of opportunity for practice, and no feedback were ranked seventh and eighth among the nine techniques. Thus, the lecture, even with provision for questions, was ranked lower than two communications media that did not permit any two way communication. It appears, however, that such strong criticism of the lecture method is unwarranted. While the lecture method is not appropriate for teaching complex skills and may not be appropriate for trying to change attitudes, it does appear to be effective for imparting factual information. When the lecture method is compared with other techniques it often is rated favorably, particularly when factual information is involved, and in fact it is very often used as a "control technique" in the evaluation of other training methods. Given the high costs associated with newer training techniques such as television, film, computer assisted instruction, and programmed instruction, the lecture method may have some significant cost advantages when the goal of training is knowledge acquisition.

In order to overcome some of the disadvantages of the lecture method, trainees may be assigned to study special materials rather than have them sit through a lecture. Such an approach permits trainees to proceed at their own rate, to make notes, and to check back on materials read previously. Thus, some active participation is involved and individual differences are taken into account. Practice and reinforcement are still lacking, however, and this technique, like the lecture, is most appropriate for having trainees acquire knowledge (factual information).

Having trainees discuss problems, issues, and other materials in groups is sometimes used to overcome the disadvantages of the lecture and special study methods. The primary advantages of the "conference" or "discussion" method, as it is called, are that it permits two way communication, which provides for active participation, feedback, and clarification of materials.[24] These factors in turn are likely to result in less frustration and greater motivation on the part of the trainee. In addition, the conference or discussion method appears to be effective for teaching complex materials, and some types of problem solving and decision making skills, as well as for changing certain attitudes.

The conference or discussion method has some disadvantages, however. It is restricted to relatively small groups, since active participation by most individuals is not likely in large groups. This is due to both a lesser opportunity and an unwillingness of individuals to participate in larger groups. Further, discussion takes time, and, thus, less information may be imparted in any given period of time than can be transmitted in a lecture. Because of these two factors, the training costs per person are likely to be higher than with the lecture method. Discussion is likely to be less organized than a lecture, because the trainees are given an opportunity to participate when they wish. Finally, there may be irrelevant discussion as many participants may try to be heard. This tendency simply magnifies the time and organization problems.

A discussion format combined with special studies is sometimes used to facilitate learning. For example, it was reported in 1973 that the Chairman of the Board of the Koppers Company met three times a month for three hours in his office with a group of ten young managers for a discussion of some previously assigned reading such as Galbraith's *The Affluent Society*.[25] The basic goal of the meetings was to provide the managers with an opportunity to see how executives at top organizational echelons thought. However, the meetings also gave the top level executives a chance to observe how the young managers thought and conceptualized materials.

The lecture can also be combined effectively with discussion. For example, in one situation in the steel industry the basic provisions of the Occupational Safety and Health Act of 1970 were communicated to managers and supervisors by means of a lecture-discussion format. The firm's safety director went over the key provisions of the new law and the foremen and supervisors were given an opportunity to ask for clarification. Later, when certain government regulations concerning the law were promulgated, this information was also provided to each foreman and supervisor by the safety director.

Programmed Instruction (PI)

In the 1950's programmed instruction (PI) was widely discussed as a revolutionary new development technique.[26] While the revolution never materialized and PI did not turn out to be the panacea that some people thought it would, it has taken its place as one form of instructional technology.

Programmed instruction involves dividing the material to be learned into small units (parts) called frames. The "frames" may be provided through different media such as sequential sections in a PI "textbook," or visually on a screen through a "teaching machine." The trainee reads the first frame, which provides certain information. This information, in turn, is used in the next frame, and subsequent frames continue to build on prior frames in the same way. The trainee typically is required to respond by answering a question, filling in a blank, or selecting a multiple choice or true/false alternative. The trainee is immediately informed whether the response is correct or incorrect. In some instances when the trainee is incorrect, he is merely informed of the error and permitted to continue. In other instances, however, the concept of branching is used. Branching means moving the trainee to other predetermined questions based on his previous responses. For example, if the trainee responds incorrectly, he may be moved back to remedial material. In very complex PI programs multiple branching may be used so that if a trainee answers a number of questions in a row correctly, he is moved to more advanced material, while a trainee who misses one question is moved to remedial material and if the first few questions are missed in the remedial section, he is sent back to even more basic material or perhaps referred to an instructor.

A major advantage of PI is that it makes use of a number of the principles of learning discussed in Chapter 6. PI is individualized, since the trainee proceeds through the frames at his own rate. Learning is active since the trainee must respond in some manner to each frame, and KOR is immediate. Reinforcement is immediate if responses are correct and the trainee derives satisfaction from responding correctly. Even if the responses are incorrect, the immediacy of KOR permits the trainee to correct any errors before incorrect information is learned. Since material to be learned is broken into small units, part learning is emphasized, and motivation may be enhanced, since the trainee proceeds at his own rate and receives immediate feedback without an "information overload." Another advantage of PI that results directly from the self-paced nature of the technique is that groups do not have to be assembled at the same time, as in the lecture method. This permits greater flexibility in assigning individual trainees and therefore may permit a better allocation of organizational resources. A final advantage of PI is that if it is implemented properly, consistent information is transmitted to each trainee since everyone works with the same materials. Of course, if program materials are erroneous, consistent but incorrect information could be transmitted and learned.

Given the extent to which PI appears to utilize principles of learning, one would expect it to be a very effective development technique. However, a review by Nash, Muczyk and Vettori of more than 100 research studies dealing with the relative effectiveness of PI as opposed to conventional techniques (primarily the lecture) in both industrial and academic settings revealed contradictory findings.[27] PI was compared to the conventional techniques in terms of training time required, materials immediately learned, and the retention of the learning. Of the studies reviewed, 32 had measures of both training time required and immediate learning, but only 26 of these studies also included a measure of retention. PI was found to provide faster learning than conventional methods in 29 of the studies reviewed, not significantly different learning time in two, and slower learning in one. Thus, in terms of training time, PI appeared to have some clear advantages over conventional methods. The results on immediate learning were less clear cut, since PI was superior to them in only nine of the studies, not significantly different in 20, and less effective in three. In terms of retention, PI was found to be equivalent to conventional techniques, since five studies found it to be superior and five inferior, with 16 finding no significant difference.

In addition to the inconclusive nature of the research on its effectiveness, there are other disadvantages to PI. First, PI is primarily effective with *factual material,* especially that which can be presented in a *logical sequence,* such as basic statistics, mathematics, or spelling. Therefore, PI may not be useful for programs dealing with human relations training and attitudinal change.[28] Second, PI may be very expensive, at least initially. One study, for example, reported that "it is not unusual for new programs to cost from $50,000 to $150,000."[29] Therefore, two of the basic contingencies mentioned in Chapter 1 influence the choice of PI. The first is organizational size in terms of "exposures," since unless there is a large enough number of trainees who will use the program, the cost of developing a PI package will be prohibitive. Second is how static or dynamic an organization is. Even if the number of trainees is large, the cost of PI may be prohibitive if the content is changing rapidly in a dynamic organization so that frequent updating and change are necessary. While these costs can be lowered considerably by purchasing PI materials developed by others, the lack of 100 per cent congruence between what any purchased program offers and what the organization wants may cause them to be less effective than needed and may even result in the occurrence of some incorrect learning. A final disadvantage of PI is that programs often are not well written or evaluated. "In sum, the recent PI literature holds no new surprises. A reasonable conclusion is still that, for appropriate material, PI is faster but probably does not lead to greater proficiency on an immediate post test. Long term retention remains an open question."[30]

One of the three basic types of management science techniques mentioned in Chapter 1—network models—has been applied in developing a PI program.[31] A PERT network was developed entailing both the writing and producing of a PI program that contained 171 events. The major activites in the network included setting the objectives of the PI program and, writing, diagramming, and validating the program. Minor, but necessary activities consisted of copying materials, making typing changes, and storing materials. The application of PERT to PI is not surprising, since both approaches start by specifying objectives and then develop a logical sequence of steps to reach these objectives. There does not appear to be any reason why PERT cannot be used to plan many other types of development programs.

Computer-Assisted Instruction (CAI)

"Computer-Assisted Instruction (CAI) refers to the use of the computer for instruction, i.e., as a means of presenting material to, and interacting with, a student."[32] It is primarily useful in teaching the same kinds of factual materials as is PI. As the definition points out, CAI is dependent upon the use of the computer. However, there are a number of different forms of CAI based upon the extent to which the computer is used. For example, based upon the degree and complexity of trainee-computer interaction, CAI has been classified as: (1) drill and practice, (2) tutorial, and (3) dialogue.[33]

Drill and practice is the simplest and most common form of CAI. In drill and practice, a trainer typically presents material to trainees, after which they go to a computer terminal and check their comprehension of the material. For example, the trainer in a basic statistics course might present the concept of the mean as an average of a set of numbers and then have the trainee go to the computer terminal to check his understanding of how the calculations should be performed. The trainee would enter a code that provides access to the memory bank of the computer. The exact sequence of events might be as presented in Figure 7–4.

The problems presented in many CAI programs will differ from time to time, since they are randomly generated from among a number of similar ones stored in the computer. The trainee is given immediate feedback as to the correctness of the response, and, while we have shown an example in which the direction of the error (too large or too small) is indicated to the trainee, this is not done in all CAI programs. On the other hand, in more sophisticated systems, even more information might be provided, such as the magnitude of the incorrect answer or perhaps even that the decimal point appears to have been misplaced. In very sophisticated systems, the program may try to identify the nature of the errors being made (such as a misplaced decimal) and shift the trainee into remedial work. Likewise, the student who is answer-

Student turns the terminal on and types in the appropriate code.

HELLO THIS YOUR FRIENDLY COMPUTER. WHICH PROGRAM DO YOU WISH?*

Mean

DO YOU NEED INSTRUCTION ON HOW TO USE THE PROGRAM?

No   (Note a "yes" response would cause instructions
           to be printed)

HERE IS THE FIRST SET OF NUMBERS: 24, 36, 72, 85. WHAT IS YOUR ANSWER?

54.25

YOUR ANSWER IS CORRECT. HERE IS THE SECOND SET OF NUMBERS: 82, 3, 45.1, 2.4. WHAT IS YOUR ANSWER?

432.67

YOUR ANSWER IS TOO LARGE. WOULD YOU LIKE TO TRY AGAIN? IF YES, MERELY TYPE THE NEW ANSWER. IF NO TYPE NO.

4.3267

YOUR ANSWER IS NOW TOO SMALL. WOULD YOU LIKE TO TRY AGAIN? IF YES MERELY TYPE THE NEW ANSWER. IF NO TYPE NO.

No

THE CORRECT ANSWER IS 43.267. WOULD YOU LIKE ANOTHER PROBLEM?

No

OK. WE ARE DONE. PLEASE TURN OFF THE TERMINAL BEFORE LEAVING. THANK YOU.

---

*The lines with all letters capitalized are the messages which the computer would type out to the trainee. The words and numbers in between these capitalized lines represent the responses which the student would type in answer to the questions coming from the computer.

Figure 7-4 *Hypothetical sequence of events for a trainee using CAI in drill and practice mode.*

ing all questions correctly might be shifted into more advanced work. Such movement, as mentioned in the discussion of PI, is referred to as "branching" and may be based not only upon the trainee's recent performance but also upon prior knowledge of his proficiency if the computer is programmed to keep continuous records on each trainee.[34] The trainee will generally not be permitted an unlimited number of trials to get the right answer. Rather, after some predetermined number of incorrect responses, the correct answer will be given and a new problem generated if the student so desires. Finally, we should note that in addition to typed responses from the computer, some CAI systems are designed so that the computer may also provide visual materials to be displayed on a screen via a slide projector or auditory messages presented to the trainee via a "random access" tape recorder.

The tutorial form of CAI is more complex than the drill and practice form. In tutorial CAI, the computer itself is doing the "teaching" rather than a human trainer — the computer is used to present *original* material rather than supplemental material as in drill and practice. Tutorial CAI makes extensive use of the branching concept of presenting different materials and questions based upon the prior responses of the trainee. In doing this, CAI has borrowed from PI, since essentially tutorial CAI is based upon the branching concept of PI with the computer simply speeding up the branching process. A tutorial system called TASKTEACH, for example, has been developed "to help trainees to learn serial tasks, from operating equipment to electronic troubleshooting."[35] The program can provide the trainee with information indicating a failure in a particular circuit of a piece of electronic equipment and the trainee can then attempt to diagnose the reason for the failure. In addition, the trainee can specify a particular malfunction in the equipment and then "test his knowledge of the symptoms it would produce."[36]

The third form of CAI, the dialogue form, is still very experimental. The hope is that eventually the trainee will be able to communicate verbally with the computer. Rather than being presented with material and then quizzed to determine understanding, the dialogue form of CAI would involve the trainee engaging in "*true conversation* with the computer."[37] This approach would go beyond the tutorial form, in that the trainee could ask for data or provide an answer at any point during the conversation.

The advantages of CAI are similar to those of PI. Such similarities are to be expected, since CAI, at least in its early formulation, merely used the computer to replace a PI textbook. As Campbell has pointed out, "Computer assisted instruction is a sophisticated descendent of programmed instruction."[38] Like PI,

CAI makes considerable use of the principles of learning, of individualization, active learning, KOR, reinforcement, part learning, and motivation. Individualization of training may be even greater in CAI than in PI. As mentioned, the computer may keep records concerning the trainee's past behavior and through branching adjust the rate of presentation and the nature of material to known characteristics of the trainee such as ability and prior knowledge. Reinforcement and motivation may be enhanced because the computer is infinitely patient, does not have inappropriate predetermined biases about the trainees, and does not ridicule the trainee when he makes a mistake as a human trainer might. Quite to the contrary, the trainee receives positive feedback for correct responses.[39] For these reasons some trainees actually prefer the computer to a human trainer.[40] Other advantages of CAI may accrue from the fact that the computer can keep records on the progress of trainees. For example, in Figure 7–4, the computer could be programmed to keep a record of each problem assigned to a trainee, the trainee's answer, whether the answer was correct or incorrect, and summary information such as how many problems were answered correctly. The instructor is then able to develop or modify existing programs and to provide individual trainees with remedial help or advanced training that is not available through existing computer programs. The record-keeping function may also provide the trainer with information concerning how learning occurs. Finally, CAI programs can "represent the teaching approaches and knowledge of the best minds in pedagogy as well as in diverse subject areas."[41]

As with PI, one would expect CAI to be a very effective development technique because it appears to draw on so many of the principles of learning. However, CAI has many of the same limitations as PI. While learning is faster than traditional methods, research is inconclusive as to whether CAI results in any greater immediate learning and retention than more traditional methods.[42] The cost of CAI is very high. One 1971 estimate, for example, placed the lower cost limit on a CAI system at $2.5 million, with large systems costing as high as $14 million.[43] However, if the number of individuals to be trained is large, the average cost per trainee may ultimately be less than with conventional training methods.[44] Finally, as with PI, CAI materials may not be well written or evaluated. A disadvantage of CAI not present in PI is that there is little research on the impact of individual interaction with a computer rather than a human trainer with respect to the motivation and satisfaction of trainees. While some people may prefer interacting with a computer rather than a human trainer, others may not, and some individuals may actually be afraid of the computer because they do not understand it.

The lack of research concerning the value of CAI poses a real problem for personnel departments in industry, since without favorable research findings, the cost of CAI has led industry to shy away from it. As Loftin stated in 1974: "At present industry has yet to commit itself to addressing CAI as anything other than an attractive but remote possibility to training employees."[45] Given this state of affairs, the reader may ask why we have devoted so much space to the topic. Our decision was based upon two factors: First, we believe that CAI has a great deal of potential and therefore will be used more frequently in industry as research demonstrates its worth. Second, CAI has become more and more frequently used in *educational* settings and therefore the "potential labor force is becoming more exposed to and more accustomed to advanced instructional technology through CAI applications."[46] Thus, in the future, there will be more individuals in business firms who are aware of CAI and willing to explore the possible use of CAI in light of its costs.

Vestibule Training

Vestibule training involves trainees learning in a nonwork environment in which conditions and equipment are *virtually identical* to what will be encountered on the job.[47] In fact, the environment and the equipment may be so similar that vestibule training *almost* becomes an on-the-job training situation. For example, in the early 1950's a group of researchers at the RAND Corporation used the vestibule method to train military personnel working in groups who were responsible for defending the United States against enemy air attacks.[48] The groups were given a number of simulated tasks to perform such as monitoring radar screens, and if an unknown aircraft was detected, dispatching an interceptor that might open fire on the unknown aircraft. In addition, they could simulate putting the whole nation on emergency alert. In this type of problem solving, it is not possible to wait for a real enemy attack in order to train people. Therefore, the researchers at RAND used vestibule training, in which they "decided not to vary either the kind of equipment (the physical environment) or such conditions as operation policies (the cultural environment)."[49] They did, however, manipulate the task conditions by creating mock attacks and simulating attack conditions to which the trainees had to respond. The researchers found that the subjects began to behave as if they were in a real life situation; they became anxious, highly involved, and learned to perform their tasks, handle information overload, etc. The trainees were also reported to be highly motivated to learn, largely due to the realism of the simulated conditions. In addition, the trainees were provided with (1) immediate KOR, which was objective, pertinent, and accurate, and (2) positive reinforcement for defending their area adequately. Both the KOR and positive reinforcement contributed to the motivation of the trainees. Quite obviously, the trainees were engaging in active learning. It should be noted that the learning in this setting was total systems-oriented. The total systems orientation and the attempt to replicate very complex real conditions so closely represents a major drawback for using such sophisticated vestibule training for industrial purposes — systems simulation is extremely costly.[50]

Another example of vestibule training that illustrates the close correspondence between this off-the-job technique and on-the-job training is provided by the training of check-out clerks in the supermarket industry. In one large supermarket chain, newly hired individuals for check-out clerk positions were assigned to a check-out counter not being used for customers at a time when the store was not busy, and the trainer pretending to be a customer came through the counter with a shopping cart full of goods. The trainee rang up the items and the trainer was able to check accuracy, speed, and customer courtesy. This example, in contrast to the RAND one, illustrates that vestibule training can be used (1) for individual skills training as well as for group and systems training, and, (2) in industrial training situations that are not cost prohibitive.

The primary advantage of vestibule training is that, like all forms of off-the-job training, the emphasis is on learning and not on results. Another significant advantage is that the problem of transferring learning is minimized because the trainee is learning under conditions very similar or virtually identical to actual job conditions. In addition, as the examples illustrate, vestibule training draws upon principles of learning such as KOR, active learning, and reinforcement. Vestibule training can also be used to teach human relations as well as other skills. For example, the trainer acting as the customer in the check-out example could pretend to become irate because the trainee was proceeding too slowly. This would show the trainee what might actually happen and also show the trainer how the trainee might react. If the trainee snaps back at the customer, the trainer might point out that this would not be acceptable behavior when an actual customer is involved and that the trainee needs to change his attitude. A final advantage of vestibule training (which again is true for most off-the-job training techniques) is that it tends more often to use individuals as trainers who are specialists in training. Such individuals are more likely to be able to draw on principles of learning that enhance the learning, give special attention to individual trainee needs, and make use of other training techniques because of their familiarity with them.

Vestibule training has certain inherent limitations and it may be poorly conducted by many firms. A primary disadvantage of much vestibule training is its cost because of the need to duplicate facilities and equipment for nonproductive purposes. Such duplication may not always be necessary, however, as is illustrated by the check-out example. Another problem, which some firms permit to occur with vestibule training, is the use of damaged or obsolete equipment for training in order to reduce the costs associated with duplication of the most modern equipment. In such cases, learning may be slower and may often result in incorrect learning and erroneous transfer of learning. Further, in vestibule training the learning environment may be different in terms of organizational rules, interpersonal relationships, and other aspects of the organizational climate than the work environment itself. For example, the pressure for production in the work environment may be so great that anxiety is induced that was not present in the training environment. These last two points indicate that vestibule training will be most effective in transferring learning to the work environment when it replicates as closely as possible the actual working conditions.

Vestibule training is likely to be justified when the risk of error is high and such errors are costly, when many people need to be trained at the same time, and when it is impossible to conduct training on the job. For example, if on-the-job training may result in injury, damage to equipment, or waste of raw materials, vestibule training may be more appropriate. For instance, in the air defense simulation it would be ludicrous to "wait" for a real enemy air attack to see how military personnel would respond.

Simulation

In a simulation, an attempt is made to replicate the system in which the trainee is ultimately expected to perform. The illustrations of vestibule training also represent examples of simulation, since they were attempts to replicate an actual work environment in training situations. As with the vestibule training examples, simulations can be used for skills, knowledge, and attitudinal training for individuals, groups, and whole systems. In this section we will discuss in order of their historical development four development techniques other than vestibule training that can be considered forms of simulation: (1) case studies, (2) role playing exercises, (3) in-basket exercises, and (4) business games. The last two techniques are both included under the simulation category in Figure 7–3. These techniques differ from vestibule training in that they either emphasize the development of human relations or decision-making skills rather than being more oriented to technical skills development as in most vestibule training. Thus, vestibule training involves transfer more through identical elements whereas simulations typically involve transfer through principle. We will now present the major advantages, disadvantages, and conditions conducive to successful training unique to each of these techniques.

Case studies. Case studies were introduced as a training technique in the 1920's at the Harvard Business School.[51] A case study simulates certain aspects of organizational problems by providing a written description of them. Given the information in the case, the trainee is typically required to identify and analyze problems and issues facing the organization and recommend courses of action. Thus, the major use of case studies is to help trainees develop decision-making skills. If the trainee is required to present his analysis to other members of a group and discussion takes place, case studies can be used to change attitudes. For example, some line managers who are negatively biased toward the behavioral sciences may change this attitude if they can see how some other trainees in a management development seminar can do a better job of analyzing a case by using certain behavioral science techniques. Case studies can also be used to see if trainees can apply appropriate techniques to complex problems. For example, a case might contain a problem that could be dealt with much more effectively if mathematical programming were used. In such a case, the trainee would first have to identify the problem and then be able to apply the technique appropriately.

Proponents of the case study method argue that learning of a lasting nature occurs because the trainees are engaged in active learning through a process of "self discovery." In addition, in group discussions of cases the trainee receives feedback about the appropriateness of his ideas and may be able to begin to generate "principles" that can be used in situations similar to those presented in the case. An advantage of this method is that simple and complex and short and long cases can be developed and therefore can be designed to meet different specific training objectives within the time available for the training.

A major limitation of the case study method is that cases are static in nature. The case is analyzed and alternatives for helping to overcome problems generated that will presumably stimulate learning. However, in many cases it is not possible to say that a particular decision alternative is the "best" among all those considered and the identification of the "best" approach to deal with problems in the case may never be possible. Further, the trainee does not have to "live" with his decisions in the sense that they are ever actually implemented. Therefore, he may not receive KOR, and interest and motivation may be lacking.[52]

When group discussion is used with cases, trainees may have an inadequate background for real analysis or an unwillingness to discuss the case thoroughly. These factors may limit the learning that takes place. The trainer can assume a very important role in case study analysis, since he can provide direction to the group. However, he needs to be careful not to provide too much direction so that he is giving answers that will negate the "self-discovery" process. On the other hand, the trainer must not provide so little direction that the group members merely "share ignorance" and learn erroneous materials.

Closely related to the case study method is a technique known as the incident technique.[53] Usually conducted in groups, trainees are provided with a brief description of a situation facing a manager that requires him to take action. Each trainee can ask the trainer for additional information, but the trainer will not voluntarily provide any information not specifically requested. Once the trainees believe they have sufficient information, when the trainer has no more information to give, or when the time allotted to the technique is up, the trainees are asked to come up with an approach for handling the problem. The problem solving approaches of the various trainees are discussed, after which the trainer usually reveals all the information he has, including what decisions were actually made in dealing with the incident and the results of these decisions if they are known. Because he must ask for information, each trainee is more actively involved in the learning process and therefore may be more motivated than in a case study discussion, in which all information that anyone will receive is provided prior to the discussion. In addition, if actual outcomes that occurred in handling the problems are made known, the trainee may be more motivated. Of course, actual results can also be made known in case studies when they are available.[54] The incident technique is sometimes intermixed in management development programs with traditional cases or role playing (which we will discuss next) to provide a "change of pace" and to emphasize to managers the importance of their being able to ferret out information by precisely phrased questions. Thus, this technique provides more explicit training than do case studies in one key facet of managerial decision making—obtaining the key *informational inputs* needed to make decisions.

Role playing. The role playing technique was developed by J. L. Moreno in the 1930's for group therapy involving mentally disturbed individuals but since has been found useful in many other situations.[55] In role playing, various members of the group (trainees and sometimes trainers as well) act out a particular part (role). Role playing may be highly structured. In such cases, the individuals playing various roles read from a script as in a play. Role playing may also be more spontaneous with only some prestructuring. In such cases, the course of action taken by individuals will be influenced considerably by the personal characteristics of those playing the roles. The reader may note that we have already described role play situations in vestibule training and case studies. The trainer who acted out the part of the customer at the check-out counter had assumed a role. Likewise, in case studies the trainee assumes the role of an organizational decision maker. (Participants in in-basket exercises and business games which we will discuss shortly, also engage in role playing.) In its "purest" form, however, role playing is used primarily for analyzing interpersonal problems, developing human relations skills, and changing attitudes.[56] Role playing can also be used to teach specific decision-making techniques, since it can help the trainee to understand both his own behavior and that of others. For example, in one organization supervisors were trained in interviewing skills by means of role playing. Each supervisor was provided with mock data on an applicant and then interviewed the trainer who played the role of the applicant. Both the trainer and other trainees provided the "interviewer" with feedback as to the appropriateness of his behavior and each supervisor was given an opportunity to "interview" again, hopefully performing more appropriately on the basis of the feedback. To help trainees gain insight into the problems, feelings, and attitudes of other individuals, role reversal can be used. For example, the production and sales managers might be asked to play one anothers' parts in handling a particular problem in which the two departments had conflicting goals. Likewise, union and management members or supervisors and subordinates are called on to reverse roles in some training situations.

Role playing is different than the case study method in certain important ways.[57] Unless the role playing is highly prestructured, problems that evolve during training are dealt with rather than those presented in advance in written form. Emotional issues rather than factual ones are dealt with more frequently, and hence trainee involvement tends to be more emotional than intellectual. Finally, role playing provides continuous feedback concerning actions taken by trainees, whereas in case studies the "real" consequences of decisions made by trainees frequently are not known. These differences are not meant to imply that role playing is either superior or inferior to case studies — these two techniques simply have different orientations.

A major disadvantage of role playing is that its success depends very heavily on the willingness of the trainees to assume the role called for. Extremely important here is that the roles appear realistic. If the trainees think that the situations lack realism they may believe that the training is "childish" and behave accordingly. For example, this happened when a male manager played the role of a female subordinate being disciplined. The manager pulled up his trousers and "pretended" to be the girl while he was being disciplined and everyone got a big laugh. However, not much was learned. Another problem with role playing is that it can be costly because only a few people may be able to be trained by a single trainer. To overcome this problem, larger groups are sometimes broken into smaller groups, each of which deals with the same role playing problem without the trainer present.[58] After the groups have completed the role playing the whole group assembles to discuss with the trainer what happened in each subgroup. Finally, trainees may become more concerned with "acting" than they are with problem solving and learning.

In-basket exercises. Modeled after an in-basket test,[59] in-basket exercises were first used in the 1950's for training managers. While the exact format of in-basket exercises will vary, they frequently involve each trainee in a group first individually assuming the role of a manager who is faced with a number of letters, memos, and notes to which he must respond in writing within a limited time period. For example, the trainee may be told that he has just returned from vacation and that he must leave on a trip in four hours, during which time he must respond in writing to all the items on his desk. To further complicate the problem the trainee might be told that it is a Saturday, no one is around to answer questions, and that no secretarial help is available. Since there are usually more items to respond to than is possible in the time provided, each trainee has to decide on which items should be given top priority. Thus, the in-basket exercise emphasizes decision-making skills rather than the learning of new facts. In addition, depending how much time pressure is applied, the trainee may find out how well he operates under stress. After each trainee has finished the exercise (i.e., the allotted time has elapsed), he is often asked to justify his decisions before the trainer and the other individuals in the training group. The decisions of the manager are evaluated and critiqued so that he receives feedback regarding his performance.

One advantage of in-basket exercises is that they are relatively easy to administer to groups of 25 to 30 manager trainees. Further, in-basket exercises are generally less costly to design than certain training tools such as CAI and business games, which we will discuss next. Thus, the cost per trainee may be relatively low. In addition they place the trainee in a time-constrained managerial decision-making situation, in which he must establish priorities quickly under stress. This is an important managerial skill in some positions and, although other training techniques such as role playing can provide stress, the in-basket is specifically designed to do so.

The limitations of the in-basket exercise are similar to those of cases. First, they are static in nature and the trainee does not really have to "live" with the consequences of his decisions. To overcome this problem, as with cases, in-basket exercises have been merged with CAI. For example, in one such program designed for training in industrial library administration, the trainee is presented with a problem which requires a series of decisions.[60] The trainee is also presented with five alternative means of resolving the problem from which he must choose. A further development of the original problem is then presented to the trainee based upon the alternative he chooses and then another five alternatives are provided to him. This sequence is finally carried out a third time. Then, the trainee meets with the trainer for an evaluation and critique session. At each decision point in this exercise, therefore, the trainee receives some information concerning the consequences of his decision.

A second limitation of in-basket exercises is that the trainer must be highly skilled in conducting the exercise and in conducting the critique. The critique, as with performance appraisals, can be so general as to be meaningless or so specific and negative that the trainee is so overloaded with information that the training may be useless. Often, it should be noted, in-basket exercises are used in off-the-job management group training programs along with cases and the incident technique to provide a "change of pace."

Business games. A relatively recently developed and highly popular managerial training technique is the business game or "simulation." The first practical business game was introduced by the American Management Association in 1957. Since that time, the number of business games or simulations have grown at a rapid rate so that today there are hundreds and perhaps thousands of such games in use.[61]

"A business simulation or game may be defined as a *sequential decision-making exercise structured around a model of a business operation, in which participants assume the role of managing the simulated operation.*"[62] The trainees, in their roles as managers, may be called upon to make decisions in various functional areas of business. For example, they may have to decide how many units to produce, how many pages of advertising to purchase, or whether to borrow money. The first set of decisions is processed either manually or by a computer and the results of these decisions returned to the trainees. Each trainee then analyzes these results, and submits another set of decisions. The results of this second set of decisions are returned, and this process is repeated until the designated end of the game. Each set of decisions usually simulates some fixed time period such as a quarter of a year. This "collapsing" of time permits the trainer to provide a longer simulated period of time in a short real time period. For example in one simulation each set of decisions represents a quarter of a year. By having the trainees submit two decision sets per week, three years of operation are simulated in a six-week period.

Some business games are noncompetitive. The model used in this type of simulation calls on trainees to compete solely against a simulated environment. Other games are competitive. Here trainees compete against other players in the game and the results of any one trainee's firm's decisions are influenced not only by its own actions but by the decisions of other trainee firms as well. In noncompetitive games, if two people are playing the game and one charges a higher price, for example, this will have no impact on the other player's sales, whereas in a competitive game the one player's higher price will influence the sales of the other player's firm.

Business games may be classified in a number of ways other than manually as opposed to computer processed, and noncompetitive as opposed to competitive. Three other classifications are of importance for understanding gaming because they are directly related to how business games may be used for training: (1) total enterprise as opposed to functional; (2) generalized vs. specific industry; and (3) individual vs. group play. A total enterprise game is one "designed to give people experience in making decisions at a top executive level and in which decisions from one functional area interact with those made in other areas of the firm."[63] These types of games are designed to have the trainees make decisions that deal basically with the overall economic operation of the business. The trainee presumably will learn to analyze complex environments and how decisions made in one functional area influence decisions made in another. For example, the trainee may come to realize that a decision to pay dividends means that there are no longer sufficient funds left to expand plant capacity. Most total enterprise games are competitively interactive.

A functional business game, on the other hand, is designed to "focus specifically on problems of decision making as seen in one particular functional area."[64] Among the most common functional areas simulated in gaming are production, marketing, and finance. The objectives in functional simulations tend to be to familiarize trainees with the activities actually carried out in the functional area, to have them make the types of decisions that might be involved in such areas, and to utilize specific analytical tools to handle problems in the functional area being simulated.

Both total enterprise and functional business games can be generalized or specific industry games. In a generalized game, no *specific* industry will be simulated — the players, for example, might be told that they are managing a firm with three undefined products and that they are competing against four other similar firms. The objectives will depend upon whether the trainee is playing a total enterprise or a functional game. However, in a specific industry game, the additional goal of providing the trainee with information concerning how a specific industry operates is also present.

Business games can be used to teach some of the same types of attitudes and skills as in role playing, since the trainees are playing the roles of managers. For example, the production manager of a firm could be asked to assume the role of a firm's sales manager in a game, and vice versa, thus helping each to better understand the problems of the other. More than one trainee may be assigned to a single game firm in our final classification of business games — group vs. individual play. When several trainees (often four to six) are assigned to one firm, they are provided training not only in decision making, but also in relating to others which hopefully helps them develop their interpersonal skills.

Group play also tends to be less expensive, because for any number of trainees, there are fewer firms' results that must be calculated either manually or by computer. On the other hand, it is easier for any particular trainee to try to "pass the buck" to other members of his firm when poor decisions are made. In general, group play is probably used more often, especially with the competitive and total enterprise games. Group play in total enterprise games is especially logical, in that those involved in making decisions at top levels of real business firms usually have to work closely with others in doing so.[65]

A primary advantage of business games is that they are much more dynamic than either cases or in-basket exercises. In the game, trainees submit decisions and they may receive feedback quickly concerning the consequences of their decisions. In addition, due to the sequential nature of the simulation, they must live with decisions made in prior time periods that in turn may help induce a greater appreciation for the need for both long- and short-range planning. Business games also draw upon many of the principles of learning such as KOR, active participation, and repetition. There is evidence that business games create a great deal of interest on the part of the player which may contribute to greater motivation to learn.

One disadvantage of business games is that participants may focus on the wrong things. For example, rather than trying to learn about the environment in which they are operating, trainees may try to find weaknesses in the game that will permit them to "win" — e.g., have earned the most profits as of the end of the game. If the trainer stresses winning, trainees may be reluctant to experiment and therefore develop less of a risk-taking attitude. Further, in a specific industry game, the trainees may focus so much on how the industry functions in the game that they forget it is only a simulation of reality in which some significant real variables may be missing or inexact. Such behavior could, of course, easily lead to incorrect learning. If the industry is a dynamic one, any simulation model that may have been developed may become quickly obsolete. In a dynamic environment, therefore, it will be more difficult to keep a specific industry game up to date. Another disadvantage of business games is that they are costly. The time to develop business games, especially computerized ones, may involve thousands of hours of labor and considerable computer time. Further, in using games, computer time, supplies, and the time of the trainer represent additional costs. The cost of games tends to be especially high when a company designs its own game to replicate its own or its industry's operating characteristics. In general, only large firms with substantial financial resources can afford to develop such simulations.

COMPARISON OF DEVELOPMENT TECHNIQUES

Given the large number of development techniques from which to choose, how can one decide which to use? Ideally, the decision would be based upon extensive research conducted by the organization to assess which techniques work best under what specific conditions. However, this type of research is often lacking because its costs may be greater than its presumed benefits or the organization simply may not have the time and resources to conduct such research. Further, in small companies there may not be enough employees needing a particular form of training to obtain an adequate sample size on which to base any research. The individual in charge of development, however, must decide which techniques to use. Frequently, he or she will rely on the opinions of "experts" or the theories and research of others. In this section we will present the findings of two studies in which training directors reported on the development techniques they regarded as the most frequently used, and effective for helping to meet various objectives. We will also provide some general observations concerning the techniques that appear most appropriate and some guidelines for making decisions about the techniques to use for meeting different objectives.

Figure 7–5 presents the findings of one survey of 112 firms in which training directors were asked to rank the frequency with which they used the training techniques illustrated in Figure 7–3.[66] The firms varied in size, and as Figure 7–5 shows, were engaged in both manufacturing and nonmanufacturing activities. The authors of the study reported that there was very little difference between manufacturing and nonmanufacturing firms in the reported frequency with which the various techniques were used. As seen in Figure 7–5, the training directors in manufacturing firms ranked only three of the 18 techniques (JIT, conference or discussion, apprenticeship) as being used to an "average" degree or above. In nonmanufacturing only two of the techniques (JIT and conference or discussion) were ranked as being used to an "average" degree

| | Type of Firm | | | |
| | Manufacturing[a] | | Non-Manufacturing[b] | |
Training Technique	Rank Order	Mean Value[c]	Rank Order	Mean Value[c]
1. Job instruction training	1	3.9	1	4.0
2. Conference or discussion	2	3.5	2	3.4
3. Apprentice training	3	3.1	6.5	2.5
4. Job rotation	4	2.8	3	2.8
5. Coaching	5	2.6	6.5	2.5
6. Lecture	6	2.4	5	2.6
7. Special study	7	2.3	4	2.7
8. Case study	8	2.1	10	2.2
9. Films	9	2.0	8.5	2.4
10. Programmed instruction	10	1.9	8.5	2.4
11. Internships and assistantships	11	1.8	11	2.0
12. Simulation	12	1.7	12	1.9
13. Programmed group exercises	13.5	1.6	16.5	1.3
14. Role playing	13.5	1.6	13	1.6
15. Laboratory training	15	1.5	16.5	1.3
16. Television	16	1.4	14.5	1.4
17. Vestibule training	17	1.2	14.5	1.4
18. Junior board	18	1.1	18	1.1

[a]Consists of 63 firms.
[b]Consists of 14 transportation, 13 finance, 10 retail and 12 "other" firms.
[c]Computed from the following values: 5 = Always; 4 = Usually; 3 = Average; 2 = Seldom; 1 = Never.

Figure 7–5 *Rank order of frequency of use of 18 training techniques by type of firm. The techniques included are those suggested by Bass and Vaughan, presented in Figure 7–3. [From Stuart B. Utgaard and Rene V. Dawis, "The Most Frequently-Used Training Techniques," Training and Development Journal, 24 (February, 1970), p. 41. Reproduced by special permission from the February 1970 Training and Development Journal. Copyright 1970 by the American Society for Training and Development Inc.]*

or above. It is interesting to note from Figure 7–5 that on-the-job techniques appeared to be more frequently used in manufacturing firms, since they occupied four of the five top rankings. The fact that the on-the-job techniques of internships and assistantships and junior boards are ranked low is not surprising, since the population with which these techniques are used is small — selected groups of managers only. These findings reinforce the view presented earlier — that on-the-job training is used more frequently than off-the-job training.

Figure 7–6 presents the findings of a second study, which obtained the "expert" opinion of training directors but which went one step further and compared their judgments to the "limited research available" concerning "adults in the employment situation."[67] The respondents were 117 training directors "who worked for the companies with the largest numbers of employees as indicated in the *Fortune* list of the top 500 corporations."[68] Thus, any inferences drawn from this study must recognize the contingency of organization size.

As can be seen from Figure 7–6, nine techniques were compared in terms of six training objectives. For acquisition of knowledge, PI was ranked as most effective and the lecture (with questions) as least effective. Based upon our earlier discussion of PI, we do not believe that the highly favorable evaluation of PI is warranted at this time. In addition, the low rating given to the lecture method relative to a number of the other techniques is not borne out by a number of other existing research studies. For example, when compared to the discussion method, the lecture has been found to be equally effective in many instances and even superior in some instances, yet the training directors in this study believed that the discussion method was significantly better than the lecture for acquisition of knowledge. Further, the training directors rated television as more effective than the lecture for knowledge acquisition, but some research comparing these two techniques has shown no significant difference between them.

The training directors saw sensitivity training, which has many of the characteristics of role playing, as the most effective method for changing attitudes. In addition, role playing, the discussion method and case studies were seen as more effective than business games, films, PI, and lecture techniques for changing attitudes. A number of research studies basically support these opinions. However, the research on the effectiveness of case studies for changing attitudes is limited, and, as mentioned earlier, in some instances business games may be used to change attitudes.

For teaching problem-solving skills, the training directors expressed the opinion that case studies, business games, role playing, and discussions were most likely to be effective. While a

Training Method	Knowledge Acquisition		Changing Attitudes		Problem Solving Skills		Interpersonal Skills		Participant Acceptance		Knowledge Retention	
	Mean	Mean Rank	Mean	Mean Rank	Mean	Mean Rank	Mean	Mean Rank	Mean	Mean Rank	Mean	Mean Rank
Case Study	3.56	2	3.43	4	3.69	1	3.02	4	3.80	2	3.48	2
Conference (Discussion) Method	3.33	3	3.54	3	3.26	4	3.21	3	4.16	1	3.32	5
Lecture (with questions)	2.53	9	2.20	8	2.00	9	1.90	8	2.74	8	2.49	8
Business Games	3.00	6	2.73	5	3.58	2	2.50	5	3.78	3	3.26	6
Movie Films	3.16	4	2.50	6	2.24	7	2.19	6	3.44	5	2.67	7
Programmed Instruction	4.03	1	2.22	7	2.56	6	2.11	7	3.28	7	3.74	1
Role Playing	2.93	7	3.56	2	3.27	3	3.68	2	3.56	4	3.37	4
Sensitivity Training (t group)	2.77	8	3.96	1	2.98	5	3.95	1	3.33	6	3.44	3
Television Lecture	3.10	5	1.99	9	2.01	8	1.81	9	2.74	9	2.47	9

Figure 7-6 Ratings of training directors on effectiveness of alternative training methods for various training objectives. [From Stephen J. Carroll, Jr., Frank T. Paine, and John J. Ivancevich, "The Relative Effectiveness of Training Methods—Expert Opinion and Research," Personnel Psychology, 25 (1972), p. 498.]

growing body of research compares case studies to business games, the research is so contradictory that it is not possible to state which may be the more effective for teaching specific kinds of problem-solving skills. It appears likely that role playing and the discussion method would also help to develop problem-solving skills because of active participation. However, when compared to case studies and business games, these two techniques are more likely to focus on human relation aspects, with case studies and games focusing attention more on the economic aspects of business operations.

For developing interpersonal skills, the training directors perceived sensitivity training and role playing as being most effective. Based upon research, these opinions appear to be justified. However, further research may show that case studies and business games are useful in this area. Case studies in which the trainees discuss human relations problems might be useful for developing interpersonal skills. Business games can be used to teach interpersonal skills when the game involves trainees making decisions as part of a group.

In terms of participant acceptance, the training directors rated discussion, case studies and business games most favorably, although the other techniques covered, except lecture and television, were also thought acceptable. Some research in this area, however, indicates that acceptance of the lecture method by managers is often as high or higher than the discussion method.

Finally, for retention of knowledge, the training directors expressed the view that PI, case studies, sensitivity training, role playing, discussions, and business games were significantly more effective than films, lectures, and television. With respect to these views, there is not a great deal of research and generally what does exist does not support the beliefs expressed by the training directors. The research conducted has primarily involved college students, and generally has indicated that the lecture and discussion techniques are comparable to one another. It is interesting to note that the techniques which the training directors believe were most effective in terms of retention all require active participation on the part of the trainees whereas those rated as least effective do not.

The preceding comments illustrate that relying on "expert" opinion can be misleading and, therefore, that the individual in charge of employee development must evaluate such opinions carefully. The comments also reinforce the following statement made by Beeland and Blumenfeld:

First, there is a multitude of training strategies available to management to choose from in pursuing their objectives. Secondly, adequate empirical evaluation of management (and nonmanagement as well) training effectiveness is a relatively rare occurrence; and demonstrated comparable effectiveness of different training strategies is virtually nonexistent.[69]

Nevertheless, if the organization cannot engage in its own evaluation, the opinion of "experts" and the theory and research of others may be useful guides in the choice of development techniques to meet particular training needs.

Based upon the discussion in this chapter and on learning principles in Chapter 6, we offer the following guides for selecting from among the various development techniques. First, an organization must carefully identify its development objectives and select those techniques that its own research and expert opinion or the theory and research of others indicate are most likely to achieve them. For example, if the objective emphasizes immediate productive results, one should select from among the on-the-job techniques, whereas off-the-job types appear preferable if learning is to be emphasized. Making the on-the-job or off-the-job decision at this point can reduce the range of alternative techniques that must be considered further. Second, the nature of the material to be covered in the training program needs to be established (Are we dealing with factual material, human relations skills, or attitudinal changes?) The answers to questions such as these permit the decision maker to reduce the range of alternatives still further. For example, if the material to be taught is of a factual nature and off-the-job training will be used, lectures, PI, CAI, films, and television appear to have some advantages over the other techniques presented in Figure 7–3. Third, the extent to which the various techniques make use of the learning principles presented in Chapter 6 should be assessed. As Figure 7–3 points out, the training techniques vary in the extent to which they make use of the principles of learning. The techniques can then be ranked according to those principles of learning that appear most important for program success. This step does not reduce the range of alternatives but merely indicates a preferred order. Fourth, the techniques need to be evaluated in terms of the number of people to be trained and whether it is important for training to take place in a group or whether individual training is desirable. For example, PI permits the trainees to work alone at their own pace, while the lecture is geared to simultaneous training of a group of trainees. Finally, the alternatives need to be evaluated in terms of the financial capability of the firm. While CAI might be the most desirable technique for a particular program from a "theoretical" learning point of view, its expense may lead a firm to develop its own PI text instead. Similarly, the expense associated with PI might induce the firm to use the lecture method, even if PI might be a theoretically more effective teaching technique. What we are advocating by specifying this sequence of steps is that the development technique selected be the most appropriate one the organization can afford to meet its program objectives.[70]

SUMMARY

In this chapter we have discussed three important training program design considerations: (1) who should conduct the training, (2) where training will take place, and (3) what specific development techniques are available. The first of these decisions involves selecting between line and staff members and between organizational and nonorganizational members who will conduct development programs. Major factors influencing this decision are expertise of the trainers, time available for training, and cost of the various alternatives. Two alternatives were presented in terms of where the training should take place: on the job or off the job. A major factor influencing this decision is whether learning or immediate production is being emphasized. The final design decision involves selecting from among a large number of development techniques those most appropriate for the accomplishment of specific program objectives. A range of techniques available for use today was evaluated in terms of their relative advantages and disadvantages, and some of the major factors that should influence the decision of which techniques to select were presented. The primary problem with respect to the choice of training techniques is that evaluative research, as to their effectiveness, is generally lacking or contradictory. Therefore, the decision maker must make a selection in light of imperfect information.

DISCUSSION AND STUDY QUESTIONS

1. Which of the following training approaches do you believe would be effective under the organizational conditions stipulated? Give your reasons why in each case.
   a. Apprenticeship training in a large firm for moderately skilled production workers, who, with proper training, can attain peak proficiency in about 10 weeks.
   b. Job rotation at General Motors.
   c. Apprenticeship training for newly hired electrical maintenance employees in a manufacturing firm with about 3000 nonmanagerial employees.
   d. Job rotation in a small four-store department store chain.
   e. Coaching of new managerial employees in a large furniture manufacturing firm.
   f. On-the-job coaching of new managerial employees in a small firm making specialized solid state electronic components.

2. Take a sheet of paper and draw a line down the middle. On the left, indicate the principles of learning indicated in Chapter 6. On the right, indicate the basic steps of the JIT method. Draw a line with an arrow at the end from each principle of learning to any step in the JIT method in which the principle is utilized. After having completed this task, be prepared to comment on the value of JIT in terms of learning theory and the principles of learning.

3. Think of a simple task that can be taught to someone else in your class within a relatively few minutes. List each step of the task on a sheet of paper, and if called on by your instructor, be prepared to "train" a classmate during the next class period as to how to perform the task. Be prepared to follow the JIT method as closely as possible. Also be sufficiently familiar with the JIT method to provide both feedback and reinforcement to any other classmate who may be called on to play the role of the trainer.

4. A large corporation is providing an off-the-job two-week management development program for its middle managers. Who should be responsible for the training program? Who should conduct the training for each of the following techniques to be used in the program?
   a. Running a generalized total enterprise business game.
   b. Discussion of a case study emphasizing financial analysis which was drawn from actual data in one of the firm's operating units.
   c. Presenting a lecture, discussion, and actual practice session on creative thinking, based on the notions from Alex Osborn's *Applied Imagination.*
   d. Conducting a role playing session in which human relations problems of a disciplinary type are to be involved.
   e. Presenting via the lecture method (permitting questions) information about the firm's new computer system, which top management wants all of its managers to become generally familiar with.

5. Which of the following training approaches do you think would be appropriate under the following conditions? Give your reasons why.
   a. Having the very complex Carnegie Tech total enterprise business game simulating the packaged detergent industry, and requiring from 100 to 300 decisions being made in each simulated period of play, being utilized with first-line production supervisors in a large company, which among other products, does manufacture detergents.
   b. Using tutorial CAI to teach all middle and lower level managers the basics of computer programming in one of this country's largest manufacturing firms.
   c. Using a film illustrating the RAND air defense systems simulation as described in this chapter under the category vestibule training to supplement this text.
   d. Utilizing the lecture method (with questions permitted) in a university or college personnel course in which this text is used.
   e. Using the lecture method in a senior level personnel course, the basic objective of which is to foster skills in

personnel decision making — e.g., interviewing, using the JIT method, etc.

   f. Using CAI to supplement this text.

6. In which of the following situations do you believe that the line manager involved should actually conduct on-the-job training for his new subordinates? Give your reasons why.

   a. A recent college graduate in business administration, after a brief orientation period, is put in charge as a first-line supervisor of a production department consisting of twenty highly skilled employees.

   b. A first line production supervisor has worked his way up in his department from a rank-and-file worker and has 32 subordinates. All tasks in the department are complex, highly skilled ones, requiring several months of training (and working) before full proficiency is usually attained.

   c. A first line supervisor in a production department has worked his way up from a rank-and-file worker in the department. He has 38 subordinates. Practically all jobs in the department are unskilled ones, and the average time required to train a new employee is four hours.

   d. A newly appointed Vice-President of Marketing, was just "raided" by a firm from one of its competitors. After two weeks on her new job, one of her subordinates is "rotated" into production, and one of the firm's production managers, in turn, is "rotated" into her department to be "broadened" and groomed for a top level executive position.

7. To what extent would you agree with each of the following statements about development? In each case, give your reasons why.

   a. "Business games may lead to dysfunctional learning because even the most complex specific industry games cannot replicate all aspects of real-life decision problems with complete accuracy; thus participants may learn 'the wrong things'."

   b. "Dialogue CAI is just a dream — computers can't be programmed to answer all questions that any individual may pose to them."

   c. "We'd take all of our first-line supervisors and have them learn the basics of computer programming by using PI, since we think they should be familiar with these basics, but with our small firm, we just can't afford PI."

   d. "All fancy development techniques such as business games, CAI, PI, role playing, etc., are simply 'frosting on the cake' — 95 per cent of the learning of our employees at all levels in the organization comes from good day-to-day on-the-job coaching by their supervisors."

   e. "Most case studies are worthless because they simply do not provide enough information for trainees to do an adequate job of analysis."

8. Which off-the-job training techniques might be used most effectively in management development to achieve the following objectives?

   a. To stress the importance of proactively seeking necessary informational inputs for decision makers to make viable decisions.

    b. To provide stress to the trainees in a decision-making situation.

    c. To learn to live with and accept one's own failures as a decision maker.

    d. To provide factual information about a series of the firm's forthcoming T.V. advertisements promoting a new product.

9. "Research evaluating the effectiveness of development techniques is in such a sad state of affairs that the training director of a firm who relies on 'common sense' and knowledge of the basic principles of learning will be more effective than the training director who both keeps up with all the new research on training effectiveness and conducts his own evaluative research as well." Comment.

10. "The state of educational technology has improved very little during the last 35 years. Lectures and discussions, and coaching subordinates in jobs are century-old techniques, and even PI, as noted in the chapter, may be traced back to the days of Quintilian between 35 and 100 A.D." Comment.

11. "A major reason why smaller firms are not generally as profitable as larger ones is that they simply can't afford the training technologies by means of which to keep their employees up with the latest, most efficient techniques for performing their jobs." Comment.

Notes

[1] Irwin L. Goldstein, *Training: Program Development and Evaluation* (Monterey, Calif.: Brooks/Cole Publishing Company, 1974), p. 139.

[2] This view is supported by Lawrence Siegel and Irving M. Lane, *Psychology in Industrial Organizations* (Homewood, Ill.: Richard D. Irwin, Inc., 1974), p. 200. They have suggested that the personnel department should be responsible for training the trainers and for developing, evaluating, and improving development programs.

[3] Bureau of National Affairs, "Planning the Training Program," *Personnel Management: BNA Policy and Practice Series* (Washington, D.C.: The Bureau of National Affairs, 1975), p. 205:102.

[4] This discussion of Bavelas' study is drawn from Norman R. F. Maier, *Psychology in Industrial Organizations* (Boston, Mass.: Houghton Mifflin Company, 1973), pp. 325–326.

[5] Bureau of National Affairs, op. cit., "On-the-Job Training," p. 205:175.

[6] Bernard M. Bass and James A. Vaughan, *Training in Industry: Management of Learning* (Belmont, Calif.: Wadsworth Publishing Company, Inc., 1966), p. 87.

[7] Much of the following material dealing with on-the-job training is based upon ibid., pp. 86–88; Goldstein, op. cit., pp. 141–143; and Martin M. Broadwell, *The Supervisor and On-the-Job Training* (Reading, Mass.: Addison-Wesley Publishing Company, 1975), pp. 37–40. We will draw heavily on the first two of these sources throughout the chapter.

[8] Bass and Vaughan, op. cit., p. 87.

[9] J. R. Hinrichs, "The Feedback Program to Make Manager Development Happen," *Personnel Journal,* 54 (September, 1975), p. 478.

[10] Bernard J. Bienvenu, *New Priorities in Training* (New York: American Management Association, 1969), p. 38.

[11]This conclusion is based upon analysis of data which we will present in Figure 7–5 and discuss later in this chapter from a study by Stuart B. Utgaard and Rene V. Dawis, "The Most Frequently Used Training Techniques," *Training and Development Journal*, 24 (February, 1970), pp. 40–43.

[12]Bass and Vaughan, op. cit., p. 88. The emphasis is ours. We should note that JIT can also be used for skills-oriented tasks performed by managers and professionals. For example, managers may have to do some of their own computer card punching from time to time and such skills can be taught by means of the JIT method. In addition, it should be noted that JIT can be used in off-the-job training situations such as so-called "vestibule" training, which we discuss later in this chapter, in which actual job conditions are *simulated*.

[13]Utgaard and Dawis, op. cit., p. 41.

[14]Bureau of National Affairs, op. cit., "Apprentice Training," p. 205: 401. Much of this section on apprenticeship training is drawn from this source, Bass and Vaughan, op. cit., pp. 89–90, and Goldstein, op. cit., pp. 142–143.

[15]Bureau of National Affairs, op. cit., "Apprentice Training," p. 205:406.

[16]Goldstein, op. cit., p. 142.

[17]Carl Heyel, ed., *The Encyclopedia of Management* (New York: Van Nostrand Reinhold Company, 1973), p. 51.

[18]This section draws heavily on Yoram Zeira, "Job Rotation for Management Development," *Personnel*, 51 (July-August, 1974), pp. 25–35, and Bass and Vaughan, op. cit., pp. 90–91.

[19]K. Brantley Watson, "The Maturing of Multiple Management," *Management Review*, 63 (July, 1974), p. 5. Much of this section is drawn from this source. Other aspects of multiple management can be found in Frederick J. Bell, "Highlights of Multiple Management," in Harwood F. Merrill and Elizabeth Marting, eds., *Developing Executive Skills* (New York: American Management Association, 1958), pp. 143–144; and John R. Craf, *Junior Boards of Executives: A Management Training Procedure* (New York: Harper and Row, 1958).

[20]Bass and Vaughan, op. cit., p. 90.

[21]Bureau of National Affairs, "Training Aids," op. cit., p. 205:151.

[22]Bass and Vaughan, op. cit., p. 94.

[23]Stephen J. Carroll, Jr., Frank T. Paine, and John J. Ivancevich, "The Relative Effectiveness of Training Methods — Expert Opinion and Research," *Personnel Psychology*, 25 (1972), pp. 495–509. Some of the key results of this study are presented in Figure 7–6, which we discuss later in the chapter.

[24]The observations concerning the discussion method are drawn from Bass and Vaughan, op. cit., pp. 97–99.

[25]"The Unstructured Management at Koppers," *Business Week*, (July 28, 1973), pp. 42–43.

[26]Two points are in order here. First, as Edward F. O'Day, et al., *Programmed Instruction: Techniques and Trends* (New York: Appleton-Century-Crofts, 1971), p. 1 have pointed out, other terms such as programmed learning, automated instruction, self-instruction, instructional technology, and teaching machines are used interchangeably with the term PI. The second point is that PI is not new. For example, Dene R. Lawson, "Who Thought of it First?: A Review of Historical References to Programmed Instruction," *Educational Technology*, 19 (October, 1969), pp. 93–96, traced the roots of PI back to the writings of Quintilian between 35 and 100 A.D.

[27]Allan N. Nash, Jan P. Muczyk, and Frank L. Vettori, "The Relative Practical Effectiveness of Programmed Instruction," *Personnel Psychology*, 24 (1971), pp. 397–418. Another excellent review of many PI studies is provided by John P. Campbell, "Personnel Training and Development," *Annual Review of Psychology*, 22 (1971), pp. 565–602.

[28]Goldstein, op. cit., p. 156. However, John W. Buckley, "Programmed Instruction in Industrial Training," *California Management Review*, 10 (Winter, 1967), pp. 71–79, has suggested that more complex forms of PI can be used to teach material that is less factual and more theoretically and problem solving oriented.

[29]Nash, et al., op. cit., p. 398.

[30]Campbell, op. cit., p. 590.

[31]Jerry F. Foster, "PERT for Programmed Instruction," *Administrative Management,* 26 (October, 1965), pp. 42–43.

[32]Marshall J. Farr, "Computer-Assisted Instruction Activities in Naval Research," *Computers and Automation,* 22 (January, 1973), p. 10. Other terms have been used to describe CAI types of activities, some with a very similar meaning and others with very different meanings. For example, the term computer assisted learning (CAL) has been used as has computer managed instruction (CMI). See, for example, Harold L. Schoen, "CAI Development and Good Educational Practice," *Educational Technology,* 14 (April, 1974), pp. 54–56, and Robert Fromer, "Distinction Between CAI and CMI Systems," *Educational Technology,* 12 (May, 1972), pp. 30–31.

[33]This classification was presented by P. Suppes, "Computer Technology and the Future of Education," in V. M. Howes, ed., *Individualizing Instruction in Science and Mathematics* (London: Macmillan, 1969), pp. 129–138.

[34]For a discussion of branching and a description of the operation of a CAI system see, "Computer-Assisted Instruction," *Inquiry,* 2(June, 1967), as reprinted in Paul S. Greenlaw and Robert D. Smith, *Personnel Management: A Management Science Approach* (Scranton, Pa.: International Textbook Company, 1970), pp. 330–345.

[35]Farr, op. cit., p. 11.

[36]Ibid.

[37]Alan B. Salisbury, "An Overview of CAI," *Educational Technology,* 11 (October, 1971), p. 49.

[38]Campbell, op. cit., p. 574.

[39]Goldstein, op. cit., p. 162.

[40]Farr, op. cit., p. 10.

[41]Ibid.

[42]Goldstein, op. cit., pp. 160–161.

[43]Edward Hartman, "The Cost of Computer Assisted Instruction," *Educational Technology,* 11 (December, 1971), pp. 6–7.

[44]See, for example, John F. Feldhusen and Michael Szabo, "A Review of Developments in Computer Assisted Instruction," *Educational Technology,* 9 (April, 1969), pp. 32–39 or Roger H. Simonsen and Kent S. Renshaw, "CAI—Boon or Boondoggle?" *Datamation,* 20 (March, 1974), pp. 90–102.

[45]Mark M. Loftin, "Whatever Happened to CAI?" *Training in Business and Industry,* 11 (June, 1974), p. 29.

[46]Ibid.

[47]We emphasize the virtually identical aspect. For example, learning to play the piano for a recital by working with a cardboard keyboard would not be similar enough to the real task to be considered vestibule training.

[48]Robert L. Chapman, et al., "The Systems Research Laboratory's Air Defense Experiments," *Management Science,* 5 (April, 1959), as reprinted in Greenlaw and Smith, op. cit., pp. 242–264.

[49]Ibid., p. 243.

[50]The use of systems training in an industrial setting has been suggested for a mail-order house. See Elias H. Porter, *Manpower Development* (New York: Harper and Row, 1964), as reprinted in Greenlaw and Smith, op. cit., pp. 265–269, This program is likely to be less costly than the one used by RAND since it is noncomputerized and appears to replicate a complex operation less closely.

[51]Malcolm P. McNair, ed., *The Case Method at the Harvard Business School* (New York: McGraw-Hill Book Company, 1954).

[52]To help overcome this problem, some "computer-assisted" cases have been developed. See for example, Daniel W. Dehayes, Jr. and William C. Perkins, "Integrating Across Functional Areas with a Computer-Assisted Case," in Richard H. Buskirk, ed., *Proceedings of the Second Annual Conference of the Association for Business Simulation and Experiential Learning* (Bloomington, Ind.: Indiana University Press, 1975), pp. 119–126.

[53]Paul Pigors and Faith Pigors, *The Incident Process: Case Studies in Management Development* (Washington, D.C.: The Bureau of National Affairs, 1955).

[54]Two notes are in order here. First, data for many critical incidents are

drawn from "real life" problems. Second, there is considerable debate as to whether actual outcomes should be provided since they may lead trainees to perceive a given course of action as correct if it was successful, when in fact other alternatives that existed might have been *even more successful*. Likewise, the trainee might reject in the future an alternative that was unsuccessful in the incident but which could be very successful under the conditions which face him.

[55]A discussion of the history of role playing and techniques used is provided by Wallace Wohlking and Hannah Weiner, "Structured and Spontaneous Role Playing: Contrast and Comparison," *Training and Development Journal*, 25 (January, 1971), pp. 8–14.

[56]Goldstein, op. cit., p. 194.

[57]Bass and Vaughan, op. cit., pp. 101–102 provide a more detailed comparison than is presented here.

[58]This approach has been used quite successfully by one of the authors in both management training programs and for undergraduate education in the behavioral sciences area.

[59]Descriptions of the in-basket test are provided by Norman O. Frederiksen, et al., "The In-basket Test," *Psychological Monographs*, 71 (1957), Whole No. 438.

[60]Martha J. K. Zachert and Veronica S. Pantelidis, "A Computer-Assisted Sequential In-basket Technique," *Educational Technology*, 11 (December, 1971), pp. 44–45.

[61]Robert Horn, *The Guide to Simulation/Games For Education and Training* (Cranford, N.J.: Didactic Systems, Inc., 1977).

[62]Paul S. Greenlaw, Lowell W. Herron and R. H. Rawdon, *Business Simulation in Industrial and University Education* (Englewood Cliffs, N.J.: Prentice-Hall, Inc., 1962), p. 5.

[63]Kalman J. Cohen and Eric Rhenman, "The Role of Management Games in Education and Research," *Management Science*, 7 (January, 1961), as reprinted in Greenlaw and Smith, op. cit., p. 280.

[64]Ibid.

[65]We should also note that the programmed group exercises approach listed in Figure 7–3 is a hybrid simulation technique that draws on case studies, role playing, programmed instruction, and sensitivity training. Ten exercises used are self-administered by the trainees, after which group discussion takes place. The advantages and disadvantages are the same as those for other simulation techniques. See Bass and Vaughan, op. cit., pp. 127–129.

[66]Utgaard and Dawis, op. cit., pp. 40–48.

[67]Carroll, Paine, and Ivancevich, op. cit., pp. 495–509. The discussion that follows is based upon this source and unless otherwise specified the references to *other research* are also from this source.

[68]Ibid., p. 496.

[69]J. L. Beeland and Warren S. Blumenfeld, "Effectiveness of a Short Supervisory Management Training Course: A Multi-Factor Evaluation Experiment," in Robert L. Taylor, et al., eds., *Proceedings of the Academy of Management 36th Annual Meeting* (Kansas City, Mo.: August 11–14, 1976), p. 19.

[70]We should emphasize that the above sequencing of steps is intended to represent only a general guide. In some cases, the sequencing may be different, due to particular factors such as cost. A small firm's personnel manager, for example, may have ruled out CAI for *all* development programs before looking at *any* particular training objective because of the cost factor.

8

EMPLOYEE DEVELOPMENT: CURRENT PROBLEMS AND ISSUES

In the previous two chapters we discussed the four basic phases of the planned organizational learning process: (1) need determination, (2) design, (3) implementation, and (4) evaluation. In this chapter we will draw upon various aspects of each of these four phases as we discuss four special types of development in organizations. First, we will look at some of the key facets of training employees who are being oriented to new jobs or new work environments. Then, we will consider two different groups of individuals who have received a great deal of attention as needing special development efforts: women for managerial and professional positions and the hard-core unemployed. Next, we will discuss two approaches in which the focus goes beyond individual development: (1) the assessment center, in which individuals are *evaluated as well as being trained,* and (2) organizational development, which incorporates individual development techniques on an organization-wide basis to facilitate organizational change as opposed to simply individual development. We will conclude our discussion of training by pointing out some of the possible dysfunctional consequences of development activities.

ORIENTATION TRAINING

As indicated in Chapter 4, when an organization selects individuals for positions, whether by recruiting new employees from outside the organization or by promoting or transferring current organization members, it is interested in choosing competent people. Just because competent people are selected, however, does not mean that development is unnecessary. In some cases, competency may mean that the individual has the aptitude to do the job but must receive specific skills training. For example, the public administrator who was hired by the retailing chain and needed special orientation training with respect to the techniques of merchandising illustrates this type of situation. Further, even when individuals are familiar with the specific task they are to perform, they must learn about aspects of the work environment such as policies and procedures, physical surroundings, and expectations of others related to their behavior.[1] Otherwise, anxiety may result that can interfere with learning and job performance. In terms of policies and procedures, for example, the employee may have questions such as: What time does work start? What do I do if I am sick? What are my vacation benefits? When is pay day? If such questions are not answered, the employee is likely to be uncertain as to what represents appropriate behavior and therefore may experience frustration and anxiety. Similarly, the employee must be familiarized with numerous physical variables relevant to his work. For example, he should be told where such facilities as the cafeteria, restrooms, and parking areas are located. Finally, the employee needs to know what is expected of him in terms of job performance. If he does not have such information, the employee will not know if his performance is acceptable in light of organizational goals. In addition to learning about policies and procedures, physical surroundings, and performance expectations, the employee needs to meet the people with whom he will be expected to interact, such as his supervisor and peers. Some of these types of learning will not need to be as extensive for employees who are transferred, demoted, promoted, or trained through job rotation as for newly hired employees, since the former will be familiar with many facets of the organizational environment. Some learning about the job and specific job environment, however, is likely to be necessary for all individuals moved into any new job. Orientation training is concerned with these aspects of familiarizing the employee with both his specific work and the job environment.

Formal provision for appropriate orientation training is necessary because organizational learning will occur whether it is planned or not. Individuals will be told how to perform their jobs by someone and they will be given information about other organizational variables. Without planned effective orientation efforts, however, the learning of erroneous information concerning policies, procedures, rules, regulations, physical surroundings, and performance expectation may take place. Two important questions that must be resolved about such formal orientation are: (1) who is to be responsible for the training and (2) what specific decisions can management make to ensure that such training will contribute to both effective individual development and the attainment of organizational objectives?

In most cases, the responsibility for employee orientation should be shared by the personnel department and the immediate supervisor, since both organizational and departmental variables are involved. For example, it is logical for personnel to handle aspects of orientation training that affect all employees, such as employee benefits. This approach will help ensure that all employees are given *consistent* interpretations of company policies by those with special expertise in such areas. On the other hand, the supervisor is usually more familiar with safety hazards in the specific work environment and generally would be called on to point them out to new employees. Even though responsibility for orientation training is shared, personnel has more responsibility for such training than line management, because it must not only conduct part of the training but also make sure that others conducting orientation training are doing so correctly. The advantages and disadvantages associated with having line or staff and insiders or outsiders conduct orientation training are similar to those indicated in Chapter 7.

A number of research studies have indicated that well-designed orientation training programs can be beneficial in terms of helping to achieve organizational objectives and contribute to employee need satisfaction. We will now discuss three such studies which have provided some insights into the kinds of problems employees face when entering new work environments and how orientation training can be used to overcome these problems.

Marion and Trieb conducted a study in 15 supermarkets of two Ohio food chains in which they related job orientation to measures of satisfaction, productivity, and certain other variables.[2] They asked employees whether the store manager had acquainted them with other people with whom they would work, had explained their own job to them and how it was related to overall store success, had informed them of store policies, and had checked to see how they were doing. They found in both companies that employees' perceptions of the extent to which they had received orientation training were significantly related to satisfaction with and loyalty to the company and positive expectations relative to work, advancement and job security.

Additional insights into important aspects of orientation training as well as specific suggestions on actions management can take to make it more effective have been provided in a study by Kotter.[3] In this study, new employees, their superiors, and their superiors' superiors were surveyed by questionnaire to identify problems they had encountered with orientation training. The questionnaire revealed that some types of problems noted in Chapter 7 often arise when line managers conduct the training. For example, supervisors were often perceived by employees as lacking the ability to train and not providing adequate feedback. Many supervisors believed that they were not sufficiently rewarded for training their subordinates. In addition, frequently a feeling of trust did not develop between the supervisor and the subordinate. Further, the subordinates often did not know what was expected from them in the way of performance, and many first assignments tended to be of a "make work" variety.

To overcome these problems four steps were taken. First, a supervisory training problem was instituted in which supervisors were made aware of the problems experienced by new employees, were taught how to coach new employees, and were provided with help in solving specific problems they were having with new employees. Second, an organizational task force, which had conducted the study, continued to function and was given some influence in deciding upon the manner in which first assignments were to be made for new employees and in how supervisors were to be evaluated and rewarded for their orientation training activities. Third, a one-day workshop for new employees and their supervisors was designed to help encourage better understanding between them and clear up any ambiguities new employees might have concerning such matters as performance criteria. Finally, a specialist in training was made responsible for monitoring and updating the orientation training process. On the basis of criteria established prior to initiating the new procedure, the following results were reported: (1) about a 30 per cent reduction in the time to train new employees, (2) a 10 per cent productivity increase, which did not diminish over time, (3) a decrease in frustration on the part of supervisors, (4) a 300 per cent increase in the number of new employees who would not consider looking for another job, and (5) an increase in job and company satisfaction. It was reported that these results led to an estimated $100,000 to $300,000 gross savings, excluding first-year costs of $40,000 and subsequent annual costs of $3000. Thus, the orientation training appears to have been justified on a cost-benefit basis.

Research into the problems of new employees and how orientation training can help overcome some of these problems has also been conducted at Texas Instruments by Gomersall and Myers.[4] These researchers found that new employees experienced a high degree of anxiety, which interfered with the training process and led to turnover. They further discovered that this anxiety was intensified by certain "initiation practices" by many of their peers and that it made many new employees reluctant to discuss problems with their supervisors. Finally, it was found that many supervisors also experienced anxiety in their dealings with new employees that resulted in communications problems.

To overcome these problems, the company initiated a special orientation training program for one group of new employees while just continuing to provide normal orientation to a "control group." The special orientation program emphasized four points. The new employees were informed that their opportunity for success was good, since company records showed that "99.6% of all persons hired or transferred into this job were eventually successful in terms of their ability to learn the necessary skills."[5] They were told about the hazing "games" of the experienced employees that attempted to frighten new workers by exaggerated stories about such matters as disciplinary action. The new employees were also informed as to both the good and bad aspects of their jobs in order to negate the effect of these distorted stories. They were instructed to ignore rumors, and the basis for some of the rumors was explained. Interestingly, some of the rumors originated from comments made by the supervisors. For example, some of the supervisors believed that a poor performer might improve his performance if he thought that most persons who left the company did so because they were fired. As a result, some of them implied that certain individuals who really left the company voluntarily to be married or because they wanted to move to another geographical location had been fired for poor performance. This behavior resulted in the false rumor that more than half the employees who left the company did so because they were fired. Employees were also asked to take the initiative in communicating with their supervisors. They were informed of the reluctance of many supervisors to talk and that each supervisor's job would be made easier if the subordinate would ask questions. It was also explained that the supervisor did expect them to ask questions and that he would not consider them "dumb" if they did so. Finally, all new employees were encouraged to get to know their own supervisor and were given specific descriptive information about him. For example, a description might have indicated that the supervisor was strict but friendly, that his hobby was fishing, and that he liked his subordinates to check with him before they went on a personal break.

The performance results of the group given the special orientation training were compared to those of the control group. The "normal" orientation training which was given to the control group "consisted of a two-hour briefing on hours of work, insurance, parking, work rules and employee services."[6] In the normal orientation training, the new employees were also warned of the consequences if they failed to conform to company expectations. While this warning was not intended to be a threat, it apparently was perceived as one and tended to increase rather than decrease employee anxiety. Performance results for the control group and the special orientation training group are presented in Figure 8–1. A number of additional groups were also given the special orientation training, with control groups receiving the normal orientation training. The results of the proficiency over time for each of these two groups is shown in Figure 8–2. As can be seen from the learning curves presented in both Figures 8–1 and 8–2, the groups that received the special anxiety-reduction orientation training learned more, as reflected by their attainment of higher competency levels, and this learning occurred at a faster rate than for the groups that received the normal

Learning Curves of Experimental and Control Groups

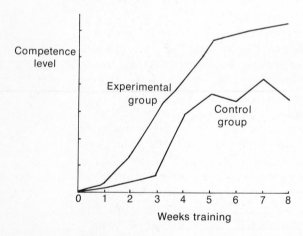

One-Month Performance Levels of Experimental and Control Groups

	Experimental Group	Control Group
Units per hour	93	27
Absentee rate	0.5%	2.5%
Times tardy	2	8
Training hours required	225	381

Figure 8–1 Orientation training performance levels and learning curves of experimental and control groups. [From Earl R. Gomersall and M. Scott Myers, "Breakthrough in On-the-Job Training," Harvard Business Review, 44 (July–August, 1966), p. 67. Copyright © 1966 by the President and Fellows of Harvard College; all rights reserved.]

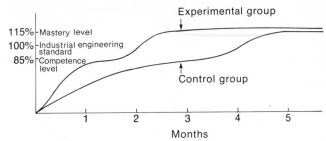

Figure 8-2 *Mastery attainment by experimental and control groups. [From Earl R. Gomersall and M. Scott Myers, "Breakthrough in On-the-Job Training," Harvard Business Review, 44 (July-August, 1966), p. 69. Copyright © by the President and Fellows of Harvard College; all rights reserved.]*

orientation training. In addition, as shown in Figure 8–1, the special group had lower absenteeism and tardiness rates, which also probably helped contribute to more rapid learning. Specifically, Gomersall and Myers reported the following gains from the special training: (1) training time was shortened by one half, (2) training costs were lowered to one third of their previous levels, (3) absenteeism and tardiness dropped to half their normal level, (4) waste and rejects were reduced to one fifth of their previous level, and (5) costs were cut as much as 15 to 30 per cent.[7] Net savings for the first year were estimated by Texas Instruments to be at least $50,000 and the reduced turnover, absenteeism, and training time were expected to result in an additional annual savings of $350,000. Thus, the decision to provide new employees with information concerning likelihood of success, rumors they might encounter, and their supervisors' personal characteristics resulted in less anxiety for new employees which in turn contributed to better and more rapid learning and lower costs. In addition, one can infer from the lower turnover, tardiness, and absenteeism rates that most new employees were more highly satisfied with their work environment.

Three other observations from this study are of interest. First, one problem with the normal orientation training was that supervisors were often so familiar with the job that they frequently gave inadequate instructions and new employees, not wanting to appear to be stupid or offend the supervisor, would not ask questions. Second, at the time of the study, Texas Instruments was experiencing rapid growth and technological change. The rapid expansion meant that a considerable number of new people were being hired, while the rapid technological change made it necessary for many current employees to be transferred and retrained, in some cases on several occasions. These conditions tended to induce anxiety for both the new and current employees and for the supervisors. Thus, from a contingency point of view, it appears that for organizations operating in a highly dynamic environment a higher degree of anxiety may exist that creates a greater need for anxiety-reduction orientation training programs than would be the case of organizations with more stable work conditions. Third, to reduce the anxiety that many supervisors appeared to have concerning their own competency, a program was instituted in which two experienced operators first oriented new supervisors to the assembly line. This approach helped in providing the supervisor with accurate information, in ensuring the operators that he was trained, and in opening communications because the supervisor was more willing to ask his subordinates for information. Thus, it appears that anxiety reduction orientation training activities can be used not only for nonmanagerial employees but for managers as well.

From this discussion we can see that well-planned formal orientation training programs can help: (1) increase the employee's rate of learning, (2) improve communications between supervisors and subordinates, (3) increase the productivity of employees, and (4) contribute to substantial dollar savings through reduced turnover, absenteeism, and training time. In spite of results such as these, orientation training is often not formally planned and conducted. In fact, introduction to the job in an appropriate manner "is a part of training which is very often neglected" and "introduction to the environment is given very little attention; in most cases, it is not even considered to be part of training."[8] Further, this lack of orientation training may exist for managers as well as for nonmanagers. As Kromer has pointed out:

> Curiously enough, however, organizations which roll out the red carpet for employees at the lower levels often allow their newly appointed managers or professionals at the higher levels in the organization to drift and fend for themselves during their first days or weeks on the job.[9]

As LaMotte has argued, orientation training may actually begin before an employee joins an organization and should be a continuous process that influences all employees as long as they remain with the organization.[10] Orientation training may begin prior to actual employment for two basic reasons. First, organizational efforts to develop a favorable image constitute a form of orientation to the company. Second, during the recruiting and selection processes, the potential employee is often given preliminary information on employee benefits, company history, job requirements and expectations, and promotional opportunities, which can be built upon in formal orientation training should the individual be hired. From a contingency point of view, orientation training will continue to be required as long as an employee remains with a firm, especially when the organizational environment is highly dynamic, leading to continuously changing work conditions.

Orientation training per se is not necessarily beneficial. Rather, such programs must be well planned, conducted, and evaluated, as was done at Texas Instruments. Lipstreu, for example, has referred to two studies that indicated that orientation training may not be worthwhile and has provided a case suggesting that orientation training may actually be harmful.[11] In this case, a bank did away with its orientation training and after six months found its employee turnover to be no greater than before and that employee attitudes toward the bank and adjustments to work actually appeared to have improved. An important but unanswered question in this case is: How good was the original orientation training? This brings us back to the point emphasized near the beginning of our discussion—individuals will become ''oriented'' regardless of what the firm does, but unplanned or ineffective orientation training may have serious dysfunctional consequences for any organization.

SPECIAL GROUPS NEEDING DEVELOPMENT

Special groups that may require unique types of training can probably be identified within any organization. For example, some organizations employ a large numbers of engineers or professionals who require continual updating of skills. Employees in other organizations, however, may be predominantly unskilled workers who are performing very routine jobs. In such a case, nonmanagerial job rotation to help reduce boredom may be appropriate. Both types of organizations need to train their employees, but the nature of the training is very different because of the different natures of the groups involved. In this section we will discuss two major groups in society which need special types of development: women assuming managerial and professional positions and the hard-core unemployed. It is generally recognized that these two groups require special development in all types of organizations—manufacturing, retailing, private nonprofit, and governmental. Historically, there have been two reasons for an interest in the development of these groups. First, in the expanding economy of the 1960's more people were needed in the work force and many individuals who had traditionally not entered the work force did so. Second, interest in ending discrimination and the establishment of affirmative action programs led many organizations to hire minority group members and women who previously had been excluded from the work force or at least had been limited in their potential for advancement to higher level positions in organizations. For example, as indicated in Chapter 4, Title VII of the Civil Rights Act of 1964 explicitly prohibited discrimination on the basis of race, religion, color, sex, or national origin. Since a large percentage of hard-core unemployed have been blacks, chicanos, and members of other minority ethnic groups, this act has not only had an impact on sex discrimination but also upon discrimination against many of the hard-core unemployed.

Women in Managerial and Professional Positions

In 1965 women represented 34 per cent of the total labor force of approximately 78 million in the United States; by 1974, this had risen to 38.5 per cent of 93 million.[12] Thus, both in absolute and percentage terms, the number of women in the total labor force increased during this period. In most instances, this increased representation has been at lower level and lower paying jobs. As reported in 1977, for example, women made up less than 6 per cent of middle management and less than 1 per cent of top management.[13] It appears, however, that more women will move into managerial and top executive positions in the future because of affirmative action programs. Further, with their increased representation in the labor force, more women will be available in organizations for promotion to managerial, professional, and top executive levels. The movement of women into these types of positions will pose problems because of the existence of a number of myths concerning their behavior, and both inappropriate male and female attitudes toward women. We will now discuss each of these types of problems and suggest some types of development activities that may be used to help overcome them.

One problem facing women entering managerial positions is that various stereotypes or myths have developed concerning them and their ability and desire to operate at this level in the business world.[14] For example, it frequently has been argued that women have higher rates of sickness, absenteeism, and turnover than do men. Some differences do exist between men and women with respect to these variables; however, they are not significant. For example, turnover rates have been found to be somewhat higher for women than for men. However, analysis of these differences has revealed that the major factors relating to turnover were number of years with the organization (those with fewer years tended to have higher turnover), age of the worker (younger workers tended to have higher turnover rates), and occupational level (higher turnover rates tended to exist in lower level positions). Since women have been overrepresented in each of these areas (i.e., less time with the organization, younger, and lower in the organization hierarchy), it is not surprising that they have had higher turnover rates than men. When men and women in professional positions have been compared, however, turnover rates have been found to be nearly identical. On the other hand, men in professional positions have tended to take longer periods of sick leave than women in comparable positions. Similarly, other stereotypes, such as the following, are *not* borne out by research: (1) women are more emotional than men, (2) women lack ability in the mathematics and scientific areas, (3) women are motivated by different factors than are men, and (4) women lack skills related to managerial success, such as objectivity, abstract thinking, and communication.

It is important that persons conducting development programs in which women are involved recognize that these stereotypes are incorrect. Otherwise, erroneous development approaches may be used. For example, if a male trainer assumes women are more emotional than men, he may try to avoid situations in the training environment that might be of an emotional nature, e.g., stressful role playing involving disciplinary problems. Since similar conditions may exist on the job, such actions on the part of the trainer may neglect an important area in the development of the trainee. Similarly, if the same trainer assumes that women lack mathematical or scientific abilities and that they cannot acquire them, he may fail to provide them with certain basic types of "operations research" techniques that they will need on the job.

The existence of stereotypes and myths about women would appear to call for training that is primarily informational in nature. Such training techniques as the lecture and PI, which are useful for imparting factual information, therefore, may appear to be appropriate for providing trainers and trainees with the facts concerning these myths. However, many of these myths are based more upon "emotionally-based" attitudes than "intellectual misinformation," and participative methods such as discussion and role playing, which are more suited to changing attitudes, may be necessary in addition to pure informational training. It is to some of these attitudinal problems that we now turn.

Women entering managerial positions face a major attitudinal problem that development programs may help to overcome. This problem is the attitudes of many males, whether subordinates, peers, or supervisors of a woman manager. Because of cultural learning, many males have developed attitudes about male-female roles that may lead them to have inappropriate predetermined role expectations concerning women. For example, males may react negatively to a woman supervisor because in this role she is violating a cultural value accepted by some individuals which specifies that women should assume positions subordinate to men but not peer or superior positions. One might think that younger, more "modern" males would hold such attitudes less than older males, but a 1971 study found that older, more experienced male employees were more willing to accept a woman as a supervisor than were younger, less experienced ones.[15] One reason for this finding may have been that younger workers saw women more as a threat to their own future advancement than did the older employees. Male peers and supervisors of women in managerial positions may feel threatened because they are not accustomed to seeing women assume assertive and dominant roles, which many such positions may require. Reactions to women assuming such roles may lead males to behave in a wide variety of ways. For example, they may attempt to treat the woman managerial peer as if she is a subordinate, or they may try to treat her as "one of the boys."

The organization can conduct development programs to help overcome such attitudinal problems, although one must recognize that changing the attitudes of certain males may be very difficult, if not impossible, to achieve. Information sessions can be used to provide factual information. Discussion sessions, which involve both men and women, can be used to explore areas of misunderstanding concerning the proper role of women managers. Role playing can also be used to help change attitudes. For example, in a conflict situation males and females might be asked to switch roles and approach the problem as they believe the other party would. Such role reversal may help expose biases on the part of both males and females. Programs of this nature can sometimes help to change male attitudes and thereby make the work environment more favorable for women managers.

Changing male attitudes alone, however, will not eliminate the problems women face in managerial positions. Women must modify their own attitudes, as well, since they have often accepted as "correct" the traditional behavior patterns and role expectations relative to male-female relationships. As Schwartz and Rago have indicated: "Full acceptance of women as professional peers or superiors requires relearning by both sexes to dispel previously learned male-female role expectations."[16]

A number of specific attitudes of some women need to be modified if they are to be successful in managerial positions. For example, there is some evidence that women in general have lower self-esteem than men.[17] From a socialization standpoint, women in our society are often trained to be more people-oriented, nonaggressive, and dependent than men. Managerial positions, however, are frequently seen as requiring task orientations, aggressiveness, and independence. Therefore, established modes of behavior of women are often in conflict with managerial role expectations. That females accept this stereotype is indicated by a study in which women and men were asked to rank nine characteristics in terms of their importance for managerial positions. Both sexes agreed that decisiveness, consistency and objectivity, emotional stability, and analytical ability were the most important *and* that men were more likely to have these characteristics than women. Thus, the basic socialization of many women contributes to a self-image that is in conflict with the image of a manager as perceived by members of both sexes. In mixed-sex groups, women may be reluctant to assume the leadership role. To the extent that women have lower self-esteem, they are more likely to doubt their own abilities and competence. There is some evidence that women may fear success in competitive situations with men and that they may, in fact, "underachieve in competitive intellectual situations when a male is present."[18] Contributing to these problems of role expectations and lower self-esteem is the fact that women wishing to enter managerial positions have very few role models to observe. This often makes it more difficult for women to establish career paths that lead to managerial positions.

Some of these attitudinal problems of women entering managerial positions may be dealt with by means of development programs. For example, a number of off-the-job techniques, such as case studies, in-basket exercises, role playing, and simulation, may be used to help the women managerial trainees gain practice in decision making. By providing positive reinforcement when appropriate, training may help to increase the self-esteem of women managerial trainees.

In addition to attitudinal training, women entering managerial positions frequently do need specific skills training, which might not be as necessary for men. For example, women may need special training in how to deal with conflict situations. This is because cultural conditioning frequently leads women to hide their hostile or aggressive feelings. In conflict situations, therefore, the woman manager is likely to have only one mode for dealing with the conflict — smoothing over — whereas her male counterpart may possess other modes of behavior as well, such as direct confrontation. Special training in managerial skills may be required by women more frequently than men because women previously have not considered managerial positions as realistic career goals and therefore have not tried to obtain training in this area. A study by Burrow, for example, revealed that women experienced a need for training in financial planning, preparing budgets, general planning, and effective decision making.[19]

Two additional points concerning "womenagement" development are important. First, it has been argued that traditional management development programs and materials are male-oriented and therefore do not fit the special needs of women.[20] Since training and development efforts need to reflect the needs of the trainees, it may be necessary to develop special materials and programs for developing women. Therefore, the program designer must decide whether existing materials can be used, or whether they need to be modified or discarded and new materials developed. Second, there is some disagreement as to whether training and development programs for women should include women only or whether men should also participate.[21] The arguments in favor of mixed groups are that women and men must learn to work together on the job and that training programs provide a nonthreatening opportunity for men to work with women and to perceive them in the role of managers. The main argument for not including men in development programs for women is that women need to deal with special problems of role expectations and self-esteem that may be inhibited by the presence of men. Our view is that it should be possible to design developmental efforts that combine programs consisting only of women when needed with mixed sessions including both sexes.

One program that provided mixed formalized training, as well as opportunities for women to learn by themselves has been described by Kanter.[22] In this program for women managerial trainees, emphasis was placed on providing women not only with managerial skills but also with more power in their actual jobs. In the organization involved both new women and men managers were to be given the responsibility of supervising a largely male blue-collar work force. This was the first time women had assumed such positions. The new men and women managers were trained together on the theory that such joint participation can be a powerful source of *peer alliances,* i.e., a camaraderie would develop and lasting friendships made between all members of the training group. Further, higher level supervisors were brought into the program and they "got to know the women trainees better than any previous group of new managers."[23] Other managers in the organization were involved in the development program and made to feel a part of it, so that they, also, would be more inclined to help the women later. Job rotation was also employed. Women were placed in a cycle of field positions between formal training activities so that they could get to know a wide variety of field personnel. They were also sent out to "interview" the few senior women managers in the organization in the hopes that "sponsor-protegé" relationships would develop there,"[24] i.e., that the senior women would take a liking to the new women trainees and give them future support in the organization. Having a chance to meet and talk with the more senior successful women in the organization also helped the new women trainees develop role models. In short, this program utilized a wide variety of development activities designed not simply to provide skills, knowledge, and attitudes necessary for effective managerial performance but also to give the new women more "political" power in the organization by providing them with role models, potential sponsors, and allies.

The Hard-Core Unemployed

A general characterization of the hard-core unemployed (HCU) has been offered by Goodman, Paransky, and Salipante, based upon a review of 192 articles dealing with training or employing members of this group. The "HCU is a member of a minority group, not a regular member of the work force, has less than a high school education, is often under 22 and of a poverty level specified by the Department of Labor."[25] In some instances individuals with criminal records may be included among the hard-core unemployed because of the difficulty such individuals often have obtaining employment.

During the 1960's, employing and training the hard-core unemployed became very fashionable. For example, the National Alliance of Businessmen set and exceeded the "goals of finding jobs for 100,000 hard-core unemployed by June, 1969 and for 500,000 by June, 1971."[26] Further, a 1969 survey of the membership of the American Society of Training Directors in Detroit found that half the firms had some sort of formal training program for the hard-core unemployed and that two thirds were involved in one way or another with the hard-core unemployed.[27] The interest in the hard-core unemployed during this period appears to have resulted from governmental and societal pressures and a tight labor market, as well as a genuine desire on the part of many companies to help the underprivileged. The existence of labor shortages is important, since some personnel managers have privately admitted that often persons designated as "hard-core unemployed" were "not really different from the general run of new hires in a tight labor market."[28] Thus, the interest in organizations hiring and developing persons designated as hard-core unemployed may fluctuate to some extent with economic conditions.

Because of their frequent low educational attainment, lack of experience in working in an organizational environment, and other background factors, the hard-core unemployed frequently need special types of development programs if they are to be able to contribute toward meeting organizational goals. More specifically, they need training that provides (1) remedial education, (2) learning specific job skills, and (3) attempts to modify certain negative attitudes.

Remedial programs are needed because of the low educational levels of many persons designated as hard-core unemployed. For example, many hard-core unemployed individuals have such poor abilities in arithmetic and English that they are classified as functionally illiterate. This has been defined to mean that they lack abilities which should have been achieved by the end of the fifth grade.[29] Therefore, the personnel department may need to sponsor remedial programs in arithmetic and English before it is possible to begin to provide specific job skills training to these persons. We say "sponsor" remedial programs because many companies have used outsiders to conduct remedial training due to the limited number of persons needing such training and the lack of expertise in providing remedial education on the part of the training staff of the organization.[30] Even so, the personnel department still has a direct responsibility in remedial education for the hard-core unemployed for at least three reasons. First, it will often be necessary for the personnel department to obtain or develop special testing procedures that will help to determine which members of the hard-core unemployed who are hired will require remedial education and what specific types of education they will need. Second, personnel may assume the responsibility of integrating remedial programs with other training activities and productive work so that the cost of remedial training is not too great relative to its benefits. A basic reason for wanting to try to rotate productive work with remedial training is that when remedial education is necessary, its potential future benefits are farther removed in time from its immediate costs than is the case with many other types of development efforts. If the organization cannot provide remedial training, it must design its selection processes to screen out those individuals who would need such training.

Finally, since the hard-core unemployed often have a low educational level and have generally never worked much before, it is quite likely that training them to acquire specific skills will be necessary. In fact, one characteristic that leads us to label an individual as hard-core unemployed is his or her lack of a saleable skill. Even before skills training can be undertaken, however, attitudinal training is likely to be needed. A basic problem that is somewhat unique to the hard-core unemployed is that they frequently have little idea what is expected in the work environment. This lack of understanding contributes to higher than normal absenteeism and tardiness rates for this group. Therefore, the hard-core unemployed individual entering the world of work must change his attitudes concerning what is acceptable work and work behavior. There are many reasons for such attitudes. For example, some young black men may lack adequate working male role models if the mother is the primary family wage earner, as has often been true. Further, the hard-core unemployed typically have low self-esteem as a result of previous educational or work failures.

To help overcome problems such as these, the personnel department needs to design development programs that will deal with both teaching skills and changing attitudes. Attitudinal change may be extremely difficult to effect as are male attitudes toward women managers. Programs that emphasize the importance of the individual and his job to other members of the organization and to the organization itself may represent one way of helping hard-core unemployed people in raising their self-esteem. For example, showing the trainee the final product and how his particular task relates to it may help convince him that what he will be doing is important. In addition, the self-esteem of these workers may be increased by having training programs proceed in small steps with constant and immediate knowledge of results (KOR) and reinforcement for desired behavior. These principles of learning have particular importance for training the hard-core unemployed because the feedback and positive reinforcement may help trainees increase their expectations of personal success.

Convincing the trainee of the importance of his job also increases the likelihood that he will come to work and be on time. Often the hard-core unemployed individual does not think it important for him to come to work as scheduled because he does not realize that other people depend on him. As Rosen and Turner have noted: "The key to developing job stability among hard-core employees, then, seems to be a matter of modifying poor work habits and developing an acceptance (and understanding) of the rigorous and systematic attendance demands made by a large business organization on its work force."[31]

Because of low educational levels and the lack of prior work experience many development techniques appear to have less application to the training of the hard-core unemployed than to other groups. For example, case studies, PI, and CAI, all of which generally require reading skills above the level attained by these individuals would not be appropriate. Showing the trainee how to do the job and providing the opportunity to practice are the most effective skills training methods. Therefore, vestibule training, which makes use of JIT, appears to be a highly appropriate development strategy. One such vestibule program that was very effective has been reported. In this program the hardcore unemployed trainees completed the program, were rated by their supervisors as turning out work comparable in terms of both quantity and quality to that of employees hired through traditional selection procedures, and had absenteeism records not significantly different from other workers.[32] Essentially, vestibule training was used. The training took place off the job with equipment quite similar to that in the actual work environment, and standard work procedures such as punching a time clock were followed in the training period. A number of reasons for the success of the program have been offered. The individuals were being trained for a specific job and they knew it. The instructors tried to help the trainees understand the reasons for what they were doing and how their behavior related to actual job requirements. The trainees were overtrained to some extent in order to increase their acceptability to the supervisors. Demonstrations were used in the job instruction and each trainee was shown his job, and given considerable practice in performing it. Tasks were broken into small parts so that recognition of accomplishments could be provided frequently. As mentioned earlier, the hard-core unemployed have a history of failure in training settings and their low self-esteem may be raised by such positive reinforcement. Special individual help was provided the trainees such as bailing them out of jail or helping them with transportation problems. Finally, strong efforts were undertaken to convince trainees that they could obtain jobs at the end of the program that were not simply "dead-end" jobs. Another interesting aspect of this study was that role playing was used to help the trainees develop greater self-confidence. Each trainee was exposed to three two-hour role playing sessions per week conducted by an expert in this technique. The trainees were called on to "act out various situations in which they confronted each other, tried to persuade each other, and had to make immediate decisions."[33] The trainees believed that these role playing experiences gave them much more confidence in working with their instructors and others.

A number of other factors that appear to be related to successful development programs for the hard-core unemployed can be identified. A study by Rosen and Turner indicated that company-run programs appear to be more effective than university-run programs.[34] A major reason for this conclusion was that the persons conducting the company-run programs were able to relate the training directly to the organization in terms of both job content and work rules and regulations. This study also supported the one just cited, in that it found that training for the hard-core unemployed needed to be job related and that attention needed to be given to personal counseling. Rosen and Turner also found that the top management of the organization needs to support actively the hiring and training of the hard-core unemployed if such programs are to be successful. Further, they concluded that the attitudes of other organization members must also be changed if the hard-core unemployed are to be successful on the job. Programs for supervisors to point out the special needs of the hard-core unemployed may be required. Similarly, training peers to change their attitudes toward the hard-core unemployed may be necessary. For example, a peer who never received any special help when he joined the firm may resent the special attention given to the hard-core worker. In such cases, using techniques such as role playing to try to help increase understanding may be beneficial, although we must recognize that some individuals' negative attitudes toward the hard-core unemployed may be so deep-rooted that no training techniques will really be effective. Efforts such as those described may increase the probabilities that members of the hard-core unemployed will be successfully integrated into the work force. However, there is some evidence indicating that training programs for the hard-core unemployed generally have not been effective. In one 1973 review of literature concerning the hard-core unemployed, for example, it was concluded that "in the studies reviewed, there is no clear indication that training significantly affects the turnover or performance of the HCU worker."[35]

There are probably a number of reasons why many development programs for the hard-core unemployed have not provided any such "clear indication" of effectiveness. First, many negative attitudes and behaviors of these individuals are extremely deep rooted, with positive change very difficult to achieve. Second, because of this difficulty, special intense developmental efforts such as those discussed are probably necessary if much hope of success is to be expected. We suspect that relatively few companies have actually gone as far in their development efforts as the "successful" organization described. In short, the effective training of the HCU and their integration into the organization poses difficult problems, which call for the intensive utilization of a number of the developmental techniques described in Chapter 7.

MULTIPLE DEVELOPMENT TECHNIQUE AND GROUP ORIENTED APPROACHES

In this section we will discuss two relatively new approaches to development: assessment centers and organizational development. These two approaches differ from the development techniques discussed in Chapter 7 in a number of ways. Many of the techniques presented in Chapter 7 can be used for either individual or group training. Both assessment centers and organizational development, however, by their very design, *must* involve groups at least during some phases of the training. Both approaches go beyond simply training an individual or group. For example, assessment centers deal with *evaluating* as well as training individuals. Organizational development, on the other hand, goes beyond focusing attention on only individuals or groups. Rather, it emphasizes changing attitudes and behaviors of individuals working together throughout the organization as a whole. Finally, these two approaches usually are used with managers rather than nonmanagerial personnel, although they have recently been adapted to all levels within organizations.

Assessment Centers

The assessment center concept had its origins prior to America's entry into World War II as a method designed and used for selecting military officers, first by the Germans, and later by the British and American military. In the 1950's the assessment center concept was adapted for industrial uses by A.T.&T. for the evaluation and selection or promotion of managers.

The basic requirements for an assessment center are presented in Figure 8–3. The assessment center is a process, not a place. Each person participating in an assessment center is evaluated, and the results of the evaluation are generally fed back to him. Participation in assessment centers usually lasts for two or more days. Finally, observers who are doing the evaluating must be trained management consultants and/or organization members who have been trained as observers and who hold positions at two or more organization levels above the persons being evaluated.

As the definition of an assessment center presented in Figure 8–3 indicates, many of the development techniques discussed in Chapter 7 are used with this approach. For example, in a typical two-day assessment center program described by Byham, the following techniques were used: business gaming, group discussion, case studies, in-basket exercise, leaderless group discussion, and role playing.[36] On the first day of the typical two-day center, the participants first had an orientation meeting. Then, as members of four-person teams they played a management game which involved forming different types of conglomerates and bartering with other teams to achieve planned objectives. Each individual had a one and a half hour interview with an assessor who examined the manager's background. Four-person groups were called on to

To be considered as an assessment center, the following minimal requirements must be met:

1. Multiple assessment techniques must be used. At least one of these techniques must be a simulation. A simulation is an exercise or technique designed to elicit behaviors related to dimensions of performance on the job by requiring the participant to respond behaviorally to situational stimuli. The stimuli present in a simulation parallel or resemble stimuli in the work situation. Examples of simulations include group exercises, in-basket exercises, and fact finding exercises.
2. Multiple assessors must be used. These assessors must receive training prior to participating in a center.
3. Judgments resulting in an outcome (i.e., recommendation for promotion, specific training or development) must be based on pooling information from assessors and techniques.
4. An overall evaluation of behavior must be made by the assessors at a separate time from observation of behavior.
5. Simulation exercises are used. These exercises are developed to tap a variety of predetermined behaviors and have been pretested prior to use to insure that the techniques provide reliable, objective and relevant behavioral information for the organization in question.
6. The dimensions, attributes, characteristics or qualities evaluated by the assessment center are determined by an analysis of relevant job behaviors.
7. The techniques used in the assessment center are designed to provide information which is used in evaluating the dimensions, attributes or qualities previously determined.

In summary, an assessment center consists of a standardized evaluation of behavior based on multiple inputs. Multiple trained observers and techniques are used. Judgments about behavior are made, in part, from specially developed assessment simulations.

Figure 8–3 *Assessment center defined. From Joseph L. Moses, et al., "Standards and Ethical Considerations for Assessment Center Operations," as developed by the Task Force on Development of Assessment Center Standards and endorsed by the Third International Congress on the Assessment Center Method, Quebec, Canada, May, 1975, p. 2.*

assume the role of management consultants in solving problems presented in four short cases. Each group, after discussing the cases, was required to develop a written analysis and sets of recommendations. Thus, the first day of activities involved mainly group decision-making problems. On the second day, the participants first participated in an in-basket exercise involving such problems as scheduling and planning activities, answering questions, and delegating responsibilities. Following the completion of the exercise, each person participated in a one-hour interview with an assessor. Next, a leaderless group discussion was conducted in which each participant was to play the role of a department head. The department heads were given the role-playing problem of meeting as a group to decide how to allocate money for salary increases among the various departments, and each participant was instructed to do the best he could for his subordinates. The participants then played the role of a management consultant called in to help a manager resolve a financial problem. Each was first asked to come up with his own recommendations; then groups were formed and a single set of recommendations had to be developed by each group. For two days after the typical assessment center was held, the "assessors meet to share their observations on each participant and to arrive at summary evaluations relative to each dimension sought and overall potential and training needs."[37]

This discussion illustrates the great deal of overlap between managerial development programs and assessment centers. Further, it has been increasingly recognized that assessment centers have uses beyond the evaluation of managerial potential. Richard Steiner, for example, has suggested the following uses of assessment centers.[38]

1. Identifying and determining immediate management potential, which aids in making selection decisions.
2. Identifying and developing individualized development programs.
3. Developing individuals just through participation in the assessment center.
4. Influencing positively employee satisfaction, job expectations, and motivation.
5. Evaluating development programs.

There is a large body of research based upon studies conducted at companies such as A.T.&T., IBM, Sears. J. C. Penney, Ford, General Electric, Standard Oil of Ohio and Kodak, which indicates that the assessment center is a valid technique for selecting managers for promotion.[39] By far the most comprehensive and important of these studies was carried out at A.T.&T. between 1956 and 1966 by Douglas Bray and his associates. In this study a large number of lower level managers participated in an assessment center, but the information about participants generated and the predictions made as to who would attain middle management positions were set aside and not used by the company. About 10 years later, the company followed up on this group to see how accurate the predictions about who would move into middle management positions were as based upon each individual's performance in the assessment center. Thus, the company engaged in a longitudinal study in which the evaluation was not biased, since the predictions were not made known to the program participants or to the organization. The accuracy of the predictions was impressive in that: "Sixty-four percent of those predicted to achieve this level *(middle-management)* actually did so, compared with only 32 percent of those who were predicted not to reach this level."[40] Other research has shown similar results. Norton, for example, has indicated that he found only one reported study which failed to validate an assessment center and that this study "was flawed by non-random sampling."[41]

In addition to being used for managerial personnel, the assessment center technique has been used and proved valid for the selection of salesmen, engineers, revenue agents, and auditors.[42] Further, it has been suggested that the assessment center may be useful for rank and file workers.[43]

Assessment centers are valid for selection purposes in that they often serve as good predictors of success on the job, which makes them particularly useful for dealing with minorities and women. This is because they may meet the nondiscrimination requirements of Title VII of the Civil Rights Act of 1964. In fact, research has shown that assessment centers are good predictors of job performance for a number of different minority group members. Further, in a consent decree with the federal government, A.T.&T. agreed to use the assessment center "as a means of judging management potential of women to facilitate their upgrading."[44] Finally, in the case of *Berry, Stokes and Lant vs. City of Omaha,* the first court test of the validity of the assessment center as a nondiscriminatory selection approach, the city was upheld in its use of the method.[45]

In addition to helping to make selection decisions, assessment centers are useful in identifying, developing, and helping to decide on individual development programs. In fact, as Byham has pointed out, the primary or highly rated secondary objective of most assessment centers is to help build individual development programs.[46] Since the individual is being evaluated on a number of specific dimensions, many different types of weaknesses can be identified and programs designed to deal with them developed. For example, the individual who does not appear to manage time effectively when working on an in-basket exercise because he does not set priorities well might be given special training in how to set priorities and manage time more wisely. The identification of specific weaknesses for future job assignments is facilitated because the assessors (if they are from within the company) hold positions in the organizational hierarchy at two or more levels above the trainee and, therefore, are quite likely to be familiar with the specific skills the individual will need in future job assignments.

Participation in an assessment center may also serve as a

development exercise in and of itself because participants may perceive this experience as a developmental one. For example, by participating in the discussion groups, the individual may learn how well he functions and relates to others in group problem solving. As Steiner has pointed out, the fact that participants in assessment centers believe that they have learned as they participated is not surprising, since many of the tools used in assessment centers are "tried and true training methodology."[47] Since most assessment centers provide both oral and written feedback of evaluation information to the participant concerning performance, many individuals in assessment centers are operating in what is, in many ways, a training environment. Even where special feedback mechanisms are not built into programs, there is evidence that "most participants gain self-insight from participating in assessment exercises and that this insight is fairly accurate."[48]

Assessment centers may be useful in influencing such variables as satisfaction, job expectations, and motivation by providing individuals with objective feedback on (1) how they performed in the assessment center and (2) their future development needs and prospects within the company. Satisfaction and motivation may also be enhanced when the individual is given an opportunity to talk candidly with the assessors, who, if individuals from within the company, hold positions above him in the hierarchy. However, if the individual is not selected for promotion or for further development after participation in an assessment center, problems may arise.

Assessment centers may also be useful for evaluating development programs. An assessment center can develop an after-training type of test for a previously conducted development program.[49] For example, using the after-only design described in Chapter 6, we might conduct a development program for managers that focuses on problem solving in groups and upon its completion, send them to an assessment center in order to see if they have learned the group problem solving techniques stressed in the program.

A final potential benefit of assessment centers is that they may constitute development programs for persons acting as assessors as well as for individuals being assessed. For example, the assessors, by observing the groups in discussion sessions, may learn more about how group norms begin to develop. This information may later help them in dealings with their own subordinates on the job. Kraut has even suggested that in the future managers may be sent to assessment centers as observers rather than to specific development courses to help them "to become more astute in behavioral observation, group dynamics and problem solving."[50]

In spite of the benefits associated with assessment centers, there are some limitations to this approach. First, assessment centers may be costly. Estimates of costs, as reported in 1974, may range from the price of a few meals to $5000 per participant, excluding staff salaries.[51] As reported in 1972, A.T.&T.'s estimated cost per participant was $500, while IBM's costs for 12 participants were about $5000 plus an additional cost of exercises and materials of about $200 to $400.[52] Any cost figures, of course, must be compared with benefits, which are much harder to determine on a dollar basis. However, one estimate made in 1976 by Kraut, if accurate only even within a very broad range, suggested that the savings derived from the use of assessment centers can be substantial.[53] He stated that the use of the assessment center for the selection of sales managers at Xerox resulted in a net benefit of $4.9 million, compared with a cost of only $340,000.

A second problem associated with assessment centers, closely related to cost, is that each organization may need to develop and validate its own assessment center. This is particularly true if the organization requires unique skills or is using the center for positions that have not previously been dealt with in assessment centers. The need for each organization to identify its own needs has been pointed out in a study by Haynes.[54] This researcher conducted some statistical analysis on several assessment center techniques and an overall performance measure (demonstrated potential for first line supervision). On the basis of this analysis as well as on an analysis of items in a battery of tests, a number of assessment center tools were identified which could be dropped since they did not provide any additional information about the participants.

Another problem centers around one of the three basic contingencies discussed in Chapter 1 — organizational size. Due to the cost of assessment centers and the need to validate them, which requires a fairly large number of participants, it is unlikely that smaller organizations can afford this evaluation-development approach. In fact, reference back to the list of companies having used the assessment center will show that they are among the largest ones in the United States. The problem can be overcome to some extent, since there are a number of consulting firms that will conduct assessment centers for organizations. For example, one company provides complete assessment center packages for smaller firms. Thus, smaller firms may utilize assessment centers which are completely externally operated. However, in many instances, very small firms will not even be able to use such services because of the costs involved. In addition, the assessment center may be most useful in rapid growth situations, because individuals who are immediately promotable can be quickly identified. Further, some individuals entering assessment centers who are not ready for immediate promotion may become promotable more quickly because the assessment center serves as a training environment.

Organization Development (OD)

In this section we will focus attention on a relatively new approach to planned organizational change — organizational development — often simply referred to as OD.[55] Organization development is difficult to define, since there have been so many different techniques and tactics referred to as OD that have been used in various organizations. However, in most cases: "Organization development is an effort (1) *planned,* (2) *organization-wide,* and (3) *managed* from the *top,* to (4) increase *organization effectiveness* and *health* through (5) *planned interventions* in the organization's 'processes,' using *behavioral science* knowledge."[56] The last two points in this definition are important because they reflect the fact that OD efforts are basically people-oriented and reflect a humanistic bias in which an attempt is made to modify the attitudes, values, and behavior of organizational members in certain specific directions. As Miner has noted, these directions include the following:

A more democratic or participative set of values that is antihierarchy, antiauthoritarian, and antiauthority. The result is a movement in the direction of democracy within the enterprise.

A greater orientation to and consciousness of the immediate peer and work group, as reflected in team building efforts.

Less individual competitiveness and less use of power. This has been called power equalization and is reflected in the strong emphasis on collaboration.

More openness and freer expression of feelings as reflected in the stress on confrontation.[57]

Another important characteristic of OD may be inferred from these dimensions and from the fact that OD efforts are organization-wide — OD focuses attention on changing the total organizational system. In essence, OD represents a systems-oriented approach in which the interactions of various individuals and groups are considered when human-oriented changes are introduced into an organization.

OD draws very heavily on the principle of active learning discussed in Chapter 6. Members of organizations participating in OD efforts are actively involved in organizational change. Further, many of the OD involvement efforts are aimed at having *groups* within the organization, rather than simply individuals, work *together* actively to learn how to function better, make decisions and relate to each other in a manner congruent with the humanistic values of OD. As Luthans has put it: "There is a sociological flavor to much of OD."[58]

With respect to the basic question concerning who should conduct the training, most OD experts emphasize that there should be an outsider, third-party "change agent," or catalyst involved in OD programs.[59] In a few cases, however, organizations have relied solely upon the expertise of their own training staffs to undertake OD activities.

While OD focuses attention on total systems change, its orientation is quite different from that involved in the systems-oriented vestibule training experiments mentioned in Chapter 7. OD attempts to change the behavior within the existing organizational system, whereas the RAND efforts attempted to replicate a real system in order to teach specific knowledge and skills.

OD has often been compared to management development. Although both are similar in that they represent development efforts, management development is geared primarily toward improving the performance of managers as individuals, while OD is concerned with improving the performance of systems that make up the total organization — work groups, departments, teams, task forces. In addition, management development and OD are complementary, and management development can be seen as a component of OD.[60] Further, it is possible to view OD as an outgrowth of some of the approaches originally used for management development such as sensitivity training.

As indicated earlier, there are many techniques used in OD efforts. The two most common of these are the so-called "managerial grid" and sensitivity training. We will now turn our attention to these specific approaches.

Managerial Grid Development

The managerial grid approach to organizational development was created by Blake and Mouton. The grid consists of two parts: (1) a conceptual model to describe managerial behavior — the managerial grid, and (2) a six-phase program for introducing change.[61] The managerial grid, presented in Figure 8–4, uses combinations of two variables to classify managerial styles: (1) concern for production and (2) concern for people. Each variable is scaled from 1 to 9, with 1 indicating low concern and 9 indicating high concern. A 1,1 managerial style represents a minimal concern for both production and people. The 1,1 manager exerts just enough effort to get the work required in his department to be done. The 1,9 managerial style indicates a high concern for people and a low concern for production. The manager using this style is

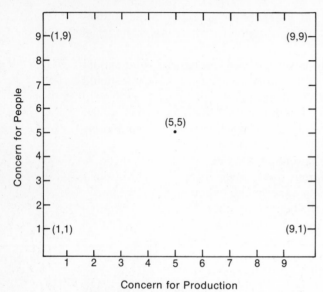

Figure 8-4 *The managerial grid.*

primarily interested in having a satisfied work group and comfortable, friendly atmosphere. Conversely, the 9,1 managerial style indicates a high concern for production and a low concern for people. The 9,1 manager is interested in getting the task done and does not care very much whether or not subordinates are satisfied. The 9,9 style, which indicates a high concern for both production and people, is regarded as the ideal situation in the grid, in which decision making is participatory and team building is emphasized. Finally, Blake and Mouton have described a 5,5 leadership style, which represents a moderate concern for both production and people.

The grid concept is used as the basis for a sequential six-phase organizational development program, which can take up to from three to five years. The first phase involves seminar training in which managers are exposed to the managerial grid concept and are given a chance to identify their own style. The managers solve problems that attempt to simulate organizational interpersonal situations. Phase two represents an on-the-job extension of phase one, in which team development of intact groups takes place "after each work group or department decides on its own 9,9 ground rules and relationships."[62] The first two phases represent more "management development" types of activities, while the next four phases are more geared toward organizational development. In phase three, interdepartmental groups begin to work together to build 9,9 relationships beyond the single work groups. The goal of phase three is to move the groups from common "win-lose" patterns of behavior to joint problem-solving activities in which groups resolve their problems on a more mature open basis. In phase four, organizational goal setting takes place. Organizational problems and goals, such as cost control and safety, are identified by special task groups composed of individuals from different segments and levels of the organization. Phase five involves goal attainment in which teams decide how to achieve the goals set in phase four. Specific problems are identified and it is determined how they can be dealt with through organization-wide activities. Finally, in phase six, the changes introduced in the first five phases are reinforced so that the organization will continue to operate in a 9,9 style. These phases, it should be noted, are not only sequential but also represent movement from a micro- to a macrofocus.

The managerial grid approach was first used by Blake and Mouton in the early 1960's at a company they called Sigma, which employed 4000 individuals, of which 800 were managers. While they have noted that it is difficult to draw direct cause and effect relationships, Blake and Mouton have indicated that following the grid program at Sigma there were both gains in productivity and profits and changes in behavior attitudes and values, such as improved superior-subordinate, group, and intergroup relations.

Since the 1960's the managerial grid has become the most popular of all OD approaches. It was reported in 1974, for example, that the grid has been accepted in whole or part by thousands of organizations, and that about 200,000 individuals had participated in in-company grid programs.[63] The grid appears to draw on certain principles of learning discussed in Chapter 6. In the Sigma program, for example, there was active involvement, which is characteristic of all OD efforts. Further, one aim of the grid is to provide for honest feedback among individuals, groups, and teams. Rather than a suppression of interpersonal conflict, in grid training such conflicts are brought out into the open. Based upon grid studies other than that at Sigma:

1. The grid has had some reported successes, some failures, and some mixed results.[64]
2. There have been criticisms of nonrigorous research methodologies used in studying the effectiveness of grid OD efforts. One author, after reviewing considerable research on grid training, for example, arrived at the conclusion that most such programs have not been evaluated at all or depend on data of a testimonial or anecdotal type.[65]

Finally, unlike sensitivity training, to which we will next turn our attention, the managerial grid was originally intended to provide a *complete* OD approach by itself. That the grid provides for involvement and humanistic change efforts across the organization may be noted in its primarily OD-oriented final four stages.

Sensitivity Training

Sensitivity training, also often referred to as T-group or laboratory training, was originally developed as a management development technique rather than an OD tool. It was pioneered in the 1940's by a group known today as the National Training Laboratory Institute for Applied Behavioral Science. The basic objective of sensitivity training in its original formulation was to help the individual achieve a variety of behavioral goals that would contribute to both more effective organizational performance and individual need satisfaction. The specific behavioral goals of sensitivity training have typically included one or more of the following: (1) increasing self-insight, by means of which the individual better understands why he behaves as he does, (2) providing a better understanding of forces, such as values and attitudes, which may facilitate or hinder group functioning and of the interpersonal dynamics existing in groups, and (3) developing skills for diagnosing individual, group, and organizational behavior.[66] Thus, a major emphasis of sensitivity training has been upon understanding oneself and others in group settings.

To achieve these goals, sensitivity training makes use of a number of training techniques — role playing, theory sessions on group dynamics, etc. The relative emphasis given to any one of these techniques may vary considerably from one sensitivity training session to the next. At the heart of *all* sensitivity training programs, however, is one special technique — the "training group," more commonly referred to as the "T-group." The T-group is a relatively unstructured, leaderless group of about 8 to 20 individuals engaged in face-to-face discussion over a one- to two-week period. The following example illustrates some of the dynamics of T-groups as used in sensitivity training.

It is the first day of the training. Twelve individuals who have never met before enter a room and sit down around a table. An individual who appears as if he were in charge of the training session enters the room and the persons sitting around the table look to him to start the session with an opening statement. However, the individual typically simply introduces himself and sits down without saying anything else except perhaps a few very general comments about the objectives of the sensitivity training program. After a period of time the participants begin to wonder what is going on. They may begin to move around in their chairs, exhibit nervous mannerisms, smile quizzically, or stare at the ceiling. Some of them may feel annoyed with the trainer. "Why doesn't he do something," they may wonder. Some participants may also wonder why the other participants don't do something. Finally, the silence may become overwhelming and someone may then suggest that the group go around the table and introduce themselves. For the moment some members of the group begin to relax; however, once everyone is introduced silence again tends to follow. Someone may now suggest that the group should decide what they should do by setting up an agenda and perhaps electing officers. (After all, they need some leadership, which the T-group trainer has failed to provide.) The group may agree with some of the participants actively trying to discuss an agenda and conduct an election with others sitting back, not participating. (Typically, in trying to formulate an agenda, group members want to discuss their own problems "back home on the job," which may be of little interest to others in the group.) The active participants may become annoyed with the nonparticipants and tell them to join in and help the group. One of the nonparticipants may tell the participants, "No, I won't participate! I don't want to be part of this group of power hungry individuals!" At this point the trainer may intervene and ask the group to assess what has happened.

This example illustrates a number of aspects of sensitivity training. First, the trainer is generally as much of an observer as a trainer. He assumes a nondirective role and intervenes in the group only when he thinks it will be beneficial for the group to engage in self-analysis, and that his intervention may help the group understand what is happening. Second, the group members often experience discomfort because of the silence or because they are challenged by someone else, and hostility between certain members may be exhibited. These emotional reactions can be used to help the participants focus on how they perceive others in the group and how others perceive them — both of which may contribute to attaining more self-insight and better understanding of the dynamics within the group. In the above example, discussion might reveal that the individual who first spoke did so because he really felt uncomfortable with the silence. However, others may have seen this as an attempt to control the group and therefore withdrew by not participating. The individuals who withdrew might be surprised to find that the active participants were hostile toward them because of their failure to participate. Third, although initially participants may want to talk about their "back home on the job" problems, our example illustrates that the trainer wants the focus in sensitivity training to be on the "here and now" and not on such problems. In his intervention he will try to get the participants to analyze what is actually going on in the group now.

Throughout the T-group sessions the trainer may intervene in a nondirective manner, trying to get the group to see for itself certain dysfunctional types of behavior exhibited in group settings and what alternative forms of behavior, such as active listening, might be more effective in particular circumstances. In some cases, the participants may then be given a chance to try out the alternative behaviors, possibly by discussing case studies with the other members of the group or by means of role playing.

It is extremely important to recognize that the trainer must play a most difficult nondirective role in the T-group. If he simply sits back and never intervenes, it is not likely that members of the group will learn much. On the other hand, if he tries to push the group into analyzing the "here and now," the group may rebel against him and refuse to discuss the current ongoing processes taking place in the group. When he intervenes, he must try not to show approval or disapproval of members' behavior. For example, in one sensitivity training group, one member of the T-group who dominated the discussion the first day was criticized for the first time early during the next day. He immediately put his arms on the table bending his head down, pulled his chair away from the table, and within a few minutes left the training room and became nauseated. For several days this individual was quite upset psychologically, and at one point the trainer found an opportunity to intervene in a nondirective manner.

> Trainer: "Are you feeling well today, Joe?"
> Participant: "No, I'm feeling very upset."
> Trainer: "Do you remember when you first began to feel this way?"
> Participant: "I guess early Tuesday morning."
> Trainer: "Would you like to know what happened just before you became upset?"
> Participant: "Well, yes, I guess so — I'm feeling so lousy."

The trainer then (from notes taken during each T-group session) indicated that the disturbed participant had said something and had been criticized by someone else. Rather than "telling" the participant that this was the first time his "leadership" had been challenged, he *asked* the participant what *he* thought had created the problem. The disturbed participant came to the conclusion himself that he must have become upset by the challenge. The trainer asked if this had ever occurred on the job. The participant indicated that it had, and an open discussion of this problem emerged in which several other participants tried to make constructive suggestions to the participant. The disturbed T-group member remained upset throughout the remainder of the (two-week) session and, as reported by his boss, for about two weeks afterwards back on the job. Finally, he "pulled himself together," and from then on, according to the testimony of the boss, seemed to "act more mature in dealing with others."

As mentioned earlier, in its original formulation sensitivity training was a management development technique rather than an OD tool, largely because sensitivity training sessions were originally conducted with participants in a single group drawn from different organizations. These are referred to as "stranger-labs," since the individuals in any group do not know the other members of the group prior to the training. The objective was to provide these individuals with insight and understanding, which they could use when they returned to their respective organizations. In addition, however, many sensitivity training programs began to emphasize the humanistic types of focus mentioned earlier. Thus, by participation in sensitivity training, individuals were instilled with the virtues of participative management and democratic organizations. However, *if* these individuals did attempt to change their behavior when they returned to their organizations, they often experienced difficulties. For one thing, subordinates were often suspicious of the new behavior, asking themselves: "What's the boss up to now?" If the upper levels of management did not accept the new values, the individual often felt frustrated because he was not permitted to use the newly acquired behavioral skills. To help overcome these problems some proponents of sensitivity training began to suggest that whole organizations, rather than selected individuals, should participate in sensitivity training. This has been done in two ways. First, numbers of groups in an organization that do *not* work with each other daily may be sent to a series of in-company sensitivity programs often called "cousin" programs, as opposed to the "stranger-labs" discussed earlier. Second, members of immediate work groups, i.e., a boss and his actual subordinates, have been put into the same T-group. Many individuals are extremely concerned about this form of training, referred to as "family" labs. As we have seen in the previous examples, T-group experiences are emotional, people may become hostile toward each other, and with the boss and one's peers present, individuals may "clam up" for fear of saying anything in a "family" lab that would hurt them later on their jobs. In short, sensitivity training has moved from a management development focus to an OD focus, and in recent years has increasingly been recognized as an OD tool.

In addition to the problem of transferring learning and gaining acceptance in the work environment, there are at least two other problems with sensitivity training. Much of the evidence supporting sensitivity training is based upon "testimonials, anecdotes, and impressions, or research focused on changes in attitudes toward and perceptions of organizational reality" rather than "measures of organizational performance."[67] As may be inferred from our previous example, trainers in sensitivity training sessions need to be highly qualified to conduct sessions that involve psychological considerations. All too often, however, the T-group trainer is not sufficiently qualified. When such is the case, some individuals may experience serious emotional trauma if their ego defense mechanisms have been stripped away in the training session and no way is provided for them to cope with such a situation. For example, in a T-group session a participant may become aware that most other participants don't like him because they think he often has a "dictatorial" manner. He may further conclude that this must be true of the people with whom he works and become extremely depressed. Such emotional upsets may also occur with "competent" trainers, and for this reason many proponents of T-group training believe that there should be a trained psychiatrist or clinical psychologist accessible should any such happenings occur.

In spite of these problems, one survey of the presidents of 74 chapters of the American Society for Personnel Administration found that they estimated sensitivity training to be moderately successful in terms of improving employee development, manager-subordinate relationships, and productivity.[68] It was also found that the frequency of use of sensitivity training increased with company size and that users generally saw benefits as exceeding costs.

A number of factors of a contingency nature appear to affect sensitivity training programs. For example, group composition in terms of personality variables may influence behavior and thereby program effectiveness, or the duration of the training may influence learning. We are especially concerned with popularized two- to three-day T-group sessions, which have been conducted by many well-meaning groups in this country. Such sessions present the serious danger that individuals may be stripped of certain defense mechanisms and become emotionally disturbed, with not enough time made available to put them, like Humpty Dumpty, "back together again." Along somewhat different lines, Sims has viewed T-group training from a contingency point of view.[69] He has noted that under dynamic conditions, a more organic type of organization is needed and that training should facilitate movement toward this type of organization. He concluded that sensitivity training is most congruent with the need for an organic organization, because it emphasizes values and attitudes, such as participation and delegation. Therefore, he has hypothesized that: "T-group training, as a means of organizational development, tends to be more effective in organic organizations facing dynamic environments, rather than in mechanistic organizations facing stable environments."[70]

OD: A Final Question

Finally, a fundamental question should be raised not only with respect to sensitivity training but to all forms of OD, including the managerial grid: Are humanistic values really desirable to promote in organizations? In Chapter 5 we indicated that some individuals have strong dependence needs, not all people want to participate in decision making, and individuals with "authoritarian personalities" have considerable difficulty in delegating responsibilities to subordinates. In light of these facts, do we really want a high degree of confrontation? Of power equalization? Of anti-hierarchical values? Of team building efforts? With basic behavioral patterns fairly well established by adulthood, these forms of behavior would pose serious difficulties for certain organizational members, and one can question whether they could be "developed" very far in the humanistic directions called for by organizational development.

DYSFUNCTIONAL CONSEQUENCES OF DEVELOPMENT

In this and the previous two chapters, we have indicated some of the dysfunctional consequences of development efforts. In this section we will briefly summarize some of these. We are particularly concerned with those possibly negative consequences that exist for all types of development.

One dysfunctional consequence of development may occur when the trainee returns to the job and meets opposition to implementing newly acquired skills, knowledge, and attitudes. As already indicated, this problem may exist following sensitivity training, if behavior is really changed. Further, that management trainees often anticipate opposition to the ideas acquired in development programs when they return to the job is reflected in such statements as: "Gee, I wish my boss had taken this course." As one person subtly put it in the final session of a program: "Do you think this was the right group for this program?" Even nonmanagers who attend development programs may experience difficulties implementing new ideas when they return to the job. Particularly under conditions of inelastic demand, they may be pressured by their peers not to use the new methods because they fear that individual productivity may rise and that the number of employees necessary to generate the level of production required by the firm will therefore fall. Further, supervisors may feel threatened by the new methods because they are not familiar with them and consequently feel they do not know as much as their subordinates. On-the-job opposition, from whatever source, to skills, knowledge, and attitudes learned in a development program is likely to create frustration and anxiety on the part of the recently trained employee. The employee can just ignore the opposition and run the risk of rejection by his peers and supervisor. On the other hand, he can give in to the pressure and not use what was learned in the development program. In either case, the employee is likely to question the worth of the developmental effort. To help overcome such problems, the personnel department needs to stimulate an environment in which the behavior, skills, and attitudes fostered by development programs are supported on the job. One way of helping to accomplish this is to make sure that employees and supervisors understand the purpose of any development program. To the extent feasible, training "from the top down" may help provide such understanding, i.e., exposing the plant manager to the training first, then his subordinates, the general foremen and finally their subordinates, the first line supervisors.

Another dysfunctional consequence of development programs that is closely related to the above problem is that some people are selected to attend certain programs and others are not selected. In management development programs it is not uncommon for those selected to be seen by others as "crown princes or princesses," as the case may be. When only some are selected, a number of problems may be created. First, the peers of the chosen ones may feel resentful and wonder why they were not selected. Persons who are not selected may lower their performance or possibly leave the organization. Second, older higher level managers may feel resentful because they had to move up the organizational hierarchy "the hard way" while younger managers are given considerable special attention. In some cases, these older managers may try to make things more difficult after the training rather than positively reinforce it on the job. Third, individuals selected may believe that they in fact have been "chosen" and therefore that they no longer have to work as hard. In addition, some of the individuals selected will not perform well in the development program and therefore will not be moved into higher level positions in the organization. The organization may need to develop new, special development efforts for these individuals to help them cope with their failure in a previous development program. While we have focused on management development, our discussion also applies to development programs for nonmanagers. For example, the individual selected to attend a program dealing with the operation of a new piece of equipment may be resented by his peers in much the same way as is the "crown prince" in a management development program.

Additionally, the organization may encourage development but not provide anything for those who are successfully trained. One organization encourages its employees to continue their educations by paying the tuition for college courses passed that contribute toward a degree or specific job related skills. In addition, the company pays for all books and other course-related materials. This approach encourages people to take courses. However, upon completion of the course or degree, the employee may find that the organization has made no provision for promotion or other rewards. As a result of this situation, a few employees who have completed their degree requirements have left the organization for better jobs. The dysfunctional consequences of this situation were further accentuated by the fact that two of these people who left were rehired a year later in higher level positions, which caused some individuals to believe that the way to get ahead in the organization was to get your degree, leave, and reapply for a higher level position. If an organization is going to encourage its employees to complete development programs, it needs to incorporate these decisions into its human resource planning.

Development programs sometimes do not teach materials that will contribute to improved job performance. For example, Miner has cited a case in which the Bell System encouraged employees to take humanities courses.[71] Later evaluation revealed that the employees increased their artistic and aesthetic values while decreasing their economic values. To the extent that these newly acquired values were transferred to the job, this employee development effort may have been dysfunctional from the organization's point of view.

SUMMARY

All organizations must engage in employee development to some extent, since employees need to be oriented to new tasks or new environments. Because the orientation period may create anxiety that interferes with learning, it is important that organizations carefully plan and evaluate their orientation training programs. In addition, all organizations employ special groups of individuals that may require special types of training. In this chapter we have described some of the problems associated with two such groups: women managers and the hard-core unemployed. We also pointed out two major types of programs that go beyond simply training an individual or group — the assessment center and organizational development. The two major approaches to organizational development are the managerial grid and sensitivity training. Finally, we noted some of the dysfunctional consequences of development.

DISCUSSION AND STUDY QUESTIONS

1. In discussing orientation training we made two points: (a) orientation training may begin before an employee actually joins an organization, and (b) some such training is often necessary for an employee as long as he remains with an organization. Professor Lucius Biddle is an internationally known authority on employee development in the School of Business Administration in a large western university located in a metropolitan area. He has been asked if he would be interested in coming to a large state university in a small college town in the midwest to consider accepting a highly prestigious chaired position in which his salary would be increased considerably. He and his wife have both been

invited to visit the state university to explore the new position, and they have accepted. Professor Biddle is 42 and the Biddles have three children, whose ages are 13, 15, and 17. During their visit, and afterwards, should the professor accept the position, what specific kinds of orientation training might be required?

2. What are some basic similarities and differences in the problems that must be faced in integrating women managers and the hard-core-unemployed into an organization?

3. "Integrating both women managers and professionals as well as the hard-core unemployed into an organization involves more than formalized developmental efforts—it represents a systems problem". Comment.

4. For what reasons do you believe that, in general, assessment center performance has proved to be a good predictor of managerial success?

5. What values do you think assessment centers may provide their participants in terms of the principles of learning discussed in Chapter 6?

6. "Sensitivity training is a highly emotional experience, and in the T-group some individuals become extremely upset and have 'nervous breakdowns.' For the organization to require individuals to participate in such a type of training is not only cruel but immoral and unethical." Comment.

7. One day the plant manager at a medium sized manufacturing facility in Michigan called her training director into her office and made the following comments: "The head of our industrial engineering department seems to have some personality problems. He's having difficulty in getting along with the general foreman in the assembly department and with the head of our quality control department. I've been reading about sensitivity training, and I think we ought to help straighten him out. Do you agree?" If you were the training director, how would you respond?

8. "The managerial grid's ideal 9,9 style of leadership is a lot of 'hogwash.' As busy as I am as a manager, to be highly concerned with both my subordinates and production — why I'd have to work a 25-hour day. Also, I remember reading that a good manager doesn't use the same leadership style all of the time — he varies his style depending on the contingencies of the situation." Comment.

9. Comment on each of the following statements:
   a. "OD is the only really effective development technique since it is the only one which explicitly incorporates a systems orientation."
   b. "Just having completed a two-week sensitivity training session, I know that I can become less 'authoritarian' on the job, but if I try to do so, both my boss and my subordinates will become suspicious of me and hostile towards me. Making matters even worse, my boss is an 'authoritarian' leader, if I ever saw one. It's just not worth trying to change my behavior."
   c. "All of the developmental approaches discussed in the chapter are more appropriate in dynamic organizations."
   d. "All of the developmental approaches in the chapter are

more appropriate in large organizations rather than small ones."

10. "The most serious dysfunctional consequence of developmental efforts is that too often neither the trainer nor the trainee is adequately rewarded for their positive contributions." Comment. If you agree with this statement (partially or in full), give some suggestions for overcoming this problem.

Notes

[1] These three dimensions of the work environment are discussed in Bernard J. Bienvenu, *New Priorities in Training* (New York: American Management Association, 1969), pp. 55–63.

[2] B. W. Marion and S. E. Trieb, "Job Orientation — A Factor in Employee Performance and Turnover," *Personnel Journal,* 48 (October, 1969), pp. 799–804 and 831. In all, 13 independent measures were related to orientation training.

[3] John P. Kotter, "Managing the Joining-Up Process," *Personnel,* 51 (July-August, 1972), pp. 46–52.

[4] Earl R. Gomersall and M. Scott Myers, "Breakthrough in On-the-Job Training," *Harvard Business Review,* 44 (July-August, 1966), pp. 62–72.

[5] Ibid., p. 66.

[6] Ibid.

[7] Ibid., p. 62.

[8] Bienvenu, op. cit., pp. 27 and 55.

[9] Ted L. Kromer, "New Employee Orientation for Managers," *Personnel Journal,* 51 (June, 1972), p. 434.

[10] Thomas LaMotte, "Making Employee Orientation Work," *Personnel Journal,* 53 (January, 1974), pp. 35–37 and 44.

[11] Otis Lipstreu, "A Systems Approach to Orientation," *Personnel Administration,* 49 (March-April, 1969), pp. 41–47.

[12] In absolute terms there were about 27 million women and 51 million men in the labor force in 1965, and 36 million women and 57 million men in 1974. These figures are drawn from U.S. Department of Labor, Bureau of Labor Statistics, *Handbook of Labor Statistics 1975 — Reference Edition* (Washington, D.C.: U.S. Government Printing Office, 1975), pp. 26–27.

[13] Gwyneth Cravens, "How Ma Bell is Training Women for Management," *New York Times Magazine,* (May 29, 1977), p 12.

[14] Much of this section is drawn from Martha G. Burrow, *Women: A Worldwide View of Their Management Development Needs* (New York: AMACOM, 1976), pp. 5–7, and William E. Reif, John W. Newstrom, and Robert M. Monczka, "Exploding Some Myths about Women Managers," *California Management Review,* 17 (Summer, 1975), pp. 72–79.

[15] This study by D. C. Basil, *Women in Management: Promotion and Prejudice* (New York: University of Cambridge Press, 1971), is cited by Marshall H. Brenner, "Management Development for Women," *Personnel Journal,* 51 (March, 1972), pp. 165–169.

[16] Eleanor Brantley Schwartz and James J. Rago. Jr., "Beyond Tokenism: Women as True Corporate Peers," *Business Horizons,* 16 (December, 1973), p. 74.

[17] The material in this section is drawn from ibid., Brenner, op. cit., and J. Stephen Heinen, Dorothy McGlauchlin, Constance Legeros, and Jean Freeman, "Developing the Woman Manager," *Personnel Journal,* 54 (May, 1975), pp. 282–286 and 297.

[18] Schwartz and Rago, op. cit., p. 71.

[19] Burrow, op. cit., p. 15.

[20] See for example, Guvenc G. Alpander and Jean E. Gutmann, "Contents and Techniques of Management Development Programs for Women," *Personnel Journal,* 55 (February, 1976), pp. 76–79 and Heinen, et al., op. cit. p. 283.

[21]Burrow, op. cit., p. 17, and Brenner, op. cit., p. 169, argue for both men and women to be included while Heinen, et al., op. cit., p. 285, argue for women only programs.

[22]Rosabeth Kanter, *Men and Women of the Corporation* (New York: Basic Books, Inc., 1977), pp. 279–280.

[23]Ibid., p. 280.

[24]Ibid.

[25]Paul S. Goodman, Harold Paransky, and Paul Salipante, "Hiring, Training and Retraining the Hard-Core Unemployed," *Journal of Applied Psychology,* 58 (1973), p. 33.

[26]James D. Hodgson and Marshall H. Brenner, "Successful Experience: Training Hard-Core Unemployed," *Harvard Business Review,* 46 (September-October, 1968), p. 148.

[27]J. L. Hausknecht, Jr., "Hard-Core and Minority Group Training Surveyed in Detroit," *Training and Development Journal,* 23 (1969), pp. 50–51.

[28]Hjalmar Rosen and John Turner, "Effectiveness of Two Orientation Approaches in Hard-Core Unemployed Turnover and Absenteeism," *Journal of Applied Psychology,* 55 (1971), p. 297.

[29]The idea of functional literacy has been discussed by Leonard Nadler, "Helping the Hard-Core Adjust to the World of Work," *Harvard Business Review,* 47 (March-April, 1970), pp. 117–126.

[30]For example, in ibid., p. 119, it was pointed out that the American Institute of Banking and the Board of Fundamental Education provided training for the hard-core unemployed for New York City banks and that Kodak had a similar program arrangement with the Board of Fundamental Education with English provided by the Adult Basic Education branch of the Rochester school system.

[31]Rosen and Tuner, op. cit., p. 300.

[32]Hodgson and Brenner, op. cit., pp. 148–155.

[33]Ibid., pp. 154–155.

[34]Rosen and Turner, op. cit., pp. 296–301.

[35]Goodman, Paransky, and Salipante, op. cit., p. 31.

[36]William C. Byham, "The Assessment Center as an Aid in Management Development," *Training and Development Journal,* 25 (December, 1971), pp. 10–22.

[37]Ibid., p. 22.

[38]Richard Steiner, "New Use for Assessment Centers—Training Evaluation," *Personnel Journal,* 54(April, 1975), pp. 236–237.

[39]An excellent review of research studies and other reviews of the literature dealing with assessment centers has been provided by Steven D. Norton, "The Empirical and Content Validity of Assessment Centers vs. Traditional Methods for predicting Managerial Success," *Academy of Management Review,* 2 (July, 1977), pp. 442–453. In addition, excellent summary information has been included in Byham, op. cit. Further, an exceptional bibliography of articles dealing with the assessment center has been provided by Steven D. Norton, "Bibliography of Published and Unpublished References on Predictors and Criteria of Managerial Success," *JSAS Catalog of Selected Documents in Psychology,* 6 (May, 1976), pp. 1–25.

[40]Allen I. Kraut, "New Frontiers for Assessment Centers," *Personnel,* 53 (July-August, 1976), p. 33. The italics are ours.

[41]Norton, "The Empirical . . . ," op. cit. p. 447. We should note, however, that other researchers have questioned the validity of assessment centers. See, for example, Richard J. Klimoski and William J. Strickland, "Assessment Centers—Valid or Merely Prescient," *Personnel Psychology,* 30 (Autumn, 1977), pp. 353–361.

[42]Ann Howard, "An Assessment of Assessment Centers," *Academy of Management Journal,* 17 (March, 1974), pp. 115–134.

[43]Douglas W. Bray and Joseph L. Moses, "Personnel Selection," in P. H. Mussen and M. R. Rosenzweig, eds., *Annual Review of Psychology,* 23 (1972), pp. 545–576.

[44]Kraut, op. cit., p. 34.

[45]Ibid., p. 30.

[46]Byham, op. cit., p. 12.

[47]Steiner, op. cit., p. 237.

[48]Byham, op. cit., p. 13.

[49]Steiner, op. cit., suggests using the assessment center in this manner.

[50]Allen I. Kraut, "A Hard Look at Management Assessment Centers and Their Future," *Personnel Journal*, 51 (May, 1972), p. 325.

[51]Howard, op cit., p. 129.

[52]Dennis P. Slevin, "The Assessment Center: Breakthrough in Management Appraisal and Development," *Personnel Journal*, 51 (April, 1972), p. 259.

[53]Kraut, "New Frontiers . . . ," op. cit., p. 35.

[54]Marion E. Haynes, "Streamlining an Assessment Center," *Personnel Journal*, 55 (February, 1976), pp. 80–83.

[55]There are a number of excellent books that deal with the topic of organization development. The two upon which we have drawn most heavily are Richard Beckhard, *Organization Development: Strategies and Models* (Reading, Mass.: Addison-Wesley Publishing Company, 1973), and J. Jennings Partin, ed., *Current Perspectives in Organization Development* (Reading, Mass.: Addison-Wesley Publishing Company, 1973). The reader who is interested in additional sources of material dealing with OD is referred to the bibliography by Kenneth L. Murrell and Peter B. Vaill, *Organization Development: A Bibliography of Sources and Applications* (Washington, D.C.: American Society for Training and Development, Organization Development Division, 1975).

[56]Beckhard, op. cit., p. 9.

[57]John B. Miner, "The OD-Management Development Conflict," *Business Horizons*, 16 (December, 1973), p. 33. "Confrontation" is generally taken to mean individuals being more open, authentic and direct in their relationships with others.

[58]Fred Luthans, *Organizational Behavior*, 2nd ed. (New York: McGraw-Hill Book Company, 1977), p. 534.

[59]Ibid.

[60]Steven Appelbaum, "Management Development and OD — Getting It Together," *Personnel Management*, 7 (August, 1975), pp. 33–35.

[61]In this section we will draw quite heavily from Robert R. Blake, Jane S. Mouton, Louis B. Barnes, and Larry E. Greiner, "Breakthrough in Organization Development," *Harvard Business Review*, 42 (November-December, 1964), pp. 133–155. More detailed information concerning the managerial grid can be obtained from Robert R. Blake and Jane S. Mouton, *The Managerial Grid* (Houston, Tex.: Gulf Publishing Company, 1964); Robert R. Blake and Jane S. Mouton, *Corporate Excellence Through Grid Organization Development* (Houston, Tex.: Gulf Publishing Company, 1968); and, Robert R. Blake and Jane S. Mouton, *Building a Dynamic Corporation Through Grid Organization Development* (Reading, Mass.: Addison-Wesley Publishing Company, 1969).

[62]Blake and Mouton, "Breakthrough in Organization Development," p. 137.

[63]Cited in Luthans, op. cit., p. 541.

[64]Don Hellriegel and John W. Slocum, Jr., *Organizational Behavior: Contingency Views* (St. Paul, Minn.: West Publishing Company, 1976).

[65]See Luthans, op. cit., p. 540.

[66]Robert A. Luke, Jr., "Matching the Individual and the Organization," *Harvard Business Review*, 53 (May-June, 1975), p. 19. See also, Edgar H. Schein and Warren G. Bennis, *Personal and Organizational Change Through Group Methods* (New York: John Wiley and Sons, Inc., 1965).

[67]John R. Kimberly and Warren R. Nielsen, "Organization Development and Change in Organizational Performance," *Administrative Science Quarterly*, 20 (June, 1975), p. 191.

[68]Jack L. Rettig and Matt M. Amano, "A Survey of ASPA Experience With Management by Objectives, Sensitivity Training and Transactional Analysis," *Personnel Journal*, 55 (January, 1976), pp. 26–29.

[69]Henry P. Sims, Jr., "The Business Organization, Environment, and T-Group Training: A New Viewpoint," *Management of Personnel Quarterly*, 14 (Winter, 1970), pp. 21–27.

[70]Ibid., p. 26.

[71]Miner, op. cit., p. 36.

IV

THE REWARDING OF
HUMAN RESOURCES

9

WAGE AND SALARY ADMINISTRATION

    Individuals are given many different types of returns for their work, such as pay, job satisfaction and status. There are several basic types of financial compensation that may be provided to the individual. First, and most basic, is the individual's salary (or wages), which we will discuss in this chapter. In a few cases, individuals have been given some choice as to the form of part of their compensation (see Chapter 10). Additionally, organizations often provide the individual with incentives based directly on some measure of personal performance, or that of the immediate work group of which he is a member. Further, rewards are given in many cases to individuals based on the performance of the organizational system as a whole. We will discuss individual and system rewards in Chapters 10 and 11 respectively. Finally, of growing importance are other types of financial returns provided to individuals as "employee benefits" such as pensions and medical insurance. Although often very costly to the firm, such benefits generally serve less as "rewards for performance" than either wages and salaries or incentives. Rather, they tend to be rewards for organizational membership. We will reserve discussing them until Chapter 12.

    In this chapter, we will first define *wages* and *salary* and indicate some of the more important distinctions between the two. Then we will focus attention on the role of money in the wage and salary administration process, and the basic objectives of wage and salary administration. Next we will discuss each of the three basic types of wage and salary determination decisions required of the organization. Finally, we will cover several other aspects of wage and salary administration such as the issue of pay secrecy and cost-benefit analysis in financial compensation.

WAGES AND SALARIES

Wages refer to compensation given to hourly paid employees, while *salary* refers to compensation paid to those paid on a weekly, biweekly, or monthly basis. While the distinction between wages and salary seems simple, there are a number of important facets of this distinction. Wage earners, for example, frequently have to punch a time clock, whereas salaried workers do not. Further, salaried workers are often given greater freedom in such matters as arriving late to work, making personal telephone calls on company time, and so forth. Salaried workers are also perceived (sometimes correctly) as being less subject to layoff than wage earners. Thus, there is often a greater status associated with being a salaried worker as opposed to a wage earner. On the other hand, hourly-paid employees receive additional compensation in the form of overtime pay, whereas salaried workers usually do not receive such pay. It is interesting to note that within the past decade the basis of pay for blue-collar workers has been changed from wages to salary at such companies as Gillette, Black and Decker, and Polaroid. The purpose of such changes was basically to treat blue-collar workers more maturely, assuming that they too have such needs as status to be met on the job.[1]

MONEY, MOTIVATION, AND SATISFACTION

Money, Pay, and Performance

The basic rationale for financial compensation, either wages or salary, is that money will somehow motivate individuals to achieve some minimum level of performance or to perform better. The function of money, however, is not clearly understood. As two researchers have pointed out: "Although it is generally agreed that money is the major mechanism for rewarding and modifying behavior in industry . . . very little is known about how it works."[2]

Some research, however, has made it possible for us to make generalizations about some of the key contingencies under which money serves as a motivator. For example, in one study of managers, those who were most highly motivated to perform well, expressed two basic attitudes:

1. They indicated that pay was important to them.
2. "They felt that good job performance would lead to higher pay for them."[3]

These two contingencies — importance of pay and pay linked to performance — seem to be basic ingredients of any successful compensation system. It should be stressed, however, that the organization may have only a limited impact on influencing how important pay is to the individual. Thus, to the extent possible, the organization should attempt to find out how important financial rewards are to individuals in the selection process.[4] Additionally, the organization can continually demonstrate to individuals through its actions that higher financial rewards are linked to better performance. Finally, it should be emphasized that other organizational variables influence the performance-pay link. For example, Lawler has indicated that for pay-performance relationships to exist, other needs must also be satisfied by effective job performance.[5] Nash and Carroll have somewhat similarly stressed that for high performance to be encouraged, such obvious but often ignored factors as the individual's simply knowing "what to do and how to do it" must be present, in addition to an individual's placing a high value on money, and his pay being related to performance.[6]

The Importance of Money

Our previous discussion raises the questions of why individuals do place value on money and why money is more important to some people than others. Different general models of motivation provide some insights into these questions. We will now discuss briefly three of these models.

A. H. Maslow developed a widely known conceptual framework which postulated that:

1. All human behavior is geared toward meeting *unsatisfied* needs.
2. There exists a *hierarchy* of five basic kinds of needs. From lower level to higher, these need types are: physiological, safety and security, love and belongingness, recognition and esteem, and self-actualization.
3. The lower level needs are the most "prepotent" and must be met first. Only then, as these become met, will the higher levels of needs begin to emerge.[7]

Money, in our exchange economy, can obviously serve to meet Maslow's lowest level of needs, physiological, e.g., hunger and thirst. Money can also very often meet higher levels of needs, such as esteem and recognition. For example, money can be used to buy a flashy sports car, which would provide us with esteem and recognition that we have reached a successful status level.

Thus, following the Maslow framework, people can have different needs satisfied by money, and to the extent that an unsatisfied need acts as a motivator, people will be motivated by money.

Research done by others such as Vroom and McClelland has attempted to provide motivational models that are more predictive than Maslow's. Vroom has viewed the individual as a decision maker, and his model places emphasis on the individual's making choices to achieve certain desired outcomes. This model emphasizes the importance of the perceived link between the individual's efforts and the probabilities of his achieving his desired outcomes (one of which may be money).[8] Here again, if money is valued highly and the performance-pay link is perceived to be strong, individuals would be predicted to choose to perform well.

One major part of the work of McClelland has been to identify individuals who have high needs to achieve. For persons with such a personality make-up, money performs a very important function. It does not, however, serve as a motivator. Rather, it functions as a feedback mechanism. That is, money is not highly valued as a medium of exchange to acquire goods and services to meet needs such as Maslow's five classes.[9] Instead, it serves as a *means* of letting the achievement-oriented person know something very important to him — how well he is achieving.

Satisfaction

In addition to the relationship between money and motivation, considerable research has been carried out to determine what variables influence the individual's satisfaction with pay. This research has been excellently summarized by others,[10] and we will simply highlight some of its key aspects.

Even if satisfaction with pay had no bearing whatsoever on employee performance, from a "humanitarian" viewpoint a firm would prefer to have satisfied employees, as long as providing such satisfaction created no negative "side effects" in the organization (e.g., too high labor costs). Although perhaps not contributing significantly to poor performance, dissatisfaction with pay may lead to two other undesirable and costly organizational outcomes — high absenteeism and turnover rates.[11]

It appears very important that organizational members *perceive* that financial remuneration has been distributed *equitably* among members of the organization.[12] We have, for example, observed college professors become extremely upset, and in some cases leave an organization, upon finding out that one of their colleagues with fewer publications was making more money than they were.

Finally, with respect to money and satisfaction (and motivation), some individuals believe that money has no intrinsic meaning by itself. Rather, they perceive of money as serving a symbolic function:

> Or, in systems terms, money serves as a perceived input into the individual's open personality system. It will lead to different behavioral and attitudinal outputs, depending both upon how he has learned previously to symbolize the "value" of money, and his current life situation.[13]

This view is congruent with the motivation theories presented earlier. For instance, for the individual with a high need to achieve, money is symbolic of achievement. For the beginning artist, who must "self-actualize" in the Maslow hierarchy by painting, money may symbolize the eventual building of a very well-equipped studio in which to work.

WAGE AND SALARY OBJECTIVES AND DECISIONS

As with many of the other personnel functions discussed, we view wage and salary determination as a multi-stage decision process aimed at meeting organizational objectives. In this area, there are three basic sequential decisions geared toward meeting objectives. These are illustrated graphically in Figure 9–1.

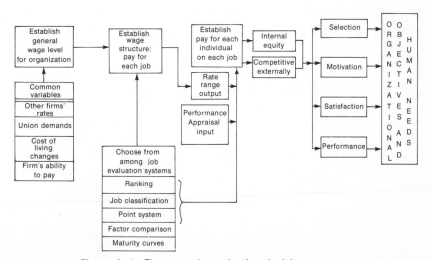

Figure 9–1 *The wage determination decision process.*

As may be noted from this figure, working from the macro- to microlevel, the organization must first establish its overall wage level, then set up a wage structure to determine the pay for each job, and finally decide on how much each individual should be paid on each job. These decisions will hopefully meet two subobjectives — maintaining internal equity and being competitive in its external labor markets. Meeting these goals will help achieve not only the motivation to perform and pay satisfaction objectives discussed previously but also the goals of being able to select competent personnel and to retain employees.[14] These four subobjectives, in turn, are directed toward meeting the firm's ultimate goals of profitability and the provision of need satisfaction to its employees.

Unfortunately, problems may arise in this decision process, in that internal equity may be incongruent with its companion external competition objective. Based on the criterion of equity, if Job A is more difficult than Job B, which is in turn more difficult than Job C, then the first should be remunerated more than the second, and this, in turn, more than the third. However, the firm must also be competitive with its external markets if it is to be able to hire and keep employees, and the value placed on jobs in an external market may be different from that arrived at in building an internally consistent and equitable wage structure. For example, a firm's internally equitable wage rates, as compared with those being paid by competition in a particular labor market may be seen in Figure 9–2, which illustrates an incongruency. The firm may have serious difficulties in hiring and retaining personnel in Job B, assuming that only the "internally-equitable" $3.75/hour rate is paid and individuals are aware of the external rates. In such cases, employees may have to be paid at the competitive rate, regardless of the fact that it is not congruent with internal equity. Such rates are sometimes referred to as "out-of-line" rates.

The degree of knowledge about other firms' rates may vary considerably from job to job. There may, for example, be several supermarkets in a small city, with *comparable jobs* for which wage information is readily available. In the same city, however,

Job	Internally Equitable Rates/Hour	Going External Labor Market Rates/Hour
A	$3.50	$3.45
B	$3.75	$4.10
C	$4.00	$4.00

Figure 9–2 Conflict between internal equity and labor market competition.

there may be only one hospital in which lab technicians are employed. The only external comparisons for personnel in such positions may be in other cities some distance away, where the cost of living may be different, thus rendering salary comparisons much more difficult to make.

It should be emphasized that simply because an incongruency between internal and external rates exists does not necessarily mean that something is wrong with the internal structure. Assuming that jobs should be paid according to their relative contribution to an organization, it is quite possible that very similar jobs in different organizations may contribute differently to profitability and therefore should be paid differently. Further, job descriptions across organizations are not uniform and what constitutes the duties actually called for in a job in one organization may be different from those called for in a job described basically the same way in another.

ESTABLISHING WAGE AND SALARY LEVELS

The first of the three key managerial decisions illustrated in Figure 9–1 is establishment of the firm's overall wage and salary levels relative to other firms. If a firm's overall wage and salary level is too low, it will not serve to meet the basic objectives illustrated in Figure 9–1. If it is too high, on the other hand, the firm's finances will be strained. We will first look at some of the key variables influencing overall wage levels and then focus attention on how information inputs may be obtained and utilized in determining the overall wage and salary structure.

Variables Affecting Wage Levels[15]

There are a number of key variables that affect a firm's overall wage level. Probably the most significant one is the amount paid by competitors for labor in each of the firm's labor markets. Although identifying labor markets sounds easy, in reality it may be difficult to determine precisely what the organization's labor markets are. In addition, a labor market will typically vary, depending upon organizational level. For example, more local markets generally exist for blue-collar workers as opposed to managers and professionals. With respect to local labor markets, the time required in getting to work seems to be an important labor market determining factor. Dunn and Rachel, for example, have referred to one study in which it was found that 80 per cent of employees in several organizations lived within 30 minutes commuting distance from their work place.[16]

Firms may face relatively little competition for prospective employees from other organizations under a variety of conditions. For example, if a firm is the only one of any size operating in a geographically isolated "company town" it may face virtually no competition for labor, especially with respect to blue-collar and clerical jobs. In times of depression, with large supplies of human resources available in comparison to demand, wage levels may be set lower than in prosperous times, when there are labor shortages and more competition for qualified employees. Further, some firms make conscious efforts to establish for themselves an image "as a good place to work" by providing security through few layoffs, excellent pensions, and other employee benefit plans. Firms having established such images may not have to be as competitive as others in their overall wage and salary levels.

Firm size, as might be expected, is another variable that may affect overall wage levels. Larger firms are generally in a position to pay a higher overall level of wages and salaries. This is not always true, however, because an extremely important variable affecting wage and salary decisions is the firm's ability to pay. We know of one firm with annual sales of about $100 million in which financial problems became so great that it could not afford to grant any salary increases to its employees, with a salary "moratorium" put into effect for six months.

The existence of a union in a firm may also have an important impact on its overall wage and salary levels. In firms having strong unions, "production workers have wage levels from 10 percent to 15 percent higher than other production workers" and this is especially true for large oligopolistic producers who can pass the higher wages on to consumers in the form of higher prices.[17] In fact, a union may force a financially weak company, whether large or small to grant wage increases. For example, one author of this text recalls sitting in on contract negotiations in the rubber industry about two decades ago. The International Rubber Workers Union had gained wage increases from the large tire producers in Akron prior to the fall of that year and then demanded the same increases for those at a smaller firm in the industry. This firm (after a strike) finally capitulated to these demands in spite of a very weak financial position, which not long thereafter forced it to sell its tire business to one of its large competitors. Finally, it should be noted that some unions have obtained "escalator clauses" for their labor contracts so that wages will be geared to the Consumer Price Index.[18]

Obtaining Wage and Salary Inputs

Most firms in the United States rely on input data from wage and salary surveys to determine wage levels. Such surveys represent a "statistical picture of what the wages for a particular geographical area, occupation, industry, or city were at a given time or are at the present time."[19] Firms may engage in wage surveys by:

1. Undertaking their own survey conducted within a local geographic area or among other firms in the industry.

2. Participating in an industry survey conducted by large corporations in the industry.

3. Obtaining data from surveys carried out by such professional organizations as the American Management Association.

4. Obtaining data from published government surveys, such as those conducted periodically by the U.S. Bureau of Labor Statistics.[20]

Such wage and salary surveys have a number of advantages. They may provide management with a good idea of how it stands in relation to prevailing wages in its labor markets. Such data can also be of use in collective bargaining with unions and can be informative to the public concerning what wages and salaries prevail in different industries and geographical areas. In general, firms are willing to reciprocate with one another in providing wage survey data.

Notwithstanding their values, a number of problems must be resolved in utilizing wage and salary surveys. For a firm to be able to utilize survey data, it must often identify only certain of its jobs to be compared with similar ones elsewhere. Here size represents a contingency, for it would be too costly for large organizations with hundreds of different jobs to compare the pay rates for all of them with those included in an industry survey. Picking a sample of only key or "benchmark" jobs, however, requires interpolation of sample data to the other jobs, which can bring about distorted views of the jobs not included.[21] Also, firms must have previously engaged in job analysis, and job descriptions must have been developed to be able to make meaningful comparisons with jobs elsewhere. A real problem also exists in that jobs with the same titles in different organizations are often really different jobs. This makes *comparability* of wage and salary data among firms very difficult. Also, the question must be raised in surveys as to whether the "prevailing" rate for any job just includes basic compensation or whether it includes any supplementary pay benefits.

Additional problems arise when a firm conducts its own survey. After it has defined its labor markets, it must determine the sample of firms it will survey. In choosing its sample, the firm must make sure it is a representative one, or else the data analyzed will be distorted. Further, firms making their own surveys must decide upon the method to be used in the survey. The firm can gather information through a mailed questionnaire or by telephone. The mailed questionnaire approach typically suffers from a low rate of response returns and the associated problem of whether the respondents are similar to the nonrespondents. Typically, however, more information can be obtained by questionnaires than by telephone surveys. Finally, from a contingency view, the cost of developing their own surveys may be too high for small firms, and they may have to resort to one or more of the other wage survey techniques indicated.

In light of the problems involved in all of the types of surveys, it is not surprising that wage and salary authorities have disagreed on the usefulness of surveys. With respect to governmental surveys, for example, Nash and Carroll have expressed the opinion that such data are not generally adequate in "amount, relevance, and timeliness,"[22] while Zollitsch and Langsner have referred favorably to the Bureau of Labor Statistics Occupational Wage Survey of specific metropolitan areas.[23] More generally, there seems to be an increasing disenchantment on the part of some compensation directors about wage surveys, and in a number of cases they may rely more on information provided through informal personal contacts with other compensation directors. Finally, it should be noted that very little is really known about exactly how wage and salary information is used to make managerial decisions.[24] However, as a tentative proposition it has been hypothesized that in nonunion firms with average profits, the going wage obtained from a survey will be the most important decision-making criterion used in determining internal wage rates.[25]

ESTABLISHING THE FIRM'S WAGE STRUCTURE

Once an organization has determined its general wage level, it must determine its wage structure — how different jobs calling for different skills should be rated (and paid) in comparison with each other. While a firm could base its internal structure completely on a wage survey or some other external criterion, such a practice is likely to be inadequate. This is because the relative worth of jobs among firms varies and, since surveys usually only include a sample of all jobs, those jobs not included in the survey would be priced without benefit of knowledge of actual labor market conditions. For such reasons, most firms establish their internal wage and salary structure by engaging in job evaluation, which is a process involving:

. . . an orderly, systematic method and procedure of ranking, grading, and weighting of jobs to determine the value of a specific job in relation to other jobs.[26]

In this section we will make some observations about job evaluation in general, discuss five different methods of job evaluation, and illustrate how the job structure developed may be translated into wages for specific jobs.

In conducting job evaluations, separate evaluations will usually be carried out for managerial, clerical, and blue-collar employees, because their work is difficult to compare. Similar jobs may also often be grouped into job families. For example, several similar secretarial jobs may be grouped together into one category. This grouping renders job evaluation simpler to carry out. Further, many authorities believe that the employees themselves should participate in the description and analysis of their jobs.[27] This view assumes that those who participate in helping to develop the system are more likely to accept it. Sometimes extensive person-to-person interviews about jobs may be carried out, but this is costly and time consuming. In unionized firms, the union may also want to participate. Unions, however, have varied considerably in their attitudes about job evaluation. This is because job evaluation is a difficult process, creating problems unions wish to avoid, and unions have historically believed that job evaluation "tends to limit bargaining and to freeze the wage structure."[28]

Paralleling our comments in Chapter 5 with respect to performance appraisal, the effectiveness of any wage and salary job evaluation method is a function both of the method and the *way* the method is carried out. In an empirical study of job evaluation systems in 1948, for example, it was found that "the particular type of system used in an organization is not nearly so important as the integrity and accuracy with which it is installed, policed, and maintained."[29]

In light of the objectives indicated in Figure 9–1, there should be a real need before a firm revises its wage and salary system. If employees seem basically satisfied with current wage and salary practices, establishing a new system may do nothing but open up a "Pandora's Box" of complaints. This results because, with a new system, some jobs may be rated lower as compared to other jobs than they had been previously and the holders of these jobs will often perceive the new system as effecting a reduction in their status as far as pay is concerned. If there are serious inequities in the firm's current wage structure, on the other hand, installation of a new system may be mandatory. Periodic review of job evaluations to detect and correct for "creeping changes" in job content will help prevent creeping inequities from occurring.

The Ranking Method

The ranking method is the oldest and simplest job evaluation scheme in existence. It provides for ranking jobs as a whole, without breaking them down into subfactors.[30] The ranking may be simple, alternation, or paired comparisons as in performance appraisal. From a contingency view, ranking is usually carried out in small firms. With large numbers of jobs, ranking is difficult, since no one person would have enough information about them all and the comparisons would become very cumbersome. Simple to understand and easy to install and modify, ranking can be easily used in small firms in which dynamic job situations exist.

On the negative side, the method is crude and highly subjective. Admission of this crudeness, however, avoids the danger of considering numbers as "highly scientific," as may be done with more sophisticated job evaluation programs. As most commonly used, ranking does not measure the *distances* between jobs. For example, it might rate three jobs as A > B > C but not account for the fact that Job A is considerably more difficult than Job B, while the latter is only slightly more difficult than Job C.

The Job Classification Method

The job classification method is a second well-known approach to job evaluation. It calls for development of a series of job grades or classifications. In the Federal Civil Service System, where it is used most widely, for example, grades have been set up from GS-1 (highly routine work) to GS-18, top executive positions. An initial step in this method is to predefine the grades that management intends should form the basic structure of the system. Sometimes grade descriptions are very briefly stated such as: "Performs routine typing and clerical duties under the close supervision of the person's superior." In other cases, however, the grades may be more fully spelled out. For example, one author, in illustrating the description of chemist positions, first looked at four factors: general characteristics of the job, direction required, typical duties and responsibilities, and responsibility for the direction of others. He then developed a brief description of each for eight classes of chemists. The lowest classification (Chemist I) called for a B.S. degree in chemistry, no experience, working under close supervision, performing a variety of routine tasks, and usually having no responsibility for directing others.[31] The highest (Chemist VIII) on the other hand, was described as involving: (1) making decisions having a "far-reaching impact on extensive chemical and related activities of the company"; (2)

receiving only general administrative direction; (3) having considerable supervisory responsibilities and/or being an individual researcher and consultant; and (4) supervising several "subordinate supervisors or team leaders."[32] Once such grades have been established, it is necessary to slot each job in the organization into a grade classification by comparing the job description as developed through job analysis to the classification descriptions.

The job classification approach is more complex than simple ranking, and judgment is required both in defining each grade and in placing each position into an appropriate grade. A description of a particular job may be written, for example, in such a way that the job may appear to fit logically into more than one classification. Like ranking, job classification is also nonquantitative and global — jobs are not broken down into various factors.[33] It is also sometimes considered necessary to have a separate classification system for managerial and professional, office, and factory employees because the nature of their jobs is so different.

The Point System

The point system, unlike ranking and grade classification, does focus attention on specific job factors. It dates back to the 1920's and is generally held to be the most popular of all job evaluation systems.

There are several steps involved in developing the point method. First, certain job variables (or factors) to be compared must be defined. Common among these are skill, responsibility, effort, and working conditions. These are the four factors in the National Metal Trades Association (NMTA) system, which is used by a number of firms.

Second, a range of points that any job can possibly have on each factor must be determined. For example, if a firm decided to use just three factors — responsibility, skill required, and education — it might set up its point ranges as follows:

1. Responsibility: 100–400 points
2. Skill: 150–200 points
3. Education: 50–200 points

Third, each factor must be broken down into a number of degrees on which jobs will be compared. For example, the education factor might be broken down into the four following degrees:

1. 50 points — grade school education required
2. 100 points — two years college or equivalent required
3. 150 points — college degree required
4. 200 points — graduate degree required

With some factors, such as education, it may be relatively easy to specify *mutually exclusive* degrees. With others, defining each degree might be quite difficult, for example, in degrees of responsibility.

Taking the numerical example presented here and defining degrees for responsibility and skill as well as education, a basic yardstick or measuring instrument could be developed, as shown in Figure 9–3.

Once this yardstick has been developed, each job can be ranked on each factor, and a total number of points for the job determined. In carrying out this step, careful attention must be given to job descriptions.

The point system has certain advantages. Unlike ranking and job classification, the method provides a breakdown into specific factors. It is also considered to be easily understood by employees, provided its basic features are communicated to them clearly.

There are, however, some limitations to the point method. A basic problem is that developing the weights of the factors and degrees involves considerable subjective judgment (which is true of all job evaluation methods). How, for example, might one justify the heavier weighting given to responsibility relative to education as shown in Figure 9–3? Further, in more ambiguously defined, organic job situations (such as engineering and research), where it is difficult to break down jobs into factors and degrees, using the point method may pose serious problems.

The Factor Comparison Method

Like the point system, the factor comparison system is based on the assumption that jobs can be broken down into such factors as skill, responsibility, and education. Unlike the point system, however, no factor and degree basic yardstick is set up. Rather, jobs are compared directly with each other on different factors.

The factor comparison method has several steps. First, a number of representative or key jobs (15 or 20) are selected for

| Factor | Degree | | | |
	1st	2nd	3rd	4th
Responsibility	100	200	300	400
Skill	150	200	250	300
Education	50	100	150	200

Figure 9–3 Hypothetical point system yardstick.

comparison. These should be widely known jobs for which current rates should be satisfactory in terms of both internal equity and external labor market conditions. Second, the jobs selected should be ranked on each factor. As a simple example, a situation in which we have only three jobs and three factors that are ranked is illustrated in Figure 9–4.

Third, we must determine what portion of the *current* wage rate for each factor for each key job chosen is worth and to rank these apportionments. To illustrate, let us use the three jobs in Figure 9–4. An apportionment of the current wages to each factor might be determined as shown in Figure 9–5.

Fourth, it is necessary to compare the factor rankings (shown in Figure 9–4) with the wage apportionment rankings shown in Figure 9–5. For purposes of simplification, we have made these two sets of rankings congruent with each other. If this occurs, there are no problems with respect to the rankings. If, however, the skill factor in Figure 9–5 had ranked second ($1.20) for Job A and first ($1.40) for Job B, these rankings would be incongruent with the factor rankings shown in Figure 9–4. In such a case, either the factor or wage rankings will have to be modified to render them congruent, which would likely be done based on subjective judgment. If this cannot be done, the jobs in which incongruencies still exist should be eliminated from consideration.

Once the two congruent rankings have been developed for each key job, a factor comparison scale, as illustrated in Figure 9–6, is developed. Then, all other jobs are fitted into the scale, factor by factor, to provide a total wage for them. For example, Job D in Figure 9–6 has been determined to be:

1. About halfway between Jobs A and B on skill and would be assigned $1.30 on this factor.
2. Ten cents higher than Job A on mental effort ($1.10).
3. Four tenths of the way between Job C and Job A ($1.14) on responsibility.

Summing these three factor values would permit us to establish the wage for Job D at $3.54/hour. All other jobs would be similarly treated by fitting them into the factor comparison scale.

	Factors		
Job	*Skill*	*Mental Effort*	*Responsibility*
A	1	1	2
B	2	3	1
C	3	2	3

Figure 9–4 Factor comparison factor rankings. A ranking of 1 is highest.

Job	Total Current Hourly Wage	Skill	Mental Effort	Responsibility
A	$3.60	$1.40 (1)	$1.00 (1)	$1.20 (2)
B	3.40	1.20 (2)	.80 (3)	1.40 (1)
C	3.00	1.00 (3)	.90 (2)	1.10 (3)

Figure 9–5 *Wage rate apportionment. The numbers in parentheses represent the ranking given the factor, with a ranking of 1 representing the highest.*

The factor comparison method has certain important advantages. It can provide a tailor-made plan for a firm and permits job factors to be specifically compared with one another. It also permits appropriate weights to be assigned to jobs where one or more factors exist to a very high degree. There is no upper limit as to how many dollars may be assigned a factor, as is the case with point systems. For example, in Figure 9–3, the maximum number of possible points was 900. Finally, factor comparison provides a dollar basis for all jobs directly; this step does not have to be taken additionally, as in the three previous methods discussed.

The factor comparison method, however, is not without its limitations. It might be very difficult to break down by factor jobs that are highly unstructured and fluid such as research scientist

	Skill	Mental Effort	Responsibility
$1.60			
1.50			
1.40	← Job A		← Job B
1.30	←————— Job D		
1.20	← Job B		← Job A
		($1.14)	←————— Job D
1.10		←————— Job D	← Job C
1.00	← Job C	← Job A	
.90		← Job C	
.80		← Job B	
.70			
.60			

Figure 9–6 *Factor comparison scale*

positions. Further, its application is limited to larger firms, both on a cost basis and on the fact that an inadequate sample of key jobs would exist in many small organizations. Further, the system is complicated, and it may be difficult to communicate to employees just how it works. Because of the complexity and time required to develop a good factor comparison method, from a contingency point of view it is more appropriate in large organizations in cases in which job content is stable.

Maturity Curves

In some scientific and engineering positions, the work is of such an organic nature that the use of traditional wage and salary approaches may pose problems. As one author has pointed out:

> Formal position analysis, preparation of position descriptions, and position evaluation were techniques which did not readily lend themselves to application in highly technical areas, particularly where jobs had ill-defined limits and the technology was very new or rapidly changing.[34]

Such was the case in many research laboratories following World War II, especially in southern California. To cope with this lack of structure, "maturity" or "career" curves were developed as either an alternative or a supplemental approach to traditional wage and salary systems.[35]

The curve approach is based on the assumption that salary growth should be related to the number of years a person has worked in a profession since receiving a college degree. By means of salary surveys, firms obtain data for various types of scientific positions. These data are used to form wage curves based upon salaries paid by years of experience coupled with performance. A family of such curves is illustrated in Figure 9–7.

Such curve data can serve several functions. It helps to plan the firm's overall wage level (as with wage surveys). It may help a firm compare its own internal wage structure with the surveys obtained outside the firm. This provides the firm with a control to make sure its salaries are not too high. Finally, it may guide salary determinations for specific individuals. To meet this objective, for example, a scientist with four years of experience in the 90th percentile performance-wise might be given a salary of $2000/month, as shown in Figure 9–7.

Typically, the curve approach has been utilized more to develop overall salary increase budgets than to determine specific raises for individuals. When the latter is done, however, effective performance appraisal is critical. This is because nowhere in the curve approach itself are direct references made to job descrip-

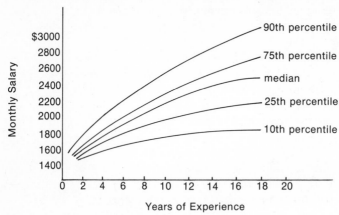

Figure 9-7 *Hypothetical set of maturity curves.*

tions or positions — its basic assumption is simply that people, as resources, become more valuable with more experience. When performance appraisal is undertaken, management will find it necessary to look at how well individuals assume responsibilities on work projects and other endeavors they have been assigned. It should also be noted that from one year to the next, a particular individual, although being evaluated on the basis of one more year's performance, may be moved up or down into a different percentile curve, depending on his performance. Thus, the curve approach, unlike the four traditional job evaluation methods discussed earlier, may involve the making of both the first and third basic wage and salary decisions indicated in Figure 9-1: determination of an overall wage rate and salary increases for specific individuals.

The advantages of the curve approach are at least twofold. As indicated, it may be very difficult to define duties and responsibilities, as required with the point or factor comparison systems. Further, a creative atmosphere for scientific research may be maintained better if position and organizational constraints associated with traditional systems are removed.

The curve approach has not been without criticism. From a technical point of view, obtaining appropriate statistical curve data can be both difficult and expensive. It is also difficult to determine the best "starting point" measure for maturity curves. Should a curve start at the receipt of the B.S. degree? If so, what about previous experience? What about advanced degrees? Questions such as these must be raised when the curve approach is utilized. Finally, the technique has been criticized as having often "moved almost totally in the direction of having the man and not the job as the basis of payment, since maturity curves explicitly consider only personal factors."[36]

Choice of a System

A firm must decide which wage and salary systems to adopt. From a contingency approach, several comments may be made concerning this decision. Factor comparison, for example, might be appropriate in large firms having many blue-collar jobs, which are highly programmed and precisely defined. However, in small firms a sample size large enough to utilize this system might not be available. For fluid, dynamic professional situations the maturity curve approach may be useful for reasons given earlier. Further, one observer has indicated that the more certain the task and technology, the more precisely defined jobs should be if workers are to gain a sense of competence from successful performance.[37] Regardless of technology it has been postulated that: "Professional and managerial jobs change quite rapidly in a dynamic economy and do not provide a stable base for factor comparison evaluation."[38]

Finally, with respect to contingencies, we find size of firm, degree of change facing the organization, and level in the organization (managerial and professional as opposed to nonmanagerial), important with respect to wage and salary administration as was also found with other personnel systems. Further, regardless of the numerical complexity of any wage and salary system, one must not become "hypnotized" by the numbers. Factor comparison wage rates and job points, for example, are no better outputs than the subjective judgmental inputs of those who designed the system.

Establishing Pay for Each Job

The ranking, job classification, and point methods do not "automatically" provide a pay rate for each job in the firm as does factor comparison. For this reason, the firm must "price" its wage structure when using such systems. For example, with the point system, total points for each job must be obtained and pay then be related to wage levels by developing a trend line, as shown in Figure 9–8. The small triangles in this figure represent current salaries before the introduction (or revision) of the system. It should be noted that each job having a different number of points would usually not be paid a different rate. Rather, for purposes of administrative simplification, jobs would be grouped into wage classes or labor grades. For example, every position shown in Figure 9–8 with total points ranging from 450 to 550 might be placed in the same classification with the same rate. Those jobs currently being paid above their newly established

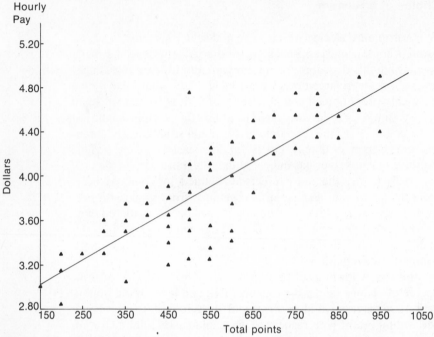

Figure 9-8 *Hypothetical trend line.*

class maximum would be considered overpaid. For example, the job with 500 points and a current wage rate of $4.75 shown on Figure 9–8 would represent such a job. However, to gain acceptance of any wage and salary system, one does not cut the pay on any such jobs. What is often done is to "red-circle" the jobs currently being paid more than the maximum for their new wage grades. This means that the individual holding such a job would be paid the same as he has been as long as he keeps the job. As attrition eliminates people from "red circled" jobs and as the overall wage level moves up, as wages and salaries generally have over the past few decades, there will be fewer red-circled positions.[39]

Rate Ranges

Generally each job is *not* assigned a single rate. Rather, rate ranges are set for each job so that individuals can progress to higher levels of pay on their jobs. Deciding how wide each rate range should be is an important managerial decision. Besides serving as a means of providing compensation increases without promotion, ranges can serve as a control mechanism to keep wages in line. There is no generally accepted criterion as to how

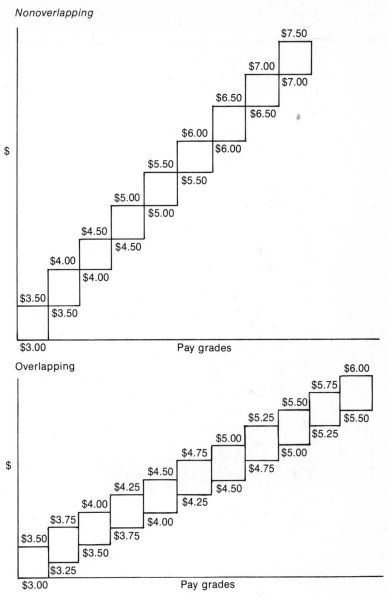

Figure 9–9. *Hourly rate ranges.*

wide ranges should be. Zollitsch and Langsner have indicated that most firms provide a spread of about 30 to 40 per cent.[40] Nash and Carroll, who have delved into the range width problem somewhat more deeply, have indicated that ranges that are too narrow may render compensation increases too small, while ranges that are too wide may represent an unnecessary amount of expenditures.[41] They have further noted that certain contingencies can guide the decision maker in the range-width choices, two of which are especially relevant to our conceptual framework. In stable, nonexpanding firms with low turnover, fewer promotional opportunities will be available and wider ranges are more appropriate, so that workers do not reach the top of their range too soon and have nowhere to go. Such individuals may become frustrated and leave the organization. As with many personnel areas, different decisions are recommended for managerial and professional employees than for blue-collar workers. Specifically, it is recommended that wider ranges be established for managerial and professional personnel, since it takes them longer to become highly competent in their positions.[42]

A second rate range decision is how much, if any, overlap should exist among ranges? Most firms do utilize overlapping ranges for two reasons. First, it permits a greater pay spread, allowing greater flexibility in "fitting rate to jobs, granting pay raises, and in transferring and promoting employees from one pay grade to another."[43] Second, it is less costly. Figure 9–9 shows an example of both overlapping and nonoverlapping systems and highlights the possible costliness of the latter. Generally, overlap may prove satisfactory as long as one range does not extend beyond the highest range.

It may be argued that having one employee in a lower-level job making more money than one in a higher paying one will create inequities. However:

1. This often does not occur because the lower job-level individuals are recognized as having certain compensating factors such as more seniority, experience, or skill.[44]

2. It is considered to create more inequities if there are inappropriate "performance-longevity differentials" within grades than between grades. This is because the most important reference group for the individual in his equity comparisons are his peers, rather than those individuals performing lower level jobs.[45]

ESTABLISHING THE INDIVIDUAL'S PAY ON EACH JOB

A basic question that must be decided by a firm is the extent to which performance appraisal data is to be used in giving "merit" increases within the rate range established for an individual's job. In using such data, management may want to consider past, present, and future performance to varying degrees. Past performance may be considered as a payment for continuing membership in the organization. Future performance, on the other hand, might be considered when "an employee who is ready to be promoted to a job for which there is no opening will receive a raise designed to prevent him from leaving before an opening occurs."[46]

In many situations, organizations have not tied wages or salary to performance appraisal. For example, one study of the Fortune 500 list of firms showed that "a majority of them do not, in fact, relate wage and salary advancement to job performance" for nonsupervisory employees.[47] More recently, at the top executive level, a lack of correlation was found between pay and financial performance in companies with one dominant business, while in firms comprised of a number of "businesses" (e.g., ITT), changes in top level compensation were linked more closely to financial measures, such as profits and earnings per share.[48]

In many organizations that do not relate "merit" increases to performance, periodic wage and salary increases are based on *automatic progression*. Under this system there are a number of salary steps for each job, and individuals' compensation moves ahead, step-by-step, at predefined times and levels as long as their performance is not unsatisfactory. For example, four consecutive steps in an executive job might be $32,300, $33,500, $34,800, and $36,200. This means, for instance, that a manager making $32,300 would automatically have his annual salary increased to $33,500 after the predetermined time for him to move up one step, and so on, assuming his performance was not unsatisfactory.

It is possible to develop a combined plan — starting an employee on an automatic raise basis up to the range midpoint, and then giving raises based on merit.[49] In the inflationary economy that has generally characterized the United States since World War II, organizations have often given "cost-of-living" wage and salary raises in addition to merit ones. One white-collar worker, for example, obtained one "generous" merit raise plus *two* cost-of-living increases in a large nationally known manufacturing firm during the inflationary year of 1974. Finally, some firms give one annual or semiannual raise that includes both cost-of-living and merit components. The whole question of what part of *any* raise is for "merit" and what part for "cost-of-living" is a very difficult one, as is the whole question of how much should be given an individual as a raise.[50]

WAGE AND SALARY ADMINISTRATION: OTHER ASPECTS

Government Legislation

Several pieces of government legislation have had an impact on wage and salary administration. Probably the most important of these is the Fair Labor Standards Act of 1938. This Act set minimum wages, maximum hours, and overtime pay. Minimum wages under the law have increased, and as of January 1978 were $2.65/hour. Workers covered under the Act must also be paid time and one half for all hours worked over 40 in any given week. Certain classes of personnel, such as managers, professional personnel, and salesmen are exempt from minimum wage and overtime provisions of the Act — leading to the use of the terms "exempt" and "nonexempt" in discussing wage and salary administration.

Of critical importance also was the civil rights legislation discussed in earlier chapters. Among this legislation was the Equal Pay Act of 1963, which explicitly forbids wage discrimination based on sex. Numerous court cases based on the Act have required employers to pay women considerable back pay due to prior discrimination. In one of the more important cases the Wheaton Glass Company of Millville, New Jersey, was required to pay over $900,000 in back pay to female inspector-packers. The United States Circuit Court of Appeals ruled that jobs need not be identical, but just "substantially equal" for the Equal Pay Act to apply. The Supreme Court refused to hear an appeal on this case so that the Circuit Court's ruling held. With the Act broadened in the summer of 1972 to cover an estimated 15 million executive, administrative, professional, and outside sales personnel, it seems likely that the push for equal pay regardless of sex will continue to grow in the future.[51]

Title VII of the Civil Rights Act of 1964 is also applicable to wage and salary administration. It is important to examine all job descriptions and classifications to "ensure that prescribed qualifications and pay scales can be justified on business grounds and that inadvertent barriers have not been erected against women and minorities."[52] Otherwise, employees may successfully win actions against the organization on the basis of discrimination under the Civil Rights Act.

Computers, Automation, and Management Science

Computers

Among personnel functions, computers probably have been used to the greatest extent and for the longest period of time in wage and salary administration. For example, among 14 personnel areas, the most respondents (78 per cent) indicated that they were using electronic data processing for wage and salary administration purposes in a 1966 study.[53] One of the prime functions which the computer has served has been in handling payroll data.

Further, various types of wage and salary analysis and controls have also been handled on computers such as the average salary for certain job classes, as indicated in Chapter 2.

Automation

The introduction of automation has had a distinct impact on wage and salary administration. It has been pointed out that conventional job evaluation methods are of limited usefulness in automated operations for at least two reasons. First, there is a considerable degree of *interdependence* among many automated jobs. This would render it

. . . insufficient to analyze only the content of an individual job "since no movement or action on the part of any one individual is meaningful except in relation to the movements of others in the same integrated system."[54]

Second, there is rarely a regular cycle of repetitive operations, and individual actions differ on differing occasions, thus making job evaluation difficult. As we will point out in the next chapter, however, special types of incentives geared directly to automated and highly mechanized operations have been developed.

Management Science

Each of the three types of management science techniques discussed in Chapter 1 has been used in wage and salary administration. The first of these is simulation. As indicated at the beginning of this chapter, individuals are compensated in many ways — they may receive individual, group, and system incentives and numerous types of employee benefits as part of their total compensation package. In most cases, however, no one

. . . really knows whether one compensation package is better than another. Direct salary figures become the ultimate criterion; the true value of stock options, profit-sharing and various deferred forms of compensation are lost in the evaluation process.[55]

To help overcome this problem, a computer simulation model called "Compsim" was developed.[56] This simulation was designed to shed light on the value of various compensation packages to any desired individuals in an organization and the associated cost of each package to the company. The simulation does this by running various compensation packages through the computer along with data on both the individual and the company. Among these input data are the individual's current and starting salary, years of service, retirement age, and tax bracket and the company's corporate tax rate, the current value of its stock, predicted future

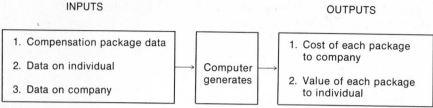

Figure 9-10 Compsim model.

stock price, and its cost of obtaining money. This model is sound with respect to basic financial theory with which the reader may be familiar — it appropriately both considers the effect of taxes and discounts the value of future benefit dollars back from the time of their payment to the present. A graphic representation of the Compsim model is found in Figure 9–10.

The network technique, PERT, has also been used in wage and salary programs to speed up getting a point system into effect.[57] The company involved had tried for almost four years to get this wage and salary system going. Then it revised its procedures of interviewing all employees, which seemed to arouse suspicions, by an approach calling for employees to fill out questionnaires outlining their jobs' characteristics. The firms also used PERT to speed up installation of the program. Parts of this PERT chart for one division of the company are shown in Figure 9–11, along with some of the events associated with this chart. With PERT supplementing its modified questionnaire efforts, the system was installed in 34 days. One of the major reasons given for PERT's usefulness in this installation was that it gave all managers a visible graphic picture of their commitment and placed the responsibility for the program's success on the shoulders of line managers, rather than staff assuming all responsibilities.

Finally, the simplex technique of linear programming has been utilized to obtain numerical values for factor-degree weights with point systems. One linear program developed by Rehmus and Wagner had as a basic goal the selection of a "factor weighting system that minimizes the discrepancy between the [current] salaries for given jobs and the factor ratings of these jobs."[58] The program included numerous constraints logical to the point system such as that no one factor could contribute more than a specified percentage of the sum of all factor weights.

Going through the mathematics of this model is beyond the scope of this book. A very simple hypothetical example following a method similar to that used by Rehmus and Wagner, however, will illustrate the basic notions underlying this linear programming approach. In our example, let us assume that there are only two

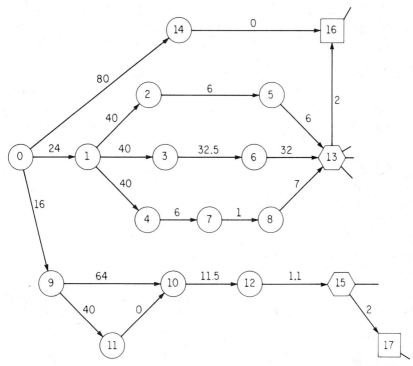

Figure 9-11 PERT chart and description of some events in PERT network.

0. All employees whose jobs are to be evaluated are identified and classified by division, department, job family, and job-summary questionnaire or job-description availability; all departments are informed of the impending salary-evaluation program.

1. Job-summary questionnaires are distributed to all employees, along with a cover letter of instructions.

4. All job-summary questionnaires for employees in the technical and scientific exempt job family and the administrative and production job family are returned to the personnel department for evaluation.

7. Evaluations are completed on all jobs in Division I that are assigned to the technical and scientific exempt job family.

8. Evaluations are completed on all jobs in Division I that are assigned to the administrative and production job family.

13. Grade structures for clerical, technical and scientific exempt, technical and scientific nonexempt, and administrative and production are completed and ready for presentation to Division I top management for review and approval.

16. Presentation of clerical, technical and scientific exempt, technical and scientific nonexempt, and administrative and production salary-evaluation results, problems, and preliminary recommendations to Division I top management.

[From Glenn H. Varney and Gerald F. Carvalho, "PERT in the Personnel Department," Personnel, 45 (January-February, 1968), pp. 52-3. © 1968 by the American Management Association and reprinted by permission from the publisher. All rights reserved.]

factors, responsibility and education, and that only two degrees have been specified for each factor. Let us also assume that we are only considering three jobs in the organization, A, B, and C, the monthly pay for which are shown in Figure 9–12. As can be seen from Figure 9–12, the current monthly salary for Job B is 75 per cent of that for Job A, while the monthly salary for Job C is only 67.5 per cent of that for Job A. Our objective will be to obtain degree weight values for both responsibility and education that, when summed for each job, will deviate the least over all jobs from the salary as a percentage of the highest paid job, Job A. Also, to add some realism, let us assume that we would like three constraints introduced into the problem:

     1. No factor-degree value may assume a value of less than 0.01.

Factor-Degree Raw Data

| Job | Factor and Degree | | Current Monthly Salary | Current Monthly Salary as a Fraction of That for Highest Paid Job |
	Responsibility	*Education*		
A	2	2	$1,600	1.000
B	2	1	1,200	.750
C	1	2	1,080	.675

Factor-Degree Weightings Obtained by the Linear Programming

| Factor | Degree | |
	1	2
Responsibility	.375	.700
Education	.050	.300

Difference From Sum of Factor-Degree Values and Current Monthly Salary Fractions

Job	Responsibility		Education		Σ		Current Fraction	Difference
A	.700	+	.300	=	1.000	−	1.000	0
B	.700	+	.050	=	.750	−	.750	0
C	.375	+	.300	=	.675	−	.675	0
								Σ = 0

Figure 9–12 *Linear programming point system example.*

2. For each of the two factors, degree 2 must be at least 0.01 greater than degree 1.

3. No factor-degree value can be weighted more than 0.70. We ran this linear program on the computer and obtained the two values for each of the two factors as is shown in Figure 9–12. As can be seen, using these values for each of the three jobs results in *no* deviations from the salary percentages, so that our objective has been met to the fullest extent possible.[59]

This method assumes that the salary relationships for the current jobs included in the program are equitable, which might well be the case for a sample of jobs, as assumed with the factor comparison method. If this is the case, we can then take the factor-degree values obtained by the linear program and use them in arriving at salaries for other jobs. For example, with the four values obtained using our simple linear program, we can determine the pay for a new fourth job, to which degree 1 has been assigned for both responsibility and education. These first degree values are 0.375 and 0.050, respectively, which sum to 0.425. This value indicates that the salary for the new job should be 42.5 per cent of that for Job A, or $1600 \times 0.425 = \$680$/month. With more factors, degrees, jobs, and perhaps constraints, a program such as the one illustrated here could provide a basis for establishing a firm's wage structure.

The simplex technique in job evaluation has also been applied outside of industry. Rodgers, for example, developed a simplex program structured differently from Rehmus and Wagner's that allocated salaries in dealing with a $12 million budget in the Diocese of Youngstown, Ohio, school system.[60] Beginning teachers were seen as the least expensive overall cost, and it was decided to maximize their salaries while still providing equitable salaries to school superintendents, principals, and other teachers. Several constraints were put into the program; e.g., "Factor 1 must be no less than $250 and no more than $1,000."[61] Thus, like all mathematical programming uses, there was an *objective* (to be maximized in this case) subject to various *constraints*.

Just how widespread the use of such programs will be is difficult to ascertain. One problem encountered is that the employees involved in the organization may have difficulties in understanding the program, so that management-employee communications may be of considerable importance.

Secrecy: Open or Closed Systems?

The question of whether salary information should be made public has attracted considerable attention in recent years. Lawler has argued that if pay data are kept secret, misperceptions will occur, and that these misperceptions will lead to dissatisfaction. More specifically, Lawler found that with pay data secrecy:

1. Employees underestimate the pay levels of their superiors.
2. They overestimate the pay of their peers and subordinates.[62]

These two findings have been corroborated by further research using a similar methodology. However, in this research there were found to be misperceptions among personnel even when salary data were given them:

1. Although 79 per cent of managers indicated that their supervisors had told them their pay *range*, only 8 per cent accurately estimated the average salary of managers at their level.
2. Even more surprisingly, those managers indicating that they were *not* told their pay ranges had a higher percentage of correct estimates of the average salaries at their level than those who said they had been told the range.[63]

Further, with respect to job satisfaction, managers who correctly estimated salaries were more dissatisfied and those who overestimated their peers' salaries were more satisfied. In short, these results refuted "the contention that the manager's satisfaction with his own pay and pay differentials are a direct function of perceptual accuracy of the compensation practices of an organization," and indicated that the "relationships between secrecy, accuracy of perception, and satisfaction is not as simple as previously implied."[64] Further, in another study it has been found that better performing managers want pay kept secret slightly more than poor performers.[65]

More recently, two organizations were studied in which pay data ranged from: (1) being completely secret; to (2) providing all salary data except telling anyone what any other person's salary actually was; to (3) a completely open system.[66] In this study, the basis for measuring performance was found to be a key variable, with a contingency approach suggested. Its findings suggested that as performance becomes more difficult to measure, secrecy is most appropriate. The reasoning for this is as follows: Without having objective measures tying pay directly to performance, such as in sales, other factors such as seniority and political power influence it. Revealing salary data under such subjective conditions simply leads to questioning and dissatisfaction.[67] The authors of this study conclude by stipulating certain contingencies essential if an open system is to function properly. For example, they indicated that:

1. Performance must be able to be measured objectively.
2. There is relatively little interdependence between jobs. Under this condition, the responsibility for performance is easier to identify.[68]

Under such conditions, with the *direct* performance-pay link *visible*, there should be few feelings of inequity.

Cost-Benefit Analysis

As indicated earlier, various forms of compensation exist. Some of these may be more cost-effective than others in terms of the financial benefits they provide the employee for each dollar spent by the organization. In one study, Hettenhouse attempted to shed light on this cost-benefit relationship. In doing so, he reported data on "typical" 50-year-old executives considering: (1) corporate income taxes; (2) individual income taxes; and (3) discounting the value of dollars to be paid or received in future years, as is done with theoretically sound financial management techniques such as present value analysis.[69] For example, he looked at the value of the current salary and bonus for an employee with annual earnings of $20,000 and at an assumed marginal *individual* federal income tax rate of 28 per cent. With federal *corporate* income taxes at 48 per cent, 48 cents of each dollar earned before taxes that is paid out as salary to any of its employees is tax deductible. To view this relationship in another way, the firm's after-tax earnings will decrease by only 52 per cent of each additional dollar it pays out in wages or salary, because of the 48 per cent deduction. Thus, in effect, each such dollar paid out represents only a 52-cent *after tax cost* to the firm.

Because of their own taxes however, the firm's employees will have to earn more than $1 to have available a dollar left for them after taxes. The executive at the marginal 28 per cent rate, for instance, must earn $1.39 in order to have a dollar after taxes. This is computed as follows:

1. $(1 - 0.28) x = \$1$; where x represents the amount to be earned before taxes to provide one dollar of income after taxes.

2. $0.72 x = \$1$,

3. $x = \dfrac{\$1}{0.72}$ and

4. $x = \$1.39$.

For the corporation, with its 52 per cent *after* tax cost required to provide the executive with each dollar he needs to earn *before* taxes to obtain his after tax dollar, 52 per cent of $1.39 or $0.72 in after tax corporate dollars must be allocated to achieve this objective.

The impact of individual income taxes may be seen more clearly by comparing this example with the executive at the 50 per cent marginal federal income tax rate. Here, the executive, being taxed marginally at 50 per cent must earn $2 more before taxes to have an additional after tax income of $1. With the corporation's tax rate remaining the same at 48 per cent, 52 per cent of this $2, or $1.04 of its after tax income will be needed to provide such an executive with an additional $1 of income after taxes.

Hettenhouse compared the $0.72 figure calculated here with

costs to the firm of providing the individual in the same 28 per cent federal income tax bracket with $1 after taxes via other compensation methods. Discounting the value of benefits to be paid in the future, for example, Hettenhouse's analysis indicated that a qualified profit sharing plan with 10 payments in retirement would cost the firm in after tax dollars only $0.33, to provide the executive with the same after-tax $1 benefit.[70] Thus it would be a much better compensation alternative from a cost-benefit point of view. In fact, looking at executives at the $50,000, $100,000, and $150,000 annual salary levels as well as at the $20,000 one, Hettenhouse found that current salary and bonus ranked no better in any case than a poor 13th of 17 possible compensation methods he evaluated.

A major question arising from such analysis is: might it not be less costly for the organization to give its employees a greater choice as to how they are to be compensated, for a form of compensation that might be highly valued for the individual might be relatively low in cost to the organization? We will pursue the answer to this question in the next chapter.

Role of the Personnel Department

If any wage and salary plan is to be effective, the personnel department must develop effective working relationships with line management, employees, and the unions. As with other personnel activities, top management support is critical. Further, one function of the personnel department is that of training line managers about wage and salary administration. Zollitsch and Langsner have expressed the belief that this is especially true for first-line supervisors. They have indicated that these supervisors ''carry the burden of most administrative activities involved in maintaining an equitable wage and salary plan.''[71] Employees look to their superiors for answers about how their pay plan works, and the supervisor must be knowledgeable in this area.

Both establishing and updating wage and salary plans are important. In general, with larger companies, the personnel department will conduct the wage and salary surveys (or obtain such data elsewhere), and submit these data to top level management for final approval of the firm's first basic decision — determination of the firm's overall wage level. Further, such data must be updated annually.

With respect to the second major wage and salary decision — establishing the wage structure for each job—personnel will often find it most desirable to gain input from line managers, employees themselves, and sometimes from unions. For example, in the company using PERT, individual employees filled out job

summary questionnaires, then the supervisors reviewed and modified the questionnaires (if necessary) and returned them to the
personnel department, job evaluations for each job were carried
out by the personnel department, and salary-evaluation results
were presented to top divisional management for final approval.
From a contingency point of view, updating job evaluations and
descriptions will be especially important in firms which are dynamic and in which the content of specific jobs changes frequently.
In such cases, employees and their supervisors may tend to bring
the change to the attention of the personnel department if the work
content is upgraded and a higher rate range is called for but not
report changes that make jobs lower ranked. Further, with respect
to the third basic decision area —establishing pay for individuals
on a job — some supervisors may tend to push for high salary
increases for their personnel.

For these two reasons, an effective wage and salary system
needs to establish some effective control mechanism. In larger
organizations, a committee of wage and salary personnel specialists, line managers, and employees often may be established to
review job evaluations and salary increases on some sort of
periodic basis. One of the primary values of committees so structured is to gain employee acceptance of any necessary updating
changes (as well as the introduction of the plan initially).

Finally, specific control techniques have been developed such
as monitoring job description data at the Northern Natural Gas
Company, discussed in Chapter 2, and the establishment of rate
ranges. Further, this company and others have used, as a control
device, the so-called "compa-ratio." The compa-ratio is defined
as:[72]

$$\frac{\text{Average of all salaries within any grade}}{\text{Midpoint of the salary range}}$$

The compa-ratio can help pinpoint wage and salary administration problems for control purposes if:

1. Salary ranges exist.
2. The midpoint of the range represents a "good competitive level
which need not, on the average, be exceeded."[73]

The determination of a compa-ratio may be illustrated with a pay
range with annual salaries as follows: $10,000, $11,000, $13,000,
$20,000. The average of these salaries is $13,500, the midpoint
$15,000, and consequently the compa-ratio is $\frac{\$13,500}{\$15,000}$, or 0.9.
With this compa-ratio falling below 1.0, it may mean that the firm
is not paying competitive wages. Such a compa-ratio, on the other
hand, may be indicative of quite a different situation such as a
group with one very senior member and three "beginners." A
compa-ratio over 1.0 may mean that wage rates are too *high* or

that the individuals in the range represent an established, experienced staff, in a stable organization with salaries generally near the top of the range. Either possibility might be the case with the following four annual salaries in a range: $12,000, $18,000, $19,000, and $20,000. Here the compa-ratio is: $\frac{\$17,250}{\$16,000} = 1.08$.

Two points of broader significance emerge from this discussion of compa-ratios. First, with ratio analysis, in general, one must look behind the actual numbers and ask why, as may be seen with the different possible interpretations of the above compa-ratios. Second, following the concept of personnel departments assuming the control function discussed in Chapter 2, we recommend that personnel generally show any possible unfavorable wage and salary problem to the manager himself, rather than going over his head, reporting the data to his superior, and putting him on the spot. Only if such discussions brought out that there were problems and the line manager involved refused to deal with them would personnel find itself in a position of having to "go over the manager's head" to higher level management.

SUMMARY

Wage and salary systems are established to meet multiple organizational goals: motivating and providing job satisfaction to its employees, and attracting and retaining its personnel. To meet these objectives, three basic sequential decisions moving from the macro to the micro are required: establishing the firm's overall wage level, determining the value of each different job, and, finally, deciding what salary (or wage) each individual on any job is to be paid. Various approaches for making equitable wage and salary decisions have been developed. Three key contingencies in deciding on any one approach are the size of the organization, the degree to which it is dynamic rather than stable, and whether we are considering managerial and professional or nonmanagerial employees. Recent issues of importance to wage and salary administration have been governmental legislation, management science, computers, and automation, secrecy with respect to pay data, and cost-benefit analysis. We will pursue the latter along with discussing several types of individual incentive plans in the next chapter.

DISCUSSION AND STUDY QUESTIONS

1. How do you think each of the following individuals might symbolize the value of money he (or she) earns in terms of the psychological theories presented in the chapter? Why?

a. The president of United Motors, America's largest automotive manufacturing firm. His salary is $800,000/year.

b. A married graduate student working on a Ph.D. degree in Business Administration who is on an assistantship which pays his tuition plus a few thousand dollars a year. (His wife has not been able to find a job).

c. The personnel manager of a company with annual sales of over $500 million. Her current salary is $65,000/year.

d. The 48-year-old wife of a $60,000 per year executive, whose four children have all graduated from college and who spends 20 hours a week making ceramic teapots, coffee mugs, vases, and other art objects and selling them through local craft outlets netting a profit about $2000 per year.

2. As indicated in the chapter, in discussing internal equity and external competition, the degree of knowledge individuals have about wages (or salaries) being paid for comparable positions elsewhere varies considerably from situation to situation. To what extent do you think that individuals in each of the following jobs could make good estimates of other firms' pay rates for jobs comparable to their own? Might they consider factors other than pay in comparing jobs? Why?

a. A salesclerk in a women's apparel store in Philadelphia.

b. A highly specialized research professor of music history who holds a chair at a large southern university. This professor is the world's outstanding authority on the works of Charles Ives (1874-1954), considered by some as America's first great composer. The professor, in addition to his research, conducts graduate seminars from time to time for small groups of students.

c. A young man who received his Ph.D. degree in management a year ago and who is now teaching personnel management and organizational behavior in a large state university in the midwest.

d. The president of the nation's third largest supermarket chain.

e. A production worker who has a highly skilled job in helping to manufacture tires at a medium sized tire and rubber company, located a little more than a hundred miles away from Akron, Ohio, this country's tire center.

3. Below are listed seven situations in which different job evaluation methods are associated with different firm situations. Indicate in each case how good you think the "fit" is between the method and the situation. Why?

a. Ranking for all positions in New York City's largest department store.

b. Ranking for all positions in a bank with 20 to 25 employees in a small midwestern town.

c. Factor comparison for production jobs in a large manufacturing firm in which job content is relatively stable.

d. Factor comparison for top managerial jobs in the same firm.

e. Maturity curves in a mass production operation.

f. Job classification for all Federal Service Commission positions.

g. The point system for all positions (except top executive ones) in a large book publishing concern.

4. Different yardsticks in point systems may have to be utilized for different classes of individuals in a firm because their work is so different. The Ajax company, however, has only the one yardstick, given below, for all of its jobs: managerial and professional, clerical, and production. Which of the following jobs do you think would be remunerated most fairly with this yardstick? Least fairly? Why? How many degrees would you assign to each factor for each job?
   a. Operations researcher
   b. Personnel manager
   c. Janitor
   d. Set-up man on the firm's production line
   e. A clerk typist in the firm's personnel department

	Degree			
Factor	1st	2nd	3rd	4th
Responsibility	75	150	225	300
Working Conditions*	100	200	300	400
Physical Effort	80	160	240	320
Mental Effort	75	150	225	300
Education	50	100	150	200

*Poorer working conditions rate more points.

5. If you were just starting in a managerial position after having just graduated from college which of the following merit raise policies would you prefer? Why?
   a. Automatic progression.
   b. Automatic progression to the midpoint, and then salary increases based solely on merit within the rate range for your job.
   c. Salary increases based solely on merit.

6. In which of the following situations do you believe that rate ranges ought to be the widest? Why?
   a. For packers at the Alpha Food Corporation, a stable, nonexpanding firm, with low turnover, that makes or processes many foods from mayonnaise to peanut butter to ice cream.
   b. For sales representative jobs at IBM.

7. None of the basic three management science approaches discussed in Chapter 1 have been applied (to our knowledge) to performance appraisal. All three — simulation, PERT, and mathematical programming — on the other hand, have been used in the personnel function of wage and salary administration. Why do you suppose this is so?

8. For which of the following jobs in a large firm manufacturing appliances do you think pay secrecy, as opposed to disclosure, is more appropriate? Why?
   a. The firm's management training director.
   b. Its regional sales manager in upstate New York.
   c. An assembler on the production line.
   d. The firm's public relations manager.

9. Dogwood Humstead is a middle level executive at the marginal income tax rate of 42 per cent. His wife, Brunettie, has just come home with a new hat, which was originally priced at $35, but which she bought on sale for $20. She tells her husband that she has just "saved him" $15. He responds: "You didn't save me anything. I had to earn more than $35 before taxes to pay for that $20 hat." Was Dogwood correct? Would Dogwood have been correct if the $35 hat had been sale-priced at only $25?

10. Manager Al and Manager Sue at the Sidal Corporation are always comparing each other's performance, and bragging whenever either of their performances is better than that of the other. Al supervises five subordinate managers, whose annual salaries are $20,000, $27,000, $28,000, $29,000, and $30,000, while Sue supervises five subordinate managers whose annual salaries are $18,000, $24,000, $25,000, $26,000, and $32,000. Al brags to Sue that he is a better manager because his compa-ratio is closer to 1.0 than Sue's. Evaluate Al's statement.

11. Rehmus and Wagner's linear programming approach attempted to arrive at a factor weighting point system that would minimize the discrepancy between the current salaries for a number of jobs and the factor ratings for these jobs. What does such a minimization assume. Is the assumption valid?

Notes

[1] For a discussion of the contingencies on which such an approach seems viable, see Robert D. Hulme and Richard V. Bevan, "The Blue-Collar Worker Goes on Salary," *Harvard Business Review*, 53 (March-April, 1975), pp. 104-112.

[2] Robert L. Opsahl and Marvin D. Dunnette, "The Role of Financial Compensation in Industrial Motivation," *Psychological Bulletin,* 66 (1966), p. 114.

[3] Edward E. Lawler, III, "The Mythology of Management Compensation," *California Management Review*, 9 (Fall, 1966), p. 14.

[4] It must be recognized, however, that an individual's desire for money may change due to changes in such factors as aspiration levels or family situations. For example, additional children might result in an individual's desiring more money. Conversely, a fortuituous financial event, such as receiving a large lottery prize, may result in the importance of money declining for an individual.

[5] Lawler, op. cit., p. 15.

[6] Allan N. Nash and Stephen J. Carroll, Jr., *The Management of Compensation* (Monterey, Cal.: Brooks/Cole Publishing Company, 1975), p. 39.

[7] A. H. Maslow, *Motivation and Personality*, 2nd ed. (New York: Harper & Row, 1970).

[8] Victor Vroom, *Work and Motivation* (New York: John Wiley & Sons, Inc., 1964).

[9] See, for example, David C. McClelland, et al., *The Achievement Motive* (New York: Appleton-Century-Crofts, 1953), or his *The Achieving Society* (Princeton, N.J.: Van Nostrand Co., Inc., 1961).

[10] See Nash and Carroll, op.cit., pp. 39ff.

[11] Edward E. Lawler, III, *Pay and Organizational Effectiveness: A Psychological View* (New York: McGraw-Hill, 1971). With respect to top executive turnover, one more recent study concluded that top executives "who change

employers report that the opportunity for more responsibility and greater challenge is more important to them than increase in compensation," and for top executives, lack of significant responsibility is the most important reason for leaving an employer. Gerard R. Roche, "Compensation and the Mobile Executive," *Harvard Business Review,* 53 (November-December, 1975), pp. 54, 56.

[12]Two notes are in order here. First, to prevent such dissatisfaction, many organzizations keep pay secret, as we will discuss later. Second, much research has been carried out in the area of "equity" theory. This field attempts, among other things, to explain "the process by which employees decide that the reward system of the organization is fair." This process "involves making comparisons of pertinent . . . inputs and desired outcomes to some standard — reality, an internal standard, or another person or group." Such groups are often referred to as "reference groups." D. W. Belcher and T. J. Atchinson, "Equity Theory and Compensation Policy," *Personnel Administration*, 33 (July-August, 1970), p. 32. For a further discussion of equity theory, see Richard M. Steers and Lyman W. Porter, *Motivation and Work Behavior* (New York: McGraw-Hill, Inc., 1975), pp. 135–179.

[13]Max D. Richards and Paul S. Greenlaw, *Management: Decisions and Behavior,* rev. ed. (Homewood, Ill.: Richard D. Irwin, Inc., 1972), p. 158.

[14]For a more elaborate list of goals that may be met in wage and salary administration, see, for example, Arthur Dick, "Job Evaluation's Role in Employee Relations," *Personnel Journal*, 53 (February, 1974), p. 117. Dick, for example, cites as one goal the reduction of "grievances over wage and salary rates."

[15]We will draw heavily in this section from Chapter 4 of Nash and Carroll, op. cit.

[16]J. D. Dunn and F. M. Rachel, *Wage and Salary Administration* (New York: McGraw-Hill, Inc., 1971), p. 200.

[17]Nash and Carroll, op. cit., p. 69.

[18]For some of the limitations of utilizing the Consumer Price Index, see Dunn and Rachel, op. cit., p. 215. One of these is that "it is virtually impossible to construct a cost-of-living index that will accurately measure general price level changes throughout the United States." Ibid.

[19]Herbert G. Zollitsch and Adolph Langsner, *Wage and Salary Administration,* 2nd ed. (Cincinnati, Ohio: South-Western Publishing Co., 1970), p. 321.

[20]Thomas L. Freas, "The Salary Survey: Know What You're Paying For," *Administrative Management,* 34 (July, 1973), p. 71.

[21]See David L. Norrgard, "The Public Pay Plan: Some New Approaches," *Public Personnel Review*, 32 (April, 1971), p. 93.

[22]Nash and Carroll, op. cit., p. 77.

[23]Zollitsch and Langsner, op. cit., p. 327.

[24]See Dunn and Rachel, op. cit., p. 205; and Nash and Carroll, op. cit., p. 93.

[25]Ibid.

[26]Zollitsch and Langsner, op. cit., p. 147.

[27]See, for example, Nash and Carroll, op. cit., p. 107.

[28]Harold D. Janes, "Issues in Job Evaluation: The Union View," *Personnel Journal,* 51 (September, 1972), p. 675. Janes indicated that there was less high dissatisfaction among union members in a study he conducted in 1971 as compared to a survey in 1968.

[29]David J. Chesler, "Reliability and Comparability of Different Job Evaluation Systems," *Journal of Applied Psychology,* 32 (October, 1948), p. 473. For a critique of this research, see Nash and Carroll, op. cit., p. 124.

[30]Sometimes criteria such as job difficulty and responsibility are considered by the evaluators; and some authorities agree that job descriptions are essential for ranking to be used. See Zollitsch and Langsner, op. cit., p. 169, and Dunn and Rachel, op. cit., p. 173.

[31]Robert B. Pursell, "Job Evaluation and Pay Plans: Engineering, Technical, and Professional Personnel," in Joseph Famularo, ed., *Handbook of Modern Personnel Administration* (New York: McGraw-Hill Book Company, 1972), p. 30–8.

[32]Ibid. pp. 30–11, 30–12.

[33]Slotting positions into grades has been found to be a real problem for

Federal Civil Service jobs, and the Federal Civil Service Commission has developed a new method for more explicitly defining criteria for assigning grades in the classification of nonsupervisory positions (GS-1–GS-15) so as to make its job classification system clearer both to federal managers and employees. This new system is called the Factor Evaluation System (FES), and is described in "FES; General Introduction, Background, and Instructions, Section VII, Instructions for the Factor Evaluation System" (Washington: U.S. Civil Service Commission, May, 1977).

[34]Edward A. Shaw, "The Curve Approach to the Compensation of Scientists," in *The Management of Scientific Manpower,* Management Report No. 76 (New York: American Management Association, 1963), p. 142.

[35]Such curves had been developed earlier by the Bell Telephone Laboratories but were especially widely used after World War II in southern California's "floating labor market." For a discussion of the use of these curves in this floating market, see Thomas H. Patten, Jr., "Maturity-Pay Curves in a Floating Labor Market: The Case of Southern California," *Quarterly Review of Economics and Business,* 7 (Fall, 1967). pp. 57–72. Patten has argued that "curves" used alone, without respect to an individual's performance, are inadequate, since they are based on the erroneous assumption that "age and/or experience should be a major factor in salary administration." Ibid., p. 69.

[36]Thomas Atchison and Wendell French, "Pay Systems for Scientists and Engineers," *Industrial Relations*, 7 (October, 1967), p. 46.

[37]John J. Morse, "A Contingency Look at Job Design," *California Management Review*, 16 (Fall, 1973), p. 72.

[38]Dunn and Rachel, op. cit., p. 309.

[39]This assumes that when across the board wage increases take place, the red-circled rate individual does not share in them until they have exceeded the red-circle figure. From that point on, the job would no longer be red circled. If such is the case, management must orient its personnel to this situation. See: Leonard R. Burgess, *Wage and Salary Administration in a Dynamic Economy* (New York: Harcourt, Brace & World, Inc., 1968), pp. 42, 44.

[40]Zollitsch and Langsner, op. cit., p. 349. They also indicated that most authorities recommend a minimum spread of 20 per cent. Ibid.

[41]Nash and Carroll, op. cit. pp. 167, 169.

[42]Ibid., pp. 169–170.

[43]Zollitsch and Langsner, op. cit., p. 349.

[44]Ibid., pp. 349–350.

[45]Nash and Carroll, op. cit., p. 171.

[46]Ibid., p. 154.

[47]William A. Evans, "Pay for Performance: Fact or Fable," *Personnel Journal,* 49 (September, 1970), p. 726.

[48]K. R. Srinivasa Murthy and Malcolm S. Salter, "Should CEO Pay be Linked to Results?" *Harvard Business Review,* 53 (May-June, 1975), pp. 66–73.

[49]See Nash and Carroll, op. cit., pp. 159–160.

[50]Two notes are in order here. For a discussion of some of the problems in determining just what a merit raise is, see Kenneth E. Foster, "What is a Merit Increase?" *Personnel,* 38 (November-December, 1961), pp. 18–25. Some research on the question of how large a raise must be to be noticeable has indicated that the size of an individual's current salary represents a key contingency, with a slight tendency for lesser percentage raises being barely perceived to be noticeable as salaries increased. See J. R. Hinrichs, "Correlates of Employee Evaluations of Pay Increases," *Journal of Applied Psychology,* 53 (December, 1969), pp. 481–489.

[51]"The Courts Back Women on Job Equality," *Business Week,* November 25, 1972, p. 44.

[52]Antonia Handler Chayes, "Make Your Equal Opportunity Program Court Proof," *Harvard Business Review,* 52 (September-October, 1974), p. 84. For an extensive analysis of progress with respect to equal pay for women, which covers not only experiences in the United States, but those abroad, see Alice H. Cook, "Equal Pay: Where Is It?" *Industrial Relations,* 14 (May, 1975), pp. 158–177.

[53]Charles E. Cassidy, "Electronic Data Processing and the Personnel Function: The Present and the Future," *Personnel Journal,* 45 (June, 1966), pp. 352–354.

[54]Julius Rezler, "Effects of Automation on Some Areas of Compensation," *Personnel Journal,* 48 (April, 1969), p. 283.

[55]Gordon Wolf and Mario Leo, "A Systems Approach to Total Compensation," *Business Management/Executive Compensation Report,* 37 (February, 1970), p. 44.

[56]Ibid., pp. 44, 46, 48.

[57]All the materials discussed with this PERT example were drawn from Glenn H. Varney and Gerard F. Carvalho, "PERT in the Personnel Department," *Personnel,* 45 (January-February, 1968), pp. 48-53.

[58]Frederick P. Rehmus and Harvey M. Wagner, "Applying Linear Programming to Your Pay Structure," *Business Horizons,* 6 (Winter, 1963), p. 92.

[59]In the Rehmus and Wagner program, with many more factors, degrees, and jobs, sums of the factor-degree values did differ slightly from the current salary fraction on certain jobs. See ibid., pp. 94-95.

[60]William A. Rodgers, "Negotiating a Salary Structure With Modeling, Simulation and Linear Programming," unpublished paper, Kent State University, August 4, 1971.

[61]Ibid., p. 10.

[62]See Edward E. Lawler, III, "Secrecy About Management Compensation: Are There Hidden Costs?" *Organizational Behavior and Human Performance,* 2 (February, 1967), pp. 184-185.

[63]George T. Milkovich and Philip H. Anderson, "Management Compensation and Secrecy Policies," *Personnel Psychology,* 25 (Summer, 1972), pp. 295-297.

[64]Ibid., p. 302.

[65]Jay R. Schuster and Jerome A. Colletti, "Pay Secrecy: Who is For and Against It?" *Academy of Management Journal,* 16 (March, 1973), pp. 35-40.

[66]Paul Thompson and John Pronsky, "Secrecy or Disclosure in Management Compensation?" *Business Horizons,* 18 (June, 1975), pp. 67-74.

[67]Two notes are in order here. First, this type of conclusion has been supported by other studies such as P. H. Thompson and G. W. Dalton, "Performance Appraisal: Managers Beware," *Harvard Business Review,* 48 (January-February, 1970), pp. 149-157. Second, these results are incongruent with the claim in the study referred to above that there is no relationship between pay satisfaction and perceptual accuracy. In the study we are discussing now, satisfaction with pay increased as salary data were made more open.

[68]Thompson and Pronsky, op. cit., p. 73.

[69]George W. Hettenhouse, "Cost/Benefit Analysis of Executive Compensation," *Harvard Business Review,* 48 (July-August, 1970), pp. 114-124.

[70]In this situation, Hettenhouse assumed in discounting future returns that the corporation has an after tax opportunity cost of 10 per cent; while the executive's after tax opportunity cost would be only 5 per cent.

[71]Zollitsch and Langsner, op. cit., p. 751.

[72]In some cases, this figure is multiplied by 100 so that an "average" compa-ratio would be 100 rather than 1. See, for example, Richard P. Rooney, "The Right Way to Pay," *Administrative Management,* 33 (October, 1972), p. 76.

[73]Ibid.

10

INDIVIDUAL INCENTIVE SYSTEMS

For many decades, American business firms have used financial incentive systems in an effort to help motivate their employees. As far back as 1890, for example, Frederick Halsey developed a wage incentive plan for production workers.[1]

A basic assumption underlying individual incentives is that, in one way or another, they will serve to spur or stimulate individuals to higher levels of performance. To the extent that this assumption is valid, the additional financial rewards obtained by the individual can meet many of his own needs, and at the same time contribute toward increased company profitability.

Our purpose in this chapter is to discuss and evaluate four basic types of individual incentives: (1) wage incentives for production and related employees, (2) suggestion systems, (3) incentives geared to top executives, managers, and professionals, and (4) the so-called "cafeteria" or flexible type of compensation approach in which individuals are given some choice as to the form of compensation they will receive. In the next chapter we will discuss certain types of system-wide incentives.

Individual incentives have varied considerably in their effectiveness. In some cases, they have served well in meeting organizational objectives and individual needs. On the other hand, many have created so many problems that they have been dropped. Thus, before establishing any particular incentive plan, management should ask the question: "Would such a plan really help meet organizational objectives and individual needs?" Although such a question may be difficult to answer, there are many situations in which management can gain cues as to the need for incentive plans. For example, if the firm's production workers are

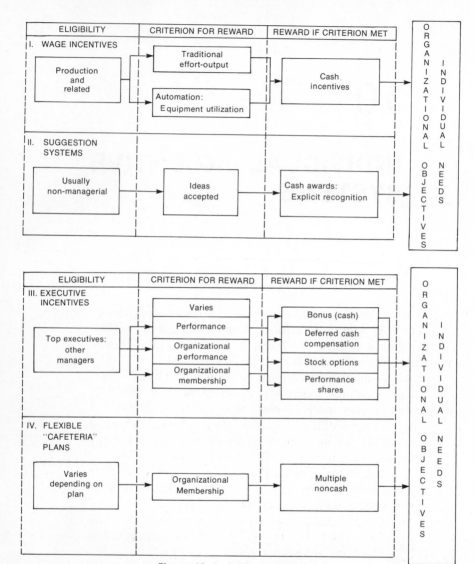

Figure 10-1 *Individual incentives.*

considered to be producing at a reasonable rate, and absenteeism and turnover are low, establishing a direct wage incentive may not only be unnecessary but might even be dysfunctional, in that it may disrupt existing wages to the point that a number of employees perceive the new incentive rates as being inequitable. On the other hand, a firm may consider it essential to establish some form of deferred compensation if it is to recruit and keep its top executives, simply because all other comparable firms provide such incentives.

If an organization decides to adopt any individual incentive system it must make three subsequent decisions. It must determine (1) which individuals are to be eligible for inclusion in the plan, (2) what the criterion (or criteria) for providing a reward will be, and (3) what the reward will be if any specific criterion has been met. These three aspects of incentive decision making are illustrated in Figure 10–1, which provides an overview of the incentives plans we will cover in this chapter.

WAGE INCENTIVES

In establishing wage incentives, management must decide how the jobs included in the plan are to be performed, what standards of performance must be met if an incentive is to be earned, and how much incentive pay the worker is to receive at different levels of performance.

Traditionally, jobs eligible for direct wage incentives have been characterized by an easily measurable output. The majority of these jobs have been in production and related work. We use the word "related" here to encompass such jobs as those of warehouse workers who are paid on an incentive basis for the number of boxes they may sort or stack during a particular time period.

In numerous companies wage incentive systems have been designed for indirect labor in production operations. These include workers who assist machine operators by providing the materials they need or helping them in other ways. For example, in one department at the American Seating Company, wage incentives were established for a number of types of indirect workers such as die-setters, crane operators, lift truck operators, and electric truckers. Here, every indirect wage incentive was related to direct labor output. Any increase in production by direct labor forced the indirect workers to increase their pace. Further, if either group slowed down, incentive earnings decreased for both groups.[2] The application of automated operations has also led to the tendency to extend incentive coverage to maintenance and other indirect jobs.[3] Finally, direct wage incentives have also been used for certain types of clerical work. This practice, however, is not common.[4]

In traditional production systems, standards of units of output can be defined, with worker effort leading to production above the standard rewarded with incentive pay. In the last few decades, however, more and more firms have turned to various degrees of automation. In automated and semi-automated situations in which there is a high degree of machine pacing it is not possible for the worker to exert more effort and thereby produce more output since the machine primarily determines the rate of production. In such situations traditional incentives based on output are not appropriate. It has been found in some highly mechanized and/or automated operations, however, that if workers pay attention to their work they can help minimize machine downtime. Since such downtime is costly, particularly in automated high capital intensive industries, some firms have developed equipment utilization incentives. Under such incentives workers are rewarded for maintaining the full practical capacity of the highly mechanized equipment.

With both traditional and the more recent automated incentives, workers may:

1. Work completely independently of each other, in which case, the incentive reward can be directly related to each individual's performance.

2. Work in interdependent crews, in which the output rate of all workers in any groups will be the *same* so that everyone must receive the same percentage incentive for any particular period of time. For example, all workers might receive 120 per cent of their base rates of pay in a given pay period.

The basic difference between these group and individual incentives is that the level of incentives for the group will be held down to the level of performance of its slowest worker. For this reason, workers may apply pressures to anyone who is "goofing-off," since this behavior would mean less incentive pay for them as well. These crew wage incentives function like individual incentives in all other respects.

Establishing Standards

Some understanding of how the development of work standards on which wage incentives are to be based is accomplished is necessary for a full understanding of how these incentives function. Setting standards involves two steps. First a methods study is performed that attempts to spell out the best way to perform each job. This may involve a motion study if the volume to be produced is high. Second, one of several available methods geared to determining how much time it should take workers to perform the job is utilized. We should emphasize that both motion and time analysis can have many advantages to the firm other than simply establishing a base for incentive systems. For example, they may provide better control over labor costs, and increase profitability as a result of improved methods design.

Motion Study

Modern motion study, a part of the "scientific management" movement, goes back to the early days of this century. Its basic objective is to find the "best" way of performing a job. Over the years, scholars and practitioners in this field have developed numerous "principles" aimed at combining, simplifying, and eliminating work elements in jobs.[5] For example, smooth simultaneous motions with both hands are much more efficient than nonsimultaneous jerky motions. This is illustrated in Figure 10–2, in which the solid arrows represent the motions of the two hands reaching for two parts, which will be taken by an operator and fastened together.

Without question, many significant improvements in the way work has been done have been achieved through the appropriate utilization of motion study. There are, however, two limitations in prescribing the so-called "best way" of performing a job. First, although some motions are obviously superior to others (as in Figure 10–2), in some cases different people may be able to perform the same task most effectively with different motions. Second, it may be more "efficient" for an operator to perform a job in one way rather than another. However, if he has to perform it over and over again using the same motions every time, it may

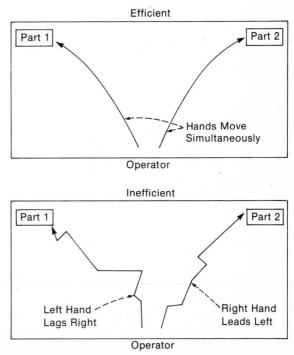

Figure 10–2 *Efficient vs. inefficient motions.*

become sufficiently more monotonous that overall production may be higher if the individual is allowed some deviation, making the job somewhat more interesting.

Determination of Standard Times

Over the years, four basic methods have been used to determine standard times upon which wage incentive plans may be built. They include the following:[6]

Traditional Time Study. This approach calls for a work measurement analyst to observe workers, measure their actual times in performing each element of a task with a stopwatch, and subsequently determine a standard time for the total task for the "average" worker. This approach is most amenable to repetitive operations where the work analyst can watch a worker perform his job enough times to get a valid sample of observations.

Macro-Synthetic Analysis (often called "standard data"). Here, if all elements of work for a new job are ones that have been previously studied, the times for each element as established in these previous studies can be taken and added together to get a total standard time for the new job.

Micro-Synthetic Analysis. This approach calls for breaking jobs down into very small basic elements (such as reach, grasp, and move), and then adding up these basic elemental times to get a total standard time for a job. Motion picture frames must be analyzed with micro-motion analysis because the elements are so small in duration. For example, in one of the more well known of these systems, *Methods-Time Measurement (MTM)*, the basic unit of time used (called a "TMU") is 0.00001 hour, and to move an object weighing up to 2.5 pounds 30 inches to an "approximate or indefinite location" calls for 24.3 TMU's or 0.000243 hours.[7]

Work Sampling. Here the analyst randomly observes tasks at which workers are engaged. A relatively large number of random observations are made. By rating operator performance for each random observation, and knowing the output produced over the time of the sampling study, time standards may be developed. This method is often used in cyclical, nonrepetitive operations, where workers could be doing any one of several possible tasks at any given time. Not knowing when any given task will be done rules out the use of traditional time study where there is a need for the repetition of tasks.

In addition to these well-known approaches, the management science technique of linear programming (simplex) has been shown feasible in setting standards. For example, this method has been used to establish standards for the erection of utility poles for an electric power company in the southeastern United States.[8] In this company, each job of installing one or more utility poles was composed of several common elements — erecting poles, installing wire, installing crossarms, etc. The number of these elements varied from job to job. These numbers were recorded along with the total *actual observed time* that it took to complete a number of these installations. A mathematical program was then developed with the following objective function:

> To arrive at a standard time for each element which, when summed for each job, will yield *total standard times* for *each* job, which, in turn when summed for all jobs will deviate the least from the sum of the *actual* observed total times for all jobs.

For example, simplifying this research, assume that the power company took observed times for the installation of only three jobs, each with only three elements as is shown in Figure 10–3*a*. If we arbitrarily assigned element times of 1 minute to install each pole, 2 minutes to install each 100 feet of wire, and 1 minute to install each crossarm, we would have element time standards which would result in total standard times deviating from total observed times by 10 minutes, as shown in Figure 10–3*b*. That the sum of these deviations can be reduced is shown in Figure 10–3*c*, in which changing the three elemental times reduced the sum of deviations to eight minutes.

The author of this program indicated that it could be used to determine standard times for jobs in which discrete work elements are basically the same except for the quantity of each type of work, which might vary from job to job. He did admit, however, that linear programming should not be used in place of "more accurate classical time study methods" except when "qualified time study personnel are not available or time and money are not available for a more detailed study."[9] We should also emphasize that this method has *not* been widely used as have the other four work measurement techniques described.

All time study methods are subjective to varying extents with respect to determining what work standards should be set for the "average" employee. Further, work sampling, macro- and microsynthetic methods, and linear programming may be very difficult for many employees to understand. For these reasons, considerable "haggling" may take place between management and workers (and unions) over standards set. In one study, it was found that of 4000 grievance cases before the American Arbitration Association in 1958, 23 per cent concerned disputes over standards.[10] This is a basic reason for our previous observation that the adoption of a wage incentive plan may not be desirable if operations in the firm are going well without incentives.

Incentive Standards: A Systems View

The introduction and updating of incentive standards may be viewed in systems terms, as many interdependent needs, objectives, and forces are in mutual interaction in these processes. An overview of these interactive relationships is shown in Figure

(a) Observations

Job	Poles	Feet of Wire (100's)	Number Cross-Arms	Actual Observed Times
1	1	4	2	9 minutes
2	2	10	4	25 minutes
3	3	6	6	28 minutes

(b) Arbitrary Element Time Standards

Job	Poles	×	Element Time	=	Wire	×	Element Time	=	Cross-Arms	×	Element Time	=	Σ of Element Time Standards	Actual Observed Times	Deviation
1	1		1	1	4		2	8	2		1	2	11	9	2
2	2		1	2	10		2	20	4		1	4	26	25	1
3	3		1	3	6		2	12	6		1	6	21	28	7
													Σ		10 minutes

(c) Example of Improved Element Times Standards*

Job	Poles	×	Element Time	=	Wire	×	Element Time	=	Cross-Arms	×	Element Time	=	Σ of Element Time Standards	Actual Observed Times	Deviation
1	1		2	2	4		1	4	2		2	4	10	9	1
2	2		2	4	10		1	10	4		2	8	22	25	3
3	3		2	6	6		1	6	6		2	12	24	28	4
													Σ		8 minutes

*Not an optimum solution: Further minimization of the sum of deviations is possible.

Figure 10–3 Linear programming time standards.

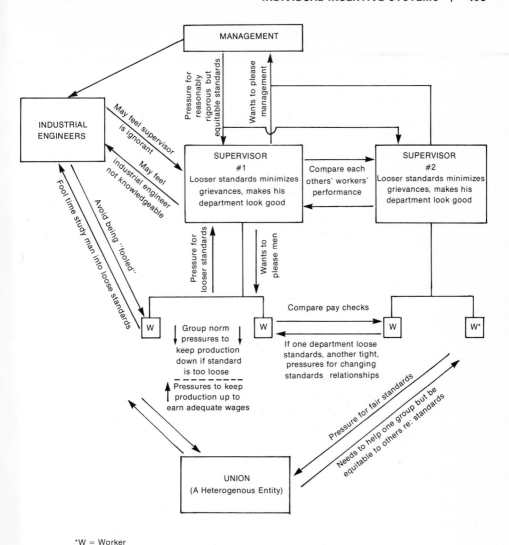

*W = Worker

Figure 10-4   Incentive standards: mutual interactions.

10-4. With traditional time study, for example, workers will often try to make the job look more difficult than it is by working at a pace slower than normal to "fool" the time study engineer into setting easy (or "loose") standards for a job. Time study engineers will try not to be fooled by workers in such a manner, and good engineers will presumably succeed in their endeavor.

In general, regardless of which time standard approach is used, workers will want relatively loose standards. However, they will not want them to be loose enough to arouse management suspicion that the standards were improperly set and thereby cause the job to be restudied. Management, in general, will want to have standards that are rigorous enough to permit competitive wage costs. On the other hand, management will want to avoid inequities in incentive standards such as very loose and very tight standards in the same plant, which could create serious human relations problems. Interestingly enough, the union (although it may generally want to obtain relatively loose standards), will want to avoid serious inequity problems as much as management. Unions are heterogeneous political entities, representing many different interests; to support one department in getting easier rates may "open the door" to dissatisfaction in other departments on the grounds that their rates, too, should be made easier.

The first-line supervisor will often prefer reasonably loose standards for his workers for two reasons. First, there will be a lower probability of his employees getting upset than would be the case if the standards are too "tight." Second, if his workers can perform at a higher percentage of standards than workers reporting to other first-line supervisors, it may make him look good by comparison.

With all these forces at play (along with the need for considerable effort to develop work standards), wage incentives from a contingency point of view appear to be most appropriate in firms in which the work of production and related employees is fairly stable, so that the whole process of updating incentives is not a major one. Further, larger organizations, regardless of job stability, may have more workers performing each job, so that the number of different standards per worker needing development is less, following the size-exposures notion expressed in Chapter 1. In addition, larger organizations may have greater computer capabilities for meeting the computational requirements involved in setting time standards and determining weekly incentive pay for each employee once the plan is in operation. For example, in one large organization, The Pennsylvania State University, a computerized janitorial work standard program was developed and used in the 1960's for performing many of the computations required utilizing traditional time study methods to set standards.[11] We will now turn our attention to the two basic types of wage incentives indicated earlier: traditional output, and equipment utilization.

Typical Incentive Plans

Traditional Output Incentives

There have been many different incentive plans designed since the Halsey plan was developed in the late 1800's. Niebel has distinguished two basic types of such plans: (1) those in which the worker shares his gains above standard with his employer, and (2) those in which he participates in all of the gains above standard.[12] Many plans in operations today are of the latter type, and we will focus our attention on two of these.[13]

Guaranteed piecework. Guaranteed piecework is very easy to understand, and earnings under this system are easy for payroll departments to calculate. With this form of incentive, a standard pay amount is established for each acceptable unit of output, e.g., 4 cents/piece. Each job also has an hourly base rate of pay. If an employee does not turn out enough pieces at the piece-rate standard to equal his hourly base rate, he is paid the hourly base rate. If he produces enough pieces to generate earnings exceeding this hourly rate, however, he is given incentive pay on a one-to-one basis. For example, if a worker's base rate of pay is $4.00/hour, and he is paid on the basis of 4 cents/piece, he will receive incentive pay of 4 cents for each piece turned out exceeding 100/hour. If he produces 101 pieces per hour his pay will be $4.04/hour; with 102 pieces, $4.08/hour; 110 pieces, $4.40/hour; and so on. This one-for-one output-earnings relationship above the guaranteed hourly base rate assumes the form of a 45 degree angle as illustrated in Figure 10–5. This system protects the new, inexperienced worker through the hourly base rate guarantee. In many cases, however, if a new worker cannot, with appropriate training, turn out enough pieces to "earn" his base rate within a reasonable time, he would be assigned to a different job that may involve a lower base rate. Further, if an experienced worker is consistently falling below this level of production, he would be subject to disciplinary action by his supervisor.

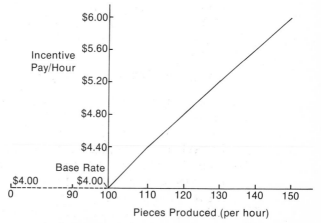

Figure 10–5 *Guaranteed piecework incentive.*

The standard hour plan. The standard hour plan is similar to guaranteed piecework in that it also provides a one-for-one relationship between output and hourly incentive earnings above the base rate, as shown in Figure 10--5. It differs, however, in that the standard is set in terms of time, rather than money. For example, a standard may be expressed as 1 hour per 100 pieces produced. With this standard, if the hourly base rate is $4.00, as in our guaranteed piecework example, and a worker turns out 110 pieces in an hour, he would be credited with 1.1 standard hours of work ($^{110}/_{100}$). Multiplying the number of standard hours earned times the base rate (1.1 × $4.00) provides the same $4.40 in earnings that a worker turning out 110 pieces in an hour would receive under guaranteed piecework. This observation raises the question: Why do some firms have guaranteed piecework plans and others standard hour plans if the results of the two are the same? The answer is that, from a contingency point of view, the two plans have one difference that may be important, especially in dynamic situations in which wage rates are changed frequently. Since piecework incentive standards are based on money, every time hourly base rates are changed, as has occurred so often in our generally inflationary economy in recent years, the piecework standard also needs changing, thus creating extra clerical work.[14] With the standard hour plan, on the contrary, the standard hours remain the same when base rates are changed. If, for example, base hourly wage rates are changed twice over a period of a year from $4.00 to $4.10 and then to $4.20, using the data in our previous examples, the changes taking place in the standard hour plan, as opposed to guaranteed piecework, are illustrated in Figure 10–6.

Finally we should note that although standards do not have to be changed when wage rates change with the standard hour plan, this plan may be more difficult for employees to understand than guaranteed piecework. For example, 2.35 standard hours per 100 pieces with an hourly base rate of $4.00 may be more difficult to grasp than the equivalent $.094/piece.

Equipment Utilization Incentives

Equipment utilization incentives have been widely used by some firms that have moved to highly mechanized or automated operations. One of the most noteworthy of such efforts has been in the steel industry. Reports of these incentives appeared at least as far back as the early 1960's, and in correspondence from the United Steelworkers late in 1975, the continued use of these incentives was reported.

The establishment of equipment utilization incentives can

Hourly Base Rate	Guaranteed Base Rate				Total Hourly Pay
	Piecerate Standard		Number of Pieces Produced		
$4.00	$.04	×	110	=	$4.40
$4.10	$.041	×	110	=	$4.51
$4.20	$.042	×	110	=	$4.62

Hourly Base Rate		Standard Hour Plan			Total Hourly Pay
		Standard Hour/ 100 Pieces	Number of Pieces Produced		
$4.00	×	1	×	110	=	$4.40
$4.10	×	1	×	110	=	$4.51
$4.20	×	1	×	110	=	$4.62

Figure 10-6 *Guaranteed piecework vs. standard hour plans when base wage rates are changed frequently. For purposes of simplification, we are assuming in the standard hour plan that 110 pieces are produced each hour by a worker and that his job involves turning out only one type of piece.*

best be illustrated by taking an example from a steel rolling mill operation. Here, taking into account maximum machine speed, human factors (fatigue), and mechanical factors (delays that can normally be expected), a "practical" measure of maximum possible production was developed.[15] A lower production level was then set at 72.5 per cent of the maximum practical possible production level, and workers were paid their base rates if they produced at this level or less. Any production above this percentage was considered incentive work, with worker pay at the maximum practical possible level equaling 137.9 per cent of the base rate. These numbers were set so that the maximum practical rate could be thought of as a norm of 1 standard hour $(1.379 \times .725 \cong 1)$. Thus,

1. If the equipment was operating at its maximum practical rate, a worker's incentive pay would be his base rate (say $4.00/hour) times $^{1.379}/_1$ or $5.52 per hour.

2. If it took 1.1 hours to carry out one standard hour's production at the same base rate, the incentive rate would be $^{1.379}/_{1.1} \times \$4.00$; or $1.254 \times \$4.00 \cong \$5.02$ per hour.

Setting 137.9 per cent as the maximum possible percentage of the hourly base rate that could be earned provided a system in which workers could earn a fairly substantial incentive (as opposed to, say, one set at only 105 per cent of their base rate), while at the same time providing incentive standards which were not too loose.

As with traditional incentives, establishing these standards involves subjective judgment, which may lead to haggling over standards. Again as with traditional incentives, a guarantee exists so that workers are not paid less than their base rate. Finally, it is frequently crews rather than individuals who are paid on incentive because of the close interdependence among different automated processes in any particular operation. In fact, in some cases, a whole operation will be on a single plant-wide incentive.

The Effectiveness of Wage Incentives

The effectiveness of wage incentives has been controversial for many years. It has been argued that incentives contribute to higher labor costs, which in some cases have even led to plant closings. On the other hand, "numerous case studies are available of companies which claim to have cut their costs by 25 to 63 percent through incentive systems, while increasing employee earnings by 10 to 70 percent."[16] With respect to equipment utilization incentives, in the steel rolling mill operation described previously, for example, after a "drive by management with the cooperation of the union to improve performance," performance in the mills went up to an average of 127 per cent of standard.[17] To what extent any increases in productivity are due to incentives per se, however, is an interesting question. Nash and Carroll have indicated that part of productivity increases associated with the introduction of an incentive plan may also be attributable to the concurrent improvement in work methods, and the establishment of specific work goals in terms of standards.[18]

The success of any wage incentive plan also depends on a number of contingencies. As we indicated earlier, the work must be measurable, and a relatively stable system where job methods are not constantly changing is most conducive to the establishment of incentives. Further, it is extremely important that management-employee relations are good. Although this observation does not seem very profound, the example of productivity increases in steel rolling mills indicates very pointedly the effect of such relations. Also, there must be: (1) a perceived relationship between effort (or attention in automated operations) and output, (2) carefully set incentive standards so that the system will not lead to serious inequities, and (3) a setting of standards so that potential incentives are high enough to be worthwhile to workers.

In many cases, employees will not resist incentives outright, but will engage in some output restrictions. That is, they will produce "above standard" but not work as hard as they might. There are at least four reasons for such behavior. In traditional incentives where physical effort is important, employees may not work as hard as they might because of simple fatigue. For this, among other reasons, some individuals have proposed an incentive plan in which there is an increasing rate of incentive reward as production increases above standard rather than a linear one-for-one relationship as shown in Figure 10–5.[19] Further, there is a belief in our culture that more experienced individuals should be paid more than less experienced ones. In many professions, this assumption is valid up to a point. The doctor, for example, gains more knowledge and experience as he practices longer. In jobs in which heavy physical effort is required, however, it may not be possible for many experienced and older workers to "keep up" with the less experienced but younger members doing the same kind of work. In such cases, work groups may apply pressures on their less experienced members not to produce so much that they will make the lower production of more experienced workers look bad. Another problem is that workers may be afraid if they produce too much they will work themselves out of a job. This fear may be real or imagined, for in some companies all additional output induced by wage incentives may be sold, while in others, increased output will result in layoffs occurring. Finally, workers may fear that their standards may be made tighter if they produce too much. In fact, management often used to tighten standards indiscriminately, and this fear is sometimes a realistic one, even today. Further, if a standard has unintentionally been set extremely loosely, management may have no other alternative than to restudy the job, because such loose rates may well create inequities and protests from other workers with tighter standards.

In light of these observations, some comments are in order concerning trends in the use of wage incentives. In the early and mid-1960's, many observers believed that automation would make work so machine-paced that there would be little direct worker effort, and that wage incentives would disappear. Work incentives are declining, but it is difficult to determine by how much. One reason for this is that it is difficult to compare different studies regarding the use of incentives because they have not all used comparable data. One report, however, which directly compared U.S. Bureau of Labor Statistics (BLS) wage studies undertaken both during the period 1963–1968 and the period 1969–1973 in 39 selected industries sheds some light on this subject:[20]

1. The total number of production and related workers included in the 1969–1973 studies increased from 4.94 million to 5.13 million, while the total number of employees on incentives decreased from 1.34 million to 1.22 million. Thus, the total number of incentive-paid workers as a percent of the total number of production workers decreased from 27 to 24 percent of the total number of production and related workers.

2. Industries (generally labor intensive) that used incentives considerably in the 1963–1968 period (e.g., hosiery) generally did so in the

1969–1973 period, although in a number of cases the percentage usage declined. Conversely, highly mechanized capital intensive industries such as cigarettes which were low users in the 1963–1968 period continued to be so in 1969–1973.

3. Automation was directly responsible for a lower usage of incentives in the previously heavy user cigar industry but, on the other hand, the percentage of total workers who were on incentives increased by 14 in basic steel. This is what one might well expect from our previous discussion of the equipment utilization incentives in this automated industry.

In summary, wage incentives have played an important role in American industry for many years. With the advent of automation and other factors, such as poor administration, their usage has declined. With over 1.2 million workers on incentives of about 5.13 million covered in the 1969–1973 period in just 39 selected industry studies, however, it appears that wage incentives will continue to play a role in American industry, especially under the contingencies discussed.

SUGGESTION SYSTEMS

The first suggestion system in the United States was introduced at the Yale and Towne Manufacturing Company in Connecticut in 1880, and one of the oldest of the successful continuing suggestion systems was developed by the National Cash Register Company in 1894.[21]

The number of plans increased especially during and after World War II. In 1942 the National Association of Suggestion Systems (NASS) was founded. The number of plans estimated to be in operation in the 1950's was around 8,000;[22] by the 1970's it was estimated that 80 per cent of the nation's 500 largest corporations had suggestion systems of one sort or another.[23] In spite of this growth, numerous suggestion systems have been abandoned. One observer in 1946, for example, estimated that "at least 90 percent of the suggestion systems installed during the past 25 years have failed."[24]

With respect to the value of suggestion systems, NASS reported that in 1973 its member firms averaged 40 suggestions/100 employees; 29.6 per cent of these suggestions were adopted; the average award per accepted suggestion was $78.65; and $5.70 in savings was obtained for every $1 spent to run these systems.[25] Further, based on this 5.70:1 ratio, it was reported in 1975 that projecting "aggregate total savings of all 1,000 NASS members, the figure is a whopping $470 million — and that's first-year savings alone."[26]

In the following discussion, we will define a suggestion system and its objectives, discuss the three basic decisions that must be made if a system is adopted, and indicate the conditions under which suggestion plans seem most effective.

Suggestion Systems: A Definition

Essentially, a suggestion system represents a contract on the part of management to buy ideas from employees. A suggestion system provides the three essentials of a legal contract: (1) an offer (publicized) by management, (2) an acceptance when an employee submits a suggestion, and (3) a consideration represented by the reward given for an accepted idea.

The statistics presented previously indicate that from the company's point of view suggestion systems may contribute substantially to profits. With regard to the individual, the monetary awards received may serve to meet many needs. The opportunity for an individual to be rewarded for being creative may contribute to his self-actualization needs, and the recognition given to successful suggestions (especially when the award is large) may help satisfy esteem needs.

Eligibility

The basic notion behind suggestions is to reward creativity above and beyond the responsibilities of the individual's job. For this reason, cash awards are usually given only to nonmanagement employees, since it is the job of managers (and professionals) to be creative, and they will be rewarded for creativity by salary increases.[27]

Criterion

Two types of suggestions are acceptable under practically all systems, those which result in the firm realizing tangible savings, and those which are good ideas and accepted but provide no tangible savings. As an example of the latter, cement posts 3 to 4 feet high were used in one firm's parking lot to separate parking areas. At dusk, they were very difficult to see, and several employees damaged car doors or fenders by scraping against the posts. One employee suggested that the posts be painted bright orange for better visibility, and the company accepted the idea as a good one even though it received no net savings from the idea.

The employee was given a nominal award for this suggestion.

Rewards

Three aspects of rewards are often included in suggestion systems. First, to foster good employee-management relations, many firms give minimum awards of $10 to $15 for intangible savings ideas and, in some cases, small tangible savings ideas. Second, many firms establish a maximum award that they will pay for any one suggestion (e.g., $10,000) in order to limit their liability. Probably most critical is the award formula for suggestions falling within these two limits. Most frequently, firms agree to pay some specified percentage for each suggestion ranging from 10 to 20 per cent of the *net* savings realized from it for the *first* year. By net savings, we mean those realized after any necessary investments have to be made. Materials and equipment purchased to implement an idea "should be prorated in the award calculation at the same amortization rate used by the accounting department on the company books."[28] For example, if an initial investment of $10,000 with an economic life of 10 years is required to implement a suggestion that will save $5000 in labor costs the first year and the award rate is 20 per cent, the award for the suggestion would be:

First year's savings	$5,000
− 1/10 of the investment (straight line depreciation)	$\underline{1,000}$
	$4,000
× 20 per cent	= $ 800 award

Some individuals believe that it is inequitable to reward individuals for only the first year's savings, and some firms have instituted supplemental awards to cover savings after the first year.[29]

Contingencies

As indicated, some suggestion systems have been very successful, while others have been abandoned. We will now turn to some of the more important conditions that contribute to the effectiveness of suggestion systems.

Organizational Size and Stability

Neither organizational size nor stability appears to affect the success of suggestion systems in the way they have with many of the other formalized systems discussed so far. Suggestion systems do not require huge expenditures to develop and maintain, and hence can be made effective with the more limited resources of smaller firms. For example, in one study covering 228 firms in five states, it was reported that in production operations, 43.5 per cent of firms with less than 250 employees had a "continuing routine usage" of suggestion systems.[30]

With respect to stability, the very essence of suggestion systems is to foster change — by developing new creative solutions for problems that will modify organizational behavior and methods to more fully meet firm objectives. Thus, suggestion systems might be viewed more positively in dynamic organizations, where there is a constant need to change, than in stable organizations, where change is less necessary to perform effectively.

Managerial Support and Employee Relations

As with all personnel programs, suggestion systems need top management's support. Also required is the support of first-line supervisors (and other lower level managers) to encourage their employees to make suggestions. Unfortunately, many first-line supervisors have not perceived suggestions from their subordinates as a positive contribution to the firm, but rather as a *threat* to themselves and have discouraged employee suggestions. Underlying this perceived threat is the notion that if their subordinates come up with ideas that they have not thought of themselves, others may think that they are not performing well. To help overcome this problem, organizations have often done two things. First, they have included as one factor to be considered in the performance appraisal of each supervisor the number and quality of suggestions submitted by his employees. To the extent that favorable supervisory appraisals contribute to higher merit raises, those supervisors who can stimulate good suggestion performance in their departments will be financially rewarded. Second, first-line supervisors and their immediate superiors are often appointed as members of the company's suggestion committee, which we will discuss later. This participation is aimed at gaining supervisor involvement and support for the suggestion system.

Also critical to the effectiveness of suggestion systems is relatively good management-employee relations. A very clear example of the importance of this variable may be illustrated by an experience in one plant.

A new and well-thought through suggestion system was instituted in September of one year; and in the ensuing two months the number of suggestions began increasing. Then, management announced that the company was going to move work performed by about one fourth of the plant's production employees to another plant in the south. With the impending layoff of the workers who performed these jobs, considerable hostility was expressed by the employees towards management. The number of suggestions then started dwindling until their number was virtually nil.

Administration of Suggestion Systems

Extremely important to the effectiveness of suggestion systems is that they be administered well. For conceptual purposes, we can view administration as encompassing two basic facets: promoting the plan and handling suggestions received from employees. In large firms these two aspects of administration will usually be handled by a suggestion director (a member of the personnel department), and with smaller companies a personnel manager (if there is one) or another member of management. In the following discussion, we will talk in terms of a single manufacturing plant large enough to have a suggestion director.

Promotion. There are many different practices that can be followed to effectively promote a suggestion system. Upon initiation of any system, it is necessary to spell out to employees all the rules of the plan with respect to eligibility and award structure. Further, continued promotion of the plan rather than "periodic bursts" is considered essential for its effectiveness, along with dignified, "varied publicity, *without* cheap ballyhoo."[31] In some cases, periodic contests or other types of special promotions are held, which have been shown to increase the number of suggestions. In 1962, for example, a month-long suggestion campaign was developed to celebrate General Motors' suggestion system's twentieth anniversary. At its Delco Remy plant in Indiana there were various promotions such as giving each employee a chance to win merchandise prizes for each suggestion accepted during the month. During the campaign, the number of suggestions submitted increased from a normal 200 to 2000 per week.[32]

In spite of the effectiveness of campaigns, there is a tendency for employees to return to their "normal" suggestion behavior after the campaign has ended. Aside from such campaigns, of considerable importance is giving publicity to suggestion awards that have been made, especially substantial ones, e.g., photographing the plant manager presenting a $500 suggestion award check to an employee for inclusion in both the plant newspaper and local news media.

Suggestions. Processing employee suggestions is a multistage decision process, the highlights of which are illustrated in Figure 10–7. Once an employee has an idea and has decided to submit it for consideration, it is transmitted (via a suggestion box, personally, or in-company mail) to the suggestion director. The director:

1. Has the suggestion immediately dated so that if another identical

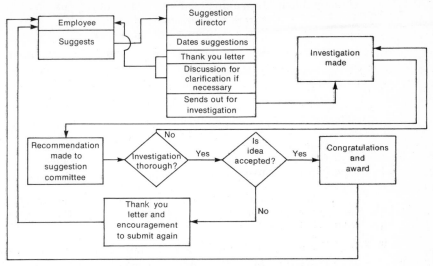

Figure 10-7 *Suggestion systems administration.*

suggestion is made, the employee with the one submitted first would be the person eligible for any award.

2. Acknowledges, with a thank you letter, receipt of the suggestion so that the employee is aware that management has received his idea and appreciates his effort.

3. May go to the suggester and try to clarify the idea, if the suggestion is poorly phrased and not possible to understand completely.

4. Transmits the suggestion to those in the organization who would have the greatest expertise to investigate the merits of the suggestion. For example, an engineer and the supervisor of the department in which the suggestion was made may be given the responsibility for evaluation of a particular suggestion.

Those investigating various suggestions will submit them with recommendations to the suggestion committee, which meets periodically (once or twice a month). The suggestion committee may send any recommendations back to the investigators if it believes a thorough analysis of a suggestion has not been made. Otherwise, it will make the final decision as to whether to accept or reject the suggestion, and the employee who submitted the idea will be appropriately notified. If the idea is rejected, a thank you letter, explaining explicitly the reasons why the suggestion was not adopted, and an encouragement to continue submitting decisions are in order. These simple but important steps can mean much in terms of conveying managerial credibility to the system, i.e., that management is serious about suggestions and does a thorough job in processing them. If the idea is accepted, a thank you and congratulatory letter along with a check for the award is transmitted to the employee. As indicated previously, giving publicity to making of the award is an effective means for promoting the system. To cite the old saying: "Success breeds success."

The *composition* of the suggestion committee is an important administrative variable. In one plant of about 2000 employees, for example:

1. The plant manager was on the committee and attended virtually all meetings to explicitly show that top management was behind the system.

2. General foremen (i.e., supervisors of the plant's first-line supervisors) were rotated on a six-month basis on the committee. This was explicitly done to involve middle management to gain their support of the system along the lines suggested earlier.

3. The suggestion director was also on the committee. In addition, two engineers were included in the membership to provide expertise in technical matters.

With such a composition, this committee not only possessed expertise with which to evaluate suggestions, but the plant manager's presence and personal involvement helped prevent unduly slow processing of suggestions by supervisors, who, among other reasons, may have felt threatened by the system.

Other Contingencies

Several other variables may affect the success of suggestion plans. In some cases, if the firm's demand is inelastic, suggesters may well suggest themselves out of a job by coming up with ideas that call for the replacement of manual effort by machines. When the company also has a wage incentive system, an employee may develop an improvement to his machine and earn more if he can successfully hide it from his supervisor than he could from a suggestion award. Finally, suggestion systems may be more successful, depending on the kinds of people working for an organization. Some research has shown, for example, that certain personal factors such as "creativity" contribute to an individual's innovativeness in a suggestion system, and that certain structural variables in the work situation such as the job he does neither "constrain nor sustain" this innovativeness.[33]

EXECUTIVE INCENTIVES

Special incentives for top executives and other upper level managers and professionals have been used successfully for many years. The well-known industrialist and former president of General Motors, Alfred P. Sloan, Jr., believed that his firm's bonus plan was a very important ingredient in its growth and success.[34]

In this section, we will discuss some executive incentive plans from each of two basic types — those providing a cash reward and those providing an equity-based award. In the cash reward group, we will cover bonuses, and deferred bonuses and compensation. In the equity-based category we will consider stock options and a relatively new approach, performance shares. Both of these provide recipients with some degree of ownership in the firm. In our discussion of cash and equity-based rewards, we will consider federal income tax legislation for the different types of incentives, which has varied in favorability to executives at different times as tax laws have been modified. We will use the terms "executive" and "upper level manager" synonymously to refer to company presidents, vice presidents, division heads, and other managers or professionals in organizations who have considerable decision-making responsibilities.

In the previous chapter, we indicated that the success of any type of compensation depends to a considerable extent on the existence of a clear connection between performance and reward. The manner in which any type of executive incentive functions, quite naturally has an important impact on this connection, as we will discuss later. Further, some authorities believe that certain industries are more suitable for executive incentives than others. Patton, for example, has contended that performance to which executive rewards may be connected most easily prevails to the greatest degree where the following conditions exist:

1. Many short-run executive decisions affect profit, such as in the 12-month automobile model cycle.
2. Decentralization is typical and individual managers have "full profit responsibility" for different divisions of the firm.
3. Quantitative tools for judging executive performance are available (e.g., market-share data and economic analysis.)[35]

As reported in 1972, almost every firm in the following industries had executive incentives: automotive, retail chains, department stores, pharmaceuticals, and chemicals.[36]

We will now discuss both cash and equity incentives together with respect to the first two basic managerial decisions concerning incentives shown in Figure 10–1 — eligibility and criterion for reward. We will then consider separately the reward given for each specific type of executive incentive. In doing so, we will examine both its motivational value and cost-benefit effectiveness.

Eligibility

Some firms have extended bonuses and stock options down to lower level managers, but generally these incentives are reserved for upper level managers. For example, under stock op-tion plans as reported in 1973, "those participating usually com-prise between 0.5% and 1.0%" of the organization's total employees.[37] Further, it has been argued that if "more than 1% of a company's total employment is included in an incentive pro-gram, the credibility of individual performance evaluations tends to suffer."[38] This is because there is more likely to be a weak visible link between lower level managers' decisions and com-pany success (such as good profit levels).

Criteria

Once a firm decides which executives are to be included in either a cash- or equity-based incentive plan, the criteria upon which the reward will be based must be determined. In develop-ing executive incentives, many different criteria have been uti-lized. The most widely used criteria for executive bonus plans are overall corporate profits and individual performance, which is generally based on a judgmental performance appraisal.[39] With stock options, the criteria may vary widely — constituting a form of bonus, being related to the executive's base salary, or simply included as a part of the firm's employment contract with the individual.[40] With performance shares, most firms have utilized cumulative growth in earnings per share of the firm's stock (EPS) as a basic criterion.[41]

Reward Systems

Current Bonus

Current bonuses for executives generally are a function of both individual performance and corporate profits. The basis for determining how much of corporate profits in any given year should be allotted to executive bonuses is usually a formula, which may be the same each year or modified from year to year.[42] Two basic kinds of formulas involve relating the incentives to a straight percentage of profits or basing them on a percentage of profit in excess of a specified return on the stockholder's invest-ment.[43]

With respect to cost-benefit analysis, current bonuses have exactly the same after tax implications to both the firm and its executives as salaries. The firm will be able to deduct the bonus as a business expense with the corporate tax rate (48 per cent) and the individual will be taxed using the same federal income tax schedule as for his current salary. One important difference between a bonus and a salary raise exists, however. If profit (or individual) performance is good in one year but becomes poor in succeeding years, the individual would receive no bonuses in those years. It is usually very difficult, however, to take away a salary increase earned by an executive in one year in any future years.

How effective are executive bonuses as stimulators of higher levels of performance? Several contingencies help provide some answers to this question. First, the bonus must be large enough to be significant. It has been argued "that a bonus that amounts to less than 15 percent of salary is hardly worth the bother."[44] One can question this argument, however, as many individuals might be happy with a 5 or 10 per cent bonus.

Also of importance is the nature of the performance-reward link. If an executive can see clearly how his performance will affect company profits, he will tend to be more highly motivated. Further, there will tend to be fewer perceptions of inequity among other members of the firm who do not receive a bonus.

Deferred Bonuses and Compensation

In some companies, provisions have been made to pay bonuses to executives, not when they earn them, but later, usually, after they have retired. A top executive, for example, may be given a $100,000 bonus to be deferred, so that he receives $20,000 of it in each of the five years following his retirement. One basic objective for providing such deferred compensation is to decrease the individual's tax burden by postponing the receipt of some compensation until after retirement when he no longer receives a large salary from the firm. Maximum marginal federal income tax rates just prior to 1969, for example, were 70 per cent, so that deferring an executive's income to postretirement years might save him considerable sums in taxes.[45] Some major changes affecting compensation, however, were made in both the 1969 and the 1976 Tax Reform Acts. In the 1969 Act, for example, a new 50 per cent maximum marginal income tax rate on "earned income" was established. Earned income generally referred to pay received for actual services rendered as opposed to that received as returns on investments, which was and still is considered "ordinary income." The whole question of just what differentiated "earned income" from "ordinary income" is complex. The important point is that deferred compensation under the 1969 Tax Reform Act was generally taxed as ordinary income with the maximum 70 per cent marginal rate, whereas if an executive had been given the bonus in the year he earned it, he would have been subjected to only the 50 per cent maximum marginal earned income rate. This made deferred compensation less attractive to highly paid executives than previously. The Tax Reform Act of 1976, however, while maintaining the 70 per cent maximum marginal tax on ordinary income, provided that deferred compensation also generally be treated at the maximum 50 per cent marginal federal income tax rate. (There are exceptions, however.) This change made deferred compensation once again taxable at the same rates as current bonuses (and salaries) and more attractive to executives. The 1976 Act also changed the name of the income subjected to the maximum 50 per cent marginal rate from earned income to "personal service income."

It is difficult to make any broad generalizations as to the cost-benefit effectiveness of deferred compensation. This is because from the executive's viewpoint, the

...exact benefit of deferred compensation depends upon a combination of factors: years to retirement, years to separation from the firm, current salary and tax bracket, anticipated income at time of retirement or separation from the firm, and present and anticipated interest rates.[46]

Also, if the deferred compensation is *guaranteed* to a manager, it is taxable in the year that it is guaranteed. From the firm's point of view: it can invest and earn a return on executives' current earnings which do not have to be paid out at present under a deferred program and can then deduct any deferred compensation as a business expense in the year it is paid out. Further, the deferred compensation does not have to be guaranteed by the company.

One can raise a question as to how effective any deferred plans may be, since, even though there may be a link from performance to reward, the link is hurt by a time lag. The reward may be provided so many years in the future that the link is barely appreciable by the employee today. Further, as is also true of other deferred plans, deferred compensation may induce executives to stay with the company until retirement. This may be dysfunctional, since in some cases, mediocre executives who would have greater difficulties finding a position with another organization may be the ones motivated to stay with the firm.

Stock Options: Qualified and Nonqualified

A stock option is a financial arrangement in which executives are rewarded by being given the option to buy company stock at a later date at a price established when the option is granted. Hopefully, the value of the stock will appreciate so that the executive can realize financial gains on the stock at a later time. A basic notion behind the stock option is that owning company stock will induce executives not only to look at short-term profits but the firm's performance in the longer run.

Two basic types of stock options have been popular from January 1964 into the 1970's. With *qualified* stock options, gains the executive realizes from the appreciation of the stock's value after being given such an option (as long as he meets numerous restrictions concerning how he can deal with his options) have been taxed only at the more favorable *capital gains* rate, rather than at either the ordinary or personal service federal income tax rates. Capital gains are taxed at only 50 per cent of ordinary income up to the maximum ordinary income tax rate of 70 per cent, with the following exception: Capital gains up to $50,000 in any year are taxed at half of the ordinary income tax rate. If an individual's capital gains exceed $50,000, he is taxed at a flat rate of 25 per cent on the first $50,000, and then at 50 per cent of the ordinary income rate for capital gains exceeding $50,000 up to the maximum ordinary income tax rate of 70 per cent. Capital gains large enough to exceed this rate continue to be taxed at 35 per cent (or 50 per cent of the 70 per cent maximum ordinary income tax rate). Although capital gains is often spoken of as a separate tax, generally individuals with such gains not exceeding $50,000 in any year do not figure it apart from their regular income tax. Rather, they simply include in their taxable income 50 per cent of their long term gains. For example, if an individual had an income in 1977 of $20,000 and sold some property that he had owned for several years for $5,000 more than he paid for it, he would add 50 per cent of the $5,000, or $2,500 to his $20,000 income for federal income tax purposes.

The second type of option is *nonqualified*. Although executives hope to be able to realize financial gains from nonqualified stock options, any gains received when this type of option is exercised do not qualify for the favorable capital gains treatment but are considered as earned income, and hence, do fall under the 50 per cent maximum tax on personal service income. On the other hand, many of the restrictions of the qualified options are absent, and the executive has more flexibility in financial maneuvering with his options.

From the 1950's until 1969, qualified stock options were industry's principal long-term compensation device.[47] In 1969, however, the Tax Reform Act, with its 50 per cent maximum tax on earned income, narrowed the difference between capital gains and current executive income, thus taking much away from the favorableness of qualifed options. Further, the stock market slides that took place in the late 1960's and into the 1970's left many executives' unexercised options worthless and gains on already exercised options wiped out. As a result, the use of qualified options declined. According to one authority: ''Whereas 93% of large companies relied on qualified options as their sole executive stock plan in 1969, only 49% did in 1972."[48] As a consequence of the new tax provisions and stock market slumps, a number of companies turned to nonqualified options during the period from 1969 to 1976.

In 1976, qualified stock options were killed by the Tax Reform Act of that year. Basically this law:

1. Blocked the establishment of any qualified stock option plan after May 20, 1976.
2. Provided that qualified stock options still outstanding, but granted under a written plan prior to May 21, 1976 could still be treated as qualified, but had to be exercised by May 21, 1981 to be treated as qualified and receive favorable capital gains tax treatment.[49]

This change in the 1976 law surprised many individuals, and there is considerable debate as to how executive compensation packages should be remodeled. Most "experts" agreed in late 1976 to the possibility that a new tax law might change tax advantages within a year or so,[50] further complicating firms' executive incentive planning processes. According to *Business Week* in 1977, "the nonqualified option is the most frequently considered compensation alternative" and deferred compensation was considered favorable by some, since the 1976 law for the first time added it to taxable income at the maximum 50 per cent marginal rate.[51] Additionally, even before the passage of the 1976 Tax Reform Act, firms had developed other alternative executive incentive approaches.

In light of this above analysis, how may stock options be evaluated as a compensation device? From a cost-benefit point of view, qualified options were rated in 1970 by Hettenhouse as either 15 or 16 lowest (depending on salary) of 17 possible compensation alternatives available to companies, and nonqualified options were rated either 10, 11, or 12.[52] Theoretically, both types of options have been intended to provide an incentive to increase long-term stock values, which is congruent with the objectives of the firm's owners (its stockholders). From a motivational point of view, however, there is often a relatively weak connection between executive performance and reward. This is because it often may not be company profits as much as the vagaries of the stock market that determine the price of the firm's stock and hence the value of the reward. The restrictions placed on qualified options have limited the ability of executives to exercise their options at times most favorable to them in light of stock market conditions — all qualified stock options had to be exercised in sequence of receipt within five years after the option was granted. Nonqualified options, on the other hand, are not subject to these sequential exercise restrictions, and the executive has 10 years in which to exercise this type of option. This makes him much freer to gain appreciation on his stock since he is less subject to the short-term vagaries of the stock market than the holder of a qualified option.

In spite of these limitations, many firms may continue to use nonqualified options for some time because other firms do and because they believe that they cannot recruit top executives without being competitive. One report in 1977, for example, indicated that nonqualified options were being used by 59 per cent of 587 large companies using extra executive compensation other than cash bonuses.[53]

Performance Shares[54]

The concept of performance shares is simple, although, as with many compensation techniques, its mechanics are complex. Its first adoption was in April, 1971 by CBS.[55] Basically, with a performance shares plan

. . . awards of company stock are made to executives at the beginning of a period that extends for several years, to be earned out over that period if a predetermined company performance objective is attained and if the executive has remained with the company.[56]

Unlike stock obtained with options, performance shares cost the executive nothing, making them favorable under both good and poor stock market conditions.

A performance shares plan provides a clearer direct connection between executive performance and rewards than do stock options plans. Although the value of the reward will be partially a function of the vagaries of the stock market, a direct performance-reward link exists, because the executive will be rewarded only if company goals are met. Normally, the company objective incorporated into performance shares plans is cumulative growth in stockholders' earnings per share (EPS).

The length of performance shares reward periods vary and, theoretically, should be related to the decision/profit cycle of the firm. Quite common are periods of from four to six years. If the reward period is too short, it will not focus attention on longer range company goals, while periods that are too long will remove one of the major benefits of performance shares — the link between performance and reward.

With respect to the EPS criterion and the size of performance shares rewards:

1. Executives generally receive no additional reward if the cumulative EPS growth objective is exceeded.
2. If this objective is not fully met but is achieved to a certain extent, scaled down rewards may be given.
3. A common range for the cumulative EPS growth objective is between 9 and 15 percent per year.

4. Awards in some companies "have been on the order of 100% of salary every two years at the chief executive officer level, scaled down to 30% or so of salary for the lowest level managers participating in the plan."[57]

It is common to pay the executive his award 50 per cent in stock and 50 per cent in cash. This split gives the executive an amount in cash needed to pay taxes on the equity reward. Thus, performance shares is not a completely equity-based plan, since cash rewards are also given. For example, if an executive receives 1000 performance shares when the company's stock is valued at $40, and the value of the stock increases to $60/share at the time of payout, he would be given 500 shares at $60, and $30,000 in cash. With performance shares, as opposed to stock options, the executive is given a cash reward and therefore does not need to finance the exercise of an option. With performance shares the executive is taxed at the maximum marginal 50 per cent personal service income rate, and the payout is fully deductible by the company when it is made (at its corporate 48 per cent tax rate).

There are certain contingencies under which performance shares seem to be most effective. In discussing the degree to which a firm is dynamic rather than static, we have often seen systems to be less effective when too much change exists (e.g., wage incentives). With respect to performance shares, both too static and too dynamic growth conditions can pose problems. If there is little cumulative EPS growth, there will be few if any rewards available, and performance shares are not likely to be effective as an incentive. Conversely, if there is too much growth, which sends a firm's stock price skyrocketing, the plan might be quite costly for the firm. For this reason, most companies have placed a maximum limit of the values of each performance share at the time of its distribution. Typically, a "performance share's worth can rise no more than 100% in a four-year plan."[58]

Another contingency is that in some companies it would be difficult to identify "appropriate and reasonable" long-term performance objectives.[59] This situation would weaken the performance-reward link. Finally, considerable criticism has surrounded performance shares by their provision of rewards to executives in periods of stock market decline when the stockholders themselves are far from being rewarded. Although the executive's reward would be less in such periods, he would still receive a reward as long as the EPS goal has been met.

CAFETERIA COMPENSATION

Since the 1960's individuals have advocated that employees be given some choice in the form of compensation they are to receive. Such a choice approach has been referred to as "flexible," "cafeteria," "supermarket" or "smorgasbord" compensation. Actually, many companies provided some choice situations before this time. For example, in the late 1950's one large retailing chain gave its employees the voluntary option of purchasing very extensive medical insurance plan coverage to supplement the basic insurance package provided at no cost to all employees. What is being advocated today is extending choice situations from choosing among a few employee insurance benefits to letting the employee choose much of his total compensation package. This alternative is not yet feasible because of certain Internal Revenue Service regulations. Further, providing each employee with thousands of different compensation choices would present prohibitive administrative problems and associated costs.

The basic idea behind cafeteria or flexible compensation is that "different people are satisfied and motivated by different things" and that participation in the design of one's own compensation "leads to a higher level of commitment to the result of the effort."[60]

In our discussion of cafeteria plans, we will examine the eligibility, criterion, and reward decisions, and then discuss the advantages and limitations of this approach.

Eligibility, Criterion, and Reward

Eligibility

Some cafeteria programs are designed especially for executives. This is true, for example, with General Electric's split dollar life insurance plan adopted for top executives in 1969.[61] In other cases, however, eligibility is much wider. In 1974, for instance, the Systems Group of TRW, Inc., started a cafeteria plan with almost 50 per cent of those eligible being "blue-collar, clerical, or other hourly employees."[62]

Criterion

Cafeteria plans are not strictly incentives in the sense that some production standard, the adoption of ideas submitted, or a profit goal is involved. Rather, the employee obtains a reward by simply choosing the form of compensation benefits he wants from among those made available. The company may pay the whole cost of the benefit or the employee may be required to pay for certain benefits desired.

Reward

Rewards in cafeteria compensation are the alternatives chosen from among available forms of compensation. However, under current Internal Revenue Service rulings, the scope of viable tax-sheltered awards is limited, thus restricting the firm's compensation strategy space and ability to more extensively improve the cost/benefit aspects. With respect to IRS rulings:

> The IRS has generally stated that in instances where an employee has the option of determining whether company expenditures will go toward direct or indirect compensation items, he is in constructive receipt of the cash equivalent and shall be taxed on that amount whether it is received in cash or not. Alternatives to this exist only when employees pay for benefits through after-tax dollars, agree to a salary decrease and have the company divert the amount of this decrease toward benefits, or eliminate the cash option and retain the trade-off in the benefit area only.[63]

In light of this constraint, we will now proceed to evaluate cafeteria compensation.

Cafeteria Compensation: An Evaluation

A number of criticisms have been raised concerning cafeteria compensation. We will examine these, and in doing so, consider their validity with respect to the well-known TRW cafeteria plan. Our observations drawn from the TRW plan experience are intended to be suggestive and may not provide accurate portrayals of other plans. We use it because little evaluative research is presently available on cafeteria plans.

It has been argued that employees are afraid to make benefit decisions that may come back to haunt them.[64] For example, an individual might reduce his medical insurance while increasing his life insurance and then incur very high medical benefits, for which he would not be covered. Somewhat relatedly, some research has shown that employee preferences may change rapidly in as short a time period as six months.[65] In the TRW plan, neither of these concerns proved valid. At the TRW Systems Group, the cafeteria plan was set up as follows:

1. Three types of insurance were included — medical, life and accident.
2. For each type the employee could retain present coverage, take more, or take less.
3. If increased coverage was desired, the individual would have to pay for the insurance at group rates.
4. If he took less, he could not take cash in return — he received a paper credit that he had to use to buy more insurance in one of the other categories.[66] This approach was used because of the IRS ruling regarding taxation if direct cash benefits are taken under cafeteria plans as indicated above.

With this system, employees were not afraid to make decisions and more than 80 per cent of them modified their benefits, with most adding some kind of coverage.[67] In this plan, there were three medical plans (low, current and improved), eight life insurance plans (low, current and six improved), and 18 supplementary accidental death and dismemberment plans not available previously. This represented a total of 432 different choices available to employees. With regard to the stability of employee preferences at the end of the first year, when employees had their first annual option to revise their benefits, fewer than 8 per cent made changes, and most of those changing chose a new medical option that had been added to the plan.[68]

Another question raised concerning cafeteria plans is that they may be costly to establish, administer, and update (annually, as with TRW). This appears to be a valid concern. Setting up the TRW plan cost $250,000, and in the first year administrative costs were approximately $50,000. Together, these approximate $300,000 total costs represented a cost of around $25/employee. Further, these costs were held down because the plan was coordinated with the Systems Group's computer-based information file. With respect to extending this plan to other smaller TRW units it was reported that "the benefits plan is impractical at small units without a computer-based manpower system."[69]

Concern has also been raised that high-risk individuals will choose benefits most valuable to them and, thus, the cost of the system will increase considerably. For example, an individual who has a chronic, high-cost medication problem would choose to obtain as favorable medical benefits as possible. This did not happen at TRW, and, in fact, with many employees increasing their coverage the "winning carrier picked up an additional $2 million in premiums."[70]

In spite of the fact that many of the concerns raised did not occur in the TRW Systems Group plan, there is little, if any, evidence that participation in cafeteria plans increases either employee satisfaction or motivation. "It remains to be demonstrated that satisfying pay preferences has any effect on employee work behavior."[71] This is logical because the all important performance-reward link is missing from cafeteria plans. Employees in the TRW plan received the benefits without having to put forth any higher levels of performance.

Additionally, because of the IRS regulations, cost/benefit improvements in terms of minimizing the summation of taxes for companies and individuals is limited. It may be possible, however, to provide an individual with more benefits that he prefers at no extra cost to the company (except administrative costs). For example, in one study of executive pay preferences, it was found that life insurance was very unattractive to executives — most executives seemed to want to "arrange on their own for what they consider adequate insurance coverage."[72] Without costing the company any more and without running into IRS tax problems, a firm could provide employees a choice of taking a smaller life insurance benefit and substituting some other benefit such as a higher pension. This would not affect either employee or company taxes, and might provide more satisfaction, although not necessarily more motivation. Further, additional benefits such as those provided by TRW Systems can be purchased more cheaply at group rates through the firm, so that even though employees have to pay for such benefits with after-tax dollars, a favorable cost-benefit situation exists.

In retrospect, it is not likely that any completely flexible cafeteria plans will be widely adopted in the United States in the near future. What seems to be emerging, however, are restricted situations in which employees voluntarily pay for more benefits, as in the TRW (and General Electric) plans.

SUMMARY

In this chapter, we have looked at four basic types of incentive plans used in industry today. We have examined eligibility, criteria, and reward decisions; contingencies, such as organizational size and dynamics; performance-reward links, which we believe are critical to motivation; trends in incentive usage; and cost/benefit analysis. A summary table illustrating many of these variables with respect to each of the plans examined is illustrated in Figure 10–8. In the following chapter, we will move on to examine system incentives utilizing a conceptual decision-making framework similar to that presented in this chapter.

DISCUSSION AND STUDY QUESTIONS

1. Which would each of the five following prefer — loose or tight work standards?
   a. Top management
   b. First-line supervisors
   c. Production workers
   d. The time study engineers
   e. The president of a firm's local union
2. Phil works under a guaranteed piecework system, in which his hourly base rate is $5; he receives $.045 for every piece of part A he turns out; and $.075 for every piece of part B. On Friday, he worked 5 hours producing part A and turned out 667 pieces, and 3 hours producing part B, turning out 210 pieces. On the same day, his friend Fran, who works in a plant across the street under a standard hour plan with the same hourly base rate of $5/hour worked eight hours, turned

Plan	Success Contingencies		Effort-Reward Link	Trend	Cost/Benefit
	Firm Size	Stability			
Wage incentives	Medium-large	Stable tasks	Strong	Declining	Current cash
Suggestion systems	Any	Dynamic in outlook	Strong	Holding strong	Current cash
Executive and professional compensation					
1. Current bonus	Any	Growth—good company profits	Varies	No great change	Current cash
2. Deferred compensation	Any	Depends on criterion	Weak	May be increasing	Varies on income—now subject to maximum 50% marginal rate*
3. Qualified option	Any	Growth in stock value	Weak	Killed by 1976 Tax Reform Act	Has varied
4. Nonqualified option	Any	Growth in stock value	Weak	May be increasing	Difficult to say†
5. Performance shares	Any	Good growth in EPS and stock value	Moderate	Increasing	Difficult to say†
Cafeteria	Medium-large	Not applicable	None	Increasing	Good: nontaxable; group rates‡

*Must also consider present value of future rewards.
†Both company tax deduction and individual "personal service" tax occur in future: present value of these two variables are important factors.
‡Benefits only: no cash considered.

Figure 10-8 Summary of incentive plan features.

out 625 pieces of part C (with 0.8 standard hours/hundred pieces or with 125 pieces constituting a standard hour); and 800 pieces of part D (0.5 standard hours required for every 100 pieces, or with 200 pieces constituting a standard hour).

a. How much money did each worker earn on Friday?

b. At what percentage of standard was each person working averaging together both the pieces each produced?

c. After doing (a) and (b), which system would you prefer — guaranteed piecework or standard hour? Why?

3. John and Betty were studying the nature of equipment utilization incentives as described in the chapter. John claimed that because they were based on standard hours, such systems were one-for-one systems. Betty disagreed. Who was right? Show specific numerical calculations to support your answer. If Betty was right, would such incentives have any different motivational impact than traditional incentives? Why? (Use the numerical data given in the chapter).

4. Under which of the following conditions would you establish a traditional incentive plan? Why?

a. In a highly automated continuous processing oil refinery.

b. In a manufacturing plant which makes products to order, and the work performed varies from product to product.

c. In a mass production operation in which job content remains fairly stable.

d. In a mass production manufacturing plant that had employed 2000 production workers, but where management has just suddenly laid off 400 production workers because it has moved this part of the operation to a southern state in which labor is cheaper.

e. In a large mass production plant which has had a traditional incentive plan, but where numerous "creeping changes" in job content have occurred so that some jobs now call for more skill and effort than they used to, whereas all wage rates have increased (in an inflationary period) by the same percentage.

5. Which of the following actions taken by a company do you believe would enhance its suggestion system? In each case, give your reasons; and indicate any problems which might arise.

a. Having a suggestion contest for 30 days in which all suggesters are given chances to win merchandise prizes.

b. Photographing the company president shaking the hands of a $5000 suggestion award winner as he hands her a check.

c. Appraising first-line supervisors partially on the basis of the suggestion performance of their employees.

d. Having the suggestion director informing an individual who submitted a suggestion three months ago that his idea involves so many complexities that, although the firm's engineering department is still working on the idea, it may still take some time before the company can decide how much a reward, if any, the individual will receive.

e. Asking all employees to print or type their suggestions so that they may be processed faster by management.

6. Jonathan Swifter has suggested a modification for his machine that would: (a) have an estimated economic life of five years, (b) require an initial investment of $4000, and (c) realize gross savings of $2000 for the first year. His firm bases its suggestion awards on 10 per cent of first years net savings. What will be Jonathan's award under this system? Should he have made the suggestion if he had known what the award would have been?

7. A top executive who is now aged 55 has been given the compensation choice by his firm of a $100,000 bonus at the end of the current year (in which his marginal federal income tax rate is 50 per cent); or as a deferred bonus consisting of a $20,000 installment at the end of each of the five years following the year in which he retires, i.e., in the years in which he is 66, 67, 68, 69, and 70. He estimates that his federal tax rates on each such installment will be 30 per cent. He further estimates that on any funds which he has to invest, he can realize a yearly after-tax rate of return of 5 per cent.

   a. Assuming that he believes he will live long enough to receive all deferred compensation, which alternative should he choose? To solve this problem, use the present value tables below.

Present Value of $1 at 5 per cent $(1 + i)^{-n}$

Years

1	.95	6	.75	11	.58
2	.91	7	.71	12	.56
3	.86	8	.68	13	.53
4	.82	9	.64	14	.51
5	.78	10	.61	15	.48

   b. Would the executive's choice be altered if his tax rate were only 20 per cent on each of his five deferred payments?

8. If you were a top executive, rank the following types of incentives in terms of benefit to you.

   a. A deferred bonus with equal payments in each of your five years after retirement. Assume your tax rate on the entire distribution would be the maximum 50 per cent personal service rate.

   b. A cash bonus equivalent in amount to the deferred compensation in (a) above and taxed at the same rate as the deferred bonus.

   c. A qualified stock option to purchase 50 shares of your company's stock at $50/share.

   d. A nonqualified stock option to purchase 50 shares of your company's stock at $50/share.

   e. Performance shares which you will obtain if your firm's cumulative EPS growth is 10 per cent/year for the next four years.

9. Pure or unlimited cafeteria compensation will never be effectively implemented in the United States. Discuss.

10. Fred and Sue are arguing over the merits of cafeteria compensation. Fred argues that some research has shown that employee preferences change rapidly, and further that many employees will be afraid to make decisions which may come back to haunt them, e.g., opting for more life insurance and less medical insurance and then having a "catastrophic" medical bill not nearly covered with their choice of level of medical insurance. Sue, on the other hand, indicates that experience has shown these concerns to be invalid, that more and more firms will adopt cafeteria compensation, which will lead to both greater employee satisfaction and motivation. Discuss.

Notes

[1]Benjamin W. Niebel, *Motion and Time Study,* 5th ed. (Homewood, Ill.: Richard D. Irwin, Inc., 1972), p. 612.

[2]Herbert G. Zollitsch and Adolph Langsner, *Wage and Salary Administration,* 2nd ed. (Cincinnati, Ohio: South-Western Publishing Co., 1970), pp. 558–559.

[3]Garth L. Magnum, "Are Wage Incentives Becoming Obsolete?" *Industrial Relations,*2 (October, 1972), p. 89.

[4]For an example of this type of incentive, see Zollitsch and Langsner, op. cit., pp. 541ff.

[5]For a comprehensive explanation of the principles of motion economy, see Niebel, op. cit., pp. 182ff. A classic work in motion study is Frank B. Gilbreth, *Motion Study* (New York: D. Van Nostrand Co., Inc., 1911).

[6]For a discussion of time study, standard data, micro-synthetic analysis, and work sampling, see, for example, Niebel, op. cit., Chapters 12–17, 18, 19, and 21, respectively.

[7]Ibid., pp. 432–433.

[8]James A. Chisman, "Using Linear Programming to Determine Time Standards," *The Journal of Industrial Engineering,* 17 (April, 1966), pp. 189–191.

[9]Ibid., p. 191.

[10]Irving A. Delloff, "Incentive Clauses, The Costly Clinkers," *Personnel,* 36 (May-June, 1959), p. 56.

[11]See Kenneth K. Kopp, "A Computer Based Janitorial Standards Program for Colleges and Universities," in Paul S. Greenlaw and Robert D. Smith, eds., *Personnel Management: A Management Science Approach* (Scranton, Pa.: International Textbook Company, 1970), pp. 392–410; or Niebel, op. cit., pp. 597ff.

[12]Niebel, ibid., p. 607.

[13]For a discussion of many of the other well known incentive plans, see ibid., pp. 609ff.; or Zollitsch and Langsner, op. cit., Chapter 17.

[14]There is disagreement as to how much extra clerical work is required under guaranteed piecework as opposed to standard hour plans. Niebel (p. 608) has spoken about "a monumental amount of clerical work to change all standards to agree with the revised hourly rates." Zollitsch and Langsner, on the other hand, have indicated that the change of wage rates under guaranteed piecework plans "may not be a serious disadvantage," (p. 478) and that such firms as Lincoln Electric (whose system incentive plan we will discuss in the next chapter) have successfully used the guaranteed piece rate for many years.

[15]Lawrence Fenninger, Jr., "The Establishment of Norms Under Incentive Systems in the Basic Steel Industry in the United States," in John T. Dunlop and Vasilli P. Diatchenko, eds., *Labor Productivity* (New York: McGraw-Hill, 1964), pp. 268–269.

[16]Garth L. Magnum, op. cit., p. 84.

[17]Fenninger, op. cit., pp. 271–272.

[18]Allen N. Nash and Stephen J. Carroll, Jr., *The Management of Compensation* (Monterey, Calif.: Brooks/Cole Publishing Company, 1975), pp. 199, 202.

[19]Charles F. James and Philip V. Rzasa, "A Pricing Analysis of the One-for-One Incentive Plans," *Personnel Journal,* 47 (June, 1968), pp. 398–401.

[20]Paul S. Greenlaw and Joseph L. Jones, Jr., "Trends in the Use of Wage Incentives," unpublished paper, Department of Management Science and Organizational Behavior, College of Business Administration, The Pennsylvania State University, 1976. The 39 manufacturing industries in this study were categorized as being heavy, medium or low users of incentives. Industry studies where there were 50 per cent or more of the workers on incentives in the 1969–1973 period were defined as high; those with 25 to 49 per cent, medium; and those under 25 per cent as low.

[21]Stanley Seimer, *Suggestion Plans in American Industry: The Role of the Foreman* (Syracuse, N.Y.: Syracuse University Press, 1959), pp. 2–3.

[22]Ibid., pp. 5, 7.

[23]Vincent G. Reuter, "A New Look at Suggestion Systems," *Journal of Systems Management,* 27 (January, 1976), p. 7.

[24]J. Alger, "Suggestion Statistics," *Production Series,* No. 165 (New York: American Management Association, 1946), p. 11.

[25]Cited in Reuter, op. cit., pp. 7–8.

[26]Milton A. Tatter, "Turning Ideas Into Gold," *Management Review,* 64 (March, 1975), p. 5. As may be observed, the number of NASS firms indicated here (1000) is only a fraction of the number of companies having plans as reported above by Seimer; and hence total savings for all companies in the U.S. would be considerably larger.

[27]For a discussion of managerial systems, see W. C. Whitwell, *Suggestion Systems Are Profitable* (Waterford, Conn.: Prentice-Hall, Inc., 1963), p. 51. Whitwell also has pointed out that some types of suggestions may not be eligible such as those which are properly a subject for collective bargaining, and personal complaints. See ibid., p. 71.

[28]Ibid., p. 92.

[29]Ibid., pp. 88–91.

[30]Reuter, op. cit., p. 8.

[31]Whitwell, op. cit., p. 110.

[32]J. Roger O'Meara, "Suggesters Wanted: Employees Please Apply," *The Conference Board Record,* 1 (December, 1964), p. 34.

[33]Abraham Pizam, "Some Correlates of Innovation Within Industrial Suggestion Systems," *Personnel Psychology,* 27 (Spring, 1974), p. 75. Other personal characteristics such as the amount of formal education or trade training have been shown to be positively related to making suggestions. William C. Cotner, "Variables Affecting Suggestion Participation," M. A. Thesis, The Pennsylvania State University, Department of Sociology, 1955, p. 19. As we would also expect from our previous discussion, foremen "who encourage employees to participate in the system have more suggesters than those who display no interest in the program" (p. 21).

[34]See Alfred P. Sloan, Jr., *My Years With General Motors* (New York: Doubleday & Company, 1963), pp. 425–428.

[35]Arch Patton, "Why Incentive Plans Fail," *Harvard Business Review,* 50 (May-June, 1972), p. 59.

[36]Ibid.

[37]George H. Foote, "Performance Shares Revitalize Executive Stock Plans," *Harvard Business Review,* 51 (November-December, 1973), p. 125.

[38]Patton, op. cit., p. 65.

[39]Philip H. Dutter, "Compensation Plans for Executives," in Joseph J. Famularo, ed. *Handbook of Modern Personnel Administration* (New York: McGraw-Hill Book Company, 1972), p. 32–10.

[40]Zollitsch and Langsner, op. cit., p. 727.

[41]Foote, op. cit., p. 127.

[42]Dutter, op. cit., p. 32–10. The pros and cons of a permanent as opposed to changeable formula from year to year are also discussed in ibid.

[43]Patton, op. cit., pp. 62ff. Patton outlines the advantages and disadvantages of each type, the discussion of which is beyond the scope of this book.

[44]Dutter, op. cit., p. 32–12.

[45]For single taxpayers, the Federal tax rate for all ordinary taxable income was 70% for all amounts over $100,000; while for married taxpayers filing joint returns, the 70 per cent maximum rate applied to all ordinary taxable income over $200,000.

[46]J. D. Dunn and F. M. Rachel, *Wage and Salary Administration* (New York: McGraw Hill, Inc., 1971), p. 331. Taking into account the present value of future cash flows by utilizing opportunity costs of 10 per cent for the firm and 5 per cent for individual executives, George W. Hettenhouse in 1970 ranked deferred pay contracts with ten payments in retirement as the best in terms of cost-benefit analysis among 17 available executive compensation methods for executives aged 50 and earning $50,000, $100,000 or $150,000. See his "Cost/Benefit Analysis of Executive Compensation," *Harvard Business Review*, 48 (July-August, 1970), p. 118.

[47]Prior to 1964 stock options which qualified for favorable capital gains treatment were called "restricted" rather than qualified stock options.

[48]Foote, op. cit., p. 121. Another survey undertaken by the McKinsey Company as reported in 1977, on the other hand, reported that 78 per cent of 587 large companies rewarding executives with extra compensation other than cash bonuses used qualified stock options. See "Tax Reform Remodels the Pay Package," *Business Week*, February 28, 1977, p. 48.

[49]Tax Reform Act of 1976, Section 603. 90 Stat. 1574.

[50]"The New Tax Law," *Business Week*, October 18, 1976, p. 132.

[51]"Tax Reform Remodels the Pay Package," op. cit., pp. 48, 51.

[52]Hettenhouse, op. cit., p. 118. This analysis was arrived at as in note 46.

[53]"Tax Reform Remodels the Pay Package," op. cit., p. 48.

[54]For the materials in this section, we have drawn heavily from Foote, op. cit.

[55]"Performance Shares: Popular — But Under Fire," *Business Week* (May 5, 1973), p. 56.

[56]Foote, op. cit., p. 122.

[57]Ibid., p. 126.

[58]"Performance Shares: Popular — But Under Fire." op. cit., p. 56.

[59]Ibid.

[60]Jay R. Schuster, "Flexible Compensation," *Personnel Administration/Public Personnel Review*, 1 (November-December, 1972), p. 13.

[61]John O. Todd, "Cafeteria Compensation: Making Management Motivators Meaningful," *Personnel Journal*, 54 (May, 1975), pp. 275–281.

[62]Berwyn N. Fragner, "Employees' 'Cafeteria' Offers Insurance Options," *Harvard Business Review*, 53 (November-December, 1975), p. 8.

[63]Thomas E. Wahlrobe, "The Cafeteria Approach to Employee Benefits," *Administrative Management*, 35 (December, 1974), p. 52.

[64]Unless otherwise noted, the criticisms indicated in this section are drawn from ibid., pp. 49–50, 52.

[65]George T. Milkovich and Michael J. Delaney, "A Note on Cafeteria Pay Plans," *Industrial Relations*, 14 (February, 1975), pp. 112–116. These researchers also found that they obtained different sets of preferences depending upon the research method used to obtain these preference expressions of employees.

[66]Fragner, op. cit., p. 8.

[67]Ibid.

[68]Ibid., p. 10.

[69]Ibid.

[70]Ibid.

[71]Milkovich and Delaney, op. cit., p. 116.

[72]Wilbur G. Lewellen and Howard P. Lanser, "Executive Pay Preferences," *Harvard Business Review*, 51 (September-October, 1973), p. 119.

11

SYSTEM INCENTIVES

In the previous chapter, we discussed four basic types of individual incentives. We will now turn our attention to three widely recognized types of incentives referred to as "group," "plant-wide," "company-wide," or "system" incentives: (1) profit sharing plans, (2) Scanlon plans, and (3) the highly systems oriented incentive plan in effect at the Lincoln Electric Company.[1]

Before discussing these, some introductory comments are in order about system incentives. The distinction between "individual" incentives discussed in the last chapter and the "system" incentives of this chapter is somewhat blurred. For example, part of the Lincoln systems approach calls for individual piecework incentives of exactly the same type as discussed in Chapter 10. In general, however, the system incentives that we will discuss here are considered to foster more "cooperative" and "collaborative" behavior among organizational members as opposed to tradition- al piecework incentives in which the individual's reward is based solely on his own effort. We will follow the same decision- sequencing framework as presented in Chapter 10 (eligibility, reward criterion, and reward) for each of the three system incen- tives we will discuss. This framework is illustrated in Figure 11–1.

As may be noted from Figure 11–1, some of these three sequential decisions require no more than a sentence to describe. For example, management at the Lincoln Electric Company sim- ply decided that all members of the organization would be eligible for participation in the yearly bonus plan except the company's Chairman of the Board of Directors and President. On the other hand, some of the other managerial decisions indicated in Figure 11–1 involve quite complex factors. Federal income taxes levied

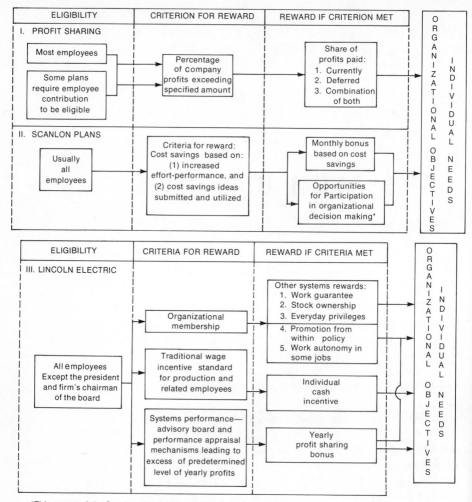

ELIGIBILITY	CRITERION FOR REWARD	REWARD IF CRITERION MET
I. PROFIT SHARING		

Most employees

Some plans require employee contribution to be eligible

→ Percentage of Company profits exceeding specified amount

→ Share of profits paid:
1. Currently
2. Deferred
3. Combination of both

| II. SCANLON PLANS | | |

Usually all employees

→ Criteria for reward: Cost savings based on: (1) increased effort-performance, and (2) cost savings ideas submitted and utilized

→ Monthly bonus based on cost savings

Opportunities for Participation in organizational decision making*

ORGANIZATIONAL OBJECTIVES — INDIVIDUAL NEEDS

ELIGIBILITY	CRITERIA FOR REWARD	REWARD IF CRITERIA MET
III. LINCOLN ELECTRIC		

All employees Except the president and firm's chairman of the board

→ Organizational membership

Traditional wage incentive standard for production and related employees

Systems performance— advisory board and performance appraisal mechanisms leading to excess of predetermined level of yearly profits

→ Other systems rewards:
1. Work guarantee
2. Stock ownership
3. Everyday privileges
4. Promotion from within policy
5. Work autonomy in some jobs

Individual cash incentive

Yearly profit sharing bonus

ORGANIZATIONAL OBJECTIVES — INDIVIDUAL NEEDS

*This aspect of the Scanlon plan is not strictly a reward contingent upon meeting a criterion. Such opportunities are an essential feature of the Scanlon plan, and are provided regardless of whether the company's savings are large enough to produce a Scanlon bonus.

Figure 11–1 *System incentives.*

on the rewards paid to individuals eligible for lump sum distributions in deferred profit-sharing plans upon retirement provide such an example. This type of plan is constrained in a number of ways by the complex Employee Retirement Income Security Act of 1974, commonly referred to as "ERISA."

In the introductory chapters of this text we indicated that there are many complex legal and economic problems that *must* be dealt with effectively by successful personnel managers today. To provide the reader with some comprehension of these complexities of today's reality, we will delve into some of the primary effects of ERISA upon deferred profit sharing plans. In all such cases, however, we will avoid technical legal "jargon." Further, when numbers are involved, we will present straightforward illustrative numerical examples. Under a deferred profit sharing plan, the individual may have to deal with income taxes on a lump sum payment of $100,000 or more given to him in the year he retires and should be aware of the fact that there are special tax methods available for dealing with such lump sums.

We should emphasize that firms are not restricted to the use of only one type of system (or individual) incentive plan. In many cases firms may have a Scanlon plan and a deferred profit sharing plan, both designed to work together to provide an attractive overall financial "package" for the organization. Further, sometimes system incentives are designed to supplement employee benefit plans, which we will discuss in Chapter 12. Perhaps the most classic example of this decision strategy is the use of deferred profit sharing plans along with pension benefits to provide individuals with considerable financial security upon retirement. We will now turn to the most widely used of the three system plans — profit sharing plans.

PROFIT-SHARING PLANS

Historical Background

Profit sharing may be defined as a financial arrangement by which a firm establishes some predetermined formula for sharing a portion of its profits with its employees. This idea of sharing profits is not new, nor is interest in profit sharing limited to the United States. For example, in 1889 an International Congress on profit sharing was held in Paris, France.[2] Procter and Gamble's profit sharing plan (the oldest still in existence in the United States) was started in 1887. Other major American corporations which have pioneered in profit sharing are Eastman Kodak (1912), and Sears, Roebuck and Company (1916).[3]

The growth of profit sharing plans was slow until recent decades. In 1940, there were only 37 qualified deferred plans in existence in the United States. "Qualified" means meeting certain requirements of the United States Internal Revenue Service to obtain favorable tax treatment, as we will explain more fully later. Since 1960, however, profit sharing has mushroomed in this country, with the number of qualified deferred plans in existence nearly doubling every five years:

Year	Number of Qualified Deferred Plans[4]
1960	24,797
1965	48,433
1970	101,842
1975	197,386

There were also approximately 100,000 current cash profit sharing plans in operation as of the end of 1975 in the United States. We have estimated that the total assets of qualified deferred profit sharing funds that have been set aside for later payment to employees were about $36 billion as of the end of 1975.[5]

As illustrated in Figure 11–1, there are three basic types of profit sharing plans: current, deferred, and a combination of the two. Under each of these arrangements an employee's share of profits is determined by two factors. The individual's pay is a factor, with persons earning more receiving larger distributions up to certain limits. The profits of the firm are a factor, since employee shares are directly related to profits, and larger sums will be available as profit sharing distributions as the firm's profits are higher. We will provide a concrete example of these two variables and other aspects of profit sharing with the very successful Sears Roebuck plan later in this chapter.

Under current plans, "profits are paid directly to employees in cash, check, or stock as soon as profits are determined (e.g., monthly, quarterly, semi-annually, or annually)."[6] Deferred plans, on the other hand, call for the accumulation of profit sharing contributions over the years into trusts, to be distributed as annuities, installments, or lump-sum distributions to the employee when he reaches retirement age,[7] or leaves the firm prior to retirement. An employee's benefits would be handled according to his beneficiary designation, should he die before becoming eligible under these conditions. Managerial decisions with respect to such deferred plans are constrained in more ways by ERISA than are current plans. In many cases, trusts with huge assets have been set up to invest the funds over the years prior to distribution to employees, and special tax benefits are provided if the firm qualifies by following numerous Internal Revenue regulations. If the deferred plan is qualified, the firm can deduct for tax purposes all profits put into its fund in the year it does so. Its employees, on the other hand, are not taxed on these sums (plus appreciation) until they actually or constructively receive them. Such a deferral represents substantial tax savings since, in many cases 20, 30, or more years pass after the firm's first profit sharing dollars are credited to an individual's account. We will not delve into the complexities of qualifying for such favorable tax treatments with deferred plans. However, there are two basic rules that such plans must abide by:

1. A firm may absolutely not use any of the funds set aside for any employee in its plan for any of its own purposes (say, financing a new large capital investment).[8]

2. A firm's plan must not discriminate in favor of any selected employees — more specifically, under ERISA, officers of the firm, shareholders or "highly compensated" employees. In addition, under

ERISA, annual additions to any individual's profit sharing account were limited to $25,000 or 25 per cent of his compensation, whichever was the lesser.[9]

The third type of profit sharing plan is the combination plan, in which some current cash benefits are provided employees, and other portions of the employee's profit share are deferred.

The deferred plans are far more complex than current plans because of their large assets and because they are subject to more provisions of ERISA. Combination plans can, of course, become involved because they encompass both the complex aspects of deferred profit sharing, and the comparatively simple mechanics of current plans. We will focus attention almost exclusively on the deferred plans because they are more complex. We do this on the assumption that if the reader is familiar with their basic aspects, he will also understand both the combined and current plans.

One point with respect to current trends in profit sharing plan development, however, does involve combination plans. With such factors as inflation and increased social security payroll deductions, many individuals have wanted more immediately available cash than previously, and a trend toward more combination plans, which provide both cash and long term security, has been reported. Further, in a number of these plans, employees have been given some choice as to how much of their profit sharing allocation will be in immediate cash and how much will constitute a deferred distribution.[10]

Deferred Plans: Eligibility

Several considerations are important with regard to eligibility in deferred plans. First, it has been a common practice to require employees to wait one year after they have been hired by a firm before they become eligible for participation in the plan. Second, to become an eligible member in a number of profit sharing plans (estimated to be from 15 to 20 per cent in 1976),[11] the employee must contribute a portion of his earnings to the plan. In some cases it is mandatory that organization employees contribute; in many other cases it is voluntary. Numerous arguments have been raised concerning the advantages of contributory as opposed to noncontributory plans.[12] For example, it has been argued that a plan with a mandatory contributory feature can have the effect of forcing habits of thrift on individuals. Further, it has been claimed that the return on profit sharing contributions is generally greater than if employees had saved money themselves, since deferred profit sharing trusts are managed by professional investors. On the other hand, being required to contribute a sum additional to social security deductions, federal withholding taxes, and perhaps state and local taxes as well may put the individual in a tight financial position. It is for this reason that fewer plans have mandatory contributory features today and more have voluntary features.

Reference to the large Sears Roebuck plan with total assets of around $2.6 billion, as of the end of 1975, will provide both an example of how management must design plans so as not to discriminate in favor of highly-paid employees to qualify for favorable tax treatment and an illustration of how employee contributions were decided upon. Under the Sears plan, effective January 1, 1978, members could agree to invest (or deposit) 2, 3, 4, or 5 per cent of their earnings up to a maximum total contribution of $750 per year. This limit meant that the maximum yearly earnings from which deposits could be deducted was $15,000.[13] This assured that all members would share fairly in company contributions, and that the fund would be kept safely within federal tax guidelines, which prohibit favoritism toward highly-paid employees. The limit also means that employees will be protected from placing themselves in cash binds in any year. Membership in the Sears plan as of 1978 was voluntary.

One final concept is important relative to deferred profit sharing plans — that of vesting. Vesting has been defined as the

> . . . *acquisition by the employee of a right (a non-forfeitable claim), according to a definite formula, to all or part of the amount in his account or in his accrued benefits, at date of severance* [from the organization] . . . .[14]

Under ERISA, there are three minimum vesting decision alternatives that can be chosen by management with respect to both pension and deferred profit sharing plans. We will discuss these vesting alternatives in the next chapter. Many firms have been more liberal in vesting in profit sharing plans than the ERISA requirements, so that this law has not imposed additional constraints upon many profit sharing plans in this respect. In the Sears plan, for example, prior to ERISA, employees enjoyed full vesting after five years, i.e., they could take all of the company's profits that had been put in their account with them if they terminated their employment after remaining with Sears for five years or more. This was more liberal from the point of view of the employees than any of the ERISA vesting alternatives; after the passage of ERISA, Sears went to full and immediate vesting (after a one year waiting period of eligibility). This move to full and immediate vesting was done for the following reasons, according to Merl Douglas, Executive Director of the Fund:

> . . . almost half our present members have less than five years service with the Company . . . . We felt that the best motivation to these people

is a full, non-forfeitable stake in the Company's success, which also carries the right to vote all the shares [of Sears stock] in their account. In addition, full and immediate vesting is simple to explain and understand, and simplifies accounting procedures. Finally, every alternative vesting schedule that was acceptable under ERISA contained at least one highly distasteful element.[15]

Finally, we should note that employees' contributions to any profit sharing plan always belong to them and may be taken from the fund, regardless of how short the individual's stay is with the company. This is true even when none of the firm's contributions to his account have yet been vested.

In summary, regarding eligibility under deferred profit sharing plans, management is constrained by ERISA and federal income tax law, but it does have certain key decisions available to it. Management can decide whether the plan is to be (mandatorily or voluntarily) contributory, and, if so, how much employees will contribute; and how fast vesting will occur within the constraints of ERISA. We will now turn our attention to the second major managerial decision regarding deferred profit sharing, that of determining the criterion for the reward.

The Criterion for Reward

The criterion for reward under current, deferred, and combination profit sharing plans will vary widely depending in no small part on the size of the company and its profits. Frequently, there will be a provision stipulating that there will be no company contributions to the plan in any year in which company profits fall below a certain dollar amount. This amount may be updated as the firm expands. In 1976, the point below which no profits would be shared in the Sears, Roebuck and Company plan was $250 million. Further, some companies provide for increasing the percentage of profit going into profit sharing in any one year as company profits increase. For example, some firms increase contributions as their profits increase by means of a kinked function criterion arrangement, as illustrated in Figure 11–2.

Profit Sharing Plans: The Rewards

In a sense, we have already indicated what the basic rewards are under profit sharing systems — some share of the firm's profits above a certain minimum.

With current plans, companies simply pay out these profit shares, deduct these payments at the corporate income tax rate, and individuals are taxed on the reward by the federal govern-

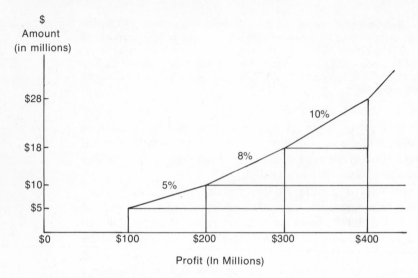

EXAMPLES: NET PROFIT BEFORE TAXES	PROFIT SHARING CONTRIBUTION
Not over $100 million	None
Over $100 million but not over $200 million	$5 million plus 5% of the excess over $100 million
Over $200 million but not over $300 million	$10 million plus 8% of the excess over $200 million
Over $300 million but not over $400 million	$18 million plus 10% of the excess over $300 million
Over $400 million	$28 million plus 12% of the excess over $400 million

Figure 11-2 *Kinked-function profit sharing example. This hypothetical example illustrates the type of plan of the Safeway Company, as reported in 1975. See* Metzger, Profit Sharing in 38 Large Companies, *p. 164.*

ment in the year they receive it as personal service income with the 50 per cent maximum marginal rate. With qualified deferred plans, on the other hand:

1. The company obtains a tax deduction immediately, to the extent that it contributes to the plan.

2. These funds are taken (along with individual contributions in contributory plans) and invested professionally so that the funds hopefully appreciate to a significant extent over the years.

3. This appreciation may be furthered by "forfeitures," which are assets that are left in the fund by those individuals who leave the firm before employer contributions to their accounts are fully vested. (These employees would receive profit sharing distributions to the extent that their accounts are vested.)

4. The reward is paid out to individuals who do remain with the company when they retire or during the years after retirement when their

incomes are at lower Federal income tax rates which tend to be favorable.

Thus, two basic functions that deferred plans can provide are: (1) tax advantages to the individual on substantial funds paid out beyond his normal compensation, and (2) security above and beyond any pension plan his firm may have.

We will now outline various alternative means by which individuals may be rewarded by deferred profit sharing plans if they stay with the firm until retirement. There are basically three different methods of paying out profit sharing rewards, and a firm may provide its employees with the option of choosing a combination of these. First, the employee can be given an annuity from his accumulated profit sharing account. In such cases, he pays income taxes on the annuity up to the 50 per cent maximum personal service rate on the funds received[16] minus any of his contributions over the years since he has already paid income taxes on his earnings earmarked for these contributions.

Second, the employee can be given his reward as a series of installments over 10 or 15 years, for example, or over a duration equivalent to his actuarial life expectancy (or the joint life expectancies of the individual and his spouse). His income taxes on these installments are treated the same as with annuities.

Finally, he may receive his reward in a lump-sum distribution when he retires. Here again, all prior contributions by the employee are subtracted for tax purposes, and extremely important, under ERISA, not immediately taxed is the "net unrealized appreciation attributable to that part of the distribution which consists of the securities of the employer corporation so distributed."[17] Thus, if the profit sharing fund transfers shares of his *own firm's stock* to the individual rather than cash, this stock is taxed only at its original acquisition cost and *not* at the current market value. For example, if the average acquisition cost of 1000 shares of the firm's stock being so distributed were $20, but the current market price were $50/share, only $20,000 rather than $50,000 would be subject to taxation in the high income distribution year. The employee would be permitted to hold the stock, sell it at his pleasure, and when he does sell it in future years, its *appreciation* would be taxed only at capital gains rates. This provision, rather evidently, makes funds like Sears (in which approximately $2 billion of its total assets of $2.6 billion were in Sears stock as of the end of 1975 and shares of stock are actually distributed to employees) much more attractive than funds that provide solely a cash distribution.

Realizing a large lump sum distribution all in one year as he retires may be better or worse for an individual than an annuity, since he may only live six months after age 65 and receive very little money from the annuity; or he may live many years, so that the total sum of his annuity payments would exceed any lump sum distribution at age 65 drawn from the same amount of money in his profit sharing account. In any event, if he receives a large lump sum distribution at retirement, say of $80,000, his income taxes, unless specially handled would be extremely high. For this reason ERISA has provided for a special means of handling lump sum distributions.

We will now briefly indicate the basic characteristics of the ERISA lump sum taxation method which provided for a gradual phasing out of capital gains. We will provide two simple numerical examples to clarify this procedure. The tax method provides for the portion of total taxable income of the lump sum distribution that is to be considered as capital gains as the total taxable amount multiplied by a fraction: (1) the numerator of which is the number of calendar years of actual participation by the employees in the plan *before* January, 1974, and (2) the denominator of which is the *total* number of calendar years of active participation in the plan. The remainder of the total taxable income (*post* January, 1974 years over total years of participation as a fraction of total taxable income) is considered as ordinary income, which is treated by a special 10-year income averaging method, but one in which all the "averaged" income is taxed in the one year in which the lump sum profit sharing distribution is made. This is a

1. Total Distribution	$110,000
2. Employee's Contributions	−10,000
3. Total Taxable Distribution	$100,000
4. Divide (3) by 10	$ 10,000
5. Figure the tax on this amount using *single person's* income tax rates	$ 2,084*
6. Multiply (5) by 10	$ 20,840
7. Multiply (6) by the percentage of years the individual was under profit sharing after January 1, 1974 (4/20 or 20 per cent in our example). This will give the special income averaged ordinary income tax.	$ 4,168

*From Single Taxpayer's 1976 Tax Table, p. 25 of the U.S. *1976 Income Tax Forms.* The 1978 Tax Tables which would actually be used for any distributions received in January, 1978 as in this example had not been developed as this book goes to press.

Figure 11–3 *Ten-year income averaging.*

special separate tax, which is in *no way related to* any of the individual's other income subject to taxation.[18]

To illustrate these characteristics, let us consider first the case of an individual who participated in a deferred profit sharing plan for 20 years from January 1, 1958 to December 31, 1977, who contributed $10,000 to the fund himself, and who received a lump sum of $110,000 in January, 1978. Sixteen of his 20 years of participation occurred prior to January 1, 1974 and 16/20 or 80 per cent of his total taxable distribution would thus be considered as capital gains. The other 20 per cent (4/20) would be considered ordinary income. His "special ten year averaging" tax would be $4168 as computed in Figure 11–3.[19] To reiterate an important point made earlier, this income-averaged ordinary income tax is a special tax, *not related* to any other taxable income for the year. In our example, however, the *other 80 per cent* of the total taxable distribution would be treated as capital gains. What the tax on this amount would be depends on what other income the individual would have in the year he receives the lump sum distribution since this is *not* a special tax and the capital gains income is *added to all* the individual's *other income* for tax purposes. Thus, if he had substantial other income, the addition of this capital gains portion of the lump sum distribution might put him in a much higher tax bracket.

Our second example may be of more direct applicability to the reader. With the phaseout of the capital gains portion, *all* lump sum rewards that the worker might receive could well be based on *post*-January 1974 profit sharing participation and, thus, taxed solely at the 10-year special income averaging ordinary income rate. In such a case, the special tax with our net $100,000 in 1976 would have been, for example, the $20,840 shown in Figure 11–3. Without this special tax, such a lump-sum payment given to the worker if he were married, filed a joint return, and had no other income, would have resulted in an income tax of $42,060[20] if he had received the $100,000 distribution in 1976 — a difference of $21,220. It should also be noted that the Tax Reform Act of 1976 made it optional for anyone to do a 10-year income average of the total taxable distribution, regardless of the number of years of his participation prior to and after January 1974.

Profit Sharing: An Evaluation, Contingencies and Management Science

Evaluation

As indicated earlier, profit sharing plans have enjoyed wide usage, and many individuals have believed them to be effective system rewards. We will now evaluate some of the major implications of profit sharing plans.

We should point out first that evaluating the effectiveness of profit sharing plans is difficult to accomplish. This is because, aside from being influenced by its employees' efforts, a firm's profits will also be affected by such factors as the business cycle or competitor strategies. Further, the vagaries of the stock market may have an important effect on the value of deferred profit sharing trust funds. As we will indicate later, however, external variables will also affect Scanlon Plan rewards (as they will most all system incentive rewards).

Recognizing these inherently difficult research limitations, some studies have shown a positive relationship between having a profit sharing plan and company success. The Profit Sharing Research Foundation, for example, compared the financial performance of several department store chains with profit sharing against a similar group without it for the period 1952–1969.[21] On all measures studied (sales, net worth, earnings per common share, dividends per common share, and market price per share), based on growth since 1952, those firms with profit sharing outperformed those without this system incentive. The sample size in this study was small (14), however, and the question must be raised: Could it not be possible that the chains which performed most successfully did so simply because they had more progressive and superior managements, that happened, among taking many other effective actions, to have decided to have profit sharing plans? The authors of this study raised this precise question and answered it as follows:

If "more competent management" is assigned as the "cause" of the superior performance (and this may well be the major factor), then one must ask himself the next logical question: "Why did 'more competent management' see fit to initiate, continue, and expand their respective profit sharing programs unless they firmly believed that profit sharing served both organizational goals and individual needs?"[22]

One tangible benefit that may be derived from profit sharing plans is that they may enhance the firm's recruiting efforts. It can be argued that this is less true today than 20 years ago, for as we saw earlier, so many firms now do have qualified deferred plans as compared to then. Still, under ERISA's provisions, the company's own stock distributions are treated so much more tax favorably that firms providing large such profit sharing distributions may have a competitive recruiting advantage over firms which do not.

It has been argued that deferred profit sharing reduces turnover. Although, as indicated previously, deferred plans have often been vested more liberally than ERISA's requirements, full and immediate vesting after one year is still not common, and the individual may gain substantially larger profit sharing sums by remaining longer with the company. This is not only because of becoming eligible for an increased amount of vesting, but also because of appreciation of assets accruing from wise fund investments and forfeitures. On the other hand, ERISA provided for a *portability provision,* by means of which, within 60 days after being separated from one firm's qualified plan, an employee may transfer without any taxation the profit sharing plan's amount that has accrued to him to either his own individual retirement account (IRA)[23] or a new employer's qualified plan if the new employer agrees.[24]

One final question must be raised with respect to profit sharing and turnover. Is it the firm's better or poorer employees who may be induced to remain with the organization because of the forfeiture of profit sharing and other types of employee benefits? Some people argue that it is often the poorer employees who cannot find a comparable job elsewhere who remain with firms, while highly capable people may be very "marketable."

One decided benefit for those individuals who belong to deferred profit sharing plans is that the benefits derived from them upon retirement may serve to meet their security needs. In some cases, deferred profit sharing plans are used as substitutes for pension plans. This is comparatively advantageous to the firm, since it only needs to make payments in profitable years, whereas contributions must be made to pension funds each year, regardless of profitability. Conversely, the fixed commitments of pension plans may provide more security to the employee than deferred profit sharing. We say "may" here because one of the major reasons for the passage of ERISA was that many firms had not put adequate funds into their pension plans to guarantee pensions and hence retirement security. With the passage of ERISA, however, firms with pension plans are required to take certain steps to make their pension plans more secure.

Profit sharing plans may be used to supplement pension funds so that a very high degree of retirement security is provided. Under ERISA, however, if an individual participates in both a defined benefit type of pension plan and a profit sharing plan, his maximum allowable benefit in any one year will be 70 per cent of the *combined* benefit maximums of the two plans, i.e., 70 per cent times 2 or 140 per cent (or a fraction or factor of 1.4).[25]

Two other points with respect to the evaluation of deferred profit sharing plans are frequently cited in discussions on the subject. First, contributory plans encourage thrift but may impose a cash strain on employees at certain times. Second, employees reaping the full benefits of qualified deferred plans often receive large sums of money that are taxed favorably. Thus, although one cannot precisely rank deferred profit sharing plans among other forms of compensation from a cost/benefit point of view, they would certainly have to be placed somewhere in the "favorable" range.

Finally, do such plans really motivate employees to higher levels of performance? In following our notion that motivation is highly correlated with the existence of a direct link between effort and reward, some current plans in small companies may provide a fairly perceptible link to employees. With deferred profit sharing rewards often time-lagged by many years and with large numbers of employees scattered over hundreds of locations in plans such as Sears', on the other hand, we would not expect to find such a link. However, the existence of such system-oriented rewards may provide more employee satisfaction with the organization and a beneficial psychological effect, legitimate ends in themselves. Such an evaluation has been phrased aptly by Katz and Kahn:

> System rewards do little to motivate performance beyond the line of duty, with two possible exceptions. As people develop a liking for the attractions of the organization, they may be more likely to engage in cooperative relations with their fellows toward organizational goals.[26]

Further, they may describe their company "as a good place to work" contributing "to a favorable climate of opinion for the system in the external environment," which may enhace recruiting efforts as described earlier.[27]

In sum, there are a number of valid reasons for firms to adopt profit sharing plans. Such plans, however, will tend to be more successful under certain contingencies. We will now examine some of these.

Contingencies

A basic contingency for successful sharing plans is that there be profits to share, at least in most years. We hypothesize that this is more important in current plans than deferred ones, since in the latter, due to forfeitures and investment appreciation, an individual's profit sharing account may increase even in years in which there have been no profits to share. Further, to be perceived positively, there is probably a certain minimum percentage of the individual's pay that must be realized on the average through profit sharing. Zollitsch and Langsner, for example, have argued that any plan which will motivate employees "will need to share enough profits so that employees will receive at least 8, 10, or 12 percent benefit beyond their annual wage or salary."[28] A somewhat related point, which has been used as an argument against the values of profit sharing, is that employees will take their profit sharing payments for granted in good years, and become dissatisfied in years in which there are few or no profits to share. This factor may be partially overcome if relevant facts about the firm's business and profits are given to employees through periodic "progress reports." Such communications and the design of plans which are understandable by employees will aid in their being viewed favorably. The example of Sears going to full and immediate vesting after the passage of ERISA because of, among other reasons, the simplicity of employee understanding of this method illustrates this point quite clearly.

Two final points concerning profit sharing plans need to be made. First, unlike many personnel programs, size or stability of the company does not appear to be a contingency influencing profit sharing plans as it would be with traditional individual incentive systems. Even if the firm is changing rapidly in a dynamic environment, profit sharing plans will not need the constant updating as would changing the tasks involved in jobs. With respect to size, in a survey reported by the Profit Sharing Research Foundation in 1969, 339 or 26.5 per cent of deferred profit sharing trusts out of a sample of 1281 such trusts encompassed a number of employees in the range 1–49; while eight such trusts covered 25,000 or more employees.[29]

Second, as we have indicated with respect to other personnel programs, profit sharing will be more effective if employee-management relations are good. As one author has phrased it, "If the organization's employee relations program is perceived as generally rational, non-manipulative and relevant to the workers' situation, considerable credibility is likely to be given to the incentive plan proposal."[30]

Management Science

Apparently, relatively little work has been done in applying management science techniques to system incentive plans. In our search for such applications, we have found only one model. This model applies to profit sharing plans only. It is a mathematical programming model that uses the specific mathematical programming technique of dynamic programming. Dynamic programming is especially geared to dealing with multistage decision problems, in which decisions have an effect on the firm, not only in the present period but in future ones as well. In discussing their profit sharing model, its authors have pointed out that the effects of any amount of profit shared with the firm's employees will be felt both in the current and in some subsequent periods. They indicated that: "Due to the dynamic nature of profit sharing it is not meaningful to maximize the [firm's] profit per period. The concept of a multiperiod planning horizon must be brought into the analysis."[31] In consequence, this model was developed to determine the amount of any period's profits that should be shared with employees to maximize the present value of the firm's profits over the whole future planning period which the firm wishes to examine. This model is more theoretical and less applied than many of the management science models presented thus far but has had as one objective, pinpointing the need for future empirical research in determining optimum profit sharing payouts.

SCANLON PLANS

The philosophy and mechanics of Scanlon plans may be traced back to Joseph N. Scanlon. Scanlon first developed and implemented his ideas while a worker in a steel mill and union worker in the 1930's during the depression. He successfully convinced his company's management to develop a collaborative approach to help solve its economic problems. These efforts attracted the attention of numerous other companies and leading academic scholars. Scanlon ultimately joined the staff of the Industrial Relations Section at M.I.T. in 1946, where he remained until his death 10 years later.[32] We refer to Scanlon plans rather than *the* Scanlon plan, since there have been numerous variations among firms in the mechanics utilized in implementing this system incentive.

Scanlon plans represent a philosophy regarding the individual and human relations and a mechanism by which this philosophy can be put into effect in organizations.

The Scanlon philosophy is one that takes a very positive view of the capabilities of the human being, stressing that individuals can and want to meet higher level needs by participation in decision making. Our own view is that this philosophy is an overly optimistic one since we do not believe that *all* people want to assume more responsibility, participate in making decisions concerning their work environment and express creative ideas.[33] In fact, even among the strongest supporters of Scanlon plans, it has been pointed out that many employees, "because of their cultural and environmental situations," have learned *not* to behave in this way, and with "competent leadership and supportive guidance . . . must be helped to unlearn the negative response."[34] As we pointed out in Chapter 4, *basic* behavioral dispositions are difficult to modify once individuals have reached adulthood, and in line with this fact, the unlearning referred to here may be very difficult, if not impossible, in some cases. Some firms have used the plan with success, however, in overcoming a wide range of problems. For example, Scanlon plans have:

1. Served as an improved substitute for traditional wage incentive plans which were functioning very poorly.

2. Mobilized strong support from virtually all workers to effect reductions in production and other costs in order for a firm to literally avoid bankruptcy.

Recognizing that the Scanlon philosophy may be overly optimistic about human capabilities but that when properly implemented may provide a successful participative decision-making incentive, we will now turn to the three management decisions regarding Scanlon plans: eligibility, criteria, and reward. Then we will specify several key contingencies for the effective utilization of such plans. Finally, we will evaluate and comment briefly on future directions with respect to Scanlon plans.

Eligibility

Only two comments need to be made with respect to employee eligibility in Scanlon plans. First, a basic notion of the Scanlon philosophy is that all employees participate and hopefully reap the benefits of the plan, although sometimes the president of a Scanlon plan firm will be excluded. Second, some firms require a 1-, 2-, or 3-month waiting period after an employee begins working before he is eligibile for the bonuses paid under Scanlon plans.

Criteria

Employees will be rewarded financially under Scanlon plans if cost savings, most commonly computed on a monthly basis, are realized by the firm. These savings may come from two sources. One means of savings may accrue from more effort on the part of employees. The other means of effecting cost savings is through the generation of employee ideas. Scanlon plans include an elaborate participative decision-making mechanism to foster this goal. There are two different types of committees set up under the Scanlon Plan — committees in each department and a plant-wide screening committee. The basic functions and interrelationships between these two types of committees are illustrated in Figure 11–4.

Production Committees

The production committees, which are usually made up of the departmental supervisor and elected employee delegates,

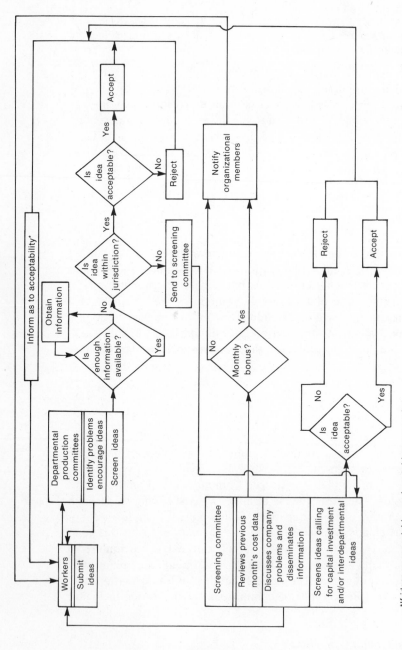

Figure 11-4 *Scanlon committees.*

*If ideas unacceptable, workers told reasons why.

meet every two to four weeks. One of their basic functions is to screen and evaluate employee ideas that fall within the jurisdiction of the department, and do not require capital investments. Ideas applying to work in more than one department or those requiring capital investments fall within the jurisdiction of the screening committee.

The second basic function of each production committee is to encourage actively employees in its department to submit suggestions. In their meetings, these committees will try to identify problems and make these problems known to the employees to "guide" creativity. This planned proaction represents one major distinction between Scanlon plans and traditional suggestion systems. Further, employees participating in Scanlon plans are not paid directly if their ideas are accepted. Even so, the Scanlon "planned proaction" appears to result in more suggestions being submitted than in traditional suggestion systems from reports in numerous case studies of plans in different companies. Certain other aspects of traditional suggestion systems, on the other hand, are equally applicable to Scanlon suggestions, e.g., prompt decisions on idea acceptance and letting employees know why any unusable suggestions have been rejected.

The Screening Committee

The screening committee is composed of the firm's or plant's chief executive officer, heads of major functional departments such as finance, and an "equal or greater number" of elected, nonmanagerial employees.[35] This committee most commonly meets once a month and performs the three functions illustrated in Figure 11–4. By being given the jobs of establishing whether there will be a bonus for the month, discussing company problems, disseminating relevant information throughout the firm (or plant), and screening ideas that have an interdepartmental impact or require capital investments, it can be seen that this committee wields considerable decision-making power.[36] With respect to the dissemination of information, for example, the committee "issues a monthly report on all the suggestions submitted to the respective Production Committees, including the name of the suggester, the suggestion, its rationale for improving productivity, and the disposition of the suggestion . . . ."[37]

The Production and Screening Committees: Learning

Regardless of whether or not we accept the optimistic assumptions about human nature indicated earlier, there can be no question but that those individuals who participate on either the production or screening committees sharpen their knowledge and skills in many ways. Thus, in a strict sense, Scanlon plan committee participation can be considered as much of a learning experience as any of the programs discussed in Chapters 7 and 8. Committee participation provides a form of leadership training. Being on a production committee, for example, places the individual in a situation in which he must learn about the firm's business (materials, supplies, overhead costs). Further, the production and screening committee problem-oriented meetings "are specific programs of training, education, and learning for personal and organizational development."[38]

Reward

The second component of the Scanlon philosophy is the provision of a reward, usually monthly, to all employees if a cost savings norm is exceeded. This is referred to as the Scanlon bonus and is shared in proportion to the individual's regular rate of pay so that those employees who hold more responsible positions in the organization will receive a larger bonus than those persons with lesser skills. For this reason, it is extremely important that wages and salaries be equitable, since if they are not, neither can the Scanlon bonus be fair.

The Scanlon norm is usually developed by analyzing total labor costs in relation to the value of the firm's output over a representative historical period (e.g., the previous two to five years). The norm is developed cooperatively by management and its employees (or their union).[39] In its simplest form, the norm equals:

$$\frac{\text{total labor costs}}{\text{total value of production}}$$

If, in any given month, total labor costs are less than would be expected under the norm, the workers and company usually share in these "savings." An example of a "typical" Scanlon bonus month for a hypothetical firm is illustrated in Figure 11–5.

References to this figure will allow further discussion of the mechanics of the Scanlon bonus. First, the reserve for future deficits is included to cover those months in which total labor costs exceed the standard. In these months, no pay is actually taken away from any employee, but a "deficit" is recorded. At the end of each year, if these reserves are greater than any deficit months, they are added to the pool and shared on the basis of

a. Scanlon ratio $\dfrac{\text{total labor costs}}{\text{total value of production}}$ 0.40/1.00

b. Value of production $200,000

c. Expected "norm" labor costs (a × b)   80,000

d. Actual total labor costs   60,000

e. Bonus "pool" (c − d)   20,000

f. Share to company—25 per cent (e × 0.25)   5,000

g. Share to employees—75 per cent (e × 0.75)   15,000

h. Reserve for future deficits (25 per cent × g)   3,750

i. Pool for monthly distribution (g − h)   11,250

j. Bonus for each employee as a percentage of his pay for the month (i ÷ d)   18.75%

Pay Example for Typical Employee

Monthly Pay	Bonus Percentage	Bonus Pay	Total Pay
$1000	18.75	$187.50	$1187.50

Figure 11–5 *Typical Scanlon bonus month calculations. (Adapted from Frost, et al.,* The Scanlon Plan for Organization Development. *p. 15, with permission of the publisher, the Michigan State University Press, 1974.)*

regular pay as with the monthly bonuses. If the reserves set aside for the year are inadequate to cover deficit months (i.e., those in which total labor costs exceed the norm), the company usually writes the deficit amount off at a loss. Hence, employees have an opportunity to "start over again" in the next year. A "typical" reserve figure is 25 per cent, but firms in which there are wider monthly fluctuations in demand patterns will usually want to provide for a higher reserve than those organizations with a relatively stable type of operation.

Second, the percentage share given to the company is frequently 25 per cent, but this will vary, depending upon the company's financial position. In an extremely financially strained company, for example, management and its employees may agree on a larger share for the firm. The converse is also true.

Third, the Scanlon factor (or ratio) must be updated from time to time as the cost structure changes, or else the bonus will be inequitable to either management or employees. A question has been raised as to the administrative complexity and feasibility of such updatings, particularly if they are frequent. The only evidence that we have been able to uncover on this point is in a letter written by Frederick Lesieur in January 1975, which indicated that "in the inflationary spirals of 1972–1974, as material costs outstripped wage increases, Scanlon ratios had to undergo frequent changes. Those involved in managing Scanlon plans found, however, that these changes were made with minimal difficulty."[40] Our own view is that firms, through the use of computers, can easily modify the ratio, as well as handle all aspects of the Scanlon bonus to the point of actually calculating employee paychecks. This assumes, of course, that management and the employees could agree on the changes.

Contingencies

Several conditions seem to be extremely important to the effective functioning of Scanlon plans. One key variable — technology — which might be expected to be important does not appear so. One of what we consider to be the two most important contingencies is that the firm's management will have to commit itself to a "tremendous change" in the firm's power structure. With the production and screening committees:

> The total effect is to move downward in the organization many decisions relating to its specific operations; moreover, this delegation or downward movement of authority and decision-making is carried out by means of formal changes in the organizational structure.[41]

As we saw earlier, the production committee members must have access to cost information that many managements would hesitate to provide workers. Further, the whole suggestion mechanism can provide a threat to supervisors and managers for the same reasons discussed with traditional suggestion systems, but moreso because of the organized, structured, and proactive nature of the suggestion process. In short, success of Scanlon plans seems to be very highly contingent on the willingness of management to actively display a "democratic" leadership and be willing to adhere to organic-oriented attitudes in actual practice.

Second, there must be the possibility of being able to obtain bonuses over a period of time for the Scanlon plan to be effective. Without this financial reward, much of the motivation built into the plan is lost. It is far from clear, however, in which types of industries such bonuses will be forthcoming, which brings us to the contingency of technology.

As indicated, Scanlon plans are based on a highly organic philosophy. There appears to be no evidence, however, that they are more effective in technologies where less certainty is present along the lines discussed in Chapter 1. Lesieur and Puckett have shown Scanlon plans to be effective both at the mass production oriented Parker Pen Company (theoretically a fairly "certain" technology amenable to mechanistic management practices) and in the highly job-shop oriented and hence less certain environment of the Pfaudler Company.[42] Katz and Kahn have raised the question as to whether Scanlon plans can survive in highly automated operations because of the sharp decline in labor costs,[43] while Bennis has reported on the adoption of a Scanlon plan at a continuous manufacturing oriented oil refinery.[44] As indicated in the last chapter, equipment utilization incentives are feasible in improving productivity in automated operations, and in fact, because of worker interdependence, are sometimes really plant-wide or system incentives. With respect to technology, in fact, we know of only one study indicating that this variable has an impact on Scanlon plans, and the technological factors so examined were so related to the particular conditions of one firm that we cannot generalize from them.[45]

Elasticity of demand, on the other hand, may well be an important Scanlon success contingency, although there is disagreement on this issue. Puckett studied 10 Scanlon plan firms, of which five represented situations in which it appeared that "price reduction based on increased efficiency could result in a significant improvement in sales,"[46] and five in which elasticity did not seem to be significant. Among these firms, he found no relationship between elasticity and Scanlon plan success. Strauss and Sayles, on the other hand, have indicated that a company must be able to increase sales to the extent of any increases in production if Scanlon plans are to succeed.[47] We agree with the latter interpretation based on theory and the fact that Puckett's sample size was small and his estimation of "elasticity" was an extremely subjective one.

Many firms that have adopted Scanlon plans have been relatively small ones with a few hundred or few thousand employees. Puckett's research indicates that "large" as well as small size firms have had successful Scanlon experiences.[48] From a theoretical point of view, however, employees in smaller operations may well be in a better position to perceive the effort-reward link than those in huge manufacturing plants. Further, the "plan may be unwieldy to administer in large companies where time consumed in operating the plan may be disproportionate to the savings gained in labor costs or where firm bigness stifles two-way communications."[49]

Finally, as is true with most personnel systems, effective administration is a basic contingency. As an almost unbelievable example of poor Scanlon administration, one firm reportedly dropped the Scanlon plan in favor of a profit sharing plan, even though it was prospering considerably. In spite of this financial prosperity, Scanlon bonus payments were negligible in this case, due to the fact that the ratio had not been updated appropriately "because the accountant felt that the bookkeeping work would have been too difficult."[50]

Evaluation and Future Directions

Evaluation

Scanlon plans have worked very successfully in some companies, but have been abandoned in others, sometimes due to poor implementation as we have seen. Implemented properly, and in light of the contingencies indicated here, Scanlon plans may serve to meet the full range of Maslow's needs hierarchy. The Scanlon bonus, if adequate, contributes to meeting many needs, including security, while participation in production or screening committees provides opportunities to meet higher level needs such as esteem and self-actualization. Simply participating in a Scanlon plan firm to the extent of suggesting ideas can, of course, also help meet self-actualization needs as can be done under traditional suggestion systems.

Supporters of Scanlon plans have also argued that the plans provide a mechanism whereby good bonuses will come about only as a result of hard work. The bonuses are related directly to production savings, not to extra profits because of a competitor's poor marketing decision or other external factors. As one book has phrased it: "There are no Santa Claus gifts or autocratic benefactor's bonuses. There are disciplined team members who are being intelligently coached to win the game."[51] Further, these efforts are *system* efforts, for the bonuses "reward not the efficiency of the individual or the group, but the gains in overall efficiency of the company as a procurement-production-marketing system."[52] It should be noted, however, that changes in Scanlon bonuses may be influenced by variables other than the combined efforts of individuals in the organizational system. Factors not completely under control of a firm such as general business conditions or competitor actions may influence the firm's sales volume, product mix, or other company characteristics. Changes in these characteristics, in turn, may affect Scanlon bonuses. For example, a change in product mix led top management at Donnelly Mirrors in Holland, Michigan, to convert its modified Scanlon formula into a profit sharing formula. As John Donnelly, Chairman of the Board of this firm, put it in 1977, "In the past year, we saw a change in product mix which left the company earning good profits and the [Scanlon] bonus falling almost to zero."[53] Thus, although Scanlon bonuses are related directly to production savings, they may be influenced by external variables in much the same way as are profit sharing distributions under both profit sharing plans and in the Lincoln plan, which we will discuss later.

Future Directions

The "future directions" of Scanlon plans encompass two aspects. First, there is the question of whether the number of such plans will grow. As just indicated, these plans do have many merits and may become even more popular in the future. In spite of the use of some important human judgments in some types of automated operations, it remains to be seen, however, whether further automation in our postindustrial society will hamper Scanlon opportunities.

There is also more attention being given to the study of Scanlon plans so as to better understand their properties and contingencies. Most of the earlier writings on Scanlon plans were in the form of case studies, and little, if any, rigorous research was carried out on the plans. More recently, however, there seems to be a renewed and more scholarly interest in Scanlon plans. For example, an organization called the Scanlon Plan Associates, has been formed and has jointly sponsored a number of research projects with the Department of Psychology of Michigan State University. Employee attitudes toward Scanlon plans, differences among organizational units' perceptions of Scanlon plans in relation to job involvement, motivation, and identification with the organization, and differences in management attitudes toward employees in Scanlon and non-Scanlon firms are among the variables which have been explored in the more recent research.[54] For example, in one study of 18 manufacturing organizations, all with at least two years experience with Scanlon plans, it was found that:

1. Managers in companies which had abandoned their Scanlon plan (8 of the 18) perceived "rank-and-file employees to demonstrate less judgment, creativity, responsibility, dependability," etc., than those in companies which maintained the plan.[55]

2. Managers in the companies which abandoned their plan had less favorable attitudes toward participative decision making than those in companies which retained the plan.

The authors of this study interpreted the results cautiously, pointing out that one could not infer from these results that managerial attitudes *caused* the abandonment of the Scanlon plans since factors associated with Scanlon plan abandonment may have "caused the observed differences in managerial attitudes."[56]

THE LINCOLN ELECTRIC PLAN

History

The Lincoln Electric Company of Cleveland, Ohio, has developed a multifaceted, highly systems-oriented and successful form of incentive management. The company is the world's leading producer of arc welding equipment and electrodes and also is well known for its electric motors production, which dates back to 1895. The company is small (approximately 2350 employees as of mid-1976).[57] Former president James F. Lincoln introduced a traditional piecework plan into the firm in 1914. During the depression, Lincoln turned down a request for a 10 per cent increase in wages, because he did not believe that meeting this request was financially feasible for the firm. Then, the company's workers responded with the request for a year-end bonus if "through increased productivity and lowered costs, the year-end profits were larger."[58] Surprisingly, the bonus was considerably larger than expected by Lincoln. Since 1934, the bonus (really a current profit sharing one) has been in effect and substantial bonuses have been realized. Lincoln's incentive management plan, however, incorporated many other interrelated mechanisms, and the total "Lincoln Plan" reflects very directly and cannot be understood without understanding the philosophical assumptions of its creator.

Lincoln's Incentive Management Philosophy

Lincoln's philosophy, put forth very clearly in his classic *Incentive Management*,[59] has psychological, religious, and economic facets. First, somewhat like Scanlon, Lincoln took an organic, positive view of the capabilities of the human being, but seemed to emphasize *latent* potential more than Scanlon. One of Lincoln's basic beliefs, for example, was the following:

The governing fact in incentive management is this: developed man will be a far abler person than he was before such development took place. . . .[He] will be a genius compared to the same individual who now under our present lack of incentive remains almost completely undeveloped.[60]

But how far can such development go? According to Lincoln:

No one can know how far man can develop his latent abilities. It is obvious that the Creator in giving to man such abilities expected them to be used. Therefore, the ultimate goal will always be a challenge to any man, no matter how far he goes in his development.[61]

Lincoln also emphasized the notion of hard work as expressed in the Protestant ethic; and believed in a "democratic" leadership style. To quote Lincoln again: "We do not distinguish between so-called management and labor. All management must labor and labor must manage."[62] Lincoln also believed, correctly or not, that crises created leaders. He believed, for example, that it was only after Christ's "crucifixion and resurrection that the disciples developed their great abilities of leadership."[63]

Lincoln's somewhat religious faith in human potential, and his highly congruent belief in democratic management was also supplemented by an economic philosophy about management and our capitalistic system. Lincoln indicated that:

1. "The real and ultimate boss of industry is the consumer."
2. The basic goal of any industry must be "*to make a better and better product to be sold to more and more people at a lower and lower price.*"
3. "Profit under incentive management is no longer an end in itself. It is a by-product."
4. Time required for production "can only be reduced by eliminating jobs that were previously needed."[64] However, as we shall see later, Lincoln believed that under incentive management, no workers needed to be laid off.
5. The owner, worker and consumer *all* must share in profits.

We will now indicate how these philosophical assumptions have been molded into a very effective incentive system.

Eligibility

With respect to eligibility, all members of Lincoln Electric except the president and chairman of the board have an opportunity to take advantage of the system's rewards. This, of course, is congruent with the democratic element of Lincoln's philosophy.

Criteria

Reward criteria are multiple under the Lincoln system of incentives. Again following Lincoln's democratic philosophy, certain rewards accrue to the individual simply by virtue of his being a member of the organization as is shown in Figure 11–1. It should be noted, however, that waiting periods are required before new employees are eligible for two of these organizational membership rewards — an employment guarantee and the option to purchase company stock.

Second is the piecework incentive mentioned earlier, which predated the profit sharing bonus by 20 years. This incentive is simply a traditional piecework system as discussed in the previous chapter. However, it has several specific features that form an integral part of the Lincoln incentive philosophy:

1. Management has guaranteed not to change the piecework rates unless job content is changed.
2. Time studies are very carefully done.
3. Certain jobs, "generally considered as 'unmeasurable,' have been closely analyzed, standardized, and included in the piece-rate incentive system."[65] This is again congruent with the democratic flavor of the Lincoln philosophy of providing as many employees an opportunity for incentives as possible.

4. Again in line with this democratic philosophy, there is an appeal procedure and employees may challenge standards that they think are unfair. Such appeals are handled by a special committee composed of the worker, his foreman, the time-study man and the personnel director. If the worker is still not convinced, the time-study man will perform the job himself, and his "reestablished time — either as originally set, higher, or lower — is then accepted as standard."[66]

5. A very careful job is done not only in time studying jobs, but in job evaluation as well. Besides being inherently equitable, these careful time study and job evaluation methods are exceptionally important for another reason. As we will show later, one of the key factors which determines how workers share in the annual (profit sharing) bonus is their basic pay. This relationship illustrates one of the ways in which the Lincoln incentive plan is such an interdependent system.

Finally, two basic systems performance mechanisms may help meet the criterion of exceeding a predetermined profit level, which determines the size of the yearly profit sharing pool. The first of these two mechanisms is an advisory board, composed of representatives elected by employees, which suggests improvements in the firm's operation. The final decision on any such suggestions is made by management.[67] This mechanism, although an important system element, does not appear as prominant as the production and screening committees in Scanlon plans.

Merit rating (or performance appraisal) is another personnel mechanism integrated into the Lincoln *system*. Twice each year, the work performance of employees is rated on four variables, each weighted equally: (1) quality of work, (2) quantity of output, (3) cooperation, and (4) dependability. This mechanism is integrated into the Lincoln incentive management system in two ways. Performance appraisals are a variable in determining how much of the profit sharing bonus pool each employee receives each year. Further, they are utilized in the firm's promotion by merit and largely from within policy.

These mechanisms are geared toward increasing profits, which are shared by employees. The criterion for profit sharing in the Lincoln plan is different from the percentage formulas illustrated in discussing deferred profit sharing plans. The Lincoln plan provides for reserves for reinvestment, and a "fair" (variable) dividend percentage for its stockholders to be deducted from its profits, with the remainder put into the yearly pool. We will indicate the relative magnitude of this reward at Lincoln Electric when we show specifically how each organizational member is rewarded. We will now turn our attention to the multiple rewards given individuals under Lincoln incentive management.

Rewards

There are three basic classes of rewards provided the individual under the Lincoln plan. For the individual piecework incentives, the rewards are simple cash payments as those discussed in the previous chapter; although these cash rewards do affect the individual's share of the Lincoln profit sharing bonus pool. There are several rewards, both financial and nonfinancial, which accrue to individuals by virtue of their organizational membership following Lincoln's democratic philosophy. Finally, there is the yearly profit sharing bonus.

Organizational Membership Rewards

Some rewards given members of the Lincoln organization are primarily psychological, with others having economic implications as well. Of the five "organizational membership" rewards shown in Figure 11–1, three may provide employee satisfaction but probably do not motivate employees to work harder to any great extent. The first of these, which follows from Lincoln's democratic philosophy, is that all organizational members are treated equally with respect to certain everyday privileges. "For example, there are no reserved employee parking spaces; there is one cafeteria (with excellent food) for all employees — workers and executives alike sit wherever spaces are available."[68]

Directly following Lincoln's philosophy, the company established in 1958 "a work guarantee policy," which provided that, after a two-year waiting period, all employees would be guaranteed at least 75 per cent of the normal work week (30 of 40 hours) and that reductions in demand would be translated into a shorter work week down to this minimum — with no one being laid off. As a matter of fact, as of July 1976, no one had been laid off at the Lincoln Electric Company since the 1958 policy was established — not even one of those employees who had not yet worked for the company for two years which was necessary to be eligible for this reward.[69]

The company also has a policy of providing all organization members with the opportunity to buy up to a certain number of shares of the firm's stock per year at "book value" rather than "market value."[70] In 1976, this maximum number was 30 shares. The company, in turn, has the option to repurchase all of the individual's stock when he leaves the company, also at book value — which it had always exercised as of mid-1976. A basic idea behind this reward is that (aside from stock dividends) the book value of the stock will typically appreciate and, when resold to the company, the employee will be taxed at the favorable capital gains rate discussed previously. There is a one-year waiting period to be eligible for this reward, and as of mid-1976, about 30 per cent of the firm's total common stock was owned by its members. Probably of more motivational value are Lincoln's two organizational membership rewards of promotion from within and granting of work autonomy. The company has traditionally followed a promotion from within policy based solely on merit. In recent years, however, a few outsiders such as sales and engineering trainees have been brought in.[71] This promotion policy may be thought of as both a reward and as a motivational tool. It may serve as such a tool by inducing employees to work harder to be qualified to move ahead in the organization. Such efforts may be linked to some extent, of course, to profits, although in the Lincoln plan one must recognize that profits are also influenced by many external variables such as competitors' actions and the state of the economy.

With respect to work autonomy in the Lincoln plan, *some* employees, where appropriate, have been given considerable latitude as to how to perform their duties. More specifically, the plan has provided for:

Independent work groups of "subcontractor shop" operations, in which employees have the opportunity to earn specified piecework rates, perform their own quality control and develop their own production procedures in completing subassembly operations within given cost, quantity, and quality parameters.[72]

Such opportunities are considered to provide some people with motivation and improve the quality of work life.

Concerning work autonomy, following an organic, democratic philosophy, certain individuals will perform better under conditions in which they have a greater say as to how their jobs will be done and when they are not required to work under rigid production methods. Some firms have "despecialized" jobs by giving the worker more tasks to perform and in some cases more complex tasks. Terms such as "job enlargement" and "job enrichment" respectively have been used to describe these decision strategies. Finally, following the notion that satisfaction *per se* is a legitimate organizational objective, contemporary authors have been interested in improving the "quality of work life" by providing workers (who can handle it) with greater "job autonomy."[73]

The Profit Sharing Bonus Mechanism

We will now turn our attention to the annual Lincoln bonus, which, as indicated previously, is a current profit sharing plan, with employee shares of the funds available being related to their pay and merit rating. Specifically, each organizational member's annual *bonus* (above and beyond his regular pay) is computed by using the following formula:

$$\text{Merit Rating Percent Score} \times \text{Annual Pay} \times \left(\frac{\text{\$ In Profit Sharing Pool}}{\text{Annual Payroll Costs}}\right).$$

For example, if an individual's merit rating is 1.10 per cent and his annual pay $12,000, there is $27 million in the profit sharing fund, and total payroll costs are $30 million, his bonus would be:

$$1.10 \times \$12,000 \times \frac{\$27,000,000}{\$30,000,000} = \$11,880$$

As may be noted, this formula is simple to calculate, and easy for employees to understand. Its equitability for each Lincoln employee, of course, depends upon the quality underlying the performance appraisal figure chosen, and good job evaluation and work standards data (where applicable) as contributors to each individual's basic yearly pay.

In our example, a bonus of 99 per cent of an employee's annual pay was given. Is such a huge bonus realistic? As reported in 1976, the bonus factor had ranged from 85 to 95 per cent during the previous five years, while since the plan's inception in 1934 there had been almost as much paid in bonuses as in regular earnings.[74] Further, in 1975 the *actual* profit sharing pool was very close to the figure shown in the example — it was approximately $27,500,000. With 2369 workers eligible for the bonus in this year, the average bonus was approximately $11,608.[75]

The thoughtful reader may raise the question: Have there been any negative *side effects* with bonuses this high? Has the firm been able to keep prices down as expressed in Lincoln's philosophy? Or, have company profits suffered with such high profit sharing bonuses? Further, are the bonuses based on competitive pay levels to start with? Or, is the Lincoln employee's normal yearly pay lower than employees in most other firms, with high percentage bonuses helping to "make up" for low regular pay? Finally, how good are its other employee benefits?

Considerable economic data have been collected over the years to provide concrete answers to these questions:

1. The firm was able to keep the prices of its products down close to 1933 levels for several decades. For example, in spite of inflationary factors, Lincoln's 200, 300, and 600 ampere electric motor driven arc welders sold for less in 1949 than in 1933. To be even more specific, the average annual price of Lincoln's 600 ampere welder was $1,288 in 1933 while only $695 in 1949.[76] It was not until the inflationary cost spirals of the 1970's that the firm was finally forced to back down on its pricing policies and increase prices to any great extent.

2. As far as company profits are concerned, the firm's return on investment was "over 10%," for example, during the difficult 1973–1975 period and the firm's profits have remained stable for several years.[77]

3. The firm has typically had a reputation of being competitive with its *basic pay* so that the bonuses have meant that Lincoln employees have been extremely well paid when their profit sharing bonuses are included in their total annual compensation. For example, Zollitsch and Langsner compared the average hourly earnings of Lincoln production

and nonsupervisory manufacturing personnel with similar data for all manufacturing industries from 1956–1968. In 1968, for example, the average hourly Lincoln wage including the bonus was $7.20, as opposed to $3.01 for all manufacturing industries.[78]

4. The employee benefit programs appear competitive with most firms. For example, the vacation policy begins with two weeks after one year's service, and goes up to four weeks after 25 years. There is "a paid medical, surgical, and hospital plan, life insurance, and retirement plan beginnning at age 60...."[79]

Further, the firm has traditionally had an excellent record on other success variables such as absenteeism and turnover. For example, Lincoln's average rate of turnover per month for the years 1934–1949 ranged from 0.574 to 1.607 per cent as compared with a range of from 3.142 to 8.000 per cent for all manufacturing industries.[80]

From almost every point of view, the Lincoln plan has been successful. Thus, we will *not* turn our attention next to contingencies contributing to the success of Lincoln plans, for there is only one such system plan. Rather, we will indicate some of the reasons why the plan has been successful — in years of depression, of World War II, of post-war inflation, and during the "inflationary recession" of the 1970's.

Reasons For Success

One basic reason for the Lincoln plan's success is that it has implemented a sound philosophy with a total system approach to motivating individuals to develop themselves and produce, present ideas, and contribute in other ways to organizational goals at very high levels. The Lincoln plan is *not* just a profit sharing plan. It does *not* just provide individual piecework incentives. It is *not* just a plan emphasizing opportunities for advancement by promotion from within policies. Rather, it is all of these aspects of personnel management interwoven into a success mosaic. Perhaps it is synergistic (synergy, in general system theory, is expressed by the notion that the whole is greater than the simple sum of its parts).[81]

The size of the firm may be another reason that has contributed to the plan's success. Lincoln Electric is small enough so that many of the interrelated effort-reward links (which we have indicated so often are important to effective incentives) are fairly easily perceptible by most all organizational members.

Another contributing factor to the effectiveness of the plan *may* be that it was installed and initially guided by a "charismatic" leader. "Charisma" is a term which has not been well researched,[82] but generally has been used to describe political figures "who have achieved very strong power positions primarily because of the extraordinary nature of their personalities alone."[83] Abraham Lincoln (on the positive side) and Adolph Hitler (on the negative side) would be examples of extremely charismatic leaders. At a much less grandiose level, two noted social scientists, Katz and Kahn, have questioned whether some charisma may need to exist in the initiation of Scanlon plans for them to be successful.[84] This raises the question that perhaps both the personalities of Joseph Scanlon (and his followers such as Frederick Lesieur) and that of James Lincoln were so dynamic as to be instrumental in attracting followers (organizational members) to their philosophies and the implementation of these philosophies in system incentive mechanisms.

The Lincoln plan seems to incorporate a wide spectrum of Maslow's five classes of needs, as described in Chapter 9. For example, the monetary rewards may meet many needs (from physiological to esteem); the guaranteed work week helps meet security needs; and election to the advisory board, for those types of people who want to participate in helping management make decisions, may serve to stimulate self-actualization. The same can also be said for those workers given a great deal of autonomy in performing their work.

Two final comments are in order concerning the Lincoln plan. First, it appears to constitute a unique open system—one which may well be irreproducible elsewhere. Second, the technology of the firm raises some questions about which organizational types are most suitable for organic and mechanistic management systems. In Lincoln's production of both electric motors and arc welding equipment, there are certain tasks conducive to organic management. Special products are manufactured that take a great deal of democratic management where the workers are given latitude in decision making. With both electric motor and arc welding equipment production, however, there is a great deal of large batch or mass production technology that is involved, and many jobs are time studied and highly standardized. Such operations are characterized by a considerable degree of certainty and are therefore theoretically conducive to mechanistic management. In all respects, however, both the Lincoln philosophy and incentive implementation mechanisms are highly organic in orientation. How Lincoln Electric has been able to foster democratic, organic-oriented management practices and the assumption of individual responsibility in production areas conducive theoretically to both organic and mechanistic approaches has been explained by Richard S. Sabo of Lincoln Electric as follows:

> Even in our high [large batch and mass] production areas, we expect everyone to produce a high quality product and the responsibility

for quality falls on the individual, not an inspection department or foreman.

I would have to summarize by saying that one of the keys to our success is that we have been able to incorporate highly-motivated people who take a great deal of pride in their work whether it be on an organic or mechanistic management task.[85]

From this discussion, the Lincoln experience suggests that even though certain technologies are more conducive to organic management practices than others, such a managerial approach can be applied to "mechanistic" conditions. Although such an application may be more difficult to achieve than under "organic" technologies, the Lincoln experience shows its feasibility when both management and its employees strongly support an organic philosophy. This conclusion parallels the one suggested earlier with the successful application of organic Scanlon plans under different technological conditions.

SUMMARY

Many different system incentives have been employed by companies in an effort to stimulate more motivation and satisfaction on the part of organizational members. Sometimes these incentives have been used to supplement individual incentives of the type discussed in Chapter 10. The most widely used of the three system incentives discussed in this chapter are profit sharing plans, of which there are three basic types — deferred, current and combination. All these plans provide for rewards to be distributed to organization members based on company profit levels (and the employees' own pay). Scanlon plans provide for current (usually monthly) bonuses to be paid to employees for increased effort or ideas which effect cost savings in the firm. There is a formalized active employee participation structure incorporated into this type of system. Finally, we discussed the unique and highly system-oriented Lincoln Electric plan, which provides for a number of interrelated rewards, some of which are primarily psychological and others economic.

DISCUSSION AND STUDY QUESTIONS

1. If you were to go to work for a company with a profit sharing plan upon graduation from college, which type of plan would you prefer — current or deferred — assuming that the firm's contribution would be the same under either type each year? Why? Assume that the company's deferred plan provides for full and immediate vesting (after a waiting period of one year).
2. Deferred qualified profit sharing plans have little motivation-

al value, and should be used only in place of a pension plan to provide employees with retirement security, because the link between effort and reward is so distant. Discuss.

3. Under which of the following conditions do you believe that a profit sharing plan would be effective?
   a. A firm whose ROI (return on investment) has been as follows over the last five years — 8%; −7%; −8%; +2%; −1%.
   b. In a small manufacturing firm with only 200 employees.
   c. In a firm in an extremely dynamic industry in which technology and job content are rapidly changing.
   d. In a large firm, with many geographically dispersed units and in which many employees may see relatively little relation between their effort and their firm's profit sharing contribution.
   e. In a firm with a deferred plan consisting largely of the firm's own common stock.

4. Why do you suppose there have been so few management science models developed to aid managers in making decisions regarding system incentives? Can you suggest any decisions which could be dealt with by utilizing either of the three types of management science models discussed in Chapter 1?

5. How would you rank the three system incentives discussed in the chapter with respect to their meeting the full range of Maslow's needs as discussed in Chapter 9 — physiological, security, belongingness, esteem and self-actualization? Give your reasons why.

6. a. The Scanlon ratio at the Acme Company is .60/1.00; or 60 per cent. In the month of January, the value of production turned out at Acme was $80,000, and total labor costs were $40,000. The Ajax company receives a 20 per cent share of the monthly bonus pool, and 20 per cent of the pool is set aside monthly as a reserve for future deficits. Janet Lanscon works at Ajax and earns $1000/month. How much, if any, bonus did she receive in January? Show all calculations. If you were Janet, would you be satisfied with this bonus?
   b. Suppose we just change one figure above — total actual labor costs from $40,000 to $48,162. In January, what would Janet's bonus be, and how satisfied do you think she would be with her bonus?

7. Under which of the following conditions do you believe that a Scanlon plan would be effective? Why?
   a. In a large mass production operation.
   b. In a job shop operation.
   c. In a firm which does not release its cost control data to first line supervisors.
   d. Under conditions of inelastic demand for a firm's products.
   e. In a continuous processing automated oil refinery.

8. Which of the following statements do you think that the late James Lincoln would agree with?
   a. "The basic objective of any firm is to make a profit, while at the same time meeting its employees security needs."

      b. "Some individuals have strong 'dependence needs'."

      c. "Consumers as well as workers and owners ought to share in the profit of a firm."

      d. "Crises create leaders."

9. To what extent to you think that the authors of the text would agree with each of the quotations in Question 8 above?

10. Which of the many system rewards in the Lincoln plan do you think contribute most to James Lincoln's philosophy that: "No one can know how far man can develop his latent abilities"?

Notes

[1]There are other "system" incentive plans which have been successfully used by a number of firms. One of the more well known of these is the Rucker-type plan, developed by Allen W. Rucker, and now being installed for firms by the consulting firm of Eddy-Rucker-Nickels Company of Cambridge, Massachusetts. See, for example, Herbert G. Zollitsch and Adolph Langsner, *Wage and Salary Administration,* 2nd ed. (Cincinnati: South-Western Publishing Co., 1970), pp. 591-595, and J. D. Dunn and F. M. Rachel, *Wage and Salary Administration* (New York: McGraw-Hill Book Co., 1971), pp. 253–255. Another newer system incentive that is becoming more popular is employee stock ownership plans (ESOPS). For a discussion and analysis of ESOPS, see, for example, *ESOPS: An Analytical Report,* prepared for the Profit Sharing Council of America by Hewitt Associates of Deerfield, Illinois, undated.

[2]Dunn and Rachel, op. cit., p. 261.

[3]Zollitsch and Langsner, op. cit., p. 571.

[4]These data were provided to the authors in a personal communication by Bert L. Metzger, President of the Profit Sharing Research Foundation in Evanston, Illinois. This organization is interested, not only in all types of profit sharing plans, but also in such other financial incentive plans as Scanlon plans, ESOPS, and employee thrift plans. Metzger has written widely in these areas and his latest work on profit sharing is *Profit Sharing in 38 Large Companies, Volume 1* (Evanston, Ill.: Profit Sharing Research Foundation, 1975). This book provides a rich amount of detail on the specific characteristics of these 38 plans. We appreciate his providing us with considerable information on profit sharing. We also appreciate his reading this section of this chapter to help ensure correctness. Full responsibility for the content, of course, is ours.

[5]This figure was arrived at as follows: Periodically the Securities and Exchange Commission publishes a total asset dollar figure for noninsured *pension funds,* but which "includes deferred profit sharing funds." Mr. Bert Metzger has indicated that of the total asset figure reported for the pension funds, approximately 25 per cent represents profit sharing funds. The total asset figure for 1975 was over \$145 billion, and 25 per cent of this figure is approximately \$36.3 billion. See *Statistical Bulletin* (Washington: Securities and Exchange Commission), 35 (April, 1976), p. 210. The astute reader will note that with approximately 197,000 qualified deferred plans in existence in 1975 with total assets of all such funds being about \$36.3 billion, the average total assets of deferred plans were only about \$184,000. At first glance this seems unbelievably low, especially when one considers that the total assets of only one company's (Sears Roebuck) deferred plan in that year were about \$2.6 billion! The reasons for this seeming anomaly are as follows: A majority of the newer plans adopted between 1970 and 1975 were those of smaller companies with relatively few employees. Also, the 95,544 plans adopted during this period (which represented 48.4 per cent of *all* existing deferred qualified plans in 1975) were so new that their fund assets had not yet had a chance to accumulate to any great extent.

[6]Dunn and Rachel, op. cit., p. 261.

[7]Under ERISA, certain tax advantages on lump sum withdrawals of assets from his firm's fund which we will discuss later, are provided the individual after he attains age 59½. See ERISA (Public Law 93–406, September 2, 1974, 88 Stat. 988). If he withdraws his assets in the fund while still an employee prior to this age he will suffer what may be a substantial tax penalty.

[8]Or, more technically, the plan must "meet the IRS requirement that an employer divest himself of any title to the contributions he will make." Bert L. Metzger, *Investment Practices, Performance, and Management of Profit Sharing Funds* (Evanston, Ill.: Profit Sharing Research Foundation, 1969), p. 137.

[9]See ERISA, 88 Stat. 939, and 982. In addition, ERISA provided for adjusting the $25,000 figure annually due to changes in the cost of living.

[10]The information in this paragraph was provided in a personal communication from Bert L. Metzger, July, 1976. A specific description of several large combined plans may be found in his *Profit Sharing in 38 Large Companies,* pp. 11–12.

[11]Personal communication from Bert L. Metzger, July, 1976.

[12]Metzger, *Investment Practices,* pp. 172–173.

[13]Taken from Sears Roebuck's "The Savings and Profit Sharing Fund of Sears' Employees," 1977, p. 9. This booklet, and permission to draw materials from it as well as other information on profit sharing plans was provided to the authors by Merl Douglas, Executive Director of The Savings and Profit Sharing Fund of Sears' Employees. We would like to express our appreciation to Mr. Douglas for his assistance, and for checking our manuscript for correctness. Full responsibility for its correctness is, of course, ours. We should also point out that a thorough description of the Sears plan may be found in Metzger, *Profit Sharing in 38 Large Companies,* pp. 171–177.

[14]Metzger, *Investment Practices,* p. 74.

[15]Excerpts of a letter from Merl Douglas, July 7, 1976.

[16]Public Law 94–455, Tax Reform Act of 1976, 90 Stat. 1554.

[17]ERISA, 88 Stat. 989.

[18]ERISA, Section 2005, 88 Stat. 989–990.

[19]We are making these calculations following the method suggested in J. K. Lasser's *Your Income Tax Guide* (New York: Simon and Schuster, 1975), Sec. 7.121, pp. 114–115. We are setting up this example so that the more complex "minimum distribution allowance" is not involved. If the reader is interested in understanding this complication, an excellent example is provided in ibid.

[20]Using tax rates derived from the Married Taxpayers Filing Joint Returns 1976 Tax Rate Schedule on p. 27 of the U.S. *1976 Federal Income Tax Forms,* assuming a maximum earned income tax rate of 50 per cent (over $52,000), and ignoring exemptions and deductions, and the possibility of regular income averaging. The 1978 rate schedule which would be technically applicable here has not been published as this book goes to press.

[21]See Bert L. Metzger and Jerome A. Colletti, *Does Profit Sharing Pay?* (Evanston, Ill.: Profit Sharing Research Foundation, 1971).

[22]Ibid., p. 84.

[23]We will discuss IRA's in the next chapter.

[24]Donald G. Carlson, "Responding to the Pension Reform Law," *Harvard Business Review,* 52 (November-December, 1974), p. 138.

[25]See ERISA, 88 Stat. 983–984 for a technical description of how this benefit maximum provision operates. We will define "defined benefit" pension plans in the next chapter.

[26]D. Katz and R. L. Kahn, *The Social Psychology of Organizations* (New York: John Wiley & Sons, Inc., 1966), p. 356.

[27]Ibid.

[28]Zollitsch and Langsner, op. cit., p. 576.

[29]Metzger, *Investment Practices,* p. 115.

[30]Peter H. Daly, "Selecting and Designing a Group Incentive Plan," *Personnel Journal,* 54 (June, 1975), p. 323.

[31]Christoph von Lanzenauer, "A Model for Determining Optimal Profit Sharing Plans," *Journal of Financial and Quantitative Analysis,* 4 (March, 1969), p. 56.

[32]Frederick G. Lesieur, ed., *The Scanlon Plan* (Cambridge, Mass.: The MIT Press, 1958), p. v. This work contains a number of essays on the early development of, philosophy behind, and mechanics of Scanlon plans.

[33]This positive philosophy, as opposed to one which assumes that most people dislike work, want to avoid responsibilities, and therefore must be threatened and coerced to produce effectively, has been put forth as "Theory Y" by Douglas McGregor in *The Human Side of Enterprise* (New York: McGraw-Hill Book Co., 1960). This theory has been cussed and discussed extensively. For research evidence indicating that a majority of managers believe that most people fall between these polar extremes (which is our belief), see Louis A. Allen, "M for Management: Theory Y Updated," *Personnel Journal,* 52 (December, 1973), pp. 1061–1067.

[34]Carl F. Frost, et al., *The Scanlon Plan for Organization Development: Identity, Participation, and Equity* (E. Lansing, Mich.: Michigan State University Press, 1974), p. 68. This work provides the most thorough and up-to-date treatment of Scanlon plans we have found. Although somewhat philosophically biased toward Scanlon plans, it does provide negative evidence as to the effectiveness of some plans, reports on most of the previous Scanlon literature, and contains an excellent bibliography. We will draw heavily upon this source, and the previous research it reports, in our discussion of Scanlon plans. For a more recent excellent summary review of Scanlon plans which agrees with our position that all people do not want participation, see A. J. Geare, "Productivity from Scanlon-type Plans," *The Academy of Management Review,* 1 (July, 1976), pp. 99–108.

[35]Frost, et al., op. cit., p. 7.

[36]In ibid. (p. 82) it is mentioned that the screening committee is not a decision-making body and that: "The president is president." Similarly, it has been pointed out that in spite of its power, although the screening committee's discussion of ideas is thorough: "After careful consideration, management makes the final decision." Fred G. Lesieur and Elbridge S. Puckett, "The Scanlon Plan Has Proved Itself," *Harvard Business Review,* 47 (September-October, 1969), p. 112.

[37]Frost, et al., op. cit., p. 90.

[38]Ibid., p. 91.

[39]Early Scanlon theorists claimed that the existence of a union was essential to the successful functioning of any such plan. More recent experience has shown that some companies without unions can develop effective Scanlon plans. The existence of a union, however, may often help facilitate the structuring of collaborative efforts between management and the employees.

[40]Cited in Richard I. Henderson, *Compensation Management* (Reston, Va.: Reston Publishing Co., 1976), p. 349.

[41]Katz and Kahn, op. cit., p. 382.

[42]Lesieur and Puckett, op. cit.

[43]Katz and Kahn, op. cit. p. 387.

[44]Warren G. Bennis, "Theory and Method in Applying Behavioral Science to Planned Organizational Change," *The Journal of Applied Behavioral Science,* 1 (October-November-December, 1965), p. 353. Bennis did not indicate how successful the plan was.

[45]R. B. Gray, "The Scanlon Plan — A Case Study," *British Journal of Industrial Relations,* 9 (1971), pp. 291–313.

[46]Elbridge S. Puckett, "Productivity Achievements — A Measure of Success," in Lesieur, ed., op. cit., p. 110.

[47]George Strauss and Leonard Sayles, "The Scanlon Plan: Some Organizational Problems," *Human Organization,* 16 (Fall, 1957), pp. 15–22.

[48]Puckett, in Lesieur, op. cit., p. 113.

[49]Zollitsch and Langsner, op. cit., p. 582.

[50]Frost, et al., op. cit., p. 146.

[51]Ibid., p. 120.

[52]Katz and Kahn, op. cit., p. 385.

[53]From a letter of August 23, 1977 from John Donnelly to Bert Metzger, President of the Profit Sharing Research Foundation, quoted in a letter to the authors, Sept. 9, 1977.

[54]See Frost, et al., op. cit., Chapter 7.

[55]Robert H. Ruh, et al., "Management Attitudes and the Scanlon Plan," *Industrial Relations,* 12 (October, 1973), pp. 285–286.

[56]Ibid., p. 288.

[57]Personal communication from Richard S. Sabo, Manager of Publicity and Education Services of the Lincoln Electric Company, July, 1976. Mr. Sabo has provided us with numerous pieces of information which we will draw on in this section concerning the Lincoln plan which were more up-to-date and/or absent from existing literature on the plan. He has also kindly read this section, checking it for accuracy and interpretation. We express our appreciation to Mr. Sabo for these efforts, while recognizing that the full responsibility for the accuracy and adequacy of this discussion of the Lincoln plan is ours.

[58]Henderson, op. cit., p. 355.

[59]James F. Lincoln, *Incentive Management* (Cleveland: The Lincoln Electric Company, 1951).

[60]Ibid., p. 4.

[61]Ibid., p. 8.

[62]Cited in Zollitsch and Langsner, op. cit., p. 590.

[63]Lincoln, op. cit., p. 6.

[64]The above four quotations are taken from ibid., pp. 9, 14, 12, and 26–27, respectively.

[65]Zollitsch and Langsner, op. cit., p. 591.

[66]Ibid.

[67]Henderson, op. cit., p. 355.

[68]Ibid., p. 356.

[69]Personal communication from Richard S. Sabo, July, 1976.

[70]For a technical discussion of the difference of common stock book value as opposed to market value, see, for example, G. W. Cooke and E. C. Bomeli, *Business Financial Management* (Boston: Houghton Mifflin Co., 1967), p. 318.

[71]Personal communication from Richard Sabo, July, 1976.

[72]Henderson, op. cit., p. 355.

[73]For a scholarly discussion of several of these interrelated facets of modern behavior theory and job design strategies, see Gerald I. Susman, *Autonomy at Work: A Sociotechnical Analysis of Participative Management* (New York: Praeger Publishers, 1976).

[74]Communication from Richard S. Sabo, October, 1976.

[75]Personal communication from Richard S. Sabo, July, 1976.

[76]Lincoln, op. cit., p. 256.

[77]Personal communication from Richard S. Sabo, October, 1976.

[78]Zollitsch and Langsner, op. cit., p. 500.

[79]Henderson, op. cit., p. 356.

[80]Compiled from Lincoln, op. cit., p. 275.

[81]See, for example, Ludwig von Bertalanffy, *Problems of Life* (New York: Harper and Brothers, 1960), p. 12. As an example, von Bertalanffy indicates that the "reflexes of an isolated part of the spinal cord are not the same as the performance of these parts in the intact nervous system." Ibid.

[82]See Edwin P. Hollander and James W. Julian, "Contemporary Trends in the Analysis of Leadership Processes," Psychological Bulletin, 71 (May, 1969), pp. 387–397.

[83]Max D. Richards and Paul S. Greenlaw, *Management: Decisions and Behavior,* rev. ed. (Homewood, Ill.: Richard D. Irwin, Inc., 1972), p. 177.

[84]Katz and Kahn, op. cit., p. 386.

[85]Personal correspondence from Richard S. Sabo, September 3, 1976.

V

THE MAINTENANCE OF HUMAN RESOURCES

12

EMPLOYEE BENEFITS

In recent years there has been a sharp increase in the number of "employee benefits" provided to organization members. We will consider as benefits such items as nonincentive-oriented "supplemental compensation," "nonwage and nonsalary types of income," and "indirect payments" to employees. It is expected that such benefits will continue to increase. In 1970, for example, a study using the Delphi technique predicted an increase in existing benefits and the introduction of many new ones.[1] From a cost standpoint, it was estimated in 1976 that in many organizations employee benefits "consume at least 30 percent of the total compensation cost for each employee, and possibly within the next decade they will reach 50 percent."[2] The two basic trends in benefits have been the introduction of new benefits and the provision of more extensive coverage of existing benefits to employees at a lesser cost to them. A notable exception to lower cost benefits are those provided by Social Security, which will continue to cost both employers and employees more and more.

The number of different types of employee benefits in existence or proposed seems almost limitless. Zollitsch and Langsner, for example, listed 197 such benefits, ranging from free beer to vaccination shots.[3] In classifying these benefits for purposes of discussion, we find Henderson's three basic categories most useful:[4]

1. *Employee services,* which include merchandise purchasing plans, social and recreational activities, counseling, and legal services.
2. *Time not worked,* which includes vacations, holidays, personal excused absences, and sabbaticals for social services.
3. *Employee security and health benefits,* which include life, health, and disability insurance, pension plans, Social Security, unemployment compensation, and guaranteed annual incomes or supplemental unemployment benefits.

In this chapter, we will first indicate some of the basic reasons why employee benefits are increasing and some of the more important implications for management decision making. Then we will briefly discuss employee services and time without pay, including changes in traditional work-week hours. Finally, we will discuss in some detail the rapidly growing, extremely costly, and generally legally established or regulated employee security and health benefits. In discussing these benefits we will focus attention on the following four key benefits: (1) Social Security, (2) other forms of income security, (3) medical insurance, and (4) pensions. We will place the greatest emphasis on pension systems because of their complexity in light of the Employee Retirement Income Security Act of 1974 (ERISA) and their enormous economic implications, not only for business firms but for the entire American economy.

Many employee benefit plans have made use of computerization because of the vast amount of financial information they require. Computerization, for example, has been used in handling individual Social Security account transactions for many years, in keeping track of and reporting periodically to employees their pension benefit rights, and to process health insurance claims.

Management science techniques and models, on the other hand, appear to have been given relatively little attention in the area of employee benefits. Testing the expected costs of various alternative benefit decisions, however, appears to be viable by the management science technique of simulation. One such effort has been reported with respect to union health and welfare funds in the construction industry. This study, although based on a model incomplete in certain respects, has illustrated how a simulation of fund reserves "can be used to generate information about fund behavior which can be of real value to trustees [of such funds] in making policy choices."[5]

PERT also appears useful in project-type employee benefit decision problems, such as implementing a new benefit plan option. This may be shown by the following occurrence.

In one year in the 1960's, one state passed a law in July providing a new pension option for its employees which they had to vote on by sometime in December of that year. The personnel director of the State University, with its main campus and numerous branch campuses scattered throughout the state, had to obtain information on the law, organize the information, provide meetings to be held at various locations to inform all university employees of the new option and its implications, provide for the printing of literature on the new option, voting forms, etc. The personnel department did not use PERT on this project, and as the employee voting deadline approached, some work on the project was put on somewhat of a "crash basis."

A year or two later, a student at the university doing his honor thesis in personnel management was given access to the files on actions taken in implementing the new law. He then "post-PERTed" the project. That is, he developed a PERT network showing all activities taken and events accomplished as the project had *actually* been carried out. Analysis of his network showed certain ways in which the personnel department could have accomplished the project more easily had they used network analysis for planning all lead times (such as for obtaining printed materials) and activities.

Although the student had the advantage of having actual past time data rather than future time estimates for his analysis, his data clearly showed a few key problem areas in the implementation of the new pension option that were known to the personnel department at the time, and could have been better overcome with network analysis. In fact, "PERTing" the installation of a new benefit plan is quite analogous to using network analysis to set up new job evaluation systems. We are not recommending "post-PERTing" as an employee-benefits technique here, since in most cases such efforts would involve costs without providing any returns. One exception would be when an organization is facing a project-type endeavor very similar to one carried out previously. In such a case, "looking backwards" at previous efforts may provide enough valuable insights into how the new project might be handled better so as to be worthwhile.

REASONS FOR INCREASED EMPLOYEE BENEFITS

There are a number of reasons for the growth of employee benefits, some of which apply to certain benefits more than others. These reasons can be both external and internal to the firm in nature. For purposes of simplification we will group the external forces that have exerted pressure on organizations to increase employee benefits into the following four categories: (1) economic, (2) governmental, (3) technological, and (4) union. Internal forces consist of management decisions that voluntarily provide employees with benefits deemed necessary for their welfare. Such voluntarily provided benefits are based on the firm's humanitarian objectives. We will now examine these two sets of forces along with some of their major interdependencies.

Historically, the great depression of the 1930's probably provided the earliest powerful force for increased employee benefits. With unemployment rates well over 10 per cent, there was a strong perceived need for economic security. Under the "New Deal" administration of President Franklin D. Roosevelt, the Social Security Act was passed in 1935. This act (both as originally enacted and later amended) provided for old age, disability and survivors benefits, health benefits, and a basis for a federal-state unemployment compensation program. The passage of the Social

Security Act also "gave private pension plans a shot in the arm. Many companies, which previously couldn't afford such plans now could use . . . [this Act] . . . as the cornerstone on which to build a private plan."[6] In this very same year, due to such factors as increasing demands for better economic conditions, the basic labor act under which union-management relations in the United States are conducted today was passed. This act, the National Labor Relations Act, or "Wagner Act," significantly increased the power of labor unions within the economy and stimulated the growth of unionism. We will discuss this legislation more fully in Chapter 14.

As the nation emerged from the depression and entered World War II in 1941, government actions and union pressures combined to provide further stimuli to the growth of employee benefits. In the pension plan area, for example, numerous forces combined in the following manner. During World War II the government froze wages and salaries. However, pensions were exempt from such a freeze. Therefore, a number of companies began to provide pensions so that by 1945, 5.6 million workers were covered.[7] Pressure to provide benefits resulted from labor shortages and strong union demands. Firms also were encouraged to provide pension benefits because of federal income tax laws. Such benefits had long been recognized as legitimate business expenses for tax purposes. Then, during the war, very high marginal corporate income taxes were put into effect. Many firms were earning high corporate profits, and taxes in the highest bracket were 93 per cent. Thus, tax-deductible pensions cost such firms only "7-cent dollars."

Once this "pension door had been opened," an even greater union push for such plans came after World War II. Four years after the end of the war, a major post-war impetus to pension growth occurred in the Inland Steel case, in which the Supreme Court in 1949 ruled that pensions could be considered a bargainable issue between unions and management.[8]

After World War II, many wartime scientific innovations were transformed into peacetime technological improvements, which increased the nation's overall productive efficiency. Coupled with union pressures for better wages, increased productivity contributed toward increasing the purchasing power of many Americans. Excessive wage demands in recent decades, of course, have helped trigger inflationary spirals and weaken the value of the dollar. Nonetheless, with the American standard of living generally increasing, the term "affluent society" came to be used to describe the American economy. At the same time, many jobs, especially in certain mass production industries, although well paid, were repetitive, monotonous, routine, and boring to many workers. Workers who performed such jobs began to look to off-the-job activities, such as civic activities and hobbies, to meet their "self-actualization" needs. In consequence, unions pressed for and obtained shorter work weeks, more vacation time, and more paid holidays.

Technology, union pressures, government intervention, and economic conditions combined in still another way to exert pressures for greater employee benefits. This technology has been *medical* technology. In recent decades, numerous new, "life-saving" forms of medical technology have been developed. In many cases they have been both very sophisticated and *costly*. In addition, inflation, such as in the 1970's, helped push up the costs of quality medical care. These forces, together with union demands, have combined to exert pressures for organizational medical insurance employee benefits to provide both broader and higher-cost coverage and for governmental intervention in the health area, which we will discuss later in this chapter.

Another factor that has made the growth of many employee benefits attractive is their favorable position in terms of cost/benefit analysis. Employer contributions to life and medical insurance programs, as well as pension plans, are deductible as business expenses, whereas individuals, if they purchased these benefits themselves, would have to do so with after-tax dollars. For example, if an individual at the 20 per cent federal income tax bracket had to pay $300 a year for a medical insurance program, his or her income taxes would not be reduced. This same benefit, if provided by the employer, on the other hand, would be tax deductible so that a large corporation could deduct 48 per cent of this sum (or $144) for tax purposes. Thus, its after-tax income, by providing the $300 benefit, would be reduced by only $156, as shown in Figure 12–1. Further, employer plans, since they insure a number of employees, can take advantage of group insurance rates that are lower than those applicable to an individual. In short, with group insurance plans, we have a combination of government regulations (tax deductibility) and the economies of scale by larger purchases of insurance operating to produce a favorable cost-benefit situation.

Finally, we have the humanitarian or social responsibility objectives of managements contributing to employee benefits. Perhaps one of the outstanding examples of this phenomenon is the Lincoln Electric Company's program discussed in the last chapter. The company, following Lincoln's own personal philosophy, has voluntarily guaranteed annual work since 1958, and had not laid off any of its workers from that time through July 1976.

	Example A No Benefits		Example B $300 Benefit	
Employee			Employee	
Income	$10,000			$10,000
Tax (20%)	−2,000			−2,000
Net	8,000			8,000
Benefit Provided	+ 0			+ 300
Total Value Provided by Firm	$ 8,000	→ Difference $+300		$ 8,300
Firm			Firm	
Income	$100,000			$100,000
Expenses Salary Benefit	− 10,000 0 $ 90,000			− 10,000 − 300 $ 89,700
Federal tax @ 48%	− 43,200			− 43,056
Net Profit	$ 46,800	→ Difference $−156		$ 46,644
Total After Tax Benefits Individual	$ 8,000			$ 8,300
Company	46,800 $ 54,800	→ Difference $+144		46,644 $ 54,944

Figure 12–1 Cost-benefit advantages in providing employee benefits.

EMPLOYEE BENEFITS AND MANAGERIAL DECISION MAKING

Numerous objectives may be met by providing employee benefits. In light of the central theme of this text that managers make decisions to meet objectives, we will now examine certain key aspects of decision making with respect to employee benefits. First, as discussed earlier, employee benefits may meet a number of employee needs. A second objective that may be met is putting the company in a better position competitively as far as recruiting new employees is concerned. Many large firms, however, have fairly similar "benefits packages," so that no strong recruiting advantage exists over their most direct competitors. The large firm may have a relative advantage over the small one, however, because it may be more difficult for small employers to provide large benefit packages. Thus, firm size may be a contingency of some importance in the employee benefits area. Good benefit programs may also help retain employees and reduce turnover. However, we must raise the same question as we did in the previous chapter in discussing profit sharing — which employees will be the ones to leave, the most desirable or those who are marginal ones?

Another supposed reason for providing employee benefits is to prevent unionization from occurring. Two questions must be asked with respect to this objective. First, to what extent can good benefits per se keep unions from organizing? Unless the total organizational system is perceived to be a favorable one (as with the Lincoln Electric Company), it is unlikely that benefits alone can keep a union out. Second, unions may bring positive values to a firm, and it may be desirable to have unionization. As indicated in the previous chapter, unions may help facilitate collaborative employer-employee relationships as under Scanlon type plans.

It is also often assumed that benefits serve the objective of motivating employees to work harder to achieve organization goals. Following the reasoning presented in previous chapters, it appears unlikely that there is generally any direct link between effort and benefits. All organization members receive benefits, regardless of how hard they work, although they may receive more benefits as their pay increases, since benefits (such as pensions) are often related to pay levels. With this lack of a direct effort-reward link, one important problem with employee benefits is that they may be taken for granted by employees, and that their often high costs may not even be appreciated by employees.

Management must make a number of decisions in the employee benefits area. Management must decide what benefits to provide. To a great extent this decision is dependent upon the firm's financial condition and size and what comparable firms are doing. The cost/benefit trade-off also needs to be considered. It should be noted that with respect to decision making, management in some cases *must* provide certain benefits in order to comply with federal and state laws. A firm covered by Social Security has no choice but to pay the required taxes to the federal government if it is to stay in business. In other situations, the firm may be in a choice situation of the following type: "If we provide benefit x we must comply with law y." For example, ERISA does not require firms to provide anyone with a pension; however, if management elects to establish a pension plan, it must comply with the sections of the law regulating pension plans.

Management also needs to decide how much information it should provide to employees about their benefits. This decision is important because it influences the employee benefits–motivation link as well as the perceived equitability of benefits. One of the basic reasons employees take benefits for granted is that management fails to describe adequately the benefits to which they are entitled and the costs of these benefits. For example:

A recent conversation with a 25-year-old, healthy, single, well-educated (Master's Degree) woman showed that after two months with her new employer she had absolutely no idea that her organization had an extensive medical benefits program, which covered not only such basic costs as hospitalization but also extensive benefits protecting her against any major medical "catastrophe." Further, she was partially financing these benefits herself by means of deductions from her monthly paycheck.

The provision of information does not guarantee that the employee will work harder or feel equitably treated since the information may be ignored or forgotten. If this is so, why bother? One basic reason is that certain benefits are not perceived as important, even if the employee is aware of them. Some employee benefits may meet some employee needs at certain times in their lives. As in our example, why should a healthy, single, 25-year-old woman really be concerned with the extensive coverage of her medical plan designed primarily to protect individuals (especially families) against medical catastrophes? She had never encountered any situation of this type before and being severely ill for a long duration was probably the farthest thing from her mind. Another type of communication problem exists because, conversely, some individuals may assume that their plan covers more than it does. In some cases, for example, older employees who are married, have families and do know that they have extensive medical insurance may remember somewhat resentfully that they had to pay $2000 in medical costs themselves for a major illness, while not paying too much attention to the fact that the company plan paid $10,000 for them. In short, a "benefit" in the eyes of management may not be a "benefit" in the eyes of the receiver.[9] This fact raises such basic questions as the following: "How far should management go in providing benefits to the extent that it does have a choice?" Can "social responsibilities" be carried too far? Are we discouraging responsibility? Is not the employee mature enough to take care of at least *some* of his own benefit needs, rather than depending on someone else — his employer — to do it for him? With some benefits, such as medical plans, we would support "catastrophe coverage," since many individuals would be financially ruined by a $20,000 medical bill in one year, for instance. To what extent the employer should provide one of the other benefits briefly mentioned earlier — free beer — we consider another question. Somewhere in between these two benefits, one may debate seriously the question of whether free company legal services are necessary, or whether it should be the responsibility of an employee as a mature adult to handle his own legal affairs. Having employees participate in choosing from among available benefits, as in "cafeteria compensation," seems to provide one means of both making individuals aware of the benefits available to them and encouraging their assumption of responsibility. In discussing "responsibility," however, we must not forget to look at the cost/benefit advantages of employer-financed benefits as mentioned earlier. Further, since it costs companies money to provide employees with information about benefits, management must consider the costs and benefits associated with providing such information.

Another important decision pertaining to benefits is whether the employee should contribute to the purchase of the benefits or the employer should pay for them completely. The former is referred to as a contributory plan and the latter as noncontributory. Arguments have been raised to support both contributory and noncontributory plans. One argument for contributory plans is that the employee will become more aware of the cost of his benefits, learn more about them, and appreciate them more if he is required to partially finance them. One further question that needs to be raised concerning how benefits are perceived by the worker is to what extent does he find that his being required to contribute is an equitable arrangement. Even with full understanding, and a perceived need for a benefit, the individual may not believe that he should have to contribute toward the financing. For example, a manager who has to contribute to his firm's pension plan while many other similar-sized firms in the same industry have noncontributory plans may perceive his situation to be less equitable.

From a pure cost point of view, it is obvious that it is to the advantage of the employee if he does not have to help finance any of his benefits, and to the advantage of the firm if he does. From a cost/benefit point of view, however, noncontributory plans that qualify as tax-deductible expenses are the most favorable. This is because the employee has to contribute his money on an after-tax basis, while the firm can deduct all of its contributions and have its after-tax income reduced by only 52 cents for every additional dollar of after-tax income that the employee would have to pay were the plan contributory. In general, the trend has been toward noncontributory insurance and pension plans.

EMPLOYEE SERVICES

In examining management's decision to provide employee services, such as cafeterias or counseling, many of the points discussed above are applicable. Further, a contingency approach is called for. Many employee services are deductible for tax purposes and, hence, favorable from a cost/benefit point of view. Other services are "nice" but costly, may be unneeded and unwanted by many employees, and may not foster the individual's responsibility for meeting his own needs. On the other hand, there may be a real need for certain services contingent upon the organization and its environment. For example, many personnel departments are called on to provide company cafeterias for employees because there are no restaurants within a reasonable distance where an employee can obtain a nutritionally well-balanced lunch at a reasonable cost. In a small "company town" where one employer predominates, there may be no public recreational facilities, so that a company swimming pool and baseball field could well be justified. In a large metropolitan area, on the other hand, there may be a wealth of easily accessible recreational facilities and the costs required to finance company facilities might well be spent for better purposes by management. In short, with continuing pressures for more employee benefits and increasing costs, employee "services" should be given careful scrutiny by personnel managers, from both a psychological and an economic point of view, for any given set of conditions.

TIME NOT WORKED

There are three basic types of time not worked for which the employee is paid. First are vacations and paid holidays, both of which provide opportunities for leisure, rest, and physical conditioning. Above and beyond the old saying "All work and no play makes Jack a dull boy" is the fact that as more and more Americans have assumed desk jobs calling for little physical effort, they need time off for activities to maintain both good physical and mental health. A classical example of the value of physical conditioning as an aid to mental sharpness and concentration was the extensive physical workouts undertaken by both Bobby Fischer and Boris Spassky during their world chess championship match in 1972.

Typically, vacation time increases with length of employment with the company. The number of paid holidays, on the other hand, is not a function of length of service. There has been an increase in pay for time not worked in both cases over the past few decades. As one example reported in 1976, the United States Steel Company, in agreement with the United Steelworkers union, was in its second-cycle of a five-year plan providing 13-week vacations for senior workers every five years, and 6-week vacations once every five years for its junior workers.[10] This plan provided that 20 per cent of the employees in each of the two groups would take their extended vacation each year. Further, the plan included payment of a vacation bonus to employees who took their vacations in months other than June, July, or August.[11] This bonus helped enable U.S. Steel to spread out the time off given to its employees to better balance its human resource needs throughout the entire year. Hence, it directly helped contribute to meeting both organizational objectives and individual needs. Unlike vacations, certain paid holidays such as Labor Day and Christmas are influenced by cultural and religious values and are provided largely as a matter of custom.

A second category of time off with pay is that of personal excused absences. These may range from jury duty (where a civic responsibility is required of the employee) to time off for a funeral of a member of the immediate family.

Another category of time not worked as a benefit is the relatively new time off *not* without pay — the four-day 10-hour a day workweek (4/40). Basically, this benefit represents a redistribution of the work week. Many smaller and medium-sized companies started to use the 4/40 approach beginning about 1970 as a benefit not found in large companies. By 1972 it was reported that 100,000 employees in 700 to 1000 organizations were on some form of the 4/40.[12] The primary benefit, as far as the employee is concerned, is having a larger concentrated segment of time for leisure and family activities each week — three consecutive days. Also, of some benefit to employees would be the need for transportation and lunches only four times per week rather than five. The importance of these costs would vary, of course, depending on geography — e.g., a professor who walks to work in a small college town and eats lunch at home as compared with a commuter from Connecticut to New York City. As far as advantages to the firm are concerned, a primary one would be the possibility of reducing costs by reducing the number of set-up times required in the operations from five to four each week.

Although some earlier literature was quite optimistic about the 4/40 week, recent research indicates that it has its disadvantages. Perhaps the greatest one is that of fatigue. However, some research indicates that fatigue is a negative factor primarily in jobs in which there is heavy physical work.[13] Further, one research study has shown that "moonlighting" (taking on a second job) has increased in 4/40 operations — in one case from 4 to 17 per cent; and in another case, while frequently increasing to 15 to 20 per cent initially, leveling off at around 10 per cent.[14] "Moonlighting" may pose problems for some individuals even if fatigue does not, because full devotion to both jobs on a continual basis may be difficult.

Other contingencies seem to have a bearing on the effectiveness of the 4/40 approach. For example, Gannon has argued that:

. . . young, single employees dislike the 4/40 approach much more than older employees because it interferes with their social life. Rather than curtail their social activities, these younger workers frequently report to their jobs after an inadequate amount of sleep and attain a low level of morale.[15]

As indicated, the initial enthusiasm for the 4/40 "benefit" has waned and some of the research has become more critical. Some critics of the 4/40 plan have also suggested an alternative approach to modifying work hours. This is referred to as flexible work hours or "flexitime." The basic notion behind this plan is to provide the worker with some choice as to when he wants to work. For example, all workers may be allowed to report to work on the hour from 7:00 to 10:00 A.M.; to work for eight hours; and then to leave between 4:00 and 7:00 P.M. Under such an arrangement all employees would be at work during the "core" period between 10:00 A.M. and 4:00 P.M. The approach originally gained popularity in European countries (especially in Switzerland) and has begun to receive support in Canada and the United States, especially among clerical workers. It was estimated in 1976, for example, that about 300,000 workers were under *some type* of flexitime plan in the United States in nearly 1000 organizations.[16] We emphasize the words "some type" because there are many variations as to the degree of flexibility provided individuals under different flexitime systems. Rather than being given wide latitude in informing their employers on a day-to-day basis as to when they want to work, many systems, in order to make it possible for management to plan and coordinate work in advance, will require employees to give two to four weeks' advance notice of their working hour choices. Further, employees may be required to commit themselves to when they want to come to work for entire work periods, such as a two-week duration. In some cases, any deviations from such schedules can be made only with the written consent of an employee's supervisor.

The approach may be perceived as a benefit by employees because of different personal preferences in "life styles" as to what working hours are most desirable for them (within the limits allowed). For example, by being relieved from an 8 to 5 schedule, flexitime may provide opportunities to make dental appointments and handle family errands more easily. Further, such an approach may help resolve such environmental problems as traffic congestion at rush hours when everyone reports to work at the same time. This was the case in Germany, at the Ottobrunn research and development plant, when flexitime was introduced in 1967.

Once the plan was instituted, this congestion problem was largely overcome and "unexpected side benefits surfaced. As it was now legitimate to arrive late for work, or rather at an hour of one's choosing, there was a remarkable drop in sick-leave calls."[17] Further, in American organizations, cost savings due to "greater productivity" (sometimes undefined) but, more tangibly, to reductions in sick leave, overtime, and absenteeism have been reported.[18]

An important contingency for the success of flexitime appears to be technology, since the plan creates obvious problems when employees whose work is interdependent are scheduled to work at different hours. Although used in many types of operations, even enthusiastic supporters of flexitime have conceded that "when flexible working hours are used in an assembly line operation, the line may have to be redesigned to include" more in-process inventory to provide more *independence* among workers.[19] Some of the most well publicized flexitime plans have proved successful only as a result of considerable investments. To put flexitime into operation, both Volvo and Saab, for example, went from the traditional assembly line to an "autonomous work group" arrangement requiring both costly modification in facilities and extensive employee training.[20] As college professors, who, when class schedules permit, sometimes practice "flexitime" and try to avoid the 8:00 A.M. and 5:00 P.M. small traffic "rush" in college towns by working at other hours, we will be interested to see to what extent this European imported employee "benefit" will continue to grow in popularity in the United States in the future.

HEALTH AND SECURITY BENEFITS

We will now turn our attention to four important types of employee health and security benefits: (1) Social Security, (2) income security (during the worker's employment), (3) medical security, and (4) retirement security (pension plans).

Social Security

The Social Security Act, which was enacted in 1935, is the basic social insurance legislation in the United States. It originally provided a monthly retirement income to those 65 or over.[21] Later, monthly income benefits to both survivors of deceased employees and to disabled employees under age 65 were added to Social Security. In 1965, the Social Security Act was further expanded to provide medical care for the aged. This part of the program is called Medicare. Medicare automatically provides hospital insurance to all elderly persons covered under Social Security. Further, it provides medical insurance to pay for doctor's bills and other related expenses on an optional, contributory basis. Monthly premiums, for example, for those who wished to take advantage of the voluntary medical insurance were increased from $7.20 to $7.70 in July, 1977.

The reader is undoubtedly familiar with Social Security, for a majority of those employed in the United States are covered by the Act; one's Social Security number is used as an identification number at many colleges, universities, and other organizations, and for federal income tax returns. For these reasons, we will simply highlight some of the major economic implications of Social Security for both management and workers.

As indicated previously, all employers covered by the Act must contribute to Social Security. Further, all employees working for employers (as opposed to the self-employed) covered by the Act must also contribute at the same rate of pay on covered earnings. This represents a no-choice system, where no decisions on the part of either the organization or its members can change their costs (or contributions). Even though management cannot choose, however, it can predict its contributions in advance and thus plan its other expenditures in light of these predictions. The current and future scheduled Social Security tax rates as a percentage of the individual's wage for both employers and employees have been established by law. These tax percentages do *not*, however, apply to the individual's *total* income but only to his income up to a certain level, called the "wage base level." In 1976, for example, both employers and employees paid a 5.85 per cent tax on income up to a maximum of $15,300, so that the tax maximum for each was $895.05. In 1977, however, the wage base was increased to a maximum of $16,500, so that the maximum tax for both employer and employee increased to $965.25, even though the tax percentage remained unchanged.

With dramatic increases in wages and living costs since the passage of the Social Security Act in 1935, benefits provided individuals have been increased numerous times. Benefits, which are generally related to average monthly wages for the years during which an individual is covered by Social Security, had increased by 1976, for example, for persons retiring at age 65 to a range of from slightly over $100/month to $364/month.[22] As of that time, however, there was grave concern among many individuals that not enough funds were being put into the Social Security system and that as a result it would become "bankrupt" within several years. This prompted passage of an amendment to

	Tax Rate (%)	Wage Base*	Employer and Employee Contribution for Maximum Wage Earner
1979	6.13	$22,900	$1403.77
1980	6.13	25,900	1587.67
1981	6.65	29,700	1975.05
1982	6.70	31,800	2130.60
1983	6.70	33,900	2271.30
1984	6.70	36,000	2412.00
1985	7.05	38,100	2686.05
1986	7.15	40,200	2874.30
1987	7.15	42,600	3045.90

*The wage base through 1981 is fixed by law; after 1981 estimated based on cost-of-living formulas.

Figure 12–2 *Social Security tax rate, wage base levels and contributions under the 1977 amendment to the Social Security Act. (Table provided by the Social Security Administration.)*

the Social Security Act late in 1977 that increased both the "wage base levels" and the percentage contributions made by both employers and employees. That contributions to be made by both employer and employee will increase considerably by 1987, as shown in Figure 12–2. The 1977 law changes will increase the costs of operating firms. These increased costs may have to be passed on to the consumer in the form of higher prices, at a time when the higher tax will decrease individuals' disposable income. The 1977 amendment, however, should help considerably in enabling the Social Security system to remain solvent.

Income Security

Social Security is certainly a basic form of income security and, in fact, unemployment compensation was provided for in the Social Security Act itself. However, with unemployment compensation and other common forms of income security the employer *can* make decisions that will affect his costs and employees are not required by federal law to make contributions.

Unemployment Compensation

Although unemployment compensation was provided for in the Social Security Act, it is a cooperative federal-state program in which employer costs and employee benefits may vary from state to state, rather than being set at a national rate as under Social Security. This cooperative feature resulted when Social

Security was being considered in 1935 because President Franklin D. Roosevelt and the Congress "feared that the United States Supreme Court would declare unconstitutional any social security legislation that imposed federal taxes for the purpose of paying unemployment benefits."[23] To lessen this danger, the Act made a provision for a federal unemployment tax on employers but no federal benefits at all to be paid to those who became unemployed — only the states could provide such benefits. Under this strong inducement, all states have by now enacted unemployment insurance laws.[24]

The whole federal-state system is based on the concept of "experience rating," which means that employers who do not lay off workers as frequently and for as long a duration as others, will pay smaller unemployment compensation taxes. Hence, managerial human resource planning decisions play a vital role in the firm's cost of unemployment compensation. Under the present system, the total federal tax the employer had to pay as of early 1978, was 3.4 per cent of each employee's wages up to a maximum annual taxable base of $6000/year, or $204. However, an employer obtained a tax credit of 2.7 per cent of this $6000 tax base (or $162). This credit or "offset" includes both any unemployment compensation taxes he paid to the state plus an additional credit for having a good "experience rating." For example, suppose an employer had maintained a policy of stable employment, had a good "experience rating," was required to pay a state experience-rated tax of only 1 per cent, and had a *taxable* payroll of $1 million. In such a case, instead of paying the 3.4 per cent tax on the $1 million ($34,000), he would have paid only 1 per cent ($10,000) to the state plus 0.7 per cent ($7000) — the difference between the 3.4 per cent federal tax and the 2.7 per cent offset ($27,000) — to the federal government. Calculations using these data are given in Figure 12–3.

As of early 1978, the employer always had to pay the 0.7 per cent to the federal government (3.4 per cent minus the 2.7 per cent offset) but with a poor experience rating could be required to pay state taxes in excess of 2.7 per cent. As reported in 1974, a majority of state tax maximum unemployment compensation wage percentages for employers with poor experience rating were 4.0 per cent or greater, and in Texas, employers who had poor ratings were subject to a state tax of as high as 8.5 per cent (on a maximum annual wage base of $4200).[25] In Pennsylvania late in 1977, the *minimum* experience rating percentage was 1 per cent with a maximum rate of 4 per cent. The difference in unemployment compensation payments required between firms with good and poor experience ratings was thus 3 per cent. An employer with a *taxable* payroll of $1 million in this illustration with "very

a. Total Federal Tax (3.4% × $1,000,000) =		$34,000
b. Less credit for state tax *actually paid* (1% of $1,000,000) =	$10,000	
c. Less additional credit that would have been paid to the state except for a good "experience rating" (1.7% × $1,000,000) =	$17,000	
d. Total credit (2.7% × $1,000,000) =		$27,000
e. Net federal tax actually due (a-d) (0.7% × $1,000,000) =		$ 7,000

The underlined figures represent the actual total taxes paid—$10,000 to the State and $7,000 to the Federal Government.

Figure 12–3 Unemployment compensation tax offset. (Drawn from Joseph M. Becker, Experience Rating in Unemployment Insurance [*Baltimore: The Johns Hopkins Press, 1972*], p. 367, and updated to reflect changes in federal law.)

good" as opposed to "very bad" experience ratings would pay a maximum difference in unemployment compensation taxes of $30,000, as calculated in Figure 12–4.

Several other points concerning unemployment compensation are in order. The weekly benefits paid to an employee who has been laid off will vary from state to state and they have tended to increase over the years. As reported in 1974, for example, the maximum weekly benefits ranged from $60 in a few states to $147 in Connecticut.[26] The maximum duration of unemployment compensation benefits as reported in 1974 was 26 weeks in most states. However, with high levels of unemployment in the 1970's, federal legislation extended the maximum duration of benefits up to 65 weeks during such periods.[27] Under the Emergency Unemployment Extension Act of 1975, for instance, the maximum of up to 65 weeks of benefits was extended throughout 1975, and in 1976, states with more than 6 per cent unemployment were provided up to 65 weeks of benefits.[28] Those increased benefits resulted in severe strains on state funds because of high unemployment rates. As reported in 1976:

State unemployment funds and reserves are rapidly being drained (at least 10 are bankrupt and 20 more on the brink) suggesting that employers will be required to generate "replenishment" funds in greater amounts.[29]

What are the implications of the current federal-state unemployment compensation program for personnel management decision making? Kaplan has emphasized that, in spite of experience rating, "smart firing" has been a little understood aspect of modern personnel management. He has suggested that even for

A. *Most Favorable Rating* (1.0%)
  a. Total Federal Tax (3.4%) × $1,000,000 = $34,000

  b. Less credit for state tax *actually* paid
    (1% of $1,000,000) = $10,000

  c. Less additional credit that would have been paid
    to Pennsylvania except for good experience rating
    (1.7% × $1,000,000) = $17,000

  d. Total Credit (2.7% × $1,000,000) = $27,000

  e. Net Federal tax actually due (a-d)
    (.7% × $1,000,000) = $ 7,000

               Total $10,000 + $7,000 = $17,000

B. *Least Favorable Rating* (4.0%)
  a. Total Federal Tax (3.4%) × $1,000,000 = $34,000

  b. Less credit for state taxes *actually paid* up to a
    maximum of 2.7% = $27,000

  c. Net Federal tax due (a-b) = $ 7,000

  d. Tax due the state (4% × $1,000,000) = $40,000

               Total $7,000 + $40,000 = $47,000

     Total Savings for a Good Rating: $47,000 − $17,000 = $30,000

Figure 12–4. *Maximum difference in unemployment taxes in Pennsylvania in 1977 depending on experience rating.*

small firms, thousands of dollars can be saved in unemployment compensation costs through stabilizing employment "by controlling hiring, controlling layoffs, and carefully scheduling production."[30] Among the cost-reduction decision-making strategies he put forth were reducing work week hours rather than laying off personnel and knowing the implications of management strategies in light of state laws.[31] To sum up, unlike uncontrollable Social Security costs, the personnel manager can make a contribution in helping to keep down his experience-rating based unemployment compensation costs.

Supplemental Unemployment Benefits (SUB) and Guaranteed Annual Work

The notion of guaranteeing income security from layoffs dates back many years before the enactment of the Social Security Act of 1935. According to one source, a "guaranteed annual wage" was negotiated between the Wallpaper Craftsmen and the

National Wallpaper Company as long ago as 1894.[32] Before describing the present status of private (as opposed to public) income security plans, some definitions are in order. "Guaranteed annual wage" has been loosely used to describe both a guaranteed income and guaranteed work. However the terms are really distinct. Guaranteed work, which is not too common in the United States today, means what the term implies. The worker is guaranteed some amount of work over a time period such as in the Lincoln Electric's work guarantee of at least 75 per cent of the normal work week. Guaranteed income, on the other hand, means guaranteeing a certain proportion of the worker's income while he is not working. Historically, this approach, after talk about a guaranteed annual wage, was first established on a major basis in the contract agreement between the United Auto Workers and the Ford Motor Company in 1955 as a Supplemental Unemployment Benefit (SUB). This benefit is supplemental to the federal-state unemployment compensation program. Hence, there are basically two different approaches to providing income security aside from unemployment compensation — SUB or guaranteed work.[33] We discussed one guaranteed work plan, that of Lincoln Electric, in the last chapter. We will now focus our attention on SUB and the comparative advantages of SUB versus guaranteed work.

As of 1974 only 13 major labor management contracts provided work guarantees of one month or more, while, in contrast, "nearly two million workers covered by 223 major contracts . . . had SUB plans."[34] The SUB plans have been found especially in certain manufacturing industries such as automotive, steel and rubber, glass and ceramic, and ladies' garments.[35] The number of workers covered by SUB appears to have decreased over the years shortly preceding this time. The *Monthly Labor Review* in 1968 estimated that 2.5 million workers were covered by SUB as compared with the reported 2 million 1974 figure.[36]

The amount of benefits granted to workers under SUB plans increased considerably in some industries. Beginning in 1968, for example, SUB payments were increased so that a Ford worker with seven years' seniority was entitled to 95 per cent of his normal pay for up to a year during layoffs.[37] In fact, the advantages of being laid off were so attractive in this industry that the principle of *juniority* was established there. Juniority required "the firm to lay off the most senior worker first when there is insufficient work."[38] It should be emphasized that these high benefits levels represented a combination of unemployment compensation plus SUB, which is a typical procedure under SUB. With SUB payments financed solely by the company, it is not surprising that the high level of SUB payments in the automobile industry could not withstand the extensive layoffs there in the 1970's:

> The unexpected huge layoffs in the automobile industry in 1974–75 resulted in the depletion of both the Chrysler and General Motors SUB fund accounts in 1975, causing the auto workers to completely depend on state unemployment benefits.[39]

The employer's contribution formulas under SUB plans have become so complex that it is beyond our scope to delve into them.[40]

Although SUB rather than guaranteed work has dominated the American industrial private income security scene, recently questions have been raised as to the relative merits of these two approaches to income security. SUB is based on the philosophy of providing benefits while not working, and in some cases may be dysfunctional. For example, a poor experience rated employer, already paying maximum state unemployment compensation rates, would benefit from increased government unemployment compensation benefits (with no employer tax increases) since it would reduce its SUB outlays.[41] This situation results because total benefits agreed to by the employer represent the sum of unemployment compensation and SUB as indicated. Also, since unemployment compensation benefits are not taxed as personal income to workers, while SUB benefits are, more unemployment compensation and less SUB would enable the employer to "provide a given amount of after-tax income maintenance for his employees through the public program at a lesser cost than through SUB."[42]

Whether guarantees based on the premise of providing work would represent a superior alternative to SUB depends on several contingencies. Essentially, however, the basic question that must be raised in evaluating any work guarantee is: "What are the costs associated with obtaining some output from excess man-hours during a downturn in 'regular' production?"[43] With many cost complexities involved in both SUB and guaranteed work, here is an area in which management science may be helpful by developing computer simulations of SUB and work guarantees, given actual cost data for particular firms. Assuming costs are not an important variable (or are similar for each alternative), one final question must be asked regarding SUB and guaranteed work: From a psychological point of view is it not more desirable to foster individual responsibility by providing some work than to provide benefits for not doing any work?

Life Insurance

Life insurance is provided by most large organizations to all members. The amount of insurance provided is usually related to income up to some maximum. A common rule of thumb is to provide insurance covering two years' income.[44] The majority of company plans are noncontributory. The tax benefits of such plans combined with the "group" economies of scale mentioned earlier make life insurance favorable from a cost/benefit point of view. Further, in some high risk jobs, individuals may not be able to buy insurance on their own, or if they are able to purchase it, the cost would be prohibitive. Such a situation makes group insurance with its broad coverage absorbing high risks almost mandatory.

Although most organizations require a physical examination of employees prior to employment, all individuals once employed are generally covered regardless of changes in their physical condition. Further, certain other features are typical of life insurance benefits. For example, employees are generally given the right to convert their group policy to an individual policy without a physical examination within a prescribed time limit after their separation from the organization.[45] Also, many insurance programs provide for accidental death and dismemberment benefits, which are in addition to those under the basic coverage. Among the directions in which group life insurance has moved is in providing life insurance benefits for the dependents of employees. With respect to such extended coverage, one can raise some of the same types of questions as raised previously about employee services. In spite of a cost/benefit advantage, should not the employee be encouraged to assume some responsibility of his own in his insurance planning, e.g., taking care of insuring his dependents? In a somewhat different vein, will the individual become complacent when he knows that he has a "nice" company package and not purchase enough additional insurance that he may really need with a wife and four children? Even at a salary of $30,000 a year, $60,000 worth of company life insurance is hardly enough by itself to take care of such a family of five potential survivors, especially if college educations are planned for the children in the future.

Medical Security

The concept of providing medical security goes back many years. Several decades ago, the privately operated Blue Cross–Blue Shield system offered hospital and surgical insurance to individuals. In recent years companies have begun to provide their employees with Blue Cross (hospitalization) and Blue Shield (surgical) insurance or similar coverage offered by other insurers owing to employee and union demands and because organizations have found group medical insurance to be favorable from a cost/benefit point of view. In recent years the benefits provided under such plans have increased greatly.

In addition to deciding which insurer to choose, the firm must make three basic decisions concerning medical coverage. The first deals with the scope of coverage. Will the firm pay for eyeglasses, hearing aids, dental insurance, additional visits to doctors' offices, and prescription drugs or just for basic surgery and hospitalization?

Second, what initial charges will the employee have to pay for any service covered? These "initial charges" are of two basic types: employee contributions for coverage, which we have discussed previously, and programs that require the employee to pay a certain amount for a particular service before the firm's plan will provide any benefits for that service. This feature, referred to as deductibility, tends to discourage persons from seeking services they do not really need and is used to control the cost of medical insurance. In some plans, for example, the plan will cover all or a proportion of the individual's medical expenses after he has first spent $100 for a particular service during a stated period of time such as a calendar year. Such a plan would be called a "$100 deductible plan." This concept is similar to $100 deductible automobile collision insurance.

Last, what is the *maximum* amount of insurance benefits the firm will provide for any particular service? The range of alternatives is virtually unlimited. For example, the company could provide up to $100 per day for a hospital room whenever the employee is hospitalized *or* it might provide up to $5000 a year for all basic hospital benefits *or* it might provide up to $25,000 for all medical benefits relating to a particular injury or illness for the employee during his entire employment with the company. Thus, the amount and the time are both discretionary variables for management.

To illustrate these decision areas, we will briefly cover certain of the basic changes which have taken place over a decade with respect to the medical insurance plan offered by one organization. This historical sketch will illustrate the basic trend of the liberalization of benefits, which has taken place in virtually all medical security plans. Then we will indicate some of the features not covered by this plan, and comment on their emergence. Finally, we will discuss the role of government in the field of medical insurance.

An Organizational Medical Plan: An Overview

The medical plan in this organization has consisted of two parts for several years: (1) a basic hospital and surgical plan and

(2) an extensive supplementary major medical plan to cover serious and extremely costly sicknesses and injuries. The plan has been a noncontributory one for protection for the employee only. If the spouse and dependent children were also covered, a monthly contribution of $5.00 was required as of 1978.

The basic hospital and medical insurance has provided benefits for hospital daily room and board charges, surgeons' fees, doctors' visits while confined to the hospital, x-rays, and other related expenses. Further, schedules of payments for various types of surgery have been established. Along with hospital daily room and board benefits, these surgical payments have been increased over the years as medical costs have gone up. For example, the scheduled fee for a tonsillectomy was increased from $40 to $60 at one time. As of July, 1977, the basic plan covered hospital expenses up to a maximum of $2000 per confinement and surgical expenses up to a maximum of $750 per operation.

The organization's major medical plan was designed to take care of medical catastrophes by covering medical charges above and beyond the basic benefits paid. Further, its benefits have been extended a number of times. At one time the major medical component was a $100 deductible/year/person for *each* accident or sickness; and it paid 80 per cent of all covered expenses for *each* such accident or illness (50 per cent for psychiatric expenses) up to specified limits which increased as medical costs increased from year to year. At one time the limit was $15,000 *per accident or sickness*. Later the plan was modified to provide $100 deductible per year per *person for all* covered expenses with the same 80 and 50 per cent coverages. There was a maximum payment over the duration of employment for this newer extended coverage, which was increased until it was $100,000 *per person* as of 1977. A hypothetical example comparing the older $15,000 maximum per sickness or accident and the newer broader coverage plan is given in Figure 12–5. The employer expenses shown in Figure 12–5 are those paid above and beyond the basic coverage. They would include such expenses as those for those hospital and surgical bills not covered in the basic plan, visits to doctors for a host of nonhospital related reasons, and prescription drugs. The handling of all claims under this system was computerized in June, 1976.

New Trends in Medical Insurance

The plan described has had two limitations. First, it pays only for medical expenses incurred as a result of injuries or illnesses which have already taken place while not covering such preventive medical expenses as annual physicals. Although annu-

Old Plan ($15,000 maximum per illness, injury)		New Plan (Only *one* $100 deductible per year and $100,000 maximum for *all sicknesses* and *injuries*)
a. Auto Accident	$20,100	$20,100
b. Deductible	− 100	− 100
	$20,000	$20,000
c. Plan pays 80%	$16,000	$16,000
d. Amount over maximum coverage	−$ 1,000	− 0
e. Plan pays	$15,000	$16,000
f. Employee pays (a-e)	$ 5,100	$ 4,100
g. Influenza	$ 200	$ 200
h. Deductible	−$ 100	− 0
	$ 100	$ 200
i. Plan Pays 80%	$ 80	$ 160
j. Employee pays (g-i)	$ 120	$ 40
k. Total Employee Payments (f+j)	$ 5,220	$ 4,140
l. Total Plan Pays (e+i)	$15,080	$16,160

Difference in Plan Payments
$16,160 − $15,080 = $1,080

Figure 12–5 *Comparison of major medical benefits under older and newer plans.*

al physical examination coverage is still relatively rare, it has been incorporated into some plans. Second, the plan did not cover prescription glasses, hearing aids, or dental expenses, which have also begun to appear in some more comprehensive plans. Dental insurance, for example, as reported in 1976 among a "broad sample of 1,600 companies has more than doubled to an estimated 19 percent" in less than three years.[46] Further, similar to basic and major medical plans, most such plans (69 per cent) in the survey specified maximum amounts payable for one person's dental expenses per year — usually $500, $750, or $1000.[47] How far companies can afford to go or should go in providing such additional benefit coverages is a question we raise once again. Further, in light of private health insurance, the question must also be asked: To what extent should government enter the field of medical insurance? We will now turn our attention to this question.

The Government and Health Insurance

Several nations have had comprehensive national health insurance plans for several decades. In the United States, the issue of such insurance has been debated seriously. In this country, such insurance was first introduced with the inclusion of Medicare in 1965 as part of Social Security, as mentioned earlier, and eight years later the federal government entered the health area again with the passage of the Health Maintenance Organization Act of 1973.[48] This Act emphasized providing medical care stressing preventive medicine. It both supported and regulated Health Maintenance Organizations (HMOs), which are typically non-profit organizations that provide services "through an affiliation of hospitals, clinics, doctors, nurses, and technicians"[49] at a fixed monthly or annual price. This act affected business organizations by requiring

. . . employers of at least 25 persons to offer an HMO plan option if they offered a traditional health benefits plan. If HMOs organized on both a group and individual practice basis operated in an employer's area, the employer would be required to offer enrollment in both types of HMOs.[50]

In spite of federal assistance to stimulate the growth of HMOs, there were certain limitations contained in the 1973 HMO Act. For example, the Act required HMOs to accept high risk patients and charge uniform fees that did not reflect a family's health status. These requirements were relaxed by amendments to the Act in 1976. Further, these 1976 amendments made it necessary for an employer to offer HMO membership as a benefit only in health maintenance organization service areas in which at least 25 of its employees resided, rather than to all employees if it employed at least 25 persons.[51]

Pension Plans

As we have already seen, the Social Security Act provides modest incomes for individuals in their retirement years. To provide greater income security during these years, many companies have developed pension plans. By providing income security so that individuals may retire with adequate incomes, those who have passed their prime may "exit" from the organization in a socially acceptable way. There need be no feelings of guilt on the part of management concerning the possibility of its retirees not being able to continue to maintain an adequate standard of living. Additionally, having individuals retire at age 65 or earlier opens the door for younger people to move into their positions, thus preventing blockages in career paths. Further, some "senior executives want to 'get out early' because of increased pace, pressure, and demands on health."[52] With such objectives in mind (as in Social Security, with retirement income payments now possible at age 62) many companies are moving more and more toward early retirement — at ages 60 or 55 in some cases.[53]

There are, however, disadvantages in forcing individuals to retire at some arbitrary age, such as 65. It has been argued that mandatory retirement may be injurious to the individual in that it may contribute to the deterioration of his physical and emotional health. Further, society may suffer when competent individuals are forced to retire at an age beyond which they can still contribute their valuable skills and experience to organizations. For these reasons, the House of Representatives introduced a bill in 1977 which would, with certain exceptions, prohibit mandatory retirement until individuals have reached 70 years of age. This bill provided such a prohibition by amending the Age Discrimination in Employment Act of 1967, discussed in Chapter 4.[54]

Pensions, especially with the passage of ERISA, are without question the most complex of all employee benefits. In this section we will: (1) discuss the scope of retirement plans, (2) expose the reader to some of the basic terms that are essential to understand pension plans, (3) discuss the typical benefits provided by "progressive" pension plans, (4) delve into the implications of ERISA for pension management, and (5) raise the basic question of whether private enterprise (especially now with ERISA) can afford to provide adequate pensions to its retirees in the future.

The Scope of Retirement Plans

The number of private pension plans continued to grow after the post–World War II spurt. In fact, we have seen approximately a doubling of the number of qualified pension plans in the United States about every five years, as shown in Figure 12–6. With respect to pension fund assets, we have estimated that as of the end of 1975, the total assets of federal, state, and local governments along with private plans were about $371 billion.[55] Further, private pension payments alone were reported in October, 1974, to be about $10 billion per year paid to more than 6 million workers.[56] Just how much the dollar significance of pensions will increase in the future is subject to speculation, but one author has

End of Year	Number of Plans
1954	18,331
1959	34,097
1964	59,536
1969	112,778
1974	237,166

Figure 12–6 Number of qualified pension plans. (From Bert L. Metzger, Profit Sharing in 38 Large Companies, Vol. 1 [Evanston, Ill.: Profit Sharing Research Foundation, 1975], p. 1.)

estimated that pension funds may have assets of $4 trillion in the year 2000,[57] which would be well over twice the total gross national product (GNP) of the United States in 1976.

Pensions: Some Basic Terms

There are several terms with which the reader must be familiar to understand how pension plans work. As with other benefits, some plans are contributory and some are noncontributory. Important in dealing with pension plans is the concept of vesting, which is an employee's nonforfeitable right to all or part of his accrued benefits when he leaves the organization. Another pension distinction of importance is the fixed or defined benefit plan as opposed to the defined contribution plan of which the money purchase plan is one type. The defined benefit plan, considered superior by many and most common, provides "a definitely determinable level of retirement income."[58] The defined contribution type of plan, on the other hand, instead of "pre-establishing a fixed level of benefits" simply calls for the employer to commit himself "to a fixed contribution into the plan each year,"[59] such as 5 per cent of each employee's compensation. The defined contribution plan, as Metzger has aptly put it, concerns itself more with the input of the plan (the employer's contribution), while the defined benefit plan focuses attention on the level of output (benefits) to be provided to the employee.[60]

Extremely important in pension financing is the concept of funding. Many years ago, a few companies simply went on a pay-as-you go basis in providing employees with pension benefits. Upon retirement each employee would receive benefits from a reserve fund or from cash on hand. This method was a haphazard one, and in poor profit years some firms were unable to meet their obligations to pay their employees the benefits due them.

A funded plan, on the other hand, sets funds aside each year to cover in advance the benefits planned for each employee in the future. This approach helps to ensure that adequate money will be available when needed. In defined benefit funding determination, actuaries estimate how much eventual pension fund needs will come to and then figure a "current service cost." This cost is "the amount of payment required annually — plus earned interest — to pay pensions to . . . [individual(s)] . . . based on their service from the time the funding starts."[61] This is not all there is to funding, however, since to have any new defined benefit plan fully funded, the firm must go back and add to current funding the amount that would have accumulated up to the present time if the plan had been in operation for all these years. Full funding was optional before ERISA. Now, however, it is required by law, both for new and existing defined benefit plans, which are not fully funded.[62] The lack of this full funding feature caused problems when some companies introduced new pension plans because they failed to provide any benefits for the past service of their older, loyal workers, who often had contributed to the firm's success over the years. Therefore, full funding is important from a humanitarian standpoint. However, this past service liability or cost, as it is called, can be extremely expensive. For example, U.S. Steel in its pension agreement with the United Steelworkers in 1951, "took on a $496-million past service liability. That was equal to 25% of its invested capital, and $1,900 per covered employee."[63] Fortunately, Internal Revenue regulations prior to the pasage of ERISA provided companies with a number of years to meet such liabilities, since financial drains of the magnitude indicated here obviously cannot be absorbed by an organization in any single year.

Pension Benefits

Numerous pension formulas have been developed for providing retirement income for retired employees. We will examine only certain basic aspects of the more common types of defined benefit plans. Such plans provide each employee with a unit of benefit for each year of service. This unit may be a specified percentage of the individual's current compensation; or his average compensation during his entire length of service or his last or highest-paid years of service (commonly three to five); or a fixed dollar amount such as $12/month for each year of service. With inflation a problem in many years over the last decade, benefits based on current or the last years' or highest years' averaging provide more realistic pension benefits than do those based on a simple average of an employee's compensation over one's career. Even with the more favorable defined benefit formulas, inflation may continue after retirement, so that the purchasing power of those benefits defined just prior to the individual's retirement may also soon be eroded.

An illustration of the more favorable highest three years formula is provided by the retirement system for state employees in Pennsylvania. Under this plan, which is a contributory one, an employee's full retirement benefits are basically determined by the formula: Average salary of three highest years × years of service × 2 per cent.[64] For example, if an individual has 35 years of service, with a highest three-year average salary of $20,000, his yearly retirement income (or annuity) would be: 35 × $20,000 × 0.02 = $14,000. For a number of years, each employee has been provided an annual statement of his contributions to the fund plus interest via a computerized system.

Two other aspects of defined benefit plans are of importance. First, in many plans, company defined benefits are "integrated" with Social Security. These plans may provide benefits only on compensation "in excess of" the Social Security wage base; "or accrue larger benefits in excess of [the wage base] cutoff point than below it."[65] Second, there are different types of annuity options commonly provided to retirees under defined benefit plans. For example, an employee may obtain a "full allowance" annuity of years times earnings times 2 per cent as in the example for as long as he lives, but annuity payments would stop upon his death, and the spouse (or other designated beneficiary) would obtain no annuity income after that time. However, some individuals would like to make it possible for their spouse or other beneficiary to continue receiving an annuity after their own death (if they should die first). Such an option would naturally cost more, since the probable life spans of two persons rather than one are now being covered, and this cost is invariably shifted from the firm to the employee. Contingent annuity options, as they are called, accomplish this by providing a smaller amount of retirement income than would a "full allowance" option as determined by any formula such as the one illustrated above. The formula amount would be reduced under a contingent annuity based on two factors: (1) the ages of the employee and his beneficiary upon retirement, and (2) the amount of the contingent annuity to be provided to the spouse should the employee die first. For example, under the Pennsylvania state system, there are options in which the surviving spouse (or other beneficiary) would:

1. Continue to receive for his or her life the *same* monthly retirement income that the employee had been receiving before his death.
2. Continue to receive only *half* of this amount. This option, of course, is less expensive than the first, so that the pension annuity would be reduced less from the "full allowance" than it would be with the first option.[66]

All of these types of benefits, however, are of no value to the employee if his plan is not adequately funded, or if he leaves the organization before retirement with few or no vested benefits. It is because numerous organizations did not adequately vest or fund their pension programs that pension reform, culminating in the passage of ERISA in 1974 took place. We will now turn our attention to this complex pension reform law.

ERISA[67]

As indicated earlier, ERISA did not require any organization to provide its employees with a pension plan. Its sole aim was to

protect the interests of those individuals covered by plans adopted by organizations. For example, prior to ERISA, existing laws
did not require vesting, and some pension plan members had no
vested rights, even those aged 60 or over.

This intent of providing income security protection has generally been considered socially desirable. However, the complexity of the law is so great that, as *Business Week* put it: "For
months, pension officers and consultants have been studying and
arguing about the text like religious scholars seeking the true
meaning of Bible passages."[68] As reported in 1976, the greatest
difficulties with ERISA were considered by some to stem "from
the odd situation that many of the regulations have not yet been
issued or are being challenged, as well as the Labor Department's
decision not to interpret some of the unclear or possibly contradictory provisions" of the law.[69] In the following sections we will
describe the major provisions of the law relevant to personnel
management and their implications for the economy, organizations and decision makers.

Scope and Coverage.   The term *Retirement Income Security*
included in ERISA's name is in some ways misleading. Although
the primary thrust of ERISA was toward pension reform, some of
its provisions also apply to profit sharing plans, as we have seen.
Since these plans also provide for retirement income security,
one might expect ERISA to cover them. Certain provisions of
ERISA, however, cover a wide variety of the employee benefit
plans which we have covered in this chapter. More specifically,
employers covered by ERISA must disclose to each covered
employee and report to the Secretary of Labor information about
"medical, surgical, or hospital care benefits, or benefits in the
event of sickness, accident, disability, death or unemployment,
or vacation benefits," or other welfare plans.[70] The vesting, funding, and many other provisions of ERISA do not cover such
employee benefit plans because they simply are not applicable.
We should also note that ERISA specifically excluded a large
segment of the population — those individuals covered by governmental plans (federal, state, and local). Many pension managers, however, have expressed the belief that before too long
employees working for government organizations will be covered
by the law.

Reporting and Disclosure.   As indicated, ERISA provided for
disclosing data to employees about their benefits and reporting
information about benefit plans to the Secretary of Labor. Additional reports with respect to certain data must be sent to the
Internal Revenue Service and Secretary of the Treasury. The
intent of these provisions has generally been considered desirable
because summary descriptions of their benefit plans provide em-

ployees with periodic data about their plans (and any plan changes) and may help improve employer-employee communications. Providing annual reports including financial statements to the federal government also helps ensure that employee benefit plans are financially sound and that the employee is going to receive the benefits promised him by the employer, which is a basic objective of ERISA.

The extensive reporting and disclosure provisions written into the law, regardless of their purpose, however, have been criticized as creating an avalanche of paperwork and high administrative costs. For example, as reported in 1975, Standard Oil of California had *102* benefit plans covering its 30,000 United States employees and 9000 annuitants.[71] This firm's benefits manager indicated that the cost of complying with the reporting and disclosure provisions "could run as high as $2.5-million to gear up for the system, and recurrent administrative costs could jump to $750,000 a year."[72] That the reporting and disclosure provisions could cause real problems for small firms was recognized by the Department of Labor, which exempted plans with fewer than 100 participants from most of the reporting and disclosure requirements, leaving them primarily the preparation of summary plan descriptions to employees. (The Secretary of Labor was given this prerogative in ERISA itself.) Along with complex reporting and disclosure systems, ERISA provided fines for corporations and fines and imprisonment for any individuals willfully violating the reporting and disclosure section of ERISA.[73] Such provisions have raised some concerns on the part of plan managers, as might be expected, and consulting firms have developed special services just to help employers and their benefits managers comply with the law.

Participation and Vesting. The participation and vesting provisions of ERISA do not apply to all benefits plans. They are primarily focused upon pension and profit sharing plans. However, *if* an employer has such a plan, the minimum requirements which must be met are fairly clear cut.

In general, ERISA provided that pension (and profit sharing) plans could not require as a condition for plan eligibility that an employee complete a period of service extending beyond the *later* of the two following dates:

(1) that at which he reaches the age 25 years; or
(2) that date on which he completes one year of service.[74]

With respect to vesting, the employer, *if* he has a plan, has three *minimum* vesting options from among which to choose.

1. Full vesting for his employees who have had at least 10 years of service.

(A) 25% Graduated Vesting

Years of Service	Nonforfeitable Percentage
5	25
6	30
7	35
8	40
9	45
10	50
11	60
12	70
13	80
14	90
15 or more	100

(B) "Rule of 45"

If years of service equal or exceed	And sum of age and service equals or exceeds	Then the nonforfeitable percentage is
5	45	50
6	47	60
7	49	70
8	51	80
9	53	90
10	55	100

Figure 12–7   *Minimum vesting rules under ERISA.*

2. A graduated vesting schedule, beginning at 25 per cent vesting after five years of service and incrementing the percentage as shown in Figure 12–7, *A*.

3. The so-called "rule of 45," which provides for 50 per cent vesting when the sum of employee's age and his number of years of service (with a minimum of five years' service) equals "45"; and grading up to a full 100 per cent vesting five years later. This grading of this rule is shown in Figure 12–7, *B*.[75]

What are the implications of such choices? First, the effect of these rules is a function of certain important organizational variables. *Business Week*, for example, reported in 1975 one estimate that indicated that "80% of all pension plans and 70% of all profit-sharing plans" already met these new eligibility and vesting standards and that even "in 1972, a survey of 491 companies indicated that, on average, the passage of a 10-year vesting rule would boost pension contributions by a scant 2%."[76] Looking more specifically at the situation for particular firms, Carlson has emphasized that vesting costs the company nothing for employees who leave the firm before becoming vested. Therefore, the new provisions of ERISA will "fall most heavily on companies that currently have the least liberal vesting provisions, particularly if these companies typically experience high turnover among employees who will now be vested but were not before."[77] In such cases, he estimated that pension costs might increase by as much as 20 per cent due to the new requirement. Carlson's statements raise an important point with respect to ERISA and personnel decision making. With respect to participation and vesting costs, ERISA-created costs to the employer will be contingent to a considerable extent on prior-to-ERISA managerial decisions. Also with respect to vesting, the employer, depending on his prior decisions, does have some latitude in decision making such as a choice from among the three minimum standard alternatives indicated earlier. According to *Business Week*, actuaries have reported that the costs among the three alternatives differ little for most companies; that the 10-year full vesting rule is the easiest to administer and communicate to employees; and that for these reasons, as of 1975, it was the most preferred method.[78] Further, one must consider not only costs but employee satisfaction. As Carlson has pointed out, the new vesting standards will help reduce job dissatisfaction to the extent that the potential loss of pension benefits in the past has discouraged employees from leaving organizations for more satisfying work elsewhere. Again, however, which employees will now be more encouraged to seek more satisfying work elsewhere? The firm's good employees may be encouraged to leave, while its marginal ones may not be able to find any better jobs elsewhere and will therefore stay.

Funding. Earlier we discussed the meaning of the term "funding." ERISA required more accelerated funding than previous law for defined benefit pension plans.[79] Under ERISA, such plans existing before January 1, 1974, were given 40 years to amortize past service liabilities, while plans initiated after this date were given only 30 years. The impact of this provision depends considerably upon the extent to which firms had funded their pension plans prior to the passage of ERISA. In general, however, considerable sums were "owed" by companies to their pension funds at the time of ERISA's enactment. *Business Week*, for example, reported just a few days prior to President Ford's signing of ERISA that the stock market decline had eaten so much into pension portfolios that total unfunded pension liabilities among American firms had reached $30 billion and that for some firms the pension liability was greater than the market value of the company.[80] In 1975, the same magazine reported that "most big companies" were already in compliance with the minimum funding standards prescribed by ERISA. However, it added that the stock market slump (which decreased the value of many pension fund assets) coupled with wage increases could lead to a "total increase in contribution levels resulting from the law" approaching 25 to 30 per cent.[81]

Fiduciary Responsibility. One of the most controversial aspects of ERISA is its provisions calling for fiduciary responsibility. A fiduciary is someone who is responsible for something valuable in trust for someone else. In ERISA, not only pension and profit sharing plans but every employee benefit plan must be set up and maintained by a written document which provides "for one or more named fiduciaries who jointly or severally shall have the authority to control and manage the operation and administration of the plan."[82] Fiduciaries under ERISA must act as "prudent men" in managing benefit monies and, when appropriate, as in pension plans, must "diversify the investments of the plan so as to minimize the risk of large losses, unless under the circumstances it is clearly prudent not to do so."[83] Fiduciaries are also personally liable if they have mismanaged monies, may be sued in civil court by plan participants, beneficiaries, other fiduciaries or the Secretary of Labor, and may be held to make good any losses resulting from such mismanagement. "Malpractice" insurance can be purchased under the provisions of ERISA to cover the liability of fiduciaries, but how effective such insurance will be is debatable. A fiduciary is also prohibited from investing more than 10 per cent of defined benefit pension fund assets in his employer's securities and is prohibited from engaging in a number of transactions such as dealing with the assets of his plan "in his own interest or for his own account."[84]

Broadening the concept of "fiduciary" under ERISA has meant that a wide variety of individuals, including personnel managers, may be liable for law suits. It is still too early to determine just what patterns the courts will follow with respect to fiduciary liability suits. There is a likelihood, however, that with the "prudent man" and "diversification" provisions of the act we will see a more conservative management of pension and profit sharing funds. This may result in a lower rate of return on investments in pension funds, thus increasing the amount the employer will need to contribute to meet the obligations of a defined benefit plan. Finally, some authorities have suggested that risks under the fiduciary responsibility provisions of ERISA may be minimized by transferring "the responsibility for fund management to an outside professional" such as a bank.[85] Others, however, have put forth the alternative strategy of having corporate managers controlling their own pension fund assets even more closely so as to minimize fiduciary responsibility risks.

Tax Provisions. The tax provisions of ERISA both for employer and employee are the same as those for profit sharing plans discussed in the previous chapter. Pension contributions are tax deductible in the year they are made by employers; employees do not pay taxes until they receive their benefits; and the special capital gain phaseout and 10-year income averaging options apply to any lump-sum distributions under pension plans.

IRA's and Portability of Vested Benefits. ERISA provided that individuals who are not covered by a pension plan (either governmental or private) may contribute 15 per cent of their annual income up to a maximum of $1500 per year into an Individual Retirement Account (IRA). The individual will *not* be taxed on this portion of his income in the year he contributes to his IRA, but only later when he utilizes the funds for retirement. Thus, the individual gets preferential tax treatment with an IRA.

When an employee with vested pension rights leaves a firm, he may (if his employer agrees) transfer the vested pension assets tax free to an IRA. Further, if the individual takes a job with a new employer, assets may be transferred tax-free to the plan of a new employer if the new and former employers so agree.[86]

Three final points are in order concerning IRA's. First, the individual is constrained as to how his IRA funds may be invested. For example, he cannot just simply invest his IRA funds in any stocks he chooses. He is limited to essentially five investment opportunities: savings institutions, mutual funds, special government retirement bonds, insurance endowment or annuity policies, and trust accounts invested in stocks and bonds.[87] Second, the IRA maximum was set fairly low, and the use of IRA's could well be expanded in use if the $1500 figure were to be raised. Under the Tax Reform Act of 1976, in fact, IRA possibilities were extended somewhat so that an employed husband or wife can make a 15 per cent IRA contribution of up to $1750 per year even though his or her spouse is unemployed. Finally, the use of IRA's has little impact on firms since they can choose whether or not to permit portability.

Keogh Plans. Since 1962, self-employed individuals have been permitted to set aside portions of their income in tax-sheltered plans similar to IRA's but called H.R. 10 or Keogh plans. ERISA increased the limits of employee contributions in Keogh plans to 15 per cent of the individual's income up to a maximum sum of $7500 per year. If an individual is part-time self-employed (such as a college professor writing a book), he can set up a Keogh plan even if he is covered by a pension on his regular job.[88] The Keogh plan increased contributions mandated by ERISA will have little or no effect on the employer, since its primary beneficiaries will be the self-employed.

Maximum Benefit Limits. Defined pension plan benefits under ERISA were limited to the lesser of $75,000 per year or 100 per cent of the employee's average compensation in his three highest "paid consecutive years of participation in the plan,"[89] while for defined contribution plans, annual additions were limited in exactly the same way as was done with deferred profit sharing plans. Further, the combined benefits for any individual if a firm has both a profit-sharing and a defined benefit pension plan were limited as described in the previous chapter. Provision was made in ERISA for adjusting annually the pension maximum dollar limits for both defined benefits and additions as the cost of living changed.

Plan Termination Insurance. ERISA established a Pension Benefit Guaranty Corporation in the Department of Labor. It is basically an insurance pension fund to which firms with defined benefit plans, but not those with "money purchase" plans, must contribute.[90] Annual premiums were originally established at a modest $1/employee/year for single employer plans and 50¢/employee/year for multi-employer plans. Should a firm's benefit plan fail, the insurance was set up to cover pension benefits up to $750/month or 100 per cent of the employee's average monthly income during his highest paid five years under the plan, whichever is the lesser. ERISA provided that this $750 per month figure would be adjusted to reflect changes in the Social Security contribution and benefit base.

One provision regarding plan termination insurance has been open to considerable criticism. If a plan fails and inadequate insurance funds are available, the government is empowered to claim up to *30 per cent of the firm's net worth*! The maximum plan termination insurance benefits indicated help cover this liability, and ERISA directed the federal insurance corporation to develop supplementary insurance to cover the maximum 30 per cent liability. Real concern, however, has existed because this liability goes beyond the plan to the firm as a whole. Some observers have expressed the hope that the "courts will deem the contingent liability to be an unlawful confiscation of shareholders' property."[91]

Just how significant plan terminations will be under ERISA is open to question. Prior to ERISA, a Treasury-Labor study in 1972 indicated that 20,000 individuals and $48.7 million in funds were affected by plan terminations which represented only about 0.08 per cent of the labor force covered by pension plans and 0.25 per cent of annual employer contributions.[92] Niland reported that an effect of ERISA was that many small plans were terminating, with 2000 such terminations having taken place by April 1975.[93] Senators Jacob Javits of New York, and Harrison A. Williams, Jr. of New Jersey, the coauthors of ERISA and among its staunchest supporters, on the other hand, cited evidence that ERISA had *not* led to more plan terminations than prior to enactment of the law. They indicated that in 1973, 4130 pension plans were terminated and that in 1975, after the passage of ERISA, the number of terminations was "smaller than the 5,000 that is commonly cited by the critics. . . . ''[94] They also reported that, in spite of the terminations in 1975, more than 33,000 applications for new plans were received by the Internal Revenue Service in that year.[95] The new (and in some firms more costly) funding requirements of ERISA did not go into effect until January 1, 1976, so that some firms may have terminated in 1975 to avoid these regulations. It is still too early to tell exactly what ultimate impact ERISA will have on plan terminations. The most recent data on plan terminations reported was about 18,000 as of late 1977.[96]

ERISA, Decision Strategies, and the Future of Private Pensions. Earlier we reported an estimate that pension assets might reach $4 trillion by the year 2000. With additional funding and vesting as mandated by ERISA, coupled with the "prudent man" rule and other factors which we will describe later, this prediction might come true. In such a case the answer to Robert Paul's question "Can Private Pension Plans Deliver?" may well be "No!"[97] Among the problems seen by Paul are the following: With a continuation of 5 to 10 per cent inflation, defined benefit pension plans of the type generally in effect will need investment returns of 10 to 13 per cent per year to "maintain costs at a level percent of payroll." The real question must be raised: "Are there such investments — sound, secure investments — that will meet the 'prudent man rule' " . . . of ERISA?[98] Another problem is that increases in salaries under defined benefit plans will create an "experience loss" unless properly constructed salary scales are used in actuarial cost projections. An experience loss means that the firm will have to "go back" and add to what it had originally planned to contribute in prior years to meet a percentage formula based on a lower "average salary" basis. Paul has estimated, for example, that under ERISA a "one-time 5 per cent increase in salaries will increase dollar pension costs by 5 per cent to 12 per cent depending on factors like the size of the past service liability and the degree to which this liability is funded."[99] Further, in a mobile society, with many individuals more loyal to their professions than their firms, mobility will tend to decrease pension costs less under ERISA with its vesting standards, since there will be fewer forfeitures. Finally, with more women in the work force, "having fewer children and spending more time working," forfeitures will decrease to an even greater extent under ERISA.[100]

Another demographic variable of importance is that the "enormous generation" born after World War II will be retiring between 2010 and 2020; the question must be raised whether or not the much smaller generation in the work force then will be able to pay the pension costs.[101] Finally, there are pressures to add automatic cost-of-living increases to pensions. Should these pressures continue, they would put further upward pressures on pension costs. Even excluding such cost-of-living pension provisions, observers such as Carlson have expressed the opinion that it will only be a matter of time before pension costs increase to 20 to 30 per cent of payroll costs. "This increase will have to be translated into price increases, which in turn will fuel more wage increases leading to even higher benefits costs. Where will this spiral end?"[102]

Management may be able to control pension costs in an inflationary economy to some extent. Among the ways in which this may be done are to:

1. Use a profit sharing plan instead of a pension plan as a means of retirement security. This approach keeps costs controllable, although individuals may not have adequate income security if a firm's profits are not good.

2. Have a combination plan that includes both the more controllable profit-sharing element and a less controllable pension element.

3. Adopt a defined contribution pension plan rather than a defined benefit plan. These plans are generally related directly to salary levels, and are not completely controllable, but they do not call for additional funding of the magnitude indicated above for defined benefit plans— where formulas call for percentages of average or highest average incomes times years of service to be paid. Defined contribution plans, however, give the individual less protection against inflation, and from this point of view may be socially less desirable.[103]

Although some companies (those which are less labor-intensive) face fewer problems than others with pensions, it appears that there is no resolution to the pension problems indicated above unless the total economic system can somehow prevent inflationary spirals. Unless this is accomplished, any alternatives such as those that keep costs down will create hardships for pensioners, while higher cost plans that are more "socially" acceptable will further fuel the flames of inflation and reduce further the purchasing power of the dollar. Just which pension strategy to choose will be a continuing problem for personnel decision makers.

Finally, it should be emphasized that rising pension costs are a problem not only for private organizations covered by ERISA, but for public administrators as well. As of 1976, the state of Massachusetts had a massive accrued pension liability of $8 billion and, in the same year, Delaware "passed a bill limiting the total retirement benefits of new state employees — including Social Security benefits — to 75% of final average pay."[104] Further, Governor Milton Shapp of Pennsylvania, concerned with the Pennsylvania state employees' retirement system described earlier, referred to the whole public pension costing and debt problem as a "time bomb ready to detonate."[105] With many pension reformers talking about extending the jurisdiction of ERISA to state and local employees, even further pressures could be placed on the public sector in the future.

SUMMARY

Employee benefits have expanded considerably over the past several decades. In some cases, one can question whether management is providing too many benefits, not only from a cost point of view but also from the viewpoint of undermining individual responsibility. Some employee services, however, appear necessary, and pay for time not worked is essential to provide employees opportunities not only to meet personal duties and civic responsibilities but also chances for rest and relaxation. Further, although not technically representing "pay for time not worked," both the 4/40 week and especially flexitime may meet both individual needs and organizational objectives under certain contingencies.

Of all employee benefits, those dealing with health and security have mushroomed the greatest. From expansion of the nation's basic Social Security program to the adoption of the complex law ERISA, pressures have been extended to both expand the scope of benefits and guarantee that employees will receive the benefits that they have been promised. Although providing health and income security represents an important social goal, the increased costs of these programs have posed severe financial problems to management. Just how our nation will resolve the problem of providing socially desirable security programs while at the same time remaining financially solvent is one of the most serious questions that must be faced in modern personnel management.

DISCUSSION AND STUDY QUESTIONS

1. Explain the growth of employee benefits in recent decades in terms of:
   a. Tecological and economic changes in the American economy during the past three or four decades.
   b. Federal Income Tax legislation.
   c. Maslow's hierarchy of needs as discussed in Chapter 9.
2. The 1977 Social Security Amendments have increased the tax rate percentages and wage bases to the point where the successful, hard working executive earning $45,000 per year may be paying more than four times as much for Social Security by 1987 as will the wage earner making only $10,000 per year. This schedule is definitely unfair to the well to do and can do nothing but discourage initiative in our free enterprise system. Discuss.

3. You are the personnel manager in a state in which the maximum unemployment compensation tax is 8 per cent and the minimum tax is 0.1 per cent (on a taxable base per worker up to $6000). If your firm's *taxable* payroll is $100,000, what total unemployment compensation tax (assuming a federal tax of 3.4 per cent with a 2.7 per cent offset as in the chapter) would your firm have to pay with the worst possible "experience rating" as opposed to the best? Do you think that the whole federal-state system is designed to foster good personnel practices? Why?

4. Paying people for not working, such as with unemployment compensation and SUB is less socially desirable than guaranteeing work that fosters individual responsibility to a greater extent. Therefore, unemployment compensation and SUB should be prohibited by law. Discuss.

5. Cautious Joe, who graduated from college a year ago, is now a management trainee with a large eastern publishing house, and had an unfortunate automobile accident when he was hit by Speedy Sam. Joe's company has both a basic surgical and hospital plan and a supplemental major medical plan. The basic plan covers employees in the organization for any hospital confinement up to $2000, and for surgical expenses per accident or sickness up to $1000. The firm's major medical plan is a $100 deductible/sickness or accident per year plan, and pays 80 per cent of all of an employee's expenses not covered by the basic plan up to a maximum of $20,000 per accident or sickness. Joe's hospitalization charges were $8000, his surgical fees $3000, and out-patient doctor's fees and prescription drugs (both covered under the major medical plan) were $400. Joe also had to pay $100 for other non-accident-related medical bills in the year he was injured. How much did the firm pay Cautious Joe in medical benefits?

6. Do you agree with the position that in general, prohibiting mandatory retirement prior to age 70 is beneficial?

7. Which of the following vesting alternatives would be considered legal under ERISA? Why?
   a. Full vesting after ten years' service.
   b. Fifty per cent vesting after 10 years' service, incremented by 5 per cent per year until full vesting is accomplished.
   c. Graduated vesting beginning at 25 per cent after five years of service, 30 per cent after six years, etc., until 50 per cent vesting is reached after 10 years of service; then 60 per cent vesting after 11 years, and 70 per cent after 12, and so forth until full vesting is achieved after 15 years of service.
   d. Fifty per cent vesting after five years' service graduated up by 10 per cent per year until full vesting is reached at the end of 10 years of service.
   e. Full vesting after four years of service.

8. With the provisions written into ERISA regarding minimal vesting standards and the "prudent man" doctrine, the answer to Robert Paul's question "Can Private Pension Plans Deliver?" may indeed be "No!" Discuss.

9. a. What would you say are the two most controversial provisions of ERISA? Why?

   b. What would you consider to be two of the least controversial provisions of ERISA? Why?

10. ERISA, although its purpose was laudable, has turned out to be nothing more than another "bureaucratic monstrosity." Discuss.

11. Benny Fitts, who received an undergraduate degree in electrical engineering, then went on to receive an M.B.A. in a highly reputable College of Business Administration, has just completed his first year as an engineer at one of this country's most thriving large computer manufacturers, and has just received from his supervisor his first performance appraisal, which was very favorable. Benny is single, aged 25, and has no immediate plans for marriage. In light of his circumstances, how do you think Benny would rank the following employee benefits in terms of desirability? Why?

    a. Social Security.

    b. A defined benefit pension plan in which he must contribute 5 per cent of his gross salary.

    c. Unemployment compensation.

    d. A major medical plan.

    e. A company cafeteria (there are no restaurants near enough to his firm's location to go to for his daily lunches).

    f. $50,000 in company paid, noncontributory life insurance.

    g. Company paid nondeductible dental insurance benefits.

12. Assume that Benny Fitts is in exactly the same situation as in question 11, except for the fact that he is married and has two very young children. With these family responsibilities, in what ways do you think Benny would perceive the value of his benefits differently?

Notes

[1] T. J. Gordon and R. E. LeBleu, "Employee Benefits, 1970–1985," *Harvard Business Review*, 48 (January-February, 1970), pp. 93–107.

[2] Richard I. Henderson, *Compensation Management: Rewarding Performance in the Modern Organization* (Reston, Va.: Reston Publishing Company, Inc., 1976), p. 283.

[3] Herbert G. Zollitsch and Adolph Langsner, *Wage and Salary Administration*, 2nd ed. (Cincinnati: South-Western Publishing Co., 1970), pp. 622–623.

[4] See Henderson, op. cit., pp. 284ff.

[5] Gordon Kaufman and Roy Penchansky, "Simulation Study of Union Health and Welfare Funds," *Industrial Management Review*, 10 (Fall, 1968), p. 159.

[6] "The Startling Impact of Private Pension Funds," *Business Week* (Jan. 31, 1959), p. 93.

[7] Ibid.

[8] Ibid.

[9] Some research studies have indicated that the accuracy of employee perceptions of benefit programs has not been good. See, for example, Alan N. Nash and Stephen J. Carroll, Jr., *The Management of Compensation* (Monterey, Cal.: Brooks/Cole Publishing Co., 1975), p. 247.

[10]Henderson, op. cit., p. 273. The junior and senior groups were determined as follows: in each steel mill, employees were divided into two equal components — the 50 per cent with greater seniority (senior) and the 50 per cent with least seniority (junior).

[11]Ibid., p. 294.

[12]Martin J. Gannon, "Four Days, Forty Hours: A Case Study," *California Management Review*, 17 (Winter, 1974), p. 74. Gannon also indicated that there are varieties of the 4/40 — e.g., 4/35 and 4/37. Ibid.

[13]Eugene J. Calvasina and W. Randy Boxx, "Efficiency of Workers on the Four-Day Workweek," *Academy of Management Journal*, 18 (September, 1975), p. 610.

[14]These two studies are reported in Gannon, op. cit., p. 77. The first study is from a classic book on the subject: Riva Poor, ed. *4 Days, 40 Hours* (Cambridge: Bursk and Poor Publishing, 1970).

[15]Gannon, op cit., pp. 76–77.

[16]Barry Stein et al., "Flextime: Work When You Want To," *Psychology Today*, 10 (June, 1976), p. 40.

[17]Alvar O. Elbing et al., "Flexible Working Hours: It's About Time," *Harvard Business Review*, 52 (January-February, 1974), p. 19. Gannon also favors flexitime and considers it sounder from a behavioral science point of view than 4/40. See Gannon, op cit., pp. 77–78.

[18]Stein et al., op cit., p. 43.

[19]Elbing et al., op. cit., p. 22.

[20]Stein et al., op. cit., pp. 43, 80. Some of the other problems encountered with flexitime are also covered in this article. For still another discussion of flexitime, see Alvar O. Elbing et al., "Flexible Working Hours: The Missing Link," *California Management Review*, 17 (Spring, 1975), pp. 50–57.

[21]Subsequently, amendments to the Act provided for smaller monthly benefits if the individual wanted to start receiving a retirement income at the age of 62.

[22]See *1976 Social Security Benefits and Medicare* (Chicago: Commerce Clearing House, Inc., 1975).

[23]Joseph M. Becker, *Experience Rating in Unemployment Insurance* (Baltimore: The Johns Hopkins University Press, 1972), p. 366.

[24]This federal-state arrangement was contained in sections 902 and 909 of the Social Security Act (49 Stat. 639, 643); and the whole unemployment compensation program subsequently was codified under the Federal Unemployment Tax Act of 1954 (FUTA). For a history of the unemployment compensation legislation see the historical notes in the *United States Code Annotated*, 26 U.S.C.A. 3302, and 26 U.S.C.A. 3309.

[25]January 1974 U. S. Department of Labor Statistics data reported in Henderson, op. cit., pp. 254–255.

[26]July 8, 1974 U.S. Department of Labor Statistics data reported in ibid., pp. 252–253.

[27]For a brief historical summary of such legislation, see the *Congressional Quarterly Almanac*, 31 (1975), p. 492.

[28]Ibid., p. 494.

[29]Philip Kaplan, "Unemployment Taxes are Variable, Controllable Expenses Which Employers Must Recognize as Growing Profit Drain," *Personnel Journal*, 55 (April, 1976), p. 171.

[30]Ibid.

[31]Ibid., p. 172.

[32]Gordon and LeBleu, op. cit., p. 93.

[33]We should indicate that there has been at least one notable exception to this dichotomy. In 1969, the United Steelworkers and basic steel agreed to a settlement that basically provided workers with a transitional quarterly earnings supplement from SUB funds to bring them up to 85 per cent of their average quarterly income in the previous year even though they were still working but at jobs paying less due to forced technological changes. See: "Protecting the Paychecks of Victims of Technology," *Business Week*, August 16, 1969, p. 98.

EMPLOYEE BENEFITS / 519

[34]Audrey Freedman, "Reexamining Income Security: SUB vs. Guaranteed Work," *The Conference Board Record*, 13 (May, 1976), p. 20.

[35]"The Labor Month in Review," *Monthly Labor Review*, 91 (January, 1968), p. III.

[36]Ibid.

[37]Ibid.

[38]Nash and Carroll, op. cit., pp. 232–233

[39]Henderson, op. cit., p. 272.

[40]For a discussion of some of these aspects, see Freedman, op. cit., pp. 20 ff.

[41]Ibid., p. 21

[42]Ibid.

[43]Ibid., p. 22

[44]Henderson, op. cit., p. 285.

[45]Ibid., p. 286.

[46]Much of the information on these plans is drawn from Mitchell Meyer, *Dental Insurance Plans* (New York: The Conference Board, Inc., 1976), p. i.

[47]Ibid.

[48]Public Law 93–222, 87 Stat., 914–1042.

[49]Henderson, op. cit., p. 288.

[50]*Congressional Quarterly Almanac*, 29 (1973), p. 507.

[51]Public Law 94–460, October 8, 1976, 90 Stat., 1951.

[52]James W. Walker, "The New Appeal of Early Retirement," *Business Horizons*, 18 (June, 1975), p. 43.

[53]See ibid., pp. 43–48 for a discussion of such aspects of early retirement as executive attitudes and early retirement guidelines.

[54]This bill (H.R. 5383, 95th Congress, 1st Session) provided the basis for a law signed by President Jimmy Carter in April, 1978, which prohibited mandatory retirement prior to age 70 except for "executives whose annual retirement benefits are at least $27,000 and tenured university teachers, who, at least until 1982, may still legally be forced to retire at age 65." *The New York Times*, April 16, 1978, Section 3, p. 1.

[55]In 1975, U.S. Government plans totaled $86 billion in assets; state and local plans, $106.5 billion; private insured, $69.4 billion; and private uninsured about $108.9 billion. This latter figure is less than that reported by the government, as about 25 per cent of the figure reported by the government represented profit sharing assets rather than pension assets, as we indicated in the previous chapter. See *Statistical Bulletin* (Washington: Securities and Exchange Commission), 35 (April, 1976), pp. 207–210.

[56]Reported in Henderson, op. cit., p. 257.

[57]Robert D. Paul, "Can Private Pension Plans Deliver?" *Harvard Business Review,* 52 (September-October, 1974), p. 32. More recently, it has been emphasized that managers and actuaries are vastly understating the costs of retirement benefits. See A. F. Ehrbar, "Those Pension Plans Are Even Weaker Than You Think," *Fortune,* 96 (November, 1977), pp. 104–114.

[58]Bert L. Metzger, *Investment Practices, Performance, and Management of Profit Sharing Trust Funds* (Evanston, Ill.: Profit Sharing Research Foundation, 1969), p. 65.

[59]Ibid.

[60]Ibid.

[61]"The Startling Impact of Private Pension Funds," op. cit., p. 95.

[62]Two notes are in order here. First, certain insurance contract plans under ERISA need not be funded, as we will indicate later. Second, the reader may be wondering how the law can require defined contribution plans to fund for past liabilities, since there are *no defined future benefits* provided by the plan as is true with defined benefit plans. The answer is as follows. Defined contribution plans are not exempt from ERISA, but "so long as the employer makes the contribution required by the plan's formula, the funding requirement. . . will be met. In effect, under this type of plan, the current payment is all that is required" since the

amount of pension benefits is uncertain "depending on the earnings of the fund to the time of the employee's retirement." Powell Niland, "Reforming Private Pension Administration," *Business Horizons*, 19 (February, 1976), p. 27.

[63]"The Startling Impact of Private Pension Funds," op. cit., p. 95.

[64]See *State Employes' Retirement System* (Harrisburg, Pa.: Commonwealth of Pennsylvania, 1976), pp. 4–5.

[65]Metzger, op. cit., p. 79.

[66]*State Employes' Retirement System*, op. cit., p. 7.

[67]Technically, ERISA (the Employee Retirement Income Security Act) is Public Law 93–406, September 2, 1974, 88 Stat. 829–1035.

[68]"Pension Reform's Expensive Ricochet, " *Business Week*, March 24, 1975, p. 144.

[69]Bea Scala, "ERISA: Administrative Nightmare," *Administrative Management*, 37 (June, 1976), p. 25.

[70]ERISA, Section 3, 88 Stat. 833. One of the many reasons given by the Congress for inclusion of such a wide array of employee benefit plans is that "they are afforded favorable preferential Federal tax treatment," as we have already noted. See, ibid, Section 2.(a), 88 Stat. 832.

[71]"Pension Reform's Expensive Ricochet," p. 149. For more detailed information on the disclosure provisions of ERISA, see, for example, Sandra Fleming, "ERISA and the Employee's Right to Know," *Personnel Journal*, 54 (June, 1975), pp. 346–349.

[72]"Pension Reform's Expensive Ricochet," op. cit., p. 149.

[73]See, for example, William I. Buppert, "Complying with ERISA Without Getting Fined," *Administrative Management*, 36 (September, 1975), pp. 20–21. Individuals, under Section 501 of ERISA (88 Stat. 891), may be fined up to $5000 and/or imprisoned for up to one year; and organizations fined up to $100,000.

[74]For exceptions to this general rule see ERISA, Section 202, 88 Stat. 853.

[75]These rules and the data on Figure 12–5(a) and (b) were drawn directly from ERISA, Section 203a, 88 Stat. 854–855.

[76]"Pension Reform's Expensive Ricochet," op. cit., p. 150.

[77]Donald G. Carlson, "Responding to the New Pension Law," *Harvard Business Review*, 52 (November-December, 1974), p. 136.

[78]"Pension Reform's Expensive Ricochet," op. cit., p. 150.

[79]Funding is not required for pension plans based on an insurance contract plan meeting several legal requirements. For these requirements see ERISA, Section 301.(b), 88 Stat. 869.

[80]"The 'Hidden' Corporate Debt," *Business Week*, August 24, 1974, pp. 46–47.

[81]"Pension Reform's Expensive Ricochet," op. cit., p. 144.

[82]ERISA, Section 402.(a), 88 Stat. 875.

[83]Ibid., Section 404.(a), 88 Stat. 877.

[84]Ibid., Section 406.(b), 88 Stat. 879.

[85]William I. Buppert, III, "ERISA: Compliance May Be Easier Than You Expect and Pay Unexpected Dividends," *Personnel Journal*, 55 (April, 1976), p. 180. See also ERISA, Section 405.(d), 88 Stat., 879.

[86]Carlson, op. cit., p. 138.

[87]For a discussion of the efforts and problems involved in savings institutions, mutual funds and insurance companies in attracting IRA funds, see "The New Personal Pension Plans," *The New York Times,* December 7, 1975, Section 3, p. 9.

[88]"Pension Reform's Expensive Ricochet," op. cit., p. 149.

[89]Carlson, op. cit., p. 139. For a more technical definition of this provision, see ERISA, Sec. 2004(b), 88 Stat. 980–981.

[90]See Carlson, op. cit., p. 137 and ibid., Section 4021.(b), 88 Stat., 1015.

[91]"Pension Reform's Expensive Ricochet," op. cit., p. 155.

[92]Ibid., p. 152.

[93]Niland, op. cit., p. 34.

[94]Jacob Javits and Harrison A. Williams, Jr., "In Defense of the Pension Reform Act," *The New York Times*, February 29, 1976, Section 3, p. 9. For other viewpoints on the effect of ERISA on plan terminations, see, for example, Ernest

Dickinson, "Backing of Paying Pensions," *The New York Times*, February 8, 1976, Section 3, pp. 1, 9; and Bea Scala, op. cit., p. 52.

[95]Javits and Williams, op. cit., p. 9.

[96]Personal communication from Dan McGill of the Wharton School.

[97]This is the title of Paul's article in the *Harvard Business Review,* op. cit.

[98]Ibid., p. 23.

[99]Ibid., p. 24.

[100]Ibid., p. 28. Forfeitures, as discussed in Chapter 11 with respect to profit sharing plans, mean monies set aside for individuals that need not be paid to them because they leave the organization before the funds are partially or fully vested and hence forfeit claims to these funds.

[101]Ibid., p. 32.

[102]Carlson, op. cit., p. 144.

[103]These are among a number of "Strategic Alternatives" suggested by Carlson, ibid., pp. 140 ff. All of these would be open to firms without pension plans under ERISA, while for companies with existing plans, ERISA would have to be taken into consideration. For example, to drop a pension plan in favor of a profit sharing one would call for encountering plan termination benefits. However, Carlson points out that *future employees* can be treated differently than present ones. Under ERISA, "a company does not have an obligation to employees who have not even been hired yet." Ibid., p. 143.

[104]"Public Pension Funds Seek Safer Grounds," *Business Week*, September 13, 1976, p. 38.

[105]Ibid.

13

OCCUPATIONAL SAFETY AND HEALTH

No matter how well an organization plans and controls its activities, some safety and health hazards will exist in the work place. These hazards may be created by (1) conditions in the work environment such as a wet floor, a poor electrical connection, dust in the air, or defective equipment or materials; (2) actions taken by the workers such as "horse play" in the work area or lack of attention; or (3) a combination of these two variables. In *some instances*, hazards will result in the occurrence of unplanned events, such as a worker carrying an expensive piece of electronic equipment, slipping, and falling on a wet floor. Unplanned events such as this may or may not cause damage to physical or human resources. For example, the employee's fall could result in any one of the four following occurrences:

1. The employee might injure himself *and* at the same time damage the expensive piece of electronic equipment he was carrying.

2. The employee might injure himself, *but not* damage the equipment.

3. The employee might *not* injure himself but damage the equipment.

4. The employee might *neither* injure himself *nor* damage the equipment.

Thus, the presence of hazards does not mean that unplanned events will occur but rather that a *potential* exists. Similarly, as illustrated here and as shown schematically in Figure 13–1, when an unplanned event does occur, it may or may not result in *damage* to physical resources or *trauma* for human resources, or both.

"Trauma," as used here, is the pathological damage of tissues by some kind of force, chemical, or other agent, or psychological shock due to stress or injury. Usually the damaging agent has a sudden, noticeable result — as in the case of crushing injuries and acid burns — for example. However, the evidence of damage often may not be seen immediately, as in the case of contact dermatitis [*skin inflammation resulting from contact with some substance*] and pneumoconiosis [*lung disorders such as black lung*].[1]

A number of aspects of Figure 13–1 and this definition of trauma deserve further discussion. First, unplanned events may result from both safety and health hazards. Generally, a "safety hazard" is said to have existed when the result of an unplanned event has been an injury and a "health hazard" when the result has been an illness (or disease). In some cases, however, the distinction between safety and health hazards is blurred. For example, coal miners work where there is a great deal of coal dust in the air, the breathing of which may contribute to nausea and headaches (illness) or, over a longer period of time, to black lung (disease). In addition, however, the dust can ignite and result in an explosion in the mine, in which miners are killed or injured. Thus, the distinction between safety and health hazards often is based upon the outcomes, not upon the hazards themselves.

As noted, the distinction between injury and illness is also sometimes blurred, and, therefore, we will use the word trauma, as defined above, to cover both injuries and illnesses. For example, if an employee in a factory breathes in dust that causes him to become dizzy and he falls and cuts his hand, it is likely to be said that an injury resulted, when in fact the employee may also have suffered an illness. The use of the word "trauma" has the additional advantage in that it covers both physical and psychological outcomes, whereas the terms injury and illness generally are used to refer to physical outcomes only. Further, "trauma" includes both the results of unplanned events that are immediately identifi-

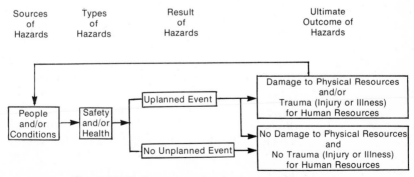

Figure 13-1 *The occupational safety and health process.*

able and those that do not appear for a number of years, as in the case of the coal miner breathing coal dust. In another example, an employee who falls off a ladder may break his leg but not discover until a number of years later that he has developed a back problem from the same fall.

As with our worker slipping and falling on the wet floor, it should be emphasized that a single unplanned event may result in more than one undesirable consequence. For example, equipment may be damaged and numerous employees may suffer trauma of both an immediate and a long-term nature. In addition, a single employee may suffer more than one undesirable consequence as a result of a single unplanned event. To illustrate, consider some of the potential outcomes of an explosion in a coal mine. Equipment such as coal cars, tracks, and mine structures may be damaged or destroyed. Some employees may suffer immediate injuries such as broken bones or they may be killed. Some employees may become ill as a result of breathing toxic fumes from a fire that resulted from the explosion. Other employees may experience long-term *psychological* problems as a result of experiencing a "close call" with death — the ultimate trauma. Still other employees may experience long-term physical problems such as broken bones that do not heal properly, amputations, and lung problems.

Notice that we have not used the word "accident" in our examples or in Figure 13–1. This is because the term has so often been used to imply that unplanned events leading to physical damage or trauma happen *purely* by chance and *without* known or identifiable causes. As Grimaldi and Simonds have noted, however:

> The majority of cases which fill safety records could be predicted and so may not be regarded as wholly accidental. Their causes and remedies already were established by countless similar earlier occurrences. Most harmful events are the result of failures to apply known principles for their control.[2]

We will sometimes use the word "accident" in this chapter because many statistics and other aspects of occupational safety and health have been reported in terms of "accidents." We will utilize the key words presented in Figure 13–1 — "hazard," "unplanned event," "damage," and "trauma" — wherever possible, however, because we believe that they more precisely define the various basic elements involved in occupational safety and health. For purposes of simplification we will also sometimes simply use the word "damage" to refer to damage to both physical resources and human resources (trauma).

In the 1970's, largely as a result of federal legislation, organizations began to show an increased interest in occupational safety and health. In addition, as more and more toxic substances have been found that are potential health hazards to employees in many industries, there has been an increasing social awareness of the problems associated with occupational health. Further, the increase in occupational injuries and deaths during the late 1960's and early 1970's also stimulated public awareness of occupational safety problems. These forces have contributed to the expansion of the role of the safety director beyond merely counting and classifying traumas and taking remedial action. Rather, the role of the safety director today involves the active creation of conditions that facilitate reducing occupational safety and health hazards to socially and economically acceptable levels. Thus, his new role is much more proactive and involves preventive as well as remedial activities.

In this chapter we will discuss a number of aspects of occupational safety and health. First, we will cover some of the historical developments relating to this subject. In this section we will deal with earlier developments with respect to occupational safety and health, legislation designed to cope with such problems, and with both the scope and measurement of contemporary occupational safety and health problems. Then we will discuss the most important piece of federal legislation regulating actions affecting occupational safety and health today — the Occupational Safety and Health Act of 1970 (OSHAct). We will discuss the major provisions of the Act, some of the problems associated with the Act and its administration, and some future trends that appear to be taking place with respect to this Act. Next, we will view occupational safety and health within an organizational context, noting the major problems which face those persons who are responsible for safety and health in the organization and some of the approaches they can use to deal with these problems. Finally, we will discuss management science techniques and computerization, which have been used in the safety and health area, and note three contingencies that influence the scope of decision making of those persons responsible for occupational safety and health within the organization.

HISTORICAL DEVELOPMENTS

In this section we will discuss some of the early historical developments and legislation associated with occupational safety and health. We will also present statistical data in order to indicate the magnitude of safety and health problems in organizations.

Early History and Legislation Up to 1970

Trauma resulting from occupational safety and health hazards has existed ever since people began to work in organized settings.[3] The earliest formalized interest in occupational safety and health often was concerned with remedial activities to "prevent" future unplanned events rather than prevention through prior control of hazards. For example, as early as 1750 B.C., the Code of Hammurabi attempted to encourage safety by providing for punishment of individuals who violated safety provisions in constructing buildings. However, there was some early interest in controlling the conditions that contributed to injuries and illnesses. For example, there are "early illustrations showing workers engaged in the grinding of vermillion, which produces a dangerous dust, wearing a primitive type of breathing apparatus."[4] In addition, in a book written in 1473, Ulrich Ellenbog noted the occupational hazards associated with being a goldsmith and metal worker and provided advice on how to avoid mercury and lead poisoning.[5] Further, in the sixteenth century, Agricola and Paracelus wrote about miners' diseases and in 1713, Ramazzini, who is regarded as the father of occupational medicine, suggested that in diagnosis doctors should ask patients about their occupations.[6]

It was not until the industrial revolution in the nineteenth century with the growth of the factory system, however, that occupational injuries and illnesses became so widespread, severe, and numerous as to constitute a serious social and economic problem. During this period it was not uncommon for factories to be poorly designed, ventilated, and illuminated. In addition, dangerous equipment was frequently poorly guarded, if it was guarded at all. Further, workers were not well trained for the conditions they encountered in the factory and they were required to work an excessive number of hours, which contributed to high levels of fatigue. These types of safety and health hazards combined to create environments conducive to the occurrence of traumas.

Despite these problems, there was only sporadic interest in employee safety and health during the nineteenth century among employers. For example, in 1825, Robert Owen, the British manufacturer, philosopher, and humanitarian, who is sometimes regarded as the "father" of personnel management, founded a community in Indiana.[7] This community included manufacturing facilities that reflected Owen's belief in a safe and healthy environment for the worker. He introduced such "innovations" as a shorter work day, the abolition of child labor, and the presence of toilet facilities in the plant. As another example, in 1888, a number of coal mining companies in Pennsylvania hired a nurse to treat miners and their families.[8] These types of efforts, which were primarily motivated by humanitarian considerations, however, were few and far between, and it is unlikely that they had any major impact on reducing injuries and illnesses. In fact, we do not know how high occupational injury and illness rates were during this period because there was no organized collection of such data.[9] It is generally accepted, however, that occupational injuries and illnesses increased after the industrial revolution began. Moreover, the ultimate loss to the unlucky individual worker was likely to be disastrous, since he lacked medical insurance and compensation benefits.

With increasing occupational injuries and illnesses during the nineteenth century it was inevitable that workers and other interested parties would react and attempt to change workers' conditions. However, from a legal standpoint in terms of safety and health, the employee had only common law to stand upon. Common law, as distinguished from statutory law, is essentially unwritten law composed of decisions handed down by judges in areas where no laws exist; or decisions interpreting laws or statutes passed by the government. In addition, as we will note in Chapter 14, the legal environment was not conducive to unions, so that concerted group actions were unlikely.

Under common law the employer had an obligation to provide his employees with:

1. A safe place to work.
2. Safe tools with which to perform the work.
3. Knowledge of any hazards that were not immediately apparent but might be encountered during performance of the work.
4. Competent fellow employees and supervisors.
5. Rules by which all could perform safely and means to ensure that rules were observed.[10]

However, when an employee experienced a trauma from his work, the burden of proof was on the employee to show that the employer was negligent. Even when employees were willing to challenge an employer and risk the loss of a job, the legal environment of the time hindered them due to three basic common law doctrines in existence:

1. The *fellow servant rule*, which exempted the employer from liability for a worker if carelessness or negligence of any of his fellow employees was involved.
2. *Contributory negligence*, which exempted the employer from any liability if the worker's own negligence contributed to the injury or illness.
3. The *assumption of risk*, which held that when an employee took a job he accepted the usual risks of the occupation and therefore the employer could not be held liable for traumas suffered.

These doctrines made it very difficult for an employee to win cases against employers. The burden of proof was on the employee, and fellow employees were usually reluctant to testify on his behalf for fear of losing their own jobs. In addition, workers frequently were poorly educated and ignorant of the law and therefore did not pursue legitimate claims because they were not aware of their rights. Further, even when they were aware of such rights, workers frequently earned so little that they could ill afford legal advice. If a worker knew his rights, had the money to obtain legal advice and decided to pursue his claim through judicial channels, he still had to take his chances with the courts. In some cases, months and even years might be involved before the court ruled on a claim. If the case was eventually won by the employee, obtaining full restitution was difficult, and legal fees often consumed major portions of any settlement. Further, as was pointed out in a 1910 report, the amount of any award was also likely to vary depending upon the individuals deciding the case as well as the type of injury. For example, "In one state, awards for loss of a hand ranged from approximately $400 to over $4000; loss of a foot $50 to $3000; and loss of an eye $290 to $2700,"[11] Owing to these types of problems, workers and the public began to pressure the government for laws to aid the worker who suffered from occupational traumas.

During the nineteenth century there were some governmental attempts to deal with safety and health problems. For example, increased concern on a nationwide basis was initially reflected in 1837 when the first United States report on occupational safety and health was issued.[12] In addition, the states began to take action. In 1867, Massachusetts passed the first major piece of legislation dealing with occupational safety and health, and in 1877, additional factory acts were passed. These pieces of legislation provided for factory inspections and for guards to be placed on dangerous pieces of machinery. In addition, specifications relating to ventilation and cleanliness were spelled out by several states. Such legislation did little to improve the lot of the worker, however, since it was generally poorly enforced. Legislative attempts of a different nature were also equally ineffective. For example, in 1885, the state of Alabama passed an ineffective employer liability law that attempted to reduce the "employer's defenses based on the common law concept of assumption of risk."[13] Other states quickly adopted similar "assumption of risk" laws. However, these laws did not prove effective because the employer could still fall back on the doctrines of the fellow servant rule and contributory negligence.

As the United States entered the twentieth century, a few organizations recognized the need for the control of safety and health hazards. For example, in 1906 the United States Steel Corporation instituted a program geared toward inspection in order to control injuries and illnesses.[14] Other *large* companies also began to develop similar types of programs. Three comments concerning these early programs are in order. First, they tended to emphasize safety to a much greater extent than health. This focus is not surprising, since injuries and the costs associated with them are generally more visible and more immediate than for illnesses. Second, these programs were probably motivated by a combination of humanitarian considerations, a realization of the economic costs and therefore potential savings, and a fear of governmentally imposed programs. Third, these programs were generally developed by only the largest organizations and therefore they did not affect the majority of the work force. Between 1907 and 1908, the industrial accident rate reached "an all time high" with approximately 30,000 workers dying from occupation related traumas.[15]

These events set the stage for the major turning point for increased interest in occupational safety and health — the passage of workmen's compensation laws. In 1908, the federal government passed a law to protect certain civil service employees; in 1909, Montana passed a law pertaining to coal miners; and in 1910, New York passed a law covering employees in eight dangerous occupations. All three of these laws were later held to be unconstitutional. However, by 1911, ten states had passed workmen's compensation laws that were upheld as constitutional; between 1912 and 1913, ten more states added such laws; by 1920, only six states lacked workmen's compensation laws; today all states have such laws that cover about 80 per cent of all workers.[16]

These laws essentially had a no-fault type of provision for the employer's liability if a worker suffered trauma on the job. The employer was required to make provision for payment of certain benefits to such an employee even though there was no evidence that the employer was in any way at fault. Such payments, which vary from state to state, include medical expenses, a portion of the worker's income for work lost due to the trauma, and additional payments in cases of dismemberment or loss of bodily functions (such as loss of an arm). Thus, workmen's compensation laws resulted in the employer accepting financial responsibility for at least a portion of any economic loss which an employee experienced due to occupational trauma. It should be noted that the initial emphasis of workmen's compensation laws was on injuries and not illnesses. However, beginning in the 1920's and early 1930's organizations became more interested in occupational health as the courts began to interpret the workmen's compensation laws in terms of occupational health as well as safety. Over the years the coverages of these laws have been extended.

For example, in July 1970 a worker in an automobile plant in Detroit was fired. Later in the day he returned to the plant and shot and killed three supervisors. He was committed to a state mental hospital after he was declared legally insane at his trial. In March 1973 the State of Michigan ruled that the worker should be paid workmen's compensation retroactive to the day on which he was fired. The state indicated that working conditions, only some of them related to physical hazards, had aggravated a preexisting but nondisabling tendency toward schizophrenia and paranoia until there was an acute, psychotic break with reality. Since psychiatric treatment was required for this job-related disability, the worker was entitled to benefits under the workmen's compensation law.[17]

The theory behind workmen's compensation was that it would motivate employers to reduce safety and health hazards because of the financial costs. It is doubtful, however, that these employer cost considerations were the direct major cause of the reductions in the number of traumas that occurred after the passage of these laws. The costs were not particularly high because insurance companies developed programs that permitted employers to spread the risk. Insurance premiums were and still are relatively low. For example, in 1972 workmen's compensation premiums as a percentage of payroll were distributed as follows in 42 states: 7 states, less than 0.500 per cent; 17, 0.500 to 0.749 per cent; 13, 0.750 to 0.999 per cent; 3, 1.000 to 1.249 per cent; and 2, 1.250 to 1.499 per cent.[18]

Nevertheless, workmen's compensation laws did contribute directly and indirectly to increased interest in occupational safety and health. While the costs of insurance premiums were not excessive, more companies saw for the first time the direct costs of safety and health problems because of the insurance premiums they were paying. Companies, therefore, became interested in reducing this cost. Insurance companies, which were now assuming a substantial portion of the dollar costs associated with occupational traumas, began to inspect employers' facilities to determine insurance premiums and to investigate accidents in insured facilities when they occurred. These efforts resulted in the insurance companies developing information useful in determining how traumas could be reduced. To encourage employers to engage in safety and health programs, the insurance companies used schedule rating, which provided for insurance premiums to be reduced according to a schedule if an insured took actions to reduce or eliminate known hazards. For example, if a company installed guards on dangerous machinery, its premiums might be reduced. Further, the insurance companies granted premium reductions for companies which had good safety and health records. This type of cost reduction is conceptually similar to the concept of "experience rating," which we discussed with respect to unemployment compensation in Chapter 12. These types of activities by the insurance companies provided employers with incentives to participate in hazards control and obtain needed expertise in this area.

Another development that increased interest in safety and health during the twentieth century was that special groups interested in occupational safety and health came into existence. For example, in 1912 a group that was the forerunner of the National Safety Council was formed. The National Safety Council still exists today as one of the more influential groups in the safety and health area. Companies began to realize because of the efforts of insurance companies, special groups and their own activities, that they could save substantial sums of money through reductions in lost time, damaged equipment, absenteeism, etc.

From the passage of workmen's compensation laws until the 1960's, occupational safety and probably also occupational health improved. However, in the 1960's injury rates increased and society became increasingly concerned with occupational health. These events resulted in the most far ranging governmental action dealing with safety and health, the passage of the Occupational Safety and Health Act of 1970 which is also referred to as the Williams-Steiger Act. We will refer to this Act as OSHAct and to the Occupational Safety and Health Administration, the agency established to administer the Act, as OSHA.

OSHAct was passed by Congress and was signed into law by President Richard M. Nixon December 29, 1970, to take effect on April 28, 1971. This act added a strong legal dimension to the earlier humanitarian and financial dimensions of occupational safety and health. The pervasiveness of this act is indicated by the fact that at the time of its passage it covered most employers engaged in interstate commerce — some 57 million workers in over 4 million business establishments. It excluded from coverage only federal, state, and municipal employers, and mining employers who were covered by other acts, although many state and municipal employers in effect became covered by OSHAct. for reasons which we will indicate later. William Steiger, one of the authors of the act, has stated that OSHAct, along with such other legislation as the Metal and Nonmetallic Mine Act and the Longshoreman's Act, covers a vast majority of the workers in the United States.[19] Because of the rights which OSHAct confers upon employees, it can be regarded as another in a series of federal laws pertaining to employee management relations. We will explore the major provisions of OSHAct later in this chapter and other legislation relating to employee management relations in the next chapter. Before looking at the major provisions of OSHAct, however, we will present some occupational safety and health statistics to indicate the contemporary magnitude of the problem upon which we are focusing our attention.

The Scope and Measurement of Occupational Safety and Health

In this section we will present and discuss in some detail data relating to occupational injuries in terms of (1) the numbers involved, (2) the amount of time lost, and (3) the dollar costs.[20] Data concerning occupational illnesses and disease cannot be presented in any detail because such data have not been collected systematically or separately in the past. There are a number of reasons for this lack of data concerning occupational health. First, it has been only within the last few years that the extent to which toxic substances can contribute to health problems has been recognized. This increased awareness has resulted from better measuring instruments to detect toxicity and from better record keeping. Improved record keeping is important because it permits locating employees who may have been exposed to health hazards in the past to see if they have since developed any particular health problems. This type of analysis, in turn, may help identify additional toxic substances. A second reason for the lack of data concerning occupational health is that illnesses and diseases often do not show up immediately. Therefore, it is frequently difficult to determine whether an illness or disease resulted from job-related activities or from other causes. In some cases illnesses and diseases have been counted as injuries, as in the case of the employee who became dizzy, fell, and cut his hand.

While there are no data available concerning occupational health, there are estimates that indicate the magnitude of the problem in this area. For example, it was estimated in 1972 that exposure at work to toxic materials may account for at least 100,000 deaths annually as well as for 390,000 additional new cases of disabling illnesses per year.[21] In addition, it was noted in 1976 that even though disabling injuries occur five times more frequently than disabling occupational illnesses, the annual mortality rate that results from disabling injuries is only one seventh of that for occupational disease.[22] Thus, the magnitude of occupational health problems is potentially very large and in the future may be of even greater importance than occupational safety.

The Numbers Involved

To give an overview of the magnitude of the problem under discussion, in 1976, for example, there were 12,500 occupational deaths, which represented an average of approximately 34 deaths per day, or 1 death about every 42 minutes. There were also 2,200,000 disabling injuries or about 6027 per day, or one injury every 0.24 minutes (one every 15 seconds).

The number of occupation-related deaths decreased from an estimated high in 1907–1908 of 30,000 to a low in 1976 of 12,500. After fairly steady declines from 1933 to 1960, however, the number of deaths rose slightly during the 1960's, averaging 14,070 per year for this decade. This increase, along with an increase in accident frequency rates, was one of the major reasons for the decision to pass OSHAct in 1970.

Until the passage of OSHAct, two rates as set forth by the American National Standards Institute (ANSI) in its "American Standard Method of Recording and Measuring Work Injury Experience, ANSI Standard Z16.1,"[23] were used on a nationwide basis as standards for recording and analyzing injury experience. These rates were based on data indicating both the *frequency* and the *severity* of disabling injuries. Four classes of disabling (also referred to as lost-time) injuries were defined: (1) deaths; (2) permanent total disabilities; (3) permanent partial disabilities; and (4) temporary total disabilities. Injuries that required medical treatment or first aid but that were in no way disabling were not included. It should be noted that these standards did cover occupational illnesses to some extent since a work injury was defined in such a way as to include an employee's exposure to environmental factors on the job to which he would not normally be exposed off the job. However, the major focus was upon occupational injuries.

Data pertaining to frequency and severity rates are presented in Figure 13–2. The basis for calculating the frequency and severity rates is as follows:

$$\text{Frequency} = \frac{\text{Number of Disabling Injuries} \times 1,000,000}{\text{Number of Employee Hours Worked}}$$

$$\text{Severity} = \frac{\text{Total Hours Charged} \times 1,000,000}{\text{Number of Employee Hours Worked}}$$

The division by the number of employees' hours worked in calculating both of these rates is done to permit comparison of firms of various sizes since larger firms typically will have more injuries in absolute terms simply because of the larger number of workers employed. The multiplication by 1,000,000 puts the rates on a lost-time or frequency basis per 1,000,000 employee hours worked. This makes it much easier to manipulate the data. For example, suppose a manufacturer has an average of 437 employees during a given year, that these employees work an average of 2000 hours

Year	Number of Units	Frequency Rates				Severity Rates	% of All Disabilities			Average Days Lost per Temp. Total Disability
		Fatal, Perm. Total	Perm. Partial Disab.	Temp. Total Disab.	All Disa- bilities		Fatal, Perm. Total	Perm. Partial Disab.	Temp. Total Disab.	
1926. . . .	1,725	.23	.93	30.71	31.87	2,500	.7	2.9	96.4	17
1927	2,089	.17	.76	25.02	25.95	1,880	.7	2.9	96.4	15
1928	2,552	.19	.71	23.62	24.52	2,030	.8	2.9	96.3	17
1929	3,603	.22	.93	24.24	25.39	2,250	.9	3.7	95.4	16
1930	4,198	.19	.78	17.50	18.47	1,970	1.0	4.2	94.8	19
1931	4,383	.17	.64	14.31	15.12	1,720	1.1	4.2	94.7	21
1932	3,937	.16	.58	12.46	13.20	1,590	1.2	4.4	94.4	21
1933	3,776	.16	.63	13.77	14.56	1,590	1.1	4.3	94.6	20
1934	3,866	.17	.69	14.43	15.29	1,700	1.1	4.5	94.4	20
1935	3,796	.15	.73	13.14	14.02	1,580	1.1	5.6	93.3	21
1936	4,093	.16	.71	12.70	13.57	1,640	1.2	5.2	93.6	22
1937	4,032	.15	.76	13.14	14.05	1,580	1.1	5.4	93.5	20
1938	4,497	.15	.65	11.38	12.18	1,530	1.2	5.3	93.5	25
1939	4,734	.14	.65	11.04	11.83	1,420	1.2	5.5	93.3	23
1940	5,163	.14	.67	11.71	12.52	1,440	1.1	5.4	93.5	22
1941	5,325	.14	.70	14.55	15.39	1,530	.9	4.5	94.6	21
1942	5,537	.15	.59	13.94	14.68	1,490	1.0	4.0	95.0	20
1943	6,060	.10	.72	13.70	14.52	1,200	.7	5.0	94.3	20
1944	5,857	.10	.80	13.56	14.46	1,210	.7	5.5	93.8	20
1945	6,262	.09	.69	12.85	13.63	1,160	.7	5.1	94.2	23
1946	6,212	.11	.77	13.28	14.16	1,280	.8	5.4	93.8	22
1947	6,634	.10	.71	12.45	13.26	1,230	.8	5.4	93.8	24
1948	6,707	.10	.69	10.70	11.49	1,120	.9	6.0	93.1	21
1949	7,185	.08	.64	9.42	10.14	1,020	.8	6.3	92.9	23
1950	6,395	.08	.57	8.65	9.30	940	.9	6.2	92.9	22
1951	6,652	.09	.53	8.44	9.06	970	1.0	5.8	93.2	23
1952	7,112	.08	.52	7.80	8.40	880	.9	6.3	92.8	23
1953	7,110	.07	.50	6.87	7.44	830	1.0	6.8	92.2	23
1954	7,018	.07	.44	6.71	7.22	800	1.0	6.1	92.9	23
1955	7,237	.08	.46	6.42	6.96	815	1.2	6.6	92.2	22
1956	7,196	.07	.40	5.91	6.38	733	1.1	6.3	92.6	25
1957	7,402	.07	.42	5.78	6.27	740	1.2	6.6	92.2	24
1958	7,512	.07	.40	5.70	6.17	744	1.2	6.6	92.2	25
1959	8,111	.07	.41	5.99	6.47	754	1.1	6.4	92.5	25
1960	7,894	.07	.38	5.59	6.04	729	1.2	6.3	92.5	26
1961	8,628	.06	.38	5.55	5.99	666	1.1	6.3	92.6	26
1962	8,824	.07	.39	5.73	6.19	694	1.1	6.3	92.6	28
1963	9,174	.06	.34	5.72	6.12	682	1.0	5.6	93.4	29
1964	9,674	.07	.35	6.03	6.45	693	1.0	5.4	93.6	27
1965	9,754	.07	.34	6.12	6.53	695	1.0	5.2	93.8	28
1966	10,017	.06	.40	6.45	6.91	689	.9	5.8	93.3	26
1967	10,161	.06	.38	6.78	7.22	672	.8	5.3	93.9	26
1968	10,576	.06	.37	6.92	7.35	665	.8	5.0	94.2	27
1969	13,627	.05	.35	7.68	8.08	640	.7	4.4	94.9	23
1970	13,121	.06	.34	8.47	8.87	667	.7	3.9	95.4	24
1971	13,371	.05	.33	8.99	9.37	611	.5	3.5	96.0	23
1972	13,223	.06	.35	9.76	10.17	655	.6	3.4	96.0	22
1973	13,923	.06	.31	10.18	10.55	654	.5	2.9	96.6	22
1974	13,557	.05	.29	9.86	10.20	614	.5	2.8	96.7	23
1975*	13,718	.06	.32	12.71	13.10	752	.4	2.4	97.2	23

*Based on Z16.1 Standard. Rates are not fully comparable from year to year due to changes in numbers of reporters and increased representation of service, trade, and government.

Figure 13-2 Injury experience of National Safety Council reporters, 1926–1975. [From National Safety Council: Accident Facts (Chicago, Ill.: National Safety Council, 1976), p. 28.]

(50 weeks times 40 hours per week), and that there are 13 lost-time injuries. The frequency rate would be $(13 \times 1,000,000)/(437 \times 2000) = 14.87$. This accident statistic would be the difficult-to-handle number 0.00001487 if we did not multiply by 1,000,000. This rate indicates that for every 1,000,000 employee hours worked the organization has experienced 14.87 injuries.

The computation of severity rates is slightly more complex than that of frequency rates. The number of injuries in each of the four classes of disabling injuries indicated must be identified along with the specific nature of each injury. The injuries are then converted to hour charges based upon a standard scale. For example, suppose that the 13 lost-time injuries for the firm as in our above example included 1 permanent total disability, 1 loss of a hand, 1 loss of an eye, and 75 lost days for the remaining injuries. From a table of time charges developed by ANSI it is found that the permanent total disability carries a time charge of 6000 hours (as does death); the lost hand, 3000 hours; the lost eye, 1800 hours; and the 75 lost days with no permanent disabilities would be charged as 75 lost days of eight hours each. Therefore, the severity rate (in hours) would be:

$$\text{Severity} = \frac{(6000 + 3000 + 1800 + 600) \times 1,000,000}{437 \times 2000} = 13,043$$

or 1630 days. Because of the high standard time charges, a single injury may cause the severity rate to fluctuate greatly. For example, if the *one* total permanent disability had not occurred but instead the employee had injured his foot and lost five days (or 40 hours) of work, the severity rate would have been reduced drastically to 6224 hours or 778 days.

With the passage of OSHAct, a new method for calculating injury and illness rates, called the incidence rate, was developed.[24] However, most companies and the National Safety Council still calculate frequency and severity rates in order to maintain the continuity of these rates for comparative purposes. The new incidence rate is defined as:

$$\text{Incidence rate} = \frac{\text{Number of recordable injuries and illnesses} \times 200,000}{\text{Number of employee exposure hours}}$$

Exposure hours is the total hours worked by all employees during the calendar year. The 200,000 figure represents the number of hours worked annually by 100 full-time employees who each work 40 hours per week, 50 weeks per year. For example, if a firm which employed 437 persons, as in our previous illustration of frequency and severity rates, had 13 recordable injuries and illnesses, its incidence rate would be $(13 \times 200,000)/(437 \times 40 \times 50) = 2.97$. As we will indicate, the recordable injuries and illnesses under OSHAct are more comprehensive than for frequency and severity rate calculations. Therefore, in the above example, it is likely that the firm would have more than 13 recordable injuries and illnesses. In 1975, the incidence rate for the private sector was 9.1, meaning 9.1 recordable injuries and illnesses occurred for each 100 employees that year on the average. OSHAct did not require the collection of data pertaining to severity because of the belief that any specification of time charges to be associated with injuries and deaths was likely to be arbitrary.

The Amount of Time Lost

The number of work hours lost due to industrial trauma has tended to be quite large. For 1976, for example, the estimated work days lost due to "accidents" was 245,000,000. This figure included 45,000,000 work days for injured workers with disabling injuries and 200,000,000 work days for other workers with nondisabling injuries and no injuries. No-injury situations can result in lost time by a worker, even though he himself is not injured, for example, by attending to others who have been injured, by becoming so emotionally upset at witnessing a "gory" injury that the noninjured employee needs to take the rest of the day off, and so on. In addition, the future work days lost due to 1976 traumas were estimated to be 120,000,000. It should be noted that these figures are estimates and that they may well understate the severity of the problem.

Dollar Costs

The total costs of work accidents in 1976, according to the National Safety Council, were $17.8 billion, of which $7.9 billion were costs such as wages lost, insurance, administrative costs, and medical costs; $7.9 billion represented costs such as the money value of time lost by workers who were not injured but were directly or indirectly involved in the accident and the cost to investigate, write up reports, and so forth. Fire losses amounted to $2 billion. The cost of these accidents per worker to industry in 1976 was $200. Both total costs and per worker costs have risen significantly and steadily from 1960 to 1976 — $4.4 billion to $17.8 billion and $65 to $200 respectively. In addition, total workmen's compensation payments rose from $2.6 billion in 1969 to $5.7 billion in 1975.

The time lost because of illness would be difficult to determine because of the problem of distinguishing occupational illnesses from "personal" illnesses which are at least not directly related to the job. For example, it is interesting to note that the $17.8 billion cost figure

. . . does not include the cost, in dollars and cents as well as productivity, of absenteeism due to alcohol, estimated to be $4 billion a year; mental illness, $3 billion a year; and drug abuse. (As for normal illness absenteeism, it is estimated to be ten times more costly than industrial accidents. A widely accepted rule-of-thumb is that when an experienced employee is incapacitated, the daily cost to his employer is one and one-half times the employee's daily wage.)[25]

OSHACT MAJOR PROVISIONS, PROBLEMS, AND PROMISE

Congress passed the OSHAct because it found "that personal injuries and illnesses arising out of work situations impose a substantial burden upon, and are a hindrance to, interstate commerce in terms of lost production, wage loss, medical expenses, and disability compensation payments."[26] The decision to pass the Act was based, in part, on the increase in injuries during the 1960's and an increased awareness that health problems could be costly. In this section we will review some of the major provisions of OSHAct and note some of the problems OSHAct and OSHA have created, along with some areas relative to OSHAct that appear to be most promising for the improvement of safety and health in the future.

OSHAct Major Provisions

The purpose of OSHAct was "to provide for the general welfare, to assure so far as possible every working man and woman in the Nation safe and healthful working conditions and to preserve our human resources."[27] To accomplish this purpose, the Act created three new organizations with various responsibilities: the Occupational Safety and Health Administration (OSHA); the Occupational Safety and Health Review Commission (OSHRC); and the National Institute for Occupational Safety and Health (NIOSH). We will now discuss the functions and responsibilities of each of these three organizations.

OSHA is an agency within the Department of Labor which is responsible for promulgating and enforcing occupational safety and health standards. To ensure enforcement of the standards, OSHAct provides for: (1) reporting by employers, (2) the inspections of organizations for safety and health hazards, and (3) investigations of accidents and allegations of hazards. The inspections and investigations are carried out by OSHA compliance officers who must, by law, issue citations that vary in penalties to organizations found to be in violation of safety or health standards.

OSHA was charged with the responsibility of setting three types of safety and health standards — interim, emergency temporary, and permanent. OSHAct required the issuance of interim standards within two years after enactment of the Act. Initially, the interim standards issued consisted of any established federal standards, such as those provided for in the Construction Safety Act, and "national consensus" standards. A national consensus standard basically referred to a standard that had been adopted by any nationally recognized standards development organization, such as the ANSI, or used extensively by a large industrial firm. Emergency temporary standards under OSHAct must be issued if it is determined (1) that grave danger exists to employees exposed to toxic or physically harmful substances or agents or from newly recognized hazards and (2) that to protect the employees an emergency standard is necessary. An emergency temporary standard takes effect immediately upon its publication in the *Federal Register* and action must be taken by OSHA to promulgate a permanent standard to replace it within six months. OSHA also has the responsibility to promulgate, modify, and eliminate permanent standards. It was expected that the original interim standards, which were essentially stopgap measures, would become permanent standards, be modified, and made permanent or be revoked.

OSHAct provided for mandatory record keeping on the part of employers. Although these records are few compared to those required for insurance purposes, it is the employer's responsibility to maintain them and to make them available to OSHA. Part of this record keeping is for the purpose of compiling of nationwide summary statistics. The OSHAct specifically provides for OSHA to:

. . . compile accurate statistics on work injuries and illnesses which shall include all disabling, serious or significant injuries and illnesses, whether or not involving loss of time from work, other than minor injuries requiring only first aid treatment and which do not involve medical treatment, loss of consciousness, restriction of work or motion, or transfer to another job.[28]

To conduct investigations and inspections OSHA is authorized:

(1) to enter without delay and at reasonable times any factory, plant, establishment, construction site or other area, workplace or environment where work is performed by an employee of an employer; and

(2) to inspect and investigate during regular working hours and at other reasonable times, and within reasonable limits and in a reasonable manner, any such place of employment and all pertinent conditions, structures, machines, apparatus, devices, equipment, and materials therein, and to question privately any such employer, owner, operator, agent or employee.[29]

The Act specifically provided that such inspections and investigations must be unannounced. Since not all 5 million work places covered by the Act could possibly be inspected, a list of four priority classes for conducting the unannounced inspections was set up. These were:[30]

1. Where a catastrophe (defined as one fatality or five or more injuries requiring hospitalization from a single incident) has occurred.

2. Where valid employee complaints were received.

3. Where "Special Emphasis Programs" were believed to be needed. Special Emphasis Programs focused attention on both:

    a. Target Industries. Here the focus has been upon the five industries with injury frequency rates more than twice that of the national average — longshoring, meat and meat products, roofing and sheet metal, lumber and wood products, and miscellaneous transportation equipment.

    b. Target Health Hazards. Here the focus has been upon the five most commonly used and hazardous of the more than 15,000 toxic substances identified by NIOSH — asbestos, carbon monoxide, cotton dust, lead and silica.

4. Random selection from all types and sizes of workplaces in all sections of the country.

It should be noted that under OSHAct if an inspection resulted from an employee complaint, the employer could not penalize the employee in any way even if the complaint proved to be invalid.

Under OSHAct, if, as a result of an inspection or investigation any OSHA compliance officer identifies an imminent danger, he must inform any affected employee and the employer of the danger. In addition, he must obtain a court order to shut down the facility until such imminent danger is corrected. An imminent danger was defined to exist when conditions "could reasonably be expected to cause death or serious physical harm immediately or before the imminence of such danger can be eliminated through the enforcement procedures otherwise provided by this Act."[31] Since most violations of OSHAct are not likely to be of the imminent danger type, the law also provides procedures for nonimminent violations. If, as a result of an investigation or inspection, violations of nonimminent dangers are found that may lead to an injury or illness, the compliance officer must issue a citation which describes the nature of the violation and sets forth a time for the abatement of the violation. The citation will also specify the penalty to be assessed, if any. A list of penalties is presented in Figure 13–3.

A company that believes a citation or penalty or both is not appropriate may appeal the decision to the Occupational Safety and Health Review Commission (OSHRC), a quasijudicial board composed of three members appointed by the President. OSHRC was established to hear and review charges of violations when requested by any employer who is charged and, when warranted, to issue corrective orders or to assess civil penalties. OSHRC may increase the penalties originally established by OSHA inspectors as well as lower them. Employers who object to an OSHRC finding may appeal the decisions through the courts. In some instances, an employer can obtain a variance from a stand-

PENALTIES-CIVIL

VIOLATION	MANDA-TORY	FINE UP TO	AND/OR IMPRISONMENT UP TO
IMMINENT DANGER, WILLFUL OR REPEATED	NO	$10,000/VIOLATION	NO
SERIOUS	YES	$1,000/VIOLATION	NO
NONSERIOUS (ROUTINE)	NO	$1,000/VIOLATION	NO
FAILURE TO CORRECT OR ABATE CITED VIOLATION	NO	$1,000/DAY	NO
FAILURE TO POST CITATION	YES	$1,000/VIOLATION	NO

PENALTIES-CRIMINAL

VIOLATION	MANDA-TORY	FINE UP TO	AND/OR IMPRISONMENT UP TO
WILLFUL VIOLATION RESULTING IN DEATH OF EMPLOYEE	YES	$10,000/CONVICTION	SIX MONTHS
SECOND CONVICTION ON VIOLATION RESULTING IN DEATH OF EMPLOYEE	YES	$20,000/CONVICTION	ONE YEAR
FALSIFICATION OF RECORDS	YES	$10,000/CONVICTION	SIX MONTHS
UNAUTHORIZED ADVANCE NOTICE OF INSPECTION	YES	$1,000/CONVICTION	SIX MONTHS
KILLING, ASSAULTING, RESISTING OSHA OFFICERS	YES	$10,000/CONVICTION	LIFE

Figure 13-3 *An OSHA listing of civil and criminal penalties. From C. Richard Anderson,* OSHA and Accident Control Through Training, *p. 8. © 1975 and published by the Industrial Press, Inc., New York, N.Y. Reprinted with Permission.*]

ard for a one-year period, renewable to a maximum of three years. Such a variance is based upon the employer's showing an inability to meet the standards because of the unavailability of personnel or equipment or time to construct alternative facilities. During the time period encompassed by the variance, the employer must make every effort to achieve compliance.

The OSHAct sought to place a great deal of emphasis on occupational health as well as safety, although in its early years less emphasis was put on health than many believed was appropriate. To deal with occupational health, the National Institute for Occupational Safety and Health (NIOSH) was created as an agency within the Department of Health, Education, and Welfare. NIOSH was empowered to carry out research and educational activities in the area of occupational safety and health. It was given the responsibility for "research experiments and demonstrations relating to occupational safety and health, including studies of psychological factors involved, and relating to innovative methods, techniques, and approaches for dealing with occupational safety and health problems."[32] NIOSH was also held responsible for making recommendations for new occupational safety and health standards. In order to gain information upon which to base such recommendations, NIOSH was given the power to issue regulations which required "employers to measure, record and make reports on the exposure of employees to substances or physical agents" that may endanger the safety or health of employees.[33] NIOSH was further required by OSHAct to publish "at least annually a list of all known toxic substances."[34] Finally, NIOSH was made responsible for training and employee education in the area of occupational safety and health.

A major reason for the passage of OSHAct was that the states had failed to set up adequate safety and health legislation. However, a major provision of OSHAct permitted the states to regain responsibility for developing and enforcing occupational safety and health standards by submitting a plan to OSHA. If any such plan is approved, much of OSHA's responsibility reverts to the state. As of April 1978, 25 states had adopted plans approved by OSHA. Under such plans the Department of Labor pays for 50 per cent of the associated total costs of the plans — e.g., inspection provision, facilities, and staff — so that the state cost is only half the total amount. Therefore, the state can economize by not adopting its own plan but by relying on the federal OSHA.

Two other aspects of state approved plans are of importance. First, states with approved plans must by law cite state and municipal employers for violations as well as private employers. Second, unlike federal OSHA inspectors, states can provide for on-site inspections without having to issue citations if violations are found. The state officials providing the "consultative assistance," however, must be employed by different administrative units in the state so that the consultative assistance is separate from state OSHA-type inspectors who must issue citations.

Finally, OSHAct specified duties for employers and employees. Each employer was required to furnish "his employees employment and a place of employment which are free from recognized hazards that are causing or are likely to cause death or serious physical harm to his employees."[35] In addition, employers were required to comply with standards promulgated under the Act. It was also each employee's responsibility to comply with any standards, rules, regulations, and orders concerning safety and health which are applicable to his own actions and conduct. However, if an employee did not comply and trauma resulted, the employer could still be assessed a penalty. The act did *not* provide for penalties to be assessed against *employees* who did not fulfill their duties under the Act in spite of the fact that it provided for penalties against the employer. The employer, under OSHAct, is clearly responsible for safety and health in the workplace.

OSHAct and OSHA: Problems and Promise

When OSHAct was passed, there was general agreement with the basic purpose of the Act of providing safe and healthy working conditions for all employees. The intent of the Act appears to have had the support of industry, unions, and other parties interested in safety and health. Some safety directors reportedly referred to the acronym OSHA as "Our Savior Has Arrived" because of their belief that OSHAct would contribute to top management's paying more attention to occupational safety and health.[36] While these groups agreed with the basic purpose of OSHAct, they were concerned about its implementation, some of its provisions, and its enforcement. Their fears often turned out to be well founded, and at the time of this writing OSHA faces many problems. As was pointed out in 1977, "Few regulators have been the target of as much vituperation and antagonism. Both labor and business have accused it of everything from triviality to harassment."[37] Further, pointing out the depths of dissatisfaction with OSHA, Eula Bingham, who was appointed by President Jimmy Carter in 1977 to head this agency, stated: "It's sad the way everybody hates OSHA."[38]

These problems, many of which OSHA created for itself, have hindered OSHA's ultimate effectiveness in achieving the goals of OSHAct. One major problem resulted from OSHA's promulgation and enforcement of the interim standards. Many of the national consensus standards were written to establish best practice conditions (ideal) and were never meant to apply to broad segments of industry. In addition, some of the interim standards did not really contribute to safety or health considerations and they seem to have been applied in a capricious and arbitrary manner. For example, the early standards required restrooms to be no more than 200 feet from any employee's work area and to be separate for men and for women.[39] Carried to its extreme, a company could have been forced to construct another restroom or move an employee's work area if such distance was 201 feet (this distance specification was eliminated in 1973). In one case, the owners of a "mom-and-pop" store were told to install a second restroom because of the requirement for separate facilities for men and women and yet the only employees in the store were the husband and his wife! This decision was subsequently overturned. The specification and enforcement of these types of standards, which did little to improve occupational safety and health, constituted a major reason for the growth of disenchantment with OSHA.

The effectiveness of OSHA has also been hindered by the fact that it is frequently the case that the direct costs of compliance with the law are greater than any fine which may be assessed if an inspection takes place. For example, in 1977 it was reported that in the prior 12 month period OSHA had levied fines of only $12.4 million for violation of all standards, yet the cost to industry to comply with only one set of standards, the OSHA noise standards, was estimated to be $13 *billion*.[40] Contributing to this problem is the fact that the likelihood of any company's being inspected is not very high. In 1976, for example, there were approximately 1300 compliance officers (of which 248 were industrial hygienists). These few officers were responsible for conducting inspections in the nearly 5 million businesses covered by OSHAct.[41] As *Business Week* stated in 1976, with the then current number of compliance officers, "the typical business establishment will see an OSHA inspector every 77 years."[42]

The implication in OSHAct that OSHA should attempt to create *completely* safe and healthy conditions has also hindered OSHA's effectiveness. Every time a compliance officer enters a business, he is looking for any possible hazard that violates existing standards. If he finds a violation, he *must* issue a citation (or at least a warning in the case of violations that would not cause injury or illness). Here we have an inherent conflict between the firm's safety director and the OSHA officer because the compliance officer to some extent is evaluated by his superiors by how many citations he issues, while the safety director is partially evaluated on not receiving citations. Compounding this problem is the fact that OSHAct specifically prohibited compliance officers from doing preliminary reviews in an organization; they must undertake a complete inspection, note all violations, issue citations, and assess fines when appropriate.

These types of problems have contributed to dissatisfaction with OSHA, and in some cases have resulted in employers challenging OSHA in the courts. For example, in 1974, the manager of a store in Texas (Gibson's Products) refused to permit two

OSHA inspectors to walk around the nonpublic areas of the store. He refused unless the inspectors had a search warrant, even though OSHAct provides for inspectors to arrive unannounced at reasonable times and to present their credentials to be given immediate entrance to conduct an inspection. OSHA sued and asked the court to order the company to let the inspectors inspect the premises based upon these provisions of OSHAct.[43] OSHA pointed out that the requirement to obtain a search warrant would greatly restrict its ability to act and therefore its effectiveness for two reasons. First, it was argued that a judge would not issue a warrant unless OSHA could demonstrate that a particular company might be in violation of the law. However, unless inspectors could enter the workplace they would not be able to obtain such proof. Second, OSHA argued that collecting the information necessary to obtain a warrant would result in the employer's becoming aware that an inspection was going to be conducted. This might permit him to "hide" hazards. Gibson's Products, on the other hand, argued that warrantless searches are unconstitutional under the Fourth Amendment of the United States Constitution. A three-judge federal panel in 1976 sided with the company's arguments. In a more significant case in Idaho, a three-judge federal panel, also in 1976, ruled that warrantless searches violated the Fourth Amendment and further that since Congress had not explicitly given OSHA the power to seek warrants, OSHA had no such power and cannot conduct inspections *with* or *without* warrants.[44]

OSHA has attempted to change both its practices and its image in recent years. As of 1977, for example, OSHA was attempting to overcome some of the objections of industry by trying "to shed its role of policeman and become a guidance counselor for industry."[45] However, to shed this image will require Congress to change the law, since it is OSHAct itself that prohibits a consultative role for OSHA inspectors and requires them to issue citations. If Congress were to change the law, the whole issue of warrantless searches would be much less important and OSHA inspectors might find themselves being welcomed by safety directors as *helpers* rather than rejected as *"prosecutors."*

In 1977, OSHA also commissioned two research groups to study occupational safety and health in hopes of showing that the total benefits of safety and health standards may outweigh their costs.[46] If the research shows that standard implementation may often be cost-beneficial, it is likely that more companies will be willing to examine the implementation of standards even when not forced to do so. Finally, it is expected that in the future OSHA will be examining health hazards much more so than it has done in the past. In 1978, for example, it was reported that OSHA was in the process of implementing a program to identify and regulate cancer-causing substances in the workplace.[47] Since these types of hazards may contribute more to deaths and injuries (illnesses) than safety hazards, the potential benefits may be even greater than from the reduction of safety hazards. Exactly what all these changes will mean for the safety director is difficult to tell, however. In the next section we will focus on some of the problems that face him as well as some of the techniques he can use in his safety and health efforts.

OCCUPATIONAL SAFETY AND HEALTH WITHIN THE ORGANIZATION

As discussed previously, organizations have a legal obligation under OSHAct (including approved state plans) to provide employees with employment and a work environment free from recognized hazards. Depending upon the size and nature of a company, someone should be assigned the responsibility on either a full- or part-time basis to deal with safety and health in general and compliance with the law in particular.[48] The size of the organization is important because smaller organizations will probably not be able to afford to hire a person to work full-time with safety and health problems and someone in the organization may be given this responsibility in addition to his other duties. Further, smaller firms may have less need for someone to deal with safety and health on a full-time basis than larger firms because, in general, they tend to have better experience in occupational safety and health — e.g., lower incidence, frequency, and severity rates. In large organizations, on the other hand, a number of individuals may be hired to deal with safety and health issues. For example, an attorney may be hired to deal with compliance under the law, an engineer to deal with technological problems, a psychologist to deal with personnel and human factors analyses, and so on.

The nature of the organization is important in the determination of the number and types of individuals that it needs to deal with safety and health problems because some industries face conditions that are inherently more potentially hazardous than others. For example, coal mining exposes individuals to a greater number of more frequent and more varied types of unsafe and unhealthy conditions than does work as a clerk in a personnel department.

We will refer to the individual in any organization who is responsible for occupational safety and health as a "safety director," although, as indicated, this individual may be responsible for other duties and only deal with safety and health issues on a part-time basis. It should be noted that although we are also using the title "safety director" to include individuals responsible for health as well as safety problems within the organization, persons who deal with health problems are often referred to as "industrial hygienists."

The safety director faces problems and must make decisions in three basic areas regarding safety and health. He must deal with OSHAct and other legal requirements related to employee safety and health. He must work with both preventive and remedial controls relative to hazards in the workplace. He must enlist the support of all organization members — top management, supervisors and workers — in safety and health efforts if these efforts are to be successful. We will now discuss each of these three areas in turn.

Compliance Problems and Approaches

One decision the safety director has to make in terms of compliance with OSHAct provisions is the extent to which the company is willing to comply. At one extreme, the company could overtly decide not to comply, as did Gibson's Products in its refusal to permit OSHA inspectors into its facility. A company could also fail to comply in a less direct fashion by not keeping its workplace clean or not properly guarding its machines, and hope that no one will be injured and that an inspection will not take place. At the other extreme, a company may attempt to comply not only with the specific provisions of the law but with the broad intent of the law as well. For example, if a company received a citation for a safety or health violation, it could provide each employee with a copy of the citation (which is not required by law) in addition to posting it prominently in each workplace as required.

Both of these extreme positions are potentially costly to the company and therefore must be weighed carefully. We believe that as a minimum, each company should comply with the provisions of OSHAct and, where reasonable and feasible, go beyond minimum compliance and attempt to comply with the broad intent of the law as well.

In complying with both the provisions and intent of OSHAct, the safety director has several alternatives. First, he may attempt to find out what types of violations the OSHA inspectors in his geographical area (or industry) typically look for and correct any such problems so that if an inspection does occur, fewer violations will be detected. Second, he may go one step further and conduct a self-evaluation (inspection) to see if his firm meets all existing OSHA standards, not just those an OSHA inspector may look for. Third, and even more proactively, he could institute some safety and health standards more rigorous than those promulgated by OSHA, though this is unlikely unless they are cost feasible and beneficial to the firm's employees.

We believe that the self-evaluation alternative offers the company an excellent OSHA compliance *starting point* for two reasons. Self-evaluation will help locate potentially hazardous conditions, which might result in unplanned events, which may in turn result in damage or trauma. The company will then be in a position to evaluate the potential cost of correcting the problem against the cost of the unplanned event occurring and to rank the hazards in terms of potential, immediacy and criticality or seriousness. We will explore the approaches and problems in determining the costs and benefits associated with hazard control and unplanned events later in this chapter. The second reason (aside from humanitarianism) for wanting to prevent a serious trauma is that if such an event occurs, the probabilities of an OSHA investigation will be increased greatly. During such an investigation (and inspection) the firm may be cited not only for the violations that led up to the unplanned event but for other violations as well. In addition to incurring the costs associated with the one serious trauma, the firm may end up paying fines and paying for further remedial actions, both of which it could have otherwise avoided.

We also reject the alternative of not complying with the law for two reasons. First, refusing to comply with the law could end up being costly to the firm in terms of legal fees as well as time spent by company officials before OSHRC hearings and possibly in court. Further, if the company loses the case, it will also, of course, have to make the corrections required by OSHA. Second, refusing to comply with the law could hurt the company in less tangible ways. For example, employees may believe that management is not interested in their well being and seek employment elsewhere or not work as hard. Similarly, a company with a poor safety and health record may develop a poor image and be seen as a less desirable place to work, which could make its recruiting efforts or labor relations more difficult, and even affect its marketing success.

The safety director needs to keep himself informed as to what current OSHA requirements are. As mentioned earlier, OSHA modifies and rescinds existing standards and issues new ones by publishing notification of such items in the *Federal Register*. In addition, changes in the law itself are published in the

Federal Register. Therefore, as an absolute minimum, the safety director should make arrangements to obtain statements from this government publication that are applicable to his organization. The safety director can also obtain information concerning OSHAct and OSHA from many different sources, such as federal and state agencies, insurance companies, trade associations, subscription services, etc.[49] Some of these sources provide information free of charge and thus are particularly helpful to smaller organizations with fewer resources. It should be noted that OSHA itself is a good source of information, for its representatives can answer employer questions. The employer need not be concerned that asking questions will prompt an inspection and possibly citations, since he can telephone an OSHA office and request the information he desires without identifying himself.

The safety director also needs to gather information to meet the record keeping and reporting requirements of OSHA.[50] The records developed to comply with workmen's compensation laws are not sufficient to meet OSHA requirements, though most firms with effective safety programs find that the minimum records required by OSHA are not sufficient for internal safety purposes. Under OSHAct, organizations with eight or more employees must keep records on injuries and illnesses, lost workdays, and so on. Some of these records must be maintained by the employer for up to five years, kept current, and reported to OSHA. The total record-keeping and reporting function is becoming increasingly complex and, as England has noted, it may require a data bank large enough to justify the use of a computer.[51] He has suggested that each firm conduct its own needs analysis to determine if computer usage is justified. A larger firm, of course, may have its own computer, whereas a smaller firm is more likely to have to purchase time from an outside computer organization. As we will discuss later, the computer can aid the safety director in other ways besides merely keeping the required safety and health records.

Control Problems and Approaches

The safety director is faced with two control problems. First, because of the interest in reducing trauma and damage to a socially and economically acceptable minimum, the safety director is faced with the problem of locating hazards and eliminating or controlling them in order to minimize unplanned events that may result in damage or trauma. Second, remedial control situations arise because, in spite of reasonable efforts, some unplanned events will occur that result in damage or trauma. We will treat the problems and approaches associated with preventive and remedial control in this section. Before dealing with these two types of control, however, it will be necessary to discuss a problem that exists in both preventive and remedial control — the assumptions concerning the factors that contribute to occupational damage and trauma.

Assumptions Concerning Factors that Contribute to Damage and Trauma

A major problem in both preventive and remedial control is the determination of what factors have the greatest potential for or contribute most to unplanned events that may result in damage or trauma. The factors that contribute to occupational safety and health hazards and thereby possibly to such unplanned events typically have been examined in two different ways. First, some individuals have taken the position that occupational injuries and illnesses are largely the result of a single factor, while others have looked for multiple variables leading to such problems. Second, it has been debated as to whether the hazards that ultimately may lead to damage are unsafe conditions, unsafe acts, or both. The assumptions made concerning each of these issues are important because they will influence the types of problems identified and therefore the types of approaches used to overcome such problems—the decisions made by the safety director in his preventive and remedial control activities.

Historically, the view that a single factor is responsible for damage is the oldest.[52] The way to prevent unplanned events under this assumption is fairly clear cut — one merely removes the unsafe act or unsafe condition leading to the damage. For example, suppose one follows the single contributing factor view and also assumes that it is unsafe acts that result in unplanned events rather than unsafe conditions. If he were to observe an employee who has had a number of accidents, he would assume that removing this employee from the workplace would result in a reduction in the number of accidents occurring. The single factor analysis view is not widely held today except in some computer models (such as traffic accident record systems) in which only one "main causal factor" can be identified.

The view that multiple variables contribute to unplanned events considers any ultimate unplanned event that directly leads to trauma or damage to be the result of a series of interrelated events. Following this view, a person who engaged in an unsafe act and was injured might not have been hurt if an unsafe condition had not been present or if an unsafe act by another individual had not been committed within some time limitation. This view would consider an automobile accident, for example, as follows: A driver, who is driving too fast (unsafe act), hits an icy spot in the road (unsafe condition), which should have been cleared by the road crews (unsafe act), his car spins and another driver coming from the other direction slams on his brakes (unsafe act) and goes into a skid and hits the first car. In this case the multiple-factor view focuses attention on the fact that ultimate damage results from an interdependent series of prior events and coincidences.

The assumption that unsafe acts are the sole contributor to damage forces one to focus on individual behavior and therefore on individual values, attitudes, needs, personality, etc., when seeking approaches to deal with control problems. Historically, proponents of the unsafe act view held that certain individuals were accident prone and that through selection procedures, such individuals could be identified and not hired, and consequently damage could be significantly reduced. Today, the theory of accident proneness has fallen into disfavor due to the fact that stable personality characteristics predictive of which employees are more likely than others to have accidents have not generally been found. This is not to say that there is no such thing as accident proneness, but rather it is not a stable enough characteristic to make consistent measurement possible.[53] Further, the number of persons involved as accident repeaters is seldom large enough to justify the expenditure of resources to use "selection as a loss control method."[54] For example, one study found that of 27,000 industrial and 8000 nonindustrial "accidents," "accident repeaters" accounted for only 0.5 per cent of the cases, while 74 per cent were associated with a large number of persons who had relatively infrequent "accident" experience.[55] It has further been pointed out that the laws of chance alone will result in some people having more accidents than others.[56]

Unfortunately, the notion that unsafe acts by the employee are the prime or sole factor contributing to most damage, whether by reason of accident proneness, negligence, or other factors, has received a great deal of support. This view was presented by H. W. Heinrich in 1931 in his pioneering work, *Industrial Accident Prevention,* in which he asserted that 88 per cent of "accidents" resulted from unsafe acts of persons, 10 per cent from unsafe mechanical or physical conditions, and that 2 per cent were unpreventable.[57] This basic relationship has continued to be accepted by a number of persons involved in occupational safety and health as well as those in traffic safety. For example, in 1970, "Goodyear's insurance carrier informed safety management that 92 percent of their accidents resulted from unsafe acts and only 8 percent from unsafe conditions."[58] The unfortunate aspect of this type of assessment is that safety and health programs may focus on only one aspect of the total problem. Thus, the belief of some safety directors seems to be: "I'll go after the 85% first and take care of the 15% after I get the carelessness thing licked. Why spend a lot of money first off on only 15% of the job? I'm not that kind of sucker."[59]

The fallacy of considering unsafe acts as the sole contributors to damage was pointed out by a study of 90,000 industrial "accidents" in Pennsylvania.[60] This study looked beyond the unsafe action and found an unsafe condition or mechanical problem underlying 89 per cent of the damages. It was further found that in 83 per cent of these cases the unsafe action consisted of continuing to work with the unsafe conditions.

The assumption that unsafe conditions are the only important contributors to damage and trauma forces one to focus solely on factors in the physical and environmental conditions (technology, machinery, noise, etc.). This results in an engineering approach to safety and health problems that attempts to reduce damages by reducing technological hazards through the redesign of machinery, equipment, and working procedures. The success of this approach has been fairly well substantiated. For example, it is known that continuous noise at 100 decibels day after day will produce permanent nerve deafness.[61] Some research has also shown that proper illumination can result in reduced "accidents."[62] However, the success in the elimination or reduction of physical hazards over the years has had the unfortunate dysfunctional consequence of leading some people to blame the employee for almost all accidents on the premise that his environmental conditions are free of hazards. As William W. Allison has stated: "Safety engineers have long felt that they must accept design concepts as logical and unalterable. Consequently they blame 85 percent of all accidents on the injured."[63]

Beginning in the late 1950's and continuing to the present, there has been an increasing recognition that safety and health problems are often the result of multiple factors which include unsafe acts, unsafe physical conditions, unsafe environmental conditions, and various combinations thereof.

Problems and Approaches in Preventive Control

As we have just indicated, the major problem in preventive control is the determination of the factors that have the greatest potential for contributing to damage and trauma in the area of safety and health. In preventive control the safety director performs three functions. First, he conducts inspections to identify situations that are potentially hazardous, whether due to unsafe conditions, unsafe acts, or both. Second, he recommends programs to eliminate or reduce the incidence of these situations.

Third, he recommends means for reducing the consequences of unplanned events when they do occur.

Unsafe conditions. The evaluation and control of unsafe conditions is essentially an engineering problem that encompasses "the four engineering aspects: design, construction, operation and maintenance."[64] Ideally, unsafe conditions will be "designed out" or provisions made for their control during the conceptual or design phase. During this phase and the construction phase the safety director will have limited input because the design and construction may be carried out in other locations and require technical engineering expertise. Some hazardous conditions not detected during the design phase may be found and corrected during construction. However, additional hazardous conditions may also be established during the construction phase because of faulty workmanship or poor materials or equipment. Further, once facilities and equipment are in operation, it may be necessary to modify them, which may also result in hazardous conditions being created. These types of problems will appear during the firm's operation, and it is in this area that the safety director can make a major contribution by inspecting to detect and eliminate or control potentially hazardous conditions. The safety director can also contribute in the maintenance area by checking company records and conducting inspections to make certain that facilities and equipment are being maintained properly.

One approach that the safety director can use for dealing with unsafe conditions is job safety analysis.[65] Job safety analysis is similar to job analysis in that it involves breaking the job down into its component parts. The potential hazards associated with each step of the job are then identified and ways to eliminate or control them are developed. In general, however, the safety director's primary activity in dealing with unsafe conditions consists of inspecting the workplace for potentially hazardous conditions.

This type of continuous effort is necessary because conditions change. Further, some of the engineering relationships we think we know may in fact be erroneous. For example, since the time of Frederick W. Taylor, jobs have been designed to use synchronized motions because of the greater efficiency that results. However, in one study it was found that the safety of machine operators was actually compromised by the "complexity of synchronized movements required of the worker."[66] Because of changing conditions and because additional research may increase our knowledge concerning unsafe conditions, the safety director needs to keep apprised of such changes through trade journals, conferences, and other sources of information if the job is to be done effectively.

Unsafe acts. The safety director will often spend much of the time trying to eliminate and reduce unsafe acts. There are basically two approaches for accomplishing this objective: (1) avoiding the placement of workers possessing certain characteristics in jobs unsuited to them from a safety and health point of view and (2) training employees to behave in safer ways.

Although the "selection" approach to safety has not proved as fruitful as the "engineering" approach, some individuals may be identified, by means of physical examinations in the selection process, who have high potential for certain types of illness or injuries, which may be aggravated by certain types of jobs. For example, a person with a history of respiratory problems should not be hired or placed in an environment in which there is constant unavoidable exposure to dust. Similarly, a person who has had a history of lower back problems should not be called on to lift heavy objects continuously.

The safety director's approaches to dealing with unsafe acts through training consist of trying to make employees aware, through safety education, of potentially hazardous situations or behaviors and how they can be avoided. In such efforts the safety (or training) director is interested both in *teaching* employees about unsafe acts and how to avoid them and in *motivating* them to avoid actively unsafe acts.

Safety directors will frequently use posters, contests, and training programs to increase employee awareness of unsafe acts and to motivate them to avoid them. Posters are perhaps the simplest technique the safety director can use to remind employees of the need to engage in safe practices.[67] Obviously, posters need to be placed where they will be seen by the employees and should be changed frequently so that employees do not become bored by them and stop paying attention to them. Further, we seriously question the effectiveness of posters (or signs) that simply convey a general safety message in no way relevant to any particular situation the employee will experience. Signs that give specific warnings of specific hazards, on the other hand, may represent a viable approach to safety. For example, a large sign indicating "HIGHLY EXPLOSIVE FUMES — NO SMOK-ING!" will tend to have a much greater impact on employee behavior than attractive, multicolored posters that simply state "WORK SAFELY."

Contests are frequently used to keep employees aware of the need for safe actions. Contests may reward individual employees or departmental units within the organization that maintain the best safety and health records. Frequently, such records are based upon frequency or incidence rates. A major problem with such contests is that there may be a letdown after a damaging or traumatic event does occur, and the company may experience a rash of incidents. Further, if the damage results from an unsafe act, there may be resentment against the person or persons responsible. Another problem with contests is that if the reward is large enough, individuals may falsify records, not report injuries, and not seek necessary medical treatment when injuries do occur. In the latter case, what might have been a minor injury could become a major one due to complications. Finally, after contests are over, even the members of the department with the best record are likely to revert to their previous patterns of behavior, as we indicated in Chapter 10 with suggestion system contests.

The safety director may conduct or have others conduct one or more training programs in an effort to keep employees aware of the need to behave safely. Some such programs may be effective, while others may be virtually worthless. As with safety posters (or signs), training that makes the individual aware of *specific dangers* he may face, as opposed to programs composed of general platitudes about the importance of being safe, are much more likely to help eliminate or reduce the number of unsafe acts. The following examples will illustrate this point:

1. We have attended weekly safety meetings in which the safety director "sermonized" to first-line supervisors on how they had to not only "think safety" but "live safety." Before such meetings were over, a number of first-line supervisors could often be caught "dozing off" — the message was irrelevant, repetitious, boring, and an overgeneralization, and it provided the supervisors with no new knowledge to provide a basis for safer behavior.

2. Safety films depicting accidents in situations *completely unlike* those prevalent in a particular firm have often been shown to the firm's supervisors in safety meetings. Here again, messages in no way related to any happenings which the supervisors themselves might face have been presented — which, in our opinion, have no benefits worth the cost of presentation.

3. The JIT method, discussed in Chapter 7, as commonly used in industry, *specifically* calls on the trainer to make the trainee aware of any potential damage or trauma that may occur in *each* step of performing the job. Here we have a specific message addressed to an immediate situation in which hazards exist — a highly effective approach if properly executed.

4. In one firm, a combination contest-training-learning experience was set up by the safety director. Supervisors from all three shifts (the plant operated on a 24-hour basis) were put into fire brigade groups. These groups set fires in a vacant lot adjacent to the plant, and contests were *continuously* held to see which group of supervisors could extinguish the fires most quickly. As a result of this (simulated) training, each supervisor in each department on each shift in the plant repetitively practiced using fire extinguishers. There would then always be someone in each department of the plant who knew what to do in case a fire should occur. This training was effective not only in that it was directed toward specific hazards the supervisors may have had to face at any time without warning, but also in that it gave them substantial *practice* in dealing with actual fires.

The number of forms safety training may take is large, and these examples are simply intended to suggest some appropriate and inappropriate forms of training. One other form of safety training that encompasses certain aspects of performance appraisal is worth mentioning. Peterson has suggested the use of job safety observation as an approach "to learn more about the work habits" of each employee.[68] This approach also acts as a feedback mechanism to check on training adequacy. It calls for the workers to be observed, their actions recorded, any unsafe acts noted, and the results reviewed with each employee. As with unsafe conditions, the safety director also needs to keep himself informed of new knowledge that may help to reduce unsafe acts. For example, one question that has been raised in recent years is whether there is a relationship between an individual's "biorhythm" and the commission of unsafe acts. In one study the records of 300 "accidents" in four factories were examined and it was found that 70 per cent of them happened on biorhythmically critical days of the individuals involved.[69] While there is still controversy concerning the validity of biorhythm as predictors, the safety director may wish to follow the literature further.

Unsafe conditions and acts. In recent years safety and health analysts have taken more of a "systems" approach and attempted to deal with unsafe conditions and acts simultaneously. These approaches have drawn on a wide variety of disciplines such as psychology, engineering, physiology, and medicine.

One well known approach utilized in systems design and in safety is called "ergonomics." Ergonomics, which is also called human factors engineering or (by the military) human engineering, "is a systems-oriented approach to safety which deals with the interaction between the worker, his job and his work environment."[70] In studying these relationships the ergonomist looks at "anatomical, physiological, and psychological capabilities and limitations of man."[71] Thus, ergonomics can be seen as an eclectic approach to total system safety. This approach includes not only design considerations but evaluation procedures as well. To illustrate, human factors engineers may analyze anatomically how far individuals can reach for levers while sitting down without losing their balance and possibly being injured. For efficiency and convenience, many facets of our society have been improved or at least studied from the ergonomic point of view. Many devices, gauges, etc., in homes, on machines in the workplace, in automobiles, in airplanes, and in spacecraft have been oriented directionally or color coded to prevent confusion and hence unsafe acts. For example, water faucets have traditionally provided for hot water coming from the left and cold water from the right so that people would not be confused when using a faucet from one facility to another and individuals expect to obtain hot water from the left and cold from the right. When a plumber in one plant inadvertently reversed the piping for one faucet in repairing it, one worker scalded his right hand by turning on the ''cold'' right faucet. Similarly, gauges and dials should be standardized so that people will not commit unsafe acts by virtue of confusion or false expectations. For example, speedometers should move to the right as a car is driven faster and vice versa, and in western society, at least, we ''automatically'' react to red as dangerous and green as safe — not only with respect to stop lights at road intersections, but on temperature gauges in automobiles or on machinery and in numerous gauges in aircraft. Human factors engineers consider these conventional population stereotypes very seriously when designing controls, knobs, gauges, and other indicators into new technology, e.g., in temperature and pressure controls in continuous production automated oil refineries.

Recognition of such factors as those considered in ergonomics brought safety and health analysts to the following point:

> This then is where we stood at the beginning of the 1970's. We had evolved to the point where we knew we must control physical conditions, environmental conditions, and the behavior of workers. We had found a variety of techniques from other disciplines and other systems that might help us do this. While experimenting with these, we also had come to the realization that what we have been doing is no longer as effective as it once was. This realization forced us to examine critically not only what we have been doing but also the fundamental concepts on which our techniques were based.[72]

Petersen has argued that in this reexamination many safety directors were about to return to a view that it is primarily human behavior which leads to damage and trauma with an emphasis on the psychological aspects of such behavior but that the appearance of OSHAct brought many of these individuals back to the view that damage is primarily due to unsafe conditions. In fact, OSHAct has seemed to place more emphasis on unsafe conditions and injuries than on unsafe acts and health considerations. There is some evidence, however, that OSHA plans to emphasize occupational health problems more fully in the future.

Although there is a recognition that damages and trauma can result from both unsafe acts and conditions, and from an interaction between the two, considerable research still needs to be carried out with respect to the interrelationships among factors that contribute to occupational safety and health. One area in which extensive research is lacking, for example, is with respect to those environmental conditions that *interact* to produce hazards,[73] i.e., two separate conditions may not be especially harmful by themselves but when placed together, they interact dangerously. For example, in the home it has been discovered only relatively recently that certain bleaches (dilute sodium hypochlorite) will react with household ammonia to create highly toxic chlorine gas, while the fumes of either chemical separately are merely annoying. With more and more new chemical substances being developed and used in industry, ensuring that they do not interact dangerously is a problem of growing concern.

Problems and Approaches in Remedial Control

In remedial control situations, the safety director faces the problems of dealing with the sources of damage and trauma just as he does in preventive control. The basic difference is that in remedial control situations an unplanned event has already resulted in damage. The safety director therefore has direct evidence as to which hazards will lead to which unplanned events and which will lead to various types of damage. In addition to investigating to determine what factors contributed to the damage, the safety director needs to determine (1) the magnitude and potential for recurrence of such events in terms of their frequency and severity; and (2) the costs or potential costs associated with the unplanned event. This information is needed so that the safety director can decide the priorities on which hazards are to be eliminated or controlled. This information will also be useful to the safety director in gaining support for safety and health programs. In this section we will deal with some approaches to these problems.

Magnitude of unplanned events. The safety director must determine the magnitude of unplanned events that have occurred. In doing so, he must determine what events are to be counted. Should he include only disabling injuries or illnesses or should he try to include also unplanned events that *might have* resulted in damage or trauma *but did not*? Under OSHAct the safety director must collect and report only certain types of injury data. However, for internal purposes he may wish to count other items as well, in order to generate interest in the magnitude of the problem and to evaluate safety and health programs.

The decision as to which data to examine in remedial control is a difficult one because the inclusion of too little data will understate the magnitude of the problem, while the inclusion of a great deal will cost more to collect and analyze and possibly may overstate the magnitude of the firm's problems. Prior to the passage of OSHAct, the most widely used statistics for deciding what to include in analyzing occupational safety and health were the ANSI Standard Z16.1 frequency and severity rates, discussed earlier in this chapter. The Z16.1 standard has been criticized for not including many unplanned events that might have led to damage and trauma because it only included lost-time accidents.[74] Further, it has been pointed out that "Z16.1 rates are not very satisfactory in evaluating the safety performance of operations having few disabling injuries, the performance of small establishments, or those with low rates."[75] Finally, the Z16.1 standard was a voluntary one, open to a great deal of interpretation. As a consequence, companies using the same standard were often using "vastly different criteria for accident reporting."[76] This situation contributed to problems of comparability among firms. Despite these problems, it may be advisable for firms to continue to collect data based upon the Z16.1 standard for some time, because there are so many historical data derived from it that can be used for comparative purposes. As indicated earlier, the safety director may wish to examine other items as well as incidence, frequency, and severity for internal reporting purposes. The desirability of such a variety of measures makes the use of the computer even more advantageous. Any one of many different approaches may be used by the safety director in a particular firm for determining the magnitude of unplanned events as long as it is logical, understandable, cost feasible, and provides useful output. Any method meeting these criteria should, however, be used over a sufficiently long period of time and with unchanging data collection methods to generate comparable measures so that past and present safety and health efforts can be evaluated. The major disadvantage in using organizationally specific methods is that comparability with other organizations is lost.

Costs of unplanned events. A number of different approaches have been developed for determining the cost of unplanned events. In this section we will present one such method in some detail — the Simonds Method.[77]

Two types of costs associated with "accidents" and injuries are included in the Simonds Method — insurance costs and uninsured costs. "The insurance cost is the cost of workmen's compensation insurance required by law in each of the 50 states."[78] Since most companies carry this insurance with an insurance firm the costs are easier to obtain than the uninsured costs. In companies which are self-insured, insurance costs would include the cost of direct payments to doctors, hospitals, beneficiaries, etc.

The Simonds Method includes 10 elements of uninsured cost:

(1) *Cost of wages paid for working time lost by workers who were not injured.*

(2) *The net cost to repair, replace, or straighten up material or equipment that was damaged in an "accident."*

(3) *Cost of wages paid for working time lost by injured workers, other than workmen's compensation payments.*

(4) *Extra cost due to overtime work necessitated by an "accident."*

(5) *Cost of wages paid supervisors while their time is required for activities necessitated by the injury.*

(6) *Wage cost due to decreased output of injured worker after return to work.*

(7) *Cost of learning period of new worker.*

(8) *Uninsured medical cost borne by the company.*

(9) *Cost of time spent by higher supervision and clerical workers on investigations or in the processing of compensation application forms.*

(10) *Miscellaneous unusual costs.*[79]

These ten elements are allocated among four types of cases: lost-time, doctor's, first-aid, and no-injury, which are defined as follows:

1. *Lost-time cases* are (a) permanent partial disabilities and (b) temporary total disabilities.

2. *Doctor's cases* are (a) temporary partial disabilities and (b) medical treatment cases requiring the attention of a physician.

3. *First-aid cases* are medical treatment cases (a) requiring only first aid and (b) resulting in property damage of less than $20 and in loss of less than eight hours of working time.

4. *No-injury cases* are unintended occurrences (a) resulting in loss of eight or more man-hours of $30 or more of property damage, (b) affording danger of personal injury, and (c) by good fortune not actually causing personal injury, or else resulting in only minor injury not requiring the attention of a physician.[80]

It should be noted that fatalities and permanent total disabilities are not included in any of the categories. This is because they are so unusual that they would generally be classified as catastrophes and therefore would be investigated separately. As we will see shortly, the no-injury cases include unplanned events, which result in damage, and which can be quite costly.

Using this information, the total uninsured cost for a given time period is then calculated as:[81]

Uninsured cost = A times the number of lost-time cases +
B times the number of doctor's cases +
C times the number of first-aid cases +
D times the number of no-injury "accident" cases

where A, B, C and D are constants which indicate the uninsured costs for each type of case.

Simonds has recommended that each firm calculate its own values for A, B, C, and D. However, if this is not feasible, the values obtained by Simonds as of February 1974 can be updated and used:[82]

A — Lost-time cases $220
B — Doctor's cases 55
C — First-aid cases 12
D — No-injury cases............................. 400

It should be noted that the number of no-injury cases would be estimated by applying a ratio such as 1:1 to the number of lost-time cases. Using such a ratio rather than attempting to count "no-injury" cases is suggested because it may be unreasonably costly to keep records on all such items. An illustration of an application of these cost data to a particular situation in 1974 is provided (applying a 1:1 ratio) below:

Insured costs	$42,500
Uninsured costs	
20 lost-time cases × $220	4,400
75 doctor's cases × $55	4,125
900 first-aid cases × $12	10,800
20 no-injury cases × $400	8,000
	$69,825

While calculations such as this may seem cumbersome and, to some extent, to lack rigor, it is recommended that the safety director use this or some similar costing analysis so that the value of the safety and health efforts can be shown. For example, if one can demonstrate to management that a particular device which will cost $5,000 can probably eliminate two lost-time accidents, three doctor's cases, five first-aid cases, and two no-injury cases per year over the next five years, it may be possible to convince management that the investment should be undertaken. We leave it to the reader as a problem at the end of this chapter to determine whether or not management should make this specific investment.

Support Problems and Approaches

Occupational safety and health, like many personnel functions, is one in which virtually every organization member is responsible to some degree for the success or failure of the organization's efforts. It is the safety director's responsibility, however, to make organization members aware of their responsibilities in the support of the firm's safety and health efforts. More specifically, the safety director needs to gain the support of three groups within the organization — top management, supervisors and nonmanagerial employees.

Top Management Support

Saying that there is need for top management support if safety and health efforts are to be successful sounds trite and trivial — yet it cannot be emphasized too much. Top management sets safety objectives and allocates funds to carry out occupational safety and health programs. Further, top management can set a climate in which the safety director gains the cooperation of supervisors and workers. For example, a great deal of support is provided if top management is willing to *"emphasize that one of the criteria for promotion is safe performance . . . whatever the individual's level in the corporate hierarchy."* [83] By showing that it cares about safety and health, top management can help to create an organizational climate that is conducive to maintaining low levels of physical damage and trauma.

The importance of top management support was pointed out in a study conducted by Yaghoub Shafai-Sahrai.[84] He studied a pair of American companies in each of 11 different industries (22 companies were studied). The firms were relatively small, ranging from 80 to 650 employees. The firms making up each study pair were of similar size and performed similar work, but differed greatly in their work-injury frequency rates, which ranged from 12 to 173. The average pair frequency rate difference was 50, the lowest being 11 and the highest 129. It was found that in the firms with the lower frequency and severity rates, top management was highly interested and involved in the company's overall safety programs and actively participated in and supported safety activities. This top management support may have had a double effect — a direct one and an indirect one by its influence on other conditions favorable to accident control.[85]

How can the safety director get the support of top management? One way is to appeal to the "humanitarian values" of top management. Since top management sets the overall direction for the firm and the firm reflects their values, this approach may gain some support for safety. A second approach for gaining top management support is to emphasize the legal requirements for occupational safety and health. This approach may contribute to interest on the part of top management but only to the extent of minimum compliance with OSHAct or state laws. The third approach for gaining top manangement support is to demonstrate that damage and trauma in the safety and health area cost money and that safety and health efforts can help to decrease these financial drains. Top managements generally respond much more quickly to cost information than to humanitarian appeals. For example, in the study of the matched pairs it was found that "the greater use of costs was one of the factors in which the pair members with better injury records differed from their 'twins.'"[86] As Ronald B. Blake stated in 1944, "The main driving force behind the industrial safety movement is the fact that accidents are expensive. Substantial savings can be had by preventing them."[87]

Supervisory Support

The supervisor's support in safety and health is extremely important since he or she is the connecting link between the objectives of top management and the worker. Further, it is the supervisor who is in the best position to influence worker behavior on a day-to-day basis. The importance of supervisory attitudes toward safety was pointed out in a 1967 study by Hannaford.[88] This study covered data from a five-year period and involved 769 male employees from 47 companies with varying safety records. The safety attitudes of supervisors were measured and it was found that supervisors with poor attitudes tended to have a much larger number of lost-time injuries per employee supervised than supervisors whose attitudes were more enthusiastic. Support for the view that a supervisor can influence an employee's desire to perform safely has also been provided in a study by Dunbar, in which it was found that "whether subordinates associate safety with their manager's safety related behavior may depend on the extent to which they perceive their manager as being interested in their general welfare. That is, through the support he or she provides, the manager may significantly influence the way subordinates think about safety."[89]

The safety director can attempt to win the support of supervisors in the same ways as were suggested for top management — humanitarian, legal, and cost. If the safety director has the support of top management, it can also be made clear to the supervisors that one element of their performance appraisal will be the safety and health record of their department. In emphasizing this point, the safety director must make certain that supervisors understand what factors contribute to a good record and that supervisors have control over the factors that enter into evaluation.

The safety director may also be able to increase supervisor interest in safety and health efforts by providing supervisors with information concerning potential safety and health hazards of which he becomes aware, whether during walks through the work area or through articles in safety journals, news releases, etc. When the safety director does become aware of a hazard, he should immediately inform the supervisor and give him an opportunity to correct it, where possible. If the safety director does not go to the supervisor first, but instead informs his superior, he will be putting the supervisor "on the spot."

The safety director can gain the support of supervisors by conducting effective training programs for them. Effective training programs may motivate supervisors by showing them the costs associated with damage and trauma, informing them about their obligations under the law, and providing them with information on how to minimize safety and health hazards. Providing information concerning the legal requirements is particularly important since the passage of OSHAct.[90] The Act requires the supervisor to know what his responsibilities are. For example, the supervisor *must* keep the records prescribed by OSHA, he *must* explain known hazards to his subordinates, and he *must* be certain that equipment is functioning properly. The safety director also can help the supervisor in setting up training programs for his subordinates.

Nonmanagerial Support

The attitude of nonmanagerial employees toward safety and health is also important in minimizing damage and trauma. Hannaford, for example, found that the number of lost-time injuries experienced by workers increased as their safety attitudes became less favorable.[91] Gaining the support of employees, as we have already noted, will be easier if safety and health efforts are supported by top management and supervisors.

The safety director can help to make employees more safety conscious by providing training programs that stress the dangers and costs of unsafe acts. As indicated earlier, for example, safety should be built into all JIT training. In addition, sponsoring programs that reward safe behavior can promote desired behaviors. For example, in those cases in which promotional channels are open for nonmanagerial employees or in which management has discretion as to how large merit raises will be, safe performance can be accounted in a way similar to that with supervisory performance appraisal. Finally, we should emphasize that the safety director needs to keep in mind that employees will behave in desired ways only if they see that the potential *rewards* for such behavior are *greater than* the potential *costs*. For example, if a blue collar worker is being pushed for higher production by a supervisor, he is on an incentive system, and he sees that higher production is possible if he removes a safety guard from his machine, he may well be motivated to do so because the probable benefits appear to him to be greater than any chance of injuries.

MANAGEMENT SCIENCE, COMPUTERS, AND CONTINGENCIES

Management Science and Computers

In making decisions with respect to safety and health, the safety director appears to be limited in the use of management science techniques. However, logarithmic learning curve analysis (see Chapter 3) and educational simulation (see Chapter 7) have been applied to the field of occupational safety and health. We will now discuss these two techniques. In addition, we will discuss computer applications in the area of safety and health.

Logarithmic Learning Curves

Greenberg has applied logarithmic learning curve analysis to the area of occupational safety and health.[92] He has pointed out that it is not valid to treat trauma and damage as if these experiences were "reborn" each year. Rather, he viewed the organization as an ongoing entity in which persons were learning over time through experience. He also noted that every time a new product is introduced, new learning must take place, even though some prior learning is carried over from prior work. To the extent that new learning is required during periods in which new products are being introduced, one would expect more occupational damage and trauma to occur. It also seems logical that this argument can be extended to cover any change in procedure, process, worker, etc. Greenberg has also pointed out that one would expect hazards to be eliminated or reduced as management becomes aware of them. Therefore, one would expect that as production continues occupational damage and trauma experience should decline, particularly if a learning curve phenomenon exists (see Chapter 3).

On the basis of his research, Greenberg reported that disabling injury and damage data in the petroleum industry indicate that an experience learning curve does in fact exist. He has indicated that results from other industries, such as coal mining, copper mining, and logging industries, indicate similar results. The existence of such a relationship implies that companies need to be particularly conscious of "accident" prevention when new products or processes are introduced or when the work force is relatively inexperienced. These are the types of conditions that exist in dynamic environments, so that it seems more likely that firms which operate under more dynamic conditions are likely to experience more safety and health problems than those in which job content is relatively stable.

Simulation

Educational simulations of many kinds have been used in safety training. In one series of experiments, a standard bench grinder was modified so that "when a switch was closed by the experimenter, a spray of water was directed at the operator's normal position in front of the grinder; this was the simulated accident."[93] A person operating the machine who was standing in an improper position would be hit by the water, reflecting a hazardous event that resulted in an injury.

Two experiments were conducted with the simulation that dealt directly with the question of the effectiveness of simulation as a safety training device. Each experiment involved four groups. Group 1 received written instructions and a demonstration of the task, both of which included coverage of safety procedures. Group 2 received the same information as Group 1 plus an explanation and demonstration of the simulated "accident." Group 3 received the same information as Group 2 *except* that the demonstration of the simulated "accident" was omitted and, instead, the subjects in this group experienced the simulated "accident" during a trial run which was part of the instruction for this group. Group 4 received the same information as Group 2 and the individuals in this group also had an opportunity to experience the simulated "accident" during training. Thus, Groups 3 and 4 both experienced the simulated "accident," while Groups 1 and 2 did not.

In the first experiment the members of each of the four groups were required to test 10 steel bars which exposed each individual to 10 potential "accident" situations. The results showed that the simulation groups that had experienced the simulated "accident" (Groups 3 and 4) had significantly fewer "accidents" than Groups 1 and 2, both initially and one week after training. The second experiment replicated the first by merely adding another retention test 4 weeks after training. The results of the second experiment paralleled the first; the basic difference was that after four weeks, retention proved to be significantly better for Group 4. The authors speculated that Group 4 was superior in both cases because it had double exposure to the simulation since it received both a demonstration of and the experiencing of a simulated "accident."

Rubinsky and Smith claimed the results indicated "that the use of accident simulation as a training method for the safe operation of a power tool is a powerful technique."[94] To achieve the best results, the following steps were suggested. First, identify any unsafe acts associated with the power tool. Second, devise a suitable simulated damage or trauma that will result from the unsafe act and modify the equipment. Third, have the trainee operate the equipment and have him experience the simulated "accident" when the unsafe act is performed. Finally, in the event the trainee does not perform an unsafe act, the simulated damage or trauma should be demonstrated by intentional improper behavior.

It should be noted that it may be difficult to justify this approach on a cost/benefit basis. As noted in Chapter 7, simulations are often costly, both in terms of development and operation, and their benefits must be weighed against their costs. It seems likely that the approach described here would be justified only when a firm has a large number of employees performing the particular task and that the task is stable over a long period of time so that the simulation does not have to be changed continually.

Computers

The safety director can use the computer in a variety of ways.[95] Insurance companies, OSHA, and state workmen's compensation laws require record keeping and reporting activities. The safety director can use the computer to store the necessary data and to generate the required OSHA reports as needed, as well as workmen's compensation reports and insurance forms, and accident and other reports used for internal purposes. By using the computer to analyze data, the safety director may become aware of problems or potential problems. For example, records with respect to worker absenteeism, turnover, trips to the first-aid station and medical claims may indicate where a hazardous situation exists. By storing historical data, the safety director may be able to "confirm problem trends based upon new discoveries."[96] He may also be able to use such information to prove that the workplace was not responsible for a particular problem or that a known problem has truly been reduced by countermeasures. The computer may further be used to schedule required maintenance automatically. Thus, the computer can be used in a number of ways to improve occupational safety and health. For example, the Sun Oil Company has used a computer-based management information system to deal with safety and health problems. This system has generated monthly reports such as the following to help locate actual or potential problem areas:

1. *A corporate report* that shows the accident frequency of the major divisions;

2. *A manufacturing division report* that summarizes the frequency of injuries or illnesses in the major categories used by the Bureau of Labor Statistics; and

3. *A facility report* (i.e., for each refinery) that shows in detail what type of accident occurred, how the employee was affected, who his supervisor was, what unsafe act occurred or unsafe condition existed, how many previous accidents this employee suffered this year, and how many days were lost.[97]

Other types of reports can be generated on an as-needed basis. While this type of system is likely to be too expensive for smaller firms, "some insurance companies now provide a computerized service for smaller companies and the cost is very low."[98]

Contingencies

The safety director needs to recognize that his decisions will be influenced by a number of contingencies. Some of these contingencies have been discussed previously and therefore will not be discussed in detail here — top management support and the impact of a dynamic environment, for example. In this section we will discuss the contingencies of firm size, the industry in which the firm operates, which influences the technology it uses, and the composition of the workforce.

Firm Size

Firm size appears to be related to the incidence rate, as shown in Figure 13–4. Very small firms and very large firms have the lowest "incidence" rates defined by OSHA. More importantly, these results tend to be fairly consistent across a wide variety of industries, as shown in Figure 13–5. A number of reasons for these findings have been suggested.[99] Smaller firms may be less accurate in their reporting, since larger firms typically engage in better record keeping. Firms with fewer than eight employees are exempt from some of the reporting requirements of OSHA. In smaller firms, managers may have closer personal contact with the operations and know when and where unsafe conditions exist. In addition, these managers may monitor the workers and processes more closely because even small losses could be disastrous to the organization. While the close contact may be lost, especially in the largest firms, these firms, on the other hand, can afford to hire specialists in occupational safety and health whose efforts may help reduce damages and traumas. In addition, the largest firms

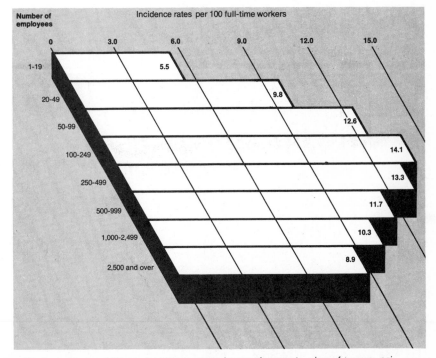

Figure 13–4 Injury and illness incidence rates by employment—size of group, private sector, United States, 1974. [From U.S. Department of Labor, Bureau of Labor Statistics: Chartbook on Occupational Injuries and Illnesses, 1974 (Washington, D.C.: U.S. Department of Labor, Bureau of Labor Statistics, 1976), p. 4.]

Incidence rates per 100 full-time workers 1/

Number of employees	Private sector 2/		Agriculture, forestry, and fisheries		Mining 3/	Contract construction		Manufacturing		Transportation and public utilities		Wholesale and retail trade		Finance, insurance, and real estate		Services	
	1974	1973	1974	1973	1974	1974	1973	1974	1973	1974	1973	1974	1973	1974	1973	1974	1973
All sizes	10.4	11.0	9.9	11.6	10.2	18.3	19.8	14.6	15.3	10.5	10.3	8.4	8.6	2.4	2.4	5.8	6.2
1-19	5.5	5.5	6.8	8.5	8.7	13.8	13.6	11.4	10.9	7.3	7.4	4.5	4.5	1.9	1.9	2.7	2.6
20-49	9.8	10.3	11.0	12.1	12.9	19.5	21.2	15.7	16.2	12.4	11.9	8.7	8.9	2.2	2.1	4.1	5.0
50-99	12.6	13.1	14.9	13.6	12.1	22.2	23.7	18.6	19.2	13.6	13.7	11.1	11.1	2.7	2.8	6.4	6.4
100-249	14.1	14.8	15.2	15.3	11.3	23.7	23.8	19.2	20.2	12.0	11.5	12.1	12.4	3.1	2.8	7.9	8.4
250-499	13.3	13.8	14.4	14.3	9.4	20.6	23.7	17.1	17.6	9.5	9.9	11.8	12.4	2.9	3.1	8.6	7.7
500-999	11.7	12.5	21.2	21.0	7.0	19.0	21.0	13.8	14.4	10.0	9.1	11.1	11.5	2.7	2.7	8.8	10.0
1,000-2,499	10.3	10.9	26.6	16.3 4/	5.4	17.9	16.8	11.6	12.2	9.1	10.4	10.7	11.7	2.6	3.3	8.4	8.1
2,500 and over	8.9	9.7	-	-	6.0	4.8	8.6	9.7	11.0	9.3	8.5	10.0	8.8	2.0	2.0	6.2	6.1

1/ The incidence rates represent the number of injuries and illnesses per 100 full-time workers, and were calculated as (N/EH) X 200,000, where

N = number of injuries and illnesses
EH = total hours worked by all employees during the calendar year
200,000 = base for 100 full-time equivalent workers (working 40 hours per week, 50 weeks per year)

2/ For 1973, incidence rates by employment - size groups for the private sector exclude data for coal and lignite mining (SIC 10 and 12) and metal and nonmetal mining and quarrying (SIC 10 and 14). The "all sizes" estimate for the private sector in 1973 includes all of mining (SIC 10 - 14).

3/ Comparable data are not available for 1973.

4/ Rate for units with 1,000 or more employees.

NOTE: Dashes indicate no data reported, or data that do not meet publication guidelines.

SOURCE: Bureau of Labor Statistics, U.S. Department of Labor

Figure 13-5 *Occupational injury and illness incidence rates, private sector, by employment size and industry division, United States, 1974 and 1973. [From U.S. Department of Labor, Bureau of Labor Statistics: Chartbook on Occupational Injuries and Illnesses, 1974 (Washington, D.C.: U.S. Department of Labor, Bureau of Labor Statistics, 1976), p. 23.]*

can generally afford to hire more competent managers. In medium-sized firms the advantages of both "smallness" and "bigness" are lacking, and therefore occupational safety and health problems occur with greater relative frequency.

Industry

As Figures 13–5, 13–6 and 13–7 indicate, incidence and frequency or severity rates vary considerably across industries. Some industries are inherently more dangerous than others. The safety director needs to be aware of these differences and the impact that different types of technology can have. In making comparisons to find out how well his company is doing, he should use data from industries or firms that have similar technologies. The type of technology is important, because as the studies of such researchers as Joan Woodward have indicated, technology influences organization structural variables, such as span of control.[100] In the study of the pairs of firms mentioned earlier it was found that higher injury rates were significantly related to wider spans of control.[101] To the extent that a firm can change its structural relationships or technology it may be able to reduce its number or rate of injuries.

Workforce Characteristics

Specific characteristics of the work force may have to be taken into account when making safety and health decisions. For example, the frequency of damage and trauma should decrease as experience increases. In fact, research generally has indicated that such occurrences do decline with experience.

Age, sex, and emotional stability also have all been shown to be related to the likelihood of damage and trauma. After an analysis of the survey of 27,000 industrial and 8000 nonindustrial "accidents" cited earlier, the following conclusions were reached:[102]

1. Young people tend to have more "accidents" than older persons. Fifty per cent of the nonindustrial "accidents" happened to people under age 24 and 70 per cent to those under the age of 35. Further, the tendency to have "accidents" passes with age. In both the industrial and nonindustrial samples the "accident" rate in the 20 to 24 age group was two and one half times higher than the 40 to 44 age group, four times higher than the 50 to 54 age group, and nine times higher than the 60 to 65 age group.

2. Men are significantly more likely to have "accidents" than women. The ratio was two to one in the nonindustrial setting and even higher in the industrial setting.

3. Accident proneness is not useful as a concept to deal with accident prevention. However, irresponsible and maladjusted individuals are significantly more likely to have "accidents" than responsible and normally adjusted individuals.

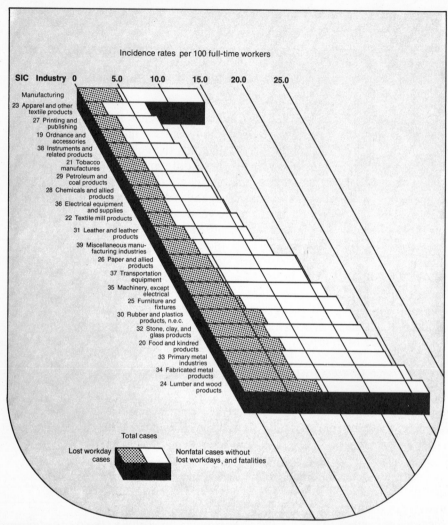

Figure 13–6 *Injury and illness incidence rates by type of manufacturing activity, United States, 1974.* [*From U.S. Department of Labor, Bureau of Labor Statistics:* Chartbook on Occupational Injuries and Illnesses, 1974 *(Washington, D.C.: U.S. Department of Labor, Bureau of Labor Statistics, 1976), p. 6.*]

In addition, in one study it was found that firms in which a high percentage of the workforce was married had better safety and health records than firms in which only a small percentage was married.[103]

There is also some evidence that occupational safety and health statistics will vary with the economic conditions that influence the nature of the workforce. As economic conditions are improved, more marginal workers are employed which has been

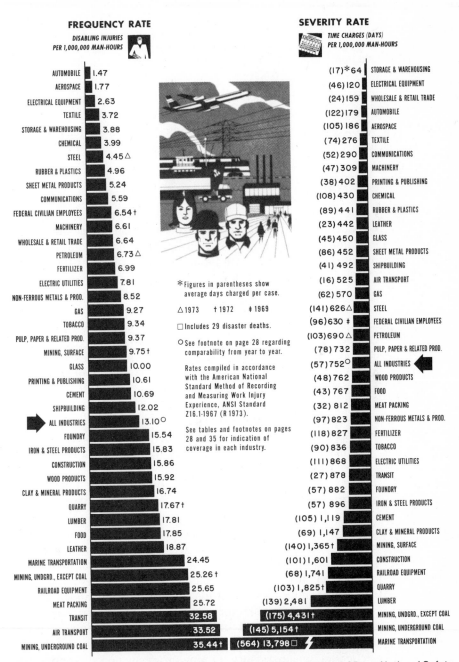

FREQUENCY RATE

DISABLING INJURIES
PER 1,000,000 MAN-HOURS

Industry	Rate
AUTOMOBILE	1.47
AEROSPACE	1.77
ELECTRICAL EQUIPMENT	2.63
TEXTILE	3.72
STORAGE & WAREHOUSING	3.88
CHEMICAL	3.99
STEEL	4.45△
RUBBER & PLASTICS	4.96
SHEET METAL PRODUCTS	5.24
COMMUNICATIONS	5.59
FEDERAL CIVILIAN EMPLOYEES	6.54†
MACHINERY	6.61
WHOLESALE & RETAIL TRADE	6.64
PETROLEUM	6.73△
FERTILIZER	6.99
ELECTRIC UTILITIES	7.81
NON-FERROUS METALS & PROD.	8.52
GAS	9.27
TOBACCO	9.34
PULP, PAPER & RELATED PROD.	9.37
MINING, SURFACE	9.75†
GLASS	10.00
PRINTING & PUBLISHING	10.61
CEMENT	10.69
SHIPBUILDING	12.02
ALL INDUSTRIES	13.10○
FOUNDRY	15.54
IRON & STEEL PRODUCTS	15.83
CONSTRUCTION	15.86
WOOD PRODUCTS	15.92
CLAY & MINERAL PRODUCTS	16.74
QUARRY	17.67†
LUMBER	17.81
FOOD	17.85
LEATHER	18.87
MARINE TRANSPORTATION	24.45
MINING, UNDGRD., EXCEPT COAL	25.26†
RAILROAD EQUIPMENT	25.65
MEAT PACKING	25.72
TRANSIT	32.58
AIR TRANSPORT	33.52
MINING, UNDERGROUND COAL	35.44†

SEVERITY RATE

TIME CHARGES (DAYS)
PER 1,000,000 MAN-HOURS

(17)＊64	STORAGE & WAREHOUSING
(46)120	ELECTRICAL EQUIPMENT
(24)159	WHOLESALE & RETAIL TRADE
(122)179	AUTOMOBILE
(105)186	AEROSPACE
(74)276	TEXTILE
(52)290	COMMUNICATIONS
(47)309	MACHINERY
(38)402	PRINTING & PUBLISHING
(108)430	CHEMICAL
(89)441	RUBBER & PLASTICS
(23)442	LEATHER
(45)450	GLASS
(86)452	SHEET METAL PRODUCTS
(41)492	SHIPBUILDING
(16)525	AIR TRANSPORT
(62)570	GAS
(141)626△	STEEL
(96)630 ‡	FEDERAL CIVILIAN EMPLOYEES
(103)690△	PETROLEUM
(78)732	PULP, PAPER & RELATED PROD.
(57)752○	ALL INDUSTRIES
(48)762	WOOD PRODUCTS
(43)767	FOOD
(32)812	MEAT PACKING
(97)823	NON-FERROUS METALS & PROD.
(118)827	FERTILIZER
(90)836	TOBACCO
(111)868	ELECTRIC UTILITIES
(27)878	TRANSIT
(57)882	FOUNDRY
(57) 896	IRON & STEEL PRODUCTS
(105)1,119	CEMENT
(69)1,147	CLAY & MINERAL PRODUCTS
(140)1,365†	MINING, SURFACE
(101)1,601	CONSTRUCTION
(68)1,741	RAILROAD EQUIPMENT
(103)1,825†	QUARRY
(139)2,481	LUMBER
(175)4,431†	MINING, UNDGRD., EXCEPT COAL
(145)5,154†	MINING, UNDERGROUND COAL
(564)13,798□	MARINE TRANSPORTATION

＊Figures in parentheses show average days charged per case.

△1973   †1972   ‡1969

□Includes 29 disaster deaths.

○See footnote on page 28 regarding comparability from year to year.

Rates compiled in accordance with the American National Standard Method of Recording and Measuring Work Injury Experience, ANSI Standard Z16.1-1967 (R 1973).

See tables and footnotes on pages 28 and 35 for indication of coverage in each industry.

Figure 13–7 1975 injury rates, reporters to National Safety Council. [From National Safety Council: Accident Facts (Chicago, Ill.: National Safety Council, 1976), p. 26.]

shown to contribute to an increase in injury rates. As Smith has pointed out:

> The cyclical nature of work injury rates was first noted around 1940, and it has been estimated that in the post-war period a two percentage-point reduction in the overall unemployment rate was associated with one additional (manufacturing) lost workday injury per million man-hours worked.[104]

This relationship may explain why frequency rates increased during the 1960's, as not only more people in general entered the workforce but more culturally disadvantaged individuals, who are least likely to be employed, found jobs.

SUMMARY

Unplanned events, which may result in trauma or damage, will occur in all organizations. The hazards that contribute to these unplanned events may result from unsafe acts or unsafe conditions or both. Organizations will be interested in reducing the hazards that contribute to unplanned events and thereby the consequences of unplanned events (trauma or damage) for humanitarian, legal, and cost reasons. Particularly since the passage of OSHAct, the legal dimension has become more important to organizations. OSHA, to some extent, acts as a constraint on management decisions in the safety and health area since it specifies actions that management must or must not take. OSHA through its requirements has also had an impact on cost considerations relative to safety and health. Even independent of OSHA related costs, organizations face costs associated with safety and health such as insurance costs or time lost, which may be quite high.

The safety director engages in preventive control to keep the occurrence of unplanned events that may result in trauma or damage to a socially and economically acceptable minimum. In performing this function he will assess the probable sources of hazards that lead to unplanned events and how to reduce or eliminate them. Since unplanned events will occur in spite of the safety director's efforts, he will also engage in remedial control activities in which he assesses the sources of hazards and how to reduce or eliminate them. In remedial work, the safety director will try to determine the magnitude and cost of unplanned events. Finally, the safety director needs to enlist the support of all organization members if safety and health programs are to be successful. To gain such support he may engage in such activities as conducting supervisory training programs and presenting cost information that illustrates to top management that effective occupational safety and health programs do indeed pay off for the firm.

DISCUSSION AND STUDY QUESTIONS

1. Which of the following statements are true? Why or why not?
   a. The primary intent of the Federal Workmen's Compensation law of 1914 was preventive—to prevent accidents before they occurred—and it was effective in doing so.
   b. State workmen's compensation laws have had as their primary intent compensating workers for traumas already having taken place, and in general these laws have been effective.
   c. One of the primary reasons for the passage of OSHAct was that workmen's compensation legislation provided inadequate payments to employees who suffered occupational traumas.
2. In this chapter we stated that, as a minimum, companies should comply with the provisions of OSHAct and, where reasonable and feasible, go beyond minimum compliance and attempt to comply with the broad intent of the law as well. Do you agree or disagree with this point of view? Why?
3. Regardless of Supreme Court decisions, do you believe that OSHAct's warrantless searches should be permitted? What do you think is the basic issue involved with respect to this question?
4. The top management of a firm has been informed by its safety director that a particular safety device, which will cost $5000, can probably eliminate 2 lost-time cases, 3 doctor's cases, 5 first-aid cases, and 2 no-injury cases during each year for the next five years.
   a. From a purely cost standpoint, using the Simonds costing method, should top management make such an investment? Why?
   b. What other considerations would influence the decision made in part (a)? Why?
   c. Why do you think the safety director has limited the potential cost reductions to the next five years?
5. Suppose you are given the following additional information pertaining to question 4:
   a. The cost of capital for the firm is 5 per cent. Assuming that the investment will be made on the first day of the year and that all savings will be realized at the end of each of the five years, including the year in which the investment is made, what decision should be made regarding the investment? Why? (Note: In solving the problem use the present value table presented in question 7 in Chapter 10).
   b. The safety director estimates that the probability of obtaining the results presented in question 4 are 0.5 in each of the next five years. In addition, he estimates that there is an 0.3 probability of eliminating only 1 lost-time case, 2 doctor's cases, 3 first-aid cases, and 1 no-injury case in each of the five years and an 0.2 probability of obtaining no reductions whatsoever in any of the five years. Neglecting the time value of money, what decision should the firm make? Why?

    c. Utilizing both present value as in part (a), and the consideration of probabilities as stipulated in part (b), what decision should the firm make? Why?

6. Joe Joseph, the safety director of the XYZ Corporation, was walking through the plant at 10:13 a.m. on his way to keeping an appointment with the plant manager at 10:15 a.m. concerning the hiring of new workers. As he walked past Sam Samson he noticed that a safety guard had been removed from the machine which Sam was operating. Evaluate the following alternatives which Joe has available to him. In each case give your reason for your evaluation.
   a. Do nothing.
   b. Tell Sam to put the safety device on the machine.
   c. Go to Sam's supervisor, a production foreman, and tell him what Sam is doing.
   d. In the meeting with the plant manager, the supervisor of production foremen, mention the situation just observed.
   Does Joe have any other alternatives beside those listed above? If so, what are they and what are their advantages and disadvantages?

7. Which of the following safety approaches do you think are effective? In each case state your reasons why.
   a. Having the safety director prepare and report a summary of all "accidents" in all departments to all supervisors attending regularly scheduled bi-weekly safety and health meetings.
   b. Modifying a suggestion system which excludes managerial and supervisory personnel, so that such personnel could obtain suggestion awards for their own suggestions which help overcome safety and health problems.
   c. Giving the supervisors an additional proportionate award of any suggestion awards that employees in their departments receive for ideas which reduce or eliminate safety and health problems. For example, if an employee receives an award of $50 the supervisor might receive $10.
   d. Developing a computer program which will generate reports providing safety and health statistics, using a costing method such as Simonds' on a monthly or bi-weekly basis.
   e. Showing films, which depict a worker on an assembly line having his hand seriously injured, to supervisors who work in an automated continuous process petroleum firm.

8. Under what conditions do you believe Greenberg's logarithmic learning curve model would be useful in helping to pinpoint safety and health problems? Why?

9. Can you think of any other educational devices for safety and health other than the two simulation examples mentioned in the chapter—fighting fires and squirting water to simulate a trauma?

10. Given the information below:
   a. Evaluate the safety records of each of the four companies.

b. Which of the four companies has the best safety record?
Why?
c. Which of the four companies has the worst safety record? Why?

Type of Accident	Company Number of Occurrences (Total hours lost)			
	A	B	C	D
Fatality	0 (0)	0 (0)	1 (6000)*	0 (0)
Permanent Total Disability	0 (0)	0 (0)	1 (6000)	0 (0)
Permanent Partial Disability	0 (0)	0 (0)	2 (1200)	2 (600)
Temporary Total Disability	1 (100)	12 (400)	8 (200)	10 (200)
Nonfatal cases without lost work days but which resulted in transfer to another job or termination of employment, or required medical treatment, or involved loss of consciousness or restriction of work or motion†	2	10	10	209
Company Data Number of Employees	50	240	300	2000
Average hours worked by each employee during the year	2000	2000	2000	2000
Type of Industry	Electrical equipment & supplies	Tobacco manufac- turers	Lumber & wood prod- ucts	Leather & leather products

*The number of total hours lost which are in parentheses and in italics come from a table of standard time changes as discussed in the chapter. The nonitalized numbers in parentheses are actual hours lost.

†The nonfatal cases are those required by OSHA to be included for incidence calculations.

Notes

[1] John V. Grimaldi and Rollin H. Simonds, *Safety Management* (Homewood, Ill.: Richard D. Irwin, Inc., 1975), p. 4. The italics are ours.

[2] Ibid., p. 5.

[3] Much of this section is drawn from ibid., pp. 28–55; Willie Hammer, *Occupational Safety Management and Engineering* (Englewood Cliffs, N.J.: Prentice-Hall, Inc., 1976), pp. 1–27; and Roland Blake, *Industrial Safety* (Englewood Cliffs, N. J.: Prentice-Hall, Inc., 1963), pp. 12–31.

[4] Frederick L. Creber, *Safety for Industry* (London: The Royal Society for the Prevention of Accidents in Association with the Queen Anne Press, Limited, 1967), p. 60.

[5] Patricia E. O'Brien, "Health, Safety and the Corporate Balance Sheet," *Personnel Journal*, 52 (August, 1973), p. 726.

[6] Donald Hunter, *The Diseases of Occupations* (London: The English Universities Press, Limited, 1974), pp. 12–13 and 24–25.

[7] Ibid., p. 116.

[8] O'Brien, op. cit., p. 726.

[9] W. Wayne Worick, *Safety Education: Man, His Machines, and His Environment* (Englewood Cliffs, N. J.: Prentice-Hall, Inc., 1975), p. 99.

[10]Hammer, op. cit., p. 15.

[11]Ibid., p. 19.

[12]Robert J. Paul, "Workers' Compensation — An Adequate Employee Benefit?" *The Academy of Management Review,* 1 (October, 1976), p. 112.

[13]Hammer, op. cit., p. 17.

[14]In fact, as early as 1892 a safety program that was fairly effective was established at the Joliet Works of the Illinois Steel Company.

[15]Paul, op. cit., p. 113.

[16]Ibid. Paul has indicated that workmen's compensation laws have generally not provided adequate protection for the worker and his family. Ibid., pp. 112–123.

[17]Hammer, op. cit., p. 22.

[18]Paul, op. cit., p. 120. We should note that some states set up their own workmen's compensation insurance system and provide employers with an opportunity to utilize the latter or private insurance carriers.

[19]William A. Steiger, "Can We Legislate the Humanization of Work?" in W. Clay Hammer and Frank L. Schmidt, *Contemporary Problems in Personnel: Readings for the Seventies* (Chicago, Ill.: St. Clair Press, 1974), p. 501.

[20]The statistics in this entire section are drawn from National Safety Council, *Accident Facts 1977* (Chicago, Ill.: National Safety Council, 1977), pp. 23–39, except where noted otherwise. It should be noted that these statistics are based upon data from reports to the National Safety Council from organizations that tend to be more safety and health conscious than employers as a whole. Therefore, these statistics probably understate the magnitude of the problem of occupational safety.

[21]The President's Report on Occupational Safety and Health (May, 1972), p. 1.

[22]Norman J. Wood, "Environmental Law and Occupational Health," *Labor Law Journal,* 27 (February, 1976), p. 152.

[23]American National Standards Institute, "American Standard Method of Recording and Measuring Work Injury Experience — ANSI Z16.1," (New York). This standard has undergone a number of revisions during the years of its use.

[24]The precise definition of incidence and statistics concerning incidence are published annually by the U.S. Department of Labor, *Occupational Injuries and Illnesses in the United States by Industry* (Washington, D. C.: U.S. Government Printing Office, latest edition).

[25]O'Brien, op. cit., pp. 725–726.

[26]The Occupational Safety and Health Act, Public Law 91–596 (December 29, 1970), Sec. 2, p. 1.

[27]Ibid.

[28]Ibid., Sec. 24(a), p. 25.

[29]Ibid., Sec. 8(a), pp. 9–10.

[30]Occupational Safety and Health Administration, "All About OSHA," pp. 9–10.

[31]The Occupational Safety and Health Act, op. cit., Sec. 13(a), p. 16.

[32]Ibid., Sec. 20(a)(1), p. 21.

[33]Ibid., Sec. 20(a)(5).

[34]Ibid., Sec. 20(a)(6).

[35]Ibid., Sec. 5(a)(1), p. 4.

[36]Fred K. Foulkes, "Learning to Live with OSHA, " *Harvard Buisness Review,* 51 (November-December, 1973), p. 64.

[37]"The Grand Scale of Federal Intervention," *Business Week* (April 4, 1977), p. 56.

[38]As quoted in "The Critics Size Up OSHA's New Chief," *Business Week* (February 28, 1977), p. 38.

[39]Foulkes, op. cit., pp. 59–60. The two examples are from this source.

[40]This problem has been pointed out by John M. Gleason and Darold T. Barnum, "Effectiveness of OSHA Sanctions in Influencing Employer Behavior: Single and Multi-Period Decision Models," *Accident Analysis and Prevention* (in press).

[41]"OSHA's New Focus: The Health of Your Employees," *Nation's Business,* 64 (May, 1976), p. 19.

[42]"Why Nobody Wants to Listen to OSHA," *Business Week* (June 14, 1976), p. 6.

[43]*Brennan v. Gibson's Products,* 407 F. Supp. 154 (1976).

[44]*Barlow's Inc. v. Usery,* 424 F. Supp. 437 (1977). The Barlow case, by covering *all* inspections, raised a broader issue than *Brennan v. Gibson's,* which dealt only with the constitutionality of warrantless searches. For this reason, *Brennan v. Gibson's* in early 1978 was in the 5th Circuit Court pending the outcome of *Barlow's Inc. v. Usery. Barlow's, Inc. v. Usery* was heard by the United States Supreme Court early in 1978 and a decision was rendered on May 23, 1978. At the Supreme Court level, with a new Secretary of Labor, this case became *Marshall v. Barlow's, Inc.* In its 5 to 3 decision in the *Barlow* case, the Supreme Court ruled that OSHA's warrantless searches violated the Fourth Amendment's ban against "unreasonable searches and seizures." On the other hand, the Court said that OSHA would not have to meet strict criminal law requirements to obtain a warrant. To quote Justice Byron R. White, "probable cause in the criminal law sense is not required" for OSHA warrants, eliminating the need for "specific evidence of an existing violation." In short, as a result of this decision, OSHA could obtain warrants fairly easily, but more time, expense, paperwork and litigation would be required. These materials were drawn from *The New York Times,* May 24, 1978, pp. 1, D21.

[45]"OSHA: Hardest to Live With," *Business Week* (April 4, 1977), p. 79.

[46]"OSHA Gets Ready to Analyze Its Rules," *Business Week* (August 8, 1977), p. 30.

[47]"OSHA Tries for A Fresh Start," *Business Week,* (April 3, 1978), p. 109.

[48]Rollin H. Simonds, "OSHA Compliance: 'Safety is Good Business.'" *Personnel,* 50 (July-August, 1973), pp. 30–38.

[49]An excellent review and description of various sources of information with respect to OSHA is provided by Theodore P. Peck, *Occupational Safety and Health: A Guide to Information Sources* (Detroit, Mich.: Gale Research Company, 1974). Some of the possible sources of information are the American Society of Safety Engineers, American Industrial Hygienists Association, National Safety Council, American National Standards Institute and *Occupational Safety and Health Reporter.* Addresses for these sources were provided by James O. Matschulat and John P. Gausch, *Organizing for OSHAct: A Management Challenge* (New York: AMACOM, 1973), p. 21.

[50]Requirements pertaining to record keeping and reporting are updated in the *Federal Register.*

[51]Gordon R. England, "OSHA Compliance: Let Your Computer Help," *Advanced Management Journal,* 41 (Spring 1976), pp. 35–41.

[52]Descriptions of these views are provided by many writers. See, for example, Dan Petersen, *Safety Management: A Human Approach* (Fairview, N.J.: Aloray Inc., 1975), pp. 17–18.

[53]This point was strongly set forth by Robert Guion, *Personnel Testing* (New York: McGraw-Hill, 1965).

[54]Petersen, op. cit., p. 252.

[55]Morris Schulzinger, *Accident Syndrome* (Springfield, Ill.: Charles C Thomas, 1956).

[56]See, for example, Alexander Mintz and Milton L. Blum, "A Re-examination of the Accident Proneness Concept," *Journal of Applied Psychology,* 33 (1949), pp. 195–211.

[57]H. W. Heinrich, *Industrial Accident Prevention* (New York: McGraw-Hill Book Company, Inc., 1950), p. 17. The first edition of this work was published in 1931.

[58]"A Research Center for Safety Management," *Management Review,* 59 (October, 1970), p. 21.

[59]Russell DeReamer, *Modern Safety Practices* (New York: John Wiley and Sons, Inc., 1958), p. 18.

[60]William W. Allison, "High Potential Accident Analysis," *Safety Maintenance,* 132 (October, 1966), pp. 22–23.

[61]E. C. Poulton, "The Environment at Work," *Applied Ergonomics,* 1 (March, 1972), p. 25.

[62]C. B. Grether, "Engineering Psychology," in Bruce L. Margolis and William H. Kroes (eds.), *The Human Side of Accident Prevention: Psychological Concepts and Principles Which Bear on Industrial Safety* (Springfield, Ill.: Charles C Thomas Publishers, 1975), p. 53, for example, cites a case in which proper illumination resulted in a 43 per cent reduction in the accident rate of a manufacturing shop.

[63]Allison, op. cit., p. 22.

[64]Grimaldi and Simonds, op. cit., p. 154.

[65]Dan Petersen, *Safety Supervision* (New York: AMACOM, 1976), p. 126.

[66]Grether, op. cit., p. 52.

[67]Grimaldi and Simonds, op. cit., p. 147.

[68]Petersen, *Safety Supervision*, op. cit., p. 131.

[69]Cited by Petersen, *Safety Management*, op. cit., p. 367. In certain other research dealing with pilots, however, no "correlation was found between accident occurrence and biorhythmic criticality or low phase of cycle." John H. Wolcott et al., "Correlation of General Aviation Accidents with the Biorhythm Theory," *Human Factors*, 19 (June, 1977), p. 283.

[70]"Ergonomics — New Angle on Employee Health and Safety," *Management Review*, 56 (September, 1967), p. 47.

[71]Richard G. Pearson and Mahmoud A. Ayoub, "Ergonomics Aids Industrial Accident and Injury Control," *Management Review*, 54 (November, 1965), p. 38.

[72]Petersen, *Safety Management*, op. cit., pp. 11–12.

[73]Poulton, op. cit., p. 25.

[74]George W. Bower, "Z16-Pro and Con," *National Safety News*, 97 (June, 1968), p. 68, stated that by recording lost-time "accident" injuries only, we "represent only .15 per cent of all accidents, on the average, that will occur in a plant." Supporting this view, William W. Allison, in "High Potential Accident Analysis," op. cit., pp. 22–23, stated that: "The disabling injuries reported under the Standard Frequency Rate System represent only one-tenth of one percent of all accidents that occur."

[75]"What is the Future of Z16.1?" *National Safety News*, 103 (May, 1971), p. 45.

[76]Kenyon B. DeGreene, *Systems Psychology* (New York: McGraw-Hill Book Company, Inc., 1970), p. 132.

[77]This discussion of the Simonds method is drawn from Grimaldi and Simonds, op. cit., pp. 391–418.

[78]Ibid., p. 409.

[79]Ibid., pp. 397–402.

[80]Ibid., p. 412.

[81]Ibid., p. 411.

[82]Ibid., p. 415.

[83]Leon Schenkelbach, *The Safety Management Primer* (Homewood, Ill.: Dow Jones-Irwin, Inc., 1975), p. 13.

[84]Cited by Simonds, op. cit., pp. 30–38.

[85]Ibid., p. 35.

[86]Grimaldi and Simonds, op. cit., p. 393.

[87]Quoted by ibid., p. 392.

[88]This study is cited by Petersen, *Safety Supervision*, op. cit., p. 87.

[89]Roger L. M. Dunbar, "Manager's Influence on Subordinates' Thinking About Safety," *Academy of Management Journal*, 18 (June, 1975), pp. 368–369.

[90]William P. Anthony, Philip Anthony, and Jack Steen, "The Supervisor's Role in the Occupational Safety and Health Act," *Supervisory Management*, 17 (October, 1972), pp. 2–8.

[91]Cited by Petersen, *Safety Supervision*, op. cit., p. 87.

[92]Les Greenberg, "Learning as a Factor in Accident Experience," *Personnel Psychology*, 24 (Spring, 1971), pp. 71–76. Greenberg also mentioned a study in which the cumulative frequency rate was plotted against cumulative seniority. A curve was obtained which approximated a hyperbola. This study suggested that when the experience factor was taken into consideration, there was a gradual decrease in the frequency rate.

[93]Stanley Rubinsky and Nelson Smith, "Safety Training by Accident Simulation," *Journal of Applied Psychology,* 57 (February, 1973), p. 69.

[94]Ibid., p. 72.

[95]England, op. cit., pp. 35–41.

[96]Ibid., p. 38.

[97]Ibid., p. 40.

[98]Ibid.

[99]Grimaldi and Simonds, op. cit., pp. 361–362.

[100]See Joan Woodward, *Industrial Organization: Theory and Practice* (London: Oxford University Press, 1965).

[101]Simonds, op. cit., pp. 37–38.

[102]Schulzinger, op. cit., as cited by Petersen, *Safety Supervision,* op. cit., pp. 117–118.

[103]Simonds, op. cit., p. 37.

[104]Robert S. Smith, *The Occupational Safety and Health Act: Its Goals and Its Achievements* (Washington, D. C.: American Enterprise Institute for Public Policy Research, 1976), p. 6.

14

EMPLOYEE MANAGEMENT RELATIONS

The purpose of this chapter is to discuss some of the relationships that exist between management and its employees. With respect to employee relations, two quite different types of situations may exist: (1) some of the organization's employees may have joined a union or (2) the organization may be completely nonunionized.

The existence of one or more unions in a firm will influence in many ways the rules under which employees operate, how the rules are set, the nature of the rules, and the types of constraints placed on management decision making. We use the term "one or more unions" because in some organizations different groups of employees may have joined different unions, so that management must deal with more than one. For purposes of simplification, we will use the term "unionized" in this chapter to describe firms in which any number of unions, small or large, exist; the term "nonunionized" will describe organizations in which no employees have joined unions.

In our society, employees make available their efforts, abilities, and time to employers in exchange for compensation and employee benefits (as discussed in Chapters 9 to 12) as well as such psychological and social rewards as meeting self-actualization needs in their work and developing interpersonal friendships with other employees on the job. Additionally, the employer-employee relationship must provide for measures relating to *individual security*.[1] Individual security deals with the employee's (1) receiving equitable treatment on the job, such as being disciplined in a fair and impartial manner, and (2) his relative claim to available work. More specifically, claims to work involve such questions as: Who gets laid off? Who is to be recalled from a layoff when work is available again? Who gets promoted? Who is to be given overtime work when it is available?[2]

Under nonunion conditions, compensation, benefits, and individual security decisions are essentially unilaterally made by management. If an employee is dissatisfied with the way he is treated, his only recourse sometimes may be to leave the firm. In other cases, he may slow down his work on the job, continue to work regardless of his dissatisfaction, or be able to persuade management to provide him with more favorable economic rewards or equitable treatment. Frequently, in nonunionized firms some policies concerning compensation and benefits as well as individual security issues are more implicit than explicit.

In unionized firms, however, policies regarding the conditions of employment indicated here are much more explicitly spelled out in written form. The employer must negotiate with the elected representatives of the employees and a written labor management contract, called a "collective bargaining agreement" is agreed upon by both management and the union. In addition to dealing with economic and individual security issues, labor-management contracts will deal with: (1) what rights management has in spelling out conditions of employment for its employees and (2) the rights that the union has in representing its members.[3]

Some of the major differences between unionized and nonunionized firms are illustrated in Figure 14–1. As may be noted here, key differences between these two situations are that in nonunionized firms efforts are frequently taken to keep unions out and "negotiations" may be undertaken by management with employees on an individual basis, whereas unionized firms negotiate collectively with their employees via the unions.

Many managements in nonunionized firms expend considerable efforts in attempting to prevent unions from organizing any of their employees. This is basically because unionization will result in management's decision making powers with respect to employee relations being constrained to a considerable extent. Unionization, however, we should emphasize, is not necessarily "bad." Unions have negotiated with firms to provide better working conditions, more equitable disciplinary procedures, etc., which, over the years, have economically and socially improved the quality of work life for millions of Americans. Further, unions in some firms may actively collaborate with management to improve the position of *both* its members *and* the organization. As indicated in Chapter 11, for example, unions have played such a collaborative role in many Scanlon plans.

We have entitled this chapter "Employee Management Relations" rather than "Union Relations" for two reasons. First, the

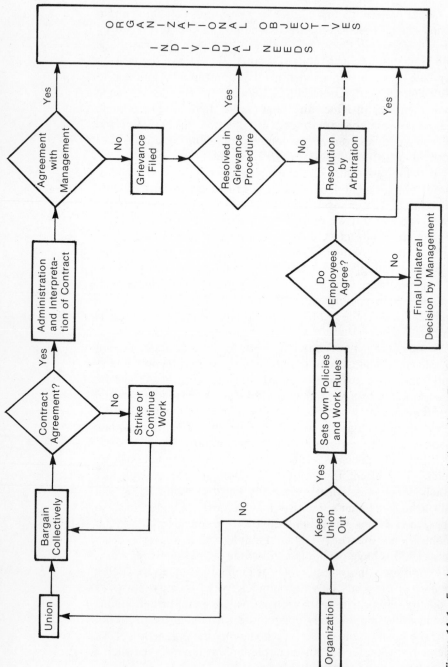

Figure 14-1 *Employee management relations. Note: The dashed arrow is intended to illustrate that arbitrators' awards may please management, the union and employees, or none of these parties.*

majority of workers in the United States do *not* belong to unions. In 1974, for example, approximately, 20,199,000 American workers were members of unions. This number represented only 21.7 per cent of the total labor force of about 93,240,000.[4] Further, union membership is heavily concentrated in a relatively small number of states. In 1974, six states accounted for more than half the total union membership in the United States — New York, California, Pennsylvania, Illinois, Ohio, and Michigan.[5] In general, membership in unions is concentrated in certain industries such as automotive and steel in those areas with the largest numbers of workers in nonagricultural establishments. Thus, for personnel managers in certain geographical areas, unionization poses much more of a concern than in other areas.

Many of the issues and ideas we will deal with in this chapter apply to both unionized and nonunionized firms, e.g., the establishment of equitable disciplinary procedures for employees. We should point out, however, that many of the materials presented in this chapter will relate directly to unionization. We give this emphasis because unions represent a very powerful minority in the United States, an elaborate body of labor law has developed to govern union management relations, and the impact of unions' behavior extends far beyond simply the workers they represent. The reader may recall, for example, the extensive energy conservation measures that had to be taken in certain states in early 1978 as the long United Mine Workers strike cut off necessary supplies of coal.

We will focus our attention on several facets of employee management relations. We will examine the legal framework in this country primarily affecting unionization in the private sector of our economy. Then we will briefly trace the history of the American labor movement. We will next provide an overview of the structure of American unions and discuss some of the reasons why workers do (and do not) join unions. We will proceed to focus attention on basic decision-making areas that the personnel or labor relations manager is responsible for relative to unionization, contract negotiations, and labor management contract administration and interpretation. Here, we will also focus attention on the general subject of equitable discipline for employees, whether they are unionized or not. Finally, we will look at management science, computers, and certain key contingencies relating to employee management relations.

UNIONIZATION: THE LEGAL FRAMEWORK

The legal environment relating to labor relations in the United States has assumed two forms: common law and statute (or statutory) law.[6] Common law, as indicated in Chapter 13, is essentially unwritten law that is based on judicial decisions interpreting existing law or resolving issues not covered by statutory law. Statutory law, on the other hand, is that written law specifically enacted by the federal government, states, and municipalities. In general, with respect to labor relations, common law "has tended to be more conservative and less adaptable to changing economic and social conditions" than statutory law.[7]

From the Nineteenth Century to the 1930's

For most of the nineteenth century, public policy toward unions was "expressed principally through judicial interpretations by state courts," with judicial decisions closely tied to English common law precedents during the first half of this period.[8] We will now examine some of the more important aspects of governmental policy from 1800 until the 1930's.

The Conspiracy Doctrine

An 1806 court case involving a group of Philadelphia shoemakers severely hampered the growth of unions by ruling that it was illegal for workers to organize in order to raise wages. The basic common law precept involved in this case was the so-called "conspiracy doctrine," which dated back to feudal times. This doctrine stipulated that it was an unlawful conspiracy to organize in order to raise wages because such efforts were a crime against society.

In 1842, the conspiracy doctrine was dealt a serious blow in the case of *Commonwealth vs. Hunt,* handed down by the Massachusetts Supreme Court. In this case, it was ruled that unions per se were not illegal but that the goals and means of unions would be scrutinized by the courts. "If both the goals and means employed were legal, then the union was legal."[9] After this decision, the criminal conspiracy doctrine fell into disuse, but state courts, which were generally opposed to unions, ruled in favor of employers in most cases involving union management controversies. For this and other reasons, unions did not really establish themselves as viable organizations until the 1880's.[10]

The Yellow Dog Contract

The demise of the "conspiracy doctrine" did not usher in a period of friendly labor management relations. Rather, emplyers sought new ways to prevent the formation of unions. One of these methods was the so-called "yellow dog contract," under which an employee "agreed to abstain from union membership as a condition of continued employment.''[11] In signed statements, employees also gave assurances to the employer that they were not members of any union and that they would not attempt to influence other individuals to join a union. Such contracts were legally enforceable in the courts and enabled managers to circumvent the *Commonwealth vs. Hunt* ruling.[12]

The Injunction

A second method used by management to keep unions from organizing was the use of injunctions. An injunction is a "court order to cease and desist from some specified action such as a strike, a boycott, or picketing."[13] Violations of such court orders represent contempt of court and are punishable accordingly.

The power of the injunction began to be used after the *Commonwealth vs. Hunt* decision to fight unionization until the passage of the Norris-LaGuardia Act in 1932.[14] Its use was dramatized in a dispute between the Pullman Company and its employees in the 1890's.[15] Due to an economic depression in 1893, this company dismissed more than half of its shop employees and reduced the wages of the remainder by as much as 40 per cent. It also refused to reduce the rent for its employees who lived in company-owned housing in a "company town." A number of sequential events then occurred that led to a major labor management controversy. A group of workers who met with company officials to object to the firm's actions were fired on the following day; the employees, who were members of the American Railway Union (ARU) struck; and the company reacted by shutting down its facilities. The ARU had members who were employed on numerous railroads, and these union members refused to work on or with any train that included a Pullman car. The railroads then indicated that they would fire any employee who refused to work; the ARU in turn announced that if a member of any crew were fired, the whole crew would quit; and rail service was virtually halted. Strikebreakers were then imported from Canada with instructions to couple United States Mail cars to any train with a Pullman car; when violence occurred, the railroad managers persuaded President Grover Cleveland to send in troops to protect the mails, and the railroad managers successfully obtained a federal court injunction to prevent interference with the mails. The strike continued, however, and the president of ARU, Eugene Debs, as well as other union officials, were arrested and convicted for not complying with the injunction. The ARU strike was lost, and the injunction, so effective in this case, continued to be relied on by management until it was subsequently outlawed.

Antitrust Legislation

A third method used by management to combat unionization was by relying on federal antitrust legislation. Such reliance began after 1890, when the Sherman Antitrust Act was passed in an attempt to prohibit corporate monopolization and business combinations that would restrain trade. The Act provided for fines and imprisonment and that offenders could also be subject to triple damages. A number of lower courts applied the Sherman Act to unions, and in 1908, the Supreme Court applied the Act to unions in a key case — the Danbury Hatters case (*Loewe vs. Lawlor*).[16] The United Hatters Union was trying to organize a union at the Loewe Hat Company, and had persuaded the American Federation of Labor (AFL) to urge its union members throughout the United States to stop buying Loewe hats. Such an activity as was undertaken by the AFL is referred to as a *secondary boycott*. A secondary boycott differs from an ordinary boycott in that it calls on workers *not directly involved* in a labor dispute themselves to refuse to buy goods from a company or companies involved in a dispute with another union. This secondary boycott resulted in lost sales for Loewe, and the firm "brought suit successfully for triple damages against the members of the hatters' union and was awarded over half a million dollars."[17] With the Supreme Court upholding the employer, the precedent for using antitrust legislation to counteract union activities such as secondary boycotts was firmly established. Unions worked to offset this use of antitrust legislation and were successful in influencing the passage of the Clayton Antitrust Act in 1914. This Act amended the Sherman Act in a way designed to exclude unions from its coverage. In both Sections 6 and 20 of the Clayton Act,[18] apparent Congressional intent was to remove unions from prosecution under the antitrust laws, and labor leaders were initially overjoyed with the passage of the Act.

Labor's reprieve from antitrust legislation was short-lived, however. In 1921, the Supreme Court ruled that Section 6 of the Clayton Act had not changed the fact that "it was the *activities* of a union that determined whether or not it was in violation of the antitrust law."[19] The case in question involved the use of a secondary boycott against the Duplex Printing Press Company,[20] which was the only nonunion producer of printing presses. In effect, the Court in this decision ruled that Congress had done nothing regarding unions with the passage of the Clayton Act. Even worse, as far as labor was concerned, the Supreme Court subsequently found strikes as well as secondary boycotts to be in restraint of trade. It was not until after the passage of the Norris-

LaGuardia Act in 1932 that unions were essentially finally excluded from antitrust legislation.[21]

Company Unions

According to Hagburg and Levine, there was another employer weapon against union organizational efforts, which was perhaps "the most effective" of all.[22] This was the "company union." Managements of numerous firms organized unions, which they controlled. An illusion of collective bargaining was created, but the union was dominated by agents of the employer. This approach became popular in the 1920's and "accounted in large part for the organizational weakness of unions during the 1920s."[23]

The 1930's Through the 1950's

The first federal law supporting the right of workers in the private sector of our economy to unionize that was subsequently upheld by the Supreme Court was the Railway Labor Act of 1926. This Act was amended to include the airlines in 1936. This act was, in many ways, the first major federal collective bargaining act and laid a basis for future federal legislation. We will not discuss this piece of legislation, however, since it dealt with only two industries.[24]

Six years later, in 1932, in the waning days of the Hoover Administration, an important law that covered business firms in general was passed — the Norris-LaGuardia or Anti-Injunction Act. This Act seriously limited the use of injunctions in labor disputes. "No peaceful or nonfraudulent union activity, including strikes and picketing," according to the Act, could be subjected to the use of injunctions.[25] Further, the Norris-LaGuardia Act made the "yellow dog contract" unenforceable in federal courts.

The Norris-LaGuardia Act required neither unions nor managements to accept or recognize one another. Instead, this Act simply permitted each party to use the same methods to achieve its ends unhampered by federal control and left the outcome of disputes to the relative skills and strengths of the parties.[26]

The National Labor Relations Act (Wagner Act)

The "New Deal" administration of President Franklin D. Roosevelt effected a number of significant pieces of legislation in the 1930's to help economic recovery from the great depression and provide improved social services to the nation such as the

Social Security Act and unemployment compensation, discussed in Chapter 12. In 1935, the National Labor Relations Act (or Wagner Act) was enacted. This law, which was decidedly prolabor is *the basic piece of federal legislation* governing union management relations in the United States today.

In the Wagner Act, it was declared to be the policy of the United States:

> . . . to eliminate the causes of certain substantial obstructions to the free flow of commerce and to mitigate and eliminate these obstructions when they have occurred by encouraging the practice and procedure of collective bargaining and by protecting the exercise by workers of full freedom of association, self-organization, and designation of representatives of their own choosing, for the purpose of negotiating the terms and conditions of their employment or other mutual aid or protection.[27]

According to Estey, only three basic techniques were necessary to effect the basic objectives of the Wagner Act: (1) giving workers a new method of organizing — by means of a secret ballot election to determine whether they wanted to be represented by a union; (2) prohibiting employers from interfering with a worker's right to join a union by spelling out five unfair labor practices on the part of the employer; and (3) establishing a quasi-judicial body, the National Labor Relations Board (NLRB), to enforce and administer the law, to decide on charges of unfair labor practices, and to administer the secret ballot elections (called "representation" elections).[28] We will now examine each of these three facets of the Wagner Act.

Under the Wagner Act, in order for the NLRB to conduct a secret ballot representation election, employees or a union had to indicate that there was sufficient interest in unionization to justify such an election. It was "early decided that if 30 percent of the workers in a bargaining unit were interested in having an election and demonstrated this interest by submitting authorization cards, petitions, or other means, an election would be held."[29] The Act provided that if a majority of the employees who voted in a representation election favored unionization, the union would be certified by the NLRB as their authorized representative.

The five unfair labor practices of employers enacted into law by the Wagner Act were the following:[30]

1. To interfere with, restrain, or coerce employees in the exercise of their rights to self-determination, e.g., threatening employees with loss of job or benefits if they should join a union.
2. To dominate or interfere in the formation or administration of any labor organization or contribute financial or other support to it, e.g., a company union.
3. To discriminate against any employee "in regard to hire or tenure of employment or any term or condition of employment to encourage or discourage membership in any labor organization,"[31] e.g., demoting or

discharging any employee because he encouraged his fellow employees to join a union.

4. To discriminate against any employee because he has filed charges or given testimony before the NLRB concerning any alleged employer violations of the Act.

5. To refuse to bargain in good faith concerning wages, hours, and other conditions of employment with any union duly chosen as a representative of its employees.

The NLRB was established as an independent agency of the federal government, and members of this board were appointed by the President of the United States with the consent of the Senate, for terms of three years. The NLRB deals only with unfair labor practice cases brought to it; its rulings serve as precedents and have the effect of law, but the NLRB cannot enforce its decisions itself — it must go to the federal courts. The NLRB has been criticized as partisan both by management and labor. In the first 40 years of its existence (1935–1975), however, "the Board's decisions and interpretations have been affirmed in full by both U.S. Courts of Appeal and the Supreme Court four times as often as they have been set aside."[32]

The Labor Management Relations Act of 1947 (Taft-Hartley Act)

The Wagner Act stimulated the growth of unionism, and both union membership and power grew in succeeding years. During World War II the federal government established wage and price controls, and organized labor gave a no-strike pledge. Immediately after the war, however, there was "an unparalleled wave of shutdowns, as workers in every major industry sought to catch up after the war years' wage and price freezes."[33] In light of these happenings, strong pressures were placed on Congress to redress the prolabor orientation of the Wagner Act, and this act was *amended* in 1947 by Congress over the veto of President Harry S Truman, by what is popularly called the Taft-Hartley Act.

The major provisions of Taft-Hartley may be grouped into four classes. First, a number of unfair *union* practices were now spelled out. Unions, for example, were prohibited from:[34]

1. Restraining or coercing employees in their exercise of their rights to join or assist a labor union or to refrain from doing so, e.g., threats of violence to nonstriking employees.

2. Causing or attempting to cause an employer to engage in discrimination against an employee in order to get him to encourage or discourage union membership, e.g., causing an employer to fire an employee because he circulated a petition to have the union's election procedures changed.

3. Refusing to bargain in good faith with the employer.

4. Engaging in some types of secondary boycotts and certain types of strikes and picketing.[35]

5. Charging excessive or discriminatory initiation fees.

6. "Featherbedding." Featherbedding was defined as causing an employer to pay for services of employees not performed.

Second, the Taft-Hartley Act banned the *closed shop,* which requires employees to become union members before they are hired.[36] The *union shop,* in which an employee must join the union within no less than 30 days after employment is still legal with the following exception. In one of the most controversial sections of the Act (Section 14(b)), states are permitted to enact "right-to-work" laws, which prohibit the union shop or any arrangements that require union members who voluntarily joined the union to maintain their union membership. In some states, *agency shops* were also outlawed in right-to-work laws. An agency shop is one in which employees do not need to join a union but must contribute financially to the union (usually the equivalent of union dues and initiation fees) as a condition of employment.

As opposed to the representation elections provided by the Wagner Act, Taft-Hartley provided for *decertification* elections, in which employees could vote on whether or not they wanted to stop being represented by their union. Further, deauthorization elections were provided that gave union employees a chance to vote on whether they wanted to have their union continue to be able to maintain a union shop. The membership of the NLRB was also increased from 3 to 5, with each member appointed for a five-year term.

Finally, the Taft-Hartley Act amended the Wagner Act with respect to the role of the federal government in resolving labor disputes. The Act created the Federal Mediation and Conciliation Service (FMCS). It also required that if either management or labor wanted to make a change in any existing contract, it must notify the other party of such an intention within 60 days prior to the expiration of the contract. Then, unless the changes have been accepted by both sides, the parties must notify the FMCS within 30 days after such notice that a labor dispute exists. The FMCS will assist management and the union in helping to resolve disputes through mediation and conciliation, although neither management nor the union are required to utilize the services of the FMCS.[37]

The Taft-Hartley Act also authorized the President of the United States, in strikes that may result in a "national emergency," after appointing a board of inquiry to report on the issues involved, to direct the Attorney General to ask for an 80-day injunction from a United States District Court requiring employees to resume or continue to work for that period. "After the injunction is issued the parties to the dispute are required during the next 60 days, to try to settle their differences with the assistance of the Federal Mediation and Conciliation Service."[38] At the end of this 60-day period, a further report from the board of inquiry must be made to the President that he, in turn, must make available to the public. This report must contain a statement of the employer's last offer.[39] This 80-day injunction period is often referred to as a "cooling off period," during which parties to the dispute would return to or continue at the bargaining table to iron out their differences.

The effectiveness of the Taft-Hartley injunction is debatable. From 1947 through 1975, the injunction was used 29 times, and in "at least nine cases, strikes occurred or were resumed after the eighty-day injunction had expired."[40] Further, employees may refuse to go back to work even though the President invokes the injunction. In the 1977–1978 coal strike, for example, members of the United Mine Workers (UMW) refused to obey President Jimmy Carter's 80-day injunction. They continued their work stoppage for a short period afterwards, until an agreement was finally reached by the UMW and the coal operators, and was voted on and accepted.

The Landrum-Griffin Act

One of the basic objectives of unionization has been to bring more democracy into firms by providing workers a mechanism by which they could participate in decisions dealing with the terms of their employment. As unions grew in size, however, certain union officials committed numerous unethical practices. These practices were investigated, most notably by the McClellan Committee from 1957–1959. The committee "produced 58 volumes of testimony, over half of which were devoted to evidence of various types of racketeering and corruption in the Teamsters Union."[41] One of the effects of this investigation was the passage of the Labor-Management Reporting and Disclosure Act of 1959, more commonly known as the Landrum-Griffin Act. This Act contained seven titles. Title I, often referred to as "Union Members' Bill of Rights," set forth certain rights that Congress believed should be guaranteed by federal law. This title applied "not only to union members but also to [other] employees covered by collective bargaining agreements."[42] The "bill of rights" provided for:

1. Equal rights for union members to attend, participate, and vote in meetings and elections subject to reasonable union rules.
2. Freedom to meet and assemble with other members, to express any views or opinions, and to express views about union business and candidates.
3. Protection from increased dues, initiation fees, and assessments, unless certain specific proper procedures were followed.

4. Protection of the right to testify, communicate with legislators, and bring suit in the courts for relief against union violation of their rights, after using reasonable remedies available within the union.

5. The right to obtain or inspect copies of collective bargaining agreements and to be informed as to the rights granted to them under the Act.

6. The right to a notice and fair hearing before being disciplined by the union (except discipline for non-payment of dues).[43]

Titles II through VI of the Landrum-Griffin Act primarily dealt with reporting requirements and other procedures to prevent abuses by union officials. For example:

1. Each union was required to file an annual financial report with the Secretary of Labor covering its assets and liabilities, income and expenses, payments and loans to union officers, etc.

2. Safeguards were provided for with respect to conducting union elections.

3. Union officials were required to be bonded, the use of union funds was restricted, and union officers who had allegedly violated their "fiduciary responsibilities" as spelled out by the Act could be sued both by unions and union members.

4. The Act made it a federal crime for a union officer or employee to embezzle or steal any of the funds of any labor organization.[44]

The final title of Landrum-Griffin made certain amendments to the Taft-Hartley Act, for example, tightening restrictions on secondary-boycott actions.[45]

The 1960's to the Present

Since the passage of the Landrum-Griffin Act, a number of attempts have been made to modify labor law; e.g., unions have exerted considerable pressure to eliminate the controversial Section 14(b) of the Taft-Hartley Act, permitting states to enact "right-to-work" laws. Additionally, more recently, President Jimmy Carter called on the 95th Congress to enact "labor-reform" legislation. This legislation provided for several changes in existing labor law. Among the more important of these were:

1. The access of union representatives to provide information to employees on company premises during working time during the period that the employees are seeking representation was to be increased.

2. Deadlines were to be set for representation elections.

3. Employers willfully violating final orders of the NLRB or federal courts with respect to unfair labor practices were to be denied federal contracts for a period of time.

4. The compensation of any worker reinstated with back pay if fired for helping in an organizing campaign (an unfair labor practice under prior law) was to be increased.

5. The number of members on the NLRB was to be increased from 5 to 7.[46]

In addition to the Carter-sponsored labor reform legislation, several other legal actions have taken place since 1960 relating to labor management relations. These actions assumed the form of Presidential Executive Orders and dealt with one portion of the public sector in this country — federal employees. Federal employees had been given the right to join unions in 1912 under provisions of the Lloyd-LaFollette Act, and, by 1961, 40 labor organizations with approximately 760,000 members represented federal employees, mostly in the postal service.[47] Executive Order 10988, issued by President John F. Kennedy in 1962, and Executive Order 11491, issued by President Richard M. Nixon in 1969, (and later amended), gave federal employees stronger rights in dealing with their employer. These employees were provided with the right to bargain collectively; mandatory procedures for handling employee grievances were ordered; a Federal Services Impasses Panel was set up to help resolve negotiating impasses; unfair labor practices were spelled out; union reporting and disclosure procedures similar to those in the private sector were required; and the Federal Mediation and Conciliation Service was given a role in mediating labor disputes. Federal employees, however, were not given the powers given organized workers in the private sector in that:

1. They were not permitted to strike.
2. The areas in which they could bargain collectively were much more narrowly circumscribed than in private-sector union management collective bargaining, e.g., Congress sets pay scales for job classifications in the federal service.
3. Both union shops and agency shops were prohibited.[48]

Following the issuance of the Executive Orders, federal employee unionization increased, until in 1975, for the first time, the number of federal employees covered by negotiated agreements exceeded 1 million.[49]

THE HISTORY OF THE AMERICAN LABOR MOVEMENT

Early Attempts at Unionism

The development of labor unions in the United States is no recent phenomenon. As far back as the 1790's, for example, craft unions "such as those of carpenters, shoemakers and printers formed separate organizations in Philadelphia, New York, and Boston."[50] With the industrial revolution and mass production assembly line operations not yet developed, the unions in existence in the United States until much later in the nineteenth century were of the craft type in which the members were highly skilled craftsmen rather than semi- or unskilled factory workers.

Prior to the Civil War, a number of craft unions were organized on a citywide basis and in 1834, for example, "city central bodies from seven cities met in New York to form the National Trades' Union,"[51] which was basically a regional union. These early American unions were often short lived, having been forced to cope with employer opposition, and the "conspiracy doctrine" mentioned earlier. Further, the unions were particularly susceptible to loss of membership or disbandment during periods of depression and unemployment. During the Civil War, many new industries were started, and new railroads brought the country closer together. Unions sought to organize employees in many of the new industries and a number of national unions were formed. Thirteen such unions appeared between 1861 and 1865,[52] and by 1879 more than 50 national unions were functioning in the United States. There were at least three important reasons for the development of national unions:

First, they were more suitable than local unions in meeting the problems associated with widening markets and migrating workmen. *Second,* they were better able to extend and preserve organization of the craft or industry. *Third,* they increased the power of local unions in the latters' struggles with employers.[53]

After having developed national unions, the next logical step in the development of unionization in the United States was the creation of *federations* of workers in different occupations. In 1869, a small group of custom tailors in Philadelphia formed a secret society called the Noble Order of the Knights of Labor. "Unlike other organizations of handicraft workers, it did not confine its membership to workers in a single trade, but spread, first as a multicraft federation, then as a general order of working men."[54] The Knights of Labor became nonsecretive, and by 1886 claimed more than 700,000 members. Due to numerous factors, however, its membership declined and it was abandoned in 1917. Historically, the Knights of Labor, although ultimately a failure, is important, since it provided the first major effort at *industrial* unionism, i.e., the inclusion of unskilled workers from factories in various industries rather than simply skilled craftsmen. The craft unions had never been successful in organizing factory workers with the advent of the industrial revolution in this country, but the Knights of Labor was able to organize these workers along with skilled craftsmen.

The AFL-CIO

The AFL

One of the primary reasons for the demise of the Knights of Labor was the successful establishment and expansion of another group, the American Federation of Labor (AFL). In 1881, six prominent craft unions established the Federation of Organized Trades and Labor Unions. In 1886, this federation joined with a group of craft unions that had split away from the Knights of Labor and formed the AFL, with Samuel Gompers as its first president. Under the leadership of Gompers, the AFL, a federation of craft unions (with the notable exception of the United Mine Workers), prospered until its membership reached more than 4 million in 1920; during the 1890–1920 period an estimated 70 to 80 per cent of all union workers were in the AFL.[55] The AFL was conservative in orientation and based on four operating principles:

1. Complete autonomy of affiliated national unions in their own internal affairs.
2. Exclusive jurisdiction for all affiliates with that jurisdiction respected by all other affiliates.
3. Avoidance of any formal political attachments but vigorous support of candidates friendly to it.
4. Exclusive reliance on collective bargaining for the improvement of wages and working conditions.[56]

Although the membership of the AFL fell off in the 1920's until it reached a low of 2.1 million in 1933 in the midst of the depression, it continued as this country's largest union.

The CIO

With the favorable labor legislation passed from 1932 to 1935 (Norris-LaGuardia and Wagner Acts), additional union growth took place in many of the nation's mass production industries such as automobile, rubber, and steel. Certain union leaders questioned the validity of organizing unions covering such workers on a craft basis, and in 1935 set up a Committee for Industrial Organization, which had as its objective working within the AFL to promote industrial unionism. AFL leaders rejected the idea of industrial unionism and this group was suspended from the AFL in 1936 and later expelled from the AFL in 1938. This group had its first constitutional convention in 1938 and was reorganized as a federation of national unions under the name of The Congress of Industrial Organization (CIO). Under the favorable New Deal legislation, the membership of the CIO increased to about 3.6 million by 1940 (with that of the AFL reaching about 4.3 million by that time).[57]

Competition and the Merger

During World War II, union membership increased, and both the AFL and CIO agreed to a no-strike pledge during the war.

After the war, with the rash of strikes and passage of the Taft-Hartley Act, there was competition among the two major unions, and each attempted to raid members from the other.[58] Further, the CIO lost nearly 1 million members when it expelled 11 of its national unions during 1949–1950 on charges of communist domination. The CIO, additionally, had attained only half of the membership of the AFL, and "it was evident that a merger of the two federations might effect substantial economies of scale, if only by eliminating duplication of effort and improving coordination."[59] Joining together, it was hoped, might also help to strengthen unionism so as to pressure Congress to eliminate some of the more disliked provisions of the Taft-Hartley Act, such as Section 14(b) (providing for the passage of state right-to-work laws).

As a result of such forces, the two unions merged in 1955, forming a new federation, the AFL-CIO, with a combined membership of slightly more than 16 million workers. In spite of its increased power with such a combined workforce, the success of the AFL-CIO has been mixed since the merger. The AFL-CIO was unable to influence the repeal of Section 14(b) of Taft-Hartley; union membership grew at a slow rate; corruption was soon found in certain national unions in the federation, culminating in the passage of the Landrum-Griffin Act in 1959; the powerful Teamsters Union was expelled from the AFL-CIO when it refused to fire its president, Jimmy Hoffa; in 1967, the United Auto Workers, with a membership of about 1.4 million members, left the AFL-CIO. On the other hand, the growth of unionism in the federal civil service (and in other public institutions) was paying off; and substantial gains were made in white-collar unionization. The relatively small growth of membership in the AFL-CIO up through 1974 is illustrated in Figure 14–2.

It was more recently reported that total AFL-CIO membership declined by 50,000 from 1975 to 1977.[60] Also very important to note is that union membership as a *percentage* of the total labor force has dropped since the 1950's, from 25.2 in 1956 to 21.7 in 1974.[61] Further, it was reported late in 1977 that there has been an increasing trend in employees "dumping" their unions by means of decertification elections as provided by the Taft-Hartley Act. For example, the number of workers lost by their unions in such elections increased from 8556 in fiscal year 1973 to 19,167 in fiscal year 1977.[62]

One reason for these trends is that most of the large firms that were "unionizable" have now already been unionized. Also, as Schmidman has hypothesized:

Demographic changes in the labor force will force organized labor to face the challenge of . . .the restructuring of appeals to the unorganized. [Among these are the] larger numbers of younger workers with higher

Year	Total, all unions	American Federation of Labor	Congress of Industrial Organizations[2]	Unaffiliated
1897	440	265		175
1900	791	548		243
1910	2,116	1,562		554
1920	5,034	4,079		955
1930	3,632	2,961		671
1933	2,857	2,127		730
1940	8,944	4,247	3,625	1,072
1945	14,796	6,931	6,000	1,865
1947	15,414	7,578	6,000	1,836
1953	17,860	10,778	5,252	1,830
1955	17,749	16,062		1,688
1960	18,117	15,072		3,045
1965	18,519	15,604		2,915
1968	20,258	15,608		4,650
1970	20,752	15,978		4,773
1974	21,643	16,938		4,705

[1]Includes members outside of the United States, primarily in Canada.
[2]Organized in 1938.
Data compiled by the Bureau of Labor Statistics from various sources.

Figure 14–2 *Labor union membership, selected years, 1897–1974 (in thousands).*[1] *[From* Brief History of the American Labor Movement, *U.S. Department of Labor, Bureau of Labor Statistics, Bulletin 1000 (Washington, D.C.: Government Printing Office, 1976), p. 52.]*

levels of educational attainment . . . . The new breed of worker/union member may be more interested in obtaining some personal satisfaction from his work than the older worker who views work as a means to an end.[63]

Before examining further reasons why employees join or refrain from joining unions, we will focus attention on the structure of American unions in this country today.

THE STRUCTURE OF AMERICAN UNIONISM

There are a number of organizations that form the overall union structure in the United States. There are three basic ones, however: (1) the AFL-CIO, which is a federation of (2) more than 150 national or "international" unions (so called because they have members in Canada as well as the United States), each of which is comprised of (3) geographic regions or districts that contain numerous local unions. Some major internationals in this country are unaffiliated (such as the United Auto Workers), but as may be noted from Figure 14–2, in 1974, approximately 78.3 per cent of the 21,643,000 union members in the United States and Canada were affiliated with the AFL-CIO, and it was reported in 1976 that about 85 per cent of the American labor movement was affiliated with the AFL-CIO.[64] In this section we will briefly examine the structure and functions of these three levels of unionism to provide the reader with a background for understanding the three basic managerial decision areas with respect to unions: the organizing of unions, contract negotiation and contract administration and interpretation.

THE AFL-CIO

At the heart of the American labor movement is the AFL-CIO, which is a federation of international unions, but in effect is a "creature" of the internationals, whose interests the AFL-CIO is designed to serve. As Estey has indicated, there is an analogy between the AFL-CIO and the United Nations.[65] Both are voluntary associations composed of free and autonomous units. The AFL-CIO, does, however, have the power to charter, and suspend or expel its international unions for reasons of misconduct.

The governing body of the AFL-CIO is its convention (held every two years), which is attended by delegates from the affiliated internationals. The delegates elect officers, discuss important issues, adopt resolutions, and may change the AFL-CIO constitution. An executive council made up of the president, secretary treasurer, and 27 vice presidents run the federation between conventions.[66] In order to function financially, the AFL-CIO receives per capita dues from each of its international affiliates.

The AFL-CIO does not engage in any collective bargaining itself. Its primary service objectives are to engage in political activities such as attempting to pressure federal, state and local governments for legislation favorable to it and to support political candidates favoring its goals in election campaigns. Unions, under federal law, are prohibited from contributing funds to political candidates. The AFL-CIO, however, has developed a "political arm" called COPE (Committee on Political Education); the national unions have COPE departments, and local unions, COPE committees. With the contribution prohibition, COPE raises funds from voluntary contributions, and helps political candidates "deemed to be friends of labor [by] . . . doorbell-ringing, precinct-walking . . . from COPE volunteers, union members."[67]

The AFL-CIO also assists the international unions in helping to organize yet unorganized employees. It also has nine trade and industrial union departments with which most international unions affiliate. One of the functions of these departments is to provide research assistance to the internationals.

The International Unions

The governing body of international unions, like the AFL-CIO, is their conventions, to which its local unions send delegates. Between conventions, the international is run by an executive board made up of its officers elected by delegates from the locals.

The international union performs a number of vital functions. Unlike the AFL-CIO, it may actively assist the local unions in contract negotiations (and also in arbitration cases arising out of the grievance procedure which we will discuss later). One of its basic functions is to organize the unorganized and attempt to maintain membership in its already unionized locals. Such organizational efforts are at times expensive, but permitting "any significant number of nonunion competitors poses a threat to the conditions of employment that can be established in unionized enterprises."[68]

International unions also set up "strike benefit" funds in order to help their locals when strikes are called; they may also provide political services to their locals as well as research and statistical data. There are basically two types of internationals — craft and industrial — paralleling this earlier distinction made by the AFL and CIO prior to their merger. In general, industrial internationals have more control over the local unions than do craft internationals. In some industrial unions, we have seen increasing centralization of power and growing importance, as there have been a large number of national contract negotiations in such industries as rubber and steel. The international, much more powerful and closer to the local unions than the AFL-CIO, is financially supported by dues paid by local union members.

The Local Union

The local union, as a member of an international in the AFL-CIO, is the basic contact between the rank and file union member and his employer. It was reported in 1975 that there were about 76,000 locals belonging to over 115 internationals in the AFL-CIO.[69] At local meetings, with each union member having one vote, local officers are elected who represent the members of the local in both contract negotiations and in the handling of any employee grievances that may arise concerning the interpretation of the union contract. In industrial unions, where all members of a manufacturing plant, for instance, are members of the same union, a president, secretary treasurer, and, if the union is large enough, a full-time business agent will be chosen by the union's membership. Within each department, employees will elect a shop steward. The primary function of the stewards is to represent the workers, and shop stewards will usually be allowed a specified amount of time each week by the employer to carry on union business during working hours. Shop stewards are extremely important in the industrial local and provide a direct

INDUSTRIAL

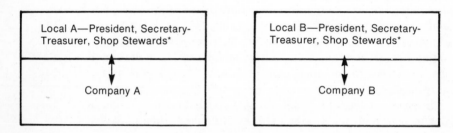

*With large locals sometimes full time paid business agent as well.

CRAFT

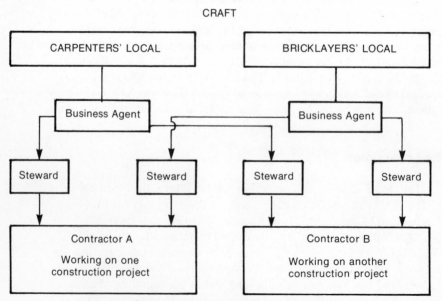

Figure 14-3 Local industrial and craft unions.

contact between the worker and his supervisor when disagreements arise.

In local craft unions, the key union official is a full-time paid business agent. He will represent members of the local in dealing with the employers of members of the craft union in a particular geographic area; a steward will be chosen to conduct union business with each employer. "Craft union stewards, furthermore, do not represent the members on the job. They represent the business agent, who is responsible for enforcing the [union employer] agreement."[70] The differences in local union relationships in industrial locals and craft locals is depicted in Figure 14–3.

Many members are somewhat apathetic, when it comes to attending local meetings and voting, although the rank and file, as Estey has put it, are the "ultimate authority" in unionism.[71] It was the rank and file workers, for example, who rejected by a 2 to 1 vote the contract agreed upon by the United Mine Workers' leadership and the coal operators in early 1978 during the longest strike in the union's history — 111 days.

Local unions must be viewed as heterogeneous political entities, representing many diverse interests of different groups within the local. Especially in industrial union locals, the local leadership may have to contend with different worker groups concerning various issues. As pointed out in Chapter 10, for example, incentive standards have sometimes been set too "loose" for certain jobs and too "tight" for others. There will be pressures on the part of the holders of the latter jobs for restudying the jobs to provide more equitable standards, while those workers whose standards have been set quite "loosely" would not be amenable to having their standards modified. With local officers elected by the rank and file members, they must, therefore, attempt to reconcile such issues to the satisfaction of the majority of the membership if they are to remain in office.[72]

Other Union or Organized Bodies

We have described the three basic levels of functioning in the AFL-CIO. There are, however, other organizational bodies within the federation, such as joint boards, conference boards, city central and state central bodies.[73] The discussion of these groups is beyond the scope of this text.

Additionally, in the United States there are a number of employee associations that have grown considerably in the 1970's. In 1974, more than 90 per cent of such association members were state and local government employees, and about half of all employee association members were teachers — about 1,200,000 in the National Education Association (NEA) and 85,000 in the American Association of University Professors (AAUP).[74] These associations are not new, but many of them recently became involved for the first time in collective bargaining. The NEA, for example, "consistently opposed any interruptions in school functions prior to 1961, but since then its position concerning the propriety of collective action has shown a definitely positive trend."[75] Finally, in 1968, the NEA passed a resolution urging its affiliates to work toward repealing state laws prohibiting strikes by public employees. During the 1970's there was increased teacher militancy, with 154 teacher strikes reported during the 1973–1974 school year.[76] Some of these were conducted by a teachers' affiliate of the AFL-CIO (the American Federation of Teachers), but many others were instigated by NEA affiliates. In consequence, by 1975, "few in the public could distinguish between the NEA and AFT affiliates, particularly in terms of their activities as bargaining agents."[77] Thus, the NEA, which was once a purely professional employee association, has taken on characteristics of and engaged in behavior comparable to unions within the structure of the AFL-CIO. Even the more conservative (and much smaller) AAUP appears to be moving in similar directions, for in 1972 it voted to pursue collective bargaining as one additional way of meeting its goals. With inflationary wage increases having been negotiated by such unions as the United Mine Workers in 1978 (about a 37 per cent increase in wages and employee benefits over a three year period), contrasted with declining enrollments and financial difficulties accompanied with relatively modest salary increases in much of higher education during an inflationary period, it will be interesting to see whether such historically conservative employee associations as the AAUP continue to move more in the direction of assuming activities like those undertaken for years by traditional unions in the United States.

REASONS FOR JOINING UNIONS

In the previous section, we have noted some of the more significant trends in union growth in the United States. We now raise the question: "Why have employees joined and continue to join unions; or conversely, why do many people *avoid* joining unions?"

One basic reason why employees join unions is that they must do so. With the union shop, the union hiring hall in the building and construction trades, and sometimes agency shops, workers have no choice but to join a union (or in the agency shop to support the union by paying the equivalent of initiation fees and union dues). By law, an exclusive bargaining unit must represent all members in the unit regardless of membership or nonmembership (or agency shop dues-paying status). A 1973 survey of union contracts covering 1000 or more workers indicated that the percentage of contracts with union security provisions was high — 72.5 per cent of the agreements provided for union shops and 9.7 per cent for agency shops.[78] These agreements accounted for about 62.2 and 13.2 per cent, respectively, of the workers covered. As might be expected, with union power stronger in certain states to help prevent the passage of state right-to-work laws, union membership as a percentage of nonagricultural employment has tended to be higher in those states without such laws providing less union security. This pattern for 1971 is illustrated in Figure 14-4.

Although many employees have joined unions because they have had to in order to obtain and keep a job, one must be careful not to infer that this is a primary reason for joining unions. This is evidenced by the fact that even in right-to-work states many unions have increased their membership. Further, before a union or agency shop can be established, a union must be formed. Thus, the real question facing management is why employees form unions in the first place and why they often join voluntarily.

There are many reasons why employees may form or join a union voluntarily. Underlying all these reasons is the question of whether or not unionism will provide individuals with payoffs or benefits exceeding the costs of joining. By payoffs and costs, we do not mean only purely economic factors. Rather, we are referring to physiological, psychological, and sociological ones as well.

Different observers have provided different lists of reasons why employees do form or join unions. Lawson, for example, has provided 15 reasons why employees form unions — from unfair and harsh treatment by supervisors to being paid substandard wages.[79]

Many important reasons why employees join unions can be classified and related to Maslow's hierarchy of needs, discussed in Chapter 9.

1. Physiological needs can be better met if unions can improve the individual's wages. Further, unions may pressure management to improve working conditions in terms of occupational safety and health. Organized labor, for example was strongly behind the passage of OSHAct.

2. Unions can help individuals meet their safety and security needs to a greater extent. For example, employees cannot be arbitrarily discharged without reason by their supervisor under virtually all union

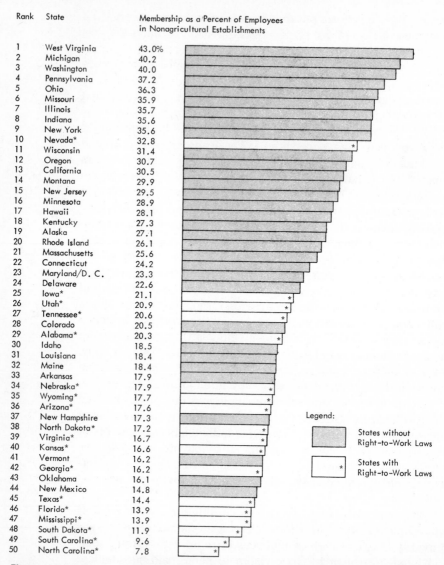

Rank	State	Membership as a Percent of Employees in Nonagricultural Establishments
1	West Virginia	43.0%
2	Michigan	40.2
3	Washington	40.0
4	Pennsylvania	37.2
5	Ohio	36.3
6	Missouri	35.9
7	Illinois	35.7
8	Indiana	35.6
9	New York	35.6
10	Nevada*	32.8
11	Wisconsin	31.4
12	Oregon	30.7
13	California	30.5
14	Montana	29.9
15	New Jersey	29.5
16	Minnesota	28.9
17	Hawaii	28.1
18	Kentucky	27.3
19	Alaska	27.1
20	Rhode Island	26.1
21	Massachusetts	25.6
22	Connecticut	24.2
23	Maryland/D. C.	23.3
24	Delaware	22.6
25	Iowa*	21.1
26	Utah*	20.9
27	Tennessee*	20.6
28	Colorado	20.5
29	Alabama*	20.3
30	Idaho	18.5
31	Louisiana	18.4
32	Maine	18.4
33	Arkansas	17.9
34	Nebraska*	17.9
35	Wyoming*	17.7
36	Arizona*	17.6
37	New Hampshire	17.3
38	North Dakota*	17.2
39	Virginia*	16.7
40	Kansas*	16.6
41	Vermont	16.2
42	Georgia*	16.2
43	Oklahoma	16.1
44	New Mexico	14.8
45	Texas*	14.4
46	Florida*	13.9
47	Mississippi*	13.9
48	South Dakota*	11.9
49	South Carolina*	9.6
50	North Carolina*	7.8

Legend:

States without Right-to-Work Laws

* States with Right-to-Work Laws

Figure 14–4 *Union membership as a proportion of nonagricultural employment by states, 1971.* [*From U.S. Department of Labor, Bureau of Labor Statistics:* Directory of National International Labor Unions in the United States, *1971, Bulletin No. 1750 (1972), p. 84.*]

contracts. Second, unions have been instrumental in helping to provide security by pressuring and obtaining such employee benefits as SUB, medical insurance, and pension plans. Finally, the seniority system provisions of contracts may provide workers with greater tenure protection from layoffs.

3. In some cases, unions have been able to meet employees' belongingness and esteem needs more fully. As Lawson has put it, many employees "believed that the union organization could relieve their

feelings of frustration and boredom by giving them a chance to achieve prestige and social recognition."[80] Active participation in a union, such as being elected shop steward or local union president, may provide individuals with considerable recognition among their fellow workers as well as helping to meet their self-actualization needs. Somewhat relatedly, with more and more companies hiring only college graduates for managerial and professional positions and no longer promoting rank-and-file workers into such jobs, many workers have come to believe (especially on assembly-line jobs) that there are no real opportunities to meet their esteem and self-actualization needs within the firm itself.

Employees may refrain from joining unions even if it would improve their economic position or working conditions because they fear a *loss* of status. This factor seems to be an important one, accounting for the reluctance of many professionals and salaried white-collar workers to join unions—they visualize a union as a "blue-collar" organization, representing hourly paid rather than salaried employees. They may also fear that there would be more constraints on their individual discretion if they joined a union. For example, unionization of professors at the Pennsylvania State University was rejected in 1977. If a union had been chosen to represent this group, professors would have had to deal with their supervisors (the department heads, who were often long-time colleagues) on a much more formal basis, since the latter would have represented "management" and would not have been members of the bargaining unit. The growth of teacher unionism and militancy, however, seems to indicate that such perceptions by professionals may be rapidly changing.

DECISION STRATEGIES WITH RESPECT TO UNIONS

There are three basic decision-making areas in which the firm may become involved with respect to unions. First, it may want to determine what strategies to take to discourage employees from voting for union representation. If the company is successful in such an endeavor, it will remain nonunionized and not become involved in the other two decision-making areas that unionized companies must face: (1) contract negotiations and (2) contract administration and interpretation. We will now consider each of these decision-making areas.

Unionization

Some firms may have no objections to becoming unionized. As indicated earlier: (1) unions are not "all bad" from the point of view of the company, but (2) unionization may constrain management decision making to a considerable extent. Further, the unionized company will face incurring the costs of employing personnel to deal with relations with the union — whether it be retaining an "outside" labor relations specialist or hiring a vice-president for labor relations (with a full-time staff).

In unionization drives the union is interested in winning the right to be the exclusive bargaining agent for all employees in any particular bargaining unit. Although there are different patterns of union strategies undertaken prior to representation elections, union activities such as the following are fairly typical.[81]

Prior to the actual beginning of a unionization drive, the union will usually attempt to obtain as much relevant information concerning the company as is possible. The union organizer will try to seek information about the employees and the community. Such information may be obtained by studying published material about the firm and by talking to local labor leaders. Once he has such information, the organizer will be ready for initial contact with the firm's employees. Union organizers often try to seek out particular employees who are strongly interested in the union and who show potential for assuming an effective leadership role. Next, the organizer will attempt to get a sufficient number of employees in the proposed bargaining unit (at least 30 per cent) to sign authorization cards or otherwise indicate their interest in unionization to have a representation election held.[82] The union organizer will typically communicate with both employees and their families, attempting to sell them on the benefits of unionization. Effective union organizers are likely to use a variety of communications methods in these efforts — letters, telephone conversations, calling at the employees' homes, etc.

Should the firm desire to prevent unionization, it will want to follow similar strategies as the union organizer — obtaining information about the union and communicating to its employees reasons why they should not unionize. Management may examine the organizing union's contracts with other companies, particularly those in the same industry; and may obtain useful information from contracts of other unions in its geographical location. Such information may (1) pinpoint weaknesses in union contracts from the employees' point of view which can be communicated to them, and (2) provide management with some idea of the relative past success of the union's representation efforts with other firms. Management can also obtain information and assistance in preventing the unionization of its firm from management consulting firms that specialize in these types of endeavor.[83] Certain professional associations may provide useful information to a management attempting to prevent unionization. For example, the National Association of Manufacturers (NAM) in late 1977 was reportedly about to announce the formation of a new committee to promote good employee relations. The aim of this committee, "is not to be antiunion but to 'educate' employers how to satisfy workers without a union."[84]

To be effective in preventing unionization, management also needs to keep appraised of possible reasons why its employees might join the union. Continually obtaining information from its supervisors and nonmanagerial employees about problem areas in the firm that might increase the probabilities of unionization may enable these problems to be resolved so that unionization drives may never even start or, once started, may be rejected by an organization's employees. In attempting to obtain such information, however, management must be careful that it is not committing an "unfair labor practice" as spelled out by the Wagner Act. Management may also obtain information about the data being provided by the organizing union to its employees.

With such information management may communicate with its employees as to reasons for remaining nonunionized. In such communications, facts about the union (e.g., a previous history of many long and bitter strikes) may be brought out that may induce those employees highly concerned with job security to reject unionization. Further, the company can present additional information as to the many employee benefits which it offers. As indicated in Chapter 12, employees often do not appreciate some of their important benefits partially because they do not understand just exactly what the organization offers. Gearing any such communications to its employees at *their* educational level is extremely important, for numerous studies have shown a tendency on the part of organizations to communicate with their employees at an educational level above that of many of their rank-and-file workers. For example, one study showed that in one firm workers understood less than 25 per cent of what their managers thought they did,[85] while in another it was found that more than half the articles from company newspapers written for employees were on a readability level above the level of 67 to 95 per cent of the adult population.[86]

Contract Negotiation

There are several important aspects of contract negotiation. In this section we will focus attention on three aspects of negotiations: (1) which company (or companies) will negotiate with which unions; (2) what types of issues typically form the *content* of collective bargaining contracts; and (3) what information and decision-making *processes* typically take place in contract negotiations.

Parties to the Negotiations

Depending upon the particular situations facing firms and unions, different patterns may exist as to who negotiates with whom. In examining this situation, we find Beal, Wickersham, and Kienast's classification of six different possible negotiation patterns most useful.[87] We will now briefly describe each of these patterns, a graphic illustration of which is provided in Figure 14–5.

The most common negotiating relationship in the United States is the simple one in which one employer negotiates a contract with one local. With large multiplant operations, on the other hand, some firms negotiate with numerous local unions from the same international. A typical example of this type of pattern would be General Motors negotiating with the United Auto Workers (UAW), with certain issues having companywide application (such as percentage wage increases) agreed to with the international, leaving local issues, such as those regarding seniority units, to be resolved between each plant and the local at that plant. Still in the one firm category is the pattern of one company negotiating contracts with several internationals. In some such cases, the different internationals dealing with the (large) firm "combine forces for bargaining purposes and negotiate with the employer on a united-front basis."[88] In the long copper strike of 1967–1968, for example, the United Steelworkers of America and more than 20 other unions tried (unsuccessfully) to seek company wide contracts.[89]

The other three patterns of negotiating involve associations of more than one employer dealing with one local, one international, or multiple-international unions. Employers in the building trades industry, for example, have typically formed associations to bargain with different locals (such as those representing carpenters and bricklayers) one at a time. A classic case of employers banding together to deal with many locals of one international is that of the Bituminous Coal Operators' Association dealing with the United Mine Workers. This pattern of negotiating is typical in cases in which there are a number of smaller companies who perceive a need for banding together against a powerful international union. Employer associations may also bargain with more than one international; e.g., in the lumber industry on the west coast, an employer association has bargained with several industrial internationals such as paper makers and wood workers.

In some industries, such as automotive and steel, "pattern

1. One employer—one local

2. One employer—one international

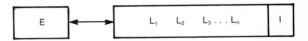

3. One employer—more than one international

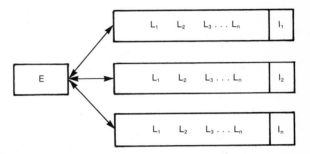

4. Employer association—one local

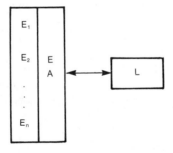

5. Employer association—one international

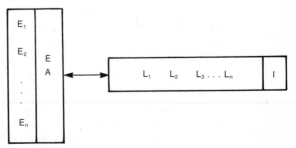

Figure 14–5 *Different contract negotiation patterns.*
Illustration continued on following page.

6. Employer association—more than one international

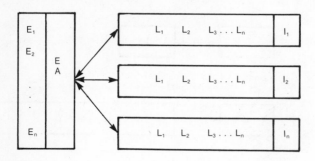

Notation

E = Employer

L = Local

I = International

EA = Employer Association

Figure 14-5 Continued.

bargaining" has existed. This is a "practice of following the lead on wages and/or some significant non-wage bargaining development established by a union and a major employer in a particular industry by other firms in that same industry."[90] In such cases, although the union (e.g., the UAW) and the major automotive firms "still preserve the appearance of separate negotiations but employers engage in constant communication and information-sharing as the nearly simultaneous negotiation sessions go forward."[91] Thus, although no multiemployer associations exist under such conditions, in fact the interfirm relationship is very close.

Contract Issues

Different authorities have classified typical issues negotiated in labor-management contracts in different ways. Davey, for example, has taken the position that although the substantive content of matters bargained about has expanded considerably over the years, in comparing an 1893 agreement between Chicago Contractors and the Lathers' union with the 1967–1970 John Deere-UAW contracts: *"Both the 1893 contract and the Deere-UAW contract cover the same basic trinity of wages, hours and other conditions of employment."*[92] Although these three essentials are contained in all collective bargaining agreements, we believe that the more elaborate classification of labor-management content clauses provided by Randle and Wortman will provide the reader with a better idea of the substantive content contained in today's typical contract. These authors have distinguished six basic types of contract clauses, emphasizing that there may be little uniformity among contracts in the specific ways in which these clauses are designed.[93]

The typical contract will contain a *preamble* and *purpose* clauses. Such clauses outline, in general, the purpose of the agreement, make pledges of goodwill, and may provide for no-strike pledges on the part of the union for the duration of the contract.

There are also security clauses. This category is rapidly becoming one of the largest in contract agreements, as might be expected in light of our discussion of the expansion of individual security employee benefits in Chapter 12. Security, in this classification, refers not only to individual security, e.g., seniority systems as well as employee benefits, but also to both management and union security. By management security we mean the rights and prerogatives that management has to run a firm as it sees fit. In nonunionized firms, this right to manage is not constrained by contracts with unions on such matters as to how overtime work must be allocated or how employees are to be disciplined. Without delving into the theoretical aspects of "the right to manage," we will simply state that firms often attempt to define and limit the scope of collective bargaining to concrete terms. "Employers wish to draw a clear line between management functions immune to contractual rule-making and those properly amenable to joint decision-making."[94] Union security, on the other hand, refers to such matters as recognition of the union and the inclusion of provisions calling for a union shop.

Next are clauses dealing with various forms of compensation, which we have discussed in previous chapters — incentive systems, job standards, and pay for vacations.

Working-conditions clauses define such matters as "the work-week, hours, overtime, shifts, Sunday and holiday work, health, hygiene, and safety."[95]

Enforcement clauses are common in labor management contracts. Very frequently, contracts spell out a grievance procedure and provide for binding arbitration if no agreement can be reached through the grievance procedure, as we will discuss later.

Finally, management and the union need to spell out the length of time the contract is to be in effect and methods of contract renewal. Labor management contracts may be negotiated for one, two, or three years, or longer. It was reported that in 1973, for example, "51 percent of the workers covered by 1339 major agreements had 3-year contracts, while the next largest group, 21 percent, were working under agreements of twenty-five to thirty-five months' duration."[96]

Decision Making Processes in Negotiations[97]

Once a firm has been unionized, the personnel or labor relations manager is confronted with two basic decision areas — preparing for and participating in contract negotiations, and dealing with grievances and arbitration. As far as contract negotiation is concerned, the personnel manager's responsibilities are continuous ones throughout the duration of the contract and are not just confined to the actual negotiations themselves. It is being increasingly recognized that much preparatory work is required between contract negotiations if the firm is to be as successful as possible in dealing with the union. Further, proactive union leaders are continuously preparing for future negotiations throughout the duration of the contract.

Unions ordinarily initiate contract negotiations with a set of demands to be incorporated into the labor management agreement. Increasingly, managements are prepared to present a series of counterdemands. Prior to this time, however, both the union and management should be actively preparing for the negotiations. This preparation involves two basic steps — engaging in an information seeking process attempting to assess the other party's strength and weaknesses, and building a factual basis for its own demands (or counterdemands). Unions also often expend considerable efforts in publicizing their demands to their workers through the steward system and by word of mouth, for ultimately it will be members of the local unions who accept or reject any agreement entered into by their bargaining representatives.

In many ways, the contract negotiation preparation efforts undertaken by management parallel those of the union. The company attempts to assess the union's strength, to anticipate what the union's demands might be (and whenever possible, cost them out), and it talks to its supervisors about problems that they have encountered in the existing contract and analyzes patterns of grievances that have arisen under the present contract. These two information sources assume that the company already has a contract and is not negotiating with a union for the first time. As Randle and Wortman have pointed out:

> Management is seldom entirely satisfied with the way the contract has functioned over the past contract period and may be able to demonstrate that specific abuses have resulted. Possibly the seniority system has affected efficiency of operations or work-stoppages or illegal slow-downs have occurred.[98]

Management, in anticipating union demands, may also examine other recent labor management agreements in its industry (or others), recognizing that the union may try to "keep up" with other union successes.

The union will, in turn, talk to its own members to see what issues are important to them, look to other recent labor-management contracts to see what their peers have obtained, analyze grievance patterns in the present contract, and assess the economic strength of the employer — trends in sales, profits, return on investment, etc. Both simulation and computerization may be effective aids in the information-gathering process.

Information such as this may provide the basis for proposals on the part of both the union and management. Usually, both parties will incorporate more in their demands and counterdemands than they realistically expect. Since the final agreement may be the result of some "pretty tall horsetrading," both union and management proposals "usually contain from the start a certain number of built-in bargaining points that are intended to be thrown away, or swapped for something else, at the last moment."[99]

The actual negotiation process varies considerably from one situation to the other. However, certain guidelines have been put forth, which, if followed, may help facilitate the negotiation process. Privacy of the negotiations seems generally to be considered advisable, with the presence of outsiders tending to inhibit negotiations.[100] Davey has suggested a number of other successful resolution conditions. Some of the more important conditions include:[101]

1. Both negotiating committees should be reasonably small which tends to decrease the probabilities of much irrelevant information being introduced.

2. One person should be in charge of conducting the negotiations for each side so that an undivided front can be maintained.

3. Exchange of demands by each side prior to actual negotiations will speed up the negotiations.

4. Negotiators for both sides should have the power to make decisive commitments. Since in most cases the union's agreement must be ratified by its membership, this may create serious problems. In fact, trends in increasing membership rejections in the past few decades have been reported. For example, the director of the Federal Mediation and Conciliation Service indicated that "by early 1962, mediator reports indicated a sharp upsurge of membership rejections."[102]

5. The negotiators should first resolve the less controversial issues and then proceed to the more difficult issues. This narrows the areas of real conflict, and hence, may make ultimate agreement usually based on compromises easier.

6. The difficult issues can be divided into those that involve monetary outlays and those which do not; the noneconomic issues may then be "negotiated individually in terms of their intrinsic merit rather than in terms of the bargaining strength"[103] of the two parties; and a decision must be made as to whether to bargain the monetary outlay issues one by one, or all together as a package.

Davey has pointed out that nearly all management negotiators and most union negotiators favor the "total economic package" approach. Often management may be indifferent as to the "mix" of wage increases as opposed to benefit increases — it is primarily concerned with the total outlay of funds it will have to make. Unions, on the other hand, may be much more interested in the monetary outlay mix. In the 111-day 1977–1978 UMW strike, for example, the miners, in rejecting an agreement between the UMW and the coal producers, probably did so more because of a concern about health insurance costs to them and pensions for retired miners than to purely wage issues.

Both management and labor must estimate the impact of their respective decisions to permit a strike. Typically, when impasses have been reached in negotiations, management must choose between accepting "excessive" union demands as opposed to the threatened loss of profits if the plant has to be shut down.[104] Further, management must decide under conditions of uncertainty, in which not only "taking a strike" but the duration of a possible strike is involved. Unions, on the other hand, also face a difficult choice: (1) accept management's not wholly satisfactory offer or (2) face the temporary loss of income during the strike and assume the even greater risks that management will replace the strikers with other workers or go out of business. Union members also face a difficult choice because their livelihoods are at stake.[105]

Under the Taft-Hartley Act, when a dispute arises over the renewal of a contract, the parties are required to notify the Federal Mediation and Conciliation Service. The FMCS is also active in the field of preventive mediation and often enters labor disputes before this notification date. Although the FMCS has *no power* to compel a settlement, it may provide a useful service in facilitating an agreement between management and the union. In fiscal year 1975, for example, the FMCS was involved in 19,540 dispute cases involving negotiating an initial contract, contract renewals, and contract reopenings.[106] As Hagburg and Levine have pointed out:

> Through the utilization of interpersonal skills, the mediator is generally able to close the gap and bring the parties closer to a mutuality of interests and the end product — a labor contract. . . . The parties in mature labor relations generally recognize that they need some help to change postures and yet "save face."[107]

Once management and labor have resolved their contract negotiation issues, with or without a strike or mediation, they must focus attention on contract interpretation and administration. We will now turn our attention to this facet of labor management relations.

Contract Interpretation and Administration

In nonunion organizations, management establishes rules for employee behavior, management enforces these rules, and if these rules are violated, management disciplines an employee as it wishes. In unionized firms, on the other hand, many rules for behavior are spelled out in the labor management contract and a formalized grievance procedure is provided for. A grievance may be filed requesting management to reverse some action (such as disciplining an employee), do something that it has not done, or change some decision affecting the workers employed. For example, an employee may believe that a supervisor has disciplined him too harshly for reporting to work 5 minutes late; or a worker may believe that management's requiring him to follow a new speeded-up work procedure is in violation of the union contract. In a vast majority of contracts, binding arbitration by a third party is spelled out as the last resort, should management and the union fail to settle the grievance by themselves. In 1973, for example, in industrial contractual agreements 6,625,100 out of 6,723,000 workers, or about 98.5 per cent were covered by both grievance processes and binding arbitration.[108]

This contract interpretation and administration process has three different aspects: (1) management's taking or intending to take an action believed by an employee or groups of employees to be unfair, (2) the establishment of a formalized grievance procedure to attempt to resolve these issues, and (3) binding arbitration. The most common type of cases brought up in the grievance procedure is disciplinary cases.[109] We will focus our primary attention on this type of case because of its relatively high frequency and also because discipline is a very important aspect of employee management relations in nonunionized as well as unionized firms. Fair and somewhat similar disciplinary procedures can and should be spelled out regardless of whether the organization is unionized or not. Further, in only an *extremely small* number of union contracts is there no reference to *both* a grievance procedure and arbitration; the same is true of provisions for a grievance procedure only but for no binding arbitration.[110] We will now discuss each of these three aspects of what some refer to as a system of "industrial jurisprudence."

Discipline: A Major Source of Grievances

Establishing rules for proper behavior and disciplining individuals for failure to behave in a certain way is common throughout society. Parents discipline their children and informal social groups may discipline their members in much the same way as supervisors discipline their subordinates in formal organizations.

Discipline is usually thought of as being applied only when other measures have failed — the "fair" and nonpunitive parent or supervisor will usually attempt to induce desired behavior by other means, and it is only when such means do not work that the child or subordinate is disciplined. Two complementary approaches to fair discipline have been put forth as having validity in business organizations, whether union organized or not. We will now discuss each of these.

The "hot-stove rule." A number of years ago, Douglas McGregor drew the analogy between touching a hot stove and being subjected to discipline.[111] If a person touches a hot stove, he is burned *immediately, with warning, consistently,* and *impersonally.* McGregor believed that individuals should be disciplined for violating organization rules and regulations in an analogous manner. Immediate discipline raises no questions as to cause and effect — the individual knows specifically what he is being disciplined for, and the act and discipline take place almost as if they constituted the same event. The "hot-stove rule" postulates that, like touching the stove, industrial discipline should be given with warning — the individual should know in advance as to how he will be punished if he engages in certain forms of behavior. *Every time* the individual touches the stove he is burned — so also should industrial discipline be consistent, so that there will not be confusion as to which types of behavior are permissible and which are not. Finally, the stove is impersonal and plays no favorites — it burns everyone who touches it. So also, according to the "hot-stove rule," should industrial discipline be impersonal. All employees should be treated the same for any particular offense so that there will be no favoritism on the part of the supervisor.

There appears to be considerable psychological merit to the general philosophy of "hot-stove rule" discipline. However, it should be recognized that the conditions under which different individuals break a particular rule may not always be exactly the same, and that in some cases, mitigating circumstances do occur which should be taken into consideration. It is with respect to some of these "mitigating circumstances," in fact, that grievances possibly leading to arbitration are filed.

Progressive discipline. In recent decades many organizations have moved toward what is called progressive discipline. This type of system consists of several steps leading from an oral warning to discharge. For example, Randle and Wortman have indicated that a progressive discipline system may involve the following six steps.

1. For the first offense, a "friendly discussion" with the violator and a warning as to why further occurrences of the offense cannot be tolerated.

2. For the second violation of the rule, a stronger oral warning to the employee.

3. For the third violation, a formal written warning.

4. For the fourth violation, a written warning, along with suspension from the job (without pay) for a few days.

5. For the fifth violation, suspension from the job without pay for a longer period of time.

6. Finally, discharge.[112]

The progressively more serious penalties are for the *same* offense. For example, if an individual comes to work 30 minutes late on one day and then, the following week is inexcusably absent from work without giving prior notice, the first step of progressive discipline would be applied to each offense, not step one for the tardiness, and step two for the unjustifiable absenteeism. Some offenses are, without question, much more serious than others, so that the steps in progressive discipline may vary by offense. The "friendly discussion" for the first 30-minute tardiness may be quite appropriate; but smoking in a highly dangerous area of a plant, where a spark might ignite an explosion, might call for discharge as the penalty for the first offense (*if* the employee who broke the rule lives to tell about it). Many union contracts provide rules for forgiveness of certain offenses if they are not repeated again within a certain period of time. For example, if an employee has been late for work four times in three months and is given a step 4 suspension from the job for a few days but then reports promptly to work every day for a period of two years, the first four offenses may then be "removed from his record," and should he be late to work again in the future, the progressive discipline would revert back to the first "friendly discussion" step again.

Finally, in unionized situations, it is extremely important that supervisors throughout a plant (or firm) are consistent in disciplining employees according to the provisions of the collective bargaining agreement. If one supervisor in one department does not discipline an employee for breaking a rule while another does, the union has good grounds for accusing management of favoritism, and in such cases, should the parties fail to resolve the disciplinary case in the grievance procedure, arbitrators will almost universally rule in favor of the union. For this reason, providing training to supervisors as to contract provisions and "shop rules" that are often appended to labor management contracts is of considerable importance.

The Grievance Procedure

This section of the chapter is entitled "Contract Administration *and Interpretation*" since the purpose of incorporating grievance procedures in labor management contracts is not only to provide for fair treatment of employees but also to serve as a vehicle for *clarifying and interpreting* any provisions of the contract vis-a-vis employee management relations which may be vague or unclear. For example, due to changing technology, management may change some work procedures — an action the company believes is congruent with the contract but which its employees and union do not.

The grievance procedure will be quite different in craft as opposed to industrial unions. In craft unions, workers are skilled individuals who know their jobs, and what the work rules are. For this reason, craft union stewards rarely argue grievances with "gang bosses" because they rarely have to, and craft unions "resort to arbitration over disputes with the employer much less frequently than industrial unions."[113]

In manufacturing operations where industrial unions exist, on the other hand, many workers are semiskilled or unskilled, may move around from one job to another, and not really have a craft in which they have expertise. In such situations, there is more confusion as to just what the work rules are and, hence, more disciplinary cases and other actions taken on the part of management that are challenged by the union.

Typically, both management and the union would like to resolve any grievances (in their favor) in the quickest and easiest way possible or, even better, prevent grievances from occurring in the first place. Sometimes employees, when discovering that a supervisor is about to call for a new work procedure that they believe is not congruent with the contract, may be able to persuade him to change his mind, so that a grievance never materializes. Further, if a grievance is filed, both parties will first try to resolve it at a lower level in the organization and then move to higher levels of discussion only if this fails.

In industrial unions, the shop stewards play a critical role in the grievance procedure. These union officials are elected by the members of their own department and are typically given time off with pay to help resolve issues between a worker and his supervisor, and if no agreement is reached they formally file a grievance.

If the shop steward is unable to resolve an issue with the supervisor and a grievance is filed, a grievance committee composed of local union officers typically meets with higher level management, e.g., the plant manager and personnel or labor relations director, to try to resolve the issue. If this procedure fails, then the grievance would be taken to an arbitrator, where a decision resolving the dispute would be handed down that is binding on both parties. For cost and other reasons, there has been a trend of both managements and unions to "avoid arbitration by working hard at settling their disagreements within the grievance procedures";[114] only a relatively few grievances ultimately work their way up to arbitration.

Arbitration

In union contracts providing for arbitration, management and the union have two basic decisions to make: (1) whether to go to arbitration (or give in to the other party's position) and (2) if arbitration is chosen, choosing a particular arbitrator.

In deciding whether to go to arbitration, which may be costly due to arbitrator's fees, and the involvement of management and union officials, both "rational" managements and unions should weigh the costs of not going to arbitration against the probable costs (depending on how the arbitrator rules) of going to arbitration. In some cases, knowledgeable labor relations managers or union officials may be able to predict fairly well what the outcome of an arbitrator's decision will be with respect to a specific case. To help the parties pick an arbitrator or arbitrators, either the private American Arbitration Association or the Federal Mediation and Conciliation Service will provide both parties with lists of professional arbitrators who are considered qualified. If management and the union have difficulty in picking an arbitrator for a particular case or series of cases, sometimes they will obtain a list of five potential arbitrators and each side will take turns in crossing off one arbitrator's name as unwanted until only one person is left. Typically management and the union will each pay 50 per cent of the fees and expenses of arbitrators.

Once an arbitrator has been chosen, a hearing date or dates will be set, and hearings that are quasijudicial in nature will be held. Witnesses may be called in and cross-examined by both management and union officials, and in some states witnesses may be subpoened.[115] For management, the labor relations or personnel manager or an outside attorney will be responsible in the hearing, whereas a union official, often someone from the international union, will be responsible for upholding the union position. We use the word "quasijudicial" because, although following procedures similar to those in civil or criminal court cases, arbitration hearings tend to be more informal.

In judging the merits of cases and rendering awards, arbitrators will often follow past precedents established by other arbitrators, but they are not legally bound to do so. It is for this reason that an informed management or union can predict with quite high probabilities in *some* cases, whether or not they will "win the case" in arbitration. In one company, for example, a fork-lift driver lied on his application form by not indicating that he was subject to epileptic seizures and was discharged by management when they found out because they were concerned that he might injure himself or others while having an epileptic seizure. The discharge was protested by the union and could not be resolved in the grievance procedure. The labor relations manager confidently forced the case into arbitration on the basis that arbitrators in previous cases regarding lying on application forms had generally ruled in favor of the employee *if* the untruth would have *no bearing* on job performance but in favor of management if the application form statement mistruth *could cause on-the-job problems*. The labor relations manager's confidence in "winning" the case based on this past precedent was justified when the arbitrator upheld the company's position.

Arbitrators may rule totally in favor of the company or union or they may render a "compromise award." In one case, for example, a truck driver (whose truck carried perishable merchandise) was suddenly discharged by his supervisor for failing to report to work on time. The supervisor had been very negligent in warning the driver about this offense, which had occurred literally dozens of times in the past. When the case went to arbitration, it was ruled that the discharge was too serious a disciplinary measure in light of the failure of the supervisor to have taken any really strong disciplinary actions previously (such as a written warning and a two day suspension without pay) and called for reinstatement of the worker but with only *partial* back pay since his behavior was also deplorable. Discharge, it should be noted, is regarded by many as "industrial capital punishment," and typically management will need a strong case to gain support of a discharge ruling by an arbitrator.

Two final points are in order concerning arbitration. First, as specified by most union contracts, the arbitrator's decision is final and binding. This has also been reinforced by United States Supreme Court decisions. The only exceptions to this would be that if there is evidence that the decision "was influenced by corruption, fraud, or other undue means," the courts will set aside an award, and in *some* cases, courts will set aside an award "if it is clear that it exceeds the authority vested in the arbitrator by the parties."[116]

Second, the arbitration of grievances has been criticized because the procedure is slow and costly. It may be several months after an employee has been discharged, for example, before the case is heard, and more time will elapse between the hearing and the rendering of the award by the arbitrator.[117]

MANAGEMENT SCIENCE, COMPUTERS, AND CONTINGENCIES

Management Science and Computers

Both managements and unions have relied on computerization in dealing with labor management relations problems. As far back as 1966 it was reported that in "the bitter fight over union coalition bargaining that has engulfed the electrical industry negotiations," the Industrial Union Department (IUD) of the AFL-CIO was testing the use of computers as a bargaining table aid in negotiations with General Electric and Westinghouse.[118] What the Industrial Union Department began doing in the mid-1960's with respect to helping to improve unions' positions in negotiations with firms was developing through computerization much better pictures of vital data concerning the organizations with which AFL-CIO unions were negotiating. For example in collective bargaining:

> . . . a union may find it necessary to develop all necessary facts about a particular corporation's financial structure, the interlocking relationships of the members of its board of directors, a history of mergers and acquisitions, and the financial facts about them; and the nature of its collective bargaining relationships, as well as the content of its various labor-management agreements.[119]

Such data as the above must be drawn from many sources, and without computerization the development of these data would be extremely time consuming. Further, as Ginsburg has pointed out, in human analysis of this type individuals "may lose sight of elusive but important trends or relationships among all the data."[120]

More recently, it was reported that both the United Steelworkers and the International Association of Machinists were using the computer in bargaining.[121] Further, in preparation for bargaining, it was found that unions "have been so well prepared that in some instances they have obtained fringe benefits and other contract gains based almost entirely on their computer output comparisons and analyses of company or industry contract provisions."[122]

Unions have also relied on computer-generated data in organizing campaigns and for political campaign purposes. The Industrial Union Department's Data Bank, for example, was designed to make available "information on contracts covering workers in other plants of the same company where the organizing drive is directed;"[123] its computer memory had stored in it, as reported in 1967, all the facts of more than 50,000 representation elections that the NLRB had supervised during the previous six years; the Industrial Union Department system was designed to be able to pinpoint the effect of its organizing efforts in different geographical areas. For example, a breakdown of membership campaigns by 13 industrial unions in 12 southern states indicated that both representation elections and the number of new workers organized in 1966 were running behind previous years' figures, which "was contrary to the impression of most union officials."[124]

With respect to political activity, the AFL-CIO's political arm, COPE, was using the computer facilities of the International Association of Machinists in preparing for the 1972 presidential election. Voter lists and union membership rolls in major industrial states were compared with the objective of discovering which union members were not registered.[125]

Some managements have also used the computer both in preparing for contract negotiations and during negotiations. In *preparing* for bargaining, 13 companies reported in 1970 that they had developed "specially devised programs to analyze the costs of anticipated demands or offers. There were four companies who had developed and were using mathematical or simulation models in preparing for bargaining."[126] This same survey also indicated that five companies were using mathematical or simulation models to analyze the impact of ultimate demand packages *during negotiations,* with one company using a "global model to develop bargaining item costs and project their effects on sales price, profit, etc."[127] Knowing the pay, seniority, age, and other characteristics of workers covered by a firm's contract with a union permits simulation to be an especially useful tool for testing union demands, particularly economic ones. For example, knowing the pay of each worker, and his or her tenure, a computerized simulation could quickly determine how much more it would cost the company if it were to accept a union's demand for four weeks paid vacation, rather than three, after 10 years of service. Noneconomic union demands, on the other hand, such as work rule changes, are much less amenable to simulation modeling.

And what about the future? *Business Week* raised the Utopian question several years ago:

Could union and management negotiators feed a computer with data supporting both labor's contract demands and the employer's financial position and prospects and let it work out the terms of an agreement?[128]

Although an appealing idea, one negotiator, when considering this question, raised the possibility that both management and labor would still have to negotiate, and perhaps go through a strike in order to agree upon just what was to be fed into the computer!

Contingencies

A major contingency concerning the way in which employee management relations will function is whether or not the firm is unionized. Unionization not only constrains managements' decisions with respect to "unfair labor practices" as spelled out in the Wagner Act, but management's decisions are also considerably influenced by union demands in the collective bargaining process. In nonunionized companies many of the decisions and approaches we have discussed throughout this text — setting rate ranges in wage and salary administration, the offering of profit sharing, pension and health insurance plans, the provision of incentive standards — are made unilaterally. With unionization, the union may be in a position to force, or at least pressure management to take action in many of these areas.

Whether a firm will be subjected to a unionization drive and, if so, what type of union is likely to gain representation by its employees are two factors also influenced by different conditions. First, one reason why employees join unions initially is that they believe their needs are not being met by management. Firms in which top management pays its employees well, provides them with opportunities for promotion and for self-actualization on the job when possible, and has adequate employee benefits (such as at the Lincoln Electric Company), are much less likely to be unionized in the first place than are firms which take less interest in their employees.

The type of technology predominating in an organization will also have an impact on both the probabilities of unionism and the type of union chosen. As pointed out earlier, firms in which skilled craft work predominates, such as in the building trades, if unionized, will be represented by craft unions, in which the number of grievances and cases taken to arbitration will be less than in mass production operations, which are typically represented by industrial unions. Further, technology *may* have an influence on the effectiveness of strikes as a weapon by unions. Although authorities disagree on the subject, we would tend to agree with the proposition that in highly automated, capital intensive industries, automated equipment may permit management to maintain uninterrupted production with supervisory personnel, if required, due to a strike by those nonmanagerial employees belonging to the union.[129] Another contingency for the extent of unionization expected is that mentioned early in the chapter — geography — with greater union concentration in the highly industrialized east, midwest, and west than in the south and southwest. Finally, organization size seems to be a factor in whether or not unions will be organized. Although, as reported in 1978, there was one *national* union with less than 100 members (steel engravers), generally speaking, "the larger the firm, the more likely it is for employees to be organized."[130] A basic reason for this is that the dollar organization costs per potential union member are generally less for larger firms than for very small ones.

SUMMARY

Employee management relations have been complicated considerably over the last century by unionization and the development of a complex legal framework in which union management relationships must operate. A major stimulus to the growth of unionism was the passage of the Wagner Act in 1935. Then, with large unions becoming extremely powerful, more of a balance in union management relations was struck with the passage 12 years later of the Taft-Hartley Act. There have been two basic structural models of unionism in existence in the United States — craft unions and industrial unions. Individuals may join unions to meet any one or more of a number of needs — from physiological to self-actualization. Three basic decision areas exist for management with respect to unions — those regarding unionization drives, contract negotiations, and contract interpretation and administration. Since the mid-1960's the computer and, to a lesser extent the management science technique of simulation, have come into play in union management decision making. Further, there are a number of contingencies that will influence whether firms will be susceptible to unionization, and if so, what type of union structure and power relationships will exist.

In many ways, this chapter encompasses *all* of the functional areas of personnel discussed throughout this text, especially when unionization is considered. An example of this relationship is illustrated in Figure 14–6. To be able to handle all of these

Chapter	Subject	Example
3	Human Resource Planning	Establishment of seniority units
4	Recruiting and Selection	Union security provisions — e.g., union hiring hall in building trades.
5	Performance Appraisal	Shop rules prescribing worker behavior often spelled out and appended to union contracts — management violation leading to grievance and possibly arbitration.
6–8	Training and Development	Union participation in designing apprenticeship programs. Educational simulation to train managers in collective bargaining.
9	Wage and Salary Administration	Wage rates negotiated in labor management contract.
10	Individual Incentives	Union participation in and grievances over time standards — sometimes union time study man checks management.
11	System Incentives	Scanlon plan effectiveness enhanced by union management collaboration.
12	Employee Benefits	SUB, health insurance, and pension benefits often negotiated with union.
13	Occupational Safety and Health	Strong union concern over employee safety and health — organized labor behind passage of OSHA.

Figure 14–6 *Functional personnel areas and employee management relations examples with emphasis on unionization.*

increasingly complex functions requires individuals of considerable stature — such as the new corporate hero, "Percy Personnel," whose trials and tribulations we will consider in our next
chapter.

DISCUSSION AND STUDY QUESTIONS

1. The legal environment with respect to unionization in the United
   States mutually interacts with actions taken by unions in a systems sense as defined in Chapter 1. That is, certain laws affect
   union behavior, which, in turn, may influence the introduction of
   new legislation, which in turn, modifies union behavior, etc.
   Discuss. Give your reasons for your answer.
2. a. Section 14(b) of the Taft-Hartley Act should be repealed be-
      cause it enables employees in states banning both union and
      agency shops who work in unionized firms to gain all the
      benefits of unionization without having to pay union dues or
      assessments that those employees who have voluntarily
      joined the union are required to pay. Discuss.
   b. A federal "right-to-work law" outlawing *all* union and agency
      shops should be enacted because in a free society, no individ-
      uals should be forced to join a union or pay union dues and
      assessments against their will. Discuss.
3. Which of the following are unfair labor practices under labor
   legislation covering the private sector in the United States?
   Which are not "unfair"? In each case, give your reasons why.
   a. The Acme Corporation wants to make sure that the union
      representing its employees is a reputable one and contributes
      $50,000 to the local union.
   b. The local union president at the Beaver Company demanded
      from management that Joel Rankin, a union member in good
      standing who had regularly paid his union dues and assess-
      ments, be discharged after Rankin had encouraged his fellow
      workers to seek a decertification election.
   c. Emil Jones believes that he has been disciplined unfairly by his
      supervisor and asks his shop steward to file a grievance in his
      behalf. While talking with the supervisor, the union steward
      becomes quite excited and uses some four letter words un-
      printable in this text.
   d. During heated contract negotiations between the Sloan com-
      pany's bargaining committee and that of its local union (assist-
      ed by the international), the vice-president of labor relations
      for the firm suggested to the international union representa-
      tive that the latter, the local union president, and himself
      "sneak off" and over a soft drink or cup of coffee try to break
      the impasse by themselves.
4. Historically, strong unions would have developed much earlier in
   the United States if it had not been for the "conspiracy doctrine,"
   and, after *Commonwealth vs. Hunt,* numerous other judicial decisions favoring management in union management disputes. Discuss. Give the reasons for your opinions.
5. With respect to union structure, which of the following statements is (or could be) true? Why?
   a. The AFL-CIO's latest strike with the major steel producers in
      the United States was a prolonged and bitter one.

    b. The Industrial Union Department of the United Mine Workers helped in the 1977–1978 coal dispute by providing computer-developed data as to the coal producers' financial strength, which was instrumental in the UMW ultimately obtaining a favorable contract.

    c. A representative of the United Auto Workers provided valuable assistance to his union when their last contract dispute with General Motors went to binding arbitration.

    d. A representative of the United Auto Workers provided valuable assistance to numerous Ford locals in binding arbitration cases arising out of grievances last year.

    e. Increased centralization of decision making in contract negotiations has taken place especially in such unions as the Bricklayers, Masons and Plasterers (AFL-CIO).

6. In which of the following cases do you think the individual involved would join the union?

    a. A university professor, whose marginal federal income tax rate is 40 per cent, whose average annual salary increases have been 5 per cent over the last five years, with an assumed annual national rate of inflation of 6 per cent over this period, and with "average" national annual wage increases of major unions assumed to be 8 to 9 per cent.

    b. A semi-skilled worker who has just been employed by a manufacturing firm represented by an industrial union that has negotiated a union shop provision in its contract in a state that has not passed a "right-to-work" law.

    c. A semi-skilled worker who has just been employed by a unionized firm in a state that has prohibited union and agency shops, but who, leaving the plant on his first full day on the job, was approached by "Big Joe," the union steward in his department and warned that if he wanted to "remain in one piece" he would join the union "as soon as possible."

7. In which of the following cases would one expect the ultimate resolution of a labor-management conflict to occur via binding arbitration?

    a. The Wilkins Company and its local union cannot agree on an overtime allocation provision in their contract negotiations.

    b. The MacDonald Construction Company has just taken a disciplinary action against one of its carpenters, which the employee believes is unfair.

    c. Joe Shultz, a member of one of the United Steelworkers of America locals, has been unexpectedly ordered to work overtime on Friday night by his supervisor when he has planned to go to the movies that night with his girlfriend, Nancy. Joe believes that the supervisor's order is in violation of the union contract.

    d. An employee of the United States Government who is a member of the American Federation of Government Employees (an AFL-CIO affiliate), believes that his supervisor has discriminated against him in giving him some work that is not part of his job, and hence violates the union contract.

    e. A unionized company with a very proactive labor relations manager who is extremely familiar with arbitrators' patterns of past rulings on almost every subject area covered by binding arbitration.

8. The Williamson Manufacturing Company, which manufactures a

variety of rubber products, has appended to its union contract a set of shop rules. One of the rules prohibits smoking in several of its departments, and for several years, "NO SMOKING" signs have been posted in each of these departments. After a few disciplinary oral warnings about three years ago, supervisors stopped enforcing the rule, even though it still is in the "shop rules." Just recently, Smith Adams, supervisor in one of these departments caught one of his employees, Will Brown, smoking in the department, gave him an oral warning, and threatened a written warning (the second step in the firm's "progressive discipline" procedure), if he caught Will smoking again. Will protested this oral warning and his shop steward filed a grievance.

  a. If this issue cannot be resolved in the grievance procedure, should management take the case to arbitration?

  b. What lessons may be learned by management from this case?

9. The ultimate reason for conflict between labor and management is lack of understanding. Therefore, it will someday be possible with improved computer technology to put the company's financial position, the union's contract demands, and the firm's counterdemands on a computer, and resolve disputes in contract negotiations without incurring strikes or, for that matter, going through the negotiating process. Discuss.

10. It is perfectly acceptable for unions in small firms to strike in order to obtain higher wages and better working conditions, because their strikes will not injure too many "innocent" third parties. However, strikes in such basic industries as coal, steel, and automotive may put workers in other industries out of work and "cripple" the economy. Therefore, they should be prohibited. Further, public employees, such as policemen, teachers, and firemen should also be prohibited from striking since such strikes can endanger the best interests of society. Discuss.

11. With higher levels of educational attainment today on the part of both workers and managers, differences between the two can be worked out on a much more "rational" basis than 50 years ago. Further, enlightened managements have offered their employees more and more benefits, as discussed in Chapter 12. Therefore, unions are no longer as necessary as they were 50 years ago and will gradually "fade away." Discuss.

12. Define each of the following terms. If any represents an "illegal" action indicate so and under what specific piece of legislation it is prohibited.

  a. "Yellow dog" contracts.

  b. Company unions.

  c. Court injunctions forcing unions to stop following a particular course of action.

  d. Secondary boycotts.

  e. Mediation.

Notes

[1]Much of this discussion is drawn from Edwin F. Beal et al., *The Practice of Collective Bargaining*, 5th ed. (Homewood, Ill.: Richard D. Irwin, Inc., 1976), pp. 16–17.

[2]Ibid., p. 16.

[3]Ibid., p. 17.

[4]Eugene C. Hagburg and Marvin J. Levine, *Labor Relations: An Integrated Perspective* (St. Paul, Minn.: West Publishing Company, 1978), p. 29.

[5]Ibid., p. 32.

[6]Marten Estey, *The Unions,* 2nd ed. (New York: Harcourt Brace Jovanovich, Inc., 1976), p. 98.

[7]Ibid.

[8]Hagburg and Levine, op. cit., p. 15.

[9]James W. Robinson, et al., *Introduction to Labor* (Englewood Cliffs, N.J.: Prentice-Hall, Inc., 1975), p. 50.

[10]See John R. Commons and Associates, *History of Labor in the United States,* Vol. 2 (New York: Augustus M. Kelley, 1966. Original edition, New York: The Macmillan Company, 1918).

[11]Robinson et al., op. cit., p. 84.

[12]Hagburg and Levine, op. cit., p. 17.

[13]Estey, op. cit., p. 100.

[14]Elias Lieberman, *Unions Before the Bar* (New York: Oxford Book Co., 1960).

[15]The details of the Pullman controversy described here are drawn from Robinson et al., op. cit., pp. 79–80.

[16]Much of this section is drawn from Estey, op. cit., pp. 102–103, and Robinson et al., op. cit., pp. 80–83.

[17]Ibid., p. 81.

[18]See Sections 6 and 20 of the Clayton Act, 38 Stat. 731 and 738.

[19]Estey, op. cit., p. 103.

[20]This case was *Duplex Printing Press Company vs. Deering,* 254 U.S. 443.

[21]See Estey, op. cit., p. 103.

[22]Hagburg and Levine, op. cit., p. 17.

[23]Ibid., p. 18.

[24]For a thorough discussion of the Railway Labor Act, see ibid., Chapter 10.

[25]Estey, op. cit., p. 105.

[26]Robinson et al., op. cit., p. 84. These authors have also pointed out that the Norris-LaGuardia Act destroyed most of the precedents in *Loewe vs. Lawlor,* including the ban on secondary boycotts.

[27]NLRA, 49 Stat. 449.

[28]Estey, op. cit., p. 108.

[29]Ibid., p. 109.

[30]These statements with regard to the five NLRA unfair labor practices are drawn from: *Federal Labor Laws and Programs,* U.S. Department of Labor, Bulletin 262/Revised September 1971 (Washington: U.S. Government Printing Office, 1971), pp. 12–15.

[31]This is the exact phraseology of Section 8 (a)(3) of the NLRA.

[32]Estey, op. cit., p. 112.

[33]"Carter's Push Was to Invoke Taft-Hartley," *New York Times,* March 12, 1978, Section 4, p. 1.

[34]This list is drawn from *Federal Labor Laws and Programs,* op. cit., pp. 15 ff.

[35]This is probably the most complex provision of the Taft-Hartley Act. For a further discussion of it, see ibid., pp. 16–17.

[36]"Prehire" agreements and requiring union membership after seven days of employment were still permitted in the building and construction industry, which was "the bastion of the closed shop." Estey, op. cit., p. 114.

[37]Except in national emergency situations as we will describe next.

[38]*Federal Labor Laws and Programs,* op. cit., p. 33.

[39]Ibid., pp. 33–34.

[40]Estey, op. cit., p. 116.

[41]Ibid., p. 118.

[42]Hagburg and Levine, op. cit., p. 204.

[43]Drawn from *Federal Labor Laws and Programs,* op. cit., pp. 39–40.

[44]For a more thorough discussion of the many complexities of Titles II-VI of the Landrum-Griffin Act, see ibid., pp. 40–50.

[45]See, for example, Hagburg and Levine, op. cit., p. 205.

[46]See 95th Congress, 1st Session, House Bill H.R. 8410; and 95th Congress, 2nd Session, Senate Bill S.2467. These two bills differed in a number of respects, and in the summer of 1978, the legislation failed passage in the Senate.

[47]Hagburg and Levine, op. cit., p. 167.

[48]For a discussion of these Executive Orders, see Hagburg and Levine, op. cit., Chapters 8 and 12. That unionization has also grown among state and local governmental employees is shown in Chapter 7 of ibid. For the text of Executive Order 11491, as amended, see Beal et al., op. cit., pp. 656–671.

[49]Hagburg and Levine, op. cit., p. 176.

[50]*Brief History of the American Labor Movement,* U.S. Department of Labor, Bureau of Labor Statistics, Bulletin 1000 (Washington: Government Printing Office, 1976), p. 1.

[51]Ibid., p. 5.

[52]Ibid., p. 7.

[53]Abraham L. Gitlow, *Labor and Industrial Society,* Rev. ed., (Homewood, Ill.: Richard D. Irwin, 1963), p. 53.

[54]Beal et al., op. cit., p. 29.

[55]*Brief History of the American Labor Movement,* op. cit., p. 14.

[56]Drawn from Robinson et al., op. cit., pp. 51–52.

[57]Ibid., p. 57.

[58]Estey, op. cit., p. 33, has indicated that the raiding was not very effective. In 1951–1952, for example, with 62,000 workers changing unions, the net result of these exchanges of members was that the AFL gained "a meager total of [only] 8,000 workers."

[59]Ibid., p. 32.

[60]"Labor's Creaking House," *Newsweek,* Dec. 12, 1977, p. 83.

[61]Hagburg and Levine, op. cit., p. 29.

[62]"The Mixed Results of Labor-Law Reform," *Business Week,* Nov. 7, 1977, p. 86.

[63]Cited from John Schmidman, *Unions in Post-Industrial Society,* Chapter 4, "A Model of Trade Unionism in Emerging Post-Industrialism," (University Park, Pa.: The Pennsylvania State University Press, 1979).

[64]Beal et al., op. cit., p. 86.

[65]Estey, op. cit., p. 39.

[66]The materials in this paragraph were drawn from Robinson, et al., op. cit., p. 67.

[67]Beal et al., op. cit., p. 86.

[68]Ibid., p. 79. Beal, et al., consider organizing the unorganized as *the* most important service provided by the international. Ibid.

[69]Robinson et al., op. cit., p. 84.

[70]Beal et al., op. cit., p. 71. This source provides a fairly detailed account of the differences between craft and industrial locals (pp. 67–76). For example, it was indicated that craft union locals seldom "find it necessary to take unresolved grievances to arbitration," and that the business agent usually settles differences directly with employers (p. 71).

[71]See Estey, op. cit., pp. 53ff.

[72]For an interesting analysis of different patterns of work group behavior in taking concerted action towards management, see Leonard R. Sayles, *The Behavior of Industrial Work Groups* (New York: John Wiley & Sons, Inc., 1958).

[73]See for example, Beal et al., op. cit., pp. 82–85.

[74]Estey, op. cit., p. 37.

[75]Hagburg and Levine, op. cit., p. 154.

[76]Beal et al., op. cit., p. 490.

[77]Ibid., p. 491.

[78]*Characteristics of Agreements Covering 1,000 Workers or More, July 1, 1973,* Bulletin 1822, U.S. Department of Labor, Bureau of Labor Statistics (Washington: Government Printing Office, 1973), p. 14.

[79]J. W. Lawson II, *How to Meet the Challenge of the Union Organizer* (Chicago: The Dartnell Corporation, 1969), p. 11.

[80]This section is drawn largely from ibid.

[81]This section is drawn largely from ibid.

[82]As indicated earlier, one of the provisions contained in the labor-reform legislation sponsored by President Carter during the 95th Congress was that of speeding up the unionization process by setting deadlines for representation elections.

[83]J. W. Lawson, op. cit., for example, founded the Southeastern Employers Service Corporation (SESCO), a private management consulting firm specializing in such fields of personnel as labor relations.

[84]"The New Chill in Labor Relations," *Business Week,* October 24, 1977, p. 33.

[85]Ralph G. Nichols, "Listening is Good Business," *Management of Personnel Quarterly,* 1 (Winter, 1962), pp. 212–217.

[86]Schuyler D. Hoslett, "Barriers to Communication," *Personnel,* 28 (September, 1951), pp. 108–114.

[87]The conceptual framework in this section is drawn from Beal, et al., op. cit., pp. 113–114.

[88]Harold W. Davey, *Contemporary Collective Bargaining,* 3rd ed. (Englewood Cliffs, N.J.: Prentice-Hall, Inc., 1972), p. 18.

[89]Ibid.

[90]Ibid. The pattern bargaining may also extend to other industries, sometimes even unrelated ones.

[91]Ibid., p. 38.

[92]Ibid., p. 102. Such items are mandatory issues for consideration in negotiations under Section 8(d) of the Taft-Hartley Act, which calls for bargaining in good faith with respect to "wages, hours, and other conditions of employment."

[93]This section draws heavily on C. Wilson Randle and Max S. Wortman, Jr., *Collective Bargaining: Principles and Practices,* 2nd ed. (Boston: Houghton Mifflin Co., 1966), pp. 80–81. For another classification of content items in collective bargaining contracts, see, for example, Beal et al., op. cit., pp. 252–257. These authors also emphasize the diversity in labor management contracts in spite of the fact that it is possible to classify contract items.

[94]Davey, op. cit., p. 103. For a more theoretical discussion of "management rights" see ibid., pp. 101ff.

[95]Randle and Wortman, op. cit., p. 81.

[96]Hagburg and Levine, op. cit., p. 56.

[97]There are many different types of negotiation processes, depending on which of the six negotiation patterns indicated is involved. In this discussion, we will think mostly in terms of one employer negotiating with one local or one international. Some of the points we will make, will, of course, be relevant to the other four bargaining patterns discussed previously.

[98]Randle and Wortman, op. cit., p. 191.

[99]Beal, et al., op. cit., p. 218.

[100]Ibid., p. 217.

[101]Davey, op. cit., p. 129. We have elaborated on some of Davey's points discussed here.

[102]Estey, op. cit., p. 53. The percentage of tentative contract rejections jumped from 8.7 in fiscal 1964 to 14.2 in fiscal 1967. From 1968–1975, however, this percentage ranged from 9.6 to 12.3, with an average percentage rate over this eight year period being 11.05. Hagburg and Levine, op. cit., p. 58.

[103]Davey, op. cit., p. 129.

[104]Beal et al., op. cit:, p. 220.

[105]Sometimes unions take strike votes at the beginning of the negotiations and unless any specific date for striking is set, the threat may hover over the negotiations and serve to strengthen the union negotiators' position. If the threat is turned into an ultimatum by setting a specific time for a strike, the uncertainty is lost and this technique will fail to strengthen the union's position. See ibid., pp. 221–224.

[106]Hagburg and Levine, op. cit., p. 93.

[107]Ibid., pp. 298–299.

[108]*Characteristics of Agreements Covering 1,000 Workers or More,* op. cit., p. 64.

[109]Of the thousands of cases arbitrated nationally each year, the common estimate is that more than one out of four involves a discipline issue. Estey, op. cit., p. 161.

[110]Only 22,400 workers out of the 6,723,000 mentioned above for 1973 worked under contracts providing a grievance procedure only; with only 75,500 working under a contract with reference to neither a grievance procedure nor arbitration. Ibid.

[111]The earliest reference to this concept which we have found is in George Strauss and Leonard R. Sayles, *Personnel: The Human Problems of Management* (Englewood Cliffs, N.J.: Prentice-Hall, Inc., 1960), pp. 288ff.

[112]Drawn from Randle and Wortman, op. cit., p. 538. It should be mentioned that some firms have fewer progressive disciplinary steps, e.g., only an oral warning, written warning, a disciplinary layoff, and discharge.

[113]Beal et al., op. cit., p. 400.

[114]Ibid., p. 418.

[115]Ibid., p. 419.

[116]Ibid.

[117]Some firms have attempted successfully to use "expedited arbitration" in which cumbersome courtroom procedures were dispensed with and by calling on an arbitrator to hear several cases sequentially on the same day. See ibid., pp. 421–422.

[118]"Computer Sits in on the Bargaining," *Business Week,* Sept. 10, 1966, p. 154.

[119]Woodrow L. Ginsburg, "Labor Turns to the Computer," *IUD Agenda,* 3 (September, 1967), p. 27.

[120]Ibid.

[121]"Bargaining by Electronics," *Business Week,* June 5, 1971, p. 78.

[122]Robert N. Pratt, "Computer Utilization in the Collective Bargaining Process," *Industrial Management Review,* 11 (Spring, 1970), p. 63.

[123]Ginsburg, op. cit., p. 29.

[124]"Computer Sits in on the Bargaining," op. cit., p. 154.

[125]"Bargaining by Electronics," op. cit., p. 78.

[126]Pratt, op. cit., pp. 60–61. We should also mention that educational simulation as discussed in Chapter 7, may be used to train managers in collective bargaining. See, for example, Morris Sackman, "Make Your Own Simulations to Train Public Administrators in Collective Bargaining," *Public Personnel Management,* 4 (July-August, 1975), pp. 231–237.

[127]Pratt, op. cit., p. 61.

[128]"Bargaining by Electronics," op. cit., p. 78.

[129]For a discussion of the arguments raised pro and con on the issue of the impact of technology and strikes, see Hagburg and Levine, op. cit., pp. 88–89. These authors take the same position that we have taken.

[130]Ibid., p. 34.

VI

EPILOGUE

15

PERCY'S PARADOXES AND THE "FEAST OF FOOLS"

In this text we have viewed the role of the personnel manager as that of a decision maker operating in a complex organizational system, which in turn functions in an even more complex societal suprasystem. We have seen that the modern personnel manager in this role must deal with a complex of interacting psychological, sociological, economic, political, and legal variables, many of which (such as governmental regulations) constrain his strategy space as a decision maker.

In most textbooks a final chapter such as this is devoted to (1) attempting to summarize the previous chapters, (2) speculating on future trends in the area under study, or (3) both of these. To summarize in this chapter all of the topics covered previously, we believe would be too repetitive and would provide nothing but a surface coverage. To extrapolate possible future trends in modern personnel management beyond the trends we have already indicated in other chapters would be overly speculative. Therefore, what we will do in this chapter is something not done in other texts. We will present materials that focus attention on some real dilemmas and paradoxes present in modern personnel management. These paradoxes are serious, but we will treat certain aspects of them in what we believe to be a humorous fashion, sometimes utilizing satire.

PERCY THE PERSONNEL MANAGER

In February 1976, *Fortune* published an article entitled "Personnel Directors Are the New Corporate Heroes."[1] This article emphasized the point made in Chapter 2 — that personnel managers are becoming more and more important in business corporations. It indicated that, according to the American Management Association, "the average compensation for personnel directors of industrial companies with sales of $500 million to $1 billion was $61,400 in 1975."[2] The *Fortune* article also stated that:

> In many companies, the personnel director's responsibilities have become so complex that they can only be shouldered by topflight business managers who have the backing of the chief executive. The people who do the job like to say that in years to come, a tour of duty in the personnel department (more likely the division of human resources) will be mandatory for any executive who aims to be chairman.[3]

Finally, in the *Fortune* article, a two-page color cartoon story emphasizing the growth of the personnel manager's stature was cleverly presented. It was entitled "The Saga of Percy Personnel." The dialogue of the cartoon was as follows:[4]

1. Holding a telephone, Percy announces to three of his colleagues: "That was the chairman of the board on the phone . . . he wants me to be the new director of personnel." His colleagues' responses were: "Oh, you poor guy!"; "Bye, bye, Percy!"; and "My deepest sympathies, old man."

2. Percy's secretary consoles him by saying: "Don't feel too badly, boss . . . maybe when you tour your new department you'll feel better."

3. Touring his new department, Percy sees his new employees carrying signs reading: "We must be heard!" "Equal opportunity for blacks." "Senior citizens are people too." "Women in higher positions." Percy's response simply is: "Oh, no!"

4. Concerned, Percy talks to his chairman of the board and asks: "Tell me, sir, what did I do wrong to deserve a fate such as this?" The chairman hands Percy a big yellow letter "P" and responds: "You don't understand my boy, this 'P' not only stands for Personnel, it also stands for Promotion and Prestige. It also means a Plumper Paycheck." Percy walks away, now looking confident, carrying a desk nameplate entitled "V.P. Human Resources," and wearing a "Superman" outfit with a red cape, blue shirt, and a big yellow letter "P" on its front. Percy wears this costume, which is illustrated in Figure 15–1, throughout the rest of the cartoon.

5. Speaking confidently to his department, Percy then declares: "As new head of this department, I expect things to be a lot different!"

6. To one of his older subordinates he indicates: " . . . for instance, I expect you to settle existing suits and avoid future ones." To another he indicates: "And your job will be to get the company in line with new pension plans."

7. Seeing workers carrying placards indicating that "promotion

Figure 15–1 *"Percy Personnel." [From Herbert E. Meyer, "Personnel Directors Are the New Corporate Heroes," Fortune, 93 (February, 1976) p. 85. This drawing is reproduced by permission of Fortune, © 1976, Time, Inc.]*

Artist: Bob Clarke

policies are putrid," "salary scales stink," "we want less," and conversely, "we want more," Percy orders that: "Furthermore, all those grievance committees will be heard, and they will get some action!"

8. Having taken such a more proactive personnel stance, he is told by the chairman of the board, "Percy, I hear that labor costs are leveling off and productivity is moving up." Further, four other executives make the following comments to him:

"Percy, we need a new vice president for marketing."

"Percy, get us a good finance director!"

"Say Perc . . . who do you think should head up our international operations?"

"Percy, what is your opinion on acquiring new subsidiaries next year?"

9. Sometime later, Percy's secretary opens the door and says to him: "Oh boss, there's a group of the department heads waiting to ask your advice." Percy, looking startled, responds: "It's hard to believe I've become THAT important!" But then, somewhat smugly grinning to himself, Percy "thinks out loud": " . . . But then, why not? This job gives me ACCESS TO and KNOWLEDGE OF every division of the company, and every one of those men owes his current job to me!"

10. Finally, as one might expect from any hero from any saga, the group of the department heads, sitting around an executive table have the head of their group, standing and carrying a large yellow letter "C" proudly announce: "Gentlemen, the vote was unanimous . . . our new chairman of the board is PERCY PERSONNEL!"

Although chairmen of the board many Percys may someday become, today they are still personnel directors and vice presidents of personnel. In such positions, they must contend with many complex forces, solve many difficult problems, and face some troublesome paradoxes. It is to some of the latter that we will now turn.

PERCY'S PARADOXES

Percy faces several paradoxes. Some deal with his own role as a personnel manager. Some deal with the larger system of which he is a member — his organization. Some deal with that complex external set of suprasystems: the federal, state, and local governments and the economy as a whole.

Percy's Own Role

The authors of this text have performed personnel work in organizations and agree with Percy's recognition that personnel jobs often do give an individual access to and knowledge of every division of an organization. Such knowledge helps give Percy a broad background, and prepares him for assuming the "generalist role" required of the top personnel manager in any firm. Is there a danger, however, that the top personnel officers of organizations will become so "generalized" in their thinking that they will no longer possess the specialized expertise required to communicate intelligently with their subordinates? As it has been put face-tiously: "A generalist is a person who knows more and more about less and less until he knows nothing about everything." (A specialist, conversely, is one who "knows more and more about less and less until he knows everything about nothing.") At any rate, zero equals zero.

More seriously, in a rapidly changing environment, charac-terized by new technologies, problems, and an explosion of knowledge, it becomes more and more difficult for anyone to take the broad generalist view required by the proactive Percy. In fact, one theme of Alvin Toffler's book *Future Shock* is that nearly every individual in our society faces the dangers of becoming "information overloaded." As Toffler has pointed out:

> Today change is so swift and relentless in the techno-societies that yesterday's truths suddenly become today's fictions, and the most high-ly skilled and intelligent members of society admit difficulty in keeping up with the deluge of new knowledge—even in extremely narrow fields.[5]

Percy, a generalist? Yes, to an extent. A specialist? Yes, to an extent. Both potentially conflicting roles must probably be played to some extent simultaneously by modern personnel man-agers, such as Percy. They must attempt to steer a nonshipwreck course between the two dangers of the rock of Scylla and whirl-pool of Charybdis. This seems trite and yet perhaps it is actually impossible to accomplish. The obvious answer is the "golden mean." But this is a generalization (made by two specialists) and in the "cruel, hard, real world," generalizations will not suffice. To avoid facing such difficult problems and answering such impossible questions as those posed above, we will simply turn the tables and ask the reader the question: "Should you be fortunate enough to become a proactive 'generalist' Percy with an annual compensation (in 1976 dollars) of $61,400 in a corporation with earnings between $500 million and $1 billion, how would you keep up with the information explosion of the 1970's and 1980's?"

The Organizational System

Assuming that Percy can effectively deal with the first paradox posed above, how can he deal with conflicting problems existing within his organization? Some of these problems may have been created by previous "sub-Percy's," who were old-timers and not proactive. Some problems may have been created by decisions made by his current top management, faced with pressures from powerful unions and the federal government. Regardless of their origin, Percy must deal with problems such as that of the role of the organization in light of the responsibilities of its own members.

As Chris Argyris has pointed out, individuals in our society tend to mature as adults in several ways in that they:

Tend to develop from a state of passivity as infants to a state of increasing activity as adults . . . .

Tend to develop from a state of dependence upon others as infants to a state of relative independence as adults . . . .

Tend to develop from being in a subordinate position in the family and society as an infant to aspiring to occupy an equal and/or superordinate position relative to their peers.

Tend to develop from a lack of awareness of self as an infant to an awareness of and control over self as an adult.[6]

Many of Percy's (and perhaps even his predecessors) efforts have been aimed at fostering maturity, independence, and self-awareness in organizations. Techniques such as skills inventories in human resource planning are designed to provide "open" personnel systems in which individuals may be promoted to higher level positions, giving them more responsibility, placing them in positions requiring more proactivity, and ones representing "equal and/or superordinate" positions in the organization, a subsystem of society. Further, many of the training and development efforts we have discussed in this text are also designed to foster maturity, growth, and the assumption of more individual responsibility. One of the main objectives of laboratory or "sensitivity" training, discussed in Chapter 8, is specifically to foster "an awareness of and control over self as an adult."

At the same time, paradoxically, many employee benefit programs that are costly in an era in which costs must be more carefully scrutinized than ever may go beyond the point of need and actually discourage the assumption of self-responsibility. In Chapter 12, we made reference to Zollitsch and Langsner's list of 197 employee services, ranging from free beer to free innoculations, and raised the question of how far firms should go in providing such services.[7] To draw from this list, should the company provide horseshoe courts? Dietetic advice? Rod and gun clubs? Volleyball teams? Table tennis? Free meals? Legal aid? Fishing jamborees? The authors of this text are not opposed to such activities as these, but is it not one's own responsibility as a mature adult to make one's own decisions in many areas in which such services are provided by organizations? We say many, because as we indicated in discussing employee benefits, there are many very desirable services that firms do provide, such as company cafeterias when no other such facilities are physically proximate to organization members. Now we have Percy's second paradox. How can he reconcile large expenditures for activities such as training and development efforts, which foster responsibility, while justifying the expenditure of considerable sums on services that the individual could be responsible for providing himself?

Governmental Legislation and Regulation

We have emphasized in numerous chapters how modern personnel managers are constrained in their decision making by governmental laws and regulations: EEOC, ERISA, OSHA. In many cases, it can be argued that such regulations have resulted primarily because Percy's own organization (and those of other Percys) have failed to meet their social responsibilities in the past. In any event, many firms have unfairly discriminated against women and blacks and other minorities and probably deserved to be constrained from doing so — even though "reverse discrimination" in light of "affirmative action" poses an unanswerable paradox itself. Firms have maintained industrial noise levels so high as to damage permanently some workers' hearing, and perhaps OSHA was necessary, and a number of firms did not fulfill their pension promises to employees, and hence, ERISA. Just how far it is necessary for the corporation functioning in a complex societal system to go to meet its "social responsibility" is a very debatable question.

A serious paradox has arisen surrounding the passage and implementation of many laws with which Percy personnel must deal. In many cases, their purposes have been sublime; but their implementation, ludicrous. OSHA, as discussed in Chapter 13, provides an example of the paradoxical combination of the sublime and the ludicrous. The aim of OSHA was noble — to protect American workers from injuries and industrial health problems. Its passage was initially hailed by many safety directors as governmental support for many of the endeavors for which they had been fighting for years. In fact, OSHA was supposed to have been referred to somewhat facetiously by some safety directors as standing for "*O*ur *S*avior *H*as *A*rrived."[8] Many of the regulations (especially initially) promulgated to enforce OSHA, however, were outright ludicrous. As Foulkes has pointed out,

> For example, one of the provisions of the act requires separate bathrooms for male and female employees. As a result, according to one well-circulated story, a Mom-and-Pop store had to install a second bathroom (a ruling subsequently overturned). In addition, early in the act's administration, there was a ban on round toilet seats (split seats were required), a ban on providing ice water to employees (a legacy from the time when ice came from rivers), and a requirement for a hook inside the bathroom.[9]

In light of such events, probably some safety managers began referring to OSHA as "*O*ur *S*atan *H*as *A*rrived."

Although some problems such as these have been resolved as OSHA has become more service-oriented, there have been and probably will continue to be many cases when Percy must plow through the paradoxes of sublime intent and ludicrous implementation with respect to governmental regulations. How many years will it be required, for example, for pension officers and consultants to continue studying the text of ERISA "like religious scholars seeking the true meaning of Bible passages?"[10] We do not know now, and the question may not be resolved for some time to come.

Our Paradoxical Economy

One of the paradoxes of many of the free industrially developed nations of the world is that we have not been able to maintain full employment while at the same time preventing inflation. As *Business Week* has argued, neither "Keynesian fiscalism nor Friedmanian monetarism" has really solved the inflationary situation because neither "is particularly comfortable with one basic fact of life in the advanced industrial countries: that wages are set in major collective bargaining agreements between unions and management."[11] As a solution for a "new economic policy mix that will make full employment more compatible with price-stability," several foreign countries as of 1976 were trying out "wage restraints prescribed or suggested by government and accepted by labor."[12]

Perhaps Percy can do little himself to deal with this paradox, but its implications for his firm are numerous. We find such paradoxes even in many "progressive" personnel management-oriented firms. For example, some organizations have required all applicants for managerial positions to have a college education so that they would be in a position to "lead more effectively," "think more analytically," and "relate to others more realistically." At the same time, however, because of economic difficulties, such firms have often been forced to cut back in their hiring of such graduates. Further, many liberal arts majors have had such difficulties in obtaining jobs in industry that they switched into programs in the more "practically-oriented" colleges of business administration. Such changes, in turn, have required university faculty cutbacks in the arts and literature — supposedly one form of education designed to help the individual "self-actualize" when paid for time not worked — a basic employee benefit discussed in Chapter 12. In addition, many undergraduate majors, even in business administration, have had difficulty finding jobs. Finally, with respect to those with advanced degrees, more paradoxes have arisen. A student in 1976 with an MBA from a good college of business administration was generally in demand by business firms and commanded a starting annual salary of $17,000 to $20,000, while many Ph.D. graduates in the humanities were driving taxicabs because they could find no other more "self-actualizing" employment. Our inflationary economy, as indicated in Chapter 12, has posed other paradoxes for Percy, not only with respect to creating the need for huge additional sums to be contributed to pension funds but also in terms of the broader societal paradox: "Can we provide socially necessary security benefits to our citizens while at the same time remaining solvent?"

Percy's paradoxes are many, and there are no easy solutions to them. Percy may be able to control some excesses such as unnecessary employee services. Even where he has no control, such as influencing his firm's Social Security contributions, Percy may utilize his predictive information about these costs in making other financial planning decisions. Finally, perhaps Percy should set aside a day for himself and all other Percys to laugh at his paradoxes and mock the authorities in our societal system over which he has little influence or control. Yes indeed! Perhaps each year at annual meetings of personnel administrators and persons interested in personnel, our proactive Percy should encourage his colleagues to celebrate a "Feast of Fools" in which they burlesque authority over which they have little to no control. Such actions might help the Percys of the world to relieve some of their frustrations as they plow through the paradoxes of modern personnel administration.

PERCY AND THE "FEAST OF FOOLS"

In this section we will briefly describe the nature of the "Feast of Fools," which can be traced to medieval times, and then indicate how Percy might use such a feast to release some of the frustrations involved in modern personnel management.

The Feast of Fools

For many centuries, celebrations have taken place in late December and early January. In medieval times, numerous celebrations, in which reveling and masquerading were carried on, were held in western Europe during the period after Christmas day and New Year's day. To keep at least the clergy from such merrymaking, the church introduced in the eleventh century, special feast days for the various ranks of the clerical community.[13] This well-meant effort backfired, however, and the clerical feasts, gradually rather than "keeping the clergy from joining the silly revels of the laity" led to "the very abuses they were to prevent."[14] The clerical celebrations were especially popular in France, and were soon turned into festivals called "Feasts of Fools."

Common to each "Feast of Fools" was an "inversion of status" among the clergy and "the performance, inevitably burlesque, by the inferior clergy of functions properly belonging to their betters."[15] For example, some clerics "hooted and sang improper ditties, and played dice upon the altar" in a reaction to the habitual "restraints of choir discipline."[16]

Although the higher clergy attempted time and time again to prevent the lower clergy from such ludicrous merrymaking, the "Feast of Fools" continued for several centuries. In fact, one form of the "Feast of Fools," the "Feast of the Ass," which originally symbolized Mary's flight into Egypt, gave rise to a song which has continued to be sung in religious contexts up to our own century. This feast, although not as revelrous as some of the "Feasts of Fools," as reported from a thirteenth century manuscript from Beauvais, France "included a drinking-bout, the bringing of an ass into the church at the singing of the Prose of the Ass . . . and the ending of certain liturgical pieces with a bray."[17] The first stanza of the famous Prose of the Ass, as it was sung in the Cathedral of Beauvais, is given in Figure 15–2. An arrange-

Latin and French	English Translation
Orientis partibus	Out from lands of Orient
Adventavit Asinus	Was the ass divinely sent.
Pulcher et fortissimus	Strong and very fair was he,
Sarcinis aptissimus	Bearing burdens gallantly.
Hez hez sire asnes hez.	Heigh, sir ass, oh heigh.

From Henry Copley Greene, "The Song of the Ass," *Spectrum*, 6 (1931), p. 535.

Figure 15–2 *"The Song of the Ass"—first stanza as it was sung at the Cathedral of Beauvais.*

ment of the song was incorporated into *Hymns Ancient and Modern* (1909); from this work it was transferred to the American Episcopal *Hymnal*.[18] The song, as reported in 1931, was also sung from the *Harvard University Hymn Book*.[19]

From medieval Beauvais has this been carried to *the* Harvard University, publisher of the reputable *Harvard Business Review* in the twentieth century, the "Song of the Ass"? Preposterous indeed. Absurd. Ludicrous. But reportedly true. Now, however, what about Percy Personnel, the "Feast of Fools," and the "Song of the Ass" in the times of modern personnel management?

Some Modern Festivities

We suggested that Percy might organize a "Feast of Fools" at annual meetings of personnel managers and others interested in personnel. We now suggest that a donkey be led into these meetings, as in our medieval cathedrals, and that all modern personnel managers sing the "Song of the Ass" as they mock the ubiquitous authorities with which they must contend. For example, we suggest that the following revelries might take place:

1. Percy might ride the donkey as the song is sung, sitting on top of a nonsplit toilet seat as originally prohibited by an OSHA official, mocking the ludicrous regulations often promulgated by governmental authorities (or nonentities).

2. Percy might be mocking the economists who cannot resolve the problem of providing full employment without inflation by "setting them back" several centuries to a barter system. Specifically, we would have Percy carrying salt on his donkey as the song is sung, since salt has been used for money by many people at different times in the past. For example, around the first century, A.D., Roman soldiers were often paid a "salarium" (salt money), from which we get our word "salary" and "He's not worth his salt."

3. Percy might mock previous Percys and board chairmen who made ludicrous decisions constraining him today as he rides the donkey while the song is sung by bringing to these nonmodern managers a

negative pension check to reward them for their disservices to the firm. To the best of our knowledge, negative pension checks are not explicitly covered in ERISA's 207 pages of statutory law. Our modern Percy, knowing that if he is not proactive now, might find himself being mocked with a $-\$2000$/month pension check in a future "Feast of Fools," may become even more proactive. If so, good for him.

4. Percy, information overloaded with economic problems, governmental regulations, and organizational paradoxes, might mock authors such as ourselves by riding on the donkey as the song is sung carrying a torch burning a brand new copy of this book which has further information overloaded him by covering such sublime subjects as the fostering of one's self-awareness in sensitivity training to such ludicrous ones as the "Feast of Fools."

But now to be serious. Would conducting an annual "Feast of Fools" do nothing more than make Percy himself a fool? In some cases, perhaps yes. But in many other cases, we think not. For centuries, humor, burlesque, and mockery have provided a fundamental socially acceptable means of releasing one's tensions and frustrations. Further, as Weiser has described the lower clergy in concluding his discussion of their conducting the "Feast of the Ass" in medieval times: "Perhaps they had, beneath the apparent lack of reverence and good taste, a spark of the genuine spirit of Saint Francis of Assisi."[20] Thus, perhaps our new corporate hero, Percy, not a superman as he was dressed in the *Fortune* cartoon, but a mere mortal, hopefully with a "spark of genuine spirit," and needing a harmless outlet for the frustrations caused by today's problems and paradoxes, may be able to draw on the wisdom of his medieval forefathers to gain a few laughs from a "Feast of Fools" as he tackles the complexity of modern personnel management.

DISCUSSION AND STUDY QUESTIONS

1. Are there any other ways in which "Percy Personnel" should be more proactive than indicated in this text? Are there any other ways in which he should be less proactive? Give your reasons why.
2. Although we did not intend Chapter 15 to be "sacrilegious," some students who have read it have believed that it was so. Do you agree with them? Why?
3. Can you conceive of any additional paradoxes which Percy faces that we did not cover in the chapter?

Notes

[1] Herbert E. Meyer, "Personnel Directors Are the New Corporate Heroes," *Fortune*, 93 (February, 1976), pp. 84–88, 140.

[2]Ibid., p. 87.

[3]Ibid., p. 140. Meyer also pointed out that although the last statement in this quotation may be an exaggeration, firms are increasingly transferring executives moving upward in organizations into personnel for a while before they move into higher level positions.

[4]The following materials were drawn from the cartoon in ibid., pp. 85–86. The quotations are taken directly from the *Fortune* article, while the description of the scenes depicted in the cartoon is ours. These quotations are reproduced by permission of *Fortune,* © 1976, Time, Inc.

[5]Alvin Toffler, *Future Shock* (New York: Random House, 1970, Bantam Books Edition), p. 157.

[6]Chris Argyris, *Personality and Organization* (New York: Harper & Row, 1957), p. 50.

[7]Herbert G. Zollitsch and Adolph Langsner, *Wage and Salary Administration,* 2nd ed. (Cincinnati: South-Western Publishing Co., 1970), pp. 622–623.

[8]Fred K. Foulkes, "Learning to Live with OSHA," *Harvard Business Review,* 51 (November-December, 1973), p. 64.

[9]Ibid., pp. 59–60.

[10]"Pension Reform's Expensive Ricochet," *Business Week,* March 24, 1975, p. 144.

[11]"The 'Wage Flaw' in Friedman and Keynes," *Business Week,* July 26, 1976, p. 65. We have not focused a section specifically on any of the paradoxes of unionism. We might reiterate a point made in the last chapter, however— unionism may be a mixed blessing. Inflationary wage pressures present serious problems for management while union pressures for better working conditions may lead to better personnel practices. Further, as indicated in our chapter on system incentives, unions may serve as a facilitative device in fostering employee management cooperation in Scanlon plans.

[12]"New Economic Weapon: Government-Prescribed Wage Restraints to Squeeze Worldwide Inflation," *Business Week,* July 26, 1976, p. 62.

[13]Francis X. Weiser, *Handbook of Christian Feasts and Customs* (New York: Harcourt, Brace and Company, 1958), p. 126.

[14]Ibid.

[15]E. K. Chambers, *The Medieval Stage,* Vol. 1 (Oxford, Great Britain: The Clarendon Press. 1903), p. 325. Chambers devotes two chapters just to the "Feast of Fools," Chapters 13 and 14, pp. 274–335.

[16]Ibid., p. 325.

[17]Karl Young, *The Drama of the Medieval Church,* Vol. 1 (London: Oxford University Press, 1933), p. 105.

[18]Henry Copley Greene, "The Song of the Ass," *Spectrum,* 6 (1931), p. 542.

[19]Ibid.

[20]Weiser, op. cit., p. 127.

NAME INDEX

Note: Page numbers in *italics* indicate figure legends.

Adorno, T. W., 213
Alfred, Theodore M., 105, 106, 118
Alger, J., 433
Allen, Louis A., 472
Allison, William W., 551, 577, 578
Alpander, Guvene G., 349
Amano, Matt M., 351
Anderson, C. Richard, *540*
Anderson, Philip H., 394
Andress, Frank J., 116
Anthony, Philip, 578
Anthony, R. N., 251
Anthony, William P., 578
Appelbaum, Steven, 351
Argyris, Chris, 638, 645
Atchison, T., 392, 393
Ayoub, Mahmoud A., 578
Azevedo, Ross, 175

Balma, M. J., 176
Baloff, Nicholas, 116
Barnes, Louis B., 351
Barnum, Darold T., 576
Basil, D. C., 349
Bass, Bernard M., 251, 252, 253, 263, 268, *269*, 278, 307, 308, 310
Bassett, Glenn A., 66, 85, 115, 116
Bassford, Gerald L., 175
Bavelas, Alex, 262, 307
Beal, Edwin F., 608, 627, 629, 630, 631
Becker, Joseph M., *493*, 518
Beckhard, Richard, 351
Beeland, J. L., 302, 310
Belasco, James A., 244, 253, 254
Belcher, D. W., 392
Bell, Frederick J., 308
Bell, Lawrence F., 230, 252
Bennis, Warren G., 351, 457, 472
Bent, Dale H., 254
Berkshire, James, 212
Berniger, Joseph, 176

Bertalanffy, Ludwig von, 473
Besco, R., 253
Bevan, Richard V., 391
Biel, William C., 230, 252
Bienvenu, Bernard J., 307, 349
Billon, S. A., 116
Bingham, Eula, 542
Bittner, Reign, 212
Black, Frederick H., Jr., 66
Black, James M., 65
Blake, Robert R., 337, 338, 339, 351
Blake, Ronald B., 561, 575
Blakeney, Roger N., 253
Blum, Milton L., 577
Blumenfeld, Warren S., 253, 302, 310
Bolles, R. C., 252
Booth, Jerome M., 174
Borgeson, Roger D., 50, 65
Boring, E. G., 252
Bower, George W., 578
Bower, Gordon H., 252
Bowers, W. Bert, 116
Boxx, W. Randy, 518
Boynton, Robert E., 64
Bradshaw, T. I., 117
Bray, Douglas W., 332, 350
Brenner, Marshall H., 349, 350
Brewer, Jack, 117
Broadwell, Martin M., 307
Bryce, William, 117
Buckley, John W., 308
Buffa, Elwood S., 222, *222*, 252
Bugelski, B. R., 252
Buppert, William I., III, 520
Burack, Elmer, 116
Burgess, Leonard R., 393
Burns, Robert K., 203, 212
Burns, Tom, 17, 30
Burrow, Martha G., 323, 349
Bush, Robert R., 254
Buskirk, Richard H., 309
Byham, William C., 330, 331, 350, 351

Calvasina, Eugene J., 518
Campbell, David M., 64
Campbell, John P., 117, *205*, 212, 252, 253, 308, 309
Carlisle, Howard M., 30
Carlson, Donald G., 471, 508, 509, 514, 520, 521
Carroll, Stephen J., Jr., *301,* 308, 310, 357, 364, 375, 391, 392, 393, 408, 433, 517, 519
Carvalho, Gerald F., *381,* 394
Carzo, Rocco, Jr., 116
Case, C. Marston, 254
Cassidy, Charles E. J., 66, 393
Cermak, Laird S., 252, 254
Chambers, B., 252
Chambers, E. K., 645
Chapman, Robert L., 309
Chapple, Elliot V., 64
Chayes, Antonia Handler, 175, 393
Cheek, Logan M., 65, 66, 117
Chesler, David J., 392
Chisman, James A., 432
Chowdhry, K., 226, 252
Claycombe, W. W., 211
Cohen, Kalman J., 310
Cole, Reno R., 116
Coleman, Charles J., 30, 44, 64, 65
Colletti, Jerome A., 394, 471
Commons, John R., 628
Connally, Gerald E., 66, 212
Cook, Alice H., 393
Cotner, William C., 433
Craf, John R., 308
Cravens, Gwyneth, 349
Creber, Frederick L., 575
Crotty, Philip, 117
Crutchfield, Richard S., 252

Dalton, Gene W., 30, 394
Daly, Peter H., 471
Davey, Harold W., 608, 613, 630
Davies, Gordon K., 176
Dawis, Rene V., *299,* 308, 310
DeGreene, Kenyon B., 578
Dehayes, Daniel W., Jr., 309
Delaney, Michael J., 434
Delloff, Irving A., 432
DeReamer, Russell, 577
Diatchenko, Vasilli P., 432
Dick, Arthur, 392
Dickman, Robert A., 176
Dickson, W. J., 30
Domm, Donald R., 252
Donnelly, John, 458, 472
Dooley, C. R., 214, 251
Doty, Jack H., 254
Douglas, Merl, 471
Drucker, Peter, 27, 30, 47, 65, 206

Dukes, Carlton, 144, 176
Dunbar, Roger L. M., 562, 578
Duncan, Robert B., 30
Dunn, J. D., 361, 392, 393, 434, 470, 471
Dunnette, Marvin D., 174, *205,* 391
Dunlop, John T., 432
Dutter, Philip H., 433, 434

Ehrbar, A. F., 519
Eilbert, Henry, 29
Eisemann, Charles W., 212
Elbing, Alvar O., 518
Ellenbog, Ulrich, 526
England, George W., 176
England, Gordon R., 548, 577, 579
Estes, W. K., 254
Estey, Marten, 588, 598, 628, 629, 630
Evans, William A., 393

Falkner, Charles H., 176
Famularo, Joseph J., 64, *220,* 251, 392, 433
Farr, Marshall J., 309
Farson, Richard F., 212
Feld, Lipman G., 175
Feldhusen, John F., 309
Fenninger, Lawrence, Jr., 432
Flanagan, John C., 202, 203, 212
Flast, Robert H., 176
Fleishman, Edwin A., 176, 237, 253
Fleming, Sandra, 520
Foote, George H., 433, 434
Foster, Jerry F., 309
Foster, Kenneth E., 393
Foulkes, Fred K., 64, 65, 576, 645
Fox, Harold W., 33, 64
Fragner, Berwyn N., 434
Freas, Thomas L., 392
Fredericksen, Norman O., 310
Freedman, Audrey, 519
Freeman, Jean, 349
French, Wendell, 393
Froelich, Herbert F., 66
Fromer, Robert, 309
Fromm, Erich, 213
Frost, Carl F., *455,* 472

Gagné, Robert M., 211, 252
Gannon, Martin J., 488, 518
Gausch, John P., 577
Geare, A. J., 472
Giblin, Edward, 175
Gilbreth, Frank B., 432
Ginsburg, Woodrow L., 621, 631

Gitlow, Abraham, L., 629
Glaser, Robert, 211
Gleason, John M., 576
Glueck, William F., 65
Goldstein, Irwin L., 217, 251, 252, 253, 307, 308, 309, 310
Gomersall, Earl R., 314, *316, 317, 317,* 349
Goodale, James G., 177
Goodman, Paul S., 325, 350
Gordon, T. J., 517, 518
Gray, R. B., 472
Greenberg, Les, 564, 578
Greene, Henry Copley, *643,* 645
Greenlaw, Paul S., *15, 23,* 29, 64, 65, 116, 117, 160, 175, 177, 206, 213, 309, 310, 392, 432, 433, 473
Greiner, Larry E., 351
Grether, C. B., 578
Grimaldi, John V., 524, 575, 578, 579
Guion, Robert, 577
Guthrie, Robert R., 65
Gutmann, Jean E., 349

Hagburg, Eugene C., 587, 614, 628, 629, 630, 631
Haire, Mason, 116
Hammer, W. Clay, 576
Hammer, Willie, 575, 576
Hannaford, Earle, 562, 563
Harrell, Thomas W., 211
Hartman, Edward, 309
Hatry, Harry, 65
Hausknecht, J. H., Jr., 350
Hawver, Dennis A., 66
Hayden, Robert J., 211
Haynes, Marion E., 335, 351
Heinen, Stephen, 349
Heinrich, H. W., 550, 577
Hellriegel, Don, 48, 65, 351
Heneman, Herbert G., III, 177
Henderson, Richard I., 116, 472, 473, 477, 517, 518, 519
Herbert, Theodore T., 228
Herrick, Robert F., 176
Herron, Lowell W., 310
Hess, Lee, 252
Hettenhouse, George W., 385–386, 394, 422, 434
Heyel, Carl, 308
Higgins, James M., 174
Highland, Richard, 212
Hilgard, Ernest R., 252
Hinrichs, J. R., 265, 307, 393
Hodgson, James G., 350
Hofstede, Geert, 64, 65
Holland, Max G., 253
Hollander, Edwin P., 473

Horn, Robert, 310
Hoslett, Schuyler, 630
Howard, Ann, 350
Howes, V. M., 309
Huber, George P., 176
Hulin, Charles I., 252
Hull, C. Hadlai, 254
Hulme, Robert D., 391
Hunt, J. G., 64
Hunter, Donald, 575

Inskeep, Gordon, 176
Ivancevich, John J., *301,* 308, 310

James, Charles F., 433
Janes, Harold D., 392
Javits, Jacob, 520, 521
Johnson, Rossall J., 64, 118
Jones, Alun, 246, 254
Jones, J. A. G., 254
Jones, John Paul, 64
Jones, Joseph L., Jr., 433
Julian, James W., 473

Kahn, R. L., 448, 457, 471, 472, 473
Kanter, Rosabeth, 350
Kaplan, Philip, 493–494, 518
Kaufman, Gordon, 517
Kaumeyer, Richard A., Jr., 117
Katz, D., 448, 457, 471, 472, 473
Kearney, William J., 212
Keller, Robert T., 30
Kelley, Harold H., 238, 253
Kendall, Lorne, 252
Kerr, Steven D., 213
Kienast, Philip K., 608
Kimberly, John R., 30, 351
King, D. C., 253
Kirkpatrick, Donald L., 238, 253
Klaus, David J., 211
Kleinmuntz, Benjamin, 149, 177
Kleinschrod, Walter A., 176
Klimoski, Richard J., 350
Knowles, Alvis R., 230, 252
Koch, S., 254
Koenig, Peter, 176
Kolb, David A., 252
Kopp, Kenneth K., 432
Kotter, John P., 314, 349
Kraut, Allen I., 334, 335, 350, 351
Krech, David, 252
Kroes, William H., 578
Kromer, Ted L., 318, 349

LaMotte, Thomas, 318, 349
Lamouria, Lloyd H., 211
Lane, Irving M., 252, 253, *262,* 307
Langsner, Adolph, 364, 375, 386, 392, 393, 394, 432, 433, 448, 465, 470, 471, 472, 473, 477, 517, 639, 645
Lanser, Howard P., 434
Lanzenauer, Christopher von, 471
Lasser, J. K., 471
Lawler, Edward E., III, *205,* 357, 383–384, 391, 394
Lawrence, Paul, 30
Lawshe, C. H., 176
Lawson, Dene R., 308
Lawson, J. W., II, 603, 604, 629, 630
LeBleu, R. E., 517, 518
Lee, Raymond, 174
Legeros, Constance, 349
Leo, Mario, 394
Lesieur, Frederick G., 455, 456, 472
Levine, Martin J., 587, 614, 628, 629, 630, 631
Lewellen, Wilbur G., 434
Lewis, Willard A., 59, 66
Lieberman, Elias, 628
Lincoln, James F., 460ff, 473
Lindsey, Robert, 175
Ling, Cyril, 29
Lippitt, Gordon L., 226, 252
Lipstreu, Otis, 318, 349
Litwin, George H., 219, 251
Locke, Edwin A., 252
Loftin, Markus M., 219, *220,* 251, 288, 309
Lorsch, Jay W., 30
Luke, Robert A., Jr., 351
Luthans, Fred, 337, 351

Magdarz, Edward F., 251
Magnum, Garth L., 432
Mahoney, Thomas A., *95,* 117
Maier, Norman R. F., 195, 212, 253, 307
Malm, F. T., 240, 253
Margolis, Bruce L., 578
Marion, B. W., 313, 349
Marks, Melvin R., 212
Martin, Elizabeth, 308
Martin, Robert A., 117
Maslow, A. H., 357–358, 391, 603
Matschulat, James O., 577
Matteson, Michael T., 253
Mayo, Elton, 30
Merck, John W., 117
Merrill, Harwood F., 308
Metzger, Bert L., *422,* 470, 471, *502,* 503, 519, 520
Meyer, H. H., 212
Meyer, Herbert E., 644

Milkovich, George T., *95,* 116, 117, 394, 434
Milton, Charles R., 65
Miner, John B., 335, 347, 351
Mintz, Alexander, 577
Mitchell, James M., 65
Moder, Joseph J., 30
Monczka, Robert M., 349
Moreno, J. L., 292
Morse, John J., 393
Morse, Wayne J., 116
Moses, Joseph L., *331,* 350
Mosher, William E., 29
Mosteller, Frederick, 254
Mouton, Jane S., 337, 338, 339, 351
Moxham, John, 246, 254
Muczyk, Jan P., 282, 308
Murrell, Kenneth L., 351
Murthy, K. R. Srinivasa, 393
Mussen, P. H., 350
Myers, Charles A., 175, 253
Myers, M. Scott, 314, *316,* 317, *317,* 349

McClelland, David C., 177, 358, 391
MacCrimmon, Kenneth R., 115, 117
McGehee, William, 251
McGill, Dan, 521
McGlauchin, Dorothy, 349
McGregor, Douglas, 193, 206, 207, 212, 472, 616
MacGuffie, John V., 66
McIntyre, James M., 252
McMurray, Robert N., 164, 177
McNair, Malcolm P., 309

Nadler, Leonard, 350
Nash, Allan N., 282, 308, 357, 364, 375, 391, 392, 393, 408, 433, 517, 519
Newstrom, John W., 349
Nichols, Ralph G., 630
Nie, Norman H., 254
Niebel, Benjamin W., 432
Niehaus, R. J., 117
Nielsen, Warren R., 351
Norrgard, David L., 392
Norton, Steven D., 333, 350

Oates, David, 254
Oberg, Winston, 207, 212, 213
O'Brien, Patricia E., 575, 576
O'Day, Edward F., 308
Odiorne, George, 239
O'Meara, J. Roger, 433
Opsahl, Robert L., 391

Ornati, Oscar A., 175
Osgood, Donald W., 43, 65

Paine, Frank T., *301*, 308, 310
Pantelidis, Veronica S., 310
Parker, Donn B., 66
Palmer, David D., 30
Paransky, Harold, 325, 350
Partin, J. Jennings, 351
Patten, Thomas H., Jr., 60, 65, 66, 393
Patton, Arch, 211, 417, 433
Paul, Robert D., 513, 519, 521
Paul, Robert J., 576
Pearson, Richard G., 578
Peck, Theodore P., 577
Pedicord, W. J., 117
Penchansky, Roy, 517
Perkins, William C., 309
Petersen, Dan, 555, 556, 577, 578
Phillips, Cecil R., 30
Pigors, Faith, 309
Pigors, Paul, 253, 309
Pizam, Abraham, 433
Poor, Riva, 518
Porter, Elias H., 309
Porter, Lyman W., 392
Poulton, E. C., 577, 578
Pratt, Robert N., 631
Pronsky, John, 394
Puckett, Elbridge S., 456, 457, 472
Pursell, Robert B., 392

Rabe, W. F., 66
Rachel, F. M., 361, 392, 393, 434, 470, 471
Rago, James J., Jr., 322, 349
Randle, C. Wilson, 608, 612, 616, 630, 631
Rawdon, R. H., 310
Reese, Timothy T., 175
Rehmus, Frederick P., 380, 383, 394
Reif, William E., 349
Renshaw, Kent S., 309
Rettig, Jack L., 351
Reuter, Vincent G., 433
Reynolds, Lloyd, 175
Rezler, Julius, 65, 394
Rhenman, Eric, 310
Rich, Joseph, 44, 64
Richards, Max D., 29, 64, 65, 116, 175, 206, 213, 392, 473
Ritzer, George, 65
Robertson, David E., 175
Robinson, James W., 628, 629
Roch, Joe, 65
Roche, Gerald R., 392
Rodgers, William A., 383, 394

Roethlisberger, F. J., 30
Rogers, Rolf E., 66
Rome, Howard, 159
Roomkin, Myron, 254
Rooney, Richard P., 394
Rosen, Hjalmar, 325, 328, 329, 350
Rosenbaum, Bernard, 176
Rosenzweig, M. R., 350
Roter, Benjamin, 220, *220*, 251
Rowland, Kendrith M., 81, 116
Rubin, Irwin M., 252
Rubinsky, Stanley, 565, 579
Rucker, Allen W., 470
Ruh, Robert H., 473
Rzasa, Philip V., 433

Sabo, Richard S., 467, 473
Sackman Morris, 631
Saint, Avice, 251
Salipante, Paul, 325, 350
Salisbury, Alan B., 309
Salter, Malcolm S., 393
Sayles, Leonard R., 64, 457, 472, 629, 631
Scala, Bea, 520
Schein, Edgar H., 351
Schenkelbach, Leon, 578
Schmidman, John, 629
Schmidt, Frank L., 576
Schmidt, Warren, H., 207, 213, 254
Schneiderman, Mark L., 177
Schneier, Craig Eric, 252
Schoen, Harold L., 309
Schrader, Albert W., 211
Schroeder, Rolfe E., 65
Schulzinger, Morris, 577, 579
Schultz, George P., 175
Schuster, Fred, 65
Schuster, Jay R., 394, 434
Schwab, Donald P., 192, 211, 212, 213
Schwartz, Eleanor Brantley, 322, 349
Scofield, Robert, 253
Scott, Robert D., 212
Seimer, Stanley, 433
Serafini, Claudio, 177
Shafai-Sahrai, Yaghoub, 561
Shapiro, Harvey, 118
Shaw, Edward A., 393
Shetty, Y. K., 30
Shister, Joseph, 175
Short, Larry E., 174
Siegel, Laurence, 252, 253, *262*, 307
Simonds, Rollin H., 524, 575, 577, 578
Sims, Henry P., Jr., 351
Slevin, Dennis P., 351
Sloan, Alfred P., Jr., 433
Slocum, John W., Jr., 48, 65, 351
Smith, Nelson, 579
Smith, Patricia, 252

Smith, Robert D., *15,* 117, 160, 177, 309, 432
Smith, Robert S., 565, 573, 579
Snelbecker, Glenn E., 252
Somers, Gerald G., 254
Sominsen, Roger H., 309
Sovereign, Michael G., 81, 116
Sperry, Len, 252
Srinivasa, K. R., 393
Stalker, G. M., 17, 30
Steel, Munro H., 253
Steen, Jack, 578
Steers, Richard M., 392
Steiger, William A., 576
Stein, Barry, 518
Steinbrenner, Jean G., 254
Steiner, Richard, 332, 334, 350, 351
Steinmetz, Lawrence L., *143,* 176
Stessin, Lawrence, 175
Strauss, George, 457, 472, 631
Strickland, William J., 350
Stringer, Robert A., Jr., 219, 251
Stockbridge, H. C. W., 252
Suppes, P., 309
Susman, Gerald I., 473
Swanson, Stephen C., 118
Swerdloff, S., 117
Sykes, James T., 65
Szabo, Michael, 309

Tannenbaum, Robert, 207, 213
Tatter, Milton A., 433
Taylor, Frederick W., 5
Taylor, Robert L., 310
Teach, Leon, 176
Thayer, Paul W., 251
This, Leslie E., 226, 252
Thompson, John D., 176
Thompson, Paul, 394
Thorp, Cary D., 175
Tiffin, J., 253
Timmons, Jeffry, 117
Todd, John O., 434
Toffler, Alvin, 637, 645
Tracey, William R., 253
Trice, Harrison M., 65, 244, 253, 254
Trieb, S. W., 313, 349
Turner, John, 325, 328, 329, 350

Utgaard, Stuart B., *299,* 308, 310

Vaill, Peter B., 351
Varney, Glenn H., *381,* 394
Vaughan, James A., 251, 252, 253, 268, *269,* 278, 307, 308, 310
Vettori, Frank L., 282, 308
Vroom, Victor H., 117, 252, 358, 391

Wagner, L. G., *56,* 64, 66
Wagner, Harvey M., 380, 383, 394
Wahlrobe, Thomas E., 434
Walker, James W., 116, 519
Wallace, William H., 194, 212
Washburne, J. N., 177
Watson, K. Brantley, 308
Weber, Max, 30
Weick, Karl, *205*
Weiner, Hannah, 310
Weiner, Youash, 177
Weiser, Francis X., 644, 645
Wendt, George R., 175
Westin, Alan F., 58, 66
White, Harold C., 64
Whitwell, W. C., 433
Whybark, D. Clay, 98, 117
Whyte, William H., Jr., 147, 176, 177
Wickersham, Edward D., 608
Williams, Harrison A., Jr., 520, 521
Wohlking, Wallace, 310
Wolcott, John H., 578
Wolf, Gordon, 394
Wonderlic, E. F., 176
Wood, Norman J., 576
Woodward, Joan, 30, 569, 579
Worick, W. Wayne, 575
Wortman, Max S., Jr., 608, 612, 616, 630, 631
Wright, Orman R., Jr., 65
Wright, T. P., 81–82, 116

Yanouzas, John N., 116
Young, Karl, 645
Young, Samuel L., 84, 116

Zachert, Martha J. K., 310
Zeira, Yoram, 308
Zollitsch, Herbert G., 364, 375, 386, 392, 393, 394, 432, 433, 448, 465, 470, 471, 472, 473, 477, 517, 639, 645

SUBJECT INDEX

Note: Page numbers in *italics* indicate figures.

Ability tests, for job applicants, 154
Accident, defined, 524
Accident analysis, 557–560
Achievement tests, for job applicants, 154
Affirmative action programs, 132–134
  and test validation, 154
  implementation of, 136
AFL, 594–595. See also *AFL-CIO; Unions.*
  competition with CIO, 595–596
  membership of, *597*
  merger of with CIO, 596
AFL-CIO. See also *Unions.*
  Committee on Political Education of, 598
  conventions of, 599
  international unions of, 599
  local unions of, 599–601, *600*
  membership of, *597*
  structure of, 598–602
  use of computers by, 621–622
Age discrimination, 134–135
Age Discrimination in Employment Act of 1967, 134, 502
Agency shop, 590, 603
Alternation ranking, 197–198, 366
American Association of University Professors, 602
American Federation of Labor. See *AFL; AFL-CIO.*
Anti-Injunction Act, 587
Antitrust legislation, and unionization, 586–587
Apprenticeship training, 272–273
Aptitude tests, for job applicants, 154–156, *155*
Arbitration, union, 619–620
Army Alpha intelligence test, 6
Assessment centers, 330–336
  defined, *331*
  disadvantages of, 335–336
  uses of, 332–334

Attitudinal training, for hard-core unemployed, 326–327
  for women, 321–322
Assumption of risk, 527
Automation, and wage and salary administration, 379
  and wage incentives, 397–398

Behaviorally anchored rating scales, for performance appraisal, 202–206, *205*
Benefits, 489–515
  and management science, 478–479
  and managerial decision making, 482–485
  and organizational objectives, 482–485
  categories of, 477
  contingencies affecting, 482–485
  cost-benefit advantages of, 481, *482*
  employee choice of. See *Cafeteria compensation.*
  employee contributions to, 484–485
  employee education about, 483–484
  employee services as, 485–486
  flexitime as, 488–489
  four-day work week as, 487–488
  guaranteed income as, 494–496
  guaranteed work as, 495–496
  health. See *Health insurance.*
  historical development of, 479–481
  holidays as, 486–487
  income security as, 491–497
  increase in, reasons for, 479–482
  life insurance as, 496–497
  medical. See *Health insurance.*
  network analysis for, 478–479
  pension. See *Pension plans.*

Benefits (*Continued*)
  personal excused absences as, 487
  retirement. See *Pension plans.*
  Social Security, 479–480, 489–491
  supplemental unemployment,
    494–496
  time not worked as, 486–489
  unemployment compensation as,
    491–494
  vacation as, 486–487
Blue Cross–Blue Shield medical
  insurance, 497
Bona fide occupational
  qualifications, 135
Bonuses, current, 418–419
  deferred, 419–420
  in Lincoln Electric plan, 464–466
  in Scanlon plans, 454–456, *455*
Boycott, secondary, 586
Branching, in programmed
  instruction, 282
Brennan vs. Gibson's Products, 577
Buckley Amendment, 169–170
Bumping, 108–110, *109*
Business games, in employee
  development programs, 295–298

Cafeteria compensation, 425–428
  criterion for, 425
  eligibility for, 425
  evaluation of, 426–428
  rewards in, 425–426
Capital gains, 421
  in deferred profit sharing, 443–445
Career curve, for wage and salary
  administration, 371–373, *372*
Career paths, 101–104
  analysis of, 102
  counseling for, 102–104
Case studies, in employee
  development programs, 291–292
Central tendency, in performance
  appraisal, 187
CIO, 595. See also *AFL-CIO; Unions.*
  competition with AFL, 595–596
  membership of, *597*
  merger of with AFL, 506
Civil Rights Act of 1964, and bona fide
  occupational qualifications, 135
  and reverse discrimination, 134
  and wage and salary
    administration, 378
  employment provisions of, 111
Classical conditioning, 232–233
Clayton Antitrust Act, 586
Closed shop, 590
Coaching, in employee development,
  278–279
Committee on Political Education, of
  AFL-CIO, 598

Common law, defined, 527, 584
Commonwealth vs. Hunt, 584
Company unions, 587
Compa-ratio, 387–388
Computer(s), and decentralized
  decision making, 55–57, *56*
  and employee development,
    245–247
  and employee management
    relations, 620–622
  and employees' right of privacy, 58
  and management science, 22–26
  and occupational health and
    safety, 565–566
  for human resource demand
    forecasting, 84–85
  for instruction, 284–288, *285*
  for performance appraisals, 190–
    191
  for personnel information decision
    systems, 53–59, *56*
  for recruiting, 141–144
  for skills inventories, 88–89
  for test interpretation, 159–161
  for wage and salary administration,
    378–379
Computer-assisted instruction,
  284–288, *285*
  dialogue, 286
  drill and practice, 284–286, *285*
  tutorial, 286
Computer fraud, 58–59
Concurrent validation, 152
Conditioning, and learning, 232–233
Congress of Industrial Organization.
  See *AFL-CIO; CIO.*
Conspiracy doctrine, and
  unionization, 584
Content validation, 153
Contingency views, 16–21
Contract negotiation. See *Union
  contract negotiation.*
Contributory negligence, 527
Cost-benefit analysis, 52–53
  in recruiting and selection,
    385–386
  in wage and salary administration,
    385–386
Cost-of-living raises, 376–377
Critical incident technique, 202–204
Critical path method, in management
  science, 23–25. See also *Program
  evaluation and review technique.*
Cross-training, 45

Danbury Hatters Case, 586
Deferred compensation, 419–420
DeFunis vs. Odegaard, 133
Delphi technique, for human
  resources demand forecasting,
  85–87

Development, employee. See
    Employee development
    programs.
  management, 337
  organizational. See Organizational
    development.
Discipline, employee, 615–616
Discrimination. See Employees,
  minority, discrimination against.
Disease, occupational. See
  Occupational injuries and disease.
Dynamic programming, 449–450

Edwards Personality Inventory, 157
Employee(s), age discrimination
    against, 135–136
  attrition of, 107
  bumping of, 108–110, 109
  development programs for. See
    Employee development
    programs.
  discipline of, 615–616
  federal, unionization of, 593
  hiring of. See Recruiting and
    selection.
  incentives for. See Incentives.
  injuries of. See Occupational
    injuries and diseases.
  layoffs of, 107–110, 109
    discriminatory, 110–112
  minority, development programs
      for, 320–327
    discrimination against, and
        seniority systems, 111–112
      in hiring, 129–137
        affirmative action programs
            for, 132–134
        and bona fide occupational
            qualifications, 135
        and reverse discrimination,
            132–134
      in promotions and layoffs,
          110–112
      legislation pertaining to, 111,
          378
      overt vs. systemic, 131
      remedying, 135–137
      reverse, 132–134
    quotas for, 132–134
  number of, effect of on personnel
      techniques, 20–21
  performance of, appraisal of. See
    Performance appraisal.
  physical examinations for, 170
  privacy rights of, and computers,
      58
    and reference checks, 169–170
  promotion of, 99–106. See also
    Promotion.
    discrimination in, 110–112

Employee(s) (Continued)
  recruitment and selection of. See
    Recruiting and selection.
  safety and health of. See
    Occupational safety and health.
  salary of. See Wages and salary;
    Wage and salary administration.
  selection of. See Recruiting and
    selection.
  seniority of. See Seniority systems.
  services to, as benefits, 485–486
  success criteria for, 121
  training of. See Employee
    development.
  transfers of, 107
  unionization of. See Union(s);
    Unionization.
  unnecessary, reduction of, 106–110
  wages of. See Wages and salary;
    Wage and salary administration.
Employee associations, 601–602
Employee benefits. See Benefits.
Employee development programs,
    214–351
  and computers, 245–247
  and learning theories, 225–237.
    See also Learning.
  and management science, 245–247
  and motivation, 225–226
  and performance appraisal, 223
  and planned organizational
    learning, 214–254
  apprenticeship training in, 272–273
  assessment centers for, 330–336,
    331
  attitudinal training in, for hard-core
      unemployed, 326–327
    for women, 321–322
  business games in, 295–298
  case studies in, 291–292
  coaching in, 278–279
  committee assignment in, 277
  comparison of, 298–304, 299, 301
  computer-assisted instruction in,
    284–288, 285
  conductors of, choice of, 256–263
    combinations of, 261–263, 262
    line managers as, 256–257, 259
    nonmanagerial employees as,
      257–258, 259
    outside consultants as, 259, 260–261
    staff as, 258–260, 259
    training of, 261–263, 262
  consultants for, 259, 260–261
  contingencies in, 247
  design of, 255–310
  design phase of, 224–237
  determining need for, 217–224
    organizational analysis in,
      218–219
    person analysis in, 220–221
    task analysis in, 219–220, 220

Employee development programs (*Continued*)

determining need for, techniques for, 221–224, *222, 224*

discussion method in, 280–281

dysfunctional consequences of, 345–347

evaluation of, 237–245

criteria for, 238–240

experimental designs for, 240–245, *241*

for hard-core unemployed, 325–329

for women, 320–325

in-basket exercises in, 294–295

incident technique in, 292

job instruction training in, 270–272

job rotation in, 273–277

lectures in, 279–281

location of, 263–268

multiple management in, 277–278

off-the-job, 266–268

techniques for, 279–298

on-the-job, 263–266

special assignments in, 277–279

techniques for, *269,* 270–279

organization development in, 336–345. See also *Organization development.*

orientation training in, 311–319

problems and issues in, 311–352

programmed instruction in, 281–284

remedial education in, for hard-core unemployed, 326

role playing in, 292–294

simulation in, 290–298

skills training in, for hard-core unemployed, 327–328

techniques for, 268–298

comparison of, 298–304, *299, 301*

effectiveness of, 300–303, *301*

guides for selection of, 303–304

most frequently used, 299–300, *299*

vs. training, 215

vestibule training in, 288–290

Employee management relations, 580–631

and computers, 620–622

and management science, 620–622

and unions, 580–583, *582.* See also *Union(s); Unionization.*

contingencies in, 622–623

Employee Retirement Income Security Act, 505–515. See also *Pension plans.*

and future of private pension plans, 513–515

and individual pension plans, 511

and profit sharing plans, 436, 440–441

Employee Retirement Income Security Act (*Continued*)

fiduciary responsibility requirements of, 509–510

funding requirements of, 509

maximum benefit limits under, 511–512

participation and vesting requirements of, 507–509, *508*

plan termination insurance under, 512

portability of vested benefits under, 511

reporting and disclosure requirements of, 506–507

scope and coverage of, 506

tax provisions of, 510

Employment interviews. See *Interviews, employment.*

Equal Employment Opportunity Act of 1972, 111

Equal Employment Opportunity Commission, establishment of, 111

investigations by, 129–130

Equal opportunity employment, and human resource planning, 110–112

and internal promotions and layoffs, 110–112

and outside hiring, 129–137

objectives and problems of, 135–137

Equal Pay Act of 1963, 378

Equipment utilization incentives, 406–408

Ergonomics, 555–557

ERISA. See *Employee Retirement Income Security Act.*

Executive incentives, 416–424, *429*

criteria for, 418

current bonuses as, 418–419

deferred bonuses and compensation as, 419–420

eligibility for, 417–418

performance shares as, 423–424

reward systems for, 418–424

stock options as, 420–423

Experience rating, for unemployment compensation, 492, *493, 494*

Factor comparison method, for wage and salary administration, 368–371, *369, 370*

Fair Credit Reporting Act, 169

Fair Labor Standards Act of 1938, 378

Family Educational Rights and Privacy Act of 1974, 169–170

Feast of Fools, 642–644

Federal employees, unionization of, 593

Federal Mediation and Conciliation Service, 590
and union contract negotiations, 614
Feedback, and learning, 230–232
Fellow servant rule, 527
Fiduciary, defined, 510
Field review, in performance appraisal, 200
Flexitime, 488–489
Flextime, 488–489
Forced choice, in performance appraisal, 199–200
Forced distribution, in performance appraisal, 199
Four-day work week, 487–488

Games, business, in employee development programs, 295–298
Guaranteed income, 494–496
Guaranteed piecework, 405, *405, 407*
Guaranteed work, 495–496
Government employees, unionization of, 593
Government legislation. See names of specific statutes.
Graphic rating, in performance appraisal, 201–202, *201*
Grievance procedure, 615, 617–619
Griggs vs. Duke Power Co., 111
and affirmative action programs, 132

Halo effect, in interviewing, 161, 187
Health, employee. See *Occupational safety and health.*
Health hazard, vs. safety hazard, 523
Health insurance, 497–501
and health maintenance organizations, 501
Blue Cross–Blue Shield, 497
government involvement in, 500–501
organizational decisions in, 497–498
trends in, 499–500
typical organizational plan for, 498–499, *500*
Health maintenance organizations, 501
Hiring. See *Recruiting and selection.*
Holidays, 486–487
Hot stove rule, 616
Human factors engineering, 555–557
Human resource forecasting, 78–99
of external demand and supply, 97–99
of internal demand and supply, 79–97

Human resource forecasting (*Continued*)
of internal demand and supply,
computer simulation for, 84–85
Delphi technique for, 85–87
logarithmic learning curve analysis for, 81–84, *82, 83,* 119
Markov model for, 93–97, *94, 95*
quantitative models for, 84–85
replacement charts for, 91–93, *92*
skills inventories for, 87–91
traditional statistical projections for, 81
Human resource planning, 69–119
and equal opportunity employment, 110–112
defined, 69
goals and objectives of, 69
model for, *70*
plan formulation in, 99–113
trends in, 73–74

Identical element theory, 235
Illness, occupational. See *Occupational injuries and disease.*
In-basket exercises, in employee development programs, 294–295
Incentives, company-wide. See *System incentives.*
employee choice of, 424–428. See also *Cafeteria compensation.*
equipment utilization, 406–408
executive, 416–424. See also *Executive incentives.*
individual, 395–434, *396*
plant-wide. See *System incentives.*
system. See *System incentives.*
types of, *396, 429*
wage, 397–410. See also *Wage incentives.*
Incident technique, in employee development programs, 292
Income, guaranteed, 494–496
Income security, 491–497
Income taxes, and wage and salary administration, 385–386
Individual Retirement Account, 511
Industrial welfare movement, 5
Injunction(s), defined, 585
Taft-Hartley, 590–591
use of against unions, 585
Injuries, occupational. See *Occupational injuries and disease.*
Insurance, health. See *Health insurance.*
life, 496–497
pension, 512
Intelligence test, Army Alpha, 6
International unions, 599

Interview, employment, 161–166
  halo effect in, 161
  multiple, 166
  nondirective, 164–165
  patterned, 163–164, *163*
  stress, 165–166
  for performance appraisal,
    191–197

Job(s), establishing pay for. See
    Wage and salary administration.
  flexible hours for, 488–489
  training for. See *Employee
    development programs.*
Job analysis, 74–78
  benefits of, 74–75
  defined, 74
  information-gathering for, 75–76
  job description in, 76–78, *77*
  job specification in, 76–78
Job applicants, basic behavioral
    patterns of, 146–147
  privacy rights of, 147–148
  recruitment of. See *Recruiting and
    selection.*
  search strategies of, 138–139
  selection of. See *Recruiting and
    selection.*
  testing of, 151–161. See also *Tests.*
Job application form, 149–151
Job classification method, for wage
    and salary administration, 366–367
Job descriptions, 76–78, *77*
Job design, 74
Job evaluations, 365–372
  factor comparison method for,
    368–371, *369, 370*
  job classification method for,
    366–367
  maturity curve for, 371–373, *372*
  point system for, 367–368, *368*
  ranking method for, 366
Job instruction training, 270–272
Job-man matching systems, 142–144
Job performance, standard times for,
    400–401
Job posting, 100–101
Job rotation, 273–277
Job safety analysis, 552
Job specifications, 76–78
Juniority, 495

Keogh plans, 511
Kinked-function profit sharing, 441,
  442
Knights of Labor, 594
Knowledge of results, and learning,
  230–232

Kuder Occupational Interest Survey,
  157–158, *158*
Kuder Preference Record, 157–158

Labor-Management Disclosure Act of
  1959, 591–592
Labor management relations. See
  Employee management relations.
Labor Management Relations Act of
  1947, 589–591
Labor market, 138–140
Laboratory training, 340–344
Landrum-Griffin Act, 591–592
Law, common, defined, 527, 584
  statutory, defined, 527, 584
Law of effect, 232
Layoffs, 107–110, *109*
  discriminatory, 110–112
Learning, active vs. passive, 233
  and conditioning, 232–233
  and feedback, 230–232
  and knowledge of results, 230–232
  and reinforcement, 232–233
  individual differences in, 226–227
  mass vs. distributed, 233–235
  motivation in, 225–226
  principles of, and employee
    development programs, 225–237
  retention of, 237
  styles in, 226–227
  transfer of, 235–236
  whole vs. part, 235
Learning curve(s), 227–230, *228*
  logarithmic, 81–84, *82, 83,* 119
  and occupational safety and
    health, 564
Learning plateaus, 227–230, *228*
Legislation. See names of specific
  statutes.
Life insurance, 496–497
Lincoln Electric plan, 459–468
  bonuses in, 464–466
  eligibility for, 461
  incentive management philosophy
    of, 460–461
  organizational membership
    rewards in, 463–464
  profit sharing bonus mechanism
    in, 464–466
  reasons for success of, 466–468
  rewards in, 462
    criteria for, 461–462
Line department, vs. staff
  department, 35–37, *36*
Line management, as conductors of
  employee development programs,
  256–257, *259*
Line-staff relationships, and
  recruitment and selection, 128–129

Linear programming, for setting standard job times, 400–401
for wage and salary administration, 380–383, *382*
Loewe vs. Lawlor, 586
Logarithmic learning curve, 81–84, *82, 83,* 119
and occupational safety and health, 564

Man-job matching systems, 142–144
Management, and employees. See *Employee management relations.*
multiple, as development technique, 277–278
scientific, 5
Management by objectives, 47–49
and performance appraisal, 206–209
Management development, 337
Management science, and computers, 22–26
and employee benefits, 478–479
and employee development, 245–247
and employee management relations, 620–622
and occupational safety and health, 563–572
and performance appraisals, 190–191
and personnel management decision making, 22–26
and profit sharing plans, 449–450
and recruiting, 140–142
and wage and salary administration, 379–383
critical path method in, 23–25
defined, 22
mathematical programming in, *23, 25, 26*
network models in, 23–26, *23, 24*
simulation in, *23,* 26
Management science models, 23–26, *23, 24, 26*
Managerial grid, 337–339, *338*
MANPLAN, 85
Markov model, 93–97, *94, 95*
descriptive functions of, 96–97
predictive functions of, 94–96
Marshall vs. Barlow's, Inc., 577
Maslow's hierarchy of needs, 357–358
and unions, 603–605
Mathematical programming, in management science, *23, 25, 26*
in recruiting, 141–142
Maturity curve, for wage and salary administration, 371–373, *372*

McClellan Committee, 591
Medical benefits, 497–501. See also *Health insurance.*
Medicare, 490
Mental alertness tests, 154–156, *155*
Merit raises, 376–377
Micro-synthetic analysis, of job performance, 400
Minnesota Multiphasic Personality Inventory, 157
Minorities. See *Employees, minority.*
Motion study, 399–400, *399*
Multiple management, as development technique, 277–278

National Education Association, 602
National Institute for Occupational Safety and Health, 541
National Labor Relations Act, 587–589
National Labor Relations Board, 588–589
Negligence, contributory, 527
Network analysis, and employee benefits, 478–479
Network models, 23–25, *23, 24*
and programmed instruction, 283–284
for recruiting, 142, *143*
for wage and salary administration, 380, *381*
Nondirective interview, 164–165
Norris-LaGuardia Act, 587

Occupational injuries and disease, causes of, theories of, 549–551
dollar costs of, 536
analysis of, 558–560
prevention of, 551–557
employee training for, 553–555
safety director's role in, 548–557. See also *Safety director.*
safety engineering for, 552
systems approach to, 555–557
rates of, 532–536, *534*
calculation of, 533–536
remedial control of, 557–560
time lost due to, 536
Occupational safety and health, 522–579
and computers, 565–566
and contingencies, 567–572
and firm size, 567–569, *567, 568*
and logarithmic learning curves, 564
and management science, 563–572
and occupation-related death rate, 532–533

Occupational safety and health (*Continued*)
and occupational injuries, 532–536. See also *Occupational injuries and disease.*
and simulation, 564–565
and type of industry, *568,* 569, *570, 571*
and workforce characteristics, 569–572
and workmen's compensation, 529–531
employers' common law obligations for, 527–528
government regulation of, in nineteenth century, 528
in twentieth century, 528–532. See also *Occupational Safety and Health Act of 1970.*
government standards for, 537–538
historical developments in, 525–537
legislation on, current. See *Occupational Safety and Health Act of 1970.*
pre-1970, 526–532
organizational support for, 560–563
safety director's role in. See *Safety director.*
scope and measurement of, 532–536
state plans for, 541
systems approach to, 555–557
Occupational Safety and Health Act of 1970, 531, 537–545
employees' duties under, 542–543
employers' duties under, 542–543
penalties under, *540*
problems involving, 542–545
provisions of, 537–542
organizational compliance with, 546–548
record-keeping requirements of, 538
state powers under, 541
Occupational Safety and Health Administration, 537–538
enforcement powers of, 539, *540*
inspections and investigations by, 538–539
limitations on, 544
problems of, 542–545
standards of, establishment of, 537–538
problems with, 542–543
Occupational Safety and Health Review Commission, 539–540
Off-the-job training, 266–268
techniques for, 279–298

Office of Federal Contract Compliance, 130
On-the-job training, 263–266
special assignments in, 277–279
techniques for, *269,* 270–279
Organization(s), change in, and personnel decision making, 18–19
degree of certainty in, and personnel decision making, 16–18
environmental certainty in, 16–18
size of, and occupational safety and health, 567–569, *567, 568*
and personnel decision making, 19–21
Organization development, 336–347
assessment of, 344–345
defined, 336
managerial grid in, 337–339, *338*
sensitivity training in, 340–344
vs. management development, 337
Organizational analysis, 218–219
Organizational climate, defined, 219
Organizational goals, suboptimization of, 71
Organizational structure, mechanistic, vs. organic, 17–18
Orientation training, 311–319
effectiveness of, 313–319
who should conduct, 313
OSHA. See *Occupational Safety and Health Administration.*
Owen, Robert, 526

Paired comparisons, 198, *198,* 366
Pattern bargaining, 610
Patterned interview, 163–164, *163*
Pension plans, 501–515
annuity options under, 505
benefits under, 504–505
decision strategies for, 513–515
defined benefit, benefits under, 504–505
vs. defined contribution, 503
defined contribution, 503
fiduciary responsibility for, 509–510
funding of, 503
government regulation of, 509
government regulation of. See *Employee Retirement Income Security Act.*
historical development of, 480
increase in, *502*
individual, 511
Keogh, 511
maximum benefit limits for, 511–512

Pension plans (*Continued*)
  participation in, government
    regulation of, 507–509
  plan termination insurance for, 512
  portability of vested benefits in, 511
  private, future of, 513–515
  rising costs of, 513–515
  scope of, 502–503
  vesting in, 503
    government regulation of,
      507–509, *508*
Percy's paradoxes, 635–642
Performance appraisal, 181–213
  and employee development
    programs, 223
  and management by objectives,
    206–209
  and management science, 190–191
  appraiser for, 191–192
  behaviorally anchored rating
    scales for, 202–206, *205*
  central tendency in, 187
  common errors in, 187
  computers for, 190–191
  contingencies in, 188–189
  critical incident technique for,
    202–204
  data for, 182–184
  essay comparison for, 202
  feedback techniques in, absolute,
    201–206
    defined, 182
    mutually interactive, 206–209
  field review for, 200
  forced choice in, 199–200
  forced distribution in, 199
  graphic rating scales for, 201–202,
    201
  interview for, 191–197
    problems in, 192–195
    strategies in, 195–197, *196*
  multiple systems for, 208–209
  nonfeedback techniques in,
    absolute, 199–200
    comparative, 197–199, *197*
    defined, 182
  objectives of, 182–184
  process of, *183*
  ranking in, 197–199, *198*
  role of personnel department in,
    189–190
  systems for, *183,* 184–187
  techniques for, 197–209
  variable-interval, 185
  weighted checklist for, 200
Performance shares, 423–424
Person analysis, 220–221
Personal excused absences, 487
Personality profiles, 157–159
Personnel department, 31–68
  and line-staff relationships, 38–41,
    128–129

Personnel department (*Continued*)
  and unemployment compensation,
    493–494
  as staff department, 35–37, *36*
  functions of, 37–38
  role of, in performance appraisal,
    189–190
    in recruiting and selection,
      128–129
    in union contract negotiations,
      612–614
    in wage and salary
      administration, 386–388
  staff parallelism in, 41–43, *42*
Personnel information decision
    systems, 53–59
  advantages of, 54–57
  implementation problems in, 57–59
  limitations of, 57–59
  scope of, 54
Personnel management, and
    government regulation, 59–61
  and management by objectives,
    47–49
  and product life-cycle, 33–34
  and program budgeting, 49–52
  as open system, 13–16, *15*
  cost-benefit analysis in, 52
  decision making in, 12–26
    and computers, 22–26, 55–57, *56*
    and management science, 22–26
    and number of employees, 20–21
    and organizational change,
      18–19
    and organizational degree of
      certainty, 16–18
    and organizational size, 19–21
    and systems, 13–21, *15*
    as open system, 13–16, *15*
    contingency views in, 17–21
    decentralization of via
      computers, 55–57, *56*
  defined, 4
  diversity in, 31–32
  effect of economic conditions on,
    34–35
  history of, 5–8
  mechanistic vs. organic, 17–18
  paradoxes in, 634–642
  scope of, 4–5
  specialization in, 32
  updating in, 19
Personnel manager, 31–35
  and economic paradoxes, 641–642
  and Feast of Fools, 642–644
  and government regulation,
    639–640
  and organization system, 638–639
  as advisor, 35–36, 37
  as auditor, 37–38
  as compliance officer, 59
  as generalist vs. specialist, 637–638

Personnel manager (*Continued*)
as policy maker, 37
as provider of services, 37
power and status of, 43–46
enhancement of, 44–46
implications of, 46
increasing, 635–636
roles of, conflicts in, 37–38
PERT. See *Program Evaluation and
Review Technique.*
Phillips vs. Martin Marietta Company,
135, 175
Physical examinations, 170
Piecework, guaranteed, 405, *405, 407*
Planned organizational learning,
need determination phase of,
217–224
organizational analysis in,
218–219
phases in, 215–216, *216*
Point system, for wage and salary
administration, 367–368, *368*
Posting, job, 100–101
Predictive validation, 151–152
Privacy, employee, and computers,
58
and reference checks, 169–170
Product life-cycle, 33–34
Profit sharing plans, 437–450
and management science, 449–450
combination, *436,* 439
contingencies in, 448–449
criterion for reward in, 441
current, 438
deferred, *436,* 438–439
eligibility for, 439–441
pay out methods in, 443–445
vesting in, 440–441
evaluation of, 445–448
history of, 437–439
in Lincoln Electric plan, 464–466
kinked-function, 441, *442*
legislation affecting, 436, 440–441
rewards in, 441–445
types of, *436,* 438–439
Program budgeting, 49–52
Program Evaluation and Review
Technique, 23–25
and programmed instruction,
283–284
and recruiting, 142, *143*
and wage and salary
administration, 380, *381*
Programmed instruction, branching
in, 282
for employee development,
281–284
Programming, dynamic, 449–450
linear, for setting standard job
times, 400–401
for wage and salary
administration, 380–383, *382*

Programming (*Continued*)
mathematical, in management
science, *23, 25, 26*
in recruiting, 141–142
Progressive discipline, 616–617
Promotion(s), 99–106
and career path analysis and
counseling, 102–105
and job posting, 100–101
Promotion systems, discriminatory,
110–112
open and closed, 105–106
Protocol method, 159
Proxy criteria, in cost-benefit
analysis, 53
Psychological tests, 151–154
discriminatory effect of, 111
validation of, 151–154
Pullman strike, 585

Quality control charts, 222–223, *222*
Quotas, for minority employees,
132–134

Racial discrimination. See
*Employees, minority,
discrimination against.*
Railway Labor Act of 1926, 587
Raises, 376–377
Range restriction, in test validation,
152
Ranking, alternation, 197–198
paired comparison, 198, *198*
Ranking method, for wage and salary
administration, 366
Ratio hiring, 132
Recruiting and selection, 120–177
ability tests for, 154
and applicants' basic behavioral
patterns, 146–147
and applicants' privacy rights,
147–148
and applicants' search strategies,
138–139
and application form, 149–151
and computers, 141–144
and equal opportunity
employment, 129–137
and labor markets, 138–140
and line-staff relationships,
128–129
and management science, 140–142
and physical examinations, 170
aptitude tests for, 154–156, *155*
as decision making under risk,
125–128, 138–140
assessment centers for, 332–333
composite approach to, 125

Recruiting and selection (*Continued*)
computerized man-job matching
systems for, 142–144
cost-benefit model for, 126–128,
126, 127
defined, 120
discriminatory, 129–137. See also
*Employees, minority,
discrimination against.*
evaluation of, 144–145
information transmission in,
138–140
interviewing in, 161–166
mathematical programming in,
141–142
mental alertness tests for, 154–156,
155
network model for, 142, *143*
objectives of, 121–122
personality profiles for, 157–159
personnel department's role in,
128–129
probabilistic nature of, 125
process of, *124*
psychological tests for, 151–154
reference checking in, 166–170,
168
selection tools for, 137–145
reliability and validity of, 121–122
sequencing of, 123, *124*, 148–149
simulation in, 140
successive hurdle approach to,
123, *124*
systems of, characteristics of,
122–128
multistage, 122–125, *124*
testing in, 154–161. See also *Tests.*
uncertainties in, 125–128
vocational interest tests for,
156–157, *157*
References, applicants', checking of,
166–170, *168*
*Regents of the University of
California vs. Bakke,* 133–134
Reinforcement, and learning,
232–233
Remedial education, for hard-core
unemployed, 326
Replacement charts, 91–93, *92*
Retirement, mandatory, 502
Retirement benefits. See *Pension
plans.*
Reverse discrimination, 132–134
Right-to-work laws, 590
and union membership, *604*
Role playing, in employee
development programs, 292–294
Rorschach Inkblot Test, 158

Safety, employee. See *Occupational
safety and health.*

Safety director, defined, 545–546
responsibilities of, 525, 546–563
for accident analysis, 557–558
for accident cost analysis,
558–560
for compliance with
Occupational Safety and
Health Act provisions, 546–548
for data collection, 557–558
for elimination of unsafe acts,
553–557
for elimination of unsafe conditions,
552, 555–557
for organizational support for
safety, 560–563
for prevention of occupational
injuries and diseases, 551–557
for remedial control of accidents,
557–560
use of computer by, 565–566
use of management science
techniques by, 563–572
Safety engineering, 552
Safety hazard, vs. health hazard, 523
Salary. See *Wages and salary; Wage
and salary administration.*
Scanlon plans, 450–459
bonus in, 454–456, *455*
contingencies in, 456–458
criterion for, 451–454
eligibility for, 451
evaluation of, 458
future directions in, 459
norm in, 454
production committees in, 451–453,
452, 453–454
ratio, 455–456, *455*
reward in, 454–456
screening committee in, *452,*
453–454
vs. suggestion systems, 453
Scientific management, 5
Secondary boycott, 586
Selection, employee. See *Recruiting
and selection.*
Seniority and equal employment
opportunities, 111
and layoffs, 108–110, *109*
and minorities, 111–112
court rulings on, 110–111
legality of, 111–112
Sensitivity training, 340–344
Sex discrimination. See *Employees,
minority, discrimination against.*
Sherman Antitrust Act, 586
Shop steward, 618
Simonds Method, of accident cost
analysis, 558–560
Simulation, and occupational safety
and health, 564–565
in employee development
programs, 290–298
in management science, *23,* 26

Simulation (*Continued*)
  in recruiting, 140
  in wage and salary administration,
    379–380, *380*
  protocol method of, 159
Skills inventories, 87–91
Skills training, for hard-core
  unemployed, 327–328
Social Security, 489–491, *491*
Social Security Act of 1935, 489–491
  and employee benefits, 479–480,
    489–491
"The Song of the Ass," *643*
Staff, as conductors of employee
  development programs, 258–260,
  259
Staff department, vs. line
  department, 35–37, *36*
Staff parallelism, 41–43, *42*
Standard hour plan, for wage
  incentives, 406, *407*
Standard times, for job performance,
  400–401
Statutory law, defined, 527, 584
Stock options, 420–423
Stress interviews, 165–166
Suboptimization, defined, 71
Suggestion systems, 410–416, *429*
  administration of, 414–416, *417*
  and employee management
    relations, 413–414
  and organizational size and
    stability, 412–413
  contingencies in, 412–416
  criterion for, 411
  defined, 411
  eligibility for, 411
  managerial support for, 413–414
  rewards in, 412
  vs. Scanlon plans, 453
Supplemental unemployment
  benefits (SUB), 494–496
Surveys, wage and salary, 362–364
Synergy, defined, 237
Synthetic validation, 152–153
System(s), and decision making,
    13–21, *15*
  closed, 13
  defined, 13
  open, control element of, 14
    defined, 13
    feedback element of, 14
    memory element of, 14
    output element of, 13–14
    personnel management as, 13–16
    15
System incentives, 435–473, *436*
  Lincoln Electric plan for, 459–468.
    See also *Lincoln Electric plan.*
  profit sharing plans as, 437–450.
    See also *Profit-sharing plans.*

System incentives (*Continued*)
  Scanlon plans as, 450–459. See
    also *Scanlon plans.*
  types of, *436*

T-group training, 340–344
Taft-Hartley Act, 589–591
Taft-Hartley injunction, 590–591
Task analysis, 219–220, *220*
Task complexity, 235
Task organization, 235
Tax(es), income, and wage and salary
  administration, 385–386
Tax Reform Act of 1969, and deferred
  compensation, 419
  and stock options, 421–422
Tax Reform Act of 1976, and deferred
  compensation, 420
  and stock options, 422
Test(s), ability, 154
  achievement, 154
  aptitude, 154–156, *155*
  Army Alpha intelligence, 6
  computerized interpretation of,
    159–161
  mental alertness, 154–156, *155*
  personality, 157–159
  psychological, 151–154
  reliability of, 121–122
  Rorschach Inkblot, 158
  sequencing of, 123, *124,* 148–149
  Thematic Apperception, 158
  validation of, 151–154
  validity of, 121–122
  vocational interest, 156–157, *157*
Thematic Apperception Test, 158
Thurstone Temperament Schedule,
  157, 158–159
Thurstone Test of Mental Ability, 155
Time study, 400
Training, employee. See *Employee
  development programs.*
Transfer-through principle, 235–236
Trauma, defined, 523–524

Unemployed, hard-core, employee
  development programs for,
  325–329
Unemployment compensation,
  491–494, *493, 494*
  amount and duration of, 493
  and experience rating, 492, *493,*
  494
  and personnel department,
  493–494
  supplemental, 491–494, *493, 494*

Unfair labor practices, under Wagner
  Act, 588–589
Unfair union practices, under
  Taft-Hartley Act, 589–590
Union(s), and employee management
    relations, 580–583, *582*
  and injunctions, 585
  and wage and salary levels, 362
  and yellow dog contracts, 584–585
  company, 587
  deauthorization elections for, 590
  decertification elections for, 590
  firm's decision strategies
    regarding, 605–620
  international, 599
  legislation against, 584–586
  legislation protecting, 587–589
  legislation regulating, 583–593
  local, 599–601, *600*
  membership of, *597*
    and right-to-work laws, *604*
    "bill of rights" for, 591–592
    by state, *604*
  organizing techniques of, 606–607
  pattern bargaining by, 610
  reasons for joining, 602–605
  reasons for not joining, 605
  reform of, legislation for, 591–592
  representation elections for, 588
  structure of, 597–602
  types of, 597
  vs. employee associations,
    601–602
Union arbitration, 619–620
Union contract, administration of,
    615–620
  arbitration provisions of, 619–620
  disciplinary provisions of, 615–617
  grievance procedure provisions of,
    615, 617–619
  interpretation of, 615–620
  provisions of, 611, 615–620
Union contract negotiation, 607–614
  decision making processes in,
    612–614
  Federal Mediation and Conciliation
    Service for, 614
  guidelines for, 613–614
  issues in, 610–611
  parties to, 608–610, *609–610*
  patterns of, 608–610, *609–610*
  personnel manager's role in,
    612–614
Union shop, 590, 602–603
Unionization, and antitrust
    legislation, 586–587
  and conspiracy doctrine, 584
  as contingency, 622–623
  contingencies in, 623
  defined, 581
  early attempts at, 593–594

Unionization (*Continued*)
  firms' techniques for preventing,
    606–607
  history of, 593–597
  legislation involving, 583–593
    nineteenth century to 1930's,
      584–587
    1930's to 1950's, 587–592
    1960's to present, 592–593
  of federal employees, 593
  scope of, 583
  unions' techniques for, 606–607
Unplanned event, defined, 522

Vacations, 486–487
Validation, and affirmative action,
    154
  concurrent, 152
  content, 153
  of psychological tests, 151–154
  predictive, 151–152
  range restriction in, 152
  synthetic, 152–153
Validity, of employee selection tools,
    121–122
Vestibule training, 288–290
Vocational interest tests, 156–157,
    157

Wage(s) and salary, and job
    satisfaction, 358–359
  and motivation, 357–358
  and organizational objectives,
    359–361, *359, 360*
  defined, 356
  establishing levels of, 361–364
    variables affecting, 361–362
  establishing structure of, 364–376
    job evaluation for, 365–372
    surveys for, 362–364
  surveys of, 362–364
Wage and salary administration,
    355–394
  and automatic progression,
    376–377
  and automation, 379
  and computers, 378–379
  and income taxes, 385–386
  and management science, 379–383
  and raises, 376–377
  career curves for, 371–373, *372*
  choosing system for, 373
  compa-ratio for, 387–388
  cost-benefit analysis in, 385–386
  data disclosure in, 383–384
  decision making in, 359–361, *359*

Wage and salary administration (Continued)
    factor comparison method for, 368–371, *369, 370*
    for classes of jobs, 364–373
    for individual jobs, 373–374, *374*
    for individuals, 376–377
    government legislation affecting, 377–378
    job evaluation for, 365–372
    linear programming for, 380, 382–383, *382*
    maturity curve for, 371–373, *372*
    network model for, 380, *381*
    point system for, 367–368, *368*
    ranking method for, 366
    rate ranges for, 374–376, *375*
    role of personnel department in, 386–388
Wage incentives, 397–410, *429*
    and automation, 397–398
    effectiveness of, 408–410
    equipment utilization, 406–408
    establishing standards for, 398–404, *399, 402, 403*
      determining standard times for, 400–401
      motion study for, 399–400, *399*
      systems view of, 401–404, *402, 403*

Wage incentives (Continued)
    guaranteed piecework as, 405, *405, 407*
    standard hour plan for, 406, *407*
    traditional output, 404–406
    typical plans for, 404–408, *405, 407*
Wagner Act, 587–589
Weighted checklist, in performance appraisal, 200
Williams-Steiger Act. See *Occupational Safety and Health Act of 1970.*
Women, discrimination against. See *Employees, minority, discrimination against.*
    employee development programs for, 320–325
Wonderlic Personnel Test, 155, *155*
Work, guaranteed, 495–496
Work sampling, 400
Work week, four day, 487–488
Workmen's compensation laws, 529–531

Yellow dog contract, 584–585